Uniform Law for International Sales under the 1980 United Nations Convention

KLUWER LAW INTERNATIONAL

Uniform Law for International Sales under the 1980 United Nations Convention

Fourth Edition

John O. Honnold

Edited and Updated by
Harry M. Flechtner

Wolters Kluwer
Law & Business

AUSTIN   BOSTON   CHICAGO   NEW YORK   THE NETHERLANDS

Published by:
Kluwer Law International
P.O. Box 316
2400 AH Alphen aan den Rijn
The Netherlands
Website: www.kluwerlaw.com

Sold and distributed in North, Central and South America by:
Aspen Publishers, Inc.
7201 McKinney Circle
Frederick, MD 21704
United States of America
Email: customer.care@aspenpubl.com

Sold and distributed in all other countries by
Turpin Distribution Services Ltd.
Stratton Business Park
Pegasus Drive, Biggleswade
Bedfordshire SG18 8TQ
United Kingdom
Email: kluwerlaw@turpin-distribution.com

Printed on acid-free paper.

ISBN 978-90-411-2753-2

© 2009 Kluwer Law International BV, The Netherlands

Printed in Great Britain.

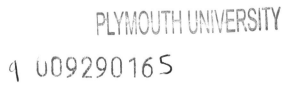

To Professor Honnold's Colleagues

of the

United Nations Commission on International Trade Law

The Vienna Diplomatic Conference

and the

United Nations International Trade Law Branch

PREFACE TO THE FOURTH EDITION
with comments on type-face conventions

Attempting a new edition of *Uniform Law for International Sales*, Professor John Honnold's classic commentary on the United Nations Convention on Contracts for the International Sale of Goods (CISG), without Professor Honnold's participation would appear to be folly, futility, or both.

The reader of this fourth edition of the treatise may conclude that, in this instance, reality corresponds to appearance. There is simply no one who can bring to this project the qualifications and experience Professor Honnold possesses. He has played, to say the least, a central role in the development, finalization, promotion, implementation and understanding of the Convention. As Secretary of the United Nations Commission on International Trade Law (UNCITRAL) from 1969–74, he led that organization's crucial initial efforts to develop the draft text of the Convention. He represented the United States at the 1980 Vienna diplomatic conference at which the text of the Convention was finalized and approved. His scholarly work on the CISG, in particular the present commentary, draws on his unique knowledge of the history and purposes of the Convention, and his almost intuitive grasp of the instrument has guided governments, tribunals, scholars and practitioners towards an enlightened international understanding of the treaty.

To the editor of this fourth edition of the treatise it is clear that Professor Honnold's spirit permeated the processes that produced the Convention and, as a result, the final product. That explains the remarkable progress of the Convention, which has been called "the most successful attempt" at uniform international commercial law.[1] His spirit combines acute intelligence; a gentle, self-effacing, sincere respect for the views of others; an energetic determination to achieve great and useful goals despite daunting obstacles; and a quintessentially international outlook engendered by a career-long drive to transcend the limitations of particular background. The editor of the current edition, clearly, is not qualified to continue the work of a giant like Professor Honnold — but who is? When the mighty are not available, the lesser must do.

---

1. Peter Schlechtriem, *Preface, in Commentary on the UN Convention on the International Sale of Goods* (CISG) at v (Peter Schlechtriem & Ingeborg Schwenzer, eds.) (2nd (English) ed. 2005).

Without a new edition, Professor Honnold's invaluable classic, which has been identified as "the most frequently cited text on the CISG,"[2] is in danger of losing the power to communicate his wisdom. Developments that Professor Honnold himself helped set into motion threaten to overtake his work. Since the third edition of *Uniform Law* appeared in 1999, the number of Contracting States to the Convention has increased significantly.[3] During this period there has also been vast growth in the number of decisions from tribunals around the globe which have applied the CISG, an explosion of new scholarly analyses of the Convention, and remarkable developments in the research infrastructure that permits access to those materials. These developments have raised many new issues, and have deepened our understanding of (or, in some instances, effectively resolved) old ones. These and other considerations demanded an updated edition of Professor Honnold's treatise.

A new edition must build on, but not obscure, Professor Honnold's work. Future scholars and practitioners would simply find it impossible to understand some Convention issues unless Professor Honnold's original analyses, reflecting his unique understanding of the Convention's development and the issues that occupied those who drafted and finalized the text, remain accessible. That is true even where subsequent developments have arguably transcended Professor Honnold's views.[4] For this reason, substantial new textual material incorporated into the fourth edition is set in bold italics: this allows the reader to distinguish the work product of the editor of this fourth edition from text preserved from earlier editions, and thus to identify the material that carries Professor Honnold's special authority. Of course the new edition also

---

2. That is the oft-repeated description in the most comprehensive and useful of English-language CISG resources — the CISG database maintained by the Pace University Institute for International Commercial Law, available on the World Wide Web at http://www.cisg. law.pace.edu. See, e.g., the Pace Website's reference to the third edition of Professor Honnold's commentary in the 'Scholarly Writings' portion of the Annotated Tex of Article 1 at http://www.cisg.law.pace.edu/cisg/text/e-text-01.html.

3. The most recent addition to the list of Contracting States, at the time this is written, is Japan.

4. A prime example is Professor Honnold's views on the unavailability of exemption under Art. 79 of the Convention where the seller has delivered non-conforming goods. See §427 *infra*. These views produced a fruitful debate with the great German CISG scholar, Professor Peter Schlechtriem, and that debate has produced results that, in practice, achieve Professor Honnold's purposes while not necessarily adopting his specific approach. Unless Professor Honnold's views are preserved, however, the discussion of this issue in, e.g., the decision of the Bundesgerichtshof, Germany, March 24, 1999, CLOUT Case No. 271, would be difficult or impossible to fathom.

makes corrections and amendments to the text of the third edition; such changes — not involving substantial new discussion — are not indicated by special type-face.

One particular change made in the fourth edition is the elimination of the summaries of cases that Professor Honnold included at the end of substantive discussion in the third edition. Such summaries — which, given the volume of case law under the Convention that is currently accessible, would now be impractical — have been rendered obsolete by wonderful new resources (often available *gratis* online) giving access not only to CISG decisions but also to a wealth of other material relevant to understanding and interpreting the Convention.

The editor of this fourth edition can render no greater service to those interested in the Convention, and to the larger international commercial community, than to make Professor Honnold's work available in renewed and updated form.

HARRY M. FLECHTNER

Pittsburgh, Pennsylvania
2009

PREFACE TO THE THIRD EDITION

Why should you (or I) bother with a third edition? One reason is the hope that a decade for reflection, stimulated by the astonishing amount of literature on the Convention, has broadened (and chastened) this writer's views. A second, and compelling, reason is the need to engage the large and growing body of decisions interpreting the Convention.

The second edition went to press shortly after the Convention's entry into force among the first eleven States; judicial and arbitral decisions applying the Convention had not yet appeared. Now, only a decade later, more than fifty States, embracing a vast majority of the world's population and commerce, have adhered to the Convention. Hundreds of decisions applying the Convention have been reported; delays intrinsic to international reporting suggest that the total number is much greater.

Do these decisions deserve our attention? Most international transactions are completed without difficulty; however, disagreements do arise involving the parties' obligations and the consequences of breach. When this occurs, counsellors need to examine both the text of the Convention and decisions applying the law. In an important transaction it may be necessary for a party in one State to consider interpretations in other States, including those where litigation may be brought — information that can be decisive in resolving the problem.

Tribunals (judicial and arbitral) have special concerns: How should they interpret and apply the Convention? Should they be concerned with decisions in other adhering States? The answer becomes clear in the light of the Convention's central objective: the promotion of international uniformity — to avoid disputes between parties in different States and to facilitate the settlement of disputes. The Convention drives this point home in Article 7(1): interpretation of the Convention shall have regard for its "international character" and "the need to promote uniformity in its application" — language that calls for tribunals to consider interpretations in other States. One goal of this book is to help tribunals respond to this mandate.

Do tribunals respond to such a mandate? The fifty states of this writer's country have separately adopted a uniform sales law — UCC Article 2. Judicial interpretations in these fifty States (as in countries that have acceded to the Convention) are not subject to central review. And yet, recognition of the importance of uniformity has led the courts of these fifty States to consider, and give weight, to the interpretations in other States.

The volume of decisions applying the Convention, at first blush, is daunting. Under the leadership of Professor Joachim Bonell, a superb collection of decisions (UNILEX), in their original languages and usually with the complete text, already extends to over 600 pages. (This and other sources will be described later.) How can this edition provide access to this mass of case-law? A second query: How much space can be given to the astonishing outpouring of writing on the Convention? (Professor Michael Will lists two thousand "or so" items.) With this embarrassment of riches, can this edition be kept within bounds?

The reader will meet these compromises: (1) The pruning of ageing material in prior editions: e.g., discussion of domestic law and historical connections with the 1964 Hague Convention. (2) Terse statement of decisions. (Paths to full opinions and future decisions, and the wealth of literature are provided immediately following the Table of Contents under these headings: "A. Case-law: Discovery Tools"; "Analyses of CISG Case-law" and "Books and Reports." In addition to these broader compilations, throughout the book writings are noted that address specific issues. Other objectives of this work are discussed in the Preface to the Second Edition, which follows.

I hope that readers will share my enthusiasm for the Convention's success in contributing to commercial relationships and international understanding.

JOHN O. HONNOLD

Kennett Square, Pennsylvania
1998

PREFACE TO THE SECOND EDITION

Uniform law for the international sale of goods at long last is now in force in each continent and is well on the way to world-wide acceptance.

Initiatives taken a half-century ago in Europe and a decade of intensive work by the United Nations Commission on International Trade Law produced unanimous agreement on a draft Convention that in 1980 was finalized and unanimously approved by a diplomatic conference of 62 States.

Then came another decade while domestic legal, commercial and governmental bodies examined the proposed uniform law, comparing it with their domestic laws and weighing the uncertainties and dangers of change against the problems of coping in international trade with a wide variety of foreign legal systems. Further delay resulted from the difficulty of getting attention and action from domestic law-making bodies that were trying to cope with current international problems that seemed more urgent, and certainly were more exciting, than a uniform law for the international sale of goods.

Surprisingly, in various parts of the world the necessary steps for adherence were gradually completed and the Convention went into force for eleven States on January 1, 1988. This decisive step stimulated action elsewhere. By March 1991 thirty States have adhered and further adoptions were nearing completion; contrary to all reasonable expectations we can now envisage the general establishment of uniform international law for the most basic transaction of international commerce.

The first edition of this book, hammered out at white heat during the year that followed the 1980 Vienna Conference, responded to pressing questions about the law's preparation and scope and provided commentary on each article of the uniform law. Work on the first edition was aided by decades of research and writing on uniform law for international sales and by intense hands-on participation in the preparation and adoption of the Convention. However, the intensity of treatment was then subject to practical limits, including the limited patience of readers who had reason to doubt that the Convention would ever go into force.

The Convention's world-wide success calls for a more intensive treatment. The writer has devoted most of the past decade to studying, lecturing and teaching about the Convention in various national settings and, like all who work in this field, has been instructed and stimulated by an amazing outpouring of legal literature and by inquiries about the Convention's response to current commercial situations.

Perhaps the most important task of this book is to present the Convention as an organic whole. One who faces a problem in international trade probably can find an applicable article of the Convention; it is much more difficult to bring all of the relevant provisions of the law to bear on the problem.

In commercial life one faces situations, not individual articles. For example, less than half of the articles of the uniform law state the parties' duties; many of the remaining articles, in various parts of the Convention, are devoted to remedies — requiring performance, avoiding the contract, measuring damages, preserving rejected goods. Rules on rights and remedies (like scissor-blades) need to work together — a point that was driven home by working with the many concrete "examples" that are used to illustrate and test the Convention's response to problems that arise in international trade. Working with these problems also revealed important resources for resolving ambiguities and for filling "gaps" by the application of policies that underlie analogous provisions. . . .

When adoption of the Convention was under consideration a natural response was to fear the worst: What were the most inept solutions that the words of the text could bear? Now, as after the birth of a child, we need to emphasize ways to nurture the new life. When the decisions embodied in the law's words permit a choice we ask this question: Which choice is more consistent with other provisions of the Convention and with its objectives? Others will develop different answers; a continuing dialogue, spanning legal and economic backgrounds, can play a vital role in the development of this epoch-making uniform international law.

JOHN O. HONNOLD

Philadelphia
March 1991

ABOUT THE AUTHOR

John O. Honnold is Schnader Professor of Commercial Law Emeritus at the University of Pennsylvania Law School. A renowned scholar of commercial law, he is former Chief of the United Nations International Trade Law Branch and Secretary of the United Nations Commission on International Trade Law "UNCITRAL"). Under his leadership UNCITRAL began the project that culminated in the United Nations Convention on Contracts for the International Sale of Goods ("CISG"), the most broadly-accepted and successful attempt to create uniform international substantive commercial law, and he represented the United States at the 1980 Vienna diplomatic conference at which the text of the CISG was approved. His treatise *Uniform Law for International Sales under the 1980 United Nations Convention* has been identified as "the most frequently cited text on the CISG." Professor Honnold is a graduate of the University of Illinois and received his law degree from Harvard Law School.

Harry M. Flechtner has been a member of the faculty of the University of Pittsburgh School of Law since 1984. He teaches contracts and commercial law subjects, and has published extensively on international and domestic commercial law, with particular emphasis on international sales law. He has been cited by the Solicitor General of the United States as "one of the leading academic authorities on the [United Nations Sales] Convention," and speaks frequently on commercial law topics at academic and professional conferences and symposia. Professor Flechtner is a four-time winner of the University of Pittsburgh Law School's Excellence-in-Teaching Award, and has received the Chancellor's Teaching Award from the University of Pittsburgh. He serves as a National Correspondent for the United States at the United Nations Commission on International Trade Law ("UNCITRAL"). He is a graduate of Harvard College, and received his J.D. from Harvard Law School and an M.A. in literature from Harvard University.

SUMMARY OF CONTENTS

[Indexing and cross-references (except for end-pages) are based on section numbers. These appear at the top and margins of the pages; pages are numbered at the bottom.]

I. OVERVIEW

II. COMMENTARY

TABLE OF CONTENTS

[Indexing and cross-references (except for end-pages) are based on section numbers. These appear at the top and margins of the pages; pages are numbered at the bottom.]

CONTENTS

II. COMMENTARY

PART I: SPHERE OF APPLICATION AND GENERAL PROVISIONS

CHAPTER I: SPHERE OF APPLICATION

CHAPTER II: GENERAL PROVISIONS

PART II: FORMATION OF THE CONTRACT

PART III: SALE OF GOODS

CHAPTER I: GENERAL PROVISIONS

CONTENTS

CHAPTER II: OBLIGATIONS OF THE SELLER

SECTION I:
DELIVERY OF THE GOODS AND HANDING OVER OF
DOCUMENTS

SECTION II:
CONFORMITY OF THE GOODS AND THIRD-PARTY CLAIMS

CONTENTS

CONTENTS

SECTION II:
TAKING DELIVERY

SECTION III.
REMEDIES FOR BREACH OF CONTRACT BY THE BUYER

CHAPTER IV: PASSING OF RISK

CONTENTS

CHAPTER V: PROVISIONS COMMON TO THE OBLIGATIONS OF THE SELLER AND OF THE BUYER

SECTION I: ANTICIPATORY BREACH AND INSTALMENT CONTRACTS

SECTION II: DAMAGES

SECTION III: INTEREST

SECTION IV: EXEMPTIONS

SECTION V: EFFECTS OF AVOIDANCE

CONTENTS

PART IV: FINAL PROVISIONS

RESEARCH RESOURCES; BIBLIOGRAPHIC NOTES AND ABBREVIATIONS

I.   Resources for Research

The text of the Convention is available from the website of its sponsoring organization, the United Nations Commission on International Trade Law (UNCITRAL), at <www.uncitral.org/pdf/english/texts/sales/cisg/CISG.pdf>. There exist a wealth of resources in aid of interpretation of the Convention, including legislative history materials (*travaux préparatoires*), scholarly commentary, and decisions from tribunals around the world that have applied the CISG. One of the most important developments associated with the Convention is the appearance of an extensive, innovative and easy-to use research infrastructure providing access (often online and *gratis*) to such materials. For elaboration, see §88 and §93 *infra*.

II.   Bibliographic Notes; Abbreviations

A.   Books and Reports

Prefatory Note: Works frequently cited are given a short title that appears in italics below, followed by fuller references.

A.B.A. Report — American Bar Association Report on the 1980 Sales Convention to the House of Delegates, 18 Int'l Law. 39 (1984).

Aix-en-Prov. Colloq. — Les Ventes Internationales de Marchandises. Paris: Economica, 1981.

AJCL UNCITRAL Symposium — "UNCITRAL's First Decade," 27 American Journal of Comparative Law 201–563 (1979).

Anson — A. G. Guest, ed. W. R. Anson's Law of Contract. 26th ed. Oxford: Clarendon, 1984.

Atiyah — P. Atiyah, The Sale of Goods. 7th ed. London: Pitman, 1985.

Atiyah, Freedom of Contract — P. Atiyah, The Rise and Fall of Freedom of Contract. Oxford: Clarendon, 1979.

Audit — B. Audit, La Vente Internationale de Marchandises, Paris: L.G.D.J., 1990.

Barrera Graf—J. Barrera Graf, La Regamentacion Uniforme de las Compraventas Internacionales de Mercaderias. Mexico: 1965.

Barrera Graf Colloquium—see *Mexico Coloq.*

Barrera-Graf Festschrift—Homenaje a Jorge Barrera Graf. México: Universidad Nac. Aut. de Mexico, 1989.

B-B Commentary—C. Bianca & M. Bonell *et al.*, Commentary on the International Sales Law: The 1980 Vienna Sales Convention. Milan: Guiffré, 1987.

Baden bei Wien Colloq.—Das UNCITRAL-Kaufrecht im Vergleich Zum österreichischem Recht, Symposium Baden-bei-Wien, April 1983. P. Doralt, ed. Wien: Manzche, 1985.

Benjamin—Benjamin's Sale of Goods, A. Guest, ed., 3d ed. London: Sweet & Maxwell, 1987.

Bielefeld Colloq.—See *Transnational Law.*

Bridge, Sale—M. G. Bridge, Sale of Goods. Toronto: Butterworths (1988).

Bridge, International Sale of Goods—Michael Bridge, The International Sale of Goods: Law and Practice (1999).

Canadian Sales Unification (1982)—Uniform Law Conference of Canada, Report No. 38, Institute of Legal Research and Reform, Edmonton, Canada: 1982.

Cheshire, F. & F.—G. Cheshire, C. Fifoot and M. Furmston, The Law of Contract. 11th ed. London: Butterworths, 1986.

Comp. Sales (I.C.L.Q.)—British Institute of International and Comparative Law. Some Comparative Aspects of the Law Relating to Sale of Goods (January 1964 London Symposium), International and Comparative Law Quarterly, Supplementary Publication No. 9 (1964).

Com. I—Report of the First Committee of the 1980 Sales Conference. A/Conf. 97/11: Published in *Records 1980 Conf., O.R.* 83–141, *Docy. Hist.* 655–724.

Contract Law Today—D. Harris & D. Tallon, eds., Contract Law Today, Anglo-French Comparisons. Oxford: Clarendon, 1989.

Corbin—A. Corbin on Contracts, St. Paul: West (1 vol. 1952, 8 vols. 1963).

Cornell Symposium—Symposium; Convention on the International Sale of Goods, Cornell International Law Journal, Vol. 21, pp. 419–589 (1988).

David, French Law—R. David, French Law, Its Structure, Sources and Methodology, Trans. M. Kindred, Baton Rouge, La.: Louisiana State University, 1972.

David, Unification — R. David, The International Unification of Private Law, International Encyclopedia of Comparative Law, vol. 2, chapter 5. Tübingen: Mohr 1971.

Dawson — J. Dawson, The Oracles of the Law. Ann Arbor: University of Michigan Law School, 1968.

Docy. Hist. — J. Honnold, Documentary History of the Uniform Law for International Sales. Deventer/Boston: Kluwer (1989).

Dölle, Kommentar — H. Dölle *et al.* Kommentar zum Einheitlichen Kaufrecht. München: Beck, 1976.

Dubrovnik Lectures — International Sale of Goods: Dubrovnik Lectures. P. Sarcevic & P. Volken, eds. New York: Oceana, 1986.

Enderlein & Maskow Commentary — Fritz Enderlein & Dietrich Maskow, International Sales Law: United Nations Convention on Contracts for the International Sale of Goods; Convention on the Limitation Period in the International Sale of Goods (1992).

Farnsworth, Contracts — E. A. Farnsworth, Contracts. Boston: Little, Brown, 1982.

Fawcett, Harris & Bridge, Sale and Conflict of Laws — James J. Fawcett, Jonathan M. Harris, Michael Bridge, International Sale of Goods in the Conflict of Laws (2005).

Feltham, JBL — J. Feltham, The United Nations Convention on Contracts for the International Sale of Goods, [1981] Journal of Business Law 346.

Finnish Reports, 1986 Comp. L. Cong. — Finnish National Reports to the Twelfth Congress of the International Academy of Comparative Law. Ed., K. Baare-Hagglund. Helsinki, IICUH: 1986. Report by Sevón, on interpretation of CISG, at 11–26.

Force Majeure (I.A.L.S.) — Some Problems of Non-Performance and *Force Majeure* in International Contracts of Sale (I.A.L.S. Colloquium, Helsinki, June 1960) Helsinki: Inst. Iur. Comp. Univ. Hensingiensis, 1961.

Freiburg Colloq. — P. Schlechtriem, ed., Einheitliches Kaufrecht and Nationales Obligationenrecht. Baden-Baden: Nomos, 1987.

Fridman — G. Fridman, Sale of Goods in Canada. 2d ed. Toronto: Carswell, 1979.

German National Reports, 1986 Comp. L. Cong. — German National Reports (Private and Civil Law Procedure), XIIth International Congress of Comparative Law, Baden-Baden: Nomos, 1987. Report by Schlechtriem at 121–149.

Giles — O. C. Giles, Uniform Commercial Law. Leyden: Sijthoff, 1970.

Graveson, C. & G. — R. H. Graveson, F. I. Cohn and D. Graveson. The Uniform Laws on International Sales Act 1967, A Commentary. London: Butterworths, 1968.

Gutteridge — H. Gutteridge, Comparative Law. 2d ed. Cambridge: University Press, 1974.

Hager — G. Hager, Die Rechtsbehelfe des Verkäufers wegen Nichtabnahme der Ware nach amerikanischem, deutschem and Einheitlichen Haager Kaufrecht. Frankfurt a.m.: Metzner, 1975.

Hague-Zagreb Essays — International Sales, C. Voskuil & J. Wade, eds. (1983).

Hamel Festschrift (1961) — Dix Ans des Conferences d'Aggregation; Etudes de Droit Commercial offertes à Joseph Hamel. Paris: 1961.

Hamel Festschrift (1974) — Dix Ans des Conferences d'Aggregation; Etudes de Droit Commercial offertes à Joseph Hamel. Paris: 1974.

Hartley — T. Hartley, A Study of the Uniform Law on the International Sale of Goods. Brussels: Commission of the European Communities, 1979.

Honnold, Documentary History — See *Docy. Hist.*

Honnold, Gen. Rep. 1986 Comp. L. Cong. — *reprinted, in substance, in Freiburg Colloq., supra*, at pp. 115–147. See General Reports, Twelfth International Congress of Comparative Law: Sydney, Melbourne (forthcoming).

Honnold, Sales — J. Honnold, Cases and Materials on the Law of Sales and Sales Financing. 5th ed. Mineola, N.Y.: Foundation, 1984.

Honnold, Life of the Law — J. Honnold, The Life of the Law, Readings on the Growth of Legal Institutions, London: Free Press; Collier Macmillan (1964).

Hjerner Festschrift — Festkrift till Lars Hjerner; Studies in International Law (Ed. J. Ramberg *et al.*). Stockholm: Norstedts, 1990.

Incoterms 1990 — International Chamber of Commerce, International Rules for the Interpretation of Trade Terms (I.C.C. Pub. No. 460, Paris 1990), (*Incoterms 1990* replaces I.C.C. Pub. No. 350 (1980)).

Incoterms Guide — International Chamber of Commerce, Guide to Incoterms (Prepared by Prof. Jan Ramberg) Paris: ICC Services, S.A.R.L., 2d ed., 1980. (Guide to Incoterms 1990 in process).

Intro. Swedish L. — S. Strömholm, ed., An Introduction to Swedish Law, Stockholm: P. A. Norstedt, 1981.

Int. Enc. Comp. L. — International Encyclopedia of Comparative Law. Tubingen: Mohr (Siebeck), multi-volume.

Kritzer Guide — A. H. Kritzer, Guide to Practical Applications of the U.N. Convention on Contracts for the International Sale of Goods, Deventer (Neth.) & Boston: Kluwer, 1989.

Kritzer Manual — A. H. Kritzer, International Contract Manual, Contract Checklists. Deventer; Boston: Kluwer, 1990 (loose-leaf).

Lausanne Colloq. — The 1980 Vienna Convention on the International Sale of Goods Lausanne Colloquium of November 1984. Institut suisse de droit comparé. Zurich: Schulthless, 1985.

Lookofsky, Understanding CISG in the USA — Joseph Lookofsky, Understanding the CISG in the USA: A Compact Guide to the 1980 United Nations Convention on Contracts for the International Sale of Goods (2nd ed. 2004).

Manual of German Law — E. J. Cohn, Manual of German Law. Br. Inst. of Int. & Comp. L., 2d ed. Oceana, 1971.

Merryman & Clark — J. Merryman & D. Clark, Comparative Law: Western European and Latin American Legal Systems. Indianapolis: Bobbs-Merrill, 1978.

Mertens & Rehbinder — H. J. Mertens & E. Rehbinder Internationales Kaufrecht: Kommentar z.d. Einheitliches Kaufgesetzen. Frankfurt: Metzner, 1975.

Mexico Coloq. — Coloquio Internacional de Derecho Mercantil, Univ. Mexico, Anuario Jurídico, Vol. X pp. 11–212 (1983).

Netherlands National Reports, 1986 Comp. L. Cong. — Netherlands Reports to the Twelfth International Congress of Comparative Law. Eds., P. H. M. Gerver, *et al.* The Hague, Asser Institute (1987). Report by van der Velden, on interpretation of CISG, at 22–45.

New Directions — UNIDROIT, New Directions in International Trade Law (Second Congress on Private Law, September 1976). Dobbs Ferry, N.Y.: Oceana, 1977.

Nicholas, French Law of Contract — B. Nicholas, French Law of Contract, London: Butterworths, 1982.

Nicholas, LQR (1988) — B. Nicholas, The Vienna Convention on International Sales Law, 105 L.Q. Rev. 201–243 (1989).

Northwestern Symposium — Symposium: Reflections on the International Unification of Sales Law, Northwestern Journal of International Law & Business, Vol. 8 pp. 531–639 (1988).

Ont. L. Ref. Com., Sales — Ontario Law Reform Commission, Report on Sale of Goods. Ontario: Ministry of the Attorney General, Ontario, Canada, 1979. 3 Vols.

O.R. — Also abbreviated as *Records 1980 Conf., infra.*

Ottawa Colloque — L. Perret & N. Lacasse, eds., Actes du Colloque sur la Vente Internationale. Montreal: W & L, 1989.

Palandt — Palandt, Bürgerliches Gesetzbuch. P. Bassenge, *et al.*, eds. 49th ed. München: C. H. Beck, 1990.

Parker Colloq. — International Sales: The U.N. Convention on Contracts for the International Sale of Goods, N. Galston & H. Smit, eds. New York: Matthew Bender, 1984.

Pelichet, 1986 PIL Convention — M. Pelichet, La Vente Internationale de Marchandises et le Conflit de Lois, Receuil des Cours, Académie de Droit international, Vol. 1987-I, Dordrecht: Nijhoff, 1988.

Pittsburgh Symposium — Symposium on the 1980 Sales Convention, University of Pittsburgh School of Law, Journal of Law & Commerce, Vol. 8, pp. 1–243 (1988).

Polish Reports, 1986 Comp. L. Cong. — Rapports Polonais Présentés au Douzième Congrès International de Droit Comparè. Wroclaw. Académie Polonaise des Sciences, 1986. Report by Rajski, on interpretation of CISG, at 45–54.

Potsdam Colloq. — Problems of Unification of International Sales Law, International Association of Legal Science, Potsdam 1979, Digest of Commercial Laws. London/Rome/New York: Oceana, 1980.

Quebec Civ. Code Revn., Obligations — Quebec, Civil Code Revision Office (Vol. XXX), Committee on the Law of Obligations, Report on Obligation. Montreal: 1975.

Quebec Civ. Code Revn., Sales — Quebec, Civil Code Revision Office (Vol. XXXI), Committee on the Contract of Sale, Report on Sale. Montreal: 1975.

Rabel, Conflicts — E. Rabel, Conflict of Laws, A Comparative Study. 2d. ed. prepared by U. Drobnig, Ann Arbor: University of Michigan Law School, 1958.

Rabel, Gesammelte Aufsätze — H. Leser, ed., Tübingen: Mohr, 1965–1967, v.2.

Rabel, Warenkauf — E. Rabel, Das Recht des Warenkaufs. Berlin: W. de Gruyter, v.1, 1936; v.2, 1958.

Rechtsvergleichung — R., Europarecht and Staatenintegration, Eds. G. Lüke *et al.*, Köln, Heymanns: 1983.

Records 1964 Conf. — Diplomatic Conference on the Unification of Law Governing the International Sale of Goods, The Hague, 2–25 April 1964, Records and Documents of the Conference (2 Vols.) The Hague: Ministry of Justice of the Netherlands, 1966.

Records 1980 Conf. — United Nations Conference on Contracts for the International Sale of Goods, Vienna, 10 March–11 April 1980, Official Records. A/CONF.97/19. United Nations, Vienna 1981, Sales No. E.81.IV.3) (*O.R.*); relevant parts reproduced in J. Honnold, Documentary History of the Uniform Law for International Sales (1989), cited as *Docy. Hist., supra.*

Register — Register of Texts of Conventions and other Instruments Concerning International Trade Law. Vol. I — Sales; International Payments. United Nations, 1971: E.71.V.3. Vol. II — Arbitration; Shipping. United Nations, 1973; E.73. V.3.

Rep. S-G — Report of the Secretary-General of the United Nations, a designation that extends to studies and recommendations prepared by the Secretariat of UNCITRAL.

Report, 1985 [1986] PIL Convention — Explanatory Report by Arthur T. von Mehren, 1985 Hague Draft Convention on the Law Applicable to Contracts for the International Sale of Goods. Hague Conference on P.I.L., 1987.

Restatement, Second of Contracts — American Law Institute, Restatement of the Law of Contracts, Second. St. Paul, Minnesota: American Law Institute Publications, 1981.

Rheinstein Festschrift — E. von Caemmerer, *et al.* eds., Ius Privatum Gentium. Festschrift für Max Rheinstein. Tübingen: J. C. B. Mohr (Paul Siebeck) 1969. 2 vols.

Sales Unification — see *Potsdam Colloq.*

Sauveplanne Festschrift — Unification and Comparative Law in Theory and Practice, Deventer: Kluwer, 1984.

Scan. Stud. — Scandinavian Studies in Law. F. Schmidt, ed., Faculty of Law Stockholm U., Stockholm: Almqvist; (Annual volumes).

Schlechtriem (1981) — P. Schlechtriem, Einheitliches UN-Kaufrecht. Tübingen: Mohr (Siebeck), 1981.

Schlechtriem, 1986 Commentary or *Schlechtriem (1986)* — P. Schlechtriem, Uniform Sales Law — The UN-Convention on Contracts for the International Sale of Goods. Vienna: Manzsche, 1986 (English translation of 1981 commentary, *supra.*)

Schlechtriem, CISG Commentary — Commentary on the UN Convention on the International Sale of Goods (CISG) (Peter Schlechtriem ed., 2nd ed. (in translation) 1998). (1st English ed. 1998).

Schlechtriem & Schwenzer, CISG Commentary (2nd English ed. 2005) — Commentary on the UN Convention on the International Sale of Goods (CISG) (Peter Schlechtriem & Ingeborg Schwenzer eds., 2nd (English) ed. 2005).

Schlesinger, et al., Comparative Law (1988) — R. Schlesinger, H. Baade, M. Damaska, P. Herzog, Comparative Law, 5th ed. Mineola, N.Y. Foundation, 1988.

Schlesinger, Formation — R. Schlesinger, *et al.*, Formation of Contract, A Study of the Common Core of Legal Systems. Dobbs Ferry, N.Y.: Oceana, 1968. 2 Vols.

Schmitthoff's Essays, — C-J Cheng, ed., Clive M. Schmitthoff's Select Essays on International Trade Law, Dordrecht etc., Nijhoff/Graham, 1989.

Schmitthoff, Sources — C. Schmitthoff, ed., The Sources of the Law of International Trade, New York: Praeger, 1964.

Schmitthoff, Festschrift — F. Fabricius, ed., Law and International Trade. Festschrift für Clive M. Schmitthoff, Frankfort a. M.: Athenäum, 1973.

Secretariat Commentary or Sec. Commy. — Commentary prepared by the U.N. Secretariat on the 1978 Draft Convention on Contracts for the International Sale of Goods. A/CONF. 97/5, *Records 1980 Conf.,* (*O.R.*), 14–66, *Docy. Hist.* 404–456.

Sources — K. Zweigert and J. Kropholler, Sources of International Trade Law, Vol. I: Private and Commercial Law. Leiden: Sijthoff, 1971.

SR — Summary Records of the meetings of the First Committee (*C.1*) of the 1980 Sales Conference: *SR.1 refers to the records of the first meeting, 10 March 1980: A/CONF. 97/C.1/SR.1;* records of succeeding meetings are cited as *SR.2*, etc. The Summary Records appear in *Records 1980 Conf. (O.R.)* 236–433, *Docy. Hist.* 457–654.

Transnational Law: Bielefeld Colloq. — The Transnational Law of International Commercial Transactions, N. Horn & C. Schmitthoff, eds. Deventer: Kluwer, 1982.

Treitel, Contract — G. Treitel, The Law of Contract. 7th ed. London: Stevens, 1987.

Treitel, Remedies (Int. Enc.) — G. Treitel, "Remedies for Breach of Contract," in International Encyclopedia of Comparative Law, Vol. 7, Ch. 16. The Hague: Mouton; Tübingen: Mohr, 1976.

Treitel, Remedies (1988) — G. Treitel, Remedies for Breach of Contract, A Comparative Account. Oxford: Clarendon, 1988.

Tunc, Commentary — A. Tunc, Commentary on the Hague Conventions of the 1st of July 1964 (ULIS and ULF) in *I Records 1964 Conf.,* 355–391.

UNCITRAL 1 — United Nations Commission on International Trade Law, Report on First Session, 1968, General Assembly, Official

Records (A/33/17). Reports on the Second and succeeding sessions are cited *UNCITRAL II*, etc. *Docy. Hist.* at p. 8 gives the U.N. document-numbers and *Yearbook* citations for these reports.

UNCITRAL Legal Guide, Industrial Works — UNCITRAL Legal Guide on Drawing Up International Contracts for the Construction of Industrial Works. United Nations, N.Y., 1988 (A/CN.9/SER.B/2, Sales No. E.87.V.10).

UNCITRAL Texts, 1986 — UNCITRAL, United Nations, N.Y., 1986. (ISBN 92-1-133284-2; includes texts of conventions and other international rules.)

UNIDROIT 1987 Congress — International Institute for the Unification of Private Law (UNIDROIT), International Uniform Law in Practice, New York: Oceana & Rome. Unidroit, 1988.

Unification Symposium 1964 — J. Honnold, ed., Unification of the Law Governing International Sales of Goods (I.A.L.S. Colloquium N.Y., 1964). Paris: Dalloz, 1966.

Vendita Int. — La Vendita Internazionale. Milan: Guiffre, 1981.

vC-S Kommentar (1990) — von Caemmerer/Schlechtriem, Kommentar zum Einleitlichen UN-Kaufrecht (P. Schlechtriem, Ed.; contributions by 10 authors). Munich: C. H. Beck (1990).

von Mehren — See *Report, 1985 [1986] Hague Convention.*

von Mehren & Gordley — A. von Mehren and J. Gordley, The Civil Law System. 2d ed. Boston: Little Brown, 1977.

von Caemmerer Festschrift (1973) — H. G. Leser & W. F. Marschall von Bieberstein, eds. Das Hagger Einheitliche Kaufgesetz und das deutsche Schuldrecht. Karlsruhe: Muller, 1973.

von Caemmerer Festschrift (1978). — H. C. Ficker *et al.*, eds., Festschrift für Ernst von Caemmerer zum 70 Geburtstag. Tübingen: Mohr, 1978.

Weidring Conf. — L. Lafili *et al.*, Survey of the International Sale of Goods. Deventer: Kluwer, 1986.

Weitnauer Festgabe — H. Ehmann *et al.*, eds. Berlin: Duncker & Humblot 1980. Privatautonomie, Eigentum and Verantwortung. Festgbe für Hermann Weitnauer.

White & Summers — J. J. White & R. S. Summers, Handbook on the Law under the Uniform Commercial Code. 3d ed. St. Paul: West, 1988.

Williston, Sales — S. Williston, The Law Governing Sales of Goods, at Common Law and under the Uniform Sales Act. 3d ed. New York: Baker, Voorhis, 1948. (This work has valuable background on the Uniform Sales Act, of which Prof. S. Williston was the draftsman.

The third edition is the last in which Prof. Williston actively participated.)

W/G 1 — UNCITRAL Working Group on the International Sale of Goods, Report on First Session, 5–16 January 1970. A/CN.9/35, I *Yearbook* 176, *Docy. Hist.* 14–40. Reports on the Second and succeeding sessions are cited *W/G2*, etc. and are reproduced in *Docy. Hist., supra.*

YB — see *Yearbook, infra.*

Yearbook — United Nations Commission on International Trade Law, Yearbook (Yearly volumes in English (E.), French (F.), Spanish (S.) and Russian (R.), Vol. 1: 1968–1970 (U.N.N.Y. 1971, Doc. A/CN.9 SER.A1970. Publications Sales Number: E.71, V.1). The various volumes are cited as I *Yearbook*, or *YB*. (*Docy. Hist.* at p. 7 gives the dates and U.N. document-numbers for these volumes).

Yntema Festschrift — American Journal of Comparative Law, XXth Century Comparative and Conflicts Law; Legal Essays in honor of Hessel E. Yntema. Leyden: Sijthoff, 1961.

Ziegel & Foster — J. Ziegel and W. Foster, eds., Aspects of Comparative Commercial Law. Montreal: McGill University; Dobbs Ferry, N.Y.; Oceana, 1969.

Zweigert & Kötz — K. Zweigert and H. Kötz, An Introduction to Comparative Law. Trans. by T. Weir. Amsterdam: North Holland, 1977.

Zweigert & Kötz II (1987) — K. Zweigert & H. Kötz, Introduction to Comparative Law, Vol. II — The Institutions of Private Law. Translated by T. Weir. Oxford: Clarendon, 1987.

B. Conventions, Statutes, Statements of Principles and General Conditions

CMEA General Conditions — General Conditions of Delivery of Goods between Organizations of the Member Countries of the Council for Mutual Economic Assistance, 1968. Reproduced in I *Register* 72 and *Sources* 172. For a later version see I. Szasz, The CMEA Uniform Law for International Sales (1985).

Finnish Sales Act (1987) — Sale of Goods Act, Finland, 27 March 1987/355 (translation, 1990, Ministry of Justice.)

French Civ. Code — The French Civil Code. Trans. with an introd. by John H. Crabb. South Hackensack, N.J.: F. B. Rothman, 1977.

GAFTA — Grain and Feed Trade Association, Baltic Exchange Chambers, 28 St. Mary AXE, London, EC3A, 8EP. (Standard Contracts are cited by number, *E.g.*, GAFTA *No. 30*, Contract for Canadian and United States Grain in Bulk.)

GDR Int. Comm. Contracts Act — German Democratic Republic, International Commercial Contracts Act (I.C.C.A.) of 1976 (German-English texts, Staatsverlag D.D.R. (G.D.R.) Berlin, 1979).

General Conditions (ECE) Durable Consumer Goods — General Conditions of Sale for the Import and Export of Durable Consumer Goods and other Engineering Stock Articles, No. 730, Prepared under the auspices of the United Nations Economic Commission for Europe, Geneva, March 1961 (U.N. Publ.61. II.E/Mim.12), *reprinted in Sources* 149–153.

General Conditions (ECE) Plant and Machinery — General Conditions for the Supply of Plant and Machinery for Export, No. 188, Prepared under the auspices of the United Nations Economic Commission for Europe, Geneva, March 1953 (U.N. Publ.ME/188 bis/53), *reprinted in Sources* 90–97. Another version of this contract: No. 188A (March 1957; Supply and Erection, *reprinted in Sources* 98–108.

General Conditions (ECE) Potatoes — General Conditions of Sale For Potatoes (1980) (ECE/AGRI/42, Sales No. E.79.II.E.30). Other general conditions in this series include: Fresh Fruit and Vegetables Including Citrus Fruit (1979) (ECE/AGRI/40; Sales No. E.79.II.E.21); Dry and Dried Fruit (1979) (ECE/AGRI/41; Sales No. E.79.II.E.15).

Hague Formation Convention (1964) — Convention Relating to a Uniform Law on the Formation of Contracts for the International Sale of Goods, Diplomatic Conference, The Hague, April 2–25, 1964. The Uniform Law on the Formation of Contracts for the International Sale of Goods (ULF) is Annex I to the Convention. The Convention and Uniform Law (ULF) are set forth *infra* as Appendix D and are reproduced in *Register* (Eng., Fr., Sp., Russ.) and in *Sources* (Eng., Fr., Ger.).

Hague Sales Convention (1964) — Convention Relating to a Uniform Law on the International Sale of Goods, Diplomatic Conference, The Hague, April 2–25, 1964. The Uniform Law on the International Sale of Goods (ULIS) appears as an Annex to the Convention. The Convention and Uniform Law (ULIS) are set forth *infra* as Appendix E and are reproduced in I *Register* (Eng., Fr., Sp., Russ.) and in *Sources* (Eng., Fr., Ger.).

Hague 1986 PIL Convention—Convention on the Law Applicable to Contracts for the International Sale of Goods, Hague Conference on Private International Law, The Hague. A Conference held at the Hague in October 1985 prepared a "Draft Convention." On December 22, 1986, the Draft Convention received its first signature (Czechoslovakia) and thereupon was termed the "*1986* Hague Convention on the Law Applicable to Contracts for the International Sale of Goods." Reproduced in Hague Conference on P.I.L., *Receuil* (Collection of Conventions) (1951–1988) 326, 15 Int. Leg. Mat. 1575.

Int. Leg. Mat.—International Legal Materials (Washington, D.C.: American Society of International Law: Bimonthly).

Israeli Contracts Law—Contracts (General Part) Law, 5733-1973, 27 Laws of the State of Israel, 5733.

Israeli Sales Law—Sales Law, 5728-1968; 22 Laws of the State of Israel 107.

Limitation Convention (1974)—Convention on the Limitation Period in the International Sale of Goods, United Nations, N.Y., June 14, 1974; Official Records, p. 101, United Nations Conference on Prescription (Limitation) in the International Sale of Goods, N.Y., 1974, A/CONF. 63/16, U.N. Pub. E.74.V.8.

Principles of European Contract Law—The Commission of European Contract Law, Principles of European Contract Law: Parts I and II Combined and Revised (Ole Lando & Hugh Beale, eds., 2003).

Swedish Contract Act—Swedish Act of June 11, 1915, on the Conclusion of Contracts and other Legal Acts in the Field of Rights of Property. Similar Acts have been enacted in Denmark (1917), Finland (1929), Iceland (1936) and Norway (1918). Translations appear in *UNIDROIT Yearbook: 1961* 191 (Eng.) and in *Sources* (Eng., Fr., Ger.).

Swedish Sales Act—Swedish Act of June 20, 1905, Relating to the Purchase and Exchange of Goods. Similar acts have been enacted in Denmark (1906), Iceland (1911, 1922), and Norway (1907). Translations appear in *UNIDROIT Yearbook: 1961* 203 (Eng.) and in *Sources* (Eng., Fr., Ger.). This Act and similar sales laws in the other Scandinavian States are in the course of being superseded by new laws influenced by the 1980 Sales Convention.

UNIDROIT Principles 2004—International Institute for the Unification of Private Law, UNIDROIT Principles of International Commercial Contracts 2004 (2004).

(U.K.) SGA (1893) — Sale of Goods Act 1893, 56 & 57 Vict. c. 71 as amended 1973. (References are usually given to the 1893 Act, since it was the basis for legislation in force in many other countries. Where relevant, reference is made to (U.K.) Sale of Goods Act 1979. Proposals for revision (See *Ont. L. Ref. Com., supra*) are sometimes discussed in reference to the section-numbers of (U.K.) SGA (1893), although the version under discussion may have different numbering.

ULF — Uniform Law on the Formation of Contracts for the International Sale of Goods (1964), annexed to the *Hague Formation Convention (1964), supra*. The Convention and ULF are set forth, *infra*, as Appendix D, and are reproduced in I *Register* (Eng., Fr., Sp., Russ.) and in *Sources* (Eng., Fr., Ger.).

ULIS — Uniform Law on the International Sale of Goods (1964), Annexed to the *Hague Sales Convention (1964), supra*. The Convention and ULIS are set forth, *infra*, as Appendix E, and are reproduced in I *Register* (Eng., Fr., Sp., Russ.) and in *Sources* (Eng., Fr., Ger.).

(U.S.A.) UCC — Uniform Commercial Code, prepared by the American Law Institute and the National Conference of Commissioners on Uniform State Laws. The UCC has been adopted (subject to local variations) by 49 of the 50 States and in part by Louisiana. The UCC has been enacted by the United States Congress for the District of Columbia and the Virgin Islands.

Vienna Convention on the Law of Treaties (1969) — U.N. Doc. A/CONF.39/27, *reprinted in* 8 Int. Legal Mat. 679 (1969) and 63 Am. J. Int. L. 875 (1969).

C. Chapters, Articles and Other

CISG-AC Opinion — CISG Advisory Council, CISG-AC Opinions, *available online at* <www.cisgac.com/default.php?sid=128>.

Ferrari, Scope of Application — Franco Ferrari, *Scope of application: Articles 4–5, in* The Draft Uncitral Digest and Beyond: Cases, Analysis and Unresolved Issues in the U.N. Sales Convention 96 (Franco Ferrari, Harry Flechtner & Ronald A. Brand eds., 2004).

Ferrari, Sphere of Application — Franco Ferrari, *The CISG's sphere of application: Articles 1–3 and 10, in* The Draft Unicitral Digest and Beyond: Cases, Analysis and Unresolved Issues in the U.N. Sales Convention 21 (Franco Ferrari, Harry Flechtner & Ronald Brand eds., 2004).

Flechtner, Manufacturers' Warranties — Harry M. Flechtner, *Enforcing Manufacturers' Warranties, "Pass Through" Warranties, and the Like: Can the Buyer Get a Refund?*, 50 Rutgers L. Rev. 397 (1998).

Rimke, Force Majeure and Hardship — Joern Rimke, *Force majeure and hardship: Application in international trade practice with specific regard to the CISG and the UNIDROIT Principles of International Commercial Contract, in* Pace Review of the Convention on Contracts for the International Sale of Goods 197 (1999–2000).

UNCITRAL Digest — UNCITRAL Digest of case law on the United Nations Convention on the International Sale of Goods, available on the UNCITRAL website at <www.uncitral.org/uncitral/en/case_law/digests/cisg.html>.

D. Periodicals

Am. J. Comp. L.	American Journal of Comparative Law
Arc. Civ. Praxis	Archiv für die Civilistsche Praxis
Ark. L. Rev.	Arkansas Law Review
Austral. Bus. L. Rev.	Australian Business Law Review
Bus. Lawyer	Business Lawyer
Camb. L.J.	Cambridge Law Journal
Can. Bus. L.J.	Canadian Business Law Journal
Can. Bar. Rev.	Canadian Bar Review
Cle. Sta. L. Rev.	Cleveland State Law Review
Colum. J. Transn. L.	Columbia Journal of Transnational Law
Colum. L. Rev.	Columbia Law Review
Cornell L. Rev.	Cornell Law Review
Dr. et Pr. Comm. Int.	Droit et Pratique du Commerce International
Duke Bar Assn. J.	Duke Bar Association Journal
Duke L.J.	Duke Law Journal
Ga. J. Int. & Comp. L.	Georgia Journal of International and Comparative Law
Harv. L. Rev.	Harvard Law Review
Int. Bus. L.J.	International Business Law Journal; Revue de Droit des Affaires Internationales (Parallel texts, English & French)
Int. Contract L. & F. Rev.	International Contract Law and Finance Review
Int. & Comp. L.Q.	International and Comparative Law Quarterly
Int. Law.	International Lawyer
Int. Rev. L. & Ec.	International Review of Law and Economics

Int. Tr. L.J.	International Trade Law Journal
J. Bus. L.	Journal of Business Law
J. Comp. Legis.	Journal of Comparative Legislation
J. D. I.	Journal du Droit International
J. Int. L. and Policy	Journal of International Law and Policy
Law & Cont. Pr. L.Q.	Law and Contemporary Problems Law Quarterly
Lloyd's Mar. & Comp. L.Q.	Lloyd's Maritime and Comparative Law Quarterly
L.Q. Rev.	Law Quarterly Review
La. L. Rev.	Louisiana Law Review
McGill L.J.	McGill Law Journal
Mich. L. Rev.	Michigan Law Review
Minn. L. Rev.	Minnesota Law Review
Mod. L. Rev.	Modern Law Review
N. Car. L. Rev.	North Carolina Law Review
Neth. Int. L. Rev.	Netherlands International Law Review
N.W.J.L. & Bus.	Northwestern Journal of Law and Business
Rabels Z.	Rabels Zeitschrift für ausländisches and internationales Privatrecht
Rev. Jur. Univ. Puerto Rico	Revista Juridica de la Universidad de Puerto Rico
Rev. Int. Dr. Comp.	Revue Internationale du Droit Comparé
Riv. Dir. Int. Pr. & Proc.	Rivista del Diritto Internazionale Privato e Processuale
Stanford J. Int. L.	Stanford Journal of International Law
S. Cal. L. Rev.	Southern California Law Review
Stanf. L. Rev.	Stanford Law Review
Tul. L. Rev.	Tulane Law Review
U.C.L.A. Rev.	University of California, Los Angeles, Law Review
U. Cin. L. Rev.	University of Cincinnati Law Review
U. Pa. L. Rev.	University of Pennsylvania Law Review
U. Pitt. L. Rev.	University of Pittsburgh Law Review
U. Queensland L.J.	University of Queensland Law Journal
U. W. Ont. L. Rev.	University of Western Ontario Law Review
UNIDROIT Unif. L. Cas.	International Institute for the Unification of Private Law, Uniform Law Cases (Rome: UNIDROIT).
UNIDROIT Unif. L. Rev.	UNIDROIT Uniform Law Review, International Institute for the Unification of Private Law (Rome: UNIDROIT).

UNIDROIT Yearbook	UNIDROIT Yearbook, International Institute for the Unification of Private Law (Rome: UNIDROIT).
U. Chi. L. Rev.	University of Chicago Law Review
Vanderbilt J. Tr. L.	Vanderbilt Journal of Transnational Law
Vand. L. Rev.	Vanderbilt Law Review
Wash. L. Rev.	Washington Law Review
Yale L.J.	Yale Law Journal

I. Overview

CHAPTER 1.

THE 1980 CONVENTION: A BRIEF INTRODUCTION

1   On April 11, 1980, a diplomatic conference of 62 States unanimously approved a Convention providing uniform law for international sales of goods — the United Nations Convention on Contracts for the International Sale of Goods (CISG). By December 11, 1986, instruments of adherence (e.g., ratification or accession) had been deposited with the Secretary-General by 11 States: Argentina, China, Egypt, France, Hungary, Italy, Lesotho, Syrian Arab Republic, United States of America, Yugoslavia and Zambia. Under Article 99 the Convention went into force a year after the deposit of the 10th instrument of adherence; for the above 11 States the Convention entered into force January 1, 1988.

At publication, over 70 States, including States from each region and embracing a large majority of the world's population (as well as its international trade in goods), have adhered to the Convention. Up-to-date information on the Convention's Contracting States, including dates of adherence and entry into force, along with any applicable reservations, is available on the website of the United Nations Commission on International Trade Law (UNCITRAL) at http://www.uncitral.org/uncitral/en/uncitral_texts/sale_goods/1980CISG_status.html. Adherence patterns of other Conventions, with less initial momentum than Convention on Contracts for the International Sale of Goods (CISG), indicate that this Convention is moving towards virtually unanimous acceptance.

2   **A. Primary Role of the Contract**

The dominant theme of the Convention is the role of the contract construed in the light of commercial practice and usage — a theme of deeper significance than may be evident at first glance. In some countries protective rules inspired by the plight of consumers could be superseded by the uniform rules developed for international commerce. To avoid any collision with such protective legislation, consumer purchases are excluded from the Convention. (See the Commentary to Arts. 2(a) and 5, *infra* §§50–55, 71.)

The Convention does not override domestic law that outlaws certain transactions or invalidates proscribed contracts and oppressive terms. See the Commentary to Article 4(a), *infra* §§64–68. Outside this narrow area the Convention protects the contractual arrangements made by the parties. (See, e.g., Ch. 2, *infra* §27.) Moreover, the parties may exclude the Convention, and the terms of their contract will prevail over inconsistent provisions of the uniform law. (See the Commentary to Art. 6, *infra* §74.) In short, like most domestic sales rules applicable to commercial contracts, the Convention's rules play a supporting role, supplying answers to problems that the parties have failed to solve by contract.

The Convention in two fundamental ways responds to the power of agreement. The Convention itself was produced by agreement. States from all parts of the world, through collaboration sustained for over a decade, reached consensus on a Convention of over a hundred articles. Then, as Contracting States, they agreed that in international sales they would substitute the Convention's rules for their domestic laws. Although we cannot know whether civilization grew from a social compact, those who saw the development of the Convention cannot doubt the power to move towards civilization by agreement.

Consistent with these origins, the Convention does not interfere with the freedom of sellers and buyers to shape the terms of their transactions. Nations can control their domestic commerce and can exclude or restrict the flow of trade. However, with the collapse of imperial and economic empires, commercial enterprises cannot compel parties in other countries to trade with them and, with the development of international competition, cannot dictate contract terms. Domestic trade may be subject to national management but international trade depends on agreement.

A highly respected legal scholar in a rhetorical flourish (later modified) announced the "Death of Contract."[1] At least for international sales this report (as Mark Twain said of a report that he had died) is "grossly exaggerated."

3   B. Major Contours of the Convention

The Convention deals with the two basic aspects of the sales transaction. Part II governs the formation of the contract; Part III governs the

---

1. Grant Gilmore, *Death of Contract* (1974). As we shall see, tort-like solutions in domestic law for problems that arise from contracts create difficult questions as to the scope of the Convention (CISG). See CISG 4 & 5 and §§69, 72–75, *infra*.

obligations of the parties under the contract. States by specific declaration (Art. 92) may exclude either Part. (In the Commentary, see the Introduction to Part II of the Convention, *infra* §131.)

Part II on Formation (Arts. 14–24) includes rules on the definiteness required of offers, the effect of communications addressed to the general public ("public offers"), the power to revoke an offer, and the requisites for a binding acceptance including rules on "acceptances" that include terms that depart from those of the offer. The "Sales" rules in Part III (Arts. 25–88) include Chapters on the seller's obligations with respect to quality of the goods and freedom of the goods from third-party claims (Ch. II), the buyer's obligations to pay for the goods (Ch. III), the allocation of risk of loss (Ch. IV), and the remedies available to both parties for breach (Ch. V).

A more precise view of the Convention can be obtained by examining the Detailed Table of Contents. Some may wish at this point to read the introductory passages that are interspersed throughout the Commentary; references to these introductions are given in a footnote.[2]

4   C. Development of the Convention

(1) Origins: The 1964 Hague Conventions

Concern for the barriers resulting from legal diversity spans the centuries[3] but we must be content to start our account with the work launched in the 1930s when the International Institute for the Unification of Private Law (UNIDROIT) requested a distinguished group of European scholars to prepare a draft of a uniform law for international sales transactions. A preliminary draft was issued in 1935. The work, suspended during the war, resumed soon after the end of hostilities. In 1951 a conference of 21 nations encouraged the continuation of the project, and in 1956 and 1963 revised drafts were sent to governments for comments. In the meantime, work was commenced on a uniform law for the formation of the contract; in 1958 a draft uniform law was circulated.

---

2. A connected presentation of the topics covered by the Convention, with references to the more significant issues, may be gained by reading *seriatim* the following: The Introductions to Parts 1–IV of the Convention, *infra* §§36, 131, 180 and 458.

3. *David, Unification*, Int. Encyc. Comp. L., Vol. 2, Ch. 5.

In April 1964 a Diplomatic Conference of 28 States met at the Hague to act on these two related drafts. After three intense weeks the Conference finalized two conventions: One set forth a Uniform Law for the International Sale of Goods (ULIS) and the other a Uniform Law on the Formation of Contracts for the International Sale of Goods (ULF). In 1972 both conventions went into effect following ratification by five States; adherents for the most part were European.[4]

5 **(2) Worldwide Sponsorship: UNCITRAL**

The 1964 Hague Conventions were of fundamental value but it became evident that success on a worldwide scale called for worldwide participation and sponsorship. In 1966 a resolution by the General Assembly of the United Nations provided for the establishment of a worldwide representative body to promote "the progressive harmonization and unification of the law of international trade." This body, UNCITRAL, had its first session in 1968; in its first decade UNCITRAL made notable progress in preparing uniform international rules for arbitration, carriage of goods by sea, negotiable instruments and the sales of goods — progress that was analyzed in a symposium issue of the American Journal of Comparative Law. References to these and other aspects of the Commission's work are given in a footnote.[5]

6 **(a) The Commission: Structure and Working Methods.**
UNCITRAL's structure has two essential elements — the number of

---

4. The development of the 1964 Hague Conventions on Sales is examined more fully in articles by the present writer, a participant in the 1964 Hague Conference. John O. Honnold, *A Uniform Law for International Sales*, 107 U. Pa. L. Rev. 299, 302, 304, (1959); John O. Honnold, *ULIS: The Hague Convention of 1964*, 30 Law & Contemp. Pr. 326 (1965); and John O. Honnold, *The Draft Convention on Contracts for the International Sale of Goods: An Overview*, 27 Am. J. Comp. L. 223 (1979). The latter is part of a symposium issue cited here as *AJCL UNCITRAL Symposium*. (This and other abbreviations of works frequently cited are given in the Bibliographic Notes.)
5. Symposium, *UNCITRAL's First Decade*, 27 Am. J. Comp. L. 201–563 (1979) (cited as *AJCL UNCITRAL Symposium*).
   The records of this work appear in the UNCITRAL *Yearbooks, Docy. Hist. 7*. The *Yearbooks* also contain bibliographic material on the various aspects of UNCITRAL's works. See, e.g., Vol. XVII at 399–408. For general information about UNCITRAL, including the texts of conventions and other international rules, see UNCITRAL (U.N.N.Y 1986, ISBN 92-1-133284-2). See also Peter Pfund, 22 Int. Law. 1157 (1988) (annual report on international unification of private law).

members is limited and the representation is worldwide. To facilitate efficiency in handling technical legal questions, the Commission's membership is limited, but that membership is allocated among the regions of the world.[6]

The full Commission meets once a year. At these sessions the Commission decides on topics for work and receives progress reports from its constituent bodies—principally Working Groups that, even with reduced size, are cross-sections of the Commission's worldwide representation. When a Working Group has completed its work on a draft Convention, the full Commission gives detailed consideration to each provision. This legislative process will be seen in a specific context when we turn to the development of the Draft Convention on Sales (*infra* §9).

7 **(b) The Representatives.** The General Assembly resolution that established UNCITRAL provided that the Member States shall appoint representatives "in so far as possible from among persons of eminence in the field of international trade." In fact, UNCITRAL representatives proved to be a wholesome mix of academic specialists in commercial and comparative law, practicing lawyers, and members of government ministries with years of experience in international lawmaking.

The Commission faced a formidable task. The representatives responded with a flexible, international approach that embraced the premise that their national interests in having an effective uniform law would not be served by bargaining (in the spirit of tariff negotiations) for the use of the maximum number of scraps of national law. Examining the development of the Convention will expose the dangers inherent in using local legal idioms; the representatives minimized this problem by deciding what result was appropriate for a series of pivotal factual examples, and by repeated review of multilingual drafts designed to embody these decisions. Since each nation has both sellers and buyers, agreeing on a solution that was fair to both parties to the contract was only rarely complicated by issues of national interest. On a few points, it was suggested that the interests of industrial and developing countries called for different rules. These issues arose in surprisingly technical settings— the time within which notice must be given that goods were defective (Arts. 39 and 44, *infra* §§254 *et seq.*), and the circumstances in which one party may suspend performance because of possible failure of

---

6. For further information on the composition of UNCITRAL see its website at http://www.uncitral.org/uncitral/en/about/origin.html.

counterperformance (Art. 71, *infra* §385). Happily, the delegates finally found acceptable solutions even for these problems.

Throughout the United Nations system, UNCITRAL became known as a businesslike and hard-working group. After a day of legislative sessions, representatives would give evenings and weekends to informal working-group sessions to resolve stubborn problems. The years of hard, successful work (and brief, notable periods of relaxation in pleasant surroundings) developed an *esprit* somewhat like that of a veteran regiment. The members jealously guarded their record of reaching decisions without a formal vote; in each case the legislative product was approved by consensus.[7]

8   **(c) The Secretariat.**   The Commission and its constituent bodies are served by a Secretariat consisting of the United Nations International Trade Law Branch. This writer cannot speak of the Secretariat with detachment. During the period (1969–1974) when he served as Chief of this Branch and as Secretary to the Commission he became deeply attached to this remarkable international team.[8]

The role of the Secretariat was established by a few basic facts of time and space. The Commission met once a year; during a two to four week session it considered the progress of programs in several complex and diverse legal fields. In the Working Groups, national representatives came together from all parts of the globe, from diverse legal and linguistic backgrounds, for annual sessions of two or three weeks. All of the representatives had primary, full-time responsibilities in their Universities or Ministries. For these reasons, progress at the legislative sessions depended on preparatory materials provided by the Secretariat. These materials included studies analyzing the divergences among the existing legal rules; reports on commercial practices to assist in making a choice among alternative solutions to pivotal factual examples; draft statutory texts formulated, at crucial spots, with clearly labeled alternatives to facilitate debate and decision with a minimum of confusion or

---

7. The Commission's working methods were analyzed more fully by the present writer in John O. Honnold, *AJCL UNCITRAL Symposium* 201, 208–211. See also E. Allan Farnsworth, *Developing International Trade Law*, 9 Calif. W. Int. L.J. 461 (1979); Erik Suy, *Achievements of the UNCITRAL*, 15 Int. Lawyer 139 (1981); Berthold Goldman, *Travaux de CNUDCI*, 106.4 J.D.I. 747 (1979).

8. This discussion is based on this writer's study in John O. Honnold, *AJCL UNCITRAL Symposium* 201, 209–210. In that study (210 n. 28) the writer, tearing off the veil of anonymity that usually conceals the Secretariat, paid individual tribute to the contributions made by his colleagues.

misunderstanding. A strong role for the U.N. Secretariat could touch sensitive political nerves, but at an early stage it was recognized that successful work depended on this help; the desire for success muted this and other divisive issues.

9   ## (3) UNCITRAL and a New Convention

At UNCITRAL's first session (1968), by common consent, high priority was given to work on uniform law for international sales. The more difficult question was whether UNCITRAL should promote adoption of the two 1964 Sales Conventions (as it did with respect to the 1958 Convention on the Recognition and Enforcement of Foreign Arbitral Awards) or whether it should prepare new legal texts.

The crucial question was this: Would it be possible to obtain widespread adoption of the 1964 Conventions? The Commission requested the Secretary-General to transmit to governments the text of the two 1964 conventions and Professor Tunc's commentary, and to ask the governments whether they intended to adhere to these Conventions and the reasons for their position.

The replies laid the foundation for the Commission's decisions at its second (1969) session. It became evident that the 1964 Conventions, despite the valuable work they reflected, would not receive adequate adherence. The basic difficulty stemmed from inadequate participation by representatives of different legal backgrounds in the preparation of the 1964 Conventions; despite efforts by UNIDROIT to encourage wider participation these Conventions were essentially the product of the legal scholarship of Western Europe.[9]

UNCITRAL thereupon established a working group of 14 States — a cross-section of UNCITRAL's worldwide representation — and requested the Working Group to prepare a text that would facilitate

---

9. An analysis of these replies, organized by Articles of the Convention, is in the *Rep. S. G.* "Analysis of Replies" I *YB* 159–176. Of the 28 states at the 1964 Hague Conference, 19 were from Western Europe. From Eastern Europe — Bulgaria, Hungary and Yugoslavia (the absence of the U.S.S.R. proved to be significant); from Latin America — only Colombia (a representative from the local embassy); from Asia — only Japan (the absence of India and Pakistan was significant); from Africa — only the U.A.R. See also the writer's discussion in John O. Honnold, *AJCL UNCITRAL Symposium* 223 at 225–226, on which the above paragraphs are based. An examination of the objections to the 1964 Conventions by the U.S. is given in Martin L. Ziontz, *A New Uniform for the International Sale of Goods*, 2 NW. J. Int. L. & Bus. 129 (1980).

"acceptance by countries of different legal, social and economic systems." Under the effective chairmanship of Professor Jorge Barrera Graf of Mexico, the working group completed this task in nine annual sessions. In 1976 the Working Group completed its work based on the 1964 Hague Sales Convention (ULIS); this was embodied in a Draft Convention on Sales — as contrasted with Formation. In 1978 the Working Group completed its work based on the 1964 Hague Formation Convention (ULF), and issued its Draft Convention on Formation. In June 1978 the full Commission completed its review of these two drafts, and combined them in a single Draft Convention that dealt both with the formation of the contract (Part II) and with the rights of the parties to the contract (Part III). This 1978 Draft Convention on Contracts for the International Sale of Goods received the Commission's unanimous approval. The General Assembly of the United Nations promptly authorized the convening of a diplomatic conference to act on the UNCITRAL draft.[10]

10   (4) The Diplomatic Conference

In March 1980, representatives of 62 States and 8 international organizations met in Vienna to finalize the UNCITRAL Draft Convention. The diplomatic conference worked for five weeks within the forbidding walls of the Hofburg; the principal sessions were held in the ornate hall that had provided the setting for the Congress of Vienna and for SALT II — international arrangements of incomparably greater political portent but (unhappily) without such worldwide representation.[11]

Nearly all the provisions in the UNCITRAL Draft Convention of 1978 were approved in substance by the Conference. Significant changes are

10. A more detailed picture of these successive drafts is given in *Docy. Hist.* 13–380. The initial members of the Working Group were Brazil, France, Ghana, Hungary, India, Iran, Japan, Kenya, Mexico, Norway, Tunisia, U.S.S.R., U.K. and U.S. Later the membership was increased to 15; new members were Austria, Czechoslovakia, the Philippines and Sierra Leone. The Working Group also profited from the participation, as observers, of several international organizations, including UNIDROIT, the Hague Conference on Private International Law, International Chamber of Commerce (ICC), Economic Commission for Europe (ECE), Council for Mutual Economic Assistance (CMEA) and Organization of American States (OAS).

11. The 62 States included all countries with significant commercial interests. The international organizations were World Bank, Bank for International Settlements, Central Office for International Railway Transport, Council of Europe, European Economic Community, Hague Conference on Private International Law, UNIDROIT, and ICC.

listed here in a footnote and are discussed in the Commentary.[12] The degree of approval of the UNCITRAL draft resulted from the fact that representatives from each region of the world had participated in preparing the draft. In addition, most delegates realized that the eighty-eight articles of the uniform sales law (Parts I–III) were closely related to each other as parts of an integrated whole; major changes in individual articles could affect the integrity of the structure. As the Conference progressed with its article-by-article discussion it became evident that the time for review of the draft as a whole would be limited, as compared with the repeated reviews that had occurred during the decade of work in UNCITRAL. See §9, *supra*. Thus, proponents of amendments had a heavy burden: they needed to show not only that a change was needed but also that a proposed amendment was clearly drafted and would not lead to untoward consequences in relation to other provisions of the law.

Through overtime work and close cooperation between language specialists of the United Nations and members of the Drafting Committee, the Convention was finalized in six official languages — Arabic, Chinese, English, French, Russian and Spanish.[13] *According to the Witness Clause at the end of the Convention, these different language versions collectively constitute "a single original" and each is "equally authentic." Discrepancies among the different language versions of the Convention's text, which inevitably arise, present interesting questions. For an example of such a discrepancy and commentary on the issues it raises see the discussion of Article 68 (infra §372.3).*

Plenary sessions met only at the beginning and end of the Conference. The text of the Convention was substantially completed by two "committees." The "committees" resembled the Plenary since all States were represented, but the committee concept permitted simultaneous work on different topics and also facilitated flexible procedures — a committee could take action by a simple majority while decisions in Plenary required a two-thirds vote.

The First Committee prepared the principal substantive provisions of the Convention (Parts I–III, Arts. 1–88) while the Second Committee

---

12. Significant substantive changes included: Art. 7(2) (filling gaps by reference to "general principles"); Art. 55 (price not stated in contract); Art. 68 (risk of loss as to goods sold during transit); Art. 71 (suspension of performance by one party because of danger of breach by the other); Art. 78 (recovery of interest for delay in payment of sums due).

13. The States elected to the Drafting Committee were Brazil, Chile, China, Czechoslovakia, Ecuador, Egypt, Finland, France, Libya, Republic of Korea, Singapore, U.S.S.R., U.K., U.S. and Zaire. The Chairman was Mr. Warren Khoo (Singapore).

prepared Part IV — Final Provisions (Arts. 89–101). These Final Provisions govern the steps necessary to bring the Convention into force and the content of permissible "declarations" (reservations) by adhering States.

The Second Committee, in response to authorization from the General Assembly, also prepared a Protocol to the 1974 Convention on the Limitation Period in the International Sale of Goods. This Protocol modified provisions of the 1974 Limitation Convention on its sphere of applicability to make the 1974 Convention conform to the 1980 Sales Convention.[14]

At the end of the Conference, the texts prepared by the First and Second Committees were voted on in Plenary, article-by-article. Under the rules of the Conference, each article required approval by a two-thirds majority. In fact, of the 88 substantive articles (Parts I–III), 74 were approved unanimously and 8 additional articles received no more than 2 negative votes. All of the other articles were approved by large majorities, but in two instances the majority fell short of two-thirds; on these articles, *ad hoc* working groups then brought in compromise versions that were approved without dissent. The Convention, as a whole, was then submitted to a roll-call vote and was approved without a dissenting vote. In short, the spirit of consensus that had developed in UNCITRAL was maintained to the end of the Diplomatic Conference.

---

14. The text of the Protocol is Annex II to the *Final Act* of the 1980 Conference. On the 1974 Limitation Convention see *infra* §§254.2 and 261.1; *AJCL UNCITRAL Symposium* 203–204, 351–352 (bibliography); Hans Smit, UNCITRAL's First Born, 23 Am. J. Comp. L. 337 (1975); Kazuaki Sono, *Unification of Limitation Period in the International Sale of Goods*, 35 La. L. Rev. 1127 (1975); Thea Krapp, *The Limitation Convention for the International Sale of Goods*, 19 J. World Trade L. 343 (1985). The 1974 Limitation Convention went into force on August 1, 1988, among ten States. By 2008, 28 States had adhered to the Limitation Convention.

CHAPTER 2.

SALIENT FEATURES OF THE 1980 CONVENTION

11   This chapter is designed to highlight some of the more significant features of the Convention. This is not a summary of the Convention; a more complete overview can be gained by examining the Detailed Table of Contents and by reading, seriatim, the brief introductions to the various parts of the Convention that appear in the Commentary, *infra* §§36, 131, 180 and 458. This chapter draws attention to aspects of the Convention that are of special significance: issues that underlie major parts of the Convention and challenging questions that will be discussed fully later. The most one can hope for here is an apéritif.

12   ## A. Scope of the Convention

(1) The Sale Must Be International

During the half-century of work that led to the present Convention there was general agreement that the uniform rules would apply only to international sales; the 1980 Convention governs contracts "between parties whose places of business are in *different* States." (See the Commentary on Art. 1, *infra* §39.) Why is the Convention's scope restricted in this manner? To many the answer will seem obvious but it may be useful to explore some of the reasons for this basic decision.

13   **(a) Reasons for Excluding Domestic Transactions.**   Although we cannot claim for law that universality of outlook that has been achieved in basic science, lawmakers have not remained so isolated that it has been necessary to await the separate invention of each legal wheel. The international use of legal ideas is illustrated by widespread acceptance of the French Code Civil; the borrowing of the work embodied in the German and Swiss codes; the adoption within Scandinavia of parallel law on various topics, including sales; and the widespread acceptance of common-law ideas, including those embodied in the (U.K.) Sale of Goods Act.

Limiting sales rules to international transactions was necessary because these rules are embodied in a Convention designed for universal adoption. In a Convention, each Contracting State undertakes (in exchange for the comparable undertaking of other States) to implement the same uniform rules. In most States, domestic transactions predominate. States can be expected to bind themselves to the same rules only in an area of shared interest — their international trade transactions.

14 **(b) The Convention as a Model for Improving Domestic Law.**   While the obligation to implement the rules of the convention is confined to the international sale, the opportunity to use the legal work embodied in the Convention is not so restricted.

This book includes references to domestic rules, and the Convention has, and in the future will surely stimulate comparative studies in this area. A number of States, including the Scandinavian States and Germany, have drawn on the Convention in revising their sales law.[1] The results of this experience will shed further light on the value of the Convention for the reform of domestic law.

The Commentary to Article 7 at *infra* §92 discusses the significance of international case law and scholarship under the Convention and the procedures for making this material generally available. Domestic law based on the Convention can also be enriched by this body of thought and experience, and students and practitioners can gain wider horizons by this contact with the world of international commerce.

15 **(2) Required Relationship between the Transaction and a Contracting Sale**

The 1964 Sales Convention directed the tribunals of Contracting States to apply its rules to any international sale even though the

---

1. See, e.g., The CISG's Impact on Legislators (Rolf Herber, The German Experience 59; Joseph Lookofsky, The Scandinavian Experience 95; Ulrich Magnus, The CISG's Impact on European Legislation 129), in *The 1980 Uniform Sales Law: Old Issues Revisited in the Light of Recent Experiences (Verona Conference 2003)* (Franco Ferrari, ed., 2003); Jan Ramberg, The New Swedish Sales Law, 28 Saggi (1997); Leif Sevón, The New Scandinavian Sales Codification and the 1980 Sales Convention, *Freiburg Colloq.* 343 (1987); John Manwaring, Reforming Domestic Sales Law: Lessons to be Learned from the International Convention on the Sales of Goods, *Ottawa Collogue* 139–170 (1989). Modern legal developments to protect consumers would need to supplement domestic rules based on the Convention. For the Convention's emphasis on freedom of contract see Art. 6, *infra* §74.

transaction and its parties had no contact with any Contracting State.[2] As we shall see in the Commentary to Article 1, the 1980 Convention rejects this "universalist" approach. Contracting States are obliged to apply the Convention only when the places of business of both the parties to the sale are in Contracting States (Art. 1(1)(a)) or when the rules of private international law lead to the application of the law of a Contracting State (Art. 1(1)(b)), and this latter ground may be excluded by reservation. (Commentary to Art. 1, *infra* §47.) These provisions do not seem too modest in view of widespread adherence to the Convention and the opportunity of parties to agree on the applicability of the Convention. (See Commentary to Art. 6, *infra* §78.)

16   B. Interpretation of the Convention

As we approach this difficult problem it may help to bear in mind two principles that will seem banal: (1) Legislation calls for an approach to interpretation that is consistent with its character and purpose. (2) The Convention has a very special function — to replace diverse domestic rules with uniform international law.

17   (1) International Character; Uniformity

The special problems of construing an international text are faced in Article 7, which lays down a series of principles for interpreting the Convention. The most basic principle is this: Interpretation shall respond to the Convention's "international character and to the need to promote uniformity in its application." Ways to effectuate this principle, examined in the Commentary to Article 7, include the following: The effort, in drafting the Convention, to avoid legal idioms that have divergent local meanings and, instead, to speak in terms of physical events that occur in international trade; the use of the legislative history of the Convention as a means of escape from preconceptions derived from domestic laws; and the dissemination and use of international case law (*jurisprudence*) and scholarly critique (*doctrine*). (Commentary to Art. 7, *infra* §§87, 88, and 92.)

---

2. ULIS 1, 2. The 1964 Conventions provide that a Contracting State by declaration may choose a narrower approach. E.g., *Hague Sales Convention (1964)* Arts. III, IV; States adhering to the Conventions have made liberal use of these articles.

18 **(2) The Convention's Texture: Capacity to Respond to New Circumstances**

Laws that may readily be amended (e.g., income tax laws and regulations) may indulge in detail but this is not feasible for laws that must endure. Most of the domestic laws on obligations and on sales have stood almost for a century and many are even older. International legislative machinery is even harder to put into motion. The Sales Convention must be read and applied in a manner that permits it to grow and adapt to novel circumstances and changing times. The Convention provides for flexibility in various ways.

19 **(a) The Contract: Practices of the Parties; Usages.** Perhaps the most important vehicle for flexibility is the role that the Convention gives to the contract. (See Overview, Ch. 1, *supra* §2; Art. 6, *infra* §75.) On points where the contract is silent, current practices and usage may apply. Under Article 9, the parties "are bound by any usage to which they have agreed and by any practices which they have established between themselves"; in addition, the parties are considered to "to have impliedly made applicable to their contract" any usage which "in international trade is widely known to, and regularly observed by . . ." such parties. Statutory norms grow old but applicable practices and usages change with changing times and respond to special circumstances and needs. (See the Commentary to Art. 9, *infra* §112.)

20 **(b) "Good Faith."** Adaptation and development are also encouraged by the statement in Article 7 that one of the factors to be considered in interpreting the Convention is the need to promote "the observance of good faith in international trade." The Commentary to Article 7 (*infra* §94) notes that using "good faith" only as a guide for interpretation is less sweeping than the general "good faith" requirements of some legal systems; nevertheless, in many situations interpretation in the light of the principle of "good faith" can avoid stultification or circumvention of specific provisions of the Convention.

21 **(c) Recourse to "General Principles" of the Convention.** Many legal systems work from the premise that solutions to legal problems can and must be found within the four comers of the Code — a premise that compels the extension by analogy of one or another of the Code's provisions. Other legal systems take a more strict view of statutes. For example, statutes like the (U.K.) Sale of Goods Act may be

regarded as islands in an ocean of uncodified common law; in this setting if the statute does not readily supply an answer the court may draw on general common-law ideas.

Which approach is more appropriate for the Convention? Under the second, narrow approach, if one looks outside the Convention one does not find a body of "common" law; instead, one faces the vagaries of private international law and a fragment of some domestic legal system. Moreover, under this approach the results of individual cases would not contribute to a uniform, growing body of case law under the Convention.

In response to this difficulty, Article 7(2) states that when questions arise concerning matters "governed by this Convention" that "are not expressly settled" in the Convention, the question is to be settled "in conformity with *the general principles*" on which the Convention is based. Only when such a general principle cannot be found may the tribunal turn to "the law applicable by virtue of the rules of private international law."

This leads to important questions: How can one establish the general principles on which the Convention is based? How diligently should a tribunal look for such principles before it turns, *via* rules of private international law, to a rule of domestic law? These questions may present the Convention's most intriguing challenge; they are explored in the setting of Article 7, *infra* §94.

21.1 **(d) New Uniform Commercial Law Initiatives.** *The further development of uniform international commercial law in harmony with the CISG is another resource that permits the Convention to adapt to changes in the commercial world. The United Nations Commission on International Trade Law (UNCITRAL), the International Institute for the Unification of Private Law (UNIDROIT) and other organizations continue efforts to develop a comprehensive system of international commercial rules. The fruits of such endeavors include projects closely related to the Sales Convention, such as the UNCITRAL-sponsored United Nations Convention on the Use of Electronic Communications in International Contracts (2005) — a treaty designed to work in tandem with the Sales Convention to deal with far-reaching developments in communications technology[3] — and the*

---

3. The text of this Convention, as well as ratification and other relevant information, is available on the UNCITRAL website at http://www.uncitral.org/uncitral/en/uncitral_texts/electronic_commerce/2005Convention.html. As this is written, this convention appears to be moving toward wide international acceptance.

UNIDROIT Principles of International Commercial Contracts — a restatement of international contract principles that first appeared in 1994 and then, in an expanded version, in 2004.[4]

22 C. Formation of the Contract: Part II of the Convention

Part II of the Convention (Arts. 14–24) addresses issues of contract formation. Questions about the existence of a contract arise more frequently in the classroom than in real life, but problems may arise after informal exchanges of letters or emails. The Convention addresses problems of contract formation such as withdrawal or revocation of an offer (Arts. 15 and 16); the point at which an acceptance becomes binding (Arts. 18–22); and the effect of an acceptance that deviates from the offer (Art. 19). As a result of Article 16, when an offeror promises (either expressly or impliedly) that the offer is irrevocable, parties grounded in the civil law need not cope with the mysteries of common-law "consideration" that may deny effect to the offeror's promise. The other articles dealing with formation of the contract adequately introduce themselves. See the Commentary to Articles 14–24, *infra*.

23 D. The Sale of Goods: Part III of the Convention

Part III (Arts. 25–88), encompassing the full range of relationships between the seller and buyer, embodies general themes that may be foreshadowed here.

24 (1) A Unified Contractual Approach to Obligations and Remedies

The Convention's unified contractual approach will seem obvious to some but others who expect liability for breach of contract to be based on fault may find the Convention's contractual approach a startling *tour de force*.

---

4. The text of the 2004 version of the UNIDROIT Principles is available on the UNIDROIT website at http://www.unidroit.org/english/principles/contracts/main.htm and through the UNILEX database at http://www.unilex.info.

25 **(a) Obligations of the Parties.** The Convention's contractual theme is announced in parallel provisions that open Chapter II (Obligations of the Seller) and Chapter III (Obligations of the Buyer): Each party must perform all of the obligations "required by the contract" (Arts. 30 and 53, *infra* §206 and §309). This emphasis on the contract continues throughout the Convention and dominates the provisions dealing with the parties' obligations concerning delivery, quality of the goods, and payment of the price. The significant point is not that the Convention mentions the contract; this is generally true of domestic sales law. What is significant is the fact that giving legal effect to the expectations of the parties (as shown by the language of the contract, the practices of the parties and applicable usages) is so consistently the theme of the Convention.[5]

26 **(b) Remedies.** The tendency in some codified systems to distinguish between remedies for different categories of breach of contract found its way into the 1964 Hague Conventions on Sales. Uniform Law for the International Sale of Goods (ULIS) divided performance by the seller into five categories, and set up a separate remedial system for each category — an approach that produced length, complexity and ambiguity. For instance, separate remedies were provided for default as to the date of delivery and the place of delivery; this distinction was difficult to apply since goods that are still en route on the date for delivery can be regarded as either at the wrong place (en route) or delivered at the wrong time. Other artificial distinctions resulted from the fragmented approach to the seller's obligations and to remedies for breach.[6]

The Convention's unified contractual approach to the parties' duties was implemented by a unified system of remedies for breach. Under Article 45 a single set of remedies applies when the seller "fails to perform any of his obligations"; similarly. Article 61 provides a single set of remedies when the buyer "fails to perform any of his obligations." The remedy does not depend on formal classifications of types of breach but on the seriousness of the breach. This approach reduced bulk and complexity.

---

5. As was noted in Overview, Ch. 1, *supra* §2, the Convention's norms serve a subsidiary role to fill gaps in the contract. See Art. 6, *infra* §574. The role of the contract is discussed in the Commentaries to Arts. 30, 31, 35, 56, 67, 70 and 79. The Convention's flexible rules on ascertaining the intent of the parties are discussed under Art. 8; the practices of the parties and usage, as extensions of the contract, are discussed under Art. 9.

6. Traditional distinctions between types of default are described in *Treitel, Remedies (Int. Enc.)* §§75–76; *Treitel, Remedies (1988)* Ch. V. The approach of ULIS is discussed more fully in the Commentaries to Arts. 45, 46 and 47 and the studies cited therein. For criticism of the 1964 approach to remedies see Ulrich Drobnig, *Dubrovnik Lectures* 317.

This unified approach to obligations and remedies at one point touched an important issue of substance. Some legal systems have traditionally restricted the seller's damage liability for defective goods to cases where the defect resulted from the seller's fault; other legal systems base damages simply on breach of contract.[7]

Under the Convention, a party's failure to perform the contract invokes the full range of remedies. For example, under Article 45 if the seller "fails to perform any of his obligations *under the contract . . .* the buyer may . . . claim damages. . . ." And the Convention's exemption from damage liability when non-performance results from an impediment (*cf. force majeure*) does *not* excuse delivery of defective goods merely because the seller is not at fault for the non-conformity.[8]

27 (2) Preservation of the Contract: Limits on Avoidance; "Cure"

We now face one of the thorniest problems in the law of contracts and sales: When will breach by one party free the other party of his obligation to perform? Students of comparative law do not credit any domestic legal system with a satisfactory approach to this problem; most of the traditional statutes dealing with the sale of goods tend to be casuistic and unresponsive to the interests at stake.[9]

In international sales the problem has special significance because of the cost of transporting goods to a distant buyer and the difficulty of disposing of rejected goods in a foreign country. These factors led to agreement on rules that can save the contract from destruction on technical and trivial grounds. One approach was a series of provisions that permit a party in breach to "cure" the deficiency in performance — Articles 34, 37 and 48.

---

7. The use of "fault" in some domestic systems to determine liability for breach of contract is discussed in *Treitel, Remedies* §§78–81; *II Zweigert & Kötz (1987)* 181–183. See also the Commentary to Arts. 45 and 79.

8. See the Commentary to Art. 79 §423, *infra*. Damages of a type that could not have been anticipated are limited in a manner reminiscent of Hadley v. Baxendale, 9 Ex. 341, 156 Eng. Rep. 145 (1854); see the Commentary to Art. 74 §403, *infra*.

9. Casuistic distinctions between "conditions" and "warranties," perpetuated by the (U.K.) SGA (1893) §§11, 13 and 30, are examined in *Benjamin* §§740–748; *Ont. L. Ref. Com., II Sales* 444–61. For Civil Law approaches see *Treitel, Remedies (Int. Enc.)* §147–149; *Treitel, Remedies (1988)* Ch. VIII and authorities cited in the Commentary to Art. 49 at §301, *infra*. The relatively modern Uniform Commercial Code is marred in this area by technical and insubstantial distinctions. See John O. Honnold, *Buyer's Right of Rejection — A Study in the Impact of Codification on a Commercial Problem*, 97 U. Pa. L. Rev. 457 (1949).

A second approach limits avoidance to breaches that are "fundamental" (Arts. 25, 49 and 64). This limitation on the right of an aggrieved party to avoid the contract is subject to a powerful tool for clarifying the position of both parties: An aggrieved party who faces non-performance (failure to deliver goods or to pay the price) may fix a final, "additional period of time of reasonable length for performance" — the famous *Nachfrist* notice adapted from German law. Failure to perform in accordance with this notice is a ground for avoidance; the aggrieved party need not establish that the breach was "fundamental." See Articles 47 and 49(1)(b) (avoidance by the buyer); Articles 63 and 64(1)(b) (avoidance by the seller).[10]

28 (3) Risk of Loss

The Sales part of the Convention devotes a separate chapter to risk of loss (Ch. IV, Arts. 66–70). These rules, applicable when the contract is silent as to when risk passes from seller to buyer, are designed to place the risk of loss on the party who is in the better position to care for or insure the goods. The rules are not complicated by concepts such as "property" but are stated in terms of physical events. For example, risk will in some circumstances pass when goods "are handed over to the first carrier" (Art. 67); when the contract does not involve carriage, risk may pass when the buyer "takes over" the goods (Art. 69). These rules are, of course, subject to special provisions on the effect of breach of contract (Arts. 69 and 70). A fuller description of the rules on risk appears in the introduction to Part III, Chapter IV, *infra* §358, and in the Commentary on Articles 66–70, *infra* §§360–383.

29 (4) Preservation of the Goods

The Convention's rules on risk of loss might have been adequate to encourage preservation of the goods except for one practical fact: The parties often have honest differences of opinion over who is in breach and who has responsibility to care for the goods. A separate section of the Convention (Ch. V, Sec. VI, Arts. 85–88) addresses the question of preservation of the goods and, in limited circumstances, provides that even an aggrieved party who may readily avoid imminent deterioration or loss has a duty to do so — with a right to full reimbursement for his expense.

---

10. A general discussion of the Convention's remedial system appears in an introduction to Part III, Ch. II, Sec. III (Arts. 45–2), *infra* §272; the rules on avoidance are discussed under Arts. 25, 34, 47, 49, 51, 63 and 64.

This part of the Convention is based on the splendid work, of both substance and form, embodied in the 1964 Hague Convention on Sale. (A fuller description of the rules on preservation of the goods appears in the introduction to Ch. V, Sec. VI, *infra*, and in the Commentary on Arts. 85–88, *infra*.)

30 **E. An Invisible Gain: The Omission of "Awesome Relics"**

(1) Domestic Antiquities and International Commerce

Ernst Rabel, whose monumental study of the comparative law of sales provided the foundation for the early work towards a uniform sales law, said that one of the gains from the new law would be to avoid the "awesome relics of the dead past that populate in amazing multitude the older codifications of sales law."[11] This book notes some of the outdated legal formulae that still complicate domestic sales law. One may delight in legal antiques and in the patina of ingenious circumlocutions that have had to substitute for fundamental reform, but these aesthetic values may not be appreciated by a modern merchant and, more especially, by his trading partner from a different legal tradition.

31 **(2) Factors that Affect the Character of the Convention**

The evolution of the 1980 Sales Convention was summarized in Overview, Chapter 1, *supra* §4. Our concern now is with factors that have affected the texture and quality of the Convention and distinguish it from domestic law.

32 **(a) The Field for Work: The International Sale.** In some legal systems many of the controlling legal formulae must do service across the broad spectrum of the law of obligations, embracing many types of contracts and also torts; in some legal systems the same rules apply to sales of goods and transactions in land. One may concede the power and utility of general legal ideas and yet doubt that provisions of such generality are appropriate for international trade.

In the domain of the common law and in some other countries separate statutes govern the sale of goods. However, many of these statutes were

---

11. Ernst Rabel, *The Hague Conference on the Unification of Sales Law*, 1 Am. J. Comp. L. 58, 61 (1952). The basic study was Ernst Rabel, Das Recht des Warenkaufs (v.l, 1936; v.2, 1958).

primarily designed for domestic transactions and in recent years have been subject to modification and interpretation to take account of the special needs of consumers. On the other hand, observers from codified systems find sales statutes of the common-law world unsatisfying because they were designed for insertion into a vast, uncodified body of common-law principles.

The 1980 Sales Convention has narrower, clearer boundaries. Confining the work to the international sale permitted a more direct and concrete mode of expression, and embodied careful, explicit choices between those areas that were embraced by the Convention, and other areas (e.g., "validity") that were expressly remitted to domestic law. The fact that the field for work was restricted to the international sale also meant that the project did not threaten any domestic legal system; the work was not burdened by the traditions that have preserved the ancient codes and statutes of domestic law.

To be sure, most of the provisions of the Convention are not innovations of 1980; the legal work spanned half a century. But during the nine years of intensive work in UNCITRAL that produced the 1978 Draft and (to a lesser extent) during the review of that draft at the 1980 diplomatic conference, the Convention benefited from suggestions based on the current practices and needs of international trade. This flow of ideas included suggestions from commercial bodies that were relayed through the national representatives. In addition, international commercial organizations, notably the International Chamber of Commerce, took an active part in the UNCITRAL proceedings and the 1980 Conference.

33 **(b) The Refining Processes of International Collaboration.**
The most powerful forces towards eliminating "awesome relics of the dead past" were intrinsic to the process of international collaboration. Proposals that embodied the idioms or traditions peculiar to a single system were subjected to polite but revealing analysis by puzzled representatives from other systems. Another powerful solvent was the process of translation; formulae that were vague or redolent of domestic legal tradition would set off alarms when they appeared in other languages. Unhappy experience with concepts in the 1964 Sales Convention that defied translation (délivrance; ipso facto avoidance) helped pave the way for UNCITRAL's use of simpler, clearer language.[12]

---

12. On the difficulties with *délivrance* see the Commentary on Art. 31, *infra* §210. As to *ipso facto* avoidance see the Commentary on Art. 26. This writer dealt further with these concepts in *AJCL UNCITRAL Symposium* 223, 228–229. For influences that discouraged the use of jargon in the French and Swiss Codes see I *Zweigert & Kötz (1987)* 85, 93, 177–178.

One device used by the Secretariat in presenting issues to UNCITRAL seemed to facilitate agreement and, perhaps, a more direct mode of expression. At points where proposed legal texts might be read differently by delegates from different legal backgrounds the crucial issues were posed initially in terms of concrete factual examples. It proved to be easier to reach agreement on the results of concrete cases than to agree on legal drafts; and starting with agreement on the substance of the rule made it easier to draft a text that was direct and clear.[13]

The process was not always successful; on occasion, the discussion emphasized competing formulas of domestic law and agreement was found only through a general rule based on the formula of wider applicability and an exception based on the competing formula. These compromises led to some of the less elegant provisions of the Convention, but were the necessary (and less than outrageous) price for international agreement.[14] More often, the international deliberative process rejected the anachronisms that complicate domestic law and produced a statutory text that is relatively straightforward and uncluttered with technical detail. The value simply of eliminating technical rules that divert attention from the transaction and its commercial setting could easily be overlooked. (Who notices obstructions that have been removed from a highway?)[15]

---

13. One example of this technique: *Rep. S-G* "Risk of Loss" paras. 64–05, V *YB* 89–94, *Docy. Hist.* 168–173. A ground-breaking use of model fact-situations in comparative legal work is demonstrated in *Schlesinger, Formation*.

14. See Gyula Eörsi, Problems of Unifying Law on the Formation of Contracts for the International Sale of Goods, *AJCL UNCITRAL Symposium* 311, 319–323 (1979). An example of such a compromise is Art. 16 on the revocability of offers.

15. See, for example, the UNCITRAL Arbitration Rules (Art. 33) which, after mentioning applicable law, reach the heart of the matter by providing: "3. In all cases, the arbitral tribunal shall decide in accordance with the terms of the contract and shall take into account the usages of trade applicable to the transaction." The practice of arbitrators in this regard is discussed in Pieter Sanders, Procedures and Practices under the UNCITRAL Rules, *AJCL UNCITRAL Symposium* 453, 464–65 (1979). See also the text of the Rules, *id.* at 489; Strohbach, Filling Gaps in Contracts, *id.* at 479. For comments by Lord Mansfield on the relative value of legal technicalities and common sense in deciding commercial cases, see *Atiyah, Freedom of Contract* 191. See also Goldstajn, *Dubrovnik Lectures* 57 (the Sales Convention crosses political, ideological and judicial barriers).

II. Commentary

Part I.

SPHERE OF APPLICATION AND GENERAL PROVISIONS
(Articles 1–13)

35   The balance of this work is a Commentary on the articles of the Convention. The uniform rules for sales transactions appear in Parts I–III of the Convention. Part I (Arts. 1–13) defines the Convention's field of application and includes other general provisions. Part 11 (Arts. 14–24) governs formation of the contract. Part III (Arts. 25–88) governs the rights and obligations of the parties to the contract of sale.

A general introduction to each Part of the Convention precedes the Commentary on individual articles.

36   INTRODUCTION TO PART I OF THE CONVENTION

Part I sets forth rules that apply throughout the Convention. Chapter I defines the Convention's field of application. Chapter II addresses other general questions, notably interpretation of the Convention and the sales contract. Each chapter calls for a brief introduction.

37   A. The Convention's Field of Application: Chapter I

Article 1 addresses two issues that control the applicability of the Convention: When is a sale "international"? What contact between the sales transaction and a Contracting State will invoke the Convention? Articles 2 and 3 exclude specified types of commodities and transactions. Articles 4 and 5 draw the line between issues that are regulated and those that are excluded; the excluded issues include the validity of the contract, the effect of the contract on the ownership rights of third persons (Art. 4) and liability for death or personal injury (Art. 5). The chapter closes with a brief but important provision (Art. 6) yielding overriding effect to the contract made by the parties.

38   **B. Interpretation and Related Questions: Chapter II**

Challenging problems of interpretation are presented by a Convention that seeks to secure uniform application by tribunals that are accustomed to applying domestic law. These problems are addressed in Article 7 — perhaps the most important provision of the Convention — and are given close attention in this study. Article 8 deals with interpretation in a different setting — the interpretation of the contract and other statements by the parties. Article 9 deals with a related issue — the added dimensions of meaning that the parties' practices and trade usages give to the contract. Article 10 defines "place of business" — a term used in various parts of the Convention. Articles 11 and 12 deal with the effect of domestic rules that contracts must be evidenced in writing.

CHAPTER I.

SPHERE OF APPLICATION
(Articles 1–6)

Article 1.
Basic Rules on Applicability: Internationality; Relation to Contracting State

39   The Overview (Ch. 2, *supra* at §12) drew attention to the limited applicability of the Convention. In brief, under Article 1 the Convention will apply only if two basic requirements are met: (1) The sale must be international, — that is, the seller and the buyer must have their "places of business in *different* States," and (2) The sale must have a prescribed relationship with one or more States that have adhered to the Convention.

Article 1[1]

(1) This Convention applies to contracts of sale of goods between parties whose places of business are in different States:
- **(a) when the States are Contracting States; or**
- **(b) when the rules of private international law lead to the application of the law of a Contracting State.**

(2) The fact that the parties have their places of business in different States is to be disregarded whenever this fact does not appear either from the contract or from any dealings between, or from information disclosed by, the parties at any time before or at the conclusion of the contract.

(3) Neither the nationality of the parties nor the civil or commercial character of the parties or of the contract is to be taken into consideration in determining the application of this Convention.

---

1. This article is substantially the same as Art. 1 of the 1978 Draft Convention. However, as we shall see, *infra* at §47, the 1980 Diplomatic Conference added Art. 95, which permits Contracting States to reject subparagraph (1)(b). ULIS 1 and 2 had more complex rules on internationality, and set no limits comparable to subparagraphs (1)(a) and (b).

On the Convention's sphere of application see, in general, Winship, *Parker Colloq.*, Ch. 1 (1984); Siehr, 52 *Rabels Z* 587 (1988); Lacasse, *Ottawa Collogue* 23–42 (1989).

40   ## A. Basic Rules on Applicability

(1) Internationality

The 1980 Convention lays down a single basic criterion of internationality: The seller and buyer must have their "places of business in different States."[2] The 1964 Conventions used the same criterion but added further tests: Did the contract "involve" international shipment? Where did "the acts constituting the offer and acceptance" take place? The deliberations in UNCITRAL showed that these additional tests did not give predictable answers; the location of the parties' places of business provided more solid footing.[3]

41   **(a) The Undisclosed Foreign Principal.**   Paragraph (2) of Article 1 addresses the following case:

Example 1A. Agent informed Seller, whose place of business was in State A, that Agent was authorized to purchase goods for a buyer but did not disclose the name or address of the person he represented. Seller and Agent concluded a sales contract; thereafter, it appeared that Agent was acting for a foreign principal, Buyer, whose place of business was in State B.

The above transaction would not be governed by the Convention. Paragraph (2) of Article 1 is based on the premise that facts implicating the internationality requirement of Article 1(1) should be available to the parties at the time of the conclusion of the contract.[4] A similar approach is taken in Article 10(a), quoted *infra* at §42, which states that the choice between multiple places of business — a choice that is important in determining applicability of the Convention — shall be based on "circumstances known to or contemplated by the parties at any time before or at the conclusion of the contract." ***As is noted below (see §66 infra),***

---

2. It is, of course, the parties' locations at the time the contract is concluded that determines whether this internationality criterion is met. See Ferrari, *Sphere of Application* at 24.

3. Development of Art. 1 in UNCITRAL: II *Yearbook* (herein "*YB*") 38–43; *Documentary History* (herein "*Docy. Hist.*") 43–48; II *YB* 51–54, III *YB* 79, 82–83, VI *YB* 88–90, 110, 50, IX *YB* 68–69; *Docy. Hist.* 57–60, 96, 99–100, 213–215, 235, 241, 300–301. The *YB* and *Docy. Hist.* citations refer to the same documents, in the same order. See also P. Kahn, La Vente Commercial Internationale 5 (Paris: Sirey, 1961); Kahn, 33 Rev. Int. Dr. Comp. 951, 959 (1981).

4. Article 1(2) is discussed in Peter Schlechtriem, Art. 1 paras. 49–52, in Schlechtriem & Schwenzer, *CISG Commentary* (2d English ed. 2005); Ferrari, *Sphere of Application* at 31–32.

agency issues are beyond the scope of the Convention. Thus, the question whether Agent or Buyer was a party to the contract of sale in the foregoing transaction would be left to applicable domestic law.[5] *Even if such law determined that Buyer was bound to the contract with Seller, the CISG would not apply because of Article 1(2).*

42 (b) Multiple Places of Business

Example 1B. Seller has places of business in both State A and State B. Buyer has a place of business in State B.

In this case, since Seller has a place of business in State A, the parties do have places of business "in different States," but they also have places of business in the same State. If seller negotiated and performed the transaction from its branch in State B, where Buyer has its sole place of business, both parties can be expected to be familiar with and follow the rules of State B. In any event, it is necessary to determine which of Seller's two places of business should be used to determine whether the sale was international.

Surprisingly, ULIS (1964) did not provide for this common problem. The 1980 Convention addresses this issue in paragraph (a) of Article 10. (Other aspects of Article 10 will be considered *infra*.) Article 10(a) provides:

> if a party has more than one place of business, the place of business is that which has the closest relationship to the contract and its performance, having regard to the circumstances known to or contemplated by the parties at any time before or at the conclusion of the contract;

Article 10(a) works from the premise that a single party (such as a corporation) may have multiple places of business, and that a selection of the applicable place of business is based on its relationship to an individual sales contract. Consequently, the Convention does not invoke any of the rules for fixing a single location or "nationality" of a corporation, such as determinations based on the place of incorporation, "domicile," or "seat" (*siège, siège social or Sitz*).[6] Article 10(a) must

---

5. See Peter Schlechtriem, Art. 1 paras. 30–31, in Schlechtriem & Schwenzer, *CISG Commentary* (2d English ed. 2005); Ferrari, *Sphere of Application* at 25–26.

6. *Accord*, Peter Schlechtreim, Art. 1 paras. 26 & 27, in Schlechtriem & Schwenzer, *CISG Commentary* (2d English ed. 2005); Ferrari, *Sphere of Application* at 29.

be construed and applied on the basis of its special role in determining the applicability of the Convention.[7]

In Example 1B, let us suppose that the making and performance of the contract are more closely related to State B than to State A. By virtue of Article 10(a), *supra*, Seller's relevant place of business is in State B. Consequently, under Article 1(1), the parties' relevant places of business are not "in different States"; the Convention does not apply.

Suppose that in Example 1B, a business in State B is incorporated in State B but is owned by a parent company incorporated in State A and the sales contract is executed between the company formed in State B and a party located in State B. Even if the corporate subsidiary in State B is closely controlled by the parent in State A the Convention would not apply to the contract. Under Article 1(1), applicability of the Convention is based on the location of the "parties" to the contract, and in this case the parties are both in the same State.[8] To avoid circumventing a State's regulatory policies it may be necessary to "pierce the corporate veil" but it is difficult to imagine circumstances in which this doctrine would apply to free a corporate subsidiary from the domestic law of its place of incorporation.

Failure to distinguish distinct legal entities in determining whether the CISG applies has already confused at least one U.S. court. In Asante Technologies, Inc. v. PMC-Sierra, Inc.,[9] the court faced a claim by a California buyer that the defendant — a U.S. corporation whose headquarters and main operations were in British Columbia, Canada (although it maintained engineering offices in Oregon) — had breached representations it made concerning computer chips it manufactured. Four of the five computer chip orders the buyer had placed, however, were directed not to the defendant, but to the defendant's U.S. distributor — a separate entity — and all billing originated from the U.S. distributor. Ignoring the fact that most (if not all) the goods involved in the dispute appear to have been purchased by a U.S. buyer from a U.S. seller (the defendant's distributor), the court applied the CISG to the buyer's claim against the manufacturer for breaching its representations concerning the chips. The court acknowledged the role of the defendant's U.S. distributor only when it analyzed, pursuant

---

7. Although ULIS (1964) had no provision like CISG Art. 10(a), a German court construed "place of business" in ULIS in accord with CISG Art. 10(a). See *Schlechtriem, German Report, 1986 Cong. Comp. L.*, 141–142, citing BGH of June 2, 1982, LM No. 6 on ULIS.
8. *Accord*, Peter Schlechtriem, Art. 1 para. 28, in Schlechtriem & Schwenzer, *CISG Commentary* (2d English ed. 2005).
9. 164 F. Supp. 2d 1142 (N.D. Cal. 2001).

to Article 10(a), whether the distributor's offices constituted a place of business of the defendant that had "the closest relationship to the contract and its performance" (see the next paragraph below); the court declared that the distributor's offices did not constitute a place of business of the defendant because the distributor was not an agent of the defendant. The larger point, which the court missed entirely, is that the actual selling party in the transactions in which the buyer acquired most (perhaps all) of the chips appears to have been the defendant's U.S. distributor — a point that, if true, would mean that those transactions were not international sales to which the CISG applies. The question whether the CISG should apply to claims of a buyer based upon breach of representations or warranties made by a manufacturer or other party located outside the buyer's state when the representing party did not sell directly to the buyer is explored in connection with Article 4, §63 infra.

In Example 1B, suppose that the seller's place of business in State B is not incorporated in State B but is a branch office of a company formed in State A and having its headquarters in State A. Determining which place of business, under Article 10(a), *supra*, "has the closest relationship to the contract and its performance" will call for weighing competing considerations. The factors in the scale are reduced by the rule of Article 10(a) that the relationship is to be determined on the basis of the circumstances known to or contemplated by both parties "before or at the conclusion of the contract"; supervision by the head office in State A that is known only to the seller is irrelevant; the same is true of facts learned by the buyer subsequent to the making of the contract.[10] The relative importance of the role of the two places of business in making and in performing the contract will be discussed *infra* at §43. However, where the balance seems close the parties would be well advised to settle the point by contract — by stating whether the Convention or specified domestic law is applicable.

The multiple places of business involved in consortia necessarily create difficult problems as to applicable law under traditional domestic law and the Convention. Usually such complex arrangements are governed by a detailed contract which should include an express provision on whether the Convention or a specified domestic legal system applies. See *Kritzer Manual* Ch. 27.

---

10. *Secretariat Commentary*, Art. 9 paras. 7–8, Official Records of the Diplomatic Conference (herein *O.R.*) 19, *Docy. Hist.* 409.

43 (c) "Place of Business"; Sojourn During Negotiations

Example 1B. Seller, in State A, entered into negotiations with Buyer in State B for a complex and important contract for the manufacture of machinery. To complete the negotiations, Seller sent senior officials and a supporting staff to the city in State B where Buyer had its headquarters. Seller's representatives rented a suite of rooms for a month; most of the negotiations and the final execution of the contract took place in that suite.

Did the suite of rooms Seller rented in State B constitute a "place of business"? If so, was this the place which had the "closest relationship to the contract and its performance" (Art. 10(a))?

For reasons explained more fully in the Commentary to Article 10, *infra* at §124, the answer to both questions should be No. "Place of business," as used in Article 1, should be construed to mean a permanent and regular place for the transacting of general business, and would not include a temporary place of sojourn during *ad hoc* negotiations.[11] This interpretation is indicated by Article 10(a) which points to the relationship between the place of business and "the contract *and its performance*." The procurement or production of goods to meet the buyer's requirements is normally of much greater significance to both parties than the place where the contract is negotiated and signed. Moreover, references to "places of business" in other parts of the Convention show that this term excludes a temporary "place" like the hotel room in Example 1B. For example, Article 31(c) provides that where the contract does not "involve carriage of the goods" (para. (a)) and the goods are not located at a place known by the parties (para. (b)), the seller's obligation to deliver consists in placing the goods at the buyer's disposal "at the place where the seller has his *place of business* at the time of the conclusion of the contract" (para. (c)). The meaning of "place of business" as a site of continuing business activity is similarly shown by provisions in Articles 24, 42(b) and 69(2).

In addition, the elusive and insubstantial nature of the place of contracting led UNCITRAL to delete provisions in Article 1(1) of ULIS that made aspects of the making of the contract relevant in determining whether a sale was international. This view is also supported by the emphasis on the place for performance in the 1980 European Economic

---

11. *Accord, Schlechtriem, 1986 Commentary* 43 (In German law a "place of business" is "an establishment of some duration and with certain authorized powers"); Peter Schlechtriem, Art. 1 para. 27, in Schlechtriem & Schwenzer, *CISG Commentary* (2d English ed. 2005); decisions cited in UNCITRAL Digest Art. 1, para. 13; Ferrari, *Sphere of Application* at 26–28. For contract language identifying the place of business, see *Kritzer Manual* Ch. 2.

Community (EEC) Convention on the Law Applicable to Contractual
Obligations (Art. 4(2)).

44 (2) The Transaction's Relation to a Contracting State

As has already been noted, an international sale is subject to the
Convention only if the transaction bears a prescribed relation to one
or more Contracting States. The Convention in Subparagraphs (1)(a)
and (1)(b) of Article 1 states two such relationships, either of which
will suffice. (These two provisions will sometimes be referred to as
"Sub (1)(a)" and "Sub (1)(b).")

45 (a) Both Parties in Contracting States (Sub (1)(a))

Under Sub (1)(a) of Article 1 the Convention applies when the places
of business of the seller and the buyer are in different Contracting States.
In such cases the Convention directs the *fora* of all Contracting States to
apply the Convention.

45.1 (i) Genesis of Sub (1)(a). There was prompt agreement that the
Convention would apply when the places of business of the seller and
buyer were in different Contracting States (Sub (1)(a)). The Convention's central objective was to reduce the legal uncertainty that plagued
trade between different legal systems — uncertainty as to which legal
system was applicable under rules of private international law (PIL) and
uncertainty that was inherent in the likelihood that the applicable
domestic law would be unknown (and often inscrutable) to at least
one of the parties. Applicability based on Sub (1)(a) responds to this
central interest in certainty in two ways: (1) applicability is not subject to
the uncertainties inherent in general rules of conflicts (PIL);[12] and (2)
uncertainties concerning unfamiliar foreign domestic law are replaced
by the applicability of a single uniform law to which the countries of
both parties (among many countries) have agreed.

The Convention's function in enhancing certainty through *uniform*
law needs to be emphasized, for in this setting one concern central to
conflicts law, the proper allocation of regulatory power among competing sovereignties, has little significance. The "regulatory" aspects of the
uniform rules are minimal, evidenced by the parties' freedom to reject

---

12. See UNCITRAL Digest Art. 1 paras. 17–18.

the Convention or modify its rules (Art. 6, §74, *infra*) and by the Convention's deference to the rules on validity under applicable domestic law (Art. 4(a), §64, *infra*).

The Convention's function in reducing the costs of legal uncertainty also supports the decision, made in Sub (1)(a), to apply the uniform rules when the parties have their places of business in different Contracting States even when important aspects of the transaction take place in a non-Contracting State. Uncertainty concerning the parties' obligations generates planning costs that center in the parties' places of business and affect the economic success of the enterprise. These enterprise costs are of concern to the parties and to the States where they have their places of business — rather than to States where aspects of the transaction occur.

There was prompt agreement on Sub (1)(a) of Article 1 but the second ground for applicability, Sub (1)(b), was sharply contested on the ground that basing applicability on rules of PIL would undermine the legal certainty that was the Convention's central goal. To meet this objection the Conference added Article 95, which permitted Contracting States to reject Sub (1)(b).[13] (The effect of an Article 95 reservation will be considered further in §47, *infra*.)

To sum up: The 1980 Convention rejected the "universalist" approach of the 1964 Conventions; Article 1(1) provides for applicability based on either of two types of connection between the sales transaction and a Contracting State: (1) In all Contracting States the Convention will apply when (Sub (1)(a)) the seller and the buyer have their places of business in different Contracting States. (2) The Convention will apply ((Sub (1)(b)) when the rules of PIL point to a Contracting State, subject to a reservation by Contracting States that they "will not be bound" by this provision.

45.2 **(ii) Sub (1)(a) and The Hague PIL Conventions.** [Omitted.]

46 **(b) Applicability Under Rules of Private International Law; Sub (1)(b): An Introduction**

Example 1D. Seller's place of business is in State A and the Buyer's place of business is in State B. State A is a Contracting State; State B is

---

13. The provision for a reservation was made only in final review by the Plenary. See *O.R.* 170 (proposal by Czechoslovakia) 229–230, *Docy. Hist.* 728.

not. Buyer brings an action against Seller in State A; State A has retained Sub (1)(b). The rules on PIL of State A point to the law of Seller's state — State A.

In this example, Sub (1)(a) is not applicable since the parties do not have their places of business in two different *Contracting* States. However, Sub (1)(b) does invoke the Convention, since "the rules of private international law lead to the application of the law of a Contracting State"; in this event Article 1(1) states that "This Convention applies."

46.1 (c) The Effect of Reservations

The Convention permits Contracting States to declare a limited number (see Article 98) of reservations making specified provisions of the Convention inapplicable to the declaring State. The permitted reservations are described in Part IV ("Final Provisions," Arts. 89–101) of the Convention. The effect of these reservations sheds light on the interpretation of the rules on applicability in Article 1. *Example 1E. Seller's place of business is in State A, a Contracting State that has exercised the option provided by Article 92 to exclude Part II on formation of the contract. Buyer's place of business is in State B, a non-Contracting State. The parties disagree over whether they made a contract — that is, whether Seller effectively revoked its offer; a provision on this question (Art. 16) appears in Part II of the Convention. This controversy is brought to a forum in State C, a Contracting State; State C has not excluded Part II. The rules of private international law of the tribunal in State C point to the law of State A. Is the forum in State C precluded from giving effect to State A's reservation excluding Part II by the fact that the forum's version of Article 1 includes Article 1(1)(b) ("Sub (1)(b)"): "When the rules of private international law lead to the application of the law of a Contracting State" the "Convention applies"?*

In this situation Article 92(2), in permitting the declaration excluding Part II, gives a clear answer: State A "is not to be considered a Contracting State within paragraph (1) of Article 1 of this Convention." Consequently, Sub (1)(b) jurisdictions like State C would reach the same result as State A and other Article 92 jurisdictions: The Convention would not apply to questions of formation when the tribunal's choice-of-law principles point to the law of a State that has made the reservation.[14]

14. This reservation was appropriately respected by decisions in Germany (Oberlandesgericht Rostock, Germany, July 27, 1995, CLOUT Case no. 228) and Hungary (Fovórosi Biróság Budapest, Hungary, May 21, 1996, CLOUT Case no. 228). See: Bonell/Ligouri,

Suppose that a State (e.g., Canada) declares under Article 93 that the Convention will not apply to one or more of its territorial units. Under Article 93(3) when a party's place of business is in such a territorial unit, that place "is considered *not to be in a Contracting State.*" Again, Contracting States that have *not* made this reservation are directed to apply the Convention in a manner that respects the decision of States that *have* made the reservation.

Similar problems can arise under Article 94 involving Contracting States "that have the same or closely related legal rules..." — for example, Scandinavian States that have adopted substantially the same law for domestic sales. Two or more States in such a group may declare that the "Convention is not to apply... where the parties have their places of business in those States," and Denmark, Finland, Iceland, Norway and Sweden have made such an Article 94 reservation. Article 94, unlike Articles 92 and 93, does not state that for transactions between parties in reserving States the States are not to be considered as "Contracting States." Nevertheless, a result comparable to that of Articles 92 and 93 must be implied.[15] For example, assume that a case involving a sale between parties in two such States is brought before a *forum* in a Contracting State outside the area. In this setting, as one would expect, the rules of PIL point to one of these States. Sub (1)(b), retained by the forum's State, says that the "Convention applies." Since the forum's State has not made a relevant reservation, Sub (1)(b) seems to say that *all* of the Convention applies so that the *forum* would apply the Convention to the transaction between the Scandinavian States. This, however, would be an inadmissible nullification of the option that Article 92 gave to those States.

In short, when a reservation is made changing the rules on applicability for that State, those rules should be applied by the *forum* of any Contracting State in a case involving parties whose places of business are in the State that made the reservation. Specifically, in cases like Example 1E, it would be basically wrong for the *forum* to apply its own rules of unrestricted applicability to parties who, by a valid reservation made by their States, are entitled to different rules.

ULR, (1997–3) 589, nn.86 & 87. For other decisions dealing with the Art. 92 reservation, see UNCITRAL Digest Art. 1 para. 19.

15. *Accord*, Peter Schlechtriem, Art. 94 para. 9, in Schlechtriem & Schwenzer, *CISG Commentary* (2d English ed. 2005); authorities cited *id.*, n. 11. *Contra*, authorities cited *id.*, n. 8.

We shall meet this problem again (§§47.4 through 47.6 *infra*) in connection with reservations under Article 95 to exclude applicability based on Article 1(1)(b).

B. Alternative Approaches to Applicability

47 **(1) The Option Not To Apply Sub (1)(b)**

At the 1980 Diplomatic Conference, some representatives proposed the deletion of sub paragraph (1)(b) of Article 1. They noted that rules of PIL might point to the law of one State with respect to formation of the contract and to the law of other States with respect to various aspects of performance. Consequently, PIL, invoked by Sub (1)(b), might lead to the applicability of only parts of the Convention whereas the Convention was designed as a unified whole. In this connection, other delegates noted that recourse to PIL became complex where countries (e.g., Czechoslovakia) had enacted a special unified code for international trade. These objections seemed also to stem from the difficulty of applying only part of a unified legal system.

A proposal to delete subparagraph (1)(b) was defeated; as a compromise, the Convention's Final Provisions (Part IV) included the following:[16]

Article 95

Any State may declare at the time of the deposit of its instrument of ratification, acceptance, approval or accession that it will not be bound by subparagraph (1)(b) or Article 1 of this Convention.

The above declaration permitted under Article 95 has been made by the following States: China, Czech Republic, Saint Vincent and the Grenadines, Singapore, Slovakia and U.S.A.[17]

---

16. Article 95 was based on a proposal Czechoslovakia made to the Conference Plenary on April 10, 1980. *Official Records* 229–230. For earlier rejection in the Second Committee see *O.R.* 439. For a general discussion see *Schlechtriem (1986)* 24–27; *B-B Commentary* 654–657 (Evans), *Cf.* Réczei, 29 Am. J. Comp. L. 513, 518–521 (1981); Peter Schlechtriem, Art. 1 paras. 41–44 & Art. 95 *passim*, in Schlechtriem & Schwenzer, *CISG Commentary* (2d English ed. 2005); Ferrari, *Sphere of Application* at 48–54.

17. Upon accession to the Convention in 1991 Canada — apparently seeking to combine its reservatory powers under Art. 93 (the "Federal State" clause) and Art. 95 — declared that one of its territorial units (British Columbia) would not be bound by Art. 1(1)(b).

We may now return to Example 1D (§46, *supra*) in which State A, the place of business of the seller, was a Contracting State but State B, where the buyer was located, was not a Contracting State. Now let us assume that State A in ratifying the Convention made the declaration permitted by Article 95. State A will now apply the Convention only to the sales covered by Sub (1)(a) — transactions between parties in two *Contracting* States. Since Sub (1)(b) is excluded, State A's rules of PIL designating the law of State A now invoke its domestic law rather than the Convention.

47.1 (2) Use of an Article 95 Reservation — Pro and Con

The factors favoring and opposing the making of an Article 95 declaration will vary from State to State; only a few general considerations can be mentioned.[18] In brief, as Example 1D suggests, in most situations an Article 95 declaration narrows the applicability of the Convention and enlarges the applicability of the domestic law of the declaring State. A Contracting State whose domestic law is ill-suited for international transactions may well prefer the wider applicability of the Convention that results from Sub (1)(b), and will choose not to make an Article 95 declaration. On the other hand, States whose domestic law is modern and well-suited to international transactions may well conclude that the Convention's greatest value is within the area defined by Sub (1)(a) — transactions between two *Contracting* States. Although (in the long run) under Sub (1)(a) in approximately half the cases the Convention will supplant the domestic law of the declaring State, in the other cases the Convention will supplant foreign law, which usually will be less accessible than the Convention and often will be archaic and ill-suited to international transactions. Moreover, this important objective — displacing foreign law with uniform international law — is not well served by Sub (1)(b). In most cases, conflict (PIL) rules will point to the State of either the seller or the buyer. As we have seen, when both the seller and buyer are in Contracting States Sub (1)(a) invokes the Convention. Thus, the relevant situation for analysis is that of Example 1D (§46, *supra*): only one of the parties to the sale is in a Contracting State. The option offered by Article 95 must of course be considered from the point of

---

In July 1992 — very shortly after the Convention entered into force with respect to Canada, this declaration was withdrawn.

18. See Volken in *Dubrovnik Lectures* 19, 29 and n. 21; *Schlechtriem, 1986 Commentary* 24–27; Winship in *Parker Colloq.*, §1.02[4].

view of Contracting States since only they can make an Article 95 declaration.

Does the Contracting State effectively displace foreign law by retaining Sub (1)(b)? No: Sub (1)(b) invokes the Convention only when conflicts (PIL) rules point to a *Contracting* State — and in the cases where Sub (1)(b) is relevant the trading partners of the Contracting States are in *non*-Contracting States. (*Non*-Contracting States can scarcely reproach Contracting States for choosing to apply their domestic law in transactions with non-Contracting States: If these States are concerned about coping with foreign domestic law they can adhere to the Convention!)

47.2 (3) The Area of Certainty Provided by Sub (1)(a)

[Omitted.]

47.3 (a) Sales between Parties in Contracting States   [Omitted.]

47.4 (4) The Effect of the Different Options

As noted above, six States have made the reservation permitted by Article 95 "*not* to be bound" by paragraph (1)(b) of Article 1 ("Sub (1)(b)"), which provides that the "Convention applies when the rules of private international law lead to the application of the law of a Contracting State." (For simplicity these will sometimes be referred to as "Reservation States" or States that have "rejected" Sub (1)(b). The significance of the latter expression is discussed at §47.5, *infra*.) Most States have not exercised the Article 95 option and *are* bound by Sub (1)(b). Interesting questions arise from the interplay of these differing choices.

As we have seen, Sub (1)(b) is irrelevant when both the seller and buyer are in Contracting States. We now turn to this general situation: One party is in a Contracting State (State A) and the other party is in a *non*-Contracting State (State B). A dispute between these parties comes before a third State (State C), a Contracting State whose rules of PIL point to State A, a Contracting State. The question will be: Does the Convention or the domestic law of State A apply to the transaction? The problem will be: What is the effect of various combinations of choices by States A and C to reject or retain Sub (1)(b)?

These cases become interesting only when State A (the place of business of one of the parties) and State C (the *forum*) have made different choices with respect to Sub (1)(b). We need to note in passing the following cases where there is no ground for dispute:

(1) When both State A and State C have *retained* Sub (1)(b), the Convention *will* apply.

(2) When both State A and State C have *rejected* Sub (1)(b) the Convention will *not* apply. Thus, if the *forum* decides that PIL points to State A the case will be governed by the domestic law of State A.

Now, at long last, we reach the interesting cases where the two Contracting States have taken different decisions about retaining Sub (1)(b). To simplify the discussion let us assume that decisions taken by the *forum* (State C) on PIL are the same as the decisions of other *fora* facing the same situation. We shall also assume, as usual, that the parties (unfortunately) have not solved the problem in their contract.

47.5 **(a) The Party's State has Retained and the Forum has Rejected Sub (1)(b)**

Example 1F. Seller is in State A, a Contracting State that has retained Sub (1)(b); Buyer is in State B, a non-Contracting State. A dispute under this contract is taken to a tribunal in State C, a Contracting State that has rejected Sub (1)(b). The PIL rules of the forum point to State A. Is the dispute governed by the Convention or by the domestic law of State A?

If we look to Article 1 as adopted by the *forum* we may find only Sub (1)(a), since State C has rejected Sub (1)(b). Thus, Article 1 as adopted by the *forum* states that the Convention applies only when the states of both parties are located in Contracting States. Using the *forum's* rules leads to strange consequences: Article 1 as adopted by the *forum* suggests that Convention would *not* apply even though State A chose to retain applicability of the Convention based on PIL and the rules of PIL point to that State. This result seems even stranger when we note that if this controversy had been taken to any of the Contracting States that have retained Sub (1)(b) (including State A) or to any of the non-Contracting States (including the buyer's State, State B), these tribunals should and probably would apply the Convention. (As noted above we are assuming that these *fora* come to the same decision on PIL as the tribunal in State C.)

These grotesque consequences force us to this conclusion: The narrower applicability of the Convention that results from rejecting Sub (1)(b) is relevant only in determining the Convention's applicability to a *party located in a State that has rejected Sub (1)(b)*. (Seller in Example

1F was not such a party since State A, where Seller was located, had chosen to *retain* applicability of the Convention based on Sub (1)(b).)

The proper effect of an Article 95 reservation becomes clearer when we consider the reason why States requested and exercised this option to reject Sub (1)(b) and thereby confine applicability to Sub (1)(a). One State observed that it would make an Article 95 reservation to protect its traders from being deprived of their familiar domestic law without the countervailing gain of supplanting the foreign law of trading partners in non-Contracting States, for example, State B in Example 1F.[19] Substituting uniform international law for such foreign law was regarded as one of the important advantages of becoming a Contracting State. Certainly Sub (1)(b) was not rejected by State C because its tribunals, acting as neutral *fora*, would find it difficult or distasteful to apply the Convention, for the Article 95 reservation is necessarily made by a Contracting State — a State that is friendly to and willing to apply the Convention.

In short, the proper approach for the *forum* in State C is to decide which State's law is indicated by the rules of PIL. Then, when PIL points to the law of a State that retained Sub (1)(b) (as in Example 1F) the *forum* should apply the Convention.[20] As we have noted, this approach gives the same result as in the *fora* of all States that have retained Sub (1)(b) and all non-Contracting States, and would eliminate the impossible problems (including *forum*-shopping) that would arise if *fora* in States like State C should improperly apply their Article 95 reservation when no party from an Article 95 reservation State is before the court.

Latent in the above solution is this question: By what authority does the forum in State C apply the Convention based on its conflicts (PIL) rules when State C has made an Article 95 reservation "*not* to be bound" by Sub (1)(b). Has it been wrong to state that an Article 95 reservation "rejects" Sub (1)(b)? When States make a reservation that they are "not bound" by Sub (1)(b) are its tribunals free to apply Sub (1)(b) if they choose?[21]

---

19. See the reasons for the Art. 95 reservation made by the U.S.A., set forth in Appendix IB to the Message from the President to the United States Senate. Treaty Doc. No. 98–9, quoted in *Parker Colloq.* at App. 1–27. This statement is also quoted in *Nicholas, LQR*, (1988) Vol. 105, p. 205 who added that this "reason, it may be thought, would apply to the United Kingdom also." Other States similarly were concerned that traders located in their States should be protected by a reservation excluding Sub (1)(b). *E.g.*, representatives from Czechoslovakia were concerned about the impact of Sub (1)(b) to deny to their traders the benefit of their codes for international trade. See Winship, *Cornell Symposium* at 508, 525.
20. Reaching the same result, Ferrari, *Sphere of Application* at 49–50.
21. See Pelichet, 1986 PIL Convention 43.

In Example 1F on what ground should the tribunal in State C, a Reservation State, apply the Convention law of State A when State C's conflicts (PIL) rules point to State A? Suppose that the dispute between the parties in Example 1F were taken to a tribunal in State N, a *non-*Contracting State, and the conflicts (PIL) rules of N (like those of State C) pointed to State A. The tribunal in State N surely should apply the Convention, since this is the law of State A that applies to this transaction. Sub (1)(b) is irrelevant in State N, a non-Contracting State; State N would apply the Convention because this is the correct application of State N's rules of PIL. This also is the reason why in Example 1F the tribunal in State C, although a Reservation State, should apply the Convention; here, too, Sub (1)(b) is irrelevant.[22]

47.6 The Party's State has Rejected Sub (1)(b)

The approach suggested above may be illustrated and tested by the following case:

Example 1G. Seller is in State A, a Contracting State that (unlike State A in Example 1F) has made an Article 95 reservation that it is "not bound" by Sub (1)(b); Buyer is in State B, a non-Contracting State. The forum is in State A which, as was just noted, is a Reservation State. The conflicts (PIL) rules of State A point to State C, a Contracting State that has retained Sub (1)(b).

Should the *forum* in State A apply the Convention to this transaction? The first step is to recognize that Article 95 does not provide that a State that makes the reservation shall apply its own domestic law; it merely frees that State from Sub (1)(b). Thus, in the present example, if the conflicts (PIL) rules of State A pointed to Buyer's State (State B), a non-Contracting State, the State A *forum* would apply the domestic (*non*-Convention) law of State B. This recourse to conflicts (PIL) is, of course, not in response to a command from Sub (1)(b) but simply in order to decide the case under the most appropriate system of law. This principle also applies if the answer to the conflicts (PIL) inquiry points to a Contracting State such as State C. In Example 1G the *forum* in State A should apply the Convention rather than the domestic law of State C.[23]

22. *Cf. Pelichet, 1986 PIL Convention* 43. Ferrari, *Sphere of Application* at 50, is in accord on the rationale in the text.
23. *Accord*, Ferrari, *Sphere of Application* at 49–50. But see Prime Start Ltd. v. Maher Forest Products, Ltd., 2006 WL 2009105 (U.S.D.C. W.D. Wa. July 17, 2006) (dicta stating that U.S. Art. 95 reservation prevents U.S. courts from applying the CISG if one party is from a non-Contracting State, even if PIL rules point to the law of a Contracting State).

This approach to Example 1G is also appropriate since it is applicable to various *fora* to which the dispute might be brought. For example, in this case the plaintiff (e.g., Seller) might choose to bring the action in Buyer's State (State B), a non-Contracting State. State B's conflicts (PIL) rules (particularly with the further success of pending measures for unification) may resemble those of State A. In that event, the conflicts (PIL) inquiry by the *forum* in State B might well point to the law of State C, — or some other similar Contracting State where, for a transaction like this, the Convention is the applicable law.

Example 1H. The facts are the same as in Example 1G in that State A (the Seller's State) made an Article 95 declaration that A "is not bound" by Sub (1)(b). However, in this case the forum is State C, a Contracting State that has retained Sub (1)(b). As in Example 1F, the conflicts, (PIL) rules of the forum point to State A.

The correct approach follows from the discussion of Example 1F. The *forum* in State C, having determined that PIL points to State A, should conclude that since State A has rejected Sub (1)(b) the law of State A for this transaction does not include the Convention; consequently the *forum* in State C should apply the domestic sales law of State A.[24]

This approach respects State A's option to reject applicability of the Convention under Sub (1)(b) when a party in that State contracts with a party in a non-Contracting State and the rules of PIL point to State A. (Reasons for exercising this option were noted at §47.1, *supra*.) Moreover, this approach would be like the approach of: (1) other States that have rejected Sub (1)(b) (like State A); (2) all non-Contracting States like State N in §47.5, *supra*.[25]

In short, the fact that States have responded differently to the option offered by Article 95 should present no serious difficulties once it is understood that the choice is exercised in the interest of parties in a State

24. Contra, Ferrari, Sphere of Application at 51–52.
25. But cf. Pelichet, *1986 PIL Convention* 43. Portions of the present text have been stimulated by helpful correspondence with Mr. Pelichet about our approaches to Sub (1)(b) and reservations under Art. 95.

The Federal Republic of Germany in ratifying the Convention (December 21, 1989) retained Sub (1)(b). The Act of Parliament enacting the Convention provided (Art. 2) that Sub (1)(b) would not apply when the rules of private international law lead to the application of the law of a State that has made a reservation under Art. 95. See *vC-S Kommentar (1990)* 762 (Schlechtriem). This action seems to be in accord with the views of the present writer. For a general commentary on Art. 1 and the Convention's sphere of applicability see *vC-S Kommentar* 44 (Herber). On Art. 95 see *id.*, 750.

that makes this choice, and that *fora* of other States should respect that choice. In addition, as we have seen (§46.1, *supra*), this result is consistent with the result of other reservations permitted by the Convention.

Two of the above examples, 1F and 1H, (perhaps unnecessarily) probed the effect of reservations excluding Article 1(1)(b) in unusual situations — litigation brought in a State where neither the seller nor buyer has its place of business.[26] In this rarified atmosphere, this writer's views have met both support and criticism.[27]

Happily, controversies involving the applicability of CISG under Article 1(1)(b), and the rare cases involving reservations to this provision, are diminishing as the number of adhering States increases.[28] The future lies with Article 1(1)(a) and its clear-cut rule: The Convention applies when the places of business of the seller and buyer are in different Contracting States.

48 ## C. Other Problems of Applicability

(1) Nationality; Civil or Commercial Character

The rules on applicability of the Convention do not refer to the nationality of the parties or to their civil or commercial character. Consequently, it was not necessary to add in paragraph (3) that these factors are not to be "taken into consideration in determining the application of this Convention."[29]

The specific rejection of a distinction between "the civil or commercial character of the parties or of the contract" should prevent any misapprehension by those who are accustomed to separate civil and commercial codes. The 1980 Convention is not of this character. True, the typical international transaction is commercial and, as we shall see.

---

26. "The expense of spirit in a waste of shame." William Shakespeare, Sonnet No. 109.

27. On the obligations of States (whether or not Contracting) to respect Art. 95 reservations excluding Sub 1(1)(b), see Schlechtriem, *CISG Commentary* (1st English ed. 1998) 27–28, §§43–44; idem., *1986 Commentary* 27 n. 56a; Bonell/Ligouri, ULR (1996–1) 153–154 nn. 37–40 (1997–2) 391–393; Evans, M., *B-B Commentary* 656–657; Winship, P., 21 Cornell Int. L.J. 487–533 (1988); Gabor, F.A. 7 N.W.J. Int'l & Bus. 696–726 (1986), 8 *id.*, 538–569 (1988). *But cf.* Ferrari, *Sphere of Application* at 15–16 nn. 201–206.

28. See Ferrari, *Sphere of Application* at 33–35.

29. The last seven words of Art. 1(3) were added at the 1980 Convention to avoid the possible implication that these factors would be irrelevant for all purposes. See, e.g., Art. 35(2)(b) (reliance on the Seller's "skill and judgment").

Articles 2(a) and 5 specifically exclude most consumer-type transactions. However, the central point, emphasized by paragraph (3), is that the traditional classifications in some legal systems between "civil" and "commercial" parties and transactions are irrelevant in determining the applicability of the Convention.[30]

(2) "Goods"

Article 1(1) provides that the Convention applies to the sale of "goods." The meaning of this term will be examined following the discussion of provisions of Articles 2 and 3 which shed light on this question. See §56 *infra*.

---

30. In rare circumstances, nationality could become relevant under Art. 1(1)(b) when a State uses nationality as a part of its rules on private international law.

Part 1 of the Convention governs the applicability of the Convention as a whole, including, of course, Part II on Formation of the Contract. Consequently, references in Part I to "contracts" (Arts. 1(1) and 3), in the setting of issues under Part II, embrace questions as to whether a contract was formed. See also the Introduction to Part II, *infra* at §131.

Article 2.
Exclusions from the Convention

49   Article 2 excludes from the Convention six specific categories. The first three (paragraphs (a)-(c)) are based on the nature of the transaction; the remaining three paragraphs (d)-(f)) are based on the nature of the goods.[1]

Article 2[2]

This Convention does not apply to sales:
(a) of goods bought for personal, family or household use, unless the seller, at any time before or at the conclusion of the contract, neither knew nor ought to have known that the goods were bought for any such use;
(b) by auction;
(c) on execution or otherwise by authority of law;
(d) of stocks, shares, investment securities, negotiable instruments or money;
(e) of ships, vessels, hovercraft or aircraft;
(f) of electricity.

50   A. Specific Exclusions

(1) Purchases for Personal, Family or Household Use

Most consumers do their shopping at stores in their own community; all of these purchases fall outside the Convention because they are not international (Art. 1, *supra* at §39). However, consumers may occasionally shop on the other side of a nearby international border or during trips abroad, or may order from foreign mail-order houses. The development of electronic commerce, particularly sales made via the Internet, undoubtedly has increased the number of international consumer sales. In some of

---

1. It has been suggested that the six categories of exclusions in Art. 2 should be divided into three (rather than two) groups by distinguishing exclusion based on the intended use of the goods (Art. 2(a)), exclusions based on the type of contracts (Art. 2(b) & (c)), and exclusions based on the kind of goods (Art. 2(d)–(f)). Franco Ferrari, *Sphere of Application* 21, 79 and authorities cited *id.*, n. 281.
2. This article is substantially the same as Art. 2 of the 1978 Draft. *Cf.* ULIS 5 (no provision comparable to paragraphs (a) and (b)).

these transactions the seller will know that the buyer is a foreigner so that the transaction would meet the Convention's requirements of internationality. (See Art. 1(2), *supra* at §41).

In UNCITRAL attention was drawn to the development of national legislation and case law designed to protect consumers; it was agreed that the Convention should not supersede these rules. Consideration was given to a provision that the Convention would not override any domestic rule that was "mandatory" or that implemented "public policy" (*ordre public*), but it was found that these concepts carried different meanings in various legal systems; the clearest and safest solution was specifically to exclude consumer purchases from the Convention.[3]

The phrase "goods *bought for personal, family or household use*" refers to the purpose of the buyer at the time of the purchase. (A similar definition in (U.S.A.) UCC 9–109 applies when the goods "are used" by the buyer for the above purposes; in CISG, "are used" was deleted so that applicability of the Convention would not depend on action taken by the buyer subsequent to the purchase.) The Austrian Supreme Court (Oberster Gerichtshof) has held, pursuant to Article 2(a), that the CISG did not apply to the sale of a Lamborghini automobile because the buyer purchased the car for personal use; the court noted that it was the buyer's *intended* use (at the time the contract was concluded) rather than the buyer's actual use of the goods that was dispositive.[4] The character of the goods is not decisive; the Convention applies to the international purchase of furniture for a business office even though this type of furniture is customarily bought by consumers.[5] ***Nor does***

---

3. *W/G 2* paras. 51, 57, IIYB 55, 56, *Docy. Hist.* 61, 62; *Sec. Commy.* para. 2, *O.R.* 16, *Docy. Hist.* 406. Some decisions rendered since CISG entered into force, however, appear unaware of the exclusion. *See, e.g.*, Bundesgericht, Switzerland, December 11, 2000, English translation available at http://cisgw3.law.pace.edu/cases/001211s1.html (applying CISG to the sale of a "fitted kitchen" to homeowners without discussing whether the transaction was excluded by Art. 2(a)); Landgericht Düsseldorf, Germany, October 11, 1995, English translation available at http://cisgw3.law.pace.edu/cases/951011g1.html (applying CISG to the sale of an electrical generator for a yacht without discussing whether the transaction was excluded by Art. 2(a)). For discussion of the latter case see Fawcett, *Harris & Bridge, Sale and Conflict of Laws* §16.85. Note that sales to consumers are covered by the Principles of European Contract Law. See Ch. 1 Section 1: Scope of the Principles (Arts. 1.01–1.07).
4. Oberster Gerichtshof, Austria, February 11, 1997, CLOUT Case no. 190, English abstract also at http://www.unilex.info/case.cfm?pid=1&do=case&id=283&step=Abstract.
5. For confirmation of this point, see Landgericht Saarbrücken, Germany, November 25, 2002, English translation available at http://cisgw3.law.pace.edu/cases/021125g1.html (applying the CISG to the sale of clothes by a clothing wholesaler to a buyer that operated a clothing store); Landgericht München, Germany, February 20, 2002, English translation

the fact that the buyer is an individual rather than a business entity necessarily mean the CISG is inapplicable: as a Swiss court has noted, "the purchase of goods by an individual for commercial or professional purposes remains subject to the Convention."[6]

The "unless" clause that concludes paragraph (a) may be illustrated as follows:

Example 2A, Seller, a dealer in photographic equipment in State A, accepted an order from Buyer, a resident of State B, for expensive and complex photographic equipment of the type normally used by professionals. In a controversy over the sale, when Seller invoked the Convention, Buyer offered evidence that he bought the equipment for his personal use as an amateur.

In this case, the seller should be able to show, under the "unless" clause of paragraph (a), that he "neither knew or ought to have known" of the buyer's purpose; in this event, the Convention would govern the sale. *The type of goods and the circumstances of the sale certainly are relevant to the question whether the seller "neither knew nor ought have known" that the goods were intended for consumer use. One decision has suggested the following approach: "If, at the time of the conclusion of the contract, the seller has no reason to think that the goods are purchased for personal, family or household use, namely, where the quantity of the goods, the delivery address or any other circumstance of the transaction are not standard for a consumer sale, the acquisition remains subject to the Convention."*[7] As to burden-of-proof see *O.R.* 239, *Docy. Hist.* 460.

Questions that turn on proof of what a person "knew" or "ought to have known" can hardly be free of doubt but advance planning can minimize the uncertainty. Sellers who distribute catalogues to international customers or who sell goods through World Wide Web sites accessible internationally may wish to include the following language on order forms (and on similar contract documents and records): "International purchases of this equipment may be governed by the United Nations Convention on Contracts for the International Sale of Goods unless the goods are bought

---

available at http://cisgw3.law.pace.edu/cases/020220g1.html (applying the CISG to sale of shoes between business entities involved in the shoe trade).

6. Tribunal Cantonal Jura, Switzerland, November 3, 2004, English translation available at http://cisgw3.law.pace.edu/cases/041103s1.html (applying the CISG to an individual buyer's purchase of "sand, palettes of masonry sand, corrugated iron sheets and a mix of gravel-sand" for use on the buyer's farm).

7. Tribunal Cantonal Jura, Switzerland, November 3, 2004, English translation available at http://cisgw3.law.pace.edu/cases/041103s1.html (citation omitted).

for personal, family or household use. If the goods are bought for such use, please check the appropriate box below." A buyer who does not make the requested indication could scarcely contend that the seller "ought to have known" of the buyer's purpose.

Although this Commentary argues that burden-of-proof issues are, except in rare instances, beyond the scope of the Convention and are governed by applicable non-Convention law (see §70.1 infra), the structure of Article 2(a) and practical considerations applicable to the allocation of the burden-of-proof suggest that the buyer has the burden of proving that it bought the goods for personal, family or household use; the seller would have the burden of proving that it did not know (and had no means of knowing) the buyer's purpose.[8] *Professor Schlechtriem is generally in accord, although he argues the burden may vary with "the nature of the goods and the position of the buyer": those circumstances, he suggests, may create a presumption of either intended commercial use or intended "personal, household or family use" which must then be rebutted by the party arguing the opposite.*[9]

51   (2) Sales by Auction

The exclusion of sales "by auction" resulted from various considerations: Auction sales present unique problems with respect to formation of the contract. The seller will not know who the buyer is (and hence whether the Convention applies under Art. 1(1)) until after the sale is "knocked down" to the highest bidder. In addition, local law often applies special regulations to auction sales.[10]

---

8. The highest German court with jurisdiction on CISG matters has suggested that Art. 2(a) of the CISG allocates burden-of-proof "tacitly." Bundesgerichtshof, Germany, January 9, 2002, English translation available at http://cisgw3.law.pace.edu/cases/020109g1.html.

9. Peter Schlechtriem, Art. 2 paras. 16–17, in Schlechtriem & Schwenzer, *CISG Commentary* Art. 2 §§16–17 (2d English ed. 2005).

10. *W/G 2* para. 58, IIYB 56, *Docy. Hist.* 62. For a case finding CISG inapplicable under Art. 2(b), see Bundesgerichtshof, Germany, October 2, 2002, English abstract available at http://www.unilex.info/case.cfm?pid=1&do=case&id=915&step=Abstract (auction sale of vegetables). Sales at a commodity exchange are not sales "by auction," but rather rapid-fire communication of offers and acceptances. *Accord*, Schlechtriem & Schwenzer, *CISG Commentary* (2d English ed. 2005). For the special problems typical of auction sales see (U.S.A.) UCC 2–328; (U.K.) SGA (1893) 58; *Ont. L. Ref. Com.*, I Sales 86–90. Professor Schlechtriem suggests that "online" auctions are excluded from the CISG by Art. 2(b). Peter Schlechtriem, Art. 2 para. 19, in Schlechtriem & Schwenzer, *CISG Commentary* (2d English ed. 2005); but see *id.*, §21 (stating that there are "good arguments" for applying the CISG to an international sales contract resulting from an "internet auction").

52   (3) Sales on Execution or Otherwise by Authority of Law

Execution and other forced sales are fundamentally different from other transactions because of the inability of the parties to negotiate the terms of the contract; in addition, the manner and effect of such forced sales are subject to special regulations.

These considerations are useful in defining the scope of this exclusion. For example, when the buyer fails to pay for the goods the seller may be empowered to "avoid" the contract and resell the goods. Similar rights may be given to the buyer when the seller delivers seriously defective goods (Arts. 49, 64, 75, 81, 88). Such resales by a party to the contract, even though authorized by the Convention, are not excluded from the Convention as sales "(c) on execution or otherwise by authority of law." The same principles apply when a secured party on default by the debtor resells the collateral at a private sale rather than by auction.[11]

53   (4) Shares and Other Securities; Money and Money Paper

The exclusion of the intangible rights listed in Article 2(d)[12] illustrates the fact, discussed more fully in §56, *infra*, that the sale of "goods" refers to moveable, corporeal things.[13] In the 1964 Hague Conventions and in UNCITRAL there was general agreement that transactions in the types of assets listed in Article 2(d) should be excluded from the law covering "sales of goods." The exclusion of "negotiable instruments" (Fr.: *effets de commerce*; Sp.: *titulos o efectos de comercio*) refers to instruments calling for the payment of money. Documents controlling the delivery of *goods* (e.g., warehouse receipts, bills of lading) are

---

11. *W/G* 2 para. 54, II YB 56, *Docy. Hist.* 62. *Cf.* (U.S.A.) UCC 9–610 (2003 version) (secured party, under specified circumstances, may resell the collateral), UCC 7–210, 7–308 (enforcement at private sale of lien of warehouseman and of carrier). In any event, such sales will usually be made to a buyer with a place of business in the same State as the seller and will fall outside the Convention since they are not international. (See Art. 1(1), *supra* at §39.).

12. For a decision refusing to apply the Convention on the basis of Art. 2(d) see Oberlandesgericht Köln, Germany, December 4, 2000 (sale of company shares).

13. Arbitration Court of the Chamber of Commerce and Industry of Budapest, Hungary, December 20, 1993, CLOUT Case no. 161, English abstract also available at http://www. unilex.info/case.cfm?pid=1&do=case&id=70&step=Abstract (CISG applies only to sales of tangible goods, and thus is inapplicable to the sale of shares of limited liability company).

subject to the Convention when they are employed to effect the delivery of goods.[14] See Arts. 30, 34, 58(1) *infra*.

54 (5) Ships, Vessels, Hovercraft, Aircraft

The 1964 Hague Conventions excluded sales "of any ship, vessel or aircraft, which is or will be subject to registration." ULIS 5 (l)(b); ULF 1 (6)(b). The reference to registration was designed to designate goods which, according to Prof. Tune's commentary, "are or will be subject to a special system of rules which, moreover, frequently resembles that for immovables." In UNCITRAL it was found that national legislation included many varieties or regulations that might (or might not) be deemed to include "registration"; the concluding phrase was therefore deleted. Consideration was given to excluding only vessels of a specified tonnage; this attempt also was abandoned.[15]

Does the exclusion of the sale of "ships, vessels" (Fr.: *navires*, *bateaux*; Sp.: *tuques, embarcaciones*)[16] extend to small pleasure craft such as sailboats and rowboats? No such restriction seems feasible for the exclusion of "aircraft."[17] UNCITRAL's inability to find a workable

---

14. See Peter Schlechtriem, Art. 1 para. 22 & Art. 2 para. 28, in Schlechtriem & Schwenzer, *CISG Commentary* (2d English ed. 2005).

15. *W/G 2* para. 55, II *YB* 56, UNCITRAL X (1977) Annex I, paras. 29–32, VIII *YB* 27; *SR. 1* para. (e); *SR. 2* paras. 5–16, *Docy. Hist.* 320.

16. For application of the Art. 2(e) exclusion of ships and vessels, see Tribunal of International Commercial Arbitration at the Russian Federation Chamber of Commerce and Industry, Russian Federation, April 6, 1998, English translation available at http://cisgw3.law.pace.edu/cases/980406r1.html; Yugoslav Chamber of Economy (arbitration proceeding), Yugoslavia, April 15, 1999, translation available at http://cisgw3.law.pace.edu/cases/990415y1.html. But see Maritime Commission at the Chamber of Commerce and Industry of the Russian Federation (arbitration proceedings), Russian Federation, December 18, 1998, English translation available at http://cisgw3.law.pace.edu/cases/981218r1.html (sale of decommissioned submarine not covered by Art. 2(e) exclusion and is governed by CISG). Some decisions appear to reflect a lack of awareness of the exclusion of ships and vessels. *See*, *e.g.*, Gerechtshof Leeuwarden, the Netherlands, August 31, 2005, English translation available at http://cisgw3.law.pace.edu/cases/050831n1.html (applying CISG to sale of six boats without discussing or mentioning Art. 2(e)); Audiencia Provincial de Baleares, Spain, June 15, 2001, English translation available at http://cisgw3.law.pace.edu/cases/010615s4.html (apparently applying CISG to sale of boats without discussing or mentioning Art. 2(e)).

17. For discussion of the aircraft exclusion, see Peter Winship, *Aircraft and International Sales Conventions*, 50 J. Air L. & Comm. 1053–1066 (1985). For a decision applying the exclusion, see Tribunal of International Commercial Arbitration at the Russian Federation Chamber of Commerce and Industry, Russian Federation, September 2, 1997, English translation available at http://cisgw3.law.pace.edu/cases/970902r1.html. But see Legfelsobb Bíróság, Hungary,

basis for distinguishing between large and small craft and the difficulty that courts would encounter in developing such a distinction suggest that Article 2(d) must be read without qualification: Sales of small pleasure craft do not fall within the Convention. Article 7(1) provides: "In the interpretation of this Convention, regard is to be had to its international character and to the need to promote *uniformity in its application....*" International uniformity in interpretation and application would be more readily achieved by an unqualified reading of Article 2(d) than by judicial attempts to narrow the scope of the provision.[18] See Nicholas, LQR (1989) 206. On the other hand, Professor Schlechtriem has suggested that this exception should not be extended to the sale of boats that under domestic law do not come under the special regulations of domestic law applicable to ships.[19] Discussion at the Diplomatic Conference is reported at *O.R.* 240–241, *Docy. Hist.* 461–62.

Providing a ship with supplies (e.g., fuel) or with equipment necessary for the voyage, although within domestic maritime law, would be subject to the Convention if other requirements of Article 1 are met.[20] On the sale of materials for ship construction, see §56, *infra.* However, under Article 90 the Convention would yield to an "international agreement" governing the rights of a seller and buyer who "have their places of business in States parties to such agreement." See §§462–464, *infra.*

55 **(6) Electricity**

The exclusion of contracts for the sale of electricity is explicit and clear-cut.[21] *See also* §56, *infra.*

September 25, 1992, English translation available at http://cisgw3.law.pace.edu/cases/ 920925h1.html (applying CISG to sale of aircraft engines).

18. *W/G* para. 55, II *YB* 56, UNICTRAL X (1977) Annex I, paras. 29–32, VIII *YB* 27; *Docy. Hist.* 320.

19. Schlechtriem, *1986 Commentary* 30. See also Peter Winship, *Aircraft and International Sales Conventions*, 50 J. Air L. & Comm. 1053 (1985). In his commentary on the CISG, Professor Schlechtriem suggests that "small rowing boats, paddle boats, and inflatables are not ships or vessels" and "interpretation should focus on whether [the watercraft] is principally intended as a means of transport (in which case it should be a ship) or as sports equipment." Peter Schlechtriem, Art. 2 para. 33, in Schlechtriem & Schwenzer, *CISG Commentary* (2d English ed. 2005). See also Ferrari, *Sphere of Application* at 92–93.

20. See McMahon, 21 J. Mar. L. & C. 305, 306 (1990). *Cf.* Legfelsobb Bíróság, Hungary, September 25, 1992, English translation available at http://cisgw3.law.pace.edu/cases/ 920925h1.html (applying CISG to sale of aircraft engines despite exclusion of sales of "aircraft" in Art. 2(e)).

21. For a critique of this exclusion, see Ferrari, *Sphere of Application* at 94–95.

56   B. "Sale of Goods"

(1) "Goods"

As we have seen, Article 1 provides that the Convention applies to contracts of "sale of goods." The Convention does not define "goods"[22] but some of the exclusions specified above in Article 2 and other provisions of the Convention provide guides for construing this basic concept. It is clear that "goods" governed by the Convention must be tangible, corporeal things,[23] and not intangible rights like those excluded by Article 2(d) above — stocks, shares, investment securities and instruments evidencing debts, obligations or the right to payment.[24] As has been noted at §53, *supra*, the point is that these documents represent *intangible rights* — a claim for payment or for receiving dividends or other payments from an enterprise.[25] Article 3(2), §60 *infra*, takes a similar approach in excluding contracts in which the preponderant part of a party's obligations "consists in the supply of labour or other *services*." Possible dispute over whether electricity is tangible (a quantum) or intangible (a wave) was avoided by the exclusion of electricity. See Article 2(f). On the other hand, a sale (e.g.) of gas is within the Convention; a motion to exclude gas was defeated.[26] *The question whether transactions in computer software constitute "sales" of "goods" that may be governed by the CISG — an increasingly significant question for modern commerce — is discussed in §56.4 infra.*

---

22. For decisions relating to the meaning of "goods" under the CISG, see UNCITRAL Digest Art. 1 paras. 8–10. For discussion of what constitutes "goods" for purposes of CISG, and a survey of authority on the issue, see Ferrari, *Sphere of Application* at 75–79.

23. See, e.g., Landgericht Flensburg, Germany, January 19, 2001, English translation available at http://cisgw3.law.pace.edu/cases/010119g1.html (sale of "goods" includes sale of livestock (sheep)).

24. Arbitration Court of the Chamber of Commerce and Industry of Budapest, Hungary, December 20, 1993, CLOUT Case no. 161, English abstract also available at http://www.unilex.info/case.cfm?pid=1&do=case&id=70&step=Abstract (CISG applies only to sales of tangible goods, and thus is inapplicable to the sale of limited liability company shares).

25. A sales contract calling for the delivery of corn, machinery or the like by handing over a bill of lading, warehouse receipt or other similar document is, of course, a contract for the sale of "goods." See Art. 34, §§217–220, *infra*; *Sec. Commy.* para. 8, *O.R.* 16, *Docy. Hist.* 406.

26. UNCITRAL X (1977) para. 35, VIII *Yearbook* 27, *Docy. Hist.* 320. *Cf. Report, 1985 Hague PIL Convention* 23 n. 22; "Delegates were clear that 'gas' constituted 'goods.' " Sale of oil is covered. See James W. Skelton, *Potential Effects of the International Sales Convention on U.S. Crude Oil Traders*, 9 Houston J. Int. L. 101 (1986).

The conclusion that "goods" refers to tangible, corporeal things means that sales of patent rights, copyrights, trademarks and "know-how" are not governed by the Convention.[27] (As we shall see, under the Convention a buyer *of goods* has rights against the seller if the goods are subject to a "right or claim of a third-party based on industrial property or other intellectual property." See Art. 42, §§267–270, *infra*).

Many provisions of the Convention also make clear that the term "goods" (French: *merchandises*; Spanish: *mercaderias*) refers to moveable tangible assets. A sale of land is excluded. Any possible doubt on this point is foreclosed by numerous provisions that are incompatible with transactions in land — e.g., quality and packaging (Art. 35), replacement or repair of defective parts (Art. 46), shipment and damage during transit (Arts. 67–69), delivery by installments (Art. 73), preservation and warehousing to prevent loss or deterioration (Arts. 85–88). It follows that a contract to construct a bridge, building or other permanent structure is not a contract for the sale of "goods." The building materials are goods[28] but materials that the builder brings to the building site normally may be removed without breaking the contract with the landowner; *cf.* (U.S.A.) UCC 2–105(1). On the other hand, the Convention would apply to an international sale of a mobile building even though the buyer might decide to affix it permanently to his land.[29]

Questions can arise from contracts relating to things that at the making of the contract are a part of or attached to land (e.g., oil, ores, trees, buildings) but which will become moveable at a later stage. Contracts requiring the seller to extract or sever corporeal objects from land and make them available to the buyer seem to be covered by Article 3(1) (§57, *infra*) as "Contracts for the supply of goods to be manufactured

---

27. *Accord, Report, Hague 1985 PIL Convention* 23, paras. 34–35. See Oberlandesgericht Köln, Germany, August 26, 1994, English translation available at http://cisgw3.law.pace.edu/cases/940826g1.html (CISG does not apply to contract to conduct and deliver a market study; "the work is embodied in a written form solely to make it intellectually graspable, and the form of the embodiment is of secondary importance to the commissioner of the study").

28. Court of Arbitration of the International Chamber of Commerce, Case No. 7153, 1992, CLOUT Case no. 26, English translation available at http://cisgw3.law.pace.edu/cases/927153i1.html.

29. Cour d'appel Grenoble, France, April 26, 1995, CLOUT Case no. 152, English translation available at http://www.cisg.law.pace.edu/cisg/wais/db/cases2/950426f2.html (sale of second-hand portable shed which the seller was to dismantle and ship to the buyer was sale of "goods" (specifically, "goods to be manufactured or produced") for purposes of CISG). See also Robert V. von Mehren & David W. Rivkin, *Contracts for the International Sale of Minerals*, 2 J. Int. Arb. 49 (1985).

or produced. . . ."[30] Legislative history (§56 n. 9, *supra*) shows that the sale of gas is covered; there is no reason to suppose that a direct underground origin for the gas affects this result. On the other hand, a contract permitting a party to come on land and mine, drill or cut timber does not call for one party to deliver goods to the other; crucial provisions of the Convention on conformity of goods (Art. 35), delivery, shipment (Arts. 31–33) and risk of loss (Arts. 66–70) do not address the special circumstances of contracts for mining or other extraction activities.[31] However, the parties by agreement may make the Convention applicable to these transactions (§81, *infra*).

56.1   (2) Exchanges of Goods: Barter Transactions

Some domestic sales laws exclude exchanges of goods. The (U.K.) Sale of Goods Act applies to transfers or property "for a *money* consideration" — a restriction that raises questions of interpretation when (e.g.) S delivers goods at a stated price to B with the understanding (as in a "trade-in" transaction) that goods that B delivers to S will reduce the price by a stated amount.[32]

The Convention does not state any restrictions as to the price. Article 53 states: "The buyer must pay the price for the goods. . . ." Articles 55–59 speak in the same general terms. This, plus the parties' freedom under the Convention to shape the transaction to meet their needs supports the view that exchanges of goods are not excluded unless the parties so choose (Art. 6 *infra*).[33] On the other hand, some

---

30. *Accord*, Cour d'appel Grenoble, France, April 26, 1995, CLOUT Case no. 152, English translation available at http://www.cisg.law.pace.edu/cisg/wais/db/cases2/950426f2.html (sale of second-hand portable shed which the seller was to dismantle and ship to the buyer was sale of "goods" (specifically, "goods to be manufactured or produced") for purposes of CISG).

31. *Cf.* (U.S.A.) UCC §2–107(1): sale of goods includes (minerals and the like only "if they are to be severed by the seller"); *Ont. L. Ref, Sales*, Vol. 3 p. 15 (Draft Act. §2.5(1)). But *cf. Bridge, Sale* 28–29.

32. *Benjamin* §§34–39. See also Winship in *Parker Colloq.* §1.02 pp. 1–24 n. 49, citing Secretariat Studies; *Ont. L. Ref. Com. Sales,* Vol. I p. 65; Proposed Act; §2.6(1) "The price may be paid in money *or otherwise.*" *Accord*, Proposed Uniform Sale of Goods Act for Canada (enacted in New Brunswick), §11(1): The price may be paid "in money *or otherwise.*" Uniform Law Conference of Canada, 1982 Proceedings, Appendix III p. 538, available at http://www.ulcc.ca/en/us/index.cfm?sec=1&sub=1s2. UCC (U.S.A.) 2–304 ("money or otherwise"). Finnish Sales Act (1987) Sec. I.

33. Decisions are split on whether CISG applies to barter transactions. For cases applying (or apparently applying) the CISG to barter and counter-trade transactions, see Tribunal of International Commercial Arbitration at the Ukrainian Chamber of Commerce & Trade,

"counter-trade" arrangements, primarily concerned with the balance of payments, may not describe the goods or other obligations of the parties with sufficient definiteness to constitute a contract of sale.[34] See §56.2 and Article 14, §133 *infra*.

56.2   (3) Framework Agreements for Future Orders and Deliveries; Franchise Agreements.

Example 2B. A supplier (S) and a distributor (D) make a "framework" agreement that will govern any orders and deliveries by S to D but does not require D to order or S to deliver any specified quantity (e.g., a particular amount, or D's "requirements," or S's "output").

This agreement, without more, does not constitute a "contract of sale" under Article 1 and is not governed by the Convention (the definiteness required of offers is discussed under Article 14 at §§134–137, *infra*); if orders are thereafter made and accepted, however, CISG may govern the resulting contracts of sale, with the "framework" agreement supplying the detailed terms of the transaction to supplement or modify the provisions of the Convention.[35] See Article 6, §§74–84. If the "framework" agreement was made before the date of the Convention's entry into

---

Ukraine, April 15, 2004, English translation available at http://cisgw3.law.pace.edu/cases/040415u5.html; Tribunal of International Commercial Arbitration at the Ukrainian Chamber of Commerce and Trade, Ukraine, October 10, 2003, English translation available at http://cisgw3.law.pace.edu/cases/031010u5.html; China International Economic and Trade Arbitration Commission [CIETAC], People's Republic of China, June 13, 1989, English translation available at http://cisgw3.law.pace.edu/cases/890613c1.html. For decisions refusing to apply the CISG to barter transactions, see Tribunal of International Commercial Arbitration at the Russian Federation Chamber of Commerce and Industry, Russian Federation, March 9, 2004, English translations available at http://cisgw3.law.pace.edu/cases/040309r1.html; Federal Arbitration Court for the Moscow Region, Russian Federation, May 26, 2003, English translation available at http://cisgw3.law.pace.edu/cases/030526r1.html. Professor Schlechtriem suggests that barter transactions are not "contracts of sale" under Art. 1. Schlechtriem, *1986 Commentary* 24 and n. 41b; Schlechtriem & Schwenzer, *CISG Commentary* Art. 1 §18 (2d English ed. 2005). See also Ferrari, *Sphere of Application* at 63–64. The present writer would agree that the complexity of some barter or counter-trade arrangements may suggest exclusion of the Convention based on the parties implied intent. See Arts. 6 and 8, *infra*.

34. See UNCITRAL Legal Guide on Drawing up Contracts in International Counter-trade Transactions (Ch. III of 1990 draft considers alternative approaches to contract. A/CN.9/332); *Kritzer Manual* Ch. 25; Loeber in *Weidring Conf.* (1986) 299–315.

35. See, for example, Bundesgerichtshof, Germany, July 23, 1997, English translation available at http://cisgw3.law.pace.edu/cases/970723g2.html (CISG is not applicable to framework agreement, but does apply to individual sale contracts entered into thereunder);

force, under Article 99 the Convention would govern orders and contracts made after that date but not before.

The arrangements and practices involved in franchise[36] and dealership relationships are too varied for thorough treatment here. Dealers sometimes sue for losses incurred in preparing for a franchise arrangement that is expected on the basis of representations that fall short of promises. These claims present some of the problems presented by outlays during negotiations that fail to ripen into contract — the problem known in some legal systems as *culpa in contrahendo*. These problems arise from such diverse settings that they are dealt with or excluded by provisions of Part II on Formation of the Contract. Other problems arise out of termination clauses in franchise agreements that are challenged as so harsh as to violate standards of conscionability — problems of contract validity that Article 4(a) leaves to domestic law. See §§64–69 (validity) and §§94–95 (good faith). In addition, close examination of the facts may show that the issue does not arise out of a "contract of sale of goods" and therefore falls outside of the scope of the Convention.

56.3 (4) Undivided Shares of Fungible Goods

Efficient handling of some types of goods (e.g., oil, grain) calls for their storage or their shipment in quantities greater than the units needed for sale. Units of such goods (e.g., bushels of No. 2 Durham wheat, barrels of No. 3 heating oil) are sufficiently uniform ("fungible")

Oberlandesgericht Düsseldorf, Germany, July 11, 1996, CLOUT Case no. 169, English translation available at http://cisgw3.law.pace.edu/cases/960711g1.html (same). Professor Schlechtriem generally agrees with this approach, although he notes "the borderline between distribution and requirement (sales) contracts may be very thin and uncertain...." Peter Schlechtriem, Art. 1 para. 16a & *Introduction to* Arts. 14–24 para. 7, in Schlechtriem & Schwenzer, *CISG Commentary* (2d English ed. 2005). See also the analysis of this issue in Fawcett, Harris & Bridge, *Sale and Conflict of Laws* §16.95; Bridge, *International Sale of Goods* §2.18. For a U.S. case on the issue, see Helen Kaminski Pty., Ltd. v. Marketing Australian Products, Inc., 1997 WL 414137 (U.S. District Court for the Southern District of New York, July 23, 1997). For other decisions on this issue, see Peter Schlechtriem, Art. 1 para. 16a nn. 28 & 29a, in Schlechtriem & Schwenzer, *CISG Commentary* (2d English ed. 2005); UNCITRAL Digest Art. 1 para. 6; Ferrari, *Sphere of Application* at 62–63 (analyzing the decisions); Multi-Juice, S.A. v. Snapple Beverage Corp., 2006 WL 1519981, 2006 U.S. Dist. LEXIS 35928 (U.S.D.C. S.D.N.Y., June 15, 2006) (refusing to apply the CISG to distribution agreement).

36. For discussion of franchise agreements and the CISG, see Ferrari, *Sphere of Application* at 62–63 text accompanying n. 160 (citing decisions). For decisions on the applicability of the CISG to franchise agreements, see UNCITRAL Digest Art. 1 para. 7.

throughout a tank or bulk carrier that contracts of sale may be framed not merely in quantities of generic goods (e.g., 1,000 bushels of No. 1 Durham wheat) but instead in terms of quantities or shares of the contents of an identified bulk ("tank #63"; "tanker North Star sailing June 1").

These transactions are clearly "contracts of sale of goods" within Article 1 and no provision excludes them from the Convention.[37] Thus, failure to deliver goods of the agreed quality or quantity, failure to receive and pay for the goods, and many related questions are governed by the Convention. The only substantial question is whether sales of quantities or shares in an identified bulk of fungible goods can satisfy the "identification" requirements of Articles 67(1) and 69(3) governing risk of loss. See §§371, 378, *infra*.

56.4   (5) Computer "Hardware" and "Software"

Computer "hardware" is clearly "goods" subject to the CISG.[38] The classification of computer software, on the other hand, has led to controversy.[39] Some software seems difficult to distinguish from an exceedingly compact book or phonograph record, the sale of which clearly could be subject to the CISG. *Some cases and commentators have distinguished between standard software and "custom-made" software,*[40] *and between software delivered on tangible media (such as a CD or*

---

37. The question would scarcely be worth mentioning but for the fact that language of the (U.K.) Sale of Goods Act has led to doubt of its applicability to such transactions. *Benjamin* §§119. *Contra, Ont. L. Ref. Com.* I, 44–45; Draft Uniform Sale of Goods Act §8, Uniform Law Conference of Canada (Proceedings, 1982) 537; (U.S.A.) UCC 2–105(4), 1–201 (definition of "fungible").

38. See, e.g., Landgericht München, Germany, May 29, 1995, English abstract available at http://www.unilex.info/case.cfm?pid=1&do=case&id=161&step=Abstract; Oberlandesgericht Koblenz, Germany, September 17, 1993, CLOUT Case no. 281, English translation available at http://cisgw3.law.pace.edu/cases/930917g1.html.

39. For decisions on the question whether the CISG applies to computer software, see UNCITRAL Digest Art. 1 para. 10. For discussion of those decisions, see Ferrari, *Sphere of Application* at 77–78.

40. Ferrari, Sphere of Application at 77–78 and decisions cited n. 267; L. Scott Primak, Computer Software: Should the U.N. Convention on Contracts for the International Sale of Goods Apply? A Contextual Approach to the Question, 11 Computer L.J. 197, 214–17 (1991); Arthur Fakes, The Application of the United Nations Convention on Contracts for the Sale of Goods to Computer, Software and Database Transactions, 3 Software L.J. 559, 582–84 (1990). The basis for this distinction appears to be that in a contract for customized software the seller's obligations may be predominantly service obligations, and thus even if contracts for standardized software are considered sales of goods, contracts for customized software would be excluded from the Convention by Art. 3(2). For discussion

diskette) and software delivered electronically over the Internet.[41] *Professor Schlechtriem rejects both distinctions, arguing that the CISG applies to sales of both standardized and custom software, irrespective of whether the software is delivered electronically or on a tangible object.*[42] *He posits, however, that the CISG is inapplicable to "mere licensing agreements" which grant only a time-limited use of software that can be rescinded in certain circumstances (such as the licensee's insolvency): in his view, only a transaction that transfers "the software in all respects except for the copyright and restrictions on its use by third parties" constitutes a "sale" within the meaning of the CISG.*[43] When dealing with software, as in other borderline areas, it seems prudent to state in the contract whether the Convention applies.

---

of whether services and labor performed by a seller in producing specially-manufactured goods should be considered in the Art. 3(2) analysis, see §60.6 *infra.*

41. E.g., Ferrari, *Sphere of Application* at 78 text accompanying n. 270. Another distinction suggested by a decision of a Danish appeals court is between a contract for the "development of a website" (which the Austrian court characterized as a service contract beyond the scope of the CISG) and a "sale of software" (which some regard as a sale of goods governed by the CISG). Østre Landsret, Denmark, March 7, 2002, commentary in English by Professor Joseph Lookofsky available at http://cisgw3.law.pace.edu/cases/020307d1.html. Professor Lookofsky characterizes the court's distinction as "elusive."

42. Peter Schlechtriem, Art. 1 para. 21, in Schlechtriem & Schwenzer, CISG Commentary (2d English ed. 2005). Compare Joseph Lookofsky, Understanding the CISG in the USA: A Compact Guide to the 1980 United Nations Convention on Contracts for the International Sale of Goods §2.5 at 19–22; Joseph Lookofsky, The 1980 United Nations Convention on Contracts of the International Sale of Goods, in International Encyclopaedia of Laws Supp. 29 §58 at 37 (R. Blainpain ed., December 2000); Frank Diedrich, The CISG and Computer Software Revisited 6 Vindobona J. Int'l Comm. L. & Arb. 55 (Supp. 2002); Frank Diedrich, Maintaining Uniformity in International Uniform Law via Autonomous Interpretation: Software Contracts and the CISG, 8 Pace U. Int'l L. Rev. 303 (1996). Recently, a U.S. court appears to have assumed (without discussion) that a sale of software would be considered a "sale of goods" and would be governed by the CISG if the other prerequisites for applying the Convention were met (the court ultimately concluded that the "internationality" requirement of CISG Art. 1 was not met, and thus that the CISG was inapplicable). See American Mint LLC v. GOSoftware, Inc., 2006 WL 42090 (U.S. District Court for the Middle District of Pennsylvania, January 6, 2006); see also the August 16, 2005 decision in this litigation, reported under the same name at 2005 WL 2021248.

43. Peter Schlechtriem, Art. 1 para. 21, in Schlechtriem & Schwenzer, *CISG Commentary* (2d English ed. 2005). Compare Fawcett, Harris & Bridge, *Sale and Conflict of Laws* §16.87 (questioning whether software transactions in the form of licenses should be considered "sales" (irrespective of whether software should be deemed "goods")); concluding that "on balance it seems correct to extend the concept of goods to intangible property that is not expressly excluded form the Convention" but that "the difficulty presented by the licensing issue . . . is by means so easily overcome").

56.5 (6) Sale of All or Part of an Enterprise

Sale of all or part of the shares of a corporation or of ownership interests in other business entities is excluded form the CISG by Article 2(d) (see §53 *supra*). Sale of the assets of an enterprise (or a part thereof) may include the transfer of "good will" and other intangibles and, sometimes, the assumption of debts; sale of equipment or "goods" such as inventory may be of secondary importance. In these cases, it appears improper to apply the Convention to a transaction as a whole (because it is not predominantly a sale of goods), and an attempt to apply CISG to a part of the transaction may not be feasible (unless the goods portion of the transaction is governed by a separate contract). *On the other hand, by analogy to mixed goods/service transactions governed by Article 3(2), the presence of intangibles and other "non-goods" should not prevent application of the Convention if the transfer of goods is the predominant part of the transaction — although the presence of real property in the transaction will undoubtedly complicate the application of the CISG.*[44]

---

44. In the U.S., this problem is solved by applying sales law to the goods portion of the transaction but not to the transfer of real estate. (U.S.A.) UCC 2–304(2). Professor Schlechtriem would not apply the CISG to the sale of assets of a business if real property, intangible rights and/or good will would make up a "considerable part" of the assets being transferred. Peter Schlechtriem, Art. 1 para. 24, in Schlechtriem & Schwenzer, *CISG Commentary* (2d English ed. 2005).

Article 3.
Goods to be Manufactured; Services

57   Paragraph (1) of Article 3 deals with the Convention's applicability to contracts for the supply of goods to be manufactured or produced; paragraph (2) deals with sales contracts that include the supply of labor or other services.

Article 3[1]

(1) Contracts for the supply of goods to be manufactured or produced are to be considered sales unless the party who orders the goods undertakes to supply a substantial part of the materials necessary for such manufacture or production.

(2) This Convention does not apply to contracts in which the preponderant part of the obligations of the party who furnishes the goods consists in the supply of labor or other services.

58   A. Goods To Be Manufactured

Paragraph (1) states the necessary premise that a modern sales law must include transactions that call for the manufacture or production of goods[2] and then addresses this question: Does the Convention extend to

---

1. This article was derived, after redrafting, from Art. 3 of the 1978 Draft. These proceedings at the Vienna Conference are recorded in *O.R.* 241–245, 270–271, 84–85; *Docy. Hist.* 462–466, 491–492, 656–657. *Cf.* ULIS 6, ULF 1(7). Proceedings in UNCITRAL: II *YB* 41, 56–57, VI *YB* 90–91, 110–111, 51, VIII *YB* 28, 38; *Docy. Hist.* 46, 62–63, 215–216, 235–236, 242, 321, 331.
2. For decisions confirming this aspect of the Convention's scope, see UNCITRAL Digest Art. 3 para. 2 n. 2. See also Handelsgericht St. Gallen, Switzerland, April 29, 2004, English translation available at http://cisgw3.law.pace.edu/cases/040429s1.html; Oberster Gerichtshof, Austria, 29 March 2004, English abstract available at http://cisgw3.law.pace.edu/cases/040329a3.html; Kantonsgericht Schaffhausen, Switzerland, January 27, 2004, English translation available at http://cisgw3.law.pace.edu/cases/040127s1.html; Oberlandesgericht Karlsruhe, Germany, December 19, 2002, English translation available at http://cisgw3.law.pace.edu/cases/021219g1.html, English abstract available at http://www.unilex.info/case.cfm?pid=1&do=case&id=909&step=Abstract; Handelsgericht St. Gallen, Switzerland, December 3, 2002, English translation available at http://cisgw3.law.pace.edu/cases/021203s1.html; Handelsgericht Aargau, Switzerland, November 5, 2002, English translation available at http://cisgw3.law.pace.edu/cases/021105s1.html; Hof van Beroep Gent, Belgium, May 15, 2002, English translation available at http://cisgw3.law.pace.edu/cases/020515b1.html; Tribunal de Commerce Namur, Belgium, January 15, 2002, English translation

contracts in which the party who receives a finished product supplies all or part of the necessary materials? *Whether services performed by the seller in producing specially ordered or customized goods implicates Article 3(2), which provides that the CISG does not apply to contracts in which the seller's obligations are preponderantly service obligations, is discussed in §60.6 infra.*

59 (1) Buyer Supplies Materials

Example 3A. Owner, in possession of unfinished textiles ("grey goods"), makes a contract with Finisher providing that Finisher will bleach and dye the goods and return them to Owner.

By virtue of paragraph (1) of Article 3, this contract does not fall within the Convention; this is true even if the contract states that the goods are owned by Finisher during the processing and are thereafter sold to Owner for an agreed price.[3] Regardless of the form of the contract, the "unless" clause of paragraph (1) is decisive: The party who ordered the goods undertook "to supply a substantial part of the materials necessary for" their manufacture or production.[4]

Questions of degree inevitably arise along the borders of the statute. Some of these questions can be suggested by an example.

Example 3B. Purchaser contracted with Manufacturer for the supply of stainless steel and agreed to supply the chromium, a necessary ingredient;

---

available at http://cisgw3.law.pace.edu/cases/020115b1.html; Oberster Gerichtshof, Austria, January 14, 2002, CLOUT Case no. 541, English translation available at http://cisgw3.law. pace.edu/cases/020114a3.html; Landgericht Hamburg, Germany, December 21, 2001, English translation available at http://cisgw3.law.pace.edu/cases/011221g1.html.

3. *Accord*, Peter Schlechtriem, Art. 3 para. 3, in Schlechtriem & Schwenzer, *CISG Commentary* (2d English ed. 2005). See Oberster Gerichtshof, Austria, October 27, 1994, CLOUT Case no. 105, English abstract also available at http://www.unilex.info/case. cfm?pid=1&do=case&id=131&step=Abstract (refusing to apply CISG where the buyer supplied the seller all raw materials for the goods (brushes and brooms)). This 1994 decision was invoked by the Austrian Oberster Gerichtshof in a later decision suggesting (but not unambiguously holding) that the CISG was inapplicable to a contract involving the "fattening of animals" — that is, (presumably) a contract in which the original owner of livestock transfers them to a feed lot for fattening and the feed lot later returns the animals to the original owner. Oberster Gerichtshof, Austria, April 17, 2002, English translation available at http://cisgw3.law.pace.edu/cases/020417a4.html. In the 2002 decision, however, the court appears to have invoked only Art. 3(2) rather than Art. 3(1) — an approach that may reflect confusion over the relationship of the two subparts of Art. 3. See §60.6 *infra*.

4. The comparable categories in various legal systems are analyzed in Lorenz, Contracts for Work on Goods and Building Contracts, VIH *Int. Enc. Comp. L.* Ch. 8 §§2–5.

the value of the chromium supplied by Purchaser comprised 15% of the total value of the materials used in manufacturing the stainless steel.

The fact that the chromium was necessary for the production does not itself lead to the exclusion of this transaction; exclusion results only when the purchaser supplies "a *substantial part* of the materials necessary" for production. We may assume that the weight or volume of the chromium would not be "substantial" in relation to all of the necessary materials, but this should not be decisive: The only commensurable relationship is one based on value.[5] How big a proportion of the value of all the materials is "substantial?" Paragraph (2) refers to "the preponderant part"; a "substantial" part would be less than preponderant. It seems that a tribunal might well conclude that 15% is "substantial" but the evaluation of such questions of degree is difficult to predict.[6] The parties to such an international transaction would be well advised to solve the question of the Convention's applicability in their contract.[7]

---

5. Professor Schlechtriem suggests that the economic value of the materials supplied by the buyer is the "starting point" in assessing whether the contribution is "substantial," but that consideration of the importance of the materials for the functioning of the goods "should not be entirely excluded." In the interest of "wide and uniform application of the Convention," however, he suggests that use of this factor to change the results of a strict "value" approach should be "rare exceptions." Peter Schlechtriem, Art. 3 para. 3a, in Schlechtriem & Schwenzer, *CISG Commentary* (2d English ed. 2005). For further discussion of the "value" approach vs. the "importance" or functionality approach, see CISG Advisory Council, CISG-AC Opinion no. 4, Contracts for the Sale of Goods to Be Manufactured or Produced and Mixed Contracts (Art. 3 CISG) paras. 2.3–2.7 (2004), available at http://www.cisg.law.pace.edu/cisg/ CISG-AC-op4.html; Ferrari, *CISG's Sphere of Application* 67–69.

6. See CISG Advisory Council, CISG-AC Opinion no. 4, Contracts for the Sale of Goods to Be Manufactured or Produced and Mixed Contracts (Art. 3 CISG) paras. 2.8–2.10 (2004), available at http://www.cisg.law.pace.edu/cisg/CISG-AC-op4.html. While generally rejecting an approach based on fixed percentages, the Advisory Council Opinion suggests that a "substantial part" of the materials may require something exceeding 50% of the value of the materials used to produce the goods. See para. 2.10. But see Ferrari, *Sphere of Application* 69 (indicating that a "substantial part" may be less than 50% of the value of the goods). For decisions on this question, see UNCITRAL Digest Art. 3 para. 2.

7. ULIS 6 made exclusion from the law depend on the supply of "an essential and substantial part of the materials." In UNCITRAL the reference to "essential" was deleted. But *cf.* Kahn, Rev. Int. Dr. Comp. 951, 955 (1981). The drafters of the French version had difficulty with the concept of "substantial" and used the phrase "*une part essentielle*." The Spanish version states "*una parte sustancial*." Peter Schlechtriem, Art. 3 para. 3a, in Schlechtriem & Schwenzer, *CISG Commentary* (2d English ed. 2005).

  Art. 6 provides that the parties "may exclude the application of the Convention . . . . . ." The Commentary to Art. 6 considers the converse — agreements that the Convention will be *applicable* — and concludes that, in cases like Example 3B, such an agreement probably

Assume that Purchaser did not supply chromium or other materials but did supply valuable technical services and "know-how" that had "substantial" value in relation to the total value of the materials. No provision of CISG excludes this transaction. Article 3(2) excludes transactions only on the basis of services provided by the *seller*.[8] At the Vienna Conference a proposal to exclude transactions on the basis of expert services supplied by the buyer was rejected.[9]

59.1 (2) Burden-of-proof under Article 3(1)

Professor Schlechtriem states that the burden of proving that a contract is excluded from the Convention under Article 3(1) is on the party claiming such exclusion.[10] For discussion of burden-of-proof in disputes governed by CISG, see §70.1 infra.

60 Contracts not Confined to the Supply of Goods

60.1 (1) Goods and Services

Example 3C. In an international contract Supplier agreed to deliver and install manufacturing machinery in Purchaser's factory and also to provide technicians to operate the machinery for a period of one year. The value of the machinery was $1,000,000 and the value of supplying the technicians was $200,000.

The above contract would not be excluded from the Convention by Article 3(2) since the "supply of labour and other services" did not comprise "the *preponderant* part of the obligations of the party who furnishes the goods." The opposite answer would result if the contract

---

would be effective. See Art. 6 *infra* at §78. *Schlechtriem, 1986 Commentary* 36 suggests that Art. 6 authorizes parties to make CISG applicable even though Art. 3(2) would otherwise exclude the contract. The discussion of Art. 6, §§78–83, *infra*, suggests a similar result based on applicable domestic law.

8. For decisions on this issue, see UNCITRAL Digest Art. 3 para. 3. For analysis of these decisions see Ferrari, *Sphere of Application* 69–70.

9. See *O.R.* 243–244; *Docy. Hist.* 464–465; Peter Schlechtriem, Art. 3 para. 3b, in Schlechtriem & Schwenzer, *CISG Commentary* (2d English ed. 2005).

10. Peter Schlechtriem, Art. 3 para. 3, in Schlechtriem & Schwenzer, *CISG Commentary* (2d English ed. 2005).

called for services with value in excess of $1,000,000.[11] For example, Article 3(2) could exclude a contract to repair a complex machine if the cost of labor is greater than that of the replacement parts. *Looking strictly to quantified economic value in assessing whether service aspects preponderate in a transaction is an approach adopted by some[12] but not all.*[13]

Does the Convention apply not only to the part of the contract dealing with the supply of goods but also to the part dealing with the supply of services? The answer should be Yes.[14] Article 3(2) applies only when the parties deal with both goods and services in a single contract. When there are significant relationships between the two aspects of the

---

11. *W/G 2* paras. 61–67, II *YB* 56–57; UNCITRAL X (1997) Annex, I, para. 43, VIII *YB* 28; *SR.* 2 paras. 30–82; SR. 4 paras. 4–10 *Docy. Hist.* 62–63, 321. For discussion of whether labor and other service costs incurred in manufacturing the machinery should be considered in the Art. 3(2) analysis, see §60.6 *infra*.

12. Fawcett, Harris & Bridge, *Sale and Conflict of Laws* §16.93 ("the case law on balance favours a quantitative monetary evaluation of the goods against services, so that if the goods are worth more than the services then the contract comes under the Convention . . . . . . The language of the Convention, however, seems more aptly to embrace the quantitative approach, however mechanical this may seem"). See also the cases cited in UNCITRAL Digest Art. 3 para. 4. These cases are analyzed by Professor Ferrari in Ferrari, *Sphere of Application* 71–74. See also Oberlandesgericht Wien, Austria, June 1, 2004, English abstract available at http://cisgw3.law.pace.edu/cases/040601a3.html; Tribunale d'appello Lugano, Switzerland, October 29, 2003, English translation available at http://cisgw3.law.pace.edu/cases/031029s1.html.

13. Peter Schlechtriem, Art. 3 para. 7a, in Schlechtriem & Schwenzer, *CISG Commentary* (2d English ed. 2005) (stating that "[a] hard and fast rule based only on a comparison of values . . . is not desirable" and that in difficult cases "intention and interest of the parties must tip the balance"); CISG Advisory Council, CISG-AC Opinion no. 4, Contracts for the Sale of Goods to Be Manufactured or Produced and Mixed Contracts (Art. 3 CISG) paras. 3.3–3.4 (2004), available at http://www.cisg.law.pace.edu/cisg/CISG-AC-op4.html (stating that the "economic value approach is correct" but suggesting that other factors should be considered "where the economic value is impossible or inappropriate to apply taking into account the circumstances of the case"; other relevant factors include "the denomination and entire content of the contract, the structure of the price, and the weight given by the parties to the different obligations under the contract"). Professor Ferrari argues that a quantitative economic value approach should be used unless it proves inconclusive, in which case factors such as the circumstances surrounding the conclusion of the contract and the purposes of the transaction should be considered. Ferrari, *Sphere of Application* 71–74. See also the cases cited in UNCITRAL Digest Art. 3 para. 5; Handelsgericht Zürich, Switzerland, July 9, 2002, English translation available at http://cisgw3. law.pace.edu/cases/020709s1.html; Kantonsgericht Schaffhausen, Switzerland, February 25, 2002, English translation available at http://cisgw3.law.pace.edu/cases/020225s1.html.

14. *Accord*, Tribunale d'appello Lugano, Switzerland, October 29, 2003, English translation available at http://cisgw3.law.pace.edu/cases/031029s1.html.

contract the Convention should apply to the entire contract. If this is not the case, the arrangement should be treated as two contracts and the Convention would apply only to the contract for goods. Because of the relationships between the supplying of goods and services it would be important for a single set of rules to apply to the entire contract. When a controversy arises, the most troublesome problems not regulated by the contract are likely to relate to remedies for breach — particularly the question whether the breach justifies avoidance of the entire contract. A unified approach to such problems may be necessary for the effective application of the Convention's provisions to the transaction in goods; pursuant to Article 3(2) the value of goods would at least equal and in most cases would exceed the value of the services.[15] Many of the provisions of the Convention are concerned with the physical aspects of goods — transport, damage, destruction, deterioration. Services do not generate these problems, but the irrelevance of these provisions of the Convention should not present difficulties. And the Convention's general approach to interpretation and enforcement of the contract would be useful for the entire transaction. (The Convention's unitary approach to the contract and its remedies was introduced in the Overview in Ch. 1 at §2 and Ch. 2 at §§24–27.)

60.2   *Severability.* Professor Schlechtriem has suggested that domestic law should decide whether a transaction involving both goods and services is one contract governed by the Convention, or two contracts with the service aspect governed by domestic law.[16] This conclusion is entitled to great weight. The present writer has held a different view but would now be inclined to agree with Schlechtriem if the approach of applicable domestic law to the question of "severability" is sufficiently flexible to give decisive weight to the question mentioned above: Will "severing" the contract prevent the effective application of the uniform international rules to the transaction in goods? If a Contracting State applies domestic rules on "severability" that ignore the effective application of the Convention to a transaction that combines goods and

15. For discussion of whether services must exceed 50% of the contract by some substantial amount in order to preclude application of the CISG, see Peter Schlechtriem, Art. 3 para. 7b, in Schlechtriem & Schwenzer, *CISG Commentary* (2d English ed. 2005); CISG Advisory Council, CISG-AC Opinion no. 4, Contracts for the Sale of Goods to Be Manufactured or Produced and Mixed Contracts (Art. 3 CISG) para. 2.8 (2004), available at http://www.cisg.law.pace.edu/cisg/CISG-AC-op4.html.

16. *1986 Commentary* 32. For a more recent pronouncement, see Peter Schlechtriem, Art. 3 paras. 5 & 7, in Schlechtriem & Schwenzer, *CISG Commentary* (2d English ed. 2005). For a different view, see Ferrari, *Sphere of Application* 74.

services, that State would scarcely be honoring its obligation to give full effect to the rules governing international sales; nor would it be obeying the mandate of Article 7(1) (§§85–86, *infra*) to interpret the Convention with regard for "its *international character* and [ ] the need to promote *uniformity in its application.*"[17] Article 3(2) is based on the premise that the Convention will apply to some transactions that embrace both goods and services; decisions as to which transactions will be covered cannot properly be made solely on the basis of principles of domestic law.

60.3   (2) Industrial Plant and Equipment; Turn-key Contracts

In discussing Article 2 at §56, *supra*, we saw that construction of an immovable building was not a sale of "goods." Even when contracts for industrial works call for the buyer to supply the land and building, some of the equipment may become a permanent part of the building while other equipment may be free-standing and readily removable. "Turn-key" contracts may also include the supplying of "know-how" and services in placing the plant in operation.

Such complex contracts should (and often do) designate the applicable law. See Art. 6 at §75, *infra*. If the contract is silent, deciding whether the Convention governs any part of the transaction calls for applying by analogy the Convention's provisions on mixed contracts in Article 3 and also consideration of the parties' implied intent (Art. 8, §§104–111, *infra*) in light of the (1) suitability of the Convention's provisions to the contract *as a whole* and (2) the feasibility of "severing" the contract to make the Convention apply to *only part* (§60.2, *supra*).[18] *Professor Schlechtriem concludes that "as a rule" CISG will not apply to turn-key contracts "because the sale of goods elements are rarely to the forefront" of such contracts.[19] A Swiss court has refused to apply the CISG to a turn-key contract involving the design, construction, installation and initial operation of a recycling plant.[20]*

17. See Khoo, *B-B Commentary* §3.1, at 43.

18. See UNCITRAL Legal Guide on the Drawing Up of International Contracts for the Construction of Industrial Works. United Nations. U. N. Sales No. E.87. V.IO 1988); *Kritzer Manual* Ch. 26.

19. Peter Schlechtriem, Art. 3 para. 8, in Schlechtriem & Schwenzer, *CISG Commentary* Art. 3 §8 (2d English ed. 2005). See also CISG Advisory Council, CISG-AC Opinion no. 4, Contracts for the Sale of Goods to Be Manufactured or Produced and Mixed Contracts (Art. 3 CISG) para. 3.5 (2004), available at http://www.cisg.law.pace.edu/cisg/CISG-AC-op4.html.

20. Handelsgericht Zürich, Switzerland, July 9, 2002, English translation available at http://cisgw3.law.pace.edu/cases/020709s1.html.

60.4   (3) Analogical use of Provisions of the Convention

In some situations tribunals may find that provisions of the Convention are helpful in solving comparable problems that fall outside its
scope. Such voluntary borrowing of solutions from specialized statutes
has been useful within domestic legal systems. For example, in the
United States the Uniform Sales Act (1906) and its successor, Article 2
of the Uniform Commercial Code (1954), state that they govern "sales"
of goods — language that literally would exclude the burgeoning field
of supplying goods through leasing (hiring or rental) arrangements.
Courts faced with the question whether the user (lessee) of the goods
was entitled to legal protection when the goods were defective, however,
found that the "sales" statutes dealt with a comparable problem and
relied on these provisions; this approach was not in obedience to statutory command but in observance of the principle that similar problems
called for similar solutions.[21] The extension of "sales" rules to "leases"
of goods has necessarily been selective; for example, some of the
"sales" rules dealing with remedies for breach are inappropriate to
transactions in which the user's investment is limited to rental payments.[22] Problems such as these led in 1987 to the addition to the
Uniform Commercial Code (UCC) of a new Article 2A-*Leases*,
immediately following Article 2-*Sales*.

"Lease" or "Sale": Form or Substance. Some transactions labeled
"lease" in substance are sales coupled with a security interest in favor of
the seller (who is labeled "lessor"). Whether the CISG applies to these
transactions should depend on substance rather than form; "chameleon
leases" may be subject to the CISG if they satisfy the other requirements
for applicability — e.g., Article 1.[23]

Tribunals, of course, are under no international obligation to use the
Convention's provisions for transactions that lie outside its scope; such
"borrowing" depends on principles of domestic *jurisprudence* and a
decision whether rules designed for domestic transactions are as suited
to international transactions as the Convention. In a larger sense, careful

21. *Honnold, Sales*; Stone, The Common Law in the United States, 50 Harv. L. Rev. 4, 12–14
(1936).
22. This difference is reflected in both case-law and in Art. 2A-Leases, which was added to
the UCC in 1987. The 1988 UNIDROIT Convention on International Financing Leasing
(Ottawa, May 28, 1988) responded to the special role of institutions that finance leasing
transactions.
23. But see Fawcett, Harris & Bridge, *Sale and Conflict of Laws* §16.89. Penetrating such
disguises in the setting of the UCC is discussed in *White & Summers* §21–3 (1995).

analogical extension of these and other international rules can make a measured, albeit modest, contribution to the reestablishment of an international law-merchant.[24]

60.5 (4) Interpretation of Rules on Scope: Certainty v. Flexibility

Measured *analogical* use of the Convention's provisions can also relieve pressure for doubtful interpretations *extending* the Convention's scope. In discussing Article 7(2), §§96–102, *infra*, we shall consider the Convention's invitation to use "the general principles on which it is based" to govern questions which, although "not expressly settled" in the Convention, arise out of matters "governed by" the Convention. This provision, which calls for analogical extension of the Convention's substantive rules to avoid "gaps" in the uniform rules for transactions falling *within the Convention's scope*, is profoundly different from principles for interpreting provisions that govern the Convention's *outer boundaries* (e.g., Articles 1–6).

As the language quoted from Article 7 shows, its call for a broad analogical approach to the Convention's substantive provisions for matters "governed by" the Convention *does not apply* to provisions such as Articles 1–6, which define the area that the Convention does not "govern." Nor does the Convention contain any provision authorizing analogical extension of its outer boundaries. Indeed, in framing the Convention such a proposal would have received short shrift and for good reason: Doubt about the Convention's outer boundaries generates uncertainty as to nearly every substantive issue that can arise in an international sale. These factors suggest that provisions defining the Convention's outer boundaries should be interpreted to achieve maximum certainty. On the other hand, as we shall see, Article 7(2) (buttressed by Articles 8 and 9, §§104–122, *infra*) calls for a more flexible approach in the development of rules to govern transactions that reside within the Convention's domain.

---

24. *Cf.* Berman, The Law of International Commercial Transactions (*Lex Mercatoria*), 2 Emory J. Int. Dispute Resolution 235, 298–310 (1988); B. Goldman, Lex Mercatoria, 3 Forum Internationale (1983). *Cf.* Goldštajn in *Dubrovnik Lectures* 55, 85–93. The present writer's commitment to the development of international *lex mercatoria* has not yet prepared him to join in proclamations that the New Dispensation has fully arrived. See Langen, Transnational Commercial Law (1973).

60.6 **(5) Seller's Services in Producing Custom-Made Goods — Relationship between Article 3(1) & Article 3(2)**

Should labor and services performed by the seller in manufacturing or producing the goods be considered in analyzing whether services constitute the "preponderant part" of the seller's obligations under Article 3(2)? This question is particularly salient if the goods are customized or otherwise "specially-made" for the buyer: in that case, the seller's production services are contemplated by (and may even be expressly described in) the contract. As we have seen, under Article 3(1) the CISG can apply to sales of goods produced for the buyer (including customized goods), provided the buyer does not supply a "substantial part of the materials necessary" for making the goods. See §§58–59 supra. But is a contract for specially-made goods in which the buyer does not supply a substantial part of the materials excluded from the Convention if the value of the manufacturing services provided by the seller (either alone or in combination with other non-manufacturing services the seller must provide under the contract) exceeds the value of the materials that the seller provided? In other words, are the scope questions raised by the fact that goods are specially manufactured for the buyer governed exclusively by Article 3(1), or does Article 3(2) also have a role to play in determining the effect of that fact on the applicability of the CISG?

Several decisions have taken into account the seller's labor and services in producing goods when determining whether the service aspect of a contract predominates under Article 3(2).[25] Article 3(2) does not expressly provide that the seller's production services should not be considered, nor does the Convention state that Article 3(1) is the exclusive source for rules relating to specially-manufactured goods. Including the seller's production labor and services in the Article 3(2) calculation, however, is problematic. The value of labor and services expended in producing goods exceeds the value of their materials in

---

25. See the decisions cited in CISG Advisory Council, CISG-AC Opinion no. 4, Contracts for the Sale of Goods to Be Manufactured or Produced and Mixed Contracts (Art. 3 CISG) 4.2 nn.43 & 44 (2004), available at http://www.cisg.law.pace.edu/cisg/CISG-AC-op4.html. See also Oberster Gerichtshof, Austria, November 8, 2005, English translation available at http://www.cisg.law.pace.edu/cisg/wais/db/cases2/051108a3.html (remanding case to determine whether service obligations predominated in a contract requiring seller to "design, produce, and deliver" a piece of machinery).

many if not most cases — creating significant uncertainty about the Convention's applicability if such labor or services "count" for purposes of Article 3(2). Even if the Article 3(2) calculation only takes into account services performed by the seller in producing specially-ordered goods, why should it matter to the coverage of the CISG whether the seller is an integrated manufacturer responsible for all or most steps in producing the goods, or a broker who arranges for production of specially-ordered goods by a third-party manufacturer? The provisions of the Convention are as well-suited to situations in which the goods are specially produced for the buyer as to sales of pre-manufactured and/or standardized goods, as Article 3(1) shows. Most authorities that have considered the question, therefore, have concluded that the seller's labor and services in producing goods should not count on the "services" side of the ledger for purposes of Article 3(2).[26]

60.7 **(6) Burden-of-proof under Article 3(2)**

Professor Schlechtriem states that the burden of proving that a contract is excluded from the Convention under Article 3(2) is on the party claiming such exclusion.[27] *For discussion of burden-of-proof in disputes governed by CISG, see §70.1 infra.*

---

26. Peter Schlechtriem, Art. 3 para. 4, in Schlechtriem & Schwenzer, *CISG Commentary* (2d English ed. 2005); CISG Advisory Council, CISG-AC Opinion no. 4, Contracts for the Sale of Goods to Be Manufactured or Produced and Mixed Contracts (Art. 3 CISG) paras. 4.1–4.4 (2004), available at http://www.cisg.law.pace.edu/cisg/CISG-AC-op4.html; Joseph Loo-kofsky, *Understanding the CISG in the USA: A Compact Guide to the 1980 United Nations Convention on Contracts for the International Sale of Goods* §2.5 at 18. See also the comment in previous editions of this book, §60.1 n. 4 ("As a result of the basic rule of Art. 3(1), *supra* at §57, labor costs in manufacturing the machinery would be irrelevant; such costs are not the 'supply of labour or other services' under Art. 3(2)."). Some of the confusion concerning whether services and labor performed in producing the goods should be considered in an Art. 3(2) analysis may stem from differences between different language versions of the official text of the CISG. See Peter Schlechtriem, Art. 3 para. 4, in Schlechtriem & Schwenzer, *CISG Commentary* (2d English ed. 2005); CISG Advisory Council, CISG-AC Opinion no. 4, Contracts for the Sale of Goods to Be Manufactured or Produced and Mixed Contracts (Art. 3 CISG) para. 4.1 (2004), available at http://www.cisg.law.pace.edu/cisg/CISG-AC-op4.html.
27. Peter Schlechtriem, Art. 3 para. 10, in Schlechtriem & Schwenzer, *CISG Commentary* Art. 3 §10 (2d English ed. 2005).

Article 4.
Issues Covered and Excluded; Validity;
Effect on Property Interests of Third Persons

61   Articles 1–3 identify the *transactions* that are subject to the Convention while Article 4 (along with Article 5) defines the *issues* to which the
Convention applies.[1] Article 4 states that the Convention "governs
only" the following: (1) "the formation of the contract" (Part II of
the Convention) and (2) "the rights and obligations of the seller and
the buyer arising from such a contract" (Part III of the Convention). As
we shall see, paragraphs (a) and (b) specifically exclude two issues that
lie on the fringes of the sales contract.

Article 4[2]

**This Convention governs only the formation of the contract of sale
and the rights and obligations of the seller and the buyer arising
from such a contract. In particular, except as otherwise expressly
provided in this Convention, it is not concerned with:**
   **(a) the validity of the contract or of any of its provisions or of any
        usage;**
   **(b) the effect which the contract may have on the property in the
        goods sold.**

62 A. Obligations "Arising from" the Contract

The general statement in Article 4 that the Convention "governs
only . . . the rights and obligations of the seller and the buyer arising
from . . ." the contract of sale will be given further content by provisions
that exclude specified issues, such as paragraphs (a) and (b) of the present article and Article 5 (liability for death or personal injury). Other
points on the line defining the issues embraced by the Convention are
fixed by the substantive provisions in Part III (Arts. 25–88).

---

1. Articles 1–3 have been said to govern the Convention's "sphere of application" whereas
Arts. 4–5 address the Convention's "scope of application." See Ferrari, *Scope of Application*
at 96.
2. This article is substantially the same as Art. 4 of the 1978 Draft. *Cf.* ULIS 8.

A subtle and important problem arises when a domestic law provides legal consequences for the very same operative facts that invoke the rules of the Convention, when the rule of domestic law bears a label other than "contract." The question whether such a domestic rule remains in effect as an alternative to the provisions of the Convention is elusive, and can best be considered in specific contexts. One example will be provided by domestic rules that bear a label such as "product liability." Article 5, *infra* at §71, which excludes from the convention liability "for death or personal injury," will provide a concrete setting for examining the above question.

63 **(1) Manufacturer's Participation in the Sale**

In recent decades some legal systems have established contractual rights for buyers against manufacturers for damage or loss caused by defects in goods which the buyer purchased from a retail dealer or other distributor. At the outset this development responded to the plight of consumers who suffer personal injury from dangerous products — an area that lies outside the Convention because of the general exclusion of consumer purchases (Art. 2(a)) and the further exclusion (Art. 5, §71, *infra*) of the liability of "the seller for the death or personal injury caused by the goods to any person." However, in some legal systems this development has made manufacturers liable, without regard to negligence, for economic loss caused by defective products purchased from a dealer or other distributor.[3]

The first edition of this work concluded that this development under the Convention was barred by the language of Article 4 that the Convention "governs only the formation of the contract of sale and the obligations of the seller and the buyer arising from such a contract."[4] Further reflection calls for reexamination in some commercial settings.

For example, some manufacturers (and similar mass distributors such as importers) provide dealers with a written "guarantee" or "warranty"

---

3. This development has included importers and similar suppliers as well as manufacturers but, for simplicity, is discussed in terms of manufacturers.

4. In one decision under the Convention a German court dismissed a buyer's claim against the manufacturer of allegedly non-conforming electric motors on the basis that the buyer had purchased the motors from a distributor and thus the manufacturer was not the "contracting partner" of the buyer. Landgericht Düsseldorf, Germany, June 23, 1994, English translation available at http://cisgw3.law.pace.edu/cases/940623g1.html, English abstract also available in UNILEX at http://www.unilex.info/case.cfm?pid=1&do=case&id=115&step=Abstract. For U.S. domestic cases rejecting this approach, see, e.g., Curtis Reitz, *Manufacturers' Warranties of Consumer Goods*, 75 Wash. U. L.Q. 357, 361 (1997).

by the manufacturer and instruct dealers to give buyers the manufacturer's "guarantee" in connection with the sale.[5] One purpose is to encourage sales because of the confidence that prospective buyers have in a guarantee to them by a well-known manufacturer. A second, less evident, purpose is to limit their responsibility (e.g.) to the replacement of defective parts for a specified limited period and thereby to bar claims for consequential damages caused by defects in the goods.

Such a "guarantee" by the manufacturer to the buyer clearly creates a contract between these parties in connection with the sale of goods.[6] The difficult problem is whether the manufacturer is a "seller" within the language of Article 4 in view of the fact that the dealer executed the contract with the buyer, delivered the goods and received the price.

Some tribunals applying the Convention, like some tribunals applying domestic laws governing the "sale of goods," may be impressed by the fact that the delivery of a "guarantee" through a local dealer was part of a larger setting in which the manufacturer played a dominant role in the sale — by franchise agreements controlling aspects of the dealer's performance and by mass-media advertising addressed to prospective buyers. Indeed, advertising appeals are typically designed to say or imply: "Go to our dealers and buy our product. If you do you will get a good product." This in substance is an offer of a unilateral contract: "If you will do X you will get Y."

Of course these facts alone do not make the manufacturer a "seller" — a contract of sale depends on the buyer's completing a transaction with a dealer. But some tribunals may conclude that when such a transaction is completed the manufacturer, although not "*the* seller," has participated with the dealer in a "contract of sale" with the buyer.[7]

The supplier's participation may be more evident — as when a representative of the manufacturer personally contacts the buyer and persuades him to purchase the manufacturer's goods from a local dealer.[8] In many cases participation by the manufacturer is more tenuous, confined to advertising[9] and possibly control of aspects of the dealer's business such as promotion methods, volume, stocking of

---

5. For discussion of such warranties in the context of domestic U.S. sales law (Art. 2 of the Uniform Commercial Code), see Flechtner, *Manufacturers' Warranties*.

6. See *id.*, at 453–54.

7. See *Benjamin* §§1037–38 (3d ed. 1987); *White & Summers* §11–7 (3d ed. 1988).

8. Benjamin, §1035 (3d ed. 1987) citing Shanklin Pier v. Detel Products, [1951] 2 K.B. 854; Ruud, 8 U.C.L.A. L. Rev. 251 (1961).

9. Ruud, *supra*, at 255; Pritchard v. Liggett & Myers, 295 F.2d 292 (3rd Cir. 1961) (explicit promise of quality in mass advertising).

repair parts, training of mechanics and, in some cases, the price to be charged.

When (as in the usual case) the buyer and dealer are in the same State the Convention would not apply to a claim against the dealer. Art. 1(1), §40, *supra*. Similarly, the Convention would not apply to a claim against even a foreign supplier if the supplier's place of business applicable to this transaction (Art. 10(a)) is in the same State as the buyer. In any event, when domestic law is favorable and the dealer is financially responsible it usually will be more convenient to confine one's claim to a local action against the dealer. The same may be true even when the claim might jeopardize the dealer's resources since the dealer may be able to bring in the manufacturer to defend the action and to satisfy any judgment. Thus, attempts to extend the Convention to foreign suppliers may be confined to special situations such as financial failure of the local dealer. Even here the rules on jurisdiction, PIL and domestic sales law in the buyer's jurisdiction may meet the buyer's needs.

In sum, it is unlikely that the Convention in the foreseeable future will play a large role in claims by buyers against manufacturers and similar remote suppliers. *That is certainly the case where the buyer's claim is not based on written warranties or other statements (e.g. representations in advertising) made by the remote supplier and directed to the buyer, and that arguably create a contractual relationship between them. If the remote supplier is not in a contractual relationship with the buyer, the supplier's liability to the buyer for defective products is not a matter of "the rights and obligations of the seller and the buyer arising from" the contract of sale, and thus it lies beyond the sphere of the Convention pursuant to Article 4.*[10] On the other hand, it seems hasty to conclude that the "buyer-seller" language of Article 4 will be an impassable barrier to applying the Convention in cases where the supplier has participated substantially (although not formally) in the sale to the buyer *by addressing written warranties or other representations of quality to the buyer. Indeed, in the Asante Technologies case*[11] *(also discussed in §42 supra) a U.S. court applied the Convention to determine a U.S. buyer's rights against a Canadian manufacturer of computer chips that the buyer had purchased from a U.S. distributor. The chips allegedly failed to conform to representations made by*

10. There appears to be no reason that a remote supplier's liability under domestic law to a buyer (or other party) for defective goods should be displaced by the Convention when that liability is not based on contractual principles.

11. Asante Technologies, Inc. v. PMC-Sierra, Inc., 164 F. Supp. 2d 1142 (N.D. Cal. 2001).

the manufacturer to the buyer. The court, however, appeared blithely unaware of any issues raised by the fact that the claim was against a party who had not sold the goods directly to the buyer, so the decision hardly stands as convincing precedent for extending the Convention to claims against remote suppliers. Domestic experience suggests that legal relations with foreign suppliers may be a field for gradual development.

64 ## B. Issues Excluded from Convention

(1) Validity

Paragraph (a) of Article 4 states that, "except as otherwise provided in this Convention," the CISG excludes issues with respect to "the validity of the contract or of any of its provisions or of any usage." *Professor Schlechtriem has suggested the following definition of a "validity" rule: "if a contract is rendered void ab initio, either retroactively by a legal act of the state or of the parties such as avoidance for mistake or revocation of one's consent under special provisions protecting certain persons such as consumers, or by a 'resolutive' condition (i.e., a condition subsequent) or a denial of approval of relevant authorities, the respective rule or provision is a rule that goes to validity and therefore is governed by domestic law and not by the CISG."*[12] *A U.S. court has adopted Professor Hartnell's test for an issue of "validity": "any issue by which the domestic law would render the contract void, voidable or unenforceable" is a matter of "validity."*[13] One obvious example of a provision that goes to "validity" is a rule of domestic law that prohibits the sale of specified products, such as heroin, and invalidates contracts relating to such illegal sales.[14] *Another is*

---

12. Peter Schlechtriem, Art. 4 para. 7, in Schlechtriem & Schwenzer, *CISG Commentary* (2d English ed. 2005).

13. Geneva Pharmaceuticals Tech. Corp. v. Barr Labs. Inc., 201 F. Supp. 2d 236, 282–83 (S.D.N.Y. 2002), quoting Helen Hartnell, *Rousing the Sleeping Dog: The Validity Exception to the Convention on Contracts for the International Sale of Goods*, 18 Yale J. Int'l L. 1, 45 (1993). See the discussion in Ferrari, *Scope of Application* at 100–01.

14. See Peter Schlechtriem, Art. 4 paras 4 & 11, in Schlechtriem & Schwenzer, *CISG Commentary* (2d English ed. 2005) ("infringements of a legal prohibition or public policy"). The substance of CISG Art. 4(a) appeared in Art. 7(1) of the W.G. "Sales" draft and Art. 6(b) of the UNCITRAL "Sales" draft, VIII *YB* 30, 31, *Docy. Hist.* 323, 324. The W.G. 9th Sess.

antitrust or unfair competition provisions that render a contract invalid.[15]
On the other hand, Article 11 of the Convention does expressly address
the formal requirements for a valid contract of sale (see §§126–127.1
infra); domestic rules imposing formal validity requirements are,
therefore, displaced by the Convention[16] *(subject to the possibility of*
a reservation — see the discussion of Article 12, §§128–29 infra). The
effect of Article 4's exclusion of validity issues "except as otherwise
provided in this Convention" is that those issues are not subject to
the gap-filling rule in Article 7(2): if no provision of the Convention
expressly addresses the validity issue, it is a so-called "external gap"
that should not be resolved by reference to "general principles" of the
CISG (even assuming relevant general principles could be located),
but rather according to applicable non-Convention law. There are
other applications of paragraph (a) that call for discussion.

65   **(a) Remedies for Fraud.**   The Convention does not interfere with
the special rights and remedies that domestic law gives to persons who
have been induced to enter into a contract by fraud.[17] (As will be suggested
under Art. 35, *infra* at §238, a very different problem of the relationship
between the Convention and domestic law is presented by an innocent
misstatement as to the quality of the goods.) Preserving domestic protection against intentional fraud could be based on the general rule of Article 4
that the Convention "governs only" the obligations "arising from [the]
contract"; the conduct that gives rise to a remedy for fraud may be distinct
from the making of the contract. This result is reinforced by paragraph (a)

(1977) considered but rejected inclusion of provisions on mistake and duress in a
UNIDROIT draft Law on Validity (LUV). VIII *YB* 105–109, *Docy. Hist.* 269–273. For
the SG Report on the UNIDROIT draft see VIII *YB* 90–93, 104–109, *Docy. Hist.* 254–
257, 268–273.

15. See Bundesgerichtshof, Germany, July 23, 1997, English translation available at http://
www.cisg.law.pace.edu/cisg/wais/db/cases2/970723g2.html (CISG did not govern validity
of sale contracts in light of EU unfair competition rules).

16. Peter Schlechtriem, Art. 4 para. 8, in Schlechtriem & Schwenzer, *CISG Commentary* (2d
English ed. 2005); UNCITRAL Digest Art. 4 para. 8; Ferrari, *Scope of Application* at 99–100.

17. *Accord*, Zurich Chamber of Commerce arbitration, Switzerland, May 31, 1996, English
translation available at http://cisgw3.law.pace.edu/cases/960531s1.html (*dicta* indicating
that the Convention does not address fraud issues); Ferrari, *Scope of Application* at 98
(stating that fraud issues are left to domestic law); Joseph Lookofsky, *In Dubio Pro Conventione? Some Thoughts about Opt-outs, Computer Programs and Preëmption under the
1980 Vienna Sales Convention (CISG)*, 13 Duke J. Comp. & Int'l L. 263, 280 (2003),
available at http://law.duke.edu/journals/djcil/articles/djcil13p0263.htm#H1N5 (stating
that fraud is a matter of validity excluded from the CISG).

which excludes issues of "validity." Even if domestic law characterizes a contract obtained by fraud as "voidable" rather than "invalid" and gives the innocent party a choice as whether to avoid the contract, these rights are not disturbed by the Convention. The crucial point is that the Convention does not address factual situations involving fraud and should not be construed as wiping out this important field of law by implication.[18] (Compare the discussion at §66 *infra*, of the relation between the Convention and domestic rules on agency.)

The fact that a domestic rule bears a label such as "validity" or "fraud" does not determine the question whether the rule is one of "validity" within the meaning of Article 4(a) of the Convention: for reasons foreshadowed at the outset of this Article and to be developed in the Commentary to Article 5, the substance rather than the label or characterization of the competing rule of domestic law determines whether it is displaced by the Convention.[19] The crucial question is whether the domestic rule is invoked by the same operative facts that invoke a rule of the Convention.[20] For example, a domestic rule of "validity" provides that a problem raised by facts A + B has result X; the Convention also addresses the problem raised by facts A + B and gives result Y. Does Article 4 provide that the

18. Accord, Joseph Lookofsky, In Dubio Pro Conventione? Some Thoughts about Opt-outs, Computer Programs and Preëmption under the 1980 Vienna Sales Convention (CISG), 13 Duke J. Comp. & Int'l L. 263, 280 (2003), also available at http://law.duke.edu/journals/djcil/articles/djcil13p0263.htm; Joseph M. Lookofsky, Loose Ends and Contorts in International Sales: Problems in the Harmonization of Private Law Rules, 39 Am. J. Comp. L. 403, 407–09 (1991). General remedies for fraud are not provided by the "good faith" provision of Art. 7(1), *infra* at §87, since this bears only on the interpretation of provisions of the Convention. The range of domestic remedies for fraud is suggested in Zweigert & Kotz II (1987) 106–110, 302, 308, 316; David, French Law 197–198. Cf. (U.S.A.) UCC 1–103 (Code supplemented by principles of fraud as part of general body of common law). See also UNIDROIT Principles of International Commercial Contracts 2004 Art. 3.8 (Fraud), available at http://www.unidroit.org/english/principles/contracts/principles2004/blackletter2004.pdf.
19. See Peter Schlechtriem, Art. 4 para. 7, *in* Schlechtriem & Schwenzer, *CISG Commentary* (2d English ed. 2005) ("What amounts to invalidity has to be analysed, however, 'autonomously', i.e. as a concept of the CISG interpreted according to the guidelines of Art. 7(1). In order to preserve or achieve a uniform application of the term 'validity,' it is not the words used in domestic law and their interpretation under domestic law, but the functions of the respective rules and provisions that are decisive" (footnote omitted)); Ferrari, *Scope of Application* at 100. ("In defining ['validity'] for purposes of the CISG, one should not resort to one's own legal background, but rather should interpret this concept, like most other CISG concepts, 'autonomously.')"
20. *Contra*, Joseph Lookofsky, *CISG Case Commentary on Preëmption in Geneva Pharmaceuticals* and *Stawski*, at nn. 21 & 30 (April 2004), available at http://www.cisg.law.pace.edu/cisg/biblio/lookofsky8.html.

Convention "is not concerned" with this problem? See §72, *infra*. To illustrate the point further, suppose that domestic law gives a "contract" label to remedies for fraudulently inducing the buyer's acceptance of goods after their return to the seller. If the Convention cannot be construed to deal with these problems (see Art. 7(2), §§95–102, *infra*), domestic remedies are not excluded merely because they are characterized as "contract" rather than "tort." In sum, access to domestic law is neither broadened or narrowed by its label or characterization.[21]

66 **(b) Competency; Authority of an Agent.** The Convention does not displace domestic rules on the effect of insanity, infancy or other disability on a party's capacity to make a contract.[22] The Convention does not address any of these difficult questions.

In the setting of international sales, a more important issue is the legal power of one person to represent another. The Convention does not address the complex issues that underlie questions of agency and authority.[23] A UNIDROIT draft dealing with this topic led to a Convention on Agency in the International Sale of Goods (Geneva 1983), 22 Int. Leg. Mat. 249. However until international rules enter into force questions of authority to act for another are left to applicable domestic law. Accordingly, references in the Convention to the acts of a party include persons for whose acts the party is responsible.[24]

67 **(c) Harsh, Unanticipated Applications.** The foregoing discussion suggests that Article 4(a), in leaving "validity" to domestic law, does not open a large door for escape from the uniform rules of Convention. Does this mean that the Convention requires the enforcement of contract

---

21. Khoo, *B-B Commentary* 47–48; *Sec. Commy. O.R.* 17, *Docy. Hist.* 407 (para. 2: Convention prevails over domestic rules of "validity").

22. See Peter Schlechtriem, Art. 4 para. 11, in Schlechtriem & Schwenzer, *CISG Commentary* (2d English ed. 2005) (CISG does not govern "the legal capacity of one of the parties to a contract and the consequences of the lack of such capacity"); cases cited in UNCITRAL Digest Art. 4 para. 3 n. 7; Ferrari, *Scope of Application* at 98 (stating that issues relating to capacity to contract are left to domestic law).

23. *Accord*, Peter Schlechtriem, Art. 4 para. 11, in Schlechtriem & Schwenzer, *CISG Commentary* (2d English ed. 2005); Ferrari, *Scope of Application* at 100–01; cases cited in UNCITRAL Digest Art. 4 para. 9 n. 24; Kantonsgericht Wallis, Switzerland, September 19, 2005, English abstract available in Unilex at http://www.unilex.info/case.cfm?pid=1&do=case&id=1083&step=Abstract; cases cited in UNCITRAL Digest Art. 4 para. 9 n. 24.

24. Nicholas, *B-B Commentary* 483–484. See *Schlesinger et al. Comparative Law (1988)* 768–793, *Zweigert & Kotz II (1987)* Ch. 9; Conell, The 1983 Geneva Convention on Agency, 32 Am. J. Comp. L. 717 (1984).

provisions that produce harsh results when conditions arise that were not anticipated when the contract was prepared? The answer depends, in part, on the approach to the interpretation of the contract, an issue that will be considered in the Commentary to Article 8, *infra* at §107.1. Related questions arise with respect to the quality of the goods required under the contract and the effect of contract provisions that, broadly construed, would cut deeply into the buyer's normal expectations. (See the Commentary to Art. 35, *infra* at §222.) Finally, reference should be made to Article 79, which exempts a party from liability for damages when an unanticipated impediment prevents him from performing. As these cross-references suggest, within this area the law is a seamless web. *Indeed, as demonstrated in the discussion of Article 79 (see §432.2 infra), domestic "hardship" doctrines (e.g., eccesiva onerosità sopravvenuta, Wegfall der Geschäftsgrundlage) are pre-empted by the Convention.*

Domestic rules that address harsh results — such as requirements of "good faith," "*Treu und Glauben*," "conscionability," or rules controlling contract clauses restricting responsibility for defective goods — *may constitute rules of validity that are not pre-empted by the Convention,*[25] but they may become inapplicable when the contract is interpreted and applied in conformity with the above provisions of the Convention. In short, failure to turn first to rules of Article 8 on construction of the contract could lead to the application of domestic law to unreal, hypothetical cases, and would restrict the scope of uniform law in violation of the rule of Article 7(1) that the Convention shall be interpreted with regard "to the need to promote uniformity in its application. . . ." See §§85–87, *infra*.

68 **(c)(1) Mistake**   *Rules addressing the effect of a party's mistake by (i.e., a misapprehension of fact when the contract was concluded) are frequently listed among the rules of validity that are outside the scope of the Convention.*[26] *Discussion of this matter in connection with the exemption provision (Art. 79) concludes that at least some mistake scenarios are expressly addressed in the Convention, and thus are within the scope of the CISG. See §§423.2, 427 & 432.2, infra.*

69 **(d) The Convention and Domestic Law: Cross-References.**
Other issues that might logically fit here have been deferred to Article 35

25. See Peter Schlechtriem, Art. 4 para. 12, in Schlechtriem & Schwenzer, *CISG Commentary* (2d English ed. 2005); Joseph M. Lookofsky, *Loose Ends and Contorts in International Sales: Problems in the Harmonization of Private Laws Rules*, 39 Am. J. Comp. L. 403, 410–12 (1991).
26. E.g., Peter Schlechtriem, Art. 4 paras. 7 & 13, in Schlechtriem & Schwenzer, *CISG Commentary* (2d English ed. 2005); Lookofsky, *The CISG in the USA* §2.6 at 24; Bridge,

so that the discussion could take a wider view of the Convention's rules on the obligations of the parties. Thus, under Article 35 consideration is given to the relationship between the Convention and domestic rules designed to preserve implied obligations as to quality of the goods (§230), rules on "unconscionability" (§235) and restrictions on the use of standard contract terms (§236).[27] The commentary on Article 29 provides occasion to discuss whether common law "consideration" doctrine constitutes a rule of validity that remains applicable to transactions governed by the Convention (§§204.1–204.4 *infra*).

70   **(2) Effect of the Contract on Property in the Goods**

Article 4 also provides that the Convention "is not concerned with: . . . (b) the effect which the contract may have on the property in the goods sold."[28] This specific provision illustrates the general rule of Article 4 that the Convention is concerned only with the "rights and obligations of the *seller and the buyer*" arising from the sales contract. In addition, problems that under some domestic systems are decided by reference to the "property" concept are governed by specific provisions of the Convention.[29]

In conformity with this principle, the Convention (Articles 41 and 42) deals with the seller's obligation to the buyer that the goods be free of third-party claims. Whether the sale to the buyer cuts off outstanding property interests of third persons is not dealt with by the Convention. Efforts to establish uniform international rules on the rights of good faith purchasers have not yet been successful; in the meantime, this question must be left to applicable domestic law.[30]

International Sale of Goods §8.03 at 297–98. Professor Franco Ferrari argues that different mistake scenarios must be distinguished in analyzing whether the Convention governs the situation. Franco Ferrari, *The Interaction between the United Nations Convention on Contracts for the International Sale of Goods and Domestic Remedies (Rescission for Mistake and Remedies in Torts)*, in 71 Rabels Zeitschrift für auslandisches und internationales Privatrecht 52 ff. (2007).

27. For other aspects of the relationship between the Convention and domestic law see Art. 5 at §72, Art, 7 at §96, Art. 16 at §145, Art. 28 at §194, Art. 46 at §281, Art. 62 at §348, and Art. 78 at §420.

28. For decisions on the exclusion of property issues, see UNCITRAL Digest Art. 4 paras. 11 & 12.

29. See Secretariat Commentary *O.R.* 17, *Docy. Hist.* 407 (para. 4). See also Ch. IV, Passing of Risk (Arts. 66–70) at §§359–383, *infra*.

30. UNDROIT has prepared a Draft Uniform Law on the Protection of the Bona Fide Purchaser of Corporeal Movables. *UNIDROIT Yearbook*, 1967–1968, Vol. I, 222. More

As we shall see, the Convention gives one party to the sales contract rights over goods held by the other party that, under domestic law, may affect the rights of third persons. For example, Article 46, §§279–286 *infra*, gives a buyer the right to require the seller to deliver goods that the seller wrongfully withholds; Article 81(2), §444 *infra*, gives a seller the right to claim restitution of goods for which the buyer fails to pay. Article 4 makes it clear that the Convention does not govern the effect of these remedial rights on the claims of third persons. However, domestic law must respect these rights as between the seller and buyer; if such rights between the parties prevail over the claims of creditors or other third parties under domestic law, domestic tribunals should give the same effect to rights established by the Convention. See *infra* at §444. *The Convention also does not govern rights to set-off debts arising in transactions governed by the Convention: set-off implicates the rights of third persons and cannot be adequately addressed using the tools the Convention supplies.*[31]

70.1   Other Matters Beyond the Scope of the Convention

Other matters beyond the validity and property issues specifically mentioned in Article 4 are outside the scope of the Convention. Indeed, Article 4 itself declares that that "[t]his Convention governs only the formation of the contract for sale and the rights and obligations of the seller and the buyer arising from such a contract."[32] *The provisions of the Convention, furthermore, generally address substantive sales law rather than the myriad of other legal issues that can arise. To take an obvious example, the Convention does not give criminal rules even for offenses arising out of an international contract for the sale of goods. A host of other legal matters, from family law to the protection of*

---

recent work has concentrated on stolen or illegally exported cultural objects. *UNIDROIT News Bulletin* (N. 81–82, January-April 1990).

31. See, e.g., Peter Schlechtriem, Art. 4 para. 22a, in Schlechtriem & Schwenzer, *CISG Commentary* (2d English ed. 2005); Ferrari, *Scope of Application* at 107–108; Harry M. Flechtner, *Remedies Under the New International Sales Convention: The Perspective From Article 2 of the U.C.C.*, 8 J.L. & Com. 53, 83 (1988); cases cited in UNCITRAL Digest Art. 4 n. 38.

32. Emphasis added. It has been argued that this phrase — in particular, the language confining the CISG "*only*" to issues of formation and the rights and obligations of the parties — cannot be read literally. See Peter Schlechtriem, Art. 4 para. 3, in Schlechtriem & Schwenzer, *CISG Commentary* (2d English ed. 2005); Ferrari, *Scope of Application* at 97.

intellectual property rights, are clearly beyond the scope of the Convention. Indeed, it is easier to describe what is covered by the Convention — in general, substantive contract law for sales — than to give a comprehensive list of all the legal issues that lie beyond its reach.

Some topics present difficult questions concerning the border between the uniform international law of the CISG and matters that (as far as the CISG is concerned) are left to the disparate regulation of individual States. For example, overlap between situations addressed by the contract law of the Convention and by domestic "tort" (delict) law can raise extremely difficult questions as to the scope and preemptive impact of the CISG.[33] Some of those questions are explored in the discussion of Article 5 (§§71–73 infra). No matter how desirable a more comprehensive system of uniform international law might be, the Contracting States to the CISG signed up only for a limited regime that focuses on substantive sales law. It is important for the proper interpretation of the Convention and to the success of future uniform law initiatives that the limits of that consent be respected.

The fact that the Convention does not in general address procedural issues[34] gives rise to some of the more challenging questions concerning the scope of the Convention.[35] One such issue is whether the damages provisions of the Convention govern the recovery of

33. Professor Joseph Lookofsky has written extensively on these issues. See Lookofsky, *The CISG in the USA* §2.6; Joseph Lookofsky, *CISG Case Commentary on Preëmption in* Geneva Pharmaceuticals *and* Stawski (April 2004), available at http://www.cisg.law.pace.edu/cisg/biblio/lookofsky8.html; Joseph Lookofsky, *In Dubio Pro Conventione? Some Thoughts about Opt-outs, Computer Programs and Preëmption under the 1980 Vienna Sales Convention (CISG)*, 13 Duke J. Comp. & Int'l L. 263 (2003), also available at http://law.duke.edu/journals/djcil/articles/djcil13p0263.htm; Joseph M. Lookofsky, *Loose Ends and Contorts in International Sales: Problems in the Harmonization of Private Law Rules*, 39 Am. J. Comp. L. 403 (1991). The matter is also addressed in Franco Ferrari, *The Interaction between the United Nations Convention on Contracts for the International Sale of Goods and Domestic Remedies (Rescission for Mistake and Remedies in Torts)*, in 71 Rabels Zeitschrift für auslandisches und internationales Privatrecht 52 ff. (2007). See also the discussion in Peter Schlechtriem, Art. 4 paras. 5 & 23a, in Schlechtriem & Schwenzer, *CISG Commentary* (2d English ed. 2005).

34. Peter Schlechtriem, Art. 4 paras. 19 & 22, in Schlechtriem & Schwenzer, *CISG Commentary* (2d English ed. 2005); Ferrari, *Scope of Application* at 107; cases cited in UNCITRAL Digest Art. 4 para. 13 nn. 41 & 42.

35. Distinguishing between procedural and substantive matters is, of course, notoriously difficult. See John Y. Gotanda, *Awarding Damages under the United Nations Convention on the International Sale of Goods: A Matter of Interpretation*, 37 Georgetown J. Int'l L. 95, 120–21 (2005). In the present context, however, the question is not whether an issue is technically characterized as procedural or substantive. After all, the Convention does not

attorney fees incurred in litigating a breach of contract claim under the Convention, a question discussed in connection with Article 74 (§408 infra).

Another thorny — and important — issue is whether the CISG governs the question of who bears the burden of proving the factual elements of the rules of the Convention. There is strong evidence in the travaux préparatoires that the drafters did not intend, in general, to deal with burden-of-proof issues. One commentator noted: "Delegations speaking on the burden-of-proof [at the Vienna Diplomatic Conference] were all quite definite that it was not the intention to deal in the Convention with any questions concerning the burden-of-proof. The consensus was that such questions must be left to the court as matters of procedural law."[36] In the same vein, a proposal to amend a draft of the Convention to add language expressly allocating the burden of proving that delivered goods were conforming was rejected because, in the words of an UNCITRAL report, "it was considered inappropriate for the Convention, which relates to the international sale of goods, to deal with matters of evidence or procedure."[37]

Despite this background, several commentators have argued that the Convention does indeed govern burden-of-proof issues.[38] Proponents of this view note that at least one provision of the CISG expressly

---

use those terms, nor does it expressly make the distinction between procedure and substance. Rather, the distinction — which *was* in the minds of the drafters of the Convention (see the discussion of the *travaux préparatoires* at the end of the current text paragraph) — is here used as an aid in determining the intended scope of CISG.

36. W. Khoo, Art. *2, in B-B Commentary* (citing United Nations Conference on Contracts for the International Sale of Goods (Vienna, March 10–April 11, 1980), Official Records, New York 1981, pp. 295–298).

37. UNCITRAL, Report of the Committee of the Whole relating to the draft Convention on the International Sales of Goods, 1977, paras. 177–178, reprinted in *Docy. Hist.* 330.

38. Peter Schlechtriem, Art. 4 paras. 5 & 22, in Schlechtriem & Schwenzer, *CISG Commentary* (2d English ed. 2005); Ferrari, *Scope of Application* at 110–13; Franco Ferrari, *Burden-of-proof under the United Nations Convention on Contracts for the International Sale of Goods (CISG)*, in Pace Review of the Convention on Contracts for the International Sale of Goods 1 (2000–2001), available at http://www.cisg.law.pace.edu/cisg/biblio/ferrari5.html; Ulrich Magnus, *General Principles of UN-Sales Law* 3 Int'l Trade & Bus. L. Ann. 33, 52 (1997), available at http://www.cisg.law.pace.edu/cisg/biblio/magnus.html text accompanying nn. 86–91 (English translation by Lisa Haberfellner of German text originally appearing in 59 Rabels Zeitschrift für ausländisches und internationales Privatrecht 469 (1995); Sonja Kruisinga, (Non-)conformity in the 1980 UN Convention on Contracts for the International Sale of Goods: A Uniform Concept? 157–86 (2004).

allocates the burden-of-proof,[39] and contend that this — along with the close relationship between the Convention's substantive rules and burden-of-proof considerations — establishes that such issues are within the scope of the CISG. They argue that the absence of either a general burden-of-proof rule in the Convention or express burden-of-proof language in the vast majority of its specific provisions constitutes an "internal gap" that is subject to Article 7(2), and that rules on burden-of-proof can be derived from general principles on which the Convention is based. They posit, for example, that the CISG contains a general principle incorporating the "rule and exception" approach under which a party invoking the benefit of a rule has the burden of proving its factual prerequisites whereas a party claiming an exception to a rule must prove the required elements of the exception.[40] The idea that the Convention governs burden-of-proof has found favor in most — but not all — of the decisions that have considered the question.[41]

Indeed, two decisions of the highest German court with jurisdiction over CISG issues — the Bundesgerichtshof (BGH) — have found that at least some burden-of-proof matters are within the scope of the CISG. In an opinion rendered in 2002 the BGH asserted that the CISG does, as an initial matter, govern burden-of-proof questions, and that it contains a general principle incorporating the "rule-and-exception" approach.[42] The result of that approach in the case before it, the court asserted, would normally have been that the buyer — which claimed the goods it received and accepted without objection had later proved defective — would bear the burden of proving that the goods were non-conforming when delivered. A lower court decision in the case, however, had invoked a rule of domestic German law to

---

39. Article 79(1) provides that a non-performing party can claim exemption from liability for damages "if he proves" that certain requirements have been met. See §§423–435.6 *infra.*

40. Peter Schlechtriem, Art. 4 para. 22, in Schlechtriem & Schwenzer, *CISG Commentary* (2d English ed. 2005); Ferrari, *Scope of Application* at 111–12; Franco Ferrari, *Burden of Proof under the United Nations Convention on Contracts for the International Sale of Goods (CISG)*, in Pace Review of the Convention on Contracts for the International Sale of Goods 1, 6 (2000–2001), available at http://www.cisg.law.pace.edu/cisg/biblio/ferrari5.html; Ulrich Magnus, *General Principles of UN-Sales Law* 3 Int'l Trade & Bus. L. Ann. 33, 52 (1997), available at http://www.cisg.law.pace.edu/cisg/biblio/magnus.html, text accompanying nn. 89–90 (English translation by Lisa Haberfellner of German original that appeared in 59 Rabels Zeitschrift für ausländisches und internationales Privatrecht 469 (1995)).

41. See the cases cited in UNCITRAL Digest Art. 4 paras. 4–7.

42. Bundesgerichtshof, Germany, January 9, 2002, English translation available at http://cisgw3.law.pace.edu/cases/020109g1.html.

reverse the burden — placing it on the seller to show that the goods were conforming at delivery — because the seller had written a letter admitting liability for the non-conforming goods. The BGH affirmed the lower court's analysis, including its application of domestic German law to determine the burden-of-proof consequences of an admission of liability:

> *[T]he CISG regulates the burden of proof explicitly (e.g., in Art. 79(1)) or tacitly (Art. 2(a)), so that consequently, recourse to the national law is blocked to that extent, and . . . the CISG follows the rule/exception principle. . . . The appeal to this Court overlooks, however, that the burden of proof rules of the CISG cannot go farther than the scope of its substantive applicability. That scope results from Art. 4(1) CISG; according to that provision, the CISG regulates exclusively the execution of the sales contract and the duties and responsibilities of the buyer and the seller resulting from that contract. The question whether and possibly which evidentiary consequences an actual admission of liability has, is not part of that scope. That question — just like the meaning of a defective mens rea, an assignment, a set-off, or similar issues — does not implicate a specific sales-law-related problem, but rather a legal aspect of a general type; there is no intimate relationship to the actual or legal aspects of the international trade in goods, which make up the regulatory subject of the CISG.[43]*

In 2004 the BGH reaffirmed that that CISG contains a general rule-and-exception principle governing burden-of-proof issues, but it again found that the facts before it raised issues that went beyond that principle.[44] A buyer who claimed to have received non-conforming goods was (the court found) late in providing the seller notice of the non-conformity as required by Article 39, and thus was in danger of losing its claim. The buyer invoked Article 40, under which a seller cannot rely on a buyer's failure to comply with Article 39 notice requirements "if the lack of conformity relates to facts of which [the seller] knew or could not have been unaware and which he did not disclose to the buyer." (See §269 infra.) The court noted that Article 40 constitutes an exception to the notice requirement and thus, under the Convention's rule-and-exception principle, the party claiming the benefit of that exception — the buyer — normally had the burden of proving the elements of Article 40.[45]

---

43. *Id.* (English translation by Alston & Bird LLP).

44. Bundesgerichtshof, Germany, June 30, 2004, English translation available at http://cisgw3.law.pace.edu/cases/040630g1.html.

45. In support of this assertion the court cited a number of decisions from outside Germany, including decisions of Dutch and Canadian courts, and rulings by Swedish and ICC arbitral tribunals. See *id.*

On the facts before the BGH, however, that burden might have required the buyer to prove whether the non-conformity arose during the seller's own manufacturing process, and thus would have confronted the buyer with "unreasonable difficulties in providing proof." The court eased those difficulties by invoking another burden-of-proof doctrine allegedly based on the Convention's general principles (rather than on domestic law) — the "proof-proximity" [Beweisnähe] principle, under which a party can be relieved of an evidentiary burden it would normally bear if there are "facts that are exclusively in [the other] party's sphere of responsibility and which therefore are, at least theoretically, better known to that party . . . . . ."[46] Applying this principle, the court found that the buyer's failure to offer proof that the seller "knew or could not have been unaware" of the defects in the goods was not sufficient to preclude application of Article 40, and thus the case was remanded for further proceedings.

As the editor of the current edition has argued elsewhere,[47] these cases demonstrate that the Convention should not be construed to govern most burden-of-proof issues; unless there is a clear textual basis for allocating the burden with regard to elements of a specific provision, such matters should be left to applicable non-Convention law. The 2002 decision of the BGH demonstrates that one cannot derive a comprehensive set of burden-of-proof rules from the Convention, and at some point recourse to otherwise-applicable law on burden-of-proof issues is inevitable. That is hardly surprising given that: (1) there are no generally-applicable express burden-of-proof rules in the Convention; (2) only an extremely small number of individual sections even arguably address burden-of-proof issues;[48]

---

46. Franco Ferrari, *Burden of Proof under the United Nations Convention on Contracts for the International Sale of Goods (CISG)*, in Pace Review of the Convention on Contracts for the International Sale of Goods 1, 6–7 (2000–2001), available at http://www.cisg.law. pace.edu/cisg/biblio/ferrari5.html.

47. See Harry M. Flechtner, Moving through Tradition Towards Universalism under the U.N. Sales Convention (CISG): Notice of Lack of Conformity (Article 39) and Burden of Proof in the Bundesgerichtshof Opinion of 30 June 2004, in Liber Memorialis Petar Šarčević: Universalism, Tradition and the Individual 459 466–70 (J. Erauw, V. Tomljenovic & P. Volken, eds., 2006).

48. Article 79(1), which expressly requires a party to "prove" certain elements in order to claim the benefits of the provision, is the only CISG article with language clearly addressing proof issues. It has been argued, however, that use of the term "unless" also indicates an allocation of the burden-of-proof. See Ulrich Magnus, *General Principles of UN-Sales Law*, 3 Int'l Trade & Bus. L. Ann. 33, 52 (1997), available at http://www.cisg.law.pace.edu/cisg/ biblio/magnus.html, text accompanying n. 87 (English translation by Lisa Haberfellner of

and (3) as was noted earlier in this sections, there is every indication that those who drafted the Convention considered burden-of-proof questions to be — in general — beyond the scope of their subject. Thus there is extremely limited data from which to derive general Convention principles on burden-of-proof. Indeed, it can be argued that the only express burden-of-proof rules in the Convention must have slipped in unintentionally.

It is little wonder, then, that even the BGH, which believes that burden-of-proof matters are within the scope of the Convention, also finds that the CISG does not contain all necessary burden-of-proof principles, and that there is no comprehensive treatment of the subject in the Convention. Thus recourse to non-Convention law is at some point inevitable, so that the gain to uniformity from bringing burden-of-proof issues within the scope of the CISG is limited.

Defining the boundaries of the Convention's treatment of burden-of-proof, furthermore, is extremely difficult. Consider the test advanced in the 2002 BGH decision: a burden-of-proof issue is beyond the scope of the Convention if it (like the issue in that case concerning the effect of an admission) "does not implicate a specific sales-law-related problem, but rather a legal aspect of a general type" and if "there is no intimate relationship to the actual or legal aspects of the international trade-in goods, which make up the regulatory subject of the CISG." This test, bristling with vague abstractions, is likely to introduce a fertile new source of non-uniformity as tribunals steeped in vastly different legal traditions attempt to determine what burden-of-proof questions have a sufficiently "intimate relationship" with the subject matter of the CISG to come within its purview.

The 2004 BGH decision demonstrates the dangers of trying to derive relevant burden-of-proof general principles from a Convention text that addresses the issue rarely and that probably was not consciously intended to address it all. (A methodology for deriving general principles of the Convention that can be used, under Article 7(2), to fill its gaps is described in §§99–102 infra.) The alleged CISG principle that

---

German original that appeared in 59 Rabels Zeitschrift für ausländisches und internationales Privatrecht 469 (1995)). The editor of the current edition has himself argued that the wording of Art. 35(2)(b) contains language expressly allocating the burden of proving a particular element of that provision. Harry M. Flechtner, *Moving through Tradition Towards Universalism under the U.N. Sales Convention (CISG): Notice of Lack of Conformity (Article 39) and Burden of Proof in the Bundesgerichtshof Opinion of 30 June 2004*, in Liber Memorialis Petar Šarčević: Universalism, Tradition and the Individual 459 467 n. 33 (J. Erauw, V. Tomljenovic & P. Volken eds., 2006).

the court invokes in its 2004 decision — the Beweisnähe principle under which the burden-of-proof can be shifted to a party that has clearly-superior access to the relevant evidence — appears to be a perfectly sensible idea at first blush. Presumably it is in fact a very sensible idea in the procedural system of the court that adopted it and of the commentators upon which the BGH relied who have advocated for such a principle,[49] *for it is a feature of domestic German jurisprudence.*[50] *There is, however, no provision of the CISG that expressly reallocates the burden-of-proof based upon a party's superior access to the evidence — hardly surprising given the extreme rarity of express references to burden-of-proof matters. Thus discovering such a general principle in the Convention may be more a matter of assuming that the CISG incorporates "sensible" notions than of a careful search for underlying concepts.*

The problem is that the Beweisnähe concept does not necessarily translate well to other procedural contexts. In a system like that in the United States, with a highly-developed pre-trial discovery procedure, it will often not make sense to relieve a party of the burden-of-proof if that party has been unable to develop sufficient evidence by means of interrogatories, document demands and depositions directed to the other side, even if the necessary evidence would be in the control of the other side. Thus shifting the burden-of-proof based on Beweisnähe-type considerations is less necessary in such systems than in systems (like Germany's) without such elaborate pre-trial discovery tools.

49. The court cited the following commentaries in support of its holding that the general principles of the Convention include the proof-proximity (*Beweisnähe*) principle: R. Hepting, "Beweislast und Beweismaβ im UN-Kaufrecht" [Burden-of-proof and Degree of Proof Under CISG], in: G. Baumgärtel/H.-W. Laumen (eds.), Handbuch der Beweislast im Privatrecht [Manual of the Burden-of-proof in Civil Law], 2nd ed., Vol. 2, Köln 1999, 28 to 30 before Art. 1 WKR; U. Magnus, UN-Kaufrecht [UN-Sales Law], in: Julius von Staudingers Kommentar zum Bürgerlichen Gesetzbuch mit Einführungsgesetz und Nebengesetzen, Berlin 1999, Art. 4 CISG 69; F. Ferrari, in: P. Schlechtriem (ed.), Kommentar zum Einheitlichen UN Kaufrecht, 3rd ed., München 2000, Art. 4 & 51. Also see Ulrich Magnus, *General Principles of UN-Sales Law*, 3 Int'l Trade & Bus. L. Ann. 33, 52 (1997), available at http://www.cisg.law.pace.edu/cisg/biblio/magnus.html, text accompanying n.91 (English translation by Lisa Haberfellner of German original that appeared in 59 Rabels Zeitschrift für ausländisches und internationales Privatrecht 469 (1995)).
50. Peter L. Murray & Rolf Stürner, *German Civil Justice* 267–68 (2004). ("Case law has recognized shifts in the burden of proof in specific circumstances. [. . .]. These allocations of burden of proof often flow from considerations of relative accessibility and practicality of proof as well as other concerns of public policy.")

Burden-of-proof principles, in other words, usually come embedded in particular litigation procedure. The Convention generally does not address procedural issues — and certainly does not create a litigation system of its own. It must be applied in the myriad of procedural contexts that exist in courts and arbitral tribunals around the world. It is thus ill-suited to be a source of implied burden-of-proof principles. That fact, coupled with travaux préparatoires indicating that burden-of-proof questions were deemed by the Convention drafters to be beyond the scope of their project, and in conjunction with the dearth of CISG provisions that expressly address burden-of-proof matters, strongly indicate that this matter should be left to applicable non-Convention law.[51]

The fact that a few CISG provisions appear to speak to the burden-of-proof question — see, in addition to Article 79(1), the discussion in §183 supra — does not bring burden-of-proof issues in general within the scope of the CISG, just as the fact that Article 11 addresses formal validity requirements does not pull validity issues in general into the Convention's sphere. To take another example, Article 11 includes a rule providing that a contract governed by the Convention "may be proved by any means, including witnesses," but this does not mean that the competency of witnesses or evidentiary matters in general are therefore governed by the CISG. Where the Convention does include an express rule on burden-of-proof or other procedural matters, of course, that rule applies in CISG transactions, and to that extent the Convention preempts the law otherwise applicable under PIL principles; but where the Convention does not provide an express rule on burden-of-proof, the matter should be referred to applicable non-Convention rules.

51. The argument for applying the "rule and exception" approach as a burden-of-proof rule implied in the Convention is stronger than the argument for other general burden-of-proof principles (such as *Beweisnähe*). For one thing, the sole Convention provision that clearly and expressly addresses burden-of-proof matters — Art. 79(1) — is consistent with the rule-and-exception approach; thus there is support in the actual text of the Convention for this principle. In addition, that approach is so obvious and sensible that it is hard to imagine non-Convention law adopting a different rule. Of course to the extent that non-Convention law universally adopts the rule-and-exception approach there is no gain to uniformity by applying it as a matter of Convention rules. And if a non-Convention law rejects the rule-and-exception approach, it probably reflects procedural considerations that would not be well served by a uniform Convention rule (see the discussion of *Beweisnähe* above). Thus the best solution is to treat burden-of-proof issues as beyond the scope of the CISG (except where the Convention expressly provides a burden-of-proof rule).

Article 5.
Exclusion of Liability for Death or
Personal Injury; "Product Liability"

71   A. Reasons for Exclusion

The strong protection that the Convention gives to the international sales contract made it necessary to limit the Convention's scope lest the Convention collide with the special protection that some domestic rules provide for the noncommercial consumer. See Ch. 1 at §2. For this reason, Article 2 provides that the Convention does not apply to sales "(a) of goods bought for personal, family, or household use...." A similar purpose underlies the present article.

Article 5[1]

This Convention does not apply to the liability of the seller for death or personal injury caused by the goods to any person.

Article 2(a) excludes certain *purchases* from the Convention; Article 5 excludes a specified *type of claim* — liability for death or personal injury — even though other aspects of the transaction may be governed by the Convention. This exclusion is significant in the following two situations.

(1) Under Article 2(a), although goods are bought "for personal, family, or household use" the Convention may apply when the seller "neither knew nor ought to have known that the goods were bought for any such use." In these unusual cases, Article 5 provides that the claim of such a buyer or any third person "for death or personal injury" falls outside the Convention, and hence will be governed by applicable domestic law.

(2) Goods not bought "for personal, family, or household use" may give rise to a claim to recover for "death or personal injury." Suppose

---

1. There was no comparable provision in the 1978 or earlier UNCITRAL drafts or in ULIS. Art. 5 was adopted at the diplomatic conference; *Com. I, O.R.* 245–246, 423; *Docy. Hist.* 466–467, 644.

that an industrial machine injures an employee of the purchaser. A claim by the purchaser to recover damages from the seller because of the injury to the employee is not governed by the Convention. (As is noted below, a claim by the employee against the seller would not be based on the "obligation of the seller and the buyer arising from" the contract of sale, and hence would be left to domestic law by Art. 4.) An interesting question that has generated controversy in commentary,[2] but apparently little in case law,[3] is whether Article 5 excludes from the Convention's coverage a buyer's claim for financial losses incurred (under non-Convention law) when the buyer's customers to whom it resold the goods make claims against the buyer in connection with personal injury or death caused by the goods.

The exclusions under Articles 2(a) and 5 have special significance in relation to the notice requirement of Article 39: A buyer "loses the right to rely on a lack of conformity of the goods" unless he gives notice to the seller within a reasonable time and, in any event, within two years after receipt of the goods. Domestic rules on liability in tort may not require such notice. The limitation period for claims in tort, furthermore, may commence, for example, only when the injury occurs or when the harm becomes known (or is evident) to the injured person; the two-year cut-off for notice under Article 39(2), in contrast, runs from the time the goods were "handed over" to the buyer.

In many countries another important feature of "product liability" is the opportunity to sue a manufacturer or distributor with whom the plaintiff had no direct contractual relationship. The Convention (Art. 4) governs "only ... the rights and obligations of the seller and buyer arising from" the "contract of sale." Thus, except for unusual cases (§63 *supra*), the Convention would not govern actions by a buyer against persons other than the seller and consequently would not interfere with domestic rules, such as product liability, that permit such actions. Moreover, as we have seen. Article 5 preserves domestic

---

2. Compare, e.g., Bridge, *International Sale of Goods* para. 2.20 with Peter Schlechtriem, Art. 5 para. 7, *in* Schlechtriem & Schwenzer, *CISG Commentary* (2nd English ed. 2005).
3. One decision applied the Convention to a buyer's claim against the seller for indemnification for liability to a sub-purchaser for an accident caused by the goods; the accident killed one of the sub-purchaser's employees and injured another. Oberlandesgericht Düsseldorf, Germany, July 2, 1993, CLOUT Case no. 49, English translation available at http://cisgw3. law.pace.edu/cases/930702g1.html. The court, however, did not focus on the question of the CISG's applicability to claims based on death or personal injury, or on the impact of Art. 5 on this issue.

rules on liability for "death or personal injury caused to any person" even for actions by the buyer against the seller.

72 ## B. Labels for Domestic Law and the Scope of the Convention

Article 4 provides that the Convention governs the "obligations of the seller and the buyer arising from (the) . . . contract. . . ." The discussion of Article 4 mentioned that a subtle issue of the relationship between the Convention and domestic law would be explored here. In schematic form the issue is as follows: Domestic law states that facts A, B, and C lead to legal result X, and gives this rule a label such as "tort" or "products liability." Under the Convention, facts A, B and C lead to legal results Y. Does the label that domestic law gives to its rule determine whether that rule is displaced by the Convention?

This issue was introduced in schematic form because the same basic issue may arise in various settings. But it may help to examine this problem in a specific setting — domestic rules of "product liability."

73 ## (1) "Product Liability"

"Product liability" differs among the various countries, and even among the fifty states of the United States, where this development (or eruption) has been unusually active. No attempt will be made to catalogue the various species of "product liability." To analyze the relationship between the Convention and domestic law, it will suffice to consider one extreme application of this doctrine.[4]

Example 5A. Seller, in State A, sold Buyer, in State B, an industrial heater for use in Buyer's factory. Seller was not negligent in manufacturing the heater, but there was a hidden flaw in the burner that led to an explosion that damaged the goods in Buyer's factory. Domestic law of "product liability" would make Seller liable to Buyer for the damage. The operative

---

4. The application of "product liability" to international sales was explored in Secretariat reports of UNCITRAL: *Rep. S-G,* "Liability for Damage," VI *YB* 255–272; *Rep. S-G,* "Liability for Damage." VIII *YB* 235–269 Rep. S-G. "Analysis of the Replies of Governments," VIII *YB* 269–287. *See also* 1977 *UNIDROIT Unif. L. Rev.* Vol. I, 192–209: Text: European Convention on Products Liability, Strasbourg January 27, 1977. Under Art. 4, *supra* at §63, attention was given to product liability rules in connection with a very different issue — the applicability of the Convention to a producer's promises to a buyer who purchased the goods from a dealer.

facts that led to liability were these: (A) The defendant "supplied" the goods; (B) The goods were defective; (C) The goods caused damage to the user. Under such "product liability" Seller is liable to Buyer even if he establishes that he (or his supplier) exercised due care in making the heater. The buyer is not required to notify the seller of the defect in the goods. Local law classifies all such "product liability" under the heading of "tort" rather than "contract."[5]

Does the Convention displace such domestic rules of "product liability?" This question has generated substantial disagreement among commentators. For example, Professor Schlechtriem (whose views are explored in detail below, Professor Lookofsky,[6] and others[7] have suggested that the domestic rules should remain applicable, concurrently with those of the CISG, in a situation like Example 5A. Others (including prior editions of this treatise), however, take the position that the Convention should preempt domestic products liability law in such circumstances.[8]

There is a strong argument that the Convention should displace domestic product liability rules in Example 5A. Whether the Convention applies is, or course, governed by the provisions of the Convention. Under Article 1 this was a "contract of sale of goods" and the transaction was not excluded by Articles 2–5.

The facts that invoke the domestic rules of "product liability" in Example 5A are the same facts that invoke the Convention. In examining Article 4 we noted that the Convention does not displace domestic remedies for fraud, but those remedies respond to facts that are different from the facts that invoke the Convention. Domestic rules that turn on substantially the same facts as the rules of the Convention must be

---

5. "Product liability" usually applies to "dangerous" goods which do physical damage to a "consumer" or his property. However, case law on occasion has extended product liability to situations like Example 5A. See *White & Summers* §11–2, discussing Seely v. White Motor Co., 403 P.2d 145 (Cal. 1965) (lost profits when truck turned over).

6. See, e.g., Joseph Lookofsky, In Dubio Pro Conventione? Some Thoughts About Opt-Outs, Computer Programs and Preëmption Under the 1980 Vienna Sales Convention (CISG), 13 Duke J. Int'l L. (No. 3 — Special Issue) 263, 286–88 (Summer 2003).

7. See the authorities cited in Peter Schlechtriem, Art. 5 para. 9 n. 16, *in* Schlechtriem & Schwenzer, *CISG Commentary* (2nd English ed. 2005).

8. See Warren Khoo, Art. 4 para. 3.3.5 and Art. 5 para. 3.2, *in B-B Commentary*; Art. 5 §1.2, *in* Enderlein & Maskow Commentary; authorities cited in Peter Schlechtriem, Art. 5 para. 9 n. 17, *in* Schlechtriem & Schwenzer, *CISG Commentary* (2nd English ed. 2005).

displaced by the Convention; any other result would destroy the Convention's basic function to establish uniform rules. (Art. 7(1).)[9]

A more difficult problem would be presented if, in a setting like Example 5A, Buyer offered to prove that the defect in the heater resulted from a lack of due care in Seller's manufacturing operations and sought recovery under domestic tort law. At stake would be the applicability of the full range of the Convention's rules — including the buyer's obligation to notify the seller (Arts. 39, 40, 44), his right to avoid the contract (Art. 49) and the measurement of damages (Arts. 74–77).

In terms of the schematic presentation set forth at §72, *supra*, the buyer would argue that his claim under domestic tort law would not be based on the same facts as a claim under the Convention for breach of contract. Under the Convention, liability would be based on two elements — (A) failure of the goods to conform to the contract (Art. 35) and (B) damage resulting from this defect (Art. 74). The claim in tort would include a third element — (C) proof of lack of due care. However, it does not necessarily follow that this third element excludes the Convention.

As we shall see, the Convention embodies a deliberate choice that the question of negligence is irrelevant to the buyer's right to recover from the seller for damage caused by non-conforming goods. One of the reasons for this choice is this: When the seller has produced defective goods (as in the present case) it is likely that the defect resulted from lack of due care in production methods. However, proof of lack of due care is expensive and the outcome of litigation is difficult to predict; to promote legal certainty, the Convention makes the seller legally responsible for defects in the goods that it sells. Thus, proof of the seller's lack of due care does not change the essential character of the claim, and access to domestic law based on such proof would make it possible to circumvent the uniform international rules established by the Convention.[10]

In examining Articles 4 and 5 we have met cases in two quite distinct categories: (1) an action to rescind the contract for fraud (e.g., false statements by the seller concerning his production capability or false financial statements supplied by the buyer) (§65) and (2) claims for

---

9. We shall have occasion to return to this principle in connection with the Convention's rules on conformity of the goods with the contract. See Art. 35, *infra* at §222. Problems of applying this principle will arise when domestic rules are invoked by facts that are, in varying degrees, similar to the facts that invoke the Convention.

10. But see Miami Valley Paper, LLC v. Lebbing Engineering & Consulting GmbH, 2006 WL 2924779 (U.S.D.C.S.D. Oh. October 10, 2006) (holding that claim of negligent misrepresentation (and claim of fraudulent inducement) in connection with a transaction governed by the CISG was not pre-empted by the Convention).

damages caused by defective goods based on domestic rules as to "product liability" or tort (the present section). Between these two poles there may well arise situations where the claim under domestic law depends on facts that differ, in varying degrees, from the facts necessary to establish a claim under the Convention. However, if it were clearly determined that claims like those in category (2), above, may not invoke domestic law, the cases that fall between these two categories should not seriously interfere with the application of the Convention.

Professor Schlechtriem concludes that the Convention supersedes domestic tort rules in actions to recover "for the *inferior value* of non-conforming goods." This type of action protects an "economic interest" which is "the essence of contractual interests." On the other hand, he argues, the Convention does not supersede actions based on "property" interests that exist "independently of contractual obligations."[11]

From these premises Professor Schlechtriem concludes that actions may be based on domestic law when defective goods "non-conforming to the contract or not" cause "property damage." Domestic law may be invoked even though "damage is recoverable under CISG, Article 74" since this action is "outside the principal domain of interests created by contracts."[12] Domestic tort rules would also apply "even if the goods themselves were destroyed by a defect giving rise to a tort action based on strict liability."[13] The preservation of overlapping CISG and

11. Schlechtriem, The Borderland of Tort and Contract, *Cornell Colloq.* 467, 469 (1988). Professor Schlechtriem has given a more recent account of his views in Peter Schlechtriem, Art. 5 paras. 10 & 12, *in* Schlechtriem & Schwenzer, *CISG Commentary* (2nd English ed. 2005). The Cornell article also mentions that an interest in "health," like property, is independent of contractual obligations; this interest seems to present no problem of overlap in view of Art. 5's exclusion of "death or physical injury."

12. Schlechtriem, The Borderland of Tort and Contract, *Cornell Colloq.* 467, 473–477 (1988). See also Peter Schlechtriem, Art. 5 para. 12, *in* Schlechtriem & Schwenzer, *CISG Commentary* (2nd English ed. 2005). Professor Schlechtriem states that a tort action would not be subject to the requirement of notice (Art. 39) or the foreseeability limit on damages (Art. 74); apparently none of the Convention's rules would be binding. It is not clear whether concurrent tort actions for "property damage" would extend to materials spoiled or defective goods produced by a machine that did not conform to the contract.

13. Schlechtriem, The Borderland of Tort and Contract, *Cornell Colloq.* 467, 474 (1988). See also Peter Schlechtriem, Art. 5 para. 12, *in* Schlechtriem & Schwenzer, *CISG Commentary* (2nd English ed. 2005). In this discussion reference was made to a "dangerous defect" but it is not clear whether this limits the scope of concurrent tort recovery; perhaps under this approach the Convention's rules would control when perishable commodities (e.g., fruit) are destroyed because they were infected with fungus or disease or were over-ripe.

domestic product liability rules for property damage caused by defective goods is necessary, Professor Schlechtriem argues, in order to preserve laws that are "part of the public order in a wider sense"; otherwise, "the conclusion of an international sales contract would amount to a partial disclaimer of tort liability."[14] Without recourse to a parallel set of domestic product liability rules in this situation, he submits, the possibility that a buyer's rights under the Convention could be cut-off by the notice requirements of Article 39 might interfere with "the passing on of respective losses from the final vendor to the party who sold to him and further on to the manufacturer . . . thereby letting fall the loss arbitrarily on those in the chain of distribution. . . ."[15] Professor Schlechtriem also notes that a "defect" that triggers product liability under domestic law is not necessarily identical to a "non-conformity" under Article 35 of the Convention, so that the preemptive scope of the CISG (if it were granted such scope) would turn on a "subtle distinction."[16] Finally he argues that the drafters probably did not intend to reverse "the incomplete preference, expressed in Article 5, [. . .] for domestic products liability law" by pre-empting such law with respect to property damage.

These views are intriguing and merit the most careful consideration. One question that calls for attention is the justification for displacing inconsistent domestic law within only part of the Convention's area of applicability. Displacing inconsistent domestic law is of the essence of establishing uniform law. In areas where appeals for domestic law were persuasive to the international legislative body the Convention carved out exceptions — for example, by excluding sales to consumers (Art. 2(a)), claims based on death or personal injury (Art. 5), and validity of the contract, any of its provisions, or usage (Art. 4(a)). Adding exceptions to the area of uniformity seems inconsistent with the compromises on scope and substance that led to international agreement. *The drafters in fact rejected a proposal to add property damage due to "products liability" to the subjects excluded from the Convention's coverage by Article 5. The premise of the debate on this matter, and indeed more generally of the exclusion of claims for personal injury or death, appears to have been that permitting the Convention to deal with that topic would exclude domestic product liability rules on the*

14. Peter Schlechtriem, Art. 5 para. 10, *in* Schlechtriem & Schwenzer, *CISG Commentary* (2nd English ed. 2005).

15. *Id.*

16. *Id.*

same topic.[17] This point highlights the fact that, if the Convention's coverage of claims for property damage caused by the goods does not displace domestic product liability laws on the question, then property damage claims are actually favored over claims for death or personal injury: property damage claimants would have their choice to proceed either under the Convention or under domestic products liability law, whichever was more favorable, whereas personal injury claimants would be relegated exclusively to domestic law because of Article 5. Such a strange set of priorities would presumably be evidenced somewhere in the drafting record.

Some of the arguments for permitting domestic product liability rules on property damage to continue to supplement the Convention's coverage of the issue appear to be mere descriptions of the inevitable interaction between uniform international law and non-uniform domestic law, and not applicable in particular to property damage claims; in other words, they are not arguments against pre-empting domestic law property damage claims, but arguments against injecting uniform international law into the midst of non-uniform domestic law. Thus the argument that property damage claims against a seller might be cut-off by the Article 39 notice rule, resulting in the interference with "the passing on of respective losses," is equally applicable to non-property damage claims for economic loss: a buyer in an international sale who resold the goods to a customer in a domestic transaction could be sued by its buyer for economic damages under domestic law, and be cut-off from passing that liability onto the international seller by Article 39. That possibility, however, is not seen as a valid argument against the Convention's pre-emption of domestic sales/contract rules with respect to the international sale.

More fundamentally, the argument that domestic product liability laws on property damage should not be displaced because they are "part of the public order in a wider sense" substitutes the opinion of commentators concerning what domestic laws are too "important" to preempt, in place of the judgment of the Convention's drafters: when the drafters were convinced that it was necessary to preserve

---

17. See *O.R.* 245–246; *Docy. Hist.* 466–467. One delegate raised the possibility that what became Art. 5 of the Convention might be interpreted so that claims for property damage "grounded on tort and not on contracts of sale" would be deemed outside the scope of the Convention — see the comments of Mr. Rognlien (Norway), *O.R.* 245, *Docy. Hist.* 466 — but he recognized that a contrary interpretation was possible, and the matter was not thereafter clarified.

*domestic law on particular subjects — as occurred in the case of con-
sumer sales (Article 2(a), personal injury/death claims (Article 5), and
even limitations on the availability of specific performance (Article
28) — they explicitly excluded those matters from the Convention.
Without such explicit guidance from the text of the Convention, having
commentators or even judges decide what domestic law is too important to preempt is a recipe for non-uniformity and infringement of the
"legislative" function. For example, in order to protect buyers from
unwittingly giving up important rights U.S. domestic sales law imposes
special requirements before parties are permitted to contract out of a
merchant seller's obligation to deliver goods fit for the "ordinary purposes" for which such goods are used.*[18] *Are these domestic rules "part
of the public order in a wider sense," and for that reason to remain
applicable with respect to a seller's obligation under Article 35(2)(a) to
deliver goods fit for their ordinary purposes? An approach that
requires such a judgment call in order to determine if the domestic
rule is pre-empted requires an extraordinarily "subtle [and difficult]
distinction."*

*A clearer, more reliable and better guide is the approach proposed
previously: domestic law is pre-empted if the facts that invoke it are the
same facts that invoke a rule of the Convention. In others words, where
the Convention has dealt with the exact circumstances at hand it presumably was intended — absent an explicit preservation of domestic
law (as with Article 28) — to bring a uniform solution to the situation
and to displace non-uniform domestic law. That result is not only
sensible, but most likely to capture the result intended by the drafters
and the fundamental purpose of the Convention — bringing uniformity to the law applicable to international sales.*

One might suppose that nothing more than generosity results from
permitting claimants to choose more favorable domestic law: this
alternative merely adds to the claimant's protection; if domestic law
is not more favorable than the Convention claimants will invoke the
Convention. However, the Convention was devised to provide a fair
balance between buyers and sellers, claimants and defendants.

A less basic point: Permitting recourse to domestic law can be unfair
since not all domestic systems permit choice between contract laws
("*non-cumul*"); under German law parties to contracts may choose

---

18. See U.C.C. §2–316(2) (requiring that disclaimers of the implied warranty of merchantability include the term "merchantability" and, if in writing, be conspicuous).

("Anspruchskonkurrenz").[19] More important, however, is the difficulty of maintaining uniformity of the international rules once a breach has been opened in the line set by the Convention's own rules on its sphere of applicability. The appeal of familiar domestic law to domestic judges is strong and should not be given further encouragement.

19. Schlechtriem, The Borderland of Tort and Contract, *Cornell Colloq.* 467, 468, 470 (1988); Nicholas, *French Law of Contract* 53.

Article 6.
The Contract and the Convention

74   The dominant theme of the Convention is the primacy of the contract. See, for example, Overview, Ch. 1 at §2, Overview, Ch. 2 at §§19, 24, Article 4 at §61, Article 31 at §207, Article 35 at §222. Of the many provisions that develop this theme, Article 6 is the most important.

Article 6[1]

The parties may exclude the application of this Convention or, subject to Article 12, derogate from or vary the effect of any of its provisions.

The most significant statement in Article 6 is that the parties may "vary the effect" of any of the Convention's provisions. This rule applies to the formation of the contract (Part II) and supplements the basic principles that the offeror is the master of its offer (Arts. 14–17) and the offeree the master of its acceptance (Art. 18(1)); in addition, the parties by agreement may set rules for the making of their future contracts. Moreover, the Convention's gamut of provisions on the obligations of seller and buyer and the remedies for breach (Part III) may be reshaped by the agreement. The breadth of the parties' freedom to modify the Convention's rules is emphasized by the one exception stated in Article 6 — the privilege of an adhering State under Articles 12 and 96 to preserve its domestic rules that require a writing.[2] (See the Commentary to Art. 12, *infra* at §128.)

This degree of freedom for the parties was made possible by excluding certain transactions and issues from the Convention. The Convention

---

1. This article is the same as Art. 5 of the 1978 Draft Convention. *Cf.* ULIS 3 (reference only to exclusion of the Convention), ULF 2.

2. It has been noted that, although not expressly so provided in Art. 6, provisions of the Convention directed to states or to courts rather than to regulating the rights and obligation of parties to an international sales contract are not subject to exclusion or modification by agreement of the parties; these include the Final Provisions in Part IV of the Convention (Arts. 89–101), Art. 7(1) (governing interpretation of the Convention) and, arguably, Art. 28 (relieving a court from the obligation to order specific performance if it would not do so under its domestic law in the circumstances). See Peter Schlechtriem, Art. 6 para. 3, *in* Schlechtriem & Schwenzer, *CISG Commentary* (2nd English ed. 2005); Markus Müller-Chen, Art. 28 para. 24, *in* Schlechtriem & Schwenzer, *CISG Commentary* (2nd English ed. 2005); UNCITRAL Digest Art. 6 para. 4.

does not apply to consumer purchases (Art. 2(a)) or to liability for death or personal injury (Art. 5). Nor does the Convention displace domestic rules with respect to the validity of the contract or prejudice the rights of third persons (Art. 4).

75   A. Exclusion or Modification

(1) Exclusion of the Convention; Designation of Domestic Law

In the preparation of both ULIS and the present Convention, it was suggested that an agreement excluding the Convention should be effective only if the agreement also designates the applicable domestic law.[3] This suggestion was not accepted;[4] if the parties merely agree that the Convention does not apply, rules of PIL would determine the applicable domestic law.[5]

76   (2) Implied Exclusion or Modification

ULIS (Art. 3) provided that total or partial exclusion of the application of the Uniform Law "may be express or implied." In UNICTRAL the reference to "implied" exclusion was deleted on the ground that this language might lead tribunals to exclude the Convention on inadequate grounds; on the other hand, UNCITRAL declined to provide that exclusion must be "express." *Thus it is possible to exclude the Convention or modify the rules contained therein impliedly*[6] — *although, as explained below (§77), this result should flow only from actual*

---

3. The UNIDROIT Draft submitted to the 1964 Hague Conference provided (§6): "The parties may entirely exclude the application of the present law provided that they indicate the municipal law to be applied to their contract." II *Records, Hague Sales Conference* 213. *Rep. S-G.* "Analysis of Governmental Comments on ULIS" paras. 68–69, 1 *YB* 168. A similar proposal was made in UNCITRAL during the early work on the Convention. See Peter Schlechtriem, Art. 6 para. 1, *in* Schlechtriem & Schwenzer, *CISG Commentary* (2nd English ed. 2005).

4. See Peter Schlechtriem, Art. 6 para. 1, *in* Schlechtriem & Schwenzer, *CISG Commentary* (2nd English ed. 2005).

5. Accord, Peter Schlechtriem, Art. 6 para. 7, *in* Schlechtriem & Schwenzer, *CISG Commentary* (2nd English ed. 2005).

6. Accord, Peter Schlechtriem, Art. 6 para. 2, 8 & 12, *in* Schlechtriem & Schwenzer, *CISG Commentary* (2nd English ed. 2005); UNCITRAL Digest Art. 6 para. 6.

agreement on this matter; an implicit exclusion or modification should be found only if such an agreement is clearly implied in fact[7] under normal rules of construction of the contract.[8]

A reference in a contract to trade terms, like *Incoterms* of the International Chamber of Commerce (ICC), should not be taken as an exclusion of the Convention,[9] any more than such a reference would exclude rules of national law. Such trade terms articulate the parties' obligations as to loading the goods, risk of loss and related matters, and are similar to contract provisions stating the parties' duties. But such trade terms ordinarily do not set forth many matters, such as the legal consequences of breach. The Convention (like domestic rules of law) and trade terms are complementary; each performs a function that cannot be well served by the other.[10]

Even detailed standard contracts or general conditions usually recognize the need for a back-up legal system to supply answers for unanticipated problems. In some cases parties may wish to provide for the settlement of disputes by an arbitral tribunal acting as *amiable compositeur or ex aequo et bono*. See the UNCITRAL Arbitration Rules, Article 33–2; UNIDROIT Principles 2004, *Preamble*. However in the absence of such a provision it is unlikely that the parties chose to divorce their contract from all systems of law.

---

7. *Dicta* in some U.S. cases suggesting that the Convention can be excluded only by "express" agreement (see, e.g., Travelers Property Cas. Co. v. Saint-Gobain Tech. Fabrics Ltd., 474 F. Supp. 2d 1075, 1081–82 (D. Minn. 2007); St. Paul Guardian Ins. Co. v. Neuromed Medical Systems & Support, GmbH, 2002 WL 465312 at *2, 2002 U.S. Dist. LEXIS 5096 at *8 (S.D.N.Y. March 26, 2002); Orbisphere Corp. v. U.S., 726 F. Supp. 1344, 1355 n. 7 (Ct. of Int'l Trade 1989)) should be considered loose language that would likely be revised if implied exclusion had actually been at issue.

8. *W/G 2* paras. 43–46, II *YB* 55; *UNCITRAL X* Annex I, paras. 56–58, VIII *YB* 29. At the diplomatic conference: *Com. I* Art. 5 para. 3(1), (v)-(vii); *SR. 3*, paras. 35–65; *SR. 4*, paras. 1–95 p. 106 n.3; *Docy. Hist.* 61, 657–658, 469–475 (*O.R.* 248–252). *Accord*, Rolf Herber, Art. 6 para. 13, *in* Schlechtriem, *CISG Commentary* (1st English ed. 1998); UNCITRAL Digest Art. 6 para. 5. In the latest English language edition of his commentary, Professor Schlechtriem argues that private international law rules, as opposed to the rules of the Convention, govern some agreements to exclude application of the Convention. Peter Schlechtriem, Art. 6 paras. 6–12, *in* Schlechtriem & Schwenzer, *CISG Commentary* (2nd English ed. 2005).

9. *Accord*, Peter Schlechtriem, Art. 6 para. 12 at 89, *in* Schlechtriem & Schwenzer, *CISG Commentary* (2nd English ed. 2005); UNCITRAL Digest Art. 6 para. 11.

10. *Cf.* Hellner, Prospects for the Unification of Sales Law at the Regional or International level: A Scandinavian View, 15 McGill L.J. 83, 92–93 (1969) p. 4; Honnold, Uniform Law and Uniform Trade Terms — Two Approaches to a Common Goal, *Trans-National Law: Bielefeld Colloq.* 161, 171.

77 **(3) Private International Law and Implied Exclusion of the Convention**

Example 6A. The places of business of Seller and Buyer are in States A and B, both of which are Contracting States. A contract of sale was signed by representatives of Seller and Buyer in State C, a non-Contracting State. The contract provided that Seller would deliver the goods to Buyer in State C. The contract had no provision designating the applicable law.

What laws should *fora* in States A and B and other Contracting States apply to the above transaction? A firm starting point is this: Since the places of business of both parties are in Contracting States, Article 1(1)(a) ("Sub (1)(a)") provides that the Convention applies unless the parties have agreed (Art. 6) to exclude the Convention.

The law designated by the "PIL" or "conflicts" rules of the various possible *fora* may be unclear or in conflict. However, let us assume that the PIL rules point to State C, a non-Contracting State.[11]

Would the above rules of PIL exclude the Convention? Article 1 of the Convention tells us that the answer is No. Subs (1)(a) and (1)(b) of Article 1 provide *alternative* grounds for applicability. A conclusion that PIL pointing to the law of a non-Contracting State bars applicability of the Convention, even though the places of business of both parties are in Contracting States, would nullify Sub (1)(a) of the Convention — the primary and universally accepted basis for the Convention's applicability. (As we have seen at §47 *supra*, Article 95 authorizes a reservation excluding applicability under Sub (1)(b); some States, including the United States, have exercised this option.)

If rules of PIL alone will not undermine applicability based on Sub (1)(a), it appears that the only basis for excluding the Convention in the above example is an agreement by the parties under Article 6.[12] The

---

11. Apart from the general lack of clarity and diversity of conflicts rules in various States, doubt about the above assumption that such rules point to State C is accentuated by the specialized Hague Conventions of 1955 and 1986 on the law applicable to international sales. Both Conventions in most situations designate the law of the place of business of the seller or buyer. See, e.g., the 1986 Hague PIL Convention Art. 8–1 and 8–2. *But cf.* Arts. 8–3, 5 and 21–1(b). In Example 6A either designation would invoke the Convention rather than the domestic law of State C.

12. Professor Schlechtriem argues that an agreement by the parties in Example 6A to apply the law of State C would be governed (e.g., with respect to its enforceability and interpretation) by the PIL rules of the forum rather than by Art. 6 or any other rules of the Convention, even if the forum was in a Contracting State to the CISG; if, however, the parties excluded the

legislative history of Article 6 outlined above (§76 at n.3) shows that, although an agreement to exclude the Convention need not be "express," the agreement may only be implied from facts pointing to *real* — as opposed to theoretical or fictitious — agreement.[13]

This view is supported by the 1986 Hague Convention on the Law Applicable to Contracts for the International Sale of Goods. This Convention gives unqualified effect to an *express* agreement choosing applicable law, but is more cautious about implied agreements. Article 7 provides:

> (1) A contract of sale is governed by the law chosen by the parties. The parties' agreement on this choice must be express or *be clearly demonstrated by the terms of the contract and the conduct of the parties, viewed in their entirety....*[14]

Similar requirements are set forth in the EEC Convention on the Law Applicable to Contractual Obligations (Rome, 19 June 1980). Article 3 provides:

> (1) The contract shall be governed by the law chosen by the parties. The choice must be expressed or *demonstrated with reasonable certainty by the terms of the contract or the circumstances of the case.*

It is not feasible to comment on the significance of the various facts that adequately evidence an implied agreement to exclude the Convention, except to suggest doubt about the significance of an agreement on the venue for arbitration. In an international transaction a single arbitrator or the chairman of a panel of three is likely to be selected from a "neutral" State having no connection with the transaction. The choice of the place where the arbitrators meet is likely to reflect practical considerations with respect to transport, meeting and translation facilities rather than a choice of applicable law.[15] See the UNCITRAL

Convention and chose the domestic sales law of a Contracting State in which a party was located, Professor Schlechtriem argues that the agreement on applicable law would be governed by the Convention. Peter Schlechtriem, Art. 6 paras. 7 & 12, *in* Schlechtriem & Schwenzer, *CISG Commentary* (2nd English ed. 2005).

13. Goldstajn, *Dubrovnik Lectures* 95 at n. 97.

14. The conflicting views reconciled in Art. 7 are reviewed in the *Explanatory Report on the 1986 Hague Sales Convention* paras. 45–49 by Professor Arthur T. von Mehren, Hague Conference on Private International Law, 1987.

15. But see Peter Schlechtriem, Art. 6 para. 8, *in* Schlechtriem & Schwenzer, *CISG Commentary* (2nd English ed. 2005) ("A contract between parties in contracting states with a jurisdiction or an arbitration clause nominating as competent a court or arbitration panel in a

Arbitration Rules (1976), Article 16 (place of arbitration) and Article 33 (applicable law).[16]

In sum: When the places of business of the seller and buyer are in different Contracting States, the applicability of the Convention mandated by Article 1(1)(a) is not undercut when rules of PIL point to a non-Contracting State. The Convention may be excluded by the parties, but only by an express agreement or an agreement that is clearly implied in fact.

77.1 **(4) Ambiguous Contracts**

Suppose the contract includes language to the following effect: "This contract is to be governed by the law of (e.g.) State X." If State X has adhered to the Convention, this question arises: Did the parties intend to invoke the CISG, or the internal, domestic law of State X?

Courts and arbitral panels have repeatedly faced this issue. A majority of tribunals have concluded that the parties intended to invoke CISG.[17] A few decisions have held that the parties chose non-CISG internal sales law.[18]

The present writer, although an advocate for CISG, ventures a surmise that the outlook of some decisions reflects patterns developed during the years when ULIS (1964) was in force in some countries of Europe; in other regions caution about the intent of the parties may be advisable.[19]

---

non-contracting state . . . may be interpreted as excluding the CISG" [contra citations omitted]); UNCITRAL Digest Art. 6 para. 9 ("The choice of a forum may also lead to the implicit exclusion of the Convention's applicability" [but citing two arbitration decisions consistent with the position taken in the text accompanying this note]).

16. See also Lebedev, The 1977 Optional Clause for Soviet-American Contracts, 27 Am. J. Comp. L. 469 (1979): Arbitrations are to be held in Sweden, with administrative and other services provided by the Stockholm Chamber of Commerce. Where the arbitration clause and the UNCITRAL Rules do not settle matters as to the conduct of the arbitration, Swedish rules may fill gaps with respect to the *conduct of the arbitration* — as distinguished from governing substantive law.

17. See UNCITRAL Digest Art. 6 para. 8 and decisions cited in nn. 20 & 21.

18. See UNCITRAL Digest Art. 6 para. 8 and decisions cited in nn. 18 & 19. In one of these cases the contract included language that, without being explicit, suggested an intent to derogate from the CISG. Ad Hoc Arbitration — Florence, Italy, April 19, 1994, CLOUT Case no. 92 (English translation of pertinent parts available at http://cisgw3.law.pace.edu/cases/940419i3.html "('Contract to be governed exclusively by Italian law'; domestic Italian law applied; one dissent)."

19. Compare the approach in Peter Schlechtriem, Art. 6 para. 14, *in* Schlechtriem & Schwenzer, *CISG Commentary* (2nd English ed. 2005) (arguing that the meaning of a choice-of-law clause referring to the law of a Contracting State is a matter of interpretation in accordance

Special caution seems advisable when the parties invoke the law of one *region* of a contracting State: for example, an agreement to apply the law of New York. True, the U.S. Constitution provides that a treaty is the "law of the land" in all 50 states. However, a reference to only one of the fifty states may suggest that the parties were not thinking of the Convention.

Despite such considerations, U.S. decisions have generally found that, where the contract is between a U.S. party and a party located in another Contracting State, choice-of-law clauses referring to the law of one particular U.S. state do not exclude the Convention.[20] It is instructive to examine one of those decisions. In Asante Technologies, Inc. v. PMC-Sierra, Inc.[21] a U.S. buyer purchased computer chips from a seller that the court determined was located (under the standards in Article 10(a) of the CISG) in another Contracting State (Canada). The buyer's standard terms, which it included with its purchase orders, specified that the sales "shall be governed by the laws of the State shown on Buyer's address on this order," and the buyer's address on the orders was shown as California. According to the seller's standard terms, however, the transactions were governed by "the laws of the Province of British Columbia and the laws of Canada applicable therein." The court held that, because each party to the sale was located in a different Contracting State, the CISG was applicable under Article 1(1)(a), and that neither party's choice-of-law clause was sufficient to exclude it: the Convention was part of the law of the jurisdictions designated by both the seller's clause (British Columbia) and, pursuant to the Supremacy Clause of the U.S.

with the rules of Art. 8 of the Convention, and suggesting some such clauses might properly be interpreted to exclude the Convention).

20. BP Oil Int'l, Ltd. v. Empresa Estatal Petroleos de Ecuador, 332 F.3d 333, 336–37 (5th Cir. 2003), CLOUT Case no. 575 (June 11, 2003); Travelers Property Cas. Co. v. Saint-Gobain Tech. Fabrics Ltd., 474 F. Supp. 2d 1075, 1081–82 (D. Minn. 2007); Am. Mint LLC v. GOSoftware, Inc., 2006 WL 42090 at *3, 2006 U.S. Dist. LEXIS 1569, at *11–12 (M.D. Pa. January 5, 2006); Am. Mint LLC v. GOSoftware, Inc., 2005 WL 2021248, at *2–*3 (M.D. Pa. August 16, 2005); Valero Mkt. & Supply Co. v. Greeni Oy, 373 F. Supp. 2d 475, 480 n. 7 (D.N.J. 2005); Asante Technologies, Inc. v. PMC-Sierra, Inc., 164 F. Supp. 2d 1142, 1149–50 (N.D. Cal. 2001), CLOUT Case no. 433 (July 30, 2001). But see Am. Biophysics Corp. v. Dubois Marine Specialties, 411 F. Supp. 2d 61, 63 (D.R.I. 2006) (holding a clause which provided, "This Agreement shall be construed and enforced in accordance with the laws of Rhode Island," sufficient to exclude the CISG from a transaction between a U.S. party and a party located in another Contracting State (Canada), but evidencing no awareness of the opposing position or authorities in support thereof).

21. 164 F. Supp. 2d 1142 (N.D. Cal. 2001), CLOUT Case no. 433 (July 30, 2001).

Constitution, the buyer's clause (California). Thus, the court found, the clauses did not exclude the Convention with sufficient clarity.[22]

By applying the Convention the court avoided the difficult determination of which (if either) party's choice-of-law clause was incorporated into the contracts and, if the seller's clause had prevailed, the challenge of applying unfamiliar foreign (British Columbian) law. The issue, however, was not the convenience of the court (although this consideration illustrates some of the advantages of applying the Convention) but the intent behind the choice-of-law clauses. Determining that intent, pursuant to the rules of Article 8,[23] is a complex challenge. Given its ambiguity and the availability of more direct and clear designations, a reference to the law of a particular U.S. state or Canadian province is an improbable choice if one is consciously attempting to invoke the Convention. It is likely that, when the standard clauses in Asante were originally drafted, the drafters (and the clients who adopted the clauses) were unaware of the Convention, possibly because it had not entered into force at that time; for that reason, they more than likely intended to refer to the internal domestic law of British Columbia or the designated U.S. state. Does that indicate an intent to exclude otherwise-applicable uniform law of which the parties were ignorant, and which may not even yet have come into existence? If these clauses were originally drafted before the Convention became effective, what is one to make of their continued use after the Convention entered into force? The intent with respect to the Convention in such circumstances is, at the least, highly ambiguous. Thus the court's decision — that the clauses did not sufficiently express a purpose of excluding the CISG — not only secured the practical advantages previously mentioned, but also is fully supportable as a construction of the contractual provisions.

22. *Id.* at 1149–50. For an appeals court opinion imposing an "affirmative opt-out" requirement for excluding the CISG, see BP Oil Int'l, Ltd. v. Empresa Estatal Petroleos de Ecuador, 332 F.3d 333, 336–37 (5th Cir. 2003), CLOUT Case no. 575 (June 11, 2003).

23. Professor Schlechtriem, who argues that the interpretation of choice-of-law clauses designating the law of a non-Contracting State is not governed by the Convention, would also apply the rules of CISG Art. 8 to the interpretation of clauses that, like those in *Asante*, designate the law of a Contracting State. See Peter Schlechtriem, Art. 6 paras. 3–4 & 7–12, *in* Schlechtriem & Schwenzer, *CISG Commentary* (2nd English ed. 2005).

78 **B. Agreements to Apply the Convention; Effectiveness**

Article 6 refers only to exclusion or modification of the Convention; there is no provision that addresses the question whether the parties may make the Convention applicable to transactions that fall outside the scope of Articles 1–5. This question may arise in at least three types of situations:

(a) The contract relates to a type of transaction or a type of commodity that is excluded by Article 2, 3 or 5.

(b) The place of business of the seller and buyer are not "in different States" as required by Article 1(1).

(c) The transaction does not bear a relationship to a Contracting State that is consistent with Article 1(1)(a) or (b).

79 **(1) Legislative History**

ULIS gave sweeping approval to agreements extending the applicability of the 1964 Sales Convention. Article 4 of ULIS provided:

> The present law shall also apply where it has been chosen as the law of the contract by the parties, whether or not their places of business or their habitual residences are in different States and whether or not such States are Parties to the Convention dated the 1st day of July 1964 relating to a Uniform Law on the International Sale of Goods, to the extent that it does not affect the application of any mandatory provisions of law which would have been applicable if the parties had not chosen the Uniform Law.

The 1980 Convention has no comparable provision. Does this mean that UNCITRAL decided that the sales contract could not invoke the Convention? The answer can be found in a brief review of the legislative history.

In 1970, UNCITRAL's Working Group on Sales deleted Article 4 of ULIS and added the following provision to Article 1: "2. The present Law shall also apply where it has been chosen as the law of the contract by the parties." The Working Group noted that ULIS, in authorizing the parties to apply the Convention (Art. 4, just quoted), added that this agreement would not affect the application of any "mandatory" provision. The Working Group recognized that some such exception was necessary but noted that the term "mandatory" was subject to varying interpretations, some of which embraced a large portion of domestic law. A final decision was deferred until further consideration could be given to this question.[24]

---

24. *W/G 2* paras. 36–42, 47–49, II *YB* 54–55, *Docy. Hist.* 60–61. The above-quoted provision was carried forward in subsequent drafts. *W/G 6* para. 16 and Annex I, VI *YB* 50, *Docy. Hist.* 241.

The Commission, in reviewing the Working Group draft, deleted the above provision that gave unqualified effect to the agreement because of concern lest contracts might apply the Convention to consumer transactions and thereby nullify domestic regulations designed to protect such purchasers. It was then proposed to return to Article 4 of ULIS, but limited to contracts between parties in different States when one of those States is a Contracting State. This proposal was rejected on the ground that it would unduly restrict parties who wished to apply the Convention. Article 4, as it stood in ULIS, was also rejected because (as the Working Group had concluded) the term "mandatory" was too vague. The upshot was a decision to omit any provision on the effect of agreements extending the applicability of the Convention. This decision by UNCITRAL's Committee of the Whole was summarized as follows:

> The Committee concludes that Article 4 raises many difficult questions of interpretation which even protracted discussions have failed to solve. Because of this, and in view of the fact that a provision on the lines of Article 4 is not strictly necessary to achieve the purpose for which it was drafted, the Committee recommends to the Commission that the article should be deleted.[25]

80 **(a) Significance of the Legislative History.** The above legislative history shows that UNCITRAL's deletion of Article 4 of ULIS was not designed to nullify agreements extending the applicability of the Convention. The actions and discussion in UNCITRAL were based on the premise that, in most situations, agreements to apply the Convention would be effective. A provision regulating the effect of agreements to apply the Convention was not included because of the drafting problem posed by divergent domestic approaches to what rules were "mandatory." In short, courts facing this issue will not be subject to a binding rule of the Convention. Instead, the point of reference will be domestic rules on the contractual freedom of the parties, derived from domestic law and applicable international conventions.[26]

International consensus favoring party autonomy is evidenced by the 1986 Hague Convention on the Law Applicable to Contracts for the International Sale of Goods. This Convention, the result of the work of over fifty States, many of them members of UNCITRAL, provides in Article 7(1): "A contract of sale is governed by the law chosen by the

---

25. *UNCITRAL X* (1977) Annex I, paras. 44–52, VIII *YB* 28; *Docy. Hist.* 321.
26. Restatement Second, Conflict of Laws §187. *Cf.* Convention on the Law Applicable to the International Sale of Goods (The Hague, 1955) Arts. 2(1), 6; I *Register* 5. *See also* Schlechtriem, *1986 Commentary* 36.

parties." The Explanatory Report authorized by the Conference states: "No delegation objected to this general proposition."[27]

Since domestic rules vary on the basic issue of the freedom of the parties to choose applicable law, it would be presumptuous to suggest final solutions to problems in this area. The most that is feasible here is to suggest aspects of the Convention that may be relevant in applying these rules of domestic law. The problem can arise in different settings; the following observations will be related to the three types of situations mentioned at §78, *supra*.

81 ## (2) Agreement to Apply the Convention in Various Settings

(a) Transactions or Issues Specifically Excluded by the Convention.
The exclusions specified in Article 2(a) (consumer purchases) and Article 5 (death or personal injury) resulted from concern over the relationship between some of the provisions of the Convention and protective rules (often of a mandatory character) of domestic law. As we have seen, the Convention does not govern the effect of contracts extending its scope. Consequently, the applicability of the Convention depends entirely on the contract; the Convention's rules would have no greater effect on protective rules of domestic law than would a contract aimed directly at those rules. If the protective rules of domestic law constitute a thorough and unified regulation the Convention might well distort the legislative pattern; on this assumption the tribunal should not apply the Convention. On the other hand, where the protective rule can readily be separated from the provisions of the Convention it may be feasible to give effect to the agreement calling for the application of the Convention.

The sales mentioned in Article 2(d), (e) and (f) (investment securities; ships; electricity) and in Article 3 (materials supplied by buyer; service contracts) were excluded because of doubts as to the appropriateness of the Convention for these specialized transactions. The parties, however, would be competent to decide this question; there seems little reason to deny them freedom to choose.

---

27. Arthur T. von Mehren, *Explanatory Report on the 1986 Sales Convention* para. 4 (Hague Conference on Private International Law, 1987). See also *id.*, para. 102; *Pilichet, 1986 PIL Convention*, 105–128. *Cf.* Cheshire & North, *Private International Law* 450–457 (11th ed. 1987).

82 **(b) Parties Located in Same State.** The discussions in UNCITRAL recognized that a sales transaction could have significant international dimensions and still not meet the Convention's strict test of internationality. For example, a contract between a seller and a buyer whose places of business are in the same State may require the seller to procure the goods by an international transaction or the buyer may contemplate reselling the goods in an international transaction; unity with respect to obligations in such "chain" transactions may be important for all parties. Early ULIS drafts that embraced such "chain" transactions were abandoned because it was impossible clearly to define this extended area. No problem of clarity arises when the parties have agreed to apply the Convention to their contract.[28]

83 **(c) International Transactions That Lack the Prescribed Contact With a Contracting State.** The Convention's rules on the relationship between the transaction and a Contracting State (Art. 1(1)(a) and (b)) are strict — particularly for States that make a declaration under Article 95 rejecting subparagraph (1)(b). (See the Commentary to Art. 1.) As we have seen, the Hague Sales Conventions of 1964 applied to international transactions even though the parties and the transaction had *no* contact with a Contracting State — an approach that was subject to objection on the ground that the Contracting States were forcing their law on parties in other States. This objection does not apply when the parties to an international sale elect to be bound by the Convention. The relevant issues may be illustrated by the following case:

   Example 6B. A sales contract between Seller (whose place of business is in State A) and Buyer (whose place of business is in State B) provided that the Convention would apply to the contract. Neither State A nor State B is a Contracting State. The Convention has gone into force.

   This agreement would present no difficulty in legal systems that give full effect to the parties' choice-of-law. What should be the fate of the agreement in States that require a "reasonable relationship" between the transaction and the legal system chosen by the parties?

   The above example is, to say the least, quite different from classroom examples of agreements that seek to invoke the law of a single, remote State. In Example 6B, the parties have referred to a set of rules approved, without dissent, by an international legislative body representing each region of the world; moreover, these rules were approved, again without

---

28. The ambiguity of these early drafts is discussed in Honnold, *A Uniform Law for International Sales*, 107 U. Pa. L. Rev. 299, 309–310 (1959).

dissent, by a diplomatic conference attended by all significant trading nations and are now in force in each continent and region of the world. The rules are readily available in the six official languages of the United Nations and are the subject of substantial international commentary. The burden on the tribunal that would result from applicability of the Convention would be much less than that involved in most cases where rules of PIL call for the application of foreign domestic law. In addition, international sales have special needs for uniform law that emphasize the need for effective party autonomy when they agree on the applicability of a uniform international rule.[29]

Suppose that a contract in an international sale provides: "This contract shall be governed by the 1980 Convention on Contracts for the International Sale of Goods." It has been suggested that this contract provision may not be effective since it does not invoke the law of the Convention as adopted by a specified State.[30] Requiring that the Convention be invoked as the law of a designated State could avoid ambiguity over whether the parties intended to have the benefit of a reservation that a few of the contracting States have made. In the unlikely event that the applicability of a reservation becomes relevant, however, the problem can be solved by deciding whether conflicts (PIL) rules applicable to the transaction invoke the law of a State that has made the reservation. (Tribunals are accustomed to resolving contract ambiguities more serious than this.) In other cases, when the parties make a general reference to the provisions of the Convention it seems reasonable to conclude that they desire the full application of the Convention. In short, there seems no adequate policy reason to frustrate the parties' wish to have their contract governed by a uniform law for international sales approved and implemented by countries in each region of the world.

84 **(d) "Mandatory" Rules.** Rules of domestic law that are "mandatory" are not disturbed when the Convention becomes applicable by virtue of an agreement by the parties. When the Convention is applicable by the action of Contracting States, the terms of the

---

29. McLachlan, *The New Hague Sales Convention and the Limits on the Choice of Law Process*, 102 L. Q. Rev. 591 (1986). See *id.*, at 592–593 for examples of conflict rules that have responded to special international circumstances. See also Brand, *Pittsburgh Symposium (1988)* 167–170 and 146–166 (choice of forum; importance).

30. See the discussion in Peter Schlechtriem, Art. 6 para. 11, *in* Schlechtriem & Schwenzer, *CISG Commentary* (2nd English ed. 2005).

Convention control the extent to which the Convention displaces domestic law; questions may arise as to whether the Convention addresses and displaces a rule of domestic law that in some States would be classified as "mandatory." (See *supra* at §79.) These questions cannot arise when the applicability of the Convention is based solely on the parties' contract unsupported by the action of Contracting States; in such cases the legal situation might be analogized to an agreement incorporating a standard contract whose terms duplicate the provisions of the Convention.

CHAPTER II.

GENERAL PROVISIONS
(Articles 7–13)

Article 7.
Interpretation of the Convention

85   Article 7 responds to the fact that a Convention establishing uniform international law performs a unique and difficult function. Paragraph (1) emphasizes that this law must be interpreted with sensitive regard for its special character and purpose; Paragraph (2) is designed to help the law adapt and grow in the light of new circumstances.

Article 7[1]

(1) In the interpretation of this Convention, regard is to be had to its international character and to the need to promote uniformity in its application and the observance of good faith in international trade.

(2) Questions concerning matters governed by this Convention which are not expressly settled in it are to be settled in conformity with the general principles on which it is based or, in the absence of such principles, in conformity with the law applicable by virtue of the rules of private international law.

86   A. International Character; Uniformity

Paragraph (1) provides that in interpreting the Convention there shall be regard for two closely-related principles — (a) the Convention's

---

1. Paragraph (1) of Art. 7 is substantially the same as Art. 6 of the 1978 Draft Convention. paragraph (2) was added at the Diplomatic Conference; see *infra* §96. ULIS had no provision like paragraph (1); the first part of paragraph (2) is based on ULIS 17, quoted *infra* §96. paragraph (1), except for the reference to good faith, duplicates provisions in the other UNCITRAL conventions. United Nations Convention on the Limitation Period in the International Sale of Goods (1974), Art. 7, V *YB* 210; United Nations Convention on the Carriage of Goods by Sea (1978), Art. 3 IX *YB* 212; 27 AJCL UNICITRAL Symposium 421.

"international character" and (b) "the need to promote uniformity in its application." How to give life to these principles deserves close attention.

87 (1) The Problem of Diverse Connotations of Legal Terms

We have reason to envy those who work in the physical sciences on phenomena that can be photographed and measured, while we must cope with disembodied concepts that have been shaped by diverse historical, economic and cultural conditions, and include concepts that have similar names but different meanings — *des faux amis.*[2]

The careful international draftsman tries to avoid abstract, disembodied concepts. For example, in the 1980 Sales Convention risk of loss passes to the buyer "when the goods are *handed over* to the first carrier" or (if the contract does not involve carriage) when the buyer "*takes over* the goods" (Arts. 67(1), 69(1)) — more stable materials than ideas such as "property" or "title." The ideal is to use plain language that refers to things and events for which there are words of common content in the various languages. But this ideal is difficult to realize, and the principles of interpretation in Article 7(1) run counter to reflexes that have been deeply implanted by our education and professional life — the reading of a legal text in the light of the concepts of our domestic legal system, an approach that would violate the requirement that the Convention be interpreted with regard "to its *international* character."

If we are deprived of our most familiar tools, what resources remain for interpreting the Convention? This question was the subject of sixteen national reports, a general report and animated discussion at the Twelfth International Congress of Comparative Law (Australia, 1986); material developed at this Congress with respect to national and international practices will be cited frequently in this work.[3] *Commentary and decisions on the CISG since the Convention has gone into force have also shed substantial light on the question.*

2. Sundburg, Uniform Interpretation of Uniform Law, 10 *Scan. Studies* 219, 221; *Giles* 34. *See also* Kastely, Rhetorical Analysis, 8 Nw. J. Int. L. & Bus. 574 (1988); Cook, 50 U. Pitt. L. Rev. I (1988).

3. See *Honnold, General Report, 1986 Comp. L. Cong.*, reproduced in substance in *Freiburg Colloq.* 115–147.

88   **(2) Legislative History**

To read the words of the Convention with regard for their "international character" requires that they be projected against an international background. With time, a body of international experience has been developing through international case law and scholarly writing. (This will be explored *infra* §92.) Another source for an international perspective on the Convention's words is its legislative history (*travaux préparatoires*) — its genetic background. Decisions construing the Convention have recognized the propriety and utility of consulting the *travaux préparatoires* when interpreting the Convention,[4] and Professor Schlechtriem has also endorsed the procedure — at least where a clear "literal interpretation" does not emerge from examining the Convention text in question.[5]

The family history of the Convention is rich and revealing. In preparing the Convention, UNCITRAL built on the work, spanning three decades, that produced the Hague Conventions of 1964 (ULIS and ULF). The deliberations in UNCITRAL would commence with an analysis of how an issue was handled in the 1964 Conventions. As we shall see, in many instances the Hague solution was retained; the discussions shed light on the common understanding of the Hague solution and the reasons for its retention. When the Hague approach was modified or rejected, the reasons for the change shed a revealing sidelight on the new provision. As the UNCITRAL draft developed, proposals to delete or amend were made and decided; the views that prevailed in making these decisions add depth to the international understandings that underlie the Convention's words.

To introduce this background material, the steps in the legislative process in UNCITRAL and at the Diplomatic Conference were summarized in the Overview, Ch. 1, at §§9, 10. In this Commentary, legislative history will be brought to bear on specific problems of interpretation.

The documents that embody this legislative history are reproduced (together with materials on other topics) in Volumes I-X of the UNCITRAL Yearbooks and in the Official Records of the 1980 Diplomatic Conference. As is common in an extended legislative process, the article-numbers of the drafts under discussion kept changing as provisions were added and deleted and as the draft's structure was

4. See UNCITRAL Digest Art. 7 2 and decisions cited n. 6.
5. See Peter Schlechtriem, Art. 7 paras. 20 & 24, *in* Schlechtriem & Schwenzer, *CISG Commentary* (2nd English ed. 2005).

reorganized. This repeated renumbering of the articles makes it very difficult to trace the development of a provision even when all the documents are at hand. Difficulties the present writer encountered in coping with these problems made it necessary to prepare a Documentary History that reproduces and introduces the relevant documents and provides references in the documents' margins to the final articles of the Convention for which the legislative deliberations were relevant.[6]

89   **(a) Domestic Law.**   In domestic law, we face a conflict over the legitimacy of legislative history. In many civil law countries, the use of legislative history has long been accepted.[7] Courts in the United States have also freely invoked the legislative history of domestic statutes and international Conventions. For example, a 1985 decision of the United States Supreme Court interpreting the Warsaw Convention on International Transportation by Air relied on the *travaux préparatoires* of the Convention and also "the weight of precedent in foreign and American courts."[8] (We shall return to the use of foreign precedent at §92, *infra*.)

Other legal systems — primarily those following judicial patterns established in England — have traditionally disavowed the use of such materials in statutory contraction: the meaning of legislation must be deduced solely from the words of the statue.[9] However, the "plain meaning" rule has not been applied with the rigor that the traditional formulae might suggest. English courts have long interpreted legislation in the light of "the defect or evil" which the statute was intended to remedy, and have considered reports of special commissions to identify the purpose of legislation that resulted from the commissions' work. And a growing body of opinion holds that the "plain meaning" doctrine

6. John Honnold, Documentary History of the Uniform Law for International Sales (Kluwer, 1989, herein, "*Docy. Hist.*"). A Table brings together the author's marginal references for each article. This Table (organizing over a thousand references) is supplemented by an Index that includes references to discussions that were not confined to a single provision.

7. The widespread and important use of legislative history (*travaux préparatoires*, or "historical" interpretation) in civil law systems is summarized, on the basis of national reports to the XIIth International Congress of Comparative Law (1986), in *Honnold, General Report, 1986 Comp. L. Cong.*, in *Freiburg Colloq.* 133. See also Schlechtriem in *German National Reports, 1986 Comp. L. Cong.*, in *Freiburg Colloq.* 140–141.

8. Air France v. Sacks, 470 U.S. 392, 400–405 (1985). *Cf.* Chan v. Korean Air Lines, 109 S. Ct. 1676 (1989). See Patterson, 22 Stanford J. Int. L. 263, 278 (1986).

9. Strömholm, Legislative Materials and Construction of Statutes, 10 *Scan. Studies* 173; *Gutteridge* 101; R. & M. Walker, English Legal System 92–93 (1976); R. Eddey, English Legal System 113–117 (1977).

stultifies the handling of statutory material and should be modified or abandoned.[10]

90 **(i) The *Fothergill* Case.** Controversy has centered on the interpretation of domestic legislation; our concern is with the interpretation of an international convention. In this setting, a slow process of development in English law took a large and decisive step in the 1980 House of Lords decision in *Fothergill v. Monarch Airlines* — a case that called for the interpretation of an Act of Parliament that gave effect to the Warsaw Convention on the liability of air carriers.[11] Under that Convention, notice must be given within seven days of "damage" (*avarie*) but no notice need be given as to "loss" with respect to baggage. A passenger failed to give this notice of the loss of part of the contents of a bag. Kerr, J., and the Court of Appeal rejected the airline's contention that the notice requirement applied to this claim. The House of Lords reversed. All five opinions conceded that "damage" would not normally refer to loss of part of the contents of baggage, but ruled that in this setting the word should be given a wider meaning. In reaching this conclusion, all of the opinions examined basic questions concerning the interpretation of statutes that implement international conventions; four of the five opinions concluded that consideration should be given to *travaux préparatoires*, and also to foreign case law and scholarly writing interpreting the Convention.[12]

These opinions stressed that they could not lay down rules to govern all future problems. One question that may still be subject to further development is this: What materials may a court consider in deciding

10. *Graveson, C. & G,* 7, 10 n.2; The (English) Law Commission, First Annual Report 1965–1966, no. 107–112; Renton et al., The Preparation of Legislation (1975) (Cmnd 6053) 135–148. The Ontario Law Reform Commission was equally divided on this point, *Ont. L. Ref. Com., I Sales* 29–30.

11. [1980] 2 All E.R. 696 (H.L.), [1980] 3 W.L.R. 209. The evolution during the preceding sixty years was summarized in the opinion by Lord Roskill. An important step in this development was the opinion by Lord Denning, M. R., in James Buchanan & Co. v. Babco Forwarding and Shipping [1977] Q.B. 208, [1977] I All E.R. 518 (C.A.) affirmed on other grounds [1978] A.C. 141 (H.L.). The Act of Parliament involved in the *Fothergill* case implemented the Warsaw Convention of 1929 as amended in 1955 at the Hague.

12. There were differences among some of these four opinions as to the use and weight to be given to these three types of interpretative aids. The fifth opinion, by Lord Fraser of Tullybelton, accepted the use in this case of scholarly writing construing the original French text of the Convention. The Convention, and the Act of Parliament implementing the Convention, provided that in the event of inconsistency between the English and French texts the original French text would prevail.

whether the language of a convention is ambiguous? In any event, it seems clear from the decision that in construing a convention, like the 1980 Sales Convention, that is finalized in several languages, the question of "clear meaning" would not be determined solely from the English text. In addition, a majority of the opinions drew attention to the rules on interpretation in the Vienna Convention on the Law of Treaties (1969).[13]

Under Article 31 of the 1969 Vienna Convention:

1. A treaty shall be interpreted in good faith in accordance with the ordinary meaning to be given to the terms of the treaty in their context and in the light of its object and purpose.

Article 32 adds:

> Recourse may be had to supplementary means of interpretation including the preparatory work of the treaty and the circumstances of its conclusion, in order to confirm the meaning resulting from the application of Article 31, or to determine the meaning when the interpretation according to Article 31: (a) leaves the meaning ambiguous or obscure; or (b) leads to a result which is manifestly absurd or unreasonable.

Under Article 32, supplementary aids, including *travaux préparatoires*, may be used when the terms of the treaty are "ambiguous or obscure" or when the language "leads to a result which is manifestly absurd or unreasonable" and also "to confirm" the meaning derived from the terms of the treaty. The opinions of Lords Diplock and Scarman indicated that, apart from the rules of the Vienna Treaty, interpretative aids could be used when there was a conflict between the literal meaning of the words and the purpose of the Convention.

In view of this development, it seems unlikely that even courts influenced by English judicial tradition will hastily decide that the words of a provision of the Convention are so clear that it is improper to look at the legislative history to ascertain the purpose of the provision. Indeed, the plausibility of the "plain meaning" approach depends upon its use within the confines of a system with established patterns for the use of language, strengthened by a symbiotic relationship between the

---

13. The Vienna Treaty of 1969, although ratified by the U.K., did not govern this case since it came into force subsequent to the Warsaw-Hague provisions that were subject to interpretation. Lord Diplock noted that the Vienna Treaty "does no more than codify the already-existing public international law." The Vienna Treaty will be in force for many States before questions of interpretation arise under the 1980 Sales Convention.

approach to drafting and to interpretation. This essential feature of the "plain meaning" tradition was stressed by Lord Diplock, who added:

> The language of an international convention has not been chosen by an English parliamentary draftsman. It is neither couched in the conventional English legislative idiom nor designed to be construed exclusively by English judges. It is addressed to a much wider and more varied judicial audience than is an Act of Parliament that deals with purely domestic law. It should be interpreted, as Lord Wilberforce put it in James Buchanan & Co., Ltd. v. Babco Forwarding & Shipping (U.K.) Ltd. [1978] A.C. 141, 152 "unconstrained by technical rules of English law, or by English legal precedent, but on broad principles of general acceptance."

We shall consider, *infra* §103, the difference between interpreting conventions in the field of public international law — the issue at the forefront of the 1969 Vienna Convention on the Law of Treaties — and the interpretation of rules regulating the relationship between sellers and buyers. In any event, the rule on interpretation in Article 7 of the 1980 Sales Convention avoids the vestige of the "plain meaning" rule of Article 31(1) of the 1969 Vienna Convention, just quoted, and in addition stresses the special role of the Sales Convention "to promote uniformity." Although the Warsaw Convention did not articulate this objective as a rule of interpretation, in the *Fothergill* case Lord Scarman made this powerful statement on interpreting a Convention to unify private law:

> Rules contained in an international convention are the outcome of an international conference; if, as in the present case, they operate within the field of private law, they will come under the consideration of foreign courts; and uniformity is the purpose to be served by most international conventions, and we know that unification of the rules relating to international air carriage is the object of the Warsaw Convention. It follows that our judges should be able to have recourse to the same aids to interpretation as their brother judges in the other contracting states. The mischief of any other view is illustrated by the instant case. To deny them this assistance would be a damaging blow to the unification of the rules which was the object of signing and then enacting the Convention. Moreover, the ability of our judges to fulfill the purpose of the enactment would be restricted, and the persuasive authority of their judgments in the jurisdictions of the other contracting states would be diminished.

91   **(b) Standards for Use.**   Legislative history (like vintage wine) calls for discretion. One who offers legislative materials as a guide to interpretation should show that they reveal the prevailing understanding of the delegates.[14] *Cf.* the Preamble, discussed in §475, *infra*.

14. Sundberg, *supra* n. 2 at 219, 237; *David, Unification* §281.

Of course, a statement by one delegate does not establish a prevailing viewpoint and silence following a statement does not establish assent. A response may require consultation with ministries that is not feasible during debate on this issue; objections are often withheld because further discussion seems unproductive and time consuming.

The *Fothergill* decision illustrated the caution that may be needed in approaching legislative history. At the Hague conference on air carrier liability, two delegates offered an amendment that would have removed the ambiguity that led to the litigation, but withdrew their amendment stating (as the minutes showed) that this was on the understanding that the existing text had the meaning expressed in their amendment. Lord Diplock's opinion considered this legislative background "for what it was worth" but noted that, based on his experience in such international conferences, he did "not attach any great significance" to this statement and added, "Machiavellism is not extinct at international conferences." On the other hand, most courts in the United States give great (and sometimes uncritical) weight to legislative history — an enthusiasm that, in the interest of uniformity in construing interpretation conventions, might well take into account the greater caution observed by courts in other countries.[15]

In evaluating legislative history, consideration must also be given to the resistance to change that develops as the long processes of deliberation near the end. Thus, an amendment offered to clarify the text may not be accepted because some delegates believe the meaning was already adequately expressed; others would be glad for the clarification but fear that the new language would create drafting problems that could not be solved in the brief time that remains. In short, the legislators placed great stress on the words of the Convention. The only legitimate role of legislative history is to shed light on the meaning of the final text. But it would be hasty to refuse to look at the legislative history on the ground that the "meaning" of the text is "clear"; the setting in which language is used in an essential aspect of its meaning.[16]

---

15. See W. R. Bishin, *The Law Finders, An Essay in Statutory Interpretation*, 38 S. Cal. L. Rev. 1 (1965). Caution about the value of legislative history: *Graveson, C. & G.*, 6; *Giles* 40–45. For examples of the use of preparatory materials in the United States, Italy and Switzerland, see *Giles* 47–48.

16. But see Peter Schlechtriem, Art. 5 paras. 20, 21 & 24, *in* Schlechtriem & Schwenzer, *CISG Commentary* (2nd English ed. 2005) (arguing that, in interpreting the Convention, *travaux préparatoires* should be consulted only if a "literal interpretation" of the Convention text in question does not yield one clear interpretation).

92 International Case Law and Scholarly Studies

Case Law. Parties to international transactions will often have a choice among the *fora* of different countries. The settlement of disputes would be complicated and litigants would be encouraged to engage in wasteful forum shopping if the courts of different countries persisted in divergent interpretations of the Convention. The Convention's requirement in Article 7(1) of regard for "uniformity in its application" calls for tribunals to consider interpretations of the Convention established in other countries.

National reporters to the 1986 International Congress on Comparative Law (§88, *supra*) reported substantial reliance on foreign decisions interpreting uniform laws and international conventions.[17] A majority of the opinions in the *Fothergill* case also concluded that consideration should be given to the judicial decisions (*jurisprudence*) in other Contracting States. Lord Scarman's opinion included this strong general conclusion: "Our courts will have to develop their jurisprudence in company with the courts of other countries from case to case, a course of action by no means unfamiliar to common-law judges."[18] *The practice of consulting foreign decisions has been strongly urged in scholarly commentary on the CISG,[19] and has actually been adopted in at least some decisions applying the Convention. Indeed, certain Italian CISG opinions represent tours de force in the technique, citing*

17. See *Honnold, General Report, 1986 Comp. L. Cong.*, in *Freiburg Colloq.* 121–124. For civil law systems see, e.g., reports from Quebec, Poland Bulgaria, Netherlands (no explicit use). For Commonwealth practice see reports from Australia, Canada, New Zealand. For England see the Fothergill decision *infra*.

18. [1980] 2 All E.R. 696, 715. *Giles* at 35–40 gives examples of reliance on foreign case law in the U.S.A., U.K., Switzerland, and Germany (F.R.G.).

19. See, e.g., Peter Schlechtriem, Art. 7 para. 14, in Schlechtriem & Schwenzer, *CISG Commentary* (2nd English ed. 2005); Franco Ferrari, *CISG Case Law: A New Challenge for Interpreters*, 17 J.L. & Com. 245, 246–48 & 259 (1998); Antonio Boggiano, *The Experience of Latin American States* in International Uniform Law in Practice/Le droit uniform international dans la pratique [Acts and Proceedings of the 3rd Congress on Private Law held by the International Institute for the Unification of Private Law (Rome 7–10 September 1997)] 47 (1988); Harry M. Flechtner, *Recovering Attorneys' Fees as Damages under the U.N. Sales Convention (CISG): The Role of Case Law in the New International Commercial Practice, with Comments on* Zapata Hermanos v. Hearthside Baking, 22 Nw. J. Int'l L. & Bus. 121, 122–23 (2002); V. Susanne Cook, *The U.N. Convention on Contracts for the International Sale of Goods: A Mandate to Abandon Legal Ethnocentricity*, 16 J.L. & Com. 257, 263 (1997).

large numbers of non-Italian decisions as guides to interpreting the Convention.[20] *Although by no means reaching this level of erudition with respect to foreign case law on the Convention, some U.S. decisions have also consulted foreign CISG cases for guidance on interpreting the Convention.*[21]

Although U.S. case law contains examples of approaches that do great honor to the mandates of Article 7,[22] *it also includes a line of*

20. See Tribunale di Vigevano, Italy, decision of July 12 2000, CLOUT case No. 378, English translation available at http://cisgw3.law.pace.edu/cases/000712i3.html; Tribunale di Rimini, Italy, decision of November 26 2002, CLOUT case No. 608, English translation available at http://cisgw3.law.pace.edu/cases/021126i3.html; Tribunale di Padova, Italy, decision of February 25 2004, English translation available at http://cisgw3.law.pace.edu/cases/040225i3.html; Tribunale di Padova, Italy, decision of March 31 2004, English translation available at http://cisgw3.law.pace.edu/cases/040331i3.html. Tribunale di Padova, Italy, decision of January 10 2006, CLOUT case No. 652, English translation available at http://cisgw3.law. pace.edu/cases/060110i3.html.

21. Barbara Berry S.A. de C.V. v. Ken M. Spooner Farms, Inc., 2006 WL 1009299, 2006 U.S. Dist. LEXIS 31262 (W.D. Wash. April 13 2006) (citing Swiss case); Chicago Prime Packers, Inc. v. Northam Food Trading Co., 320 F. Supp.2d 702 (N.D. Ill., May 21 2004), *aff'd*, 408 F.3d 894 (7th Cir., May 23 2005) (citing Dutch, German and Italian cases); Amco Ukrservice v. American Meter Co., 312 F. Supp. 2d 681 (U.S.D.C.E.D. Pa., March 29 2004) (citing German cases); Usinor Industeel v. Leeco Steel Products, Inc., 209 F. Supp. 2d 880 (U.S.D.C.N.D. Ill., March 27 2002) (citing an Australian case); St. Paul Guardian Insurance Co. v. Neuromed Medical Systems & Support, GmbH, 2002 WL 465312 (U.S.D.C.S.D.N.Y., March 26 2002) (citing two German CISG decisions that had been discussed in a commentary on German CISG case law; also citing non-CISG German decision concerning interpretation of "CIF" term); Medical Marketing International, Inc. v. Internazionale Medico Scientifica, S.R.I., 1999 WL 311945 (U.S.D.C.E.D. La., May 17 1999) (citing German case). See also TeeVee Toons, Inc. v. Gerhard Schubert GmbH, 2006 WL 2463537 at *6 n.1 (U.S.D.C.S.D.N.Y. August 23 2006) (citing the 3rd edition of the present treatise and its collection of foreign cases relating to the "reasonable time" for giving notice of lack of conformity under Art. 39(1) of the Convention, but noting that "those foreign decisions do not bind this Court"); Multi-Juice, S.A. v. Snapple Beverage Corp., 2006 WL 1519981, 2006 U.S. Dist. LEXIS 35928 (S.D.N.Y. June 1 2006) (citing the UNCITRAL CISG Case Law Digest); Shuttle Packaging Systems, L.L.C. v. Tsonakis, 2001 WL34046276 at *8 (U.S.D.C.W.D. Mich., December 17 2001) (noting that court had considered unspecified foreign CISG decisions brought to its attention by the parties); Zapata Hermanos Sucesores, S.A. v. Hearthside Baking Co., 2001 WL 1000927 at *4 (U.S.D.C.N.D. Ill., August 28 2001), *rev'd*, 313 F.3d 385 (7th Cir., November 19 2002), *cert. denied*, 124 S. Ct. 803 (December 1 2003) (same). *Cf.* MCC-Marble Ceramic Center, Inc. v. Ceramica Nuova d'Agostino, S.p.A., 144 F.3d 1384, at 1389 n. 14 (11th Cir., June 29 1998) (stating that court had found source of information concerning foreign CISG decisions, but had not located any pertinent foreign cases).

22. From the perspective pf interpretational methodology one of the most successful treatments of the CISG in U.S. case law is Amco Ukrservice v. American Meter Co., 312 F. Supp. 2d 681, at 686–87 (E.D. Pa., March 29 2004). For an analysis of the decision see

cases incorporating what may be the most brazen flouting of those mandates to be found in the corpus of CISG decisions. An early U.S. federal court of appeals opinion stated, without benefit of supporting reasoning or authority, that "[c]aselaw interpreting analogous provisions of Article 2 of the Uniform Commercial Code ('UCC'), may also inform a court where the language of the relevant CISG provisions tracks that of the UCC."[23] This statement flatly contradicts Article 7(1), which requires that the Convention be interpreted from an <u>international</u> perspective, and it threatens the very purpose of the CISG — to replace divergent national sales law with uniform international rules for international sales transactions. It has nevertheless been repeated in a disturbing number of subsequent U.S. CISG decisions,[24] and actually put into action in several.[25] The most egregious example is a federal district court opinion in which, after noting that the CISG was the governing law and had a provision specifically addressing the issue at hand (Article 79, governing exemption from liability where impediments interfere with performance (force majeure)), the court proceeded to analyze the situation by — never mentioning the CISG again![26] It asserted that decisions under Article 2 of the UCC could guide its analysis, and spent several pages

---

Harry M. Flechtner, *The CISG in U.S. Courts: The Evolution (and Devolution) of the Methodology of Interpretation, in* Quo Vadis CISG? Celebrating the 25th Anniversary of the United Nations Convention on Contracts for the International Sale of Goods 91, 97–98 (Franco Ferrari, ed. 2005).

23. Delchi Carrier SpA v. Rotorex Corp., 71 F.2d 1024, 1028 (2nd Cir., December 6 1995).

24. Chicago Prime Packers, Inc. v. Northam Food Trading Co., 408 F.3d 894, 898 (7th Cir., May 23 2005); Schmitz-Werke GmbH v. Rockland Industries, Inc., 2002 WL 1357095 (4th Cir., June 21 2002); Raw Materials Inc. v. Manfred Forberich GmbH, 2004 WL 1535839 at *3 (U.S.D.C.N.D. Ill., July 7 2004); Chicago Prime Packers, Inc. v. Northam Food Trading Co., 320 F. Supp. 2d 702, at 709 ff. (U.S.D.C.N.D. Ill., May 21 2004), *aff'd*, 408 F.3d 894 (7th Cir., May 23 2005); Chicago Prime Packers, Inc. v. Northam Food Trading Co., 2003 WL 21254261 at *4 (U.S.D.C.N.D. Ill., May 29 2003), *aff'd*, 408 F.3d 894 (7th Cir., May 23 2005); Claudia s.n.c. v. Olivieri Footwear Ltd., 1998 WL 164824 at *4 (U.S.D.C.S.D.N.Y., April 7 1998).

25. Citing the statement, several cases have actually been guided by decisions construing UCC Art. 2 in their application of the CISG. See Chicago Prime Packers, Inc. v. Northam Food Trading Co., 408 F.3d 894, 898 (7th Cir., May 23 2005); Chicago Prime Packers, Inc. v. Northam Food Trading Co., 2003 WL 21254261 at *4 (U.S.D.C.N.D. Ill., May 29 2003), *aff'd*, 408 F.3d 894 (7th Cir., May 23 2005); Delchi Carrier SpA v. Rotorex Corp., 71 F.2d 1024, 1031 (2nd Cir., December 6 1995).

26. See Raw Materials Inc. v. Manfred Forberich GmbH, 2004 WL 1535839 at *3–*6 (U.S.D.C.N.D. Ill., July 7 2004).

analyzing such decisions.[27] *The editor of the current edition of this treatise has opined,*

> Not one word of this discussion would have to be changed if UCC Article 2 had actually been the applicable law. A more flagrant and depressing example of a court ignoring its obligations under CISG Article 7(1) [...] is hard to imagine. ... Indeed, its patently improper approach to interpreting and applying the CISG may well bring international disrepute on the CISG jurisprudence of U.S. courts as a whole — which, with respect to at least some U.S. decisions, is unfortunate. The only good that could come of the [...] decision, in this author's view, is if it became an example of what to avoid when interpreting the CISG.[28]

The practice of using domestic U.S. sales law cases as a guide to interpreting the CISG, and the decisions that have employed the technique, have been roundly condemned by scholars[29] *— to no effect, thus far, in the courts. This may reflect an increasing tendency among U.S. judges to look primarily to other (U.S.) judicial opinions for guidance in their decisions. Thus it may well be that, until an American court issues a published opinion condemning this violation of a U.S. treaty obligation, the pernicious practice of consulting decisions on U.C.C. Article 2 for guidance in construing the Convention will persist.*

The use of foreign decisions as a method to bring uniformity and an international perspective to efforts to interpret the CISG raises the following issue: what impact should foreign decisions have on a tribunal's application of the Convention? Clearly decisions on the CISG do not "bind" tribunals in other jurisdictions.[30] The opinions in the

27. *Id.*

28. Harry M. Flechtner, *The CISG in U.S. Courts: The Evolution (and Devolution) of the Methodology of Interpretation, in* Quo Vadis CISG? Celebrating the 25th Anniversary of the United Nations Convention on Contracts for the International Sale of Goods 91, 107 (Franco Ferrari, ed. 2005).

29. *Id.* at 103–107; Joseph Lookofsky & Harry Flechtner, *Nominating* Manfred Forberich: *The Worst CISG Decision in 25 Years?* 9 The Vindobona Journal of International Commercial Law and Arbitration 199 (2005); Albert H. Kritzer, Editorial Remarks: Comments on *Raw Matrials Inc. v. Manfred Forberich*, http://cisgw3.law.pace.edu/cases/ 040706u1.html. *See also* Peter Schlechtriem, Art. 7 para. 13 n. 22a, *in* Schlechtriem & Schwenzer, *CISG Commentary* (2nd English ed. 2005).

30. *E.g.*, Peter Schlechtriem, Art. 7 para. 14 at pp. 98–99, *in* Schlechtriem & Schwenzer, *CISG Commentary* (2nd English ed. 2005); Franco Ferrari, *CISG Case Law: A New Challenge for Interpreters*, 17 J.L. & Com. 245, 259 (1998); Harry M. Flechtner, *Recovering Attorneys' Fees as Damages under the U.N. Sales Convention (CISG): The Role of Case Law in the New International Commercial Practice, with Comments on* Zapata Hermanos v. Hearthside Baking, 22 Nw. J. Int'l Law & Bus. 121, 124 (2002); Harry M. Flechtner, *The Several Texts of the CISG in a Decentralized System: Observations on Translations,*

Fothergill case suggest that a preponderant body of binding precedent in other Contracting States would be given great weight; otherwise, foreign decisions would be considered for the persuasive force of their reasoning.[31] *That approach has found favor.*[32] *The reviser of this current edition of this treatise has suggested some factors that may help to determine the deference that a foreign decision is due.*[33] *One of those factors is the extent to which the foreign decision itself comports with the mandates of Article 7(1), including the requirement to have*

Reservations and Other Challenges to the Uniformity Principle in Article 7(1), 17 J.L. & Com. 187, 211 (1998).

31. Lord Diplock's opinion drew attention to the fact that in some countries the decisions of even appellate courts were not "binding." The opinions did not consider whether attention should be given to the *probability* that other courts would follow such decisions — a view that would conform to Oliver Wendell Holmes's famous dictum: "The prophesies of what the courts will do in fact, and nothing more pretentious, are what I mean by the law." Holmes, *The Path of the Law*, 10 Harv. L. Rev. 457, 461 (1897). Lord Wilberforce's opinion in *Fothergill* doubted the value of decisions that were not made by a State's highest court, and also mentioned the inadequate reporting of decisions in some countries. Ways to facilitate the access to international case law and to evaluate its impact on future cases are considered *infra* §93. For discussion of the level of the court rendering a decision as a factor influencing the weight the decision should be accorded, see Harry M. Flechtner, *Recovering Attorneys' Fees as Damages under the U.N. Sales Convention (CISG): The Role of Case Law in the New International Commercial Practice, with Comments on* Zapata Hermanos v. Hearthside Baking, 22 Nw. J. Int'l Law & Bus.121, 143–44 (2002).

Since the dramatic breach with tradition of 1966, the House of Lords no longer regards that it is "bound" by its own decisions; the significant point is that the likelihood of an explicit overruling is exceedingly remote. It is true that, for historical reasons, many civil law systems hold to the theory that courts are not "bound" by precedent but students of these legal systems report that court decisions — and especially a body of case law — have predictive value that is not significantly different from that in some common-law systems. For example, Ernst Rabel has remarked that, in practice, "one must look for the difference between the German . . . and American systems of precedent with a magnifying glass. Riegert, *The West German Civil Code*, 45 Tul. L. Rev. 69–71 (1970); *von Mehren & Gordley* 1135 n. 21, 1156 n. 106 & 108 (France), 1157 N. 109 (Germany); *Merryman & Clark* 560–562 (Columbia), 571–587 (Mexico). For an arresting suggestion that strict adherence to precedent in England responded to the need for certainty created by the lack of a statutory framework — a need not felt in codified legal systems — see Goodhart, *Precedent in English and Continental Law*, 197 L.Q. Rev. 40, 61–63 (1934).

32. Peter Schlechtriem, Art. 7 para. 14 at pp. 98–99, *in* Schlechtriem & Schwenzer, *CISG Commentary* (2nd English ed. 2005).

33. Harry M. Flechtner, *Recovering Attorneys' Fees as Damages under the U.N. Sales Convention (CISG): The Role of Case Law in the New International Commercial Practice, with Comments on* Zapata Hermanos v. Hearthside Baking, 22 Nw. J. Int'l Law & Bus.121, 140–46 (2002).

regard for the international character of the Convention.[34] *That is a most important consideration. The fact that a number of decisions might ignore this mandate and, perhaps out of ignorance of alternative views, adopt an interpretation colored by domestic law should not be sufficient to impose that interpretation on others. Permitting that would allow de facto unilateral amendment of the Convention, and subvert the political processes that produced the CISG and, as a result, its legitimacy. This point, indeed, underlies another consideration in determining the weight to be accorded a foreign decision — the extent to which tribunals from a diversity of other jurisdictions adopt the same approach (i.e., a genuinely international consensus on the approach).*[35]

Use of foreign judicial decisions in the past has been inhibited by difficulties in obtaining and evaluating this material, which may be in a language unknown to counsel and the court. Special measures to meet this problem will be discussed in §93, *infra*. In addition, substantial aid can be derived from international scholarly writing reporting and analyzing case-law (*jurisprudence*) under the Convention. The intense interest in the Convention and its extraordinarily wide adoption has generated a vast body of international literature, a substantial portion of which focuses on decisions applying this uniform law.

Scholarly Writing. Courts on the Continent of Europe and in the United States (*inter alia*) give weight to scholarly writing (*doctrine*). This receptivity, at least in the United States, has responded to the wide range of materials, in addition to statutes and past decisions, that have become relevant to judicial development of the law. Although English judges have been reluctant to use scholarly writing,[36] the need for uniformity in interpreting international conventions led to a more liberal approach. In the *Fothergill* case all of the opinions gave careful attention (but varying weight) to scholarly writing on the Warsaw Convention. Lord Diplock's approach was perhaps the most cautious:

> To a court interpreting the Convention subsequent commentaries can have persuasive value only: they do not come into the same authoritative category as that of the institutional writers in Scots law. It may be that greater reliance than is usual in the English courts is placed upon the writings of academic lawyers by courts of other European states where oral argument by counsel plays a relatively minor role in the decision-making process. The persuasive effect of learned commentaries, like the

34. *Id.* at 145–46.
35. *Id.* at 144.
36. See *Honnold, General Report, 1986 Comp. L. Cong.*, in *Freiburg Colloq.* 125–127, citing report by M. Clarke. Varying degrees of flexibility were reported from other parts of the Commonwealth, especially Canada.

arguments of counsel in an English court, will depend upon the cogency of their reasoning. Those to which your Lordships have been referred contain perhaps rather more assertion than ratiocination, but for the most part support the construction favoured by your Lordships.[37]

On the other hand, the statement by Lord Scarman, quoted *supra* at §90, looks towards the development of a more unified international approach to the process of interpreting international conventions.

The importance of consulting scholarly writings as a technique to fulfill the mandates in Article 7(1) to have regard for the Convention's international character and the need for uniformity in its application has in fact been recognized both in commentary[38] and in decisions applying the CISG.[39]

93   (4) Access to International Materials

The success of the Convention has been a stimulus for the development of resources that facilitate access to international legal materials, in particular decisions of courts and arbitral tribunals. These resources build on a prior foundation: UNIDROIT has long performed a service to the international legal community by publishing case law interpreting important conventions that unify rules of private law.[40] At its 1988 session, UNCITRAL established procedures for gathering and disseminating decisions applying the Sales Convention and other uniform laws prepared by the Commission.[41] *This led to the dissemination of abstracts or summaries of such decisions in the six official languages*

37. [1980] 1 All E.R. 696, 708. For the reliance on scholarly writing in other countries see *Honnold, General Report, 1986 Comp. L. Cong.,* in *Freiburg Colloq.* 125–127.

38. See, e.g., Peter Schlechtriem, Art. 7 para. 14 at 99, *in* Schlechtriem & Schwenzer, *CISG Commentary* (2nd English ed. 2005); Harry M. Flechtner, *The CISG in U.S. Courts: The Evolution (and Devolution) of the Methodology of Interpretation,* in Quo Vadis CISG? Celebrating the 25th Anniversary of the United Nations Convention on Contracts for the International Sale of Goods 91, 92–93 (Franco Ferrari, ed. 2005); Vivian Grosswald Curran, Book Review, 15 J.L. & Com. 175, 176–77 (1995) (reviewing Claude Witz, *The Interpretative Challenge to Uniformity* (1995).

39. See UNCITRAL Digest Art. 7 para. 2 and decisions cited n. 7.

40. From 1956 UNIDROIT published decisions interpreting uniform laws in its Yearbook, from 1960 in Uniform Law Cases, and from 1973 in UNIDROIT's Uniform Law Review. On the importance of such case law see 1 *Zweigert & Kötz* 22. On limited access to foreign case law, see *Giles* 35–36.

41. UNCITRAL, Report on Twenty-First Session (1988) (A/43/17), XIX *YB* 15–16, Ch. X, paras. 98–109. Each State that is a party to the Convention is requested to designate a "national correspondent" to obtain and send to the UNCITRAL Secretariat the full text

*of the U.N. through the system of "Case Law on UNCITRAL Texts,"
or CLOUT.*[42] *At the time this is written there are over 700 CLOUT
abstracts, most covering decisions on the Convention. Institutions
other than UNCITRAL have also created rich assemblages of information on the Convention and made them available gratis through the
Internet. UNILEX, a project sponsored by the Centre for Comparative
and Foreign Law Studies in Rome, is a database (available at http://
www.unilex.info) containing the text of the CISG, information on
ratification of the Convention, bibliographies covering the Convention, and information on a large number CISG decisions from a variety
of countries, including (in most cases) both the original text of the
decision and an English summary.*[43]

*There is also the extraordinary CISG website maintained by the
Institute of International Commercial Law at Pace University School
of Law, http://www.cisg.law. pace.edu, an extremely comprehensive
and useful tool for obtaining information in English on foreign
CISG decisions. The website currently has entries for over 1800
CISG-related cases from 33 countries, as well as from a number of
standing arbitration tribunals and several international courts. The
great majority of the entries include either English summaries or, in
many cases, full translations of the decisions. Cases can be searched by
the CISG article(s) to which they refer, by the country in which the
decision was rendered, or by terms appearing in the full text of the
website's treatment of the case. If a decision is the subject of a CLOUT
abstract, the abstract is reprinted in the website's case treatment.
Each case treatment also includes much other information, including
bibliographic information on commentaries that have discussed the
decision (often with links to the text of those commentaries) and information on other English summaries or translations of the decisions
(including links to UNILEX entries for the decision — see above for
information on UNILEX). The website also has a wealth of other
resources concerning the CISG, including the text of the CISG, information and links to the drafting history (travaux préparatoires), and a
vast bibliography covering CISG commentary. The Pace CISG website*

---

of the decisions in their original languages; the Secretariat will make these decisions accessible to any interested person, upon request and payment of the cost of the service. [The
channels for gathering the decisions were examined in *Honnold, General Report, 1986
Comp. L. Cong.*, in *Freiburg Colloq.* 128–129.

42. For information on the CLOUT system, and access to CLOUT abstracts, see the World
Wide Web site of UNCITRAL, http://www.uncitral.org/uncitral/en/case_law.html.

43. UNILEX also covers the UNIDROIT Principles of International Commercial Contracts.

is part of the "Autonomous Network of CISG Websites," which links sites focusing on the Convention in a variety of countries and languages.[44]

UNCITRAL has created another resource designed to facilitate access to the body of international decisions on the CISG contained in these and other CISG resources. The "UNCITRAL Digest of Case Law on the United Nations Convention on the International Sale-of-Goods" provides an article-by-article textual guide to decisions applying the CISG. It is available in the six official U.N. languages through the "Case Law (CLOUT)" section of UNCITRAL website (http:// www.uncitral.org/uncitral/en/index.html). References to relevant parts of the Digest and to the decisions to which the Digest refers are included throughout the current edition of this treatise.

The resources described here make it not just possible, but highly practicable, to consult CISG decisions of courts and arbitral tribunals from around the world, along with the travaux préparatoires for the Convention and the efforts of a world wide community of scholarly commentators. They provide simple and easy access — particularly for Anglophones — to a rich corpus of international materials, much of which would have been, for practical purposes, inaccessible not that long ago. They make it possible for judges, arbitrators, lawyers and legal scholars to fulfill the ambitious but essential mandate of Article 7(1): to bring to interpretation of the Convention an international perspective, and regard for uniformity as it is applied in the incredibly diverse tribunals responsible for deciding disputes governed by the CISG. It is to be hoped that these resources will not only survive and flourish, but also continue to evolve, and will act as a model for the development of similar resources for other areas of international law unification.

94   B. Interpretation of the Convention to Promote Good Faith in International Trade

(1) Evolution of the "Good Faith" Provision

Paragraph (1) of Article 7 concludes with the statement that in interpreting the Convention there shall be regard for promoting "the observance of good faith in international trade" — a point that did not appear

---

44. For information on the network, see http://www.cisg.law.pace.edu/network.html#cp.

in the rules on interpretation of other earlier UNCITRAL Conventions. At a late stage in the preparation of the Sales Convention this language was adopted as a compromise between two divergent views: (a) Some delegates supported a general rule that, at least in the formation of the contract, the parties must observe principles of "fair dealing" and must act in "good faith"; (b) Others resisted this step on the ground that "fair dealing" and "good faith" had no fixed meaning and would lead to uncertainty.

The first important step towards a "good faith" provision was taken by the Working Group in preparing a separate Draft Convention on Formation of the Contract. Article 5 of the Draft included the following: "In the course of the formation of the contract the parties must observe the principles of fair dealing and act in good faith." In 1978 the Commission, in its final review of the draft Convention, decided that a "good faith" provision should not be confined to formation of the contract; at the same time, the Commission decided that an obligation of "good faith" should not be imposed loosely and at large, but should be restricted to a principle for interpreting the provisions of the Convention. This compromise was generally accepted and was embodied in the concluding words of Article 7(1).[45]

National legislation has imposed requirements of "good faith" that are broader than the principle of interpretation stated in Article 7(1). The (U.S.A.) Uniform Commercial Code states: "Every contract or duty within this Act imposes a duty of good faith in its performance or enforcement."[46]

This general requirements of "good faith" is not typical of common-law statutory drafting; the UCC at this point reveals the unstated influence of some of the civil law codes. The German Civil Code (§242) states: "The debtor is bound to effect performance according to the requirements of good faith, giving consideration to common usage." (Other examples are cited in the next footnote.) And

---

45. *W/G 9* paras. 70–87, IX *YB* 66–67, *Docy. Hist.* 298–299; *Com. I*, Art. 6; *SR. 5* (action and discussion at the Diplomatic Conference), *O.R.* 254–259, *Docy. Hist.* 475–480.

46. (U.S.A.) UCC §1–203. In most parts of the Code "good faith" has the limited meaning of "honesty in fact in the conduct or transaction concerned" (§1–201(19)). However, the obligation of "good faith" that is applicable to merchants in sales transactions includes 'the observance of reasonable commercial standards of *fair dealing* in the trade' (§2–103(1)(b)). See Farnsworth, Good Faith Performance and Commercial Reasonableness Under the UCC, 30 U. Chi. L. Rev. 666 (1963); Summers, "Good Faith" in General Contract Law and the Sales Provisions of the UCC, 54 Va. L. Rev. 195 (1968); *Restatement, Second of Contracts* §205.

common-law jurisdictions may be increasingly receptive to such legal ideas. The Ontario Law Reform Commission, on the basis of a comparative study, concluded that a revision of the Sale-of-Goods Act should include a general good faith requirement.[47]

As we have just seen, the Convention rejects "good faith" as a general requirement and uses "good faith" solely as a principle for interpreting the provisions of the Convention.[48] What content should be given to "good faith" as an aid to interpretation? The Convention's goal "to promote uniformity" should bar the use of purely local definitions and concepts in construing the international text. (See *supra* at §87.)[49] But this objection does not apply to "good faith" principles that reflect a genuine consensus — a "common core" of meaning — in a diversity of domestic law. One may hope that the scholarship in this area will be developed further with special reference to the application of "good faith" principles to issues that arise in international trade.[50]

95 **(2) Possible Areas for Interpretation to Promote "Good Faith"**

For reasons that will be developed later, "good faith" probably would be promoted by a liberal application of provisions like Articles 19(2) and 21(2), which require a party to inform another who is known to be subject to a misapprehension. (See *infra* §100.) The Article 7(1) good faith mandate has been cited by a U.S. court in support of a "liberal

---

47. *Ont. L. Ref. Com., I Sales* 163–171; *Dawson*, 461, 465–466, 475–479; Kessler and Fine, Culpa in Contrahendo, Bargaining in Good Faith, and Freedom of Contract: A Comparative Study, 77 Harv. L. Rev. 401 (1964); Israeli Sales Law §6; Draft, Netherlands Civil Code, Book 6, Ch. 5, Sec. 3, Art. 1 ("Reasonableness and equity").

48. *Accord* Peter Schlechtriem, Art, 7para. 7, *in* Schlechtriem & Schwenzer, *CISG Commentary* (2nd English ed. 2005) ("The maxim of 'observance of good faith in international trade' [. . .] concerns the interpretation of the Convention only and cannot be applied directly to individual contracts . . .").

49. See Peter Schlechtriem, Art. 7 paras. 7, 18, *in* Schlechtriem & Schwenzer, *CISG Commentary* (2nd English ed. 2005).

50. See Bonell, Some Critical Reflections on the New UNCITRAL Draft Convention (1978) II UNIDROIT Unif. L. Rev. 2, 10. *Cf.* Schlesinger, The Common Core of Legal Systems, *Yntema Festschrift* 65; Statute of the International Court of Justice, Art. 38(1)(c): the "general principles of law recognized by civilized nations"; Cohn, 23 Int. & Comp. L.Q. 520, 521 (1974). Although ULIS did not refer to "good faith" it has been suggested that a similar concept (*Treu and Glauben*) was one of the "general principles" invoked by ULIS 17. *Dölle, Kommentar* (Wahl) Art. 17 at 55–57.

approach" to the Convention's contract formation rules.[51] One who demands performance within an additional period (Arts. 47 & 63) may not, in good faith, refuse to accept the performance that he requested. (See the Commentary to Art. 47, *infra* §291.) Delay in compelling specific performance or avoiding a contract after a market change, or construing ambiguous acts as acceptance — situations that could permit a party to speculate at the other's expense — may well be inconsistent with the Convention's provisions governing these remedies when they are construed in the light of the principle of good faith. (See the discussion of the time for acceptance, *infra* §144 and Art. 46, *infra* §285.)[52] A German court has held that it would violate the good faith interpretation mandate of Article 7(1) to require a buyer to give notice of avoidance where the seller had "unambiguously and definitely" declared its intention not to perform its obligations.[53] These illustrations, of course, are incomplete and tentative.

Professor Schlechtriem has suggested that "good faith in international trade" should be construed in the light of the Convention's many references to standards of reasonableness — a standard that is so pervasive as to establish this as one of "the general principles on which [the Convention] was based."[54] What is "reasonable" can appropriately be determined by ascertaining what is normal and acceptable in the relevant trade. This approach is analogous to and is supported by Article 9, which provides that contractual obligations include "practices established by the parties and usages . . . in the particular trade." A similar linkage among "good faith," reasonableness and trade usage is found in (U.S.) UCC 2–103(1)(b): " 'good faith' in the case of a merchant means honesty in fact and the observance of reasonable commercial standards of fair dealing in the trade."

---

51. Geneva Pharmaceuticals Technology Corp. v. Barr Labs., Inc., 201 F. Supp. 2d 236, 281 (S.D.N.Y. May 10 2002).
52. See also *Secretariat Commentary*, Art. 6, para. 3, *O.R.* 18, *Docy. Hist.* 408.
53. Oberlandesgericht München, Germany, September 15 2004, CLOUT case No. 595.
54. *Schlechtriem (1986)* 39. See also Peter Schlechtriem, Art. 7 para. 30 n. 50 at 104, *in* Schlechtriem & Schwenzer, *CISG Commentary* (2nd English ed. 2005). For references to reasonableness or the reasonable person see Arts. 8(2), 16(b) (reasonable reliance), 18(2) (reasonable time), 34 (unreasonable inconvenience or expense), 38(3) (reasonable opportunity for examination), 39(1) (reasonable time, 48(1) (unreasonable delay, inconvenience or expense), 48(2) (reasonable time), 49(2) (reasonable time), 60(a) (acts reasonably expected), 63(1) (reasonable time), 72 (reasonable time for notice), 75 (reasonable time and manner), 76(2) (reasonable substitute), 79(1) (reasonable expectations), 79(4) (reasonable time), 85 (reasonable steps), 86(1) (same), 86(2) (unreasonable inconvenience or expense), 88(1) (unreasonable delay), 88(2) (unreasonable expense; reasonable measures to sell).

96   C. Gap-filling: "General Principles" v. Domestic Law

(1) Evolution of the Approach to Gap-filling

Article 7(2) addresses the following problem: A matter that is "governed by" the Convention presents a question that is not "expressly settled in it." How should such questions be decided?

Paragraph (2) was added at a late stage as a compromise between divergent views. The view that prevailed in the 1964 Sales Conventions was stated as follows in Article 17 of ULIS:

> Questions concerning matters governed by the present Law which are not expressly settled therein shall be settled in conformity with the general principles on which the present Law is based.

This provision reflects the approach established for civil law codes which were designed to displace the entire body of pre-existing law. To discourage the revival of outmoded and non-uniform rules of the *ancien régime*, solutions must be anchored in an article of the code — an approach that led to creative extension by analogy of the code's provisions to meet the myriad of new problems that arose during the following centuries.[55]

In common-law systems abrupt legal change has usually come through narrow, specific statutes that resemble islands surrounded by an ocean of case-law. On the other hand, case-law has developed in a manner that resembles the analogic development of the civil codes: the principles on which the older cases were based are enlarged or reshaped in the course of applying them to new situations.

Even ambitious legislation like the (U.S.A.) Uniform Commercial Code is not a self-contained body of law. At the outset (§1–103) this "code" states that, unless displaced by its "particular provisions," the "principles of law and equity [a phrase understood to refer to the general body of case-law] . . . shall *supplement* its provisions." The vital role of these supplemental principles in the development of the "Code" has been documented in an impressive study of over a thousand pages.[56]

It is not surprising that the "general principles" provision of ULIS 17 encountered criticism in UNCITRAL. Nor were all of the critics from common-law systems; delegates from some countries with codes

55. See Rabel, 1 Am. J. Comp. L. 58, 60 (1952); *von Mehren & Gordley* 1137 at n. 35.

56. H. Hillman, J. McDonell & S. Nickles, Common Law and Equity under the Uniform Commercial Code (1985) and supplements.

stemming from civil law roots had also developed traditions that emphasized legislative detail and strict construction.

In the UNCITRAL Working Group, objections to ULIS 17 that had been voiced (unsuccessfully) at the Hague Conference were pressed with added vigor: The "general principles" on which the law was based had never been articulated; ULIS 17 injected an unacceptable degree of uncertainty. Supporters of ULIS 17 replied that filling "gaps" by turning to domestic law would involve even greater uncertainty. The rules of private international law were neither clear nor uniform; hence there would be doubt and dispute over which law was applicable. In addition, the domestic law would be foreign to one of the parties, and in most cases would be unsuited to the problems of international trade. Finally, referring gap-filling to the diverse rules of domestic law would never lead to a uniform solution, whereas recourse to the general principles of the Convention in international case law would develop common answers for the questions that arise within the scope of the law.[57]

In 1970 the Working Group recommended that Article 17 of ULIS be replaced by a provision that the law shall be interpreted with regard "to its international character and the need to promote uniformity" (See Art. 7(1) *supra* at §85). This position was maintained throughout the balance of the proceedings in UNCITRAL. The Commission rejected further proposals to include modified versions of ULIS 17 and also rejected the counter-proposals that problems resulting from "gaps" should be decided under domestic law indicated by the rules of private international law.[58]

The 1980 Conference developed a compromise that became paragraph (2) of Article 7. In response to those who feared that courts might turn too quickly to national law, the first part of paragraph (2) reproduced the "general principles" rule of ULIS 17. On the other hand, in response to those who doubted that general principles of the Convention could always be found, paragraph (2) added that "in the absence of such principles" open questions are to be settled "in conformity with the law applicable by virtue of the rules of private international law."[59]

57. *W/G 1* paras. 56–72, I *YB* 181–183, *Docy. Hist.* 19–21; *W/G 2* paras. 126–137, II *YB* 62, *Docy. Hist.* 68.
58. *UNCITRAL X* Annex I, paras. 137–147, VIII *YB* 34–35, *Docy. Hist.* 327–328.
59. *O.R.* 255–257, *Docy. Hist.* 426–428.

97   **(2) The Nature of "Gaps"; Solutions in Domestic Law**

The Overview (Ch. 2, §18) drew attention to the inability of any statute to address and solve all the circumstances and problems that will arise. This is especially true for the 1980 Convention since it cannot be revised frequently and must embrace the gamut of transactions and conditions that will arise in a diverse and developing international economy.

Draftsmen of national codes have recognized this problem. Portalis in his preliminary discourse on the French Civil Code observed that the legislator must take "a large view of the matter" by "principles rich in implication" rather than details. "We shall leave some gaps, and they will be filled in due course by experience. National codes are created in time; indeed, people do not really create them at all."[60]

This development occurred under the French Civil Code, unaided by explicit authorization to fill gaps. Other statutes have expressly granted this authority. For example, the Uniform Commercial Code states (§1–102(1)) that it is to be "liberally construed and applied to promote its *underlying purposes and policies*." Under the Austrian General Civil Code "Where a case cannot be decided either according to the literal text or the plain meaning of a statute, regard shall be had to the statutory provisions concerning similar cases and to the principles which underlie other laws regarding similar matters."[61] On the other hand, in 1978 this approach was rebuffed by the House of Lords in *Buchanan & Co. v. Babco Forwarding and Shipping.*[62] In the Court of Appeal, Lord Denning, in construing an act of Parliament that implemented an international convention, had concluded that the legislation was subject to a "gap," and that English courts should follow the approach of

---

60. See *von Mehren & Gordley* 54–56. Portalis's proposal that the Code explicitly provide for application "according to equity . . . . . . ," rejected in France, was adopted in Louisiana. See Stone, The So-called Unprovided-for Case, 53 Tul. L. Rev. 93, 94–95 (1978).

61. *Schlesinger, Comparative Law* 602. The most far-reaching provision is Art. 1 of the Swiss Civil Code: In the absence of other specified sources "the judge shall decide . . . according to the rule which he would establish as legislator." *Id.* at 603; *Zweigert & Kötz II (1987)* 197–182. On the pressure for analogical extension of the code that results from the theory that courts may not develop the law, see Merryman, The Italian Style III; Interpretation, 18 Stanf. L. Rev. 583 (1966). For a perspective study of the conflicting "civil law" and "common-law" approaches see Nickles, Problems of Sources of Law Under the UCC, 31 Ark. L. Rev. at 16–46 (1977), 31 *id.* 171 and 34 *id.* 1 (1980).

62. [1978] A.C. 141 (H.L.) affirming on different grounds [1977] Q.B. 208 (C.A.), [1977] I All E.R. 518. The case involved an Act of Parliament that implemented the CMR Convention on the liability of carriers transporting goods by road.

courts on the Continent, including the European Economic Community (EEC) Court of Justice, and fill the gap so as to carry out the purpose of the legislation. A majority of the House of Lords, in affirming the decision of the Court of Appeal, commented adversely on the "gap-filling" approach. The legislation in question did not contain a provision on interpretation; a court construing the Sales Convention should be led by Article 7(2), *supra*, to take a broader view of the process of interpretation.

98 ## (3) The Area for Gap-Filling: "Matters Governed by" the Convention

(a) Areas excluded.   Article 7(2) provides for the use of general principles of the Convention only with respect to unsolved questions "concerning *matters governed by* this Convention." In examining Article 4 (*supra* at §64), we saw that the Convention governs only some of the issues that may arise in an international sale. Thus, the Convention specifically excludes issues concerning the validity of the contract (Art. 4(a)) and the effect of the contract on the property in the goods (Art. 4(b)). Nor does the Convention govern rights based on fraud or the capacity of an agent to bind the principal — vital but complex bodies of law which this Convention could neither supplant nor restate; unification in these areas must await the completion of separate conventions. (See Art. 4, *supra* at §65–66.) Since these areas are not "governed" by the Convention they are beyond the reach of "Gap fill-ing" under Article 7(2).[63] *Many matters are not expressly excluded by Article 4, but nevertheless are outside the scope of the CISG simply by virtue of the Convention's subject matters — i.e., it is a Convention on Contracts for the International Sale-of-Goods, and not intended to create a comprehensive legal system to deal with all legal areas. Thus, to take an obvious example mentioned earlier (see §70.1 supra), the Convention is not designed as a criminal code and does not preempt applicable national criminal rules: criminal issues are simply not a matter governed by the Convention.*

Other areas of law have a more complex relationship with the subject matter of the Convention. We have already explored the rela-tionship between the Convention and rules on "product liability" (see §73 supra), where the Convention overlaps with (and thus partially displaces) national laws dealing with the subject. The relationship between the Convention's subject matter scope and rules of procedure

63. *Cf. David, Unification* §368 (topic outside ULIS 2).

is also a complex one. Clearly the CISG is not intended to be a code of procedure: it does not give rules for many of the vital issues such a code must address, such as the jurisdiction of courts, the manner of prosecuting lawsuits, evidentiary questions, and the like. Thus, as has been recognized by many authorities, procedural issues are generally outside the scope of the Convention,[64] and applicable national rules on these matters continue to apply in proceedings in which the Convention is governing substantive law. This conclusion is not changed by the fact that particular rules of the Convention address "procedural" matters, just as the fact the Convention addresses some "product liability" issues does not mean the Convention displaces all domestic product liability rules. Thus the Convention does not render national rules of evidence generally inapplicable merely because Article 11 provides that a contract of sale "may be proved by any means, including witnesses."[65] Of course specific domestic evidentiary rules may be displaced by the express rule in Article 11 — if, for example, a domestic rule required that the existence or terms of a contract could be proven only by written evidence,[66] or if it disqualified witness testimony for such purposes.

Drawing the line between a matter of procedure that is beyond the scope of the Convention (and thus is subject to national law, and not amenable to Gap filling under Article 7(2) by reference to the "general principles" of the Convention) can be a difficult undertaking — just as distinguishing those national "product liability" rules that are pre-empted by the Convention is a challenge. The "procedural" line has already been examined in connection with the question whether the CISG governs burden of proof questions; the reviser of the current edition of this treatise believes that burden of proof is, except where expressly addressed, beyond the Convention's scope, but others argue

64. Peter Schlechtriem, Art. 4 paras. 19 & 22, *in* Schlechtriem & Schwenzer, *CISG Commentary* (2nd English ed. 2005); Ferrari, *Scope of Application* at 107; cases cited in UNCITRAL Digest Art. 4 para. 13 nn.41 & 42.

65. MCC-Marble Ceramic Center, Inc. v. Ceramica Nuova D'Agostino, S.p.A., 144 F.3d 1384, 1389 n. 13 (11th Cir., June 29 1998) ("The CISG provides that a contract for the sale of goods need not be in writing and that the parties may prove the contract 'by any means, including witnesses.' CISG, Art. 11. Nevertheless, a party seeking to prove a contract in such a manner in federal court could not do so in a way that violated in the rule against hearsay. . . . A federal district court applies the Federal Rules of Evidence because these rules are considered procedural, regardless of the source of the law that governs the substantive decision.").

66. The reservation authorized by Art. 96 of the Convention may preserve even such domestic rules. See the discussion of Art. 12 *infra*.

that the matter is one "governed by" the CISG and resolvable pursuant to Article 7(2) by reference to the Convention's general principles. (See §70.1 supra.) The line distinguishing procedural matters beyond the reach of the Convention also comes into play in connection with the question whether the Convention authorizes the recovery of attorney fees incurred in successfully pursuing litigation under the CISG (see §408 infra). It must be noted that, just as is the case when the Convention's displacement of "product liability" rules is at issue, the label that domestic places on a particular rule ("procedural" vs. "substantive"; "tort" vs. "contract") does not determine whether the rule is or is not displaced by the CISG. Indeed, whether a particular issue is or is not "procedural" is not really the issue: the Convention does not expressly exclude "procedural" questions, and never even uses the term. Indeed, distinguishing clearly between "procedure" and "substance" has been notoriously difficult.[67] The question is whether a particular matter was intended to be governed by the Convention, and the procedure vs. substance distinction is just one of the tools that can help determine that intent. The fact that that the tool can be difficult to handle is not a sufficient reason to eschew it, particularly when the drafters of the Convention themselves employed it in determining what was the proper subject matter of the Convention.[68]

99 ## (4) General Principles on which the Convention is Based: Examples and Problems

(a) Reliance on Representations of Other Party: Domestic Law ("estoppel" etc.) v. "General Principles" of Convention.
We now face a significant problem that can best be considered in a specific factual setting.

Example 7A. In a transaction governed by the Convention, Buyer ordered Type A fiberboard from Seller. After this fiberboard had arrived but before Buyer put it to use Buyer asked Seller whether the material had

---

67. See John Y. Gotanda, *Awarding Damages under the United Nations Convention on the International Sale of Goods: A Matter of Interpretation*, 37 Geo. J. Int'l L. 95, 121–23 (2005).

68. During the drafting of the Convention a proposal to add language that would have expressly allocated the burden of proof concerning conformity of delivered goods was rejected because "it was considered inappropriate for the Convention, which relates to the international sale of goods, to deal with matters of evidence or procedure." UNCITRAL, Report of the Committee of the Whole relating to the draft Convention on the International Sales of Goods, 1977, paras. 177–178, *Docy. Hist.* 330.

been tested for resistance to fire. Seller consulted its records and, by an innocent error, transmitted to Buyer the results of tests of Type B, which was fireproof. Buyer, relying on this report, used the materials in constructing a building. Thereafter, Buyer learned of Seller's error and had to reconstruct the building. Is Seller responsible to Buyer for the added costs?

Since Seller's statement occurred after the making of the contract and the delivery of the goods, it might be difficult to conclude that the seller failed to "deliver goods which are of the . . . quality . . . required by the contract" (Art. 35) or (by the same token) that the buyer's loss was "a consequence of the breach" (Art. 74). The buyer might contend that, under Article 29, the contract had been "modified" by "agreement of the parties," but not all courts would so characterize the above exchange of communications that followed the delivery of the goods. To be sure, a court might well extend the concept of "agreement" to include a supplementary representation by the seller on which the buyer relies. But this, in substance, would be an analogical extension of Article 35 to carry out the "general principle" on which this provision was based, even though the court might not refer to Article 7(2).

In the above problem should one conclude that the seller's responsibility for his representation about the goods was not "governed" by the Convention? In this event the tribunal must seek (via the rules of private international law) some rule of domestic law dealing with responsibility for representations. In the common-law world this might lead to the doctrine of "estoppel," which bars a person from contradicting a representation on which another person has reasonably relied. If this were a transaction within the United States, "estoppel" would be available to supplement the provisions of the Uniform Commercial Code. However, in international transactions reference to domestic law has special problems — the uncertainties of the rules of private international law, the difficulty of ascertaining foreign law and the possible incongruity between pieces of domestic law and the overall plan of the Convention.

Is there a "general principle" underlying the Convention that would make one party responsible to the other for his representations that relate to the contract but are not explicitly a part of the agreement? As we have seen, the representation made in Example 7A may fall just outside Article 35, which defines the seller's responsibility for quality. Is Article 35 based on a larger premise — that one party should be entitled to rely on expectations created by the other?[69]

---

69. See Peter Schlechtriem, Art. 7 para. 30 at 104, *in* Schlechtriem & Schwenzer, *CISG Commentary* (2nd English ed. 2005) (stating that the "long lists of general principles"

One must be cautious about such an extension of an article of the Convention. Article 35 refers to conformity with "the contract": Would application of the Article's provisions outside the technical area of the "contract" violate a decision that the Convention should not touch non-contractual representations?

To answer this question, we need to examine other provisions of the Convention. For example, we find that Article 16(2)(b) protects a party who "has acted in reliance" on an offer in the reasonable belief that it was irrevocable. Article 29(2) provides that when a contract in writing requires that any modification also be in writing, "*a party may be precluded by his conduct* from asserting such a provision to the extent that the other party has *relied on that conduct.*" And under Article 47, a buyer who (in effect) invites late performance by the other party must accept the invited performance. In sum, various provisions of the Convention are inconsistent with a technical and narrow view of "contract" and evince a broader view of the relationship between the parties to a sales transaction.

Our principal purpose here is not to solve Example 7A but to illustrate the problems and possibilities presented by Article 7(2). Further light may be cast on this article by considering whether other groups of provisions evince a "general principle."

100 **(b) Communications.**   A theme that underlies numerous articles of the Convention is the duty to communicate information needed by the other party — a recognition that the consummation of a sales transaction involves interrelated steps that depend on cooperation. Article 19(2) requires an offeror to draw the offeree's attention to modifications in an offeree's acceptance to which the offeror objects. Article 21(2) requires an offeror to inform an offeree of a delay in the transmission of an acceptance if the offeror concludes that the acceptance arrived too late. Article 26 provides that avoidance of a contract must be notified to the other party. Article 39(1) requires the buyer to notify the seller of defects in the goods so the seller can test the goods to ascertain whether they are defective and take steps to cure the defects. Under Article 48(2) the buyer must respond to an inquiry as to whether he will accept late performance. Article 65 requires a buyer to respond to a request for

recited by commentators include the following: "estoppel or (equivalently) the prohibition of a *venire contra factum proprium* (contradictory behaviour) or, similarly, the protection of a party's reasonable reliance, caused by the other party"); UNCITRAL Digest Art. 7 para. 10 and decisions cited therein.

missing specifications for the goods. When the parties make a contract covering goods that are then in transit, under Article 68 the seller is obliged to disclose transit damage that has occurred. Communication of needed information is required if a party suspends performance because of impending failure of counter performance (Arts. 71(3) & 72(2), or because of excuse arising from a supervening impediment (Art. 79(4)). And under Article 88(1), a party intending to resell goods of which the other party has failed to take possession must give reasonable notice of this intent.

Although numerous specific situations are covered by the above articles, it would have been difficult to anticipate and specify all of the circumstances in which communications are needed. These provisions may well evince a general principle calling for communication of information that is obviously needed by a trading partner in situations that are closely analogous to those specified in the Convention.[70] (Provisions evincing a duty to co-operate are listed at §§323 and 342 (n.2).)

101 **(c) Mitigation.**   The Convention also includes several specific provisions that respond to the principle that one party should take steps to avoid deterioration of goods and thus avoid unnecessary hardship on the other party, even when that party has sent defective goods or otherwise has failed to perform the contract. Article 77 lays down the general rule that a party who relies on a breach of contract must take reasonable measures to mitigate the loss resulting from the breach. This general principle for the reduction of waste is applied in specific situations: The seller must take reasonable steps to preserve goods when the buyer is late in taking delivery (Art. 85), and the buyer has a similar duty to preserve non-conforming goods which he intends to reject (Art. 86). Situations may well arise that call for the application of the general principle that underlies these specific provisions.[71]

---

70. See the decision of the Bundesgerichtshof, Germany, October 31 2001, CLOUT case No. 445 (English translation available at http://cisgw3.law.pace.edu/cases/011031g1.html) (finding that parties are under an obligation to exchange information needed for performance pursuant to a Convention general principle of good faith). *Cf.* Bateson, The Duty to Co-operate, [1960] J. Bus. L. 187. For the suggestion that cooperation was one of the "general principles" invoked by ULIS 17 see Riese, 29 *Rabels Z* 1, 66 (1965); *Mertens & Rehbinder*, Art. 54 at 13. P. 218; Cohn, 23 Int. & Comp. L.Q. 520, 527 (1974).

71. See Peter Schlechtriem, Art. 7 para. 30 at 104, *in* Schlechtriem & Schwenzer, *CISG Commentary* (2nd English ed. 2005) (stating that the "long lists of general principles" recited by commentators include the following: "a general duty to avoid or mitigate losses and disadvantages"); UNCITRAL Digest Art. 7 para. 17 and decisions cited therein.

102 **(d) General Approach: Boldness v. Restraint.** As Professor Schlechtriem has noted (and catalogued), "Commentators recite long lists of general principles"[72] for purposes of Gap filling under Article 7(2). Case law has also posited a number of such Convention general principles.[73] The modest number of examples given (§§99–101) illustrate an approach that was designed to reconcile the two competing values embodied in Article 7(2): (1) That the Convention should be developed in the light of its "general principles" and (2) that this development would be subject to limits. This approach responds to the reference in Article 7(2) to the principles on which the Convention "is based" by requiring that general principles to deal with new situations be moored to premises that underlie specific provisions of the Convention. Thus, like the inductive approach employed in case law development, the first step is the examination of instances regulated by specific provisions of the Convention. The second step is to choose between these two conclusions: (a) The Convention deliberately rejected the extension of these specific provisions; (b) The lack of a specific provision to govern the case at hand results from a failure to anticipate and resolve this issue. If the latter alternative applies, the third step is to consider whether the cases governed by the specific provisions of the Convention and the case at hand are so analogous that a lawmaker would not have deliberately chosen discordant results for the group of similar situations. In this event, it seems appropriate to conclude that the general principle embracing these situations is authorized by Article 7(2). In sum, the approach involves the analogical application of multiple specific provisions of the Convention.[74]

The language of Article 7(2) reflects the decision to narrow the scope of ULIS 17 (§96, *supra*) which authorized tribunals to find (or create)

National reports to the 1986 Comparative Law Congress approved most of the above general principles and suggested, in addition, (1) Action in accordance with standards of a reasonable or businesslike person; (2) The protection of reliance and (3) Preservation of the contract. See *Honnold, General Report, 1986 Comp. L. Cong.*, in *Freiburg Colloq.* 139–140, and *German National Reports* 121–149 (Schlechtriem). *See also* Magnus, 53 *Rabels Z* at 142 (1989) (in German).

72. See Peter Schlechtriem, Art. 7 para. 30 at 104, *in* Schlechtriem & Schwenzer, *CISG Commentary* (2nd English ed. 2005).

73. See UNCITRAL Digest Art. 7 paras. 7–23 and decisions cited therein.

74. Hellner, Gap filling by Analogy, *Hjerner Festschrift* 219. Leading scholars of statutory interpretation in a common-law setting strongly support analogical reasoning from "instances where the statute unquestionably applies." H. Hart & A. Sacks, Legal Process (10th ed. 1958), quoted in W. Eskridge & P. Frickey, Legislation (1988), also citing L. Fuller, 71 Harv. L. Rev. 630, 662.

general principles to settle every problem that is not governed expressly by the Convention. More important, the approach illustrated above calls for the development of the Convention subject to the discipline imposed by analyzing the provision of the Convention and by examining the closeness of the analogy between the cases governed by those provisions and the case at hand.

Article 7(2) presents a delicate balance between (1) developing the Convention's general principles and (2) recourse to domestic law — a choice that inevitably will be influenced by the traditions and mindset of the tribunal. As we have seen (§96), civil law practice is generally hospitable to the first alternative and common law to the second. Which is more compatible with the objectives of the Convention?

This writer, although nurtured in the common law, has come to believe that international unification calls for us to reexamine our traditional approach. Invoking domestic law under the Convention has more serious consequences than invoking common-law principles to solve problems under a statute in a common-law jurisdiction. Even in dealing with a statute designed to unify law among the states of a common-law country, references to general common-law principles do not seriously undermine the statute's objective to achieve uniformity for the common-law principles stem from common roots. Within the Commonwealth, respect for decisions in England and in other Commonwealth jurisdictions limits the degree of disharmony; in the United States a strong unifying influence is exerted by the periodic Restatements of the law.[75] This degree of unity is not found among the domestic laws of the many States of diverse legal systems that have adopted the Convention. Nor will references to domestic law contribute to a body of international case-law under the Convention. Thus, a generous response to the invitation of Article 7(2) to develop the Convention through the "general principles on which it is based" is necessary to achieve the mandate of Article 7(1) to interpret the Convention with regard to "the need to promote *uniformity in its application.*" It is important, however, that this approach not be extended in a fashion that distorts the meaning or operation of the Convention, or that fails to acknowledge the diversity of the legal systems within which the CISG operates. The methodology for

---

75. On regard for case-law in other Commonwealth jurisdictions see *Honnold, General Report, 1986 Comp. L. Cong.*, in *Freiburg Colloq.* 121–122. On the unifying impact of the Restatements see Honnold, The Life of the Law, Ch. 4, pp. 145–183 (1964).

identifying general principles described herein guards against this possibility. Thus, as argued above (see §70.1 *supra*), the suggestion that burden of proof questions are governed by the Convention and should be resolved by reference to general principles of the CISG does not reflect the apparent intention of the drafters, does not have an adequate basis in the Convention, and produces an inflexible approach that would not work well in the different litigation systems of Contracting States.

In cases of doubt, a proposed application of a general principle may be tested against applicable trade usages (Art. 9, *infra*, at §112) and against contract practices and modern rules of law specially designed for international transactions. Later in this book, examples of modern contract practices serve to illustrate the Convention's general rules on risk of loss (Art. 67) and on exemption from damages when performance is prevented by an impediment (Art. 79). In addition, the rules of interpretation of Article 7(1), *supra*, call for guidance based on the experience of other Contracting States.

In sum, a response to the Convention's invitation to consider its "general principles" before turning to domestic law can minimize the confusion inherent in conflicts rules and avoid the uncritical and wooden application of scraps of domestic law that were developed without regard for the special needs of international trade. The "general principles" alternative offered by Article 7(2) can help the Convention, through international case law and scholarly writing to live as uniform law that responds to changing circumstances.[76] Other examples of this approach are given *infra* §§148–151, 156 (n.5), 177, 342 (n.2).

103   ## D. Special Role of the Sales Convention

(1) Interpretation of the Sales Convention and the Rules on Interpretation of Treaties in the 1969 Vienna Convention

Students of public international law may wonder why this discussion of the interpretation of the Sales Convention has not given more attention to the 1969 Vienna Convention on the Law of Treaties and its

---

76. See *Graveson, C. & G.* 8, quoting Scarman, J.: A code must be the exclusive law within its field or otherwise it is "in danger of failing to develop or reform"; Diamond, Codification of the Law of Contract, 31 Mod. L. Rev. 361, 384 (1968).

important rules on the interpretation of treaties.[77] To what extent are these rules applicable to the Sales Convention?

The question calls for distinctions between different types of Conventions and, more precisely, between different parts of the same Convention. The 1969 Vienna Convention is concerned with the obligations of Contracting States to each other. The 1980 Sales Convention, of course, creates such obligations among the Contracting States — primarily to give legal effect to the rules on international sales that are set forth in Parts I-III of the Convention (Arts. 1–88).

The obligations of the Contracting States to each other are centered in Part IV — Final Provisions. These include: procedures for adherence; rules on reservations whereby a Contracting State may limit its obligations under the Convention; rules governing denunciation of the Convention. All of these provisions of the 1980 Sales Convention should be construed in the light of the 1969 Vienna Convention.

Most of the provisions of the Sales Convention (Arts. 1–88; Parts I-III) deal with a very different matter — the obligations not of States but of the parties to a contract for the sale of goods. With respect to these provisions the Sales Convention states its own rules of interpretation (Art. 7, *supra*). Not surprisingly, these rules call for a more flexible approach than would be acceptable for rules defining the obligations of States. This flexibility is epitomized by the fact that virtually all of the provisions of Parts I-III (Arts. 1–88) yield to the contract made by the seller and buyer; in short, the heart of the Sales Convention is the contract of sale. Moreover, as we shall see, the Sales Convention provides that (unless the parties agree otherwise) contracts between sellers and buyers may be made orally (Art. 11) and are to be interpreted against a wide range of circumstances, including negotiations, past practices and trade usages (Arts. 8(3), 9(2)). In contrast, the 1969 Vienna Treaty provides that a "treaty" must be "in written form" (Art. 2-1(a)) and lays down elaborate rules on the authority to represent a State (Arts. 7–8) and on how a State may express its consent to be bound (Arts. 11–17). Consistent with this level of formality, the rules on the interpretation of treaties (Arts. 31–33) reflect the magnitude and complexity that are associated with the obligations of States. These rules are not appropriate for sales contracts and are quite different from the rules of interpretation in Article 7 of the Sales Convention.

---

77. Vienna Convention on the Law of Treaties (1969), U.N. Doc.A/CONF. 39/27. p. 289, reprinted in 63 Am. J. Int. L. 875. The Convention's rules on the interpretation of treaties appear in Part III, Sec. 3; at Arts. 31–33. Art. 31 was quoted *supra* at §90.

In sum, rules of interpretation in the 1969 Vienna Treaty are pertinent to the obligations under the 1980 Sales Convention that the Contracting States undertake to each other, but are not pertinent to the rules relating to the mutual obligations of the parties to the contract of sale.[78]

103.1 (2) The Character and Texture of the Rules

There is perhaps one principle of statutory interpretation that has general support: One must take account of the character and texture of the law. For example, a code that lays down general principles to cover a wide variety of transactions and is expected to endure, calls for an approach very different from tax laws and similar legislation that is written in great detail and is subject to frequent legislative adjustment.

Even international conventions differ widely in their legislative texture. As we have just seen (§103), public law conventions that seek to control the conduct of governments in sensitive areas have led to stricter rules of interpretation than uniform rules for private commercial transactions. Nor are private-law conventions all cut from the same cloth. Some deal with a narrow issue (e.g., the 1958 Convention on Recognition and Enforcement of Arbitral Awards) or with a relatively narrow and specialized field (e.g., conventions on the liability of a specific type of carrier). These specialized laws may include detailed provisions that leave little room for interpretation.

What is the character of the Sales Convention? Even here we must draw distinctions for different parts of this law have different textures providing different degrees of lee-way for interpretation.

Some of the more "sharp-edged" provisions deal with the Convention's sphere of application: E.g., Articles 1(1)(a), 2 and 5 (*supra* §§45, 47, 49–55, 71–73). In this area precise drafting and strict construction are useful: doubt about the applicability of the Convention produces uncertainty as to all of the problems governed by the Convention. Comparable precision, for the same reason, characterizes Part IV, Final Provisions (Arts. 89–101) on the date of entry into force, reservations, and the like.

---

78. Article 7 of the Sales Convention embodies mutual obligations of the Contracting States as to how their tribunals will construe the Convention. Hence, the 1969 Vienna Convention would be pertinent to a question concerning the construction of Art. 7, but the 1969 Convention would not govern the interpretation of the articles dealing with the obligations of the parties to the sales contract, for these articles are to be construed according to the principles (properly construed) of Art. 7. *Cf.* Lord Diplock in *Fothergill*, [1981] A.C. 251, 282–283.

Most of the rest of the Convention has a very different scope and texture. The substantive sales provisions (Parts I-III, Arts. 14–88), in nine printed pages (*O.R.* 179–188) state principles for resolving the wide range of problems that may arise in the making and performance of sales contracts. The Contracting States vary widely, and their international trade includes transactions of almost infinite variety: — as to types of goods (ranging from raw materials to computers), arrangement for transport, payment, documentation and compliance with government requirements at point of origin and receipt, single-delivery and long-term transactions, and so on. . . .

This does not suggest that the international sales law could or should have been drafted with greater detail; detailed rules for some situations would have created problems of classification and of doubt about the applicability of the Convention's general principles. See §26, *supra*. In addition, during the life of the Convention the problems resulting from excessive detail will increase with the development of new commodities and commercial arrangements. Such a general code has a long life expectancy. Preparing the present uniform law required over a decade; substantial world-wide adoption has required a further decade. If serious problems should develop UNCITRAL could prepare a protocol of amendment but most, if not all, of the provisions of the present uniform law probably must serve for several decades in a world of accelerating change.

103.2   (3) Texture of the Convention and Approaches to Interpretation

The above facts do not suggest that the domestic tribunals of the world have a free hand in adjudicating cases that are subject to the Convention. Although this uniform law (like national codes that have endured) was drafted in terms of general rules, these rules embody important choices — choices that can be appreciated fully only in the setting of the legislative history in which alternatives were proposed, discussed and rejected. Fidelity to these choices is the essence of the commitment that Contracting States make to each other: We will apply these uniform rules in place of our own domestic law on the assumption that you will do the same.

Consistent with this basic obligation of fidelity, the Convention's general rules for a diverse, complex and developing field should not be applied narrowly but should be given full effect to achieve their underlying purpose as shown by the structure of the Convention and its legislative history.[79]

At this point several of Article 7's rules of interpretation converge: (1) Regard for the Convention's "international character" requires sensitive response to the purposes of the Convention in the light of its legislative history rather than the preconceptions of domestic law (§88, *supra*); (2) Response to "the need to promote *uniformity* in . . . *application*," which (together with point (1), *supra*) calls for consideration of interpretations developed in other countries through adjudication (*jurisprudence*) and scholarly writing (*doctrine*) (§93 *supra*); (3) Regard for "the observance of *good faith* in international trade," a principle that in conjunction with point (1), *supra* and point (4), *infra*, can resist stultification and circumvention of the Convention's rules (§§94–95, *supra*); and (4) Questions not expressly settled by the Convention should be answered, when possible, "in conformity with the *general principles* on which it is based," an approach that reinforces regard for both the Convention's "*international* character" (point (1), *supra*) and "the need to promote *uniformity* in application (point (2), *supra*) by minimizing recourse to divergent rules of domestic law (§102, *supra*)."

---

79. The importance of "purposive" or "teleological" interpretation was stressed in the reports to the Twelfth International Congress of Comparative Law (*supra* §87). See *Honnold, General Report, 1986 Comp. L. Cong.,* in *Freiburg Colloq.* 138. *National Reports to I.C.L. Cong.*: Schlechtriem, in German National Reports, *1986 Comp. L. Cong.* 140, 142; van der Velden, in *Netherlands National Reports, 1986 Comp. L. Cong.* 21–45.

Article 8.
Interpretation of Statements or Other
Conduct of a Party

104   Article 7 dealt with interpretation of the *Convention*; the present
Article deals with the interpretation of the statements and conduct of
the *parties*.

Article 8[1]

**(1) For the purposes of this Convention statements made by and
other conduct of a party are to be interpreted according to his intent
where the other party knew or could not have been unaware what
that intent was.**

**(2) If the preceding paragraph is not applicable, statements made
by and other conduct of a party are to be interpreted according to
the understanding that a reasonable person of the same kind as the
other party would have had in the same circumstances.**

**(3) In determining the intent of a party or the understanding a
reasonable person would have had, due consideration is to be given
to all relevant circumstances of the case including the negotiations,
any practices which the parties have established between themselves, usages and any subsequent conduct of the parties.**

105   A. The Function and Scope of Article 8

In discussing Article 7 (§103.1, *supra*), attention was drawn to the
need to apply rules for *statutory* construction with close attention to the

---

1. Article 8 is substantially the same as Art. 7 of the 1978 Draft Convention, which was
closely based on a provision in the Working Group's 1977 "Formation" draft. *W/G 8* paras.
155–168 and Annex I (Art. 14), VIII *YB* 86–87, 90, *Docy. Hist.* 287–288, 291; *W/G 9* paras.
11–47 and Annex (Arts. 4 of Formation Draft), IX *YB* 62–64, *Docy. Hist.* 294–296. In 1978
the Commission merged the "Formation" and "Sales" drafts, and placed the present
provision in Part I of the Convention. As a consequence, the rules on interpretation of the
offer and acceptance became applicable to statements and conduct after formation of the
contract. *UNCITRAL XI*, Annex I paras. 38–41 (summary of discussion of Art. 4 of Formation Draft, renumbered Art. 7 of the 1978 Draft Convention), IX *YB* 33–34, *Docy. Hist.*
367–368. *Cf.* ULF 4(2) and 1972 UNIDROIT Draft of a Law on Validity of Contracts (LUV)
Arts. 3–5. See VIII *YB*, 104–105 (text of LUV with Secretariat analysis), *Docy. Hist.*
268–269.

character of the statute and the texture of the statutory provision in question. This principle applies with even greater force to Article 8's rules for the interpretation of *contracts*. Article 7 on interpretation of the Convention was drafted by the body that drafted the language of the Convention to which Article 7 applies; the provisions of Article 8 on the interpretation of contracts apply to language used by others — private parties acting in a remarkably wide variety of situations. The settings range from brief telephone, email or fax communications for small or routine purchases to detailed contracts negotiated for large and complex transactions. The provisions of Article 8 apply and are relevant to these various types arrangements but have special significance for agreements that have not resulted from detailed negotiations; even detailed agreements are often modified by informal communications.[2] Article 8 is also applicable to questions of interpretation that arise under the contract when the contract is made by an exchange of communications and also when the parties join in executing a single instrument.[3] And, since Article 8 is broadly applicable to "statements made by and other conduct of a party," it reaches post-contract communications and actions, many of which have legal effect and may raise significant problems of interpretation.[4]

2. Some domestic rules for sales of goods were designed to counteract patterns of interpretation that developed under a pre-commercial static economy typified by transactions in land — unusual and important arrangements prepared cautiously and in detail; at that stage, sales of goods involved simple items purchased after inspection. Steps toward relaxing rigid patterns for construing such contracts are found (e.g.) in the English Sale of Goods Act 1893, §14 (implied obligations of merchantable quality). See *Benjamin* (3d ed.) §779–790; Llewellyn, 52 Harv. L. Rev. 725 and 873 (1939).

3. Often an instrument executed by the parties is prepared by one party and, in effect, accepted by the other. In this setting paragraph (2) applies; the party who prepared the instrument is the one who "made" the statement. When both parties participate fully in preparing the instrument, paragraph (2) is not applicable since it distinguishes between one who makes a statement and the one who receives it, but such an instrument is subject to the general rules of interpretation in paragraph (3).

4. Communications mentioned in the Convention include: notification of avoidance (Art. 26, *infra* §187); modification or termination of an agreement (Art. 29, *infra* §200); notification that goods are defective or that performance will be interrupted (Arts. 39, 48, 68, 71, 72, 79, 88). Communication that call for interpretation also may occur in settings not mentioned in the Convention.

106 B. Basic Approaches to Interpretation: Subjective Intent v. Objective Meaning

In preparing the present article, UNCITRAL had to face and reconcile conflicting theories about the fundamental nature of the process of contracting. According to one early theory, a person should be bound by contract only when he subjects his "will" to the terms of the contract. In some legal systems this contributed to the view that one's obligation was defined by his "intent" or "consent," or that making a contract required a "meeting of the minds."[5]

The image of a meeting of two minds is attractive but it raises practical difficulties. When a dispute arises over the "meaning" of a contract, the contending parties are scarcely reliable witnesses as to what was in their minds when they made the contract. Moreover, language is such an imprecise medium that shades of differences of understanding are latent in many of the agreements on which commerce depends; a purely "subjective" approach could undermine protection for reasonable reliance on expectations created by another.

These difficulties led many jurists and legal systems to reject "intent" as a basis for the contract. This view was vigorously expressed by Oliver Wendell Holmes: "The law has nothing to do with the actual state of the parties' minds. In contract, as elsewhere, it must go by externals, and judge parties by their conduct."[6] Some legal systems, while clinging to the "subjective" or "mutual intent" theory, have limited this approach to prescribed categories, and have devised remedies to protect a "speaker" when the "hearer" knew or should have known of the ambiguity.[7] However, for the most part, current references to "will" as the basis for contract resemble the echoes of distant thunder from a storm that has passed.

---

5. *Corbin* §106; *von Mehren & Gordley* 850–872; Hoff, Error in the Formation of Contracts in Louisiana: A Comparative Analysis, 53 Tul. L. Rev. 329, 335 (1979) (comparison of civil law of Louisiana and France, and of common law).

6. Holmes, The Common Law 242 (Howe ed. 1963). *Corbin* (§106) was less unqualified: when a common intent or meaning can be found, it should be given effect. See also Farnsworth, "Meaning" in the Law of Contracts, 76 Yale L.J. 939, 947 (1967). For David Hume's criticism of the "intent" or "will" theory, see *Atiyah, Freedom of Contract* 53.

7. Hoff, *supra* n. 5 at 338, 342–353 (error in corpore, error in substantia), 374 (French law may call for compensation of an unerring party for loss based on reliance). "Speaker" refers to one who makes a statement, whether written or oral; "hearer" is the one to whom the statement is made.

107 **(1) The Approach of Article 8**

Paragraph (1) is built on the "subjective" approach: Interpretation is to be based on a speaker's "intent" — but only "where the other party knew or could not have been unaware" of the intent. However, because of the practical barriers to proving identity between the intent of the two parties (particularly when they are involved in a controversy) most problems of interpretation will be governed by paragraph (2) which follows the "objective" approach: Statements by a speaker (Party A) "are to be interpreted according to the understanding that a *reasonable person* of the same kind as the *other party*" (Party B) "*would have had* in the same circumstances."

A decision by a U.S. federal appeals court demonstrates the application of Article 8(1) while also illustrating the kind of unusual circumstances in which the provision comes into play. In MCC-Marble Ceramic Center, Inc. v. Ceramica Nuova d'Agostino, S.p.A.,[8] a Florida tile retailer purchased ceramic tiles from an Italian producer. The U.S. buyer had signed the seller's purchase order forms, which were in Italian (a language the buyer did not understand). The buyer complained orally about the quality of the tiles in some deliveries, and withheld some payments. When the seller refused further shipments, the buyer sued, claiming damages both for delivery of defective goods and for failure to make further deliveries. Seller defended by invoking a clause on the back of the signed purchase order form that required written 10-day notice of complaints about the quality of delivered goods (the buyer had not given such written notice) and a clause permitting the seller to cancel all contracts upon default in payment. The buyer alleged that, although it signed the purchase order forms, the parties did not intend the terms on the reverse side to bind the buyer, despite a statement just below the signature line stating that the buyer agreed to the provisions on the reverse of the form. In support of its position, the buyer produced affidavits by the commercial agent who had represented the seller in its dealings with the buyer and by another agent of the seller who had acted as translator during the negotiations, both (along with an affidavit of the buyer's president) supporting the buyer's position. The affidavits, however, cited no objective manifestations at the time the purchase order forms were signed suggesting that the buyer was not to be bound by the terms on the reverse of the form;

8. 144 F.3d 1384 (11th Cir. June 29 1998), *cert. denied* Ceramica Nuova D'Agostino, S.p.A. v. MCC-Marble Ceramic Center, Inc., 526 U.S. 1087 (April 26 1999).

neither of the seller's representatives that gave affidavits were, at the time the affidavits were given, employed any longer by the seller. The trial court granted the seller summary judgment because, it held, the clauses on the reverse of the seller's forms bound the buyer, thus precluding its claims. The lower court rejected the buyer's argument that its affidavits raised a factual issue under CISG Article 8(1) concerning the parties' 'subjective intent' with regard to the seller's form clauses: Article 8(1), it held, did not apply because the buyer was not urging an interpretation, but rather a contradiction, of the expressions of the parties.

On appeal, the Eleventh Circuit found that Article 8(1) was applicable because it governed the meaning of the buyer's conduct in signing the seller's forms. Given the priority that Article 8(1) gives a party's subjective intent, provided such intent was known to the other side, the court held that the evidence from the affidavits given by the seller's (former) representatives was sufficient to raise a factual issue as to whether the parties shared a non-manifested subjective intent to free the buyer from the clauses on the reverse of the seller's form. Although it expressed skepticism that the buyer's evidence of a subjective intent would be found credible at trial, it held that the evidence was sufficient to preclude summary judgment. The court also strongly emphasized that it was the affidavits from the seller's (former) representatives, and not the fact that that the buyer did not know the language of the form it signed, the created a sufficient prima facie argument that the buyer had a subjective intent, known to the seller, not to be bound by the form clauses.

The application of Article 8(1) by the 11th Circuit in MCC-Marble depended on two special factors: 1) the existence of affidavits from persons who represented the seller in its transactions with the buyer which supported the buyer's factual argument for a shared subjective intent departing from the understanding that a reasonable person would have had of the parties' intentions; 2) the fact that the issue came up for review on a summary judgment motion, which the buyer could defeat merely by demonstrating that its evidence raised an issue of material fact that might be resolved at trial in its favor.[9] The former factor is unusual indeed.[10] And, as the court itself noted, the second

---

9. See 144 F.3d at 1386 ("Summary judgment is appropriate when the pleadings, depositions, and affidavits reveal that no genuine issue of material fact exists and the moving party is entitled to judgment as a matter of law.").

10. See 144 F.3d at 1391 ("This is not to say that parties to an international contract for the sale of goods cannot depend on written contracts or that parol evidence regarding subjective

factor meant that the buyer was by no means assured of prevailing at trial. Thus the decision tends to confirm that Article 8(1) will come into play only in rather rare circumstances, and most issues relating to interpretation of the parties' intent will be resolved under the objective standards of Article 8(2).[11]

107.1 **(a) Article 8(2) and Protective Legislation.** Article 8(2) places the burden on one who prepares a communication or who drafts a con-tract to communicate clearly to a reasonable person in the same position as the other party. This provision has roots in the classic rule that doubts are to be resolved against the drafter (*contra proferentem*), but the appli-cation of this principle has special significance in international sales. When the parties are based in different language and legal settings, the party who makes a proposal must avoid using expressions that are obscure, or, even worse, are "false friends" (*des faux amis*) with one "clear" meaning to the one who writes and a different "clear" meaning to the one who reads. These problems, intrinsic to language, rise to a higher power in our area through the use of legal terms with different meanings in different legal cultures (e.g., "warranty," "condition," "disclaimer," "trust") and mercantile terms with divergent meanings in different areas or settings. CISG Article 8(2) does not, of course, give binding effect to what the listener or reader (Party B) personally under-stood but, instead, to the understanding of "a *reasonable* person *of the same kind*" as the "other party" — a principle that responds to the fact that only the one who communicates has an opportunity to consider and choose among alternative modes of expression and also takes account of a drafter's opportunity to hide an unpleasant meaning through "the intellectual superiority of the legal virtuoso."[12]

---

contractual intent need always prevent a party relying on a written agreement from securing summary judgment. To the contrary, most cases will not present a situation (as exists in this case) in which both parties to the contract acknowledge a subjective intent not to be bound by the terms of a pre-printed writing. In most cases, therefore, Art. 8(2) of the CISG will apply, and objective evidence will provide the basis for the court's decision. [Citing prior edition of this Commentary.] Consequently, a party to a contract governed by the CISG will not be able to avoid the terms of a contract and force a jury trial simply by submitting an affidavit which states that he or she did not have the subjective intent to be bound by the contract's terms.").

11. *Accord*, Martin Schmidt-Kessel, Art. 8 paras. 10, 17 & 19, *in* Schlechtriem & Schwenzer, *CISG Commentary* (2nd English ed. 2005).

12. Ludwig Raiser, *in* The Law of Standard Terms of Business (*Das Recht der ABG*) 284 (1935), as quoted in *Zweigert & Kötz II* (1987) 12. Concern over the danger of meanings unclear to one of the parties underlay UNCITRAL's rejection (§118, *infra*) of proposals

Article 8(2) has interesting points of contrast and similarity in relation to various types of domestic protective laws. Some of these laws apply only to sales to consumers as defined in Article 2(a), §50, *supra*, and consequently are outside the scope of the Convention. However, some protective legislation may overlap with CISG. See §§232, 236, *infra*. Hence a preliminary analysis of these laws in relation to Article 8(2) can provide helpful background for problems that we shall meet later.

One type of domestic legislation denies effect to contract terms on the ground that they impose excessively harsh consequences even though these contract terms were (or should have been) understood by the other party.[13] Article 8(2) is quite different, for it is concerned only with the interpretation of the contract. A second type of domestic law denies full effect to standard terms and form contracts prepared by one party on the ground that the other party may not grasp their full import; this type is closely related to Article 8(2). A third type restricts the effect of standard terms or forms on the ground that their use is so widespread that they deny contractual freedom to the other party. Other laws are difficult to classify for they may reflect concern for both clarity and fairness, or the basis for the law may be unclear.[14]

Determining the basis and impact of these domestic laws is important in deciding whether they are displaced by the Convention. The first and third types, above, do not invade the area of interpretation occupied by Article 8 and are preserved by Article 4, which states that the Convention "is not concerned with: (a) the *validity* of the contract or of any of its provisions . . ."[15]

The relationship between the second type of domestic law and the Convention will be explored in more detail in discussing Article 35 on

---

based on ULIS 9(3) to give binding effect to the meaning "usually" given to expressions "commonly used in the trade concerned."

13. E.g., (U.S.A.) UCC 2–718(1): A term in a sales contract "fixing unreasonably large liquidated damages" for breach of contract "is void as a penalty."

14. (U.S.A.) UCC 2–302, authorizing courts to refuse to enforce "unconscionable" contracts or clauses, is accompanied by an Official Comment that states that the provision is directed at "one-sided" contracts but adds: "The principle is one of the prevention of oppression and unfair surprise . . . and not of disturbance of allocation of risks because of superior bargaining power." This lack of clarity has been sharply criticized. Leff, Unconscionability — The Emperor's New Clause, 115 U. Pa. L. Rev. 485 (1967). *Cf.* Hillman, 67 Cornell L. Rev. I (1981).

15. The Convention's statement in Art. 4(1) that it "*is not concerned*, with (a) validity is subject to an important limitation: 'except as otherwise expressly provided in this Convention." This limitation eliminates conflict with express provisions (such as Art. 8(2)) that might otherwise be considered as dealing with questions of "validity."

conformity of goods to the contract (§§230–234, *infra*), *but the interplay between Article 8(2) and domestic laws governing the application of a party's standard terms ("boilerplate")—an issue that has arisen in decisions applying the Convention—deserves comment here. The German Bundesgerichtshof has held that Article 8(2), rather than domestic law, governed whether a party's standard terms, referenced in but not included with an offer, were incorporated into the party's contract; the court denied effect to those terms on the footing that "a reasonable person of the same kind as" the offeree would not have understood the terms to be part of the parties' agreement.*[16] *This decision represents an appropriate use of Article 8(2) in lieu of domestic law of the second type described above. Asking whether a "reasonable person of the same kind as" one party would have understood that the other party's standard terms were part of the agreement, as per Article 8(2), seems a pertinent inquiry for the kind of issues raised by the use of standard terms—i.e., whether, given the realities of the transaction between the parties, a party was put on actual fair notice of the other party's standard terms and not unreasonably burdened in discovering their content; or, on the hand, whether the standard terms were interjected in a manner and/or form that did not reasonably encourage (that may even have been designed to discourage) understanding and real bargaining. A malleable general standard such as the "reasonable person," however, must be employed with great care in this area: the temptation to incorporate domestic law approaches under the "reasonableness" rubric—what could appear more "reasonable" than what one is accustomed to under familiar domestic law?—must be recognized and resisted.*

The above suggestion that under Article 8(2) ambiguity in a statement is to be resolved against the party who formulated this statement has considerable significance in view of the wide disparities between the modes of expression and expectations in the different areas and types of enterprises that may meet in international trade. Although this interpretation of Article 8(2) may be disputed,[17] it will at least be prudent for a

---

16. Bundesgerichtshof, Germany, October 31, 2001, CLOUT case No. 445, English translation available at http://cisgw3.law.pace.edu/cases/011031g1.html. For discussion of decisions applying the standards of Art. 8(2) to the incorporation of boilerplate terms into a contract see UNCITRAL Digest Art. 8 paras. 23–24.

17. This interpretation of Art. 8(2) apparently is not accepted by Farnsworth in *B-B Commentary* 99–100, §§2.4–2.5. In accord with the position taken in the text accompanying this note, however, see, e.g., Martin Schmidt-Kessel, Art. 8 para. 47, *in* Schlechtriem & Schwenzer, *CISG Commentary* (2nd English ed. 2005).

party in formulating a proposal or other statement to take care that it not be given a different understanding by (Art. 8(2)) "a reasonable person of the same kind as the *other* party."

108   C. Formation of the Contract: The "Peerless" Case

The most famous common-law case in this area grew out of a contract to sell 125 bales of Surat cotton which was to arrive in Liverpool "*ex Peerless* from Bombay." Unknown to the parties, there were two ships named "Peerless" that sailed from Bombay to Liverpool. Party A (the seller and "speaker") owned cotton on a "Peerless" that arrived in December and intended to offer this cotton to Party B; Party B (the buyer) had in mind a "Peerless" that arrived two months earlier. The buyer refused to accept the cotton when it arrived in December and the seller sued for damages for breach of contract. The court held for the buyer; no contract had been made because of the parties' misunderstanding.[18]

This early decision has received more attention than its practical importance would justify. Nevertheless, a series of examples based on the facts of the "Peerless" case can illustrate possible applications of Article 8.

Example 8A. On January 1, Party A in Bombay cabled Party B in London: "Offer 1,000 bales of Surat cotton at $150 per bale, for shipment from Bombay on the next sailing of the 'Peerless'." Party B consulted published shipping schedules and found that a ship named "Peerless," that ordinarily carried only coal, was scheduled to leave Bombay for arrival in Liverpool on February 1, but that a general cargo ship, also named, "Peerless," was scheduled to leave Bombay for arrival in Liverpool on May 1. B cabled: "Accept Offer." The seller (A) shipped the cotton on the general cargo ship "Peerless" that arrived, as scheduled, on May 1. B rejected the cotton on the ground that B expected the cotton to arrive on the earlier "Peerless."

In this case, a tribunal might conclude that B "knew of or could not have been unaware" that A was referring to the "Peerless" on which A in fact shipped the cotton. On this assumption, paragraph (1) of Article 8

---

18. Raffles v. Wichelhaus, 2 Hurl. & C. 906, 159 Eng. Rep. 375 (1864). See *Corbin* §104, *Benjamin* §216: Corbett, Contractual Error in Roman and Modern Law, 3 Can. Bar. Rev. 281, 284 (1925); Young, Equivocation in the Making of Agreements, 64 Colum. L. Rev. 619. 646 (1964). Cases like the "Peerless" can still arise: Oswald v. Allen, 417 F.2d 43 (2d Cit. 1969).

holds party B to the offer as understood by Party A. Unlike the result in the early "Peerless" case, a contract was formed and the buyer (Party B) was contractually bound to accept the cotton that arrived in May.[19]

Example 8B. Party A in Bombay cabled Party B in London an offer like the one stated in Example 8A and B replied "accept offer." Shipping schedules available in Bombay listed one general cargo ship named the "Peerless," scheduled to reach Liverpool in May. Published shipping schedules available in London listed one general cargo ship called the "Peerless"; this was a different ship than the one listed in Bombay and was scheduled to arrive in February. B accepted the offer reasonably expecting the sugar to arrive in February. A shipped on the "Peerless" that arrived in May; B rejected the goods for their failure to arrive, as he expected, in February.

On these facts, a tribunal could conclude that "a reasonable person of the same kind" and "in the same circumstances" as B would have understood A's offer as referring to the "Peerless" that arrived in February. On this assumption it could be argued that paragraph (2) of Article 8 binds the offeror (Party A) to the offer as understood by Party B — shipment on the February "Peerless." Under this view, a party who makes a statement has a duty to communicate in a manner that would be understood by a reasonable person in the position of the other party; the risk of misunderstanding falls on the speaker or writer.

Suppose it is argued that B's reply, "I accept," was a "statement" that, pursuant to Article 8(2), should be interpreted according to the "understanding" that A would reasonably give to this reply. Under this approach the two parties, without negligence on either side, had a basic misunderstanding as to the agreement; consequently, no contract would be formed as in the *Peerless* case and example 8C, *infra*. However, this approach fails to give effect to the provision of Article 8(2) which draws a distinction between one who initiates an ambiguous statement and one who is misled by it. This distinction is important when one party presents an ambiguous offer-form which the other party accepts under a

---

19. Example 8A and other examples that might involve paragraph (1) will seldom arise in practice. To make the situation plausible. we might suppose that B expected that A would ship as he did. but that after a drop in the cotton market B sought to escape from the contract by relying on the ambiguity in the contract. (Compare the discussion of "good faith" in the Commentary to Art. *7, supra* at §94.)

reasonable misapprehension of its meaning. To cope with such questions Article 8(2) leads to the conclusion that A is bound to B's reasonable understanding of A's offer.[20]

Example 8C. Party A in Bombay made an offer like the one stated in Example 8A. Party A intended to ship from Bombay on a "Peerless" scheduled to reach Liverpool in May. Published shipping schedules available in both London and Bombay listed two general cargo ships named "Peerless" scheduled for departure from Bombay: one would reach Liverpool in February and the other in May. Most persons in the position of A and B would have consulted these schedules, but neither did so. B had heard of a "Peerless" scheduled to arrive in February; on the assumption that this was the ship to which A referred, B accepted the offer, and rejected the cotton that arrived in May.

On these facts, a tribunal could conclude that under Article 8(2) a reasonable person in B's position would have seen that A's offer was ambiguous and consequently B's "understanding" of A's offer did not bind A. On the assumption that the time of arrival was important to the parties, there was a basic misunderstanding in their exchange of communications and the offeree (B) did not assent to the A's offer. (See Art. 18, *infra,* on the requirements for acceptance.) Consequently, as in the actual "Peerless" case, there was no contract; B would not be bound to accept goods tendered by A in May and A would not be bound to ship goods for arrival in February.

Happily, cases like the "Peerless" (like ghosts and flying saucers) are more discussed than seen. And, in the rare instances when they do appear, the full setting of the transaction (see Article 8(3), *infra)* may render the situation less elusive than the sketchy facts of the above examples.[21]

---

20. But *cf.* Farnsworth in B-B Commentary 100, 925, para. 4.

21. Article 8 is concerned only with *interpreting* statements and conduct. In some settings, as in contract formation, Art. 8 occupies one corner of a vast field that in some legal systems comes under the heading of "mistake." The consequences of ignorance (or "mistake") about surrounding circumstances or future events are not governed by Art. 8. Where unforeseen obstacles prevent a party from performing, he may be exempt from damages by Art. 79, *infra* §243. Other types of "mistake" that may justify nonperformance or rescission may lie outside the specific provisions of the Convention. See §240, *infra.*

109 **D. Interpretation in the Light of Surrounding Circumstances**

Paragraph (3) (unlike Paragraph (2)) states rules of interpretation that, *inter alia*, apply to statements embodied in an agreement formulated by both parties. (See §105 n.3, *supra*.) Article 8(3) cuts through technical rules that might bar access to relevant materials: "Due consideration" is to be given to "*all relevant circumstances* of the case," including (a) negotiations, (b) practices established between the parties (Art. 9(1)), (c) usages (Art. 9(2)) and (d) the parties' subsequent conduct.

Let us suppose that one party contends that the agreement, although not expressing result "X," should be construed to reach this result. May a tribunal consider evidence that this party proposed that the contract state result "X" but that this proposal was rejected? Under Article 8(3), such negotiations are "relevant" to the interpretation of the agreement and should be given "due consideration"; of course, they are not conclusive.

110 **(1) Other Agreements: The "Parol Evidence Rule"**

Jurists familiar with the common law will be intrigued by the relationship between Article 8(3) and the "parol evidence rule." This so-called "rule" (as aptly named as the Holy Roman Empire) has been used to bar the consideration of any agreement (whether or not "parol") that contradicts a contemporary or subsequent writing "intended by the parties as a final expression of their agreement"; the rule also bars a prior agreement in relation to a writing which was intended "as a complete and exclusive statement of the terms of the agreement." (The quoted phrases are taken from the relatively mild version of the "parol evidence rule" of (U.S.A.) UCC 2–202.)[22]

Article 8 does not directly address the "parol evidence rule"; references to this and other technical domestic rules would have cluttered the draft and would have mystified jurists from legal systems that have no such rule. But the language of Article 8(3) that "due consideration is to be given to *all relevant* circumstances of the case" seems adequate to override any domestic rule that would bar a tribunal from considering the relevance of other agreements. ***Indeed, the Convention's failure to***

---

22. The problems of interpretation that have arisen under (U.S.A.) UCC 2–202 are discussed in *White & Summers* §§2-9-2-12, and in law review articles cited therein. For case law apart from the UCC see *Corbin* §573 *et seq.*; *Treitel, Contract* 150 *et seq.*

accord exceptional status to written agreements (it expressly rejects an emphasis on written contracts in Article 11), and in particular the lack of any presumption that written contracts are intended to supersede prior agreements not reflected therein, should by itself be sufficient to eliminate the parol evidence rule's extraordinarily cumbersome machinery for determining the parties' intent with respect to a written contract — e.g., the "appearance" test, the "would certainly" test, and the like.[23] *That machinery is probably the most significant (and most troublesome) aspect of U.S. parol evidence rules. There is now a strong (but not quite unanimous) line of decisions by U.S. courts declaring that the parol evidence rules is inapplicable in transactions governed by the CISG. For example, that was the conclusion of the federal 11th Circuit Court of Appeals in the* **MCC-Marble** *case describe earlier (see §107 infra);*[24] *the court relied on Article 8(3) for this conclusion.*

Jurists interpreting agreements subject to the Convention can be expected to continue to give special and, in most cases, controlling effect to detailed written agreements *in line with the parties' likely intent (as determined under Article 8) and with the credibility of the evidence.* And contract terms (often called "integration clauses") that any contemporaneous or prior agreement shall be without effect would be supported by Article 6, which gives effect to the contract,[25] *although it would be contrary to the informality principle in Article 11 to require a written merger clause before a written contract could be intended to discharge prior agreements.*[26] But Article 8(3) relieves tribunals from domestic rules that might bar them from "considering" any evidence

---

23. See Harry M. Flechtner, *The U.N. Sales Convention (CISG) and* MCC-Marble Ceramic Center, Inc. v. Ceramica Nuova D'Agostino, S.P.A.: *The Eleventh Circuit Weighs in on Interpretation, Subjective Intent, Procedural Limits on the Convention's Scope, and the Parol Evidence Rule,* 18 J.L. & Com. 259, 277–81 (1999); Harry M. Flechtner, *More U.S. Decisions on the U.N. Sales Convention: Scope, Parol Evidence, "Validity" and Reduction of Price under* Art. 50, 14 J.L. & Com. 153, 158–59 (1995).

24. For other decisions stating that the parol evidence rule does not apply in transactions governed by the Convention, see the decisions cited in UNCITRAL Digest Art. 8 n. 39. For an apparently contrary *dicta,* see Beijing Metals & Minerals Import/Export Corp. v. American Business Center, Inc., 993 F.2d 1178, 1183 n. 9 (5th Cir. 1993).

25. *Accord* MCC-Marble Ceramic Center, Inc. v. Ceramica Nuova d'Agostino, S.p.A., 144 F.3d 1384 (11th Cir. June 29 1998), *cert. denied* Ceramica Nuova D'Agostino, S.p.A. v. MCC-Marble Ceramic Center, Inc., 526 U.S. 1087 (April 26 1999).

26. *Contra,* UNIDROIT (International Institute for the Unification of Private Law), Principles of International Commercial Contracts 2004, cmt. to Art. 2.1.17 at 64 (2004) ("in the absence of a merger clause, extrinsic evidence supplementing or contradicting a written contract is admissible").

between the parties that is relevant. This added flexibility for interpretation is consistent with a growing body of opinion that the "parol evidence rule" has been an embarrassment for the administration of modern transactions.[27]

A lawyer preparing for trial at common law may note that the parol evidence rule has its greatest significance in restricting the role of juries in the field of contract interpretation. The Convention, of course, does not interfere with domestic rules on the allocation of authority between the judge and jury, *a procedural matter clearly beyond the Convention's scope. Thus the CISG* would not interfere with the decision to exclude from a jury evidence of prior or contemporaneous agreements if (in the apparently circular language of UCC 2–202) "the *court* finds" (after giving due consideration to all relevant circumstances) that the writing was "intended also as a *complete and exclusive* statement of the terms of the agreement."[28]

111 ## (2) Reflected Light: Conduct Subsequent to the Agreement

Article 8(3) authorizes "due consideration" for conduct subsequent to the agreement since this may shed light on the intentions and expectations of the parties. Under UCC 2–207(3) "conduct by both parties which recognizes the existence of a contract is sufficient to establish a contract for sale...." And UCC 2–208(1) states that under some circumstances a "course of performance accepted or acquiesced in without objection shall be relevant to determine the meaning of the agreement." On the other hand, English case law has been hostile to evidence of subsequent conduct — an approach that has met resistance and criticism.[29]

---

27. The English Law Commission has recommended abolition of the parol evidence rule. Law Commission, Working Paper No. 70, Law of Contract, The Parol Evidence Rule (1976). *Accord, Ont. L. Ref. Com., I Sales* 110–117. For a comparative study see *Zweigert & Kötz II (1987)* 91–93 (French Civil Code Rule similar to the "parol evidence rule" is inapplicable to commercial transactions; no comparable rule in Germany). For indications of increasing flexibility in American law see *Farnsworth, Contracts* 451–474.

28. See McCormick, *The Parol Evidence Rule as a Procedural Device for Control of the Jury*, 41 Yale L.J. 365 (1932).

29. *Ont. L. Ref. Com., I Sales* 117–118, supporting *Friedman* 251 and Lord Denning, M. R., in Port Soudan Cotton Co. v. Chettiar and Sons [1977] 2 Ll. Rep. 5, 11 (C.A.).

Article 9.
Usages and Practices Applicable to Contract

112   A. The Role of Usages and Practices

The world's commerce embraces an almost infinite variety of goods and transactions; a law cannot embody the special patterns that now are current let alone those that will develop in the future.

Many of these patterns may be reflected in the contract; but there are practical limitations on the ability of the parties to envisage and answer every possible question. Many transactions must be handled quickly and informally. Even when there is time to prepare detailed documents, an attempt to anticipate and solve all conceivable problems may generate disagreements and prevent the making of a contract; moreover, the most basic patterns may not be mentioned because, for experienced parties, they "go without saying." (In the course of collaborating with an exporter in writing out the understandings that underlay a standard export transactions we both were amazed at the number and scope of basic assumptions that were not mentioned in the detailed documents.)

For these reasons, one of the most important features of the Convention is the legal effect it gives to commercial usages and practices.[1]

113   B. Usages and Practices under the 1980 Convention

Article 9[2]

(1) The parties are bound by any usage to which they have agreed and by any practices which they have established between themselves.
(2) The parties are considered, unless otherwise agreed, to have impliedly made applicable to their contract or its formation a usage

---

1. Goldstajn, Usages of Trade, *Dubrovnik Lectures* 55; *id.*, Commercial Usages as the Source of the Law of International Trade, in Mélanges Fragistas (Thessaloniki 1967) 391, 400–402 (1967); Jokela, The Role of Usages in the Uniform Law on International Sales, 10 *Scan. Studies* 81; Farnsworth, Usage and Course of Dealing, *Sauveplanne Festschrift* 81; Thieffry in *Ottawa Colloque* 93–104 (in French; usages and arbitration); David Hume and tacit understandings or "conventions" see *Atiyah, Freedom of Contract* 56.
2. Article 9 is the same as Art. 8 of the 1978 Draft Convention, except that at the diplomatic conference, for the sake of clarity, the phrase "or its formation" was added to paragraph (2): *O.R.* 265, *Docy. Hist.* 486. *Cf.* ULIS Art. 9, ULF Arts. 4(2), 5(3), 6(2), 8(1), 11, 13.

of which the parties knew or ought to have known and which in international trade is widely known to, and regularly observed by, parties to contracts of the type involved in the particular trade concerned.

Article 9 deals with three situations: (1) Usages to which the parties have agreed (Article 9(1); (2) Practices that the two parties have established between themselves (Art. 9(1)); and (3) Usages that become part of the contract based on the criteria stated in Article 9(2).

114   **(1) Usages to which the Parties have Agreed**

(a) Standards of Agreement.   ULIS (Art. 9(1)) provided that the parties "shall be bound by any usage they have *expressly or impliedly* made applicable to their contract." Article 9(1) of the Convention omitted the phrase "expressly or impliedly," and thereby avoided any inference that abnormal rules are applicable to the construction of the contract. A provision in the contract that trade terms (F.O.B., C.I.F., and the like) are governed by ICC's "Incoterms" would be a clear and common illustration of an agreement expressly making a specified usage applicable to the contract. References that are less explicit might well invoke usages if the court concludes that such was the intent of the parties, in accordance with the Convention's rules of interpretation in Article 8, *supra* at §109.[3]

(b) Agreement on Trade Terms.   When a contract uses a technical term drawn from chemistry tribunals scarcely need statutory authorization to consult standard works that give the generally understood meaning of the term. The same approach is appropriate for the technical terms of commerce. The basic definition of a trade term in a standard work like *Incoterms* is a better guide to international understanding than definitions in domestic law[4] or language in a domestic judicial opinion.

---

3. *See* Martin Schmidt-Kessel, Art. 9 para. 7, *in* Schlechtriem & Schwenzer, *CISG Commentary* (2nd English ed. 2005); UNCITRAL Digest Art. 9 para. 7 and decisions cited therein. *See also* Bonell, The Relevance of Courses of Dealing, Usages and Customs in the Interpretation of International Commercial Contracts, *New Directions* 109 (decisions applying Incoterms cited at n.72); Eisemann, *Incoterms and the British Export Trade*, 1965 J. Bus. L. 114; Honnold in *Schmitthoff, Sources* 70; Honnold, Uniform Law and Uniform Trade Terms in *Transnational Law* 161.

4. For example, the definitions of trade terms in U.S. domestic sales law (see §§2–319 through 2–324 of the UCC) are notoriously outmoded and "out-of-synch" with international

Giving weight to the basic provisions of widely-accepted commercial definitions could be supported simply as an intelligent approach to interpretation of the contract without invoking the rules on "usage" in Article 9.

However, some "definitions" of trade terms include details regarding the performance of the parties that may not be "widely known to, and regularly observed by, parties to contracts of the type involved *in the particular trade concerned.*" Article 9(2). These details become binding under Article 9(1) by express incorporation (e.g., "sale C.I.F. Buyer-sport, Incoterms 2000") or in trades where the parties regularly use and rely on this set of trade definitions (Art. 9(2)). On the other hand, proposals to give effect to trade definitions that did not meet the above standard set forth in Article 9(2) were rejected. See §118, *infra*.

116   **(2) Practices Established between Two Parties**

Expectations that have the force of contract can be established by patterns of conduct established by the seller and the buyer. Under Article 9(1) the parties are bound by the "practices which they have established between themselves."[5]

"Practices" are established by a course of conduct that creates an expectation that this conduct will be continued. Article 8(2) (§104 *supra*) provides that the "conduct of a party" (Party A) is to be "interpreted according to the understanding that a reasonable person of the same kind as the other party (Party B) would have had in the same circumstances." Under Article 9(1) a course of conduct by A in past transactions may create an expectation by B that will bind A in a future contract. ***There is a considerable body of CISG decisions addressing the frequency, duration and circumstances of conduct required before***

---

usage. See John A. Spanogle, *Incoterms and UCC* Art. 2 — *Conflicts and Confusions*, 31 Int'l Law. 111 (1997). Recognizing this problem, the drafters of the 2003 proposed revisions to UCC Art. 2 (which revisions have not, at the time this is written, been adopted by any jurisdiction) eliminated all such definitions of trade terms. See the Official Comment to §2–319 of the proposed revisions (declaring that the meaning of "shipping terms such as 'FOB,' 'CIF,' or the like, absent any express agreement to the meaning of the terms, must be interpreted in light of any applicable usage of trade and any course of performance or course of dealing between the parties").

5. For examples of such binding practices drawn from existing CISG decisions, see UNCITRAL Digest Art. 9 para. 6.

a practice can be said to be "established" between parties.[6] Of course A will not be bound if he notifies B of a change before B enters into a new contract; further reliance by B may also become unreasonable when circumstances change. *A U.S. decision has also wisely held that the meaning of a term according to practices established between the parties "controls that term's meaning in the face of a conflicting customary usage of the term."*[7] In short, the reference in Article 9(1) to practices established by the parties is one example of many situations in which binding expectations may be based on conduct. See Articles 19(2), 21(2), 35(2)(b), 47(2), 73(2).

117 ## (3) Binding Trade Usages: Article 9(2)

(a) Inapplicable Concept of Usage.
"Usage" and similar legal ideas have been used in settings that are fundamentally different from the trade usages to which Article 9 refers. "Custom" or "customary law" has sometimes been invoked as a source of law without regard to the intent of the parties. In those settings, "custom" is strictly confined; to bind "a plurality of persons" the custom must be "long established," or even "ancient."[8]

Even more remote from our current problem is "custom" as a source of public international law that binds States. Governments have sometimes viewed such "custom" as inconsistent with their sovereignty and with principles on which their regimes were based. Echoes of these fears were heard in UNCITRAL in early discussions of trade usage but it became evident that construing sales contracts in the light of the expectations current in international trade does not impair the sovereignty of States.

---

6. See the decisions discussed in UNCITRAL Digest Art. 9 para. 7. See also the discussion in Martin Schmidt-Kessel, Art. 9 para. 8, *in* Schlechtriem & Schwenzer, *CISG Commentary* (2nd English ed. 2005).

7. Treibacher Industrie, A.G. v. Allegheny Technologies, Inc., 464 F.3d 1235, 1239 (11th Cir. September 12 2006). *Compare* Martin Schmidt-Kessel, Art. 9 para. 10, *in* Schlechtriem & Schwenzer, *CISG Commentary* (2nd English ed. 2005) ("party intent inferred from practices is presumed to take precedence over trade usages under Art. 9(2)").

8. Allen, Law in the Making, Ch. II and 133 (7th ed. 1964) (discussion of whether custom must date from A.D. 1189); Note, 55 Colum. L. Rev. 1192, 1199 (1955); Honnold, The Influence of the Law of International Trade on Commercial Law, in *Schmitthoff, Sources* 70, 79.

118 **(b) Trade Term Definitions and Usage Standards.** As has been mentioned (§115, *supra*), definitions of trade terms (e.g., Incoterms) may be (and often are) made binding by express agreement (Art. 9(1)). One of the issues that was discussed repeatedly in framing Article 9 was the applicability of such definitions as international trade usage. ULIS (1964) had provisions on practices and usage similar to CISG Article 9 but added the following (ULIS Article 9(3), ULF Article 13(2)):

> Where expressions, provisions or forms of contract commonly used in commercial practice are employed, they shall be interpreted according to the meaning usually give to them in the trade concerned.

Proposals were made in UNCITRAL and at the Diplomatic Conference to include a similar provision; these proposals were resisted on the ground that phrases like "meaning usually given" might subject parties in some areas to practices with which they were not familiar. Article 9(2) had responded to these concerns since usages bound only those "which the *parties knew or ought to have known*" in addition to the requirement that the usage be "widely known to, and regularly observed by, parties to contracts *of the type involved in the particular trade concerned.*" These cumulative requirements did not appear in the proposals for a third paragraph, based on ULIS 9(3), designed to give special effect to trade terms and contract forms. Opposition to these proposals included concern for the problems of parties in developing countries: details embodied in definitions of trade terms and in forms of contract accepted and appropriate in developed, industrialized regions might not be known or appropriate in other parts of the world.[9] *For this reason, a line of U.S. cases[10] proclaiming that the Incoterms definitions of trade terms are incorporated into the Convention pursuant to Article 9(2), and thus are*

9. Rejection of proposals to introduce provisions like ULIS 9(3) on trade terms and standard contracts — UNCITRAL: VIII *YB* 31, *Docy. Hist.* 324 (paras. 84–86); 1980 Conference: *O.R.* 267–269, 202–203, *Docy. Hist.* 488–490, 737–738. Concern for effect in certain regions: *O.R.* 263, 266, *Docy. Hist.* 484 (para. 73), 487 (para. 26). *See also* Bonell, *B-B Commentary* §1.42, 105–106; *Schlechtriem, 1986 Commentary*, 42–43 and n. 130; Eörsi, *Parker Colloq.*, §2.06, p. 2–21; Goldstajn, *Dubrovnik Lectures*, 55, 61; Jacubowski, 2 *New Directions* 549 (1977).

10. BP Oil Int'l, Ltd. v. Empresa Estatal Petroleos de Ecuador, 332 F.3d 333, 337 (5th Cir. June 11 2003); China North Chemical Industries Corp. v. Beston Chemical Corp., 2006 WL 295395, at *6 (U.S.D.C.S.D. Tex. February 7 2006); St. Paul Guardian Ins. Co. v. Neuromed Med. Sys. & Support, GmbH, 2002 WL 465312, at *3–4 (S.D.N.Y. March 26 2002). See also other decisions cited in UNCITRAL Digest Art. 9 para. 17.

binding (presumably in all details) on parties who have employed such terms even if they have not referred to the Incoterms definitions, overstates the authority that those definitions should have under the Convention.[11]

In sum, definitions of trade terms can bind the parties even though they have not been incorporated into the agreement under Article 9(1), but only when their regularity of observance meets the standards of Article 9(2). World-wide legal effect for some details in definitions of trade terms and forms of contract must await the wider homogenization of international practice than has yet been achieved.

119   **(c) Trade Usage Under the Convention.** As we have seen, Article 9(2) applies only to a trade usage "of which the parties knew or ought to have known" and which "in international trade is widely known to, and regularly observed by, parties to contracts of the type involved in the particular trade concerned." This language invokes a pattern of conduct only if it is so "widely known" and "regularly observed" that it can be assumed to be a part of the expectations of the parties.[12]

120   **(d) Usage of Trade in Domestic Law.** Similar principles of contract interpretation have been widely accepted in domestic law.[13] The approach of modern case law has been articulated in the (U.S.A.) Uniform Commercial Code (§1–205(2)), which defines "usage of trade" as "any practice or method of dealing having such regularity

---

11. *Compare* Martin Schmidt-Kessel, Art. 9 para. 26, *in* Schlechtriem & Schwenzer, *CISG Commentary* (2nd English ed. 2005) (Incoterms "do not (generally and to date) represent a trade usage in their entirety" although "individual provisions of these rules can readily be deemed trade usages" and "even if not applicable by virtue of agreement or trade usage, they are still interpretation material to be considered under Art. 8(3)" [citations omitted]).

12. For discussion of this "party-expectation" or "intent" oriented approach to trade usages under Art. 9(2), see Martin Schmidt-Kessel, Art. 9 para. 12, *in* Schlechtriem & Schwenzer, *CISG Commentary* (2nd English ed. 2005).

13. (U.K.) SGA (1893) §55 (*Graveson C. and G.* 54: the comparable provisions of ULIS 9 were "in accordance with English law"); Swedish Sales Act (1905) Art. 1 ("customs of trade or other usages"); Houin, Sale of Goods in French Law, in *Comparative Aspects of Sales (I.C.L.Q.)* 16, 17–18 (1964); Ginsburgs, International Trade Custom, 5 J. Int. L. and Policy 325, 328–332 (1975) (reliance on trade usage by Foreign Trade Arbitration Commission of the U.S.S.R. Chamber of Commerce and Industry); Israeli Contracts Law §26; Israeli Sales Law §5.

of observance in a place, vocation or trade as to justify an expectation that it will be observed with respect to the transaction in question."[14] Such usages (like established practices, *supra* at §116) "give particular meaning to and supplement or qualify" terms of the agreement, according to UCC §1–205(3). Tribunals construe general provisions of the contract in the light of applicable usage since words commonly used in commerce ("draft," "order," "bill," "average") carry a heavy and complex burden of meaning based on the practices with which these words have been associated.[15] A contract provision (like a fish out of water) loses its life when it is removed from its setting.

120.1   **(e) Standards for Usage: Time and Place.**   As we have seen, the Convention gives effect to a usage only if, on an objective basis, it constitutes a part of the contractual expectations of the parties. This premise sheds light on several important questions.

We have discussed the inapplicability of the view that custom, invoked as regulatory law, must be "ancient" or of "long standing." Under Article 9(2), the usage must have been "regularly observed" for a period of time that would justify the conclusion that the parties "knew or ought to have known" of it.

Must the usage be "international?" This question can lead to confusion but the Convention clarifies the issue. Under Article 9(2) the usage must be one which "in international trade is widely *known to*, and regularly *observed by*, parties" to such transactions. A usage that is of local origin (the local practices for packing copra or jute, or the delivery dates imposed by arctic climate) may be applicable if it is "widely known to, and regularly observed by" parties to international transactions involving these situations.[16]

---

14. The same language is continued in the 2001 revisions to Art. 1 of the UCC, which have been adopted by a number of states as this is written. See §1–303(c) of the revised version.
15. Honnold, Letters of Credit, Custom, Missing Documents and the Dixon Case, 53 Colum. L. Rev. 504, 508 (1953). See also the Official Comment 2 to UCC §2–202 (written contracts "are to be read on the assumption that the course of prior dealings between the parties and the usages of trade were taken for granted when the document was phrased. Unless carefully negated they have become an element of the meaning of the words used.").
16. See Martin Schmidt-Kessel, Art. 9 para. 18, *in* Schlechtriem & Schwenzer, CISG Commentary (2nd English ed. 2005); UNCITRAL Digest Art. 9 para. 11 and decisions cited therein. See also Jokela, The Role of Usages in the Uniform Law on International Sales, 10 *Scan. Studies* 83, 93–94. But *cf.* Berman and Kaufman, The Law of International Commercial Transactions, 19 Harv. Int. L.J. 221 (1978) (doubt that Convention admits of local customs).

An example suggests that judges and arbitrators have been careful in applying the requirements of Article 9(2). In various legal systems, letters of confirmation sent in a commercial context are deemed to have binding effect if the other party fails to respond. The binding effect of the recipient's silence may range from incorporating terms into an already-formed contract (as is the case under U.S. law[17] as well as the law of other jurisdictions) to the creation of a contract.[18] A number of reported decisions address whether the practice of treating a party's silence as consent to a commercial letter of confirmation should be deemed a binding trade usage under Article 9(2). The decisions generally appear to reflect care to insure that the practice was likely part of the parties' expectations, attention to the circumstances of the individual transaction, and an ability to escape the gravitational pull of familiar domestic doctrines.[19]

121   (4) Practices and Usages: Relationship to Contract Provisions

As we have seen, Article 9 gives effect to the fact that the parties' established practices and usages of the trade constitute an important part of the parties' expectations. The parties by contract can negate these expectations.[20] See Article 6 at §74, *supra*. However, when the parties do not clearly address and negate implicit expectations based on practices and trade usages the relationship between these implicit expectations and the terms of the contract present delicate problems of interpretation.

Answers to this question must be consistent with the rule of Article 8(3) that in interpreting statements of the parties (including contract provisions) due consideration is to be given to "all relevant circumstances

17. See UCC §2–207(2) (providing for the incorporation, between merchants, of additional non-material terms found in a written confirmation of an already-formed contract, unless the other party objects).

18. For discussion of domestic law approaches in this area see *Notes* to Art. 2:210 in The Commission of European Contact Law, Principles of European Contract Law: Parts I and II Combined and Revised 186–187 (Ole Lando & Hugh Beale, eds. 2000); Martin Schmidt-Kessel, Art. 9 paras. 22 & 24, *in* Schlechtriem & Schwenzer, *CISG Commentary* (2nd English ed. 2005).

19. See UNCITRAL Digest Art. 9 para. 16 and decisions cited therein. See also Martin Schmidt-Kessel, Art. 9 paras. 22–24, *in* Schlechtriem & Schwenzer, *CISG Commentary* (2nd English ed. 2005).

20. See UNCITRAL Digest Art. 9 para. 10 and authority cited n. 21.

of the case including ... any *practices* which the parties have established between themselves, *usages* and any subsequent conduct of the parties." This provision reflects the fact that established practices and usages often create expectations that are so basic that they "go without saying" in making a contract — as is true of a buyer's expectation that the goods will be free of unusual defects (Art. 35(2)(a)) and that he will own the goods (Art. 41). One may not readily conclude that contract provisions were understood to negate such basic expectations.[21]

122 **(5) Practice and Usage and the Convention**

Suppose that a usage specifies a time or place for delivery or a time for the transfer of risk that differs from the rules of Articles 31, 33 or 67. Which is applicable? Under Article 6 (*supra* at §74), "The parties may ... derogate from or vary the effect" of the provisions of the Convention. An applicable practice or usage has the same effect as a contract.[22] Under Article 9(1) practices established by the parties become part of the contract and under Article 9(2) the parties "are considered, unless otherwise agreed, to have *impliedly made applicable to their contract*" those usages that meet the specified criteria. There is one limitation: A practice or usage is invalid if a contract term to the same effect would be invalid under applicable domestic law.[23] Article 4 states that the Convention "is not concerned with: (a) the *validity* of the contract or of any of its provisions or of any *usage*." (See the Commentary to Art. 4, *supra* at §61.) This provision, of course, does not give effect to domestic rules on the circumstances that make a usage applicable; this question is governed by Article 9 of the Convention.

Occasionally domestic legislation or case-law jurisprudence declares that a commercial usage is so firmly established that it has the force of

21. Goldstajn, *Dubrovnik Lectures*, 55, 79; Farnsworth, *Sauveplanne Festschrift* 81, 83–89; Honnold, 53 Colum. L. Rev. 504 (1953). *But cf.* Backus & Harfield, 52 Colum. L. Rev. 589 (1952).

  Some practices and usages are so basic to the parties' expectations that they can survive a standard "integration" clause stating that the writing executed by the parties comprises the entire agreement between them. See *Farnsworth, Contracts* 513.

22. See Martin Schmidt-Kessel, Art. 9 paras. 10 & 14, *in* Schlechtriem & Schwenzer, *CISG Commentary* (2nd English ed. 2005); UNCITRAL Digest Art. 9 para. 10 and decisions cited n. 20; Cour d'appel Grenoble, France, October 21 1999, CLOUT case No. 313, English translation available at http://cisgw3.law.pace.edu/cases/991021f1.html.

23. See Martin Schmidt-Kessel, Art. 9 para. 5, *in* Schlechtriem & Schwenzer, *CISG Commentary* (2nd English ed. 2005); UNCITRAL Digest Art. 9 para. 2.

law and is binding on the parties without proof that the usage meets the standards of Article 9(2). If such a rule is inconsistent with a provision of the Convention does it, like customs established in accordance with Article 9(2), prevail over the Convention?[24] The answer must be no. CISG Article 9(2) governs the circumstances in which a usage may be part of the contract and thereby prevail over provisions of the Convention; the crucial point is that factual compliance with these international standards must be established for each case. Many of the rules of domestic law may be thought to be supported by commercial usage;[25] giving effect to domestic law on this ground would be inconsistent with the standards established by Article 9(2) and would undermine the Convention's central goal to establish uniform law for international trade.

---

24. See, for example, rules derived from usage that a party under specified circumstances who fails to respond to a commercial letter of confirmation will be bound by its contents. Esser, Commercial Letters of Confirmation in International Trade: Austrian, French, German and Swiss Law and Uniform Law under the 1980 Sales Convention, 18 Georgia J. Int. & Comp. L. 427 (1988); *Schlechtriem, 1986 Commentary* 42 and n.129; Heiz, Validity under CISC and Swiss Contract Law, 20 Vanderbilt J. Tr. L. 639 (1987).
25. Many of the rules of (USA) Uniform Commercial Code are supported as consistent with commercial usage.

Article 10.
Definition of "Place of Business"

123   A. Multiple "Places of Business"

The Convention refers to a party's "place of business" in several Articles: 1, 12, 20(2), 24, 31(c), 42(1)(b), 57(1)(a), 69(2) and 96. A commercial enterprise may maintain a central office and various branch offices; in applying the above provisions of the Convention it may be necessary to choose among multiple places of business. For example, Article 1 provides that the Convention is applicable only if the seller and the buyer have their places of business "in different States." In that setting, paragraph (a) of Article 10 was quoted and discussed (see the Commentary to Art. 1, *supra* at §42); the discussion need not be repeated here.

124   (1) The Transitory Agent

During the preparation of the Convention, some delegates were concerned lest "place of business" be construed to extend to a hotel room or other temporary place where a traveling agent might conduct negotiations.[1] Referring to a "permanent" place of business presented drafting difficulties, and most delegates concluded that temporary sojourns would not establish a "place of business." The term that corresponds to "place of business" in the official French text is *établissement* and in the official Spanish text is *establecimiento* — words that seem to be inconsistent with a temporary stopping place.[2] Moreover, as was noted under Article 1 (*supra* at §43), Article 10(a) points to the place of business "which has the closest relationship to the contract *and its performance*"; the Convention's use of "place of business" in the

---

1. See, e.g., *Records 1980 Conference*, Analysis of Comments and Proposals: (Comment by ICC), *O.R.* 73, *Docy. Hist.* 394. This problem was discussed under Art. 1, *supra* at §43.

2. Consideration of the various official language versions is appropriate to promote the Convention's goal, expressed in Art. 7(1) (see §86 *supra*), of "uniformity in its application." *Accord*, Paul Volken, *The Vienna Convention: Scope, Interpretation, and Gap filling*, in Dubrovnik Lectures 19, 41. For general background see Hadari, *Choice of National Law Applicable to the MNE*, 1974 Duke L.J. 1 (1974).

context of Articles 24, 31(c), 42(b) and 69(2) shows that this term refers to a place for the continuing conduct of business. See §43, *supra*.[3]

125   B. No "Place of Business"

Paragraph (b) of Article 10 provides:

Article 10[4]

For the purposes of this Convention ...
(b) if a party does not have a place of business, reference is to be made to his habitual residence.

Parties to international sales transactions will usually have a "place of business"; paragraph (b) was included to avoid a gap in the law when this is not the case.

---

3. See Peter Schlechtriem, Art. 1 para. 27 & Art. 10 para. 2, *in* Schlechtriem & Schwenzer, *CISG Commentary* (2nd English ed. 2005).
4. Article 10 is substantially the same as Art. 9 of the 1978 Draft. Paragraph (b) follows ULIS 1(2) and ULF 1(2). See *Sec. Comm. O.R.* 19, *Docy. Hist.* 409.

Article 11.
Inapplicability of Domestic Requirement
that Contract be in Writing

126 A. Domestic Rules: "Statues of Frauds"

In 1677 the English Parliament (29 Car. II, c. 3) enacted a Statute of Frauds which required a signed writing for the enforcement of a wide variety of transactions including the sale-of-goods (§17)—a requirement that was embodied in the (U.K.) Sale of Goods Act (1893) (§4), was closely followed in the (U.S.A.) Uniform Sales Act (1896) (§4), and formed the basis for an elaborate statute of frauds included in the Uniform Commercial Code (§2–201).

More recently the tide has been running against such formal requirements. In 1954 Britain repealed this part of the Sale-of-Goods Act—a step that has been followed by many of the other countries that had adopted this Act.[1]

Many civil codes imposed formal requirements for the making of contracts, but these requirements were usually made inapplicable to commercial transactions.[2]

Formal requirements in domestic law cannot be relied upon to bar enforcement of an international contract, particularly in litigation before a foreign tribunal. Conflict rules are particularly diverse on this point. One approach, of diminishing vitality, considers statutes of frauds as "evidentiary" and "procedural"—a view that tends to invoke the law of the *forum*. Modern authorities, even in common-law areas, regard

---

1. Law Reform (Enforcement of Contracts) Act 1954 (SGA §4 had not been applicable in Scotland). *See also* Sutton, Formation of Contract: Unity in International Sales of Goods, 16 U.W. Ont. L. Rev. 113, 148–150 (1977) (Art. 11 approved from Australian perspective); *Ont. L. Ref. Com.*, *I Sales* 107–110. *Zweigert & Kötz II (1987)* 45–60 consider this development as part of a general retreat from formalism.

2. For a survey of domestic law formality requirements in the contract law of States of the European Union see n. 4 to Art. 2:101 in The Commission of European Contact Law, Principles of European Contract Law: Parts I and II Combined and Revised 142–143 (Ole Lando & Hugh Beale, eds. 2000). A review of the rules of many countries appears in Cigoj, International Sales, Formation of Contracts, 23 Neth. Int. L. Rev. 257, 270–272 (1976); *Zweigert & Kötz II (1987)*, *supra*.

these rules as "substantive" but in international transactions there will often be doubt as to which law applies.[3]

127   ## B. The Convention

The 1964 Hague Conventions rejected such formal requirements, an approach that was followed in the 1980 Convention.

Article 11[4]

A contract of sale need not be concluded in or evidenced by writing and is not subject to any other requirement as to form. It may be proved by any means, including witnesses.

The significance of the Article 11 rule dispensing with form requirements is illustrated, rather ironically, by a case litigated in U.S. courts during the early period of the Convention's effectiveness in which the parties (Canadian seller, U.S. buyer) realized too late that the Convention, as opposed to U.S. domestic sales law, was applicable.[5] The dispute involved an alleged contract entered into over the telephone, and the parties ended up litigating all the way to the Oregon Supreme Court a difficult question under the UCC Article 2 Statute of Frauds (§2–201). Because of Article 11, of course, the matter is a non-issue under the Convention, and recognizing the Convention's applicability could have saved the parties substantial time and money.

3. The Convention on the Law Applicable to International Sale of Goods (The Hague, 15 June 1955) does not apply to "the form of the contract" (§5). I *Register* 5. On the other hand, the *Hague 1986 PIL Convention*, Art. 11, states rules on which law is applicable to formal validity, subject to possible reservation under Art. 21-1(c). Under (U.S.A.) UCC 1–105, the Statute of Frauds (§2–201) is among the provisions that is applicable when the transaction bears "a reasonable relation" to the enacting State.

4. This article is the same as Art. 10 of the 1978 Draft and, in substance, is the same as ULIS 15 and ULF 3. The second sentence responds to the rule in some countries that a contract may be made without formality but must be proved by written evidence — e.g., proof by witnesses may be excluded. *Zweigert & Kötz II (1987)* 48–56. The legislative history of Art. 11 is presented in connection with Art. 12, §128–129, *infra*.

5. GPL Treatment, Ltd. v. Louisiana-Pacific Corp., 894 P.2d 470 (Or. Ct. App. August 12 1995), *aff'd*, 914 P.2d 682 (Or. S.C. April 11 1996). For extended discussion of the litigation, see Harry M. Flechtner, *Another CISG Case in the U.S. Courts: Pitfalls for the Practitioner and the Potential for Regionalized Interpretation*, 15 J. L. & Com. 127 (1995).

Many authorities declare that the freedom-of-form rule in Article 11 establishes a general principle of the Convention which can be employed, pursuant to Article 7(2), to settle questions within the scope of the CISG that the Convention does not expressly address.[6] In the UNCITRAL proceedings this question arose: Would Article 11 nullify regulations that required certain contracts to be in writing in order to assist in the enforcement of exchange controls and other regulatory programs? This question is answered by the scope of the Convention as defined in Article 4: the Convention "governs only . . . the rights and obligations of the seller and the buyer arising from" the sales contract. (See the Commentary to Art. 4, *supra* at §61). Consequently, the Convention would not interfere with the imposition of sanctions for evasion or violation of a regulatory program; Article 11 merely removes any impediment to enforcement between the parties based on any domestic "requirement as to form."[7]

Article 11 does not bar the parties from imposing formal requirements.[8] An offeror may require that an acceptance must be in writing, so that an oral "acceptance" is not an "assent" to the offer. (See Arts. 18 and 19, *infra* §§157, 165.) Such requirements are often contained in offers.[9] In addition, pursuant to Article 29 (*infra* §200), the parties by a contract in writing may require "any modification or termination by agreement" to be in writing.

A Contracting State, by a "declaration" ("reservation") under Article 96, may protect its formal requirements from Article 11. See Article 12 (discussed in §§128–129 *infra*).

Government procurement. Contracts for the purchase of supplies for a government present special problems of administration, such as the authority of government employees to create financial obligations for the public, and the possibility of favoritism, waste and fraudulent claims

---

6. Peter Schlechtriem, Art. 7 para. 30 at 104, *in* Schlechtriem & Schwenzer, *CISG Commentary* (2nd English ed. 2005); see UNCITRAL Digest Art. 11 para. 2 and decisions cited therein.

7. *Sec. Comm.* draft Art. 10, para. (2) *O.R.* 20, *Docy. Hist.* 410. See Baker, *Enforcement of Contracts Violating Foreign Exchange Laws*, 3 Int. Tr. L.J. 247 (1977), *Giles* 65.

8. See Peter Schlechtriem, Art. 11 paras. 16–17, *in* Schlechtriem & Schwenzer, *CISG Commentary* (2nd English ed. 2005).

9. *General Conditions (Economic Commission for Europe) Plant and Machinery*, No. 188, §2.1. *Accord*, No. 188A, §2.1; No. 574, §2.1. *Contra*, *id.* Potatoes (1980), Fresh Fruit and Vegetables (1979), Dry and Dried Fruit (1979); Art. 7 of all of these general conditions provides that the contract may be "formed orally." *See also* Cigoj, *supra* n. 2, at 272 and n. 67.

to public funds. As a consequence, legislation may impose special requirements for the approval, manner of execution and form for procurement contracts made by governmental units.[10] Sales of government property, such as agricultural commodities acquired under a price support program, often pose fewer governmental problems and may be subject to fewer or no special regulations; the same may be true of contracts made by publicly owned corporations that perform functions such as the supply of electricity or transport.[11]

A procurement contract made with a seller in the same State (the most common setting) would not meet the requirement of internationality of Article 1 (§§40–43, *supra*). When these requirements are met, the fact that the Convention does not deal with problems of authority of an agent or other representative to bind the principal (§§65–66, 98, *supra*) will avoid conflict with many laws on government procurement.[12] A more difficult problem is posed by a procurement contract that would bind the government except for the requirement that it be in written form.

One view is that domestic regulations requiring government procurement contracts to be in written form remain applicable, at least in some cases, despite Article 11. Article 4(a) (§§61–64, supra) states that the "Convention is not concerned with (a) the validity of the contract," so that, arguably, regulations rendering a procurement contract invalid unless in a particular form would not be pre-empted by the Convention. Even in this view, however, the fact that a law states a formal requirement in terms of "validity" does not necessarily preserve the requirement from being overridden by Article 11; in this and many other settings achieving the Convention's central goal of uniform application (Art. 7, §§85–87, *cf.* 72–73, *supra*) requires that the relationship between the Convention and domestic law be decided on the basis of the substance of the domestic rule rather than its form. Thus, it would be necessary to consider whether the law in question was addressed to a special problem posed by government procurement; if so, the law probably should not *(in this view)* be affected by Article 11. *According to this analysis,* formal requirements that are applicable only to government procurement or that are more strict than for comparable private contracts

10. Turpin, Public Contract, VII *Int. Enc. Comp. L.* Ch. 4, §43 n. 250.
11. See Turpin, n. 7 *supra*, §4.
12. See Peter Schlechtriem, Art. 11 para. 15, *in* Schlechtriem & Schwenzer, *CISG Commentary* (2nd English ed. 2005). *See also* J. Whelan, Federal Government Contracts 39–56 (1985); Principles of Government Contract Law (Fed. Acq. Inst., Off. Mgt. & Budget, 1980); J. Zenserle & J. McHale (N.Y., Bender, 1985); UNCITRAL, Model Law on Procurement.

probably should be unaffected by Article 11. This conclusion would also be supported by applicability of the government's regulations to procurement contracts made and performed abroad, and circumstances showing special needs for formal requirements in government contracting.[13]

An alternative analysis, however, suggests that Article 11 overrides formality requirements for government procurement contracts when such requirements go to the validity (under domestic law) of the contract. Note that Article 4(a) does not exclude all questions of validity from the Convention's scope: it merely declares that, "except as otherwise expressly provided in this Convention" the CISG is not concerned with validity. Article 11 arguably is an express provision addressing a validity question, declaring that a contract governed by the Convention is valid even if it is not in a particular form — i.e., it "need not be concluded in or evidenced by writing and is not subject to any other requirement as to form." By this view, and subject to Article 12 (see §§128–129 infra), government procurement contracts need not meet domestic law form requirements in order to be valid when the Convention governs.[14] This conclusion is buttressed by the idea that States who were concerned to preserve formality requirements relating to government procurement were free to do so by making a reservation under Article 96 (see §§128–129 infra); those that failed to do so presumably were willing to forego such protections. As noted previously, however, the fact that the Convention does not address agency issues, and thus does not supplant domestic law governing agency questions, limits the impact of Article 11 on special domestic requirements for procurement contracts.

127.1 C. Rejection of Part II, Formation of Contract: A Problem?

An Unnecessary Concern: In ratifying CISG, four Scandinavian States (Denmark, Finland, Norway and Sweden) exercised the privilege, provided by Article 92, not to be bound by Part II, Formation of the Contract. (These States had agreed among themselves on uniform rules for contract formation.) Article 11, above, provides that a contract of sale

---

13. See works cited by Turpin, n. 7, *supra*.
14. *Accord*, Peter Schlechtriem, Art. 11 paras. 11 & 15, *in* Schlechtriem & Schwenzer, *CISG Commentary* (2nd English ed. 2005).

may be concluded without a writing or other formality — a provision dealing with contract formation. Could one imagine that, to give full effect to the rejection of Article II, Formation of Contract, Article 11 might be considered a part of Article II and therefore not applicable to the above four Scandinavian States? *The answer should be no. This argument has been rejected in case law;*[15] *the domestic laws of the Scandinavian States that made the Article 92 reservation, furthermore, apparently do not require a writing or other formality for commercial sales of goods and thus are not in conflict with Article 11.*[16]

127.2 D. "Hybrid" Contracts

Contracts that include a sale-of-goods aspect along with elements that are not properly so characterized present special challenges to the application of Article 11. We have already examined questions concerning the general applicability of the Convention to such "hybrid" or "mixed" contracts in connection with Article 3 (see §§60–60.6 supra). With regard to mixed sales/service contracts, Article 3 appears to require that the contract be treated either as wholly governed by the Convention or, if the service element constitutes the "preponderant part" of the seller's obligations, as wholly beyond the scope of the CISG. This suggests that, if the Convention is applicable to a hybrid goods/services transaction, Article 11 should apply to the contract as a whole; thus any domestic formality requirements applicable to service contracts would be supplanted. For example, U.S. Statute of Frauds rules requiring a writing for contracts that cannot be performed within one year (or some other specified period) from their formation should not apply to a contract governed by the Convention, even if the contract includes service obligations extending more than a year from the time of contract formation. In the case of other kinds of mixed contracts, the same approach might not be proper. Suppose a single contract requires a party to transfer both goods and real property to the buyer. Should domestic formality requirements applicable to

---

15. Oberlandesgericht München, Germany, March 8 1995, CLOUT case No. 134, additional English abstract available in UNILEX at http://www.unilex.info/case.cfm?pid=1&do=case&id=119&step=Abstract.

16. See n. 4(a) to Art. 2:101 in The Commission of European Contact Law, Principles of European Contract Law: Parts I and II Combined and Revised 142 (Ole Lando & Hugh Beale, eds. 2000); §127.1 of the third edition of this treatise.

sales of real property remain applicable to the real-estate portion of the transaction? In other words, should the transaction be divided into two parts (sale of goods and sale of real estate), and the freedom-from-form-requirements rule of Article 11 applied only to the sales part?[17] *Professor Schlechtriem suggests the answer is yes.*[18] *That conclusion appears justified given the particularly strong association of real property issues with local law, and the Convention's express declaration in Article 4(b) that, unless otherwise expressly provided, it is not concerned with "the effect which the contract may have on the property in the goods sold."*

17. In the case of hybrid goods/real property sales, that "divvying up" approach is adopted in U.S. domestic law. See UCC §2–304(2).

18. Peter Schlechtriem, Art. 11 para. 7, *in* Schlechtriem & Schwenzer, *CISG Commentary* (2nd English ed. 2005).

Article 12.
Declaration by Contracting State Preserving Its Domestic Requirements as to Form

128   **A. The Conflict**

Laws of the U.S.S.R. imposed strict formal requirements for the making of foreign trade contracts. In the UNCITRAL proceedings representatives of the U.S.S.R. indicated that preserving these requirements was of great importance to protect established patterns for the making of foreign trade contracts. Most delegates, however, felt strongly that formal requirements were inconsistent with modern commercial practice — particularly in view of the speed and informality that characterized many transactions in a market economy.[1]

129   **B. The Resolution: A Reservation Under Article 96**

The result was a compromise. In Part IV (Final Provisions), Article 96 authorizes a Contracting State "whose legislation requires contracts of sale to be concluded in or evidenced by writing" to make a "declaration" that Article 11 (and certain other provisions of the Convention affecting formal requirements) "does not apply where any party has his place of business in that State." Article 12 articulates the effect of a declaration under Article 96.

Article 12[2]

Any provision of article 11, article 29 or Part II of this Convention that allows a contract of sale or its modification or termination by agreement or any offer, acceptance or other indication of intention to be made in any form other than in writing does not apply where

1. Early discussion in UNCITRAL leading to Arts. 11 and 12; II *YB* 48–49, 60–61, VI *YB* 96, 111–112, 53–54, VIII *YB* 94–95, 76; *Docy. Hist.* 53–54; 66–67, 221, 236–237, 244–245, 258–259, 277.
2. This article is substantially the same as Art. 11 of the 1978 Draft. Art. 12, in substance a repetition of Art. 96, was inserted immediately following Art. 11 to draw attention to the fact that Art. 11 might be affected by a reservation. Discussion in UNCITRAL leading to Arts. 12 and 96: IX *YB* 70–71, VIII *YB* 33–34, *Docy. Hist.* 302–303, 366–367, 326–327. The 1980 Conference: *O.R.* 74, 20, 271–275, 90–92, *Docy. Hist.* 395, 410, 492–496, 662–664.

any party has his place of business in a Contracting State which has made a declaration under article 96 of this Convention. The parties may not derogate from or vary the effect of this article.

The final text, above, followed rejection of a proposal that the formalities of one "declaring" State (including matters such as registration, etc.) would govern both parties to the contract. This proposal was rejected on the ground that it would extend formal requirements beyond prevailing law, which depended on agreement of the parties, or conflicts (PIL) rules of the forum.

The crucial language of the compromise (which admittedly is difficult to parse) provides that any provision of Articles 11, 29 or Part II of the Convention that allows a transaction "in a form other than in writing does not apply where any party has his place of business in a Contracting State which has made a declaration under article 96 of this Convention."

At the time this is written, the following States have made declarations under Articles 12 and 96: Argentina, Belarus, Chile, China, Hungary, Latvia, Lithuania, Paraguay, Russian Federation and Ukraine.[3] The language of Articles 12 and 96 has led to uncertainty; perhaps concrete examples will help:

Example 12A. Seller (S), in State S, claims that S and Buyer (B), in State B agreed on a sale of a tractor by S to B. The agreement was not embodied in a writing. State B requires a signed writing, and has made a declaration under Articles 12 and 96 rejecting Article 11, *supra*, that dispenses with such formalities. State S does not require a writing or other formalities. Seller (S) shipped the tractor to B, whose place of business was in State B, a "reservation" State requiring a written agreement. B refused to receive or accept the tractor or to pay, on the ground that the alleged agreement was not in writing. The above basic, but incomplete, facts need to be considered in different situations.

Case A. S sued B in State B, *whose PIL principles led to the application of the law of State B to the transaction.* Witnesses testified that S and B had agreed on the sale. Nevertheless, in the absence of further facts (e.g., a request by B for shipment, or B's acceptance of delivery of the tractor that would create an estoppel) it seems that the tribunal in B would dismiss S's suit. This is the typical case envisaged by Articles 12

---

3. Estonia initially made an Art. 96 reservation, but it withdrew that declaration (as permitted by Art. 97(4)) in 2004. See UNCITRAL, Status: 1980 — United Nations Convention on Contracts for the International Sale of Goods, http://www.uncitral.org/uncitral/en/uncitral_texts/sale_goods/1980CISG_status.html.

and 96. Suppose the law of State B requires not only a written agreement but also additional formalities such as registration in a specified public office in State B. When the Convention applies, should fora in State B (or anyplace else) refuse to enforce a written agreement because it has not been so filed? This added formality is not preserved by State B's Article 96 reservation because Articles 12 and 96 derogate only from the provisions of the Convention that permit an agreement "in any form other than in writing."[4]

Case B. Alternatively, suppose S sued B in State S, whose conflicts rules point to the application of the law of State S. As in Case A, there are no further facts (e.g., a request for shipment or acceptance of the tractor that would create an estoppel). *In the first editions of this treatise it was argued that, because the tribunal's PIL rules point to the laws of State S, the form requirements of State B should be inapplicable, and thus the oral contract would be enforceable.[5] To find otherwise, it was argued, "would make the formal requirements of the [Article 96] declaring State more widely applicable than under present law." It would also be contrary to the wording of Article 12, which says only that the Convention's freedom-of-form rules "do not apply" if one party is located in a State that has made an Article 96 reservation, but does not provide for the automatic application of the form rules of the reserving State. The third edition of this treatise adopted a different position: it argued that the form requirements of State B, although inapplicable under the tribunal's conflicts rules, should nevertheless prevent enforcement of the oral agreement because "(1) 'any party' [a phrase used in Article 12] could refer to the application of Article 12 to both parties to the transaction, and (2) the acceptance by the Convention of the need, felt by some States, for protection against claims unsupported by a written agreement."[6] The reviser of the current edition believes that the position adopted in the first editions of the treatise rather than the analysis proposed in the third edition is correct because it more accurately reflects the drafting history and purposes of*

---

4. *Accord*, Peter Schlechtriem, Art. 12 para. 5, *in* Schlechtriem & Schwenzer, *CISG Commentary* (2nd English ed. 2005).

5. See, e.g., §129 of the 2nd edition (1991) of this treatise. This position is also consistent with the approach taken in several decisions (see UNCITRAL Digest Art. 12 para. 4 and decisions cited in n. 7) as well as the view advocated by Professor Schlechtriem (see Peter Schlechtriem, Art. 12 para. 2, *in* Schlechtriem & Schwenzer, *CISG Commentary* (2nd English ed. 2005)).

6. Section 129 of the 3rd edition of this treatise. See also UNCITRAL Digest Art. 12 para. 4 and decisions cited in n. 8.

Articles 96 and 12. To apply State B's domestic law form requirements where the tribunal's PIL principles would not lead to the application of the law of State B, furthermore, would create a perverse incentive for States to make a declaration under Article 96 in order to extend the influence of that State's laws; this would further undermine the Convention's goal of achieving uniform international sales law.

Case C. Suppose that the forum's conflicts rules point to the law of State S, which has not made an Article 96 reservation, but that the domestic law of State S would require the contract to be in written form. Should the forum apply the domestic form requirements of State S and refuse to enforce the oral contract? In these circumstances Professor Schlechtriem (among many others) argues that Article 11 comes back into play, and the contract is enforceable regardless of form.[7] That position is appealing from a policy perspective. As Professor Schlechtriem notes, "[o]therwise, rules as to form would be applicable which would not apply at all unless that Contracting State [i.e., State S in the current example] had made a reservation."[8] In other words, since State S, which ratified the Convention without the Article 96 reservation, thereby indicated that it was willing to forego its domestic form requirements for international sales, why should the Article 96 reservation of a different State (State B) bring those form requirements back into play?

The problem with this approach, as sensible as its result appears, is that it is impossible to reconcile it with the text of Article 12. Article 12 provides that, where "any party" to a sale governed the CISG has its place of business in an Article 96 reservatory State, then any rule of the Convention that permits a contract to be in non-written form "does not apply." Thus because Buyer in Example 12A is located in a State that made an Article 96 reservation, the rule of Article 11 permitting non-written contracts "does not apply" to the transaction. The result is a gap in the Convention on the question of written-form requirements — either an external gap (because, as result of Articles 96 and 12, the matter is beyond the scope of the Convention in this case) or an internal gap; in the latter case, there is no source of Convention "general principles" that would, under Article 7(2), permit non-written contracts because the relevant aspects of Article 11 are inapplicable to the case. Thus whether the gap is deemed external or internal, the

---

7. Peter Schlechtriem, Art. 12 para. 3, *in* Schlechtriem & Schwenzer, *CISG Commentary* (2nd English ed. 2005).
8. *Id.*

result is the same: the matter must be referred to the non-Convention law applicable under PIL rules, just as it was in Case A above (where it led, non-controversially, to the application of the domestic form rules of State B[9]). Therefore, if PIL rules point to the law of State S, and State S has an applicable domestic law that would require the contract to be in writing, that domestic form requirement applies in the case under consideration.

The conclusion in the prior sentence, however, must be parsed carefully. Just because State S has a domestic rule requiring a contract of sale to be in writing does not mean that rule is necessarily applicable (as a matter of State S's domestic law) to a contract that is otherwise governed by the Convention. In the United States, for example, §2–201 of the UCC requires a writing for sales contracts where the price is $500 or more, but the reviser of the current edition of this treatise would argue strongly that this provision is not intended to and should not be applied when the transaction is otherwise governed by the Convention rather than by Article 2 of the UCC. Thus if the United States were State S in the case under consideration, there is (arguably) no applicable domestic law requiring a writing, and the oral contract should be enforced if conflicts rules lead to the application of U.S. law. It should be emphasized, however, that this is a question of domestic law, not the Convention. If the domestic law of State S, properly interpreted (as per domestic law), includes an applicable rule requiring the contract between S and B to be in written form, it should be applied in the case under consideration.

In short, the view espoused by many that the freedom-of-form rule in Article 11 applies where one party is located in an Article 96 reservatory State but PIL rules lead to the application of the law of a non-reserving Contracting State simply contradicts Article 12: this article provides that, where "any party" is located in a reserving State, the Article 11 rule "does not apply." To achieve the result for which others argue, Article 12 would have to be amended so that it comes into play only "where any party has his place of business in a Contracting State that has made a declaration under Article 96 of this Convention and the rules of private international law lead to the application of the law

---

9. A tribunal would also clearly have to resort to conflicts rules if both State B and State S had made an Art. 96 reservation, the each State's domestic form requirements differed in a relevant way (e.g., one State requires the entire agreement to be written, while the other requires only material terms to be in writing).

of that State." The drafters of the Convention and the States that ratified it, however, did not include the underlined language.

It is worth noting that the result argued for here — employing the domestic form requirements of a non-reservatory State when Article 12 is triggered and PIL principles point to the law of the non-reserving State — is not simply the product of the "plain meaning" approach to the text of Article 12. The reviser of the current edition of this treatise is no partisan of the "plain meaning" approach, and Professor Honnold appears to have shared this view. The interpretation espoused here is not advanced because the text of Article 12 is so clear that contrary indications concerning the meaning of that text should be ignored: if, for example, the history of the Convention indicated that the drafters and Contracting States intended Article 11 to apply in the case under consideration, the reviser might well consider the text of Article 12 as the product of careless drafting. There are, however, simply no such indications in the drafting history of the CISG or in the rest of the text of the Convention.

The only real argument against the construction of Article 12 advanced here is that another view (Professor Schlechtriem's) leads to a more sensible result. A preference for a different result, of course, is not a sufficient reason to ignore the meaning of a text. A widely-accepted canon of interpretation declares that a reasonable or sensible reading is to be preferred over a nonsensical one; the interpretation proposed here, however, yields a result that can be justified: applying the domestic law form requirements of State S, even though it did not make an Article 96 reservation, arguably reflects the norm of reciprocity. In other words, if State B insists on its domestic form requirements (through the Article 96 reservation) when PIL rules lead to the application of its law, the domestic form requirements of State S can fairly be applied when PIL rules point its way. The reviser of the current edition does not find this "tit-for-tat" justification appealing or particularly in keeping with the Convention's general spirit of international cooperation, but a similar reciprocity-oriented rationale appears to lie behind the Article 95 reservation (which prevents application of the Convention if one party is located in a non-Contracting State). Thus this rationale cannot be said to be outside the Convention's ethos. Since the proper interpretation of the words used in Article 12 leads to the view advocated here, mere commentators are not endowed with the power to change what was agreed to by the sovereign Contracting States, even if they would prefer a different result.

Article 13.
Telegram and Telex as a "Writing"

130   The Convention imposes no formal requirements with respect to the notices, requests or declarations to which it refers.[1] All such communications may be made orally (face-to-face or by telephone) or by other means.

The Convention refers to "writing" in Article 21(2) ("letter or other writing containing a late acceptance") and in Article 29(2) (contract in writing that requires written modification or agreement).[2] These provisions are supplemented by the following definition:

Article 13[3]

For the purposes of this Convention "writing" includes telegram and telex.

The Convention's few references to a "writing" do not require a signature or other validating mark or sign. Hence, no problem regarding signatures arises in connection with communication by telegram or telex.

Article 13 was drafted prior to substantial commercial use of electronic transmission of facsimiles (FAX), the making of contracts by electronic data exchange (EDI), or the use of email. The statement in Article 13 that "writing" *includes* telegram and telex does not fix the outer limits of this term as used in Articles 21(2) and 29(2) of the Convention; electronic developments such as FAX, EDI and email do not present more serious problems of verification than "telegram and telex" and should be assimilated to the definition of "writing" in Article 13.

Questions can arise as to whether electronic communications can satisfy the requirements of a "signature" under domestic statutes of

---

1. See Arts. 39(1), 43(1), 46(2) & (3), 47(2), 48(2) & (3), 63(1), 67(2), 71(3), 79(4), and 88(1).

2. *Cf.* Art. 18(2) ("oral" offer must be accepted immediately); Art. 24 (in defining when an offer, acceptance or declaration of assent "reaches" a party, there is a distinction between statements made "orally" and those "delivered").

3. Article 13 was added at the Diplomatic Conference. *O.R.* 269, 424, *Docy. Hist.* 490, 645. The discussion emphasized the application of this provision to the modification of agreements by telegram or telex.

frauds.[4] However, this question does not arise under the Convention since references to "writing" in Articles 21(2) and 29(2) do not require a "signature." Whether electronic communications satisfy domestic formal requirements preserved by a declaration (reservation) under Article 96 (see Art. 12 at §§128–129, *supra*) depends on the domestic law preserved by the reservation. As we have seen (§129, *supra*), domestic formality requirements in States that have not made an Article 96 reservation (e.g., the U.S.A.) may be applicable in transactions with parties in States that have made a reservation under Article 96.

The United Nations Convention on the Use of Electronic Communications in International Contracts[5] ("CUECIC") is an UNCITRAL text, issued in November 2005, that addresses many of the contract law issues raised by modern means of communication. Although not limited to contracts for the sale of goods,[6] CUECIC was expressly designed to work in tandem with the CISG,[7] and its application together with the Sales Convention would insure the proper operation of the Sales Convention in e-commerce. Article 8(1) of CUECIC provides: "A communication or contract shall not be denied validity on the sole ground that it is in the form of an electronic communication." Article 9(2) of CUECIC provides: "Where the law requires that a communication or contract should be in writing, or provides consequences for the absence of a writing, that requirement is met by an electronic communication if the information contained therein is accessible so as to be usable for subsequent reference." Article 9(3) of CUECIC provides for the satisfaction of signature requirements using electronic communications. Although CUECIC has not yet entered into force at the time this is written (effectiveness requires ratification or accession by three States), interest in this convention appears high.

---

4. Ways of meeting this problem are discussed in a thorough study: The Commercial Use of Electronic Data Interchange — A Report and Model Trading Partner Agreement, 45 Bus. Law. 16451749 (1990). For other recent studies in this field see the Introduction to Part II, Formation of the Contract at §132.1, *infra*.

5. Text available on the UNCITRAL website at http://www.uncitral.org/pdf/english/texts/electcom/06-57452_Ebook.pdf.

6. See CUECIC Art. 1.

7. See Art. 20(1) of CUECIC.

Part II.

FORMATION OF THE CONTRACT

(Articles 14–24)

INTRODUCTION TO PART II OF THE CONVENTION

131 ## A. Relation Between Part II and Other Parts of the Convention

Part II of the Convention, Formation of the Contract, is subject to the rules of Part I (Arts. 1–13) on the scope and interpretation of the Convention,[1] but is independent of Part III (Arts. 25–88) which deals with the obligations of the parties to the contract. Article 92 (Part IV) permits a Contracting State to declare that it will not be bound either by Part II or by Part III. This reflects aspects of the Convention's history that were described in the Overview (Ch. 1, *supra* at §4) — the completion in 1964 of two Conventions, one on Formation (ULF) and one on Sales (ULIS), and UNCITRAL's decision to prepare a single Convention, subject to an option to adhere to only Part II on Formation or Part III on Sales.[2] *Although no State has yet availed itself of the opportunity provided in Article 92 to declare that it is not bound by Part III ("Sale of goods") of the CISG, the Scandinavian States have declared that they are not bound by Part II of the Convention ("Formation of contract"). See §127.1 supra. As a result the reserving States, under Article 92(2), are not considered "Contracting States" with respect to matters governed by Part II. As is explored in greater depth in the discussion of Article 92 (see §467 infra), the Article 92 declarations by Denmark, Finland, Iceland, Norway and Sweden will in certain circumstances prevent the application of Articles 14–24 to issues of contract formation.*

---

1. See Peter Schlechtriem, *Introduction to* Arts. 14–24 para. 1, *in* Schlechtriem & Schwenzer, *CISG Commentary* 176 (2nd English ed. 2005); UNCITRAL Digest Part 2 paras. 14–15.
2. On the interpretation of references to "the contract" in Art. 1 in the setting of Part II of the Convention, see the Commentary to Art. 1, *supra* at §48 n.16.

132   **B. Structure of Part II**

(1) Summary and Scope

The first four articles (14–17) deal with the offer — the minimum criteria for an offer (Art. 14), and the withdrawal (Art. 15), revocation (Art. 16) or termination (Art. 17) of an offer. The next five articles (18–22) deal with acceptance — "acceptances" that do not match the offer (Art. 19), the period allowed for acceptance (Arts. 20 and 21), and withdrawal of an acceptance (Art. 22). The two final articles (Arts. 23 and 24) relate to the time when a contract is concluded.

Although Part II of the CISG contains a coherent and extensive system of rules addressing contract formation, some matters relating to the formation of an international sales contract are beyond the Convention's scope. As noted earlier (§66 supra), the CISG does not govern issues of agency, authority or capacity: thus whether a party had the authority to make or accept an offer on behalf of another, or whether a person's age or mental condition disables him or her from entering into a contract, are matters beyond the scope of the CISG; they remain subject to applicable non-Convention law as determined under rules of private international law.

The effect of the death of the offeror or offeree or the commencement of insolvency proceedings before a contract has been concluded or the commencement of insolvency proceedings raises issues relating to the scope of Part II. For example, U.S. domestic contract law denies effect in some circumstances to an acceptance made after the offeror has died.[3] The CISG contains nothing expressly addressing this situation. If the matter is within the scope of the Convention, the silence of the text could be interpreted as a rejection of the rule, or it might be treated as an "internal gap" which under Article 7(2) should be filled by reference to the Convention's general principles; only in the absence of relevant general CISG would applicable non-Convention law be invoked to resolve the issue. On the other hand, if the matter is beyond the scope of the Convention then the issue should be subject directly to applicable non-Convention law. Professor Schlechtriem advocates the latter approach,[4] and his position has much to

---

3. See John Edward Murray, Jr., *Murray on Contracts* §42(E) at 124–125 (4th ed. 2001).
4. Peter Schlechtriem, Art. 15 paras. 7–8 and Art. 17 para. 6, in Schlechtriem & Schwenzer, *CISG Commentary* (2nd English ed. 2005). If the issue is deemed to fall into an "internal gap" subject to Art. 7(2), Professor Schlechtriem suggests that there are no relevant general principles

recommend it. The issue of the effect of the offeror's death on unaccepted offers, for example, appears analogous to capacity issues that are clearly beyond the scope of the CISG, and resolving the issue under applicable non-Convention law finds support in the drafting history of the CISG.[5]

132.1 ## (2) "Offer" and "Acceptance" in Statutory Drafting and Contract Formation

As the above summary indicates, most of the provisions of Part II are concerned with "offer" and "acceptance," an emphasis more consistent with traditional patterns of contract formation than with current practices in international trade. Nonetheless, rules on offer and acceptance are still needed when the only relevant facts are two communications — one that may (or may not) be an "offer" and one that may (or may not) be an "acceptance." In this setting different rules are needed for each communication: An "offer" may be made at any time but the time for "acceptance" is limited (Arts. 18–21); "offers" in some circumstances may be revoked or expire but an effective "acceptance" closes a contract (Arts. 16, 18(2)). *These rules have been applied not only to the formation of the original international sales contract but also to the conclusion of subsequent agreements affecting that original contract, such as agreements to modify or terminate it.*[6]

However, serious problems arise if one assumes that contracts can be made only if they fit this two-step formula. For example, a typical export sale may be instituted by an exchange of letters, emails or other communications (including *a pro-forma* invoice), none of which may be an "offer" or "acceptance." Thereafter, communications will discuss descriptions and prices of the goods, the expected dates and methods of shipment, and the methods of payment — perhaps by the buyer's arrangement for the issuance of a letter of credit and its confirmation by a bank near the seller; a contract may not be intended to be closed before the letter of credit is confirmed and in some cases only when the

---

to be derived from the CISG, and thus the issue would still be subject to applicable non-Convention law. *Id.* Art. 15 para. 8. For contrary views, see the commentary cited *id.* n. 16.

5. See Peter Schlechtriem, Art. 15 paras. 7–8, in Schlechtriem & Schwenzer, *CISG Commentary* (2nd English ed. 2005) (noting that the CISG drafters opted not to retain a ULF rule that addressed the effect of the death or incapacity of the offeror, and concluding that this rejection "leaves one to conclude that those matters fall outside the scope of the Convention *ratione materiae*").

6. See UNCITRAL Digest Part 2 para. 2 and decisions cited nn. 2 & 3.

seller ships the goods and presents the necessary documents (invoice, bill of lading, insurance policy and draft) to the confirming bank.[7] In short, in many transactions it is difficult or impossible to isolate an "offer" and "acceptance."[8]

The Convention does not compel the stretching or amputation of a living understanding to fit the Procrustean bed of "offer" and "acceptance." Under Article 18(1) a contract may be concluded any "statement" or "conduct" that indicates "assent to an offer." See §§158–160, *infra*. In addition, Article 8(3) gives effect to "understanding" that is derived from "all relevant circumstances of the case including the negotiations, any practices which the parties have established between themselves, usages and any subsequent conduct of the parties."[9] In short, the Convention and its general principles accommodate both the simple exchange of two communications and also the development of a contract when it is impossible to isolate an "offer" and "acceptance."[10]

This flexibility is becoming increasingly important with the development and expanding use of electronic means of communications and programmed systems for making commercial arrangements by "Electronic Data Interchange (EDI)." To help commerce cope with these problems, UNCITRAL has undertaken a variety of initiatives. In 1996, UNCITRAL adopted the Model Law on Electronic Commerce, and a Guide to enactment of the Model Law (A/51/17). *Legislation influenced by this model law has been enacted in a large number of States, including the United States (the Uniform Electronic*

---

7. See §339.2 *infra* and the Prototype Export Transaction in J. Honnold, Sales & Sales Financing 310–339 (5th ed. 1984).

8. *Schlechtriem (1986)* 48 and references at notes 150–151; Eörsi, *Lausanne Colloquium* 43–44, *cf.* 1 Schlesinger, *Formation* 1585.

9. Article 8 is placed in Part I of the Convention and subsequently applies to Part II on Formation as well as to Part III.

10. See Peter Schlechtriem, *Introduction to* Arts 14–24 paras. 2, 3 & 5, *in* Schlechtriem & Schwenzer, *CISG Commentary* (2nd English ed. 2005). *Cf.* UNCITRAL Digest Part 2 paras. 5–6. In UNCITRAL's 1978 review of the Working Group Draft Convention on Formation an amendment was proposed to articulate the principle stated above. Some objected that in some domestic systems a contract "cannot be formed without the existence of an offer or an acceptance"; others stated that no amendment was needed since the principle "was self-evident." Sponsors then withdrew the proposal "because of the extreme difficulty of formulating an acceptable text" (paras. 103–104). IX YB 38–39, *Docy. Hist.* 372–373. In this writer's view the substance of the proposal had been implicit in Arts. 8(3) and 18 mentioned above.

Article 23, *infra*, on the time of completion of the contract, rounds out provisions that address problems that arise from claims that an acceptance is too late (e.g., Art. 18(2)), and does not suggest that a contract can not exist if it is impossible to determine "the moment" when it was made.

Transactions Act, adopted in 47 states and the District of Columbia).[11]
In 2001 UNCITRAL promulgated the Model Law on Electronic Sig-
natures, which has been enacted by several States.[12] *And, as discussed*
earlier (see §130 infra), in 2005 the United Nations Convention on the
Use of Electronic Communications in International Contracts
("CUECIC"), an UNCITRAL project, was issued. CUECIC in
particular, when it becomes applicable, may have a significant impact
the legal status and effect of electronic communications under the
CISG, particularly in the area of contract formation addressed in
Part II. The impact of CUECIC will be addressed in the analysis of
individual substantive provisions of Part II of the Convention.

Other specific issues relating to the scope and application of the
contract formation rules in Part II of the Convention are discussed
in connection with individual Convention provisions. See the analysis
of the application of the Convention to framework agreement (§56.2
supra); the discussion of pre-contractual liability (culpa in contra-
hendo) in transactions governed by the CISG (§§145–151 infra);
the examination of contract formation by failure to respond to a
commercial confirmation (§160 infra); and the incorporation of
standard terms under the Convention (§§236–237 infra).

132.2 ## C. Derogating from or Opting Out of the Convention's Contract Formation Rules

Under Article 6 (supra §§74 et seq.) the parties can, subject to Article
12, derogate from any provision of the CISG, or opt out of the Con-
vention entirely. The power to derogate or opt out, obviously, encom-
passes the contract formation rules in Part II (Articles 14–24), but
exercising this power presents special conceptual challenges. Derogat-
ing from or opting out of other parts of the Convention, such as the
"Sale of Goods" provisions of Part III (Articles 25–88), generally
requires an agreement between both parties, as suggested by the
reference to plural "parties" in Article 6. The point of the rules in

---

11. See UNCITRAL, Status: 1996 — UNCITRAL Model Law on Electronic Commerce, http://www.uncitral.org/uncitral/en/uncitral_texts/electronic_commerce/1996Model_status. html.

12. See UNCITRAL, Status: 1996 — UNCITRAL Model Law on Electronic Signatures, http://www.uncitral.org/uncitral/en/uncitral_texts/electronic_commerce/2001Model_status. html.

CISG Part II, however, is to determine whether the parties have a contract. How can you decide whether the parties have changed or made inapplicable the contract formation rules of the Convention before determining whether the parties have an agreement at all? The conceptual problem is particularly acute — threatening circular logic — where recognition of the parties' power to determine or change the applicable contract formation rules would result in failure to conclude a contract: if the parties have no agreement, how did they opt out or derogate?

The problem does not arise if the parties have entered into a pre-sale framework agreement (see supra §56.2) providing that specified (or all) provisions of Part II will not apply to future dealings between them. Is this rare scenario the only way to derogate from or opt out of the Convention's contract formation rules? Suppose, for example, an offer states that it can be revoked if the revocation is dispatched before the offeror receives an acceptance. Is this an effective derogation from Article 16(1) (supra §140), so that a revocation received after the offeree dispatches an acceptance (but sent before the offeror received the acceptance) prevents conclusion of a contract? Or suppose the offer provides that the transaction will be governed by specified domestic law rather than the Convention — an attempt to opt out of the Convention, including Part II, in toto. In both these situations, the policy that the offeror is master of the offer and can determine its terms, along with the fact that the offeree is on notice of the non-applicability of the Convention's contract formation rules, may argue in favor of recognizing the offer's unilateral attempt to derogate from or opt out of the rules of Part II of the CISG. On the other hand, an offeror clearly should not have the power, unilaterally, to derogate from the rule in Article 18(1) that the offeree's silence or inactivity does not by itself constitute acceptance; otherwise, the whole purpose of that rule would be subverted.

Can the offeree also "unilaterally" derogate from or opt out of the Convention's contract formation rules? Suppose an offeree transmits a rejection of the offer, but the rejection states that it does not terminate the offer. Is this an effective derogation from Article 17 (supra §§152 et seq.), so that the offer remains open despite the rejection? Or suppose the offeree transmits a purported acceptance that attempts to opt out of CISG Part II completely. Such attempts at "unilateral" derogation or opt out by the offeree could constitute "different terms" that, under Article 19 (supra §§165 et seq.), might or might not prevent contract formation, depending on whether they are deemed "material." Alternatively, perhaps the "different or additional" terms referred to in Article 19 encompass only those that would affect the parties' rights after the contract was formed. Under the latter approach, changes in contract formation rules would be outside the scope of Article 19, although an attempt to opt out of the Convention generally would still be covered (at least to the extent it specified the law applicable after a contract was concluded). Working out proper results in this and the multitude of other scenarios involving attempts to derogate from or opt out of the contract formation rules of the CISG presents significant challenges.

Article 14.
Criteria for an Offer

133   The basic criterion for an offer, under prevailing law and the Convention, is whether one party has indicated to another "the intention...to be bound in case of acceptance." In applying this standard, two subsidiary factors need to be taken into account—the number of people addressed and the definiteness of the proposal. These standards are set forth in this opening article of Part II:

Article 14[1]

    (1) A proposal for concluding a contract addressed to one or more specific persons constitutes an offer if it is sufficiently definite and indicates the intention of the offeror to be bound in case of acceptance. A proposal is sufficiently definite if it indicates the goods and expressly or implicitly fixes or makes provision for determining the quantity and the price.

    (2) A proposal other than one addressed to one or more specific persons is to be considered merely as an invitation to make offers, unless the contrary is clearly indicated by the person making the proposal.

134 A. Indication of Intent to be Bound

    When one party is in doubt over whether the other intends to be bound or merely to open negotiations the question can usually be resolved quickly by phone or wire.[2] Moreover, doubts suggested by the bare text of the parties' statements will often be dissipated when (as Art. 8 requires) those statements are interpreted in their full context, including "the negotiations, any practices which the parties have established between themselves, usages and any subsequent conduct of the parties."

---

1. Art. 14 is the same as Art. 12 of the 1978 Draft Convention. *Cf.* ULF 4. Legislative history of Arts. 14 and 55; 1 YB 194, VI YB 73–74, VIII YB 48–49, IX YB 38–39, *O.R.* 21, 275–277, 292–295; *Docy. Hist.* 32, 151–152, 341–342, 372–373, 411, 496–498, 513–516.
2. The Convention's numerous provisions calling for communications to enable a party to know where the other stands suggest a "general principle" (Art. 7(2), *supra* at §100) that a party may not take advantage of ambiguity when an inquiry could readily remove the doubt. See also the "good faith" provision in Art. 7(1), *supra* at §95.

In short, the parties' understanding is a question of fact that is individual to each transaction; the general guides in Article 14 for interpreting the parties' intent, to which we now turn, play subordinate and supporting roles.

135 **(1) Communications to an Indefinite Group: "Public Offers"**

Article 14 incorporates the generally-accepted premise that a party may make an offer to as large a group as it wishes.[3] However, a communication addressed to a large group, if construed as an offer, can involve practical difficulties and hazards. For example, sellers often give wide distribution to catalogues describing a line of goods and indicating prices. Some months may be required for the preparation, printing, and distribution of the catalogue, although modern means of communication and e-commerce practices have in many cases minimized such delays. Nevertheless, some goods may become unavailable because of heavy demand, shortage of materials, or other production difficulties, and cost increases may call for readjustment of prices. If supply or production difficulties are widespread, or if the general price-level rises sharply, the seller may face a flood of orders. If these orders should be "acceptances" of an "offer," the result could be ruin for the seller and a windfall for the buyers. In these settings a "reasonable person" (Art. 8(2)) would not think that a catalogue or price list "indicates an intention ... to be bound" (Art. 14(1)) and courts have been reluctant to construe communications to create such hazards.[4]

These practical considerations are reflected in Article 14(2): If a proposal is not "addressed to *one or more specific persons*," it is not an offer "unless the contrary is *clearly indicated* by the person making the proposal."[5]

---

3. I *Schlesinger, Formation* 101–103 (general report); 647–679 (reports on the law of U.S.A., Eng., Australia, Can., N.Z., France, Ger., Switz., India, Italy, Poland and Rep. So. Af.). The most famous common-law decision is *Carlill v. Carbolic Smoke Ball Co.*, (1893) 1 Q.B. 256 (C.A.) which gave legal effect to an advertisement offering a specified sum to anyone who caught influenza after using a "smoke ball."

4. I *Schlesinger, Formation* 668 (F.R.G. and Switz.), 678 (So. Af.); *Corbin* §§25, 28; Restatement Second of Contracts §26; *Farnsworth, Contracts* 129.

5. *W/G* 8 paras. 52–54, VIII *Yearbook*, 78; *W/G* 9 paras. 163–173, IX *Yearbook* 73, 74; *UNCITRAL XI* Annex I, paras. 75–78, IX *Yearbook* 37. *Docy. Hist.*, 279–280, 305–306, 371.

136   **(a) "Specific Persons."**   Even if a proposal is addressed to "one or more specific persons" it is not an offer unless under the basic test of paragraph (1) it "indicates the intention of the offeror to be bound in case of acceptance." This test may be decisive when the line between paragraph (1) and paragraph (2) is difficult to draw.

To take a common case: Supplier mails a catalogue to 500 prospective buyers; each envelope is addressed to a specific person. Is this a proposal "addressed to one or more specific persons" and therefore governed by paragraph (1)? The answer should be No. The purpose underlying the dividing line between paragraphs (1) and (2) is to avoid the hazards latent in widespread communications mentioned at §135. To this end, the phrase "addressed to one or more specific persons" should refer to communications that are *restricted* to the addressees; a seller who mails out a catalogue normally intends as wide a distribution as possible and would be glad for the addressee to pass the catalogue on to others. Thus, such a mailing to named addressees should be governed by paragraph (2): the intent "to be bound in case of acceptance" must be "clearly indicated."[6]

137   **B. Definiteness of an Offer and the Scope of Party Autonomy**

(1) The Goods: Designation and Quantity

137.1   **(a) The Role of Article 14: Defining an Offer v. Validity of Contract.**   The provisions on definiteness in Article 14(1) are drafted in terms of the question whether a "proposal" constitutes an "offer." We turn first to the question whether a communication should be *construed* as an offer (§§137.2–.4). Later (§137.5) we shall consider whether these provisions control the *validity* of agreements.

As we have seen (§§134–36 *supra*), the "public offer" provisions of Article 14 are concerned only with the question whether a communication should be *interpreted* as an offer: Under Article 14(2) a clear intent

---

6. If such a catalogue distribution were held to be "addressed to one or more specific persons," the catalogue may not constitute an offer under the basic "intent to be bound" test of para. (1). And even if the catalogue was an "offer," orders for goods listed in the catalogue may not be timely under Art. 18(2), which requires acceptance within a reasonable time, due account being taken of the *circumstances of the transaction . . . .*" See Art. 18, *infra* at §161.

to make a public offer is given full effect. What is the purport of the other provisions of Article 14?

137.2   **(b) Description of the Goods: Specifications made by the Seller.**   Article 14(1) states that "a proposal is sufficiently definite if it *indicates the goods*." Does a proposal "indicate the goods" if it states that the buyer will later "specify the form, measurement, or other features of the goods?" This does not make a contract too indefinite: Article 65 (§357, *infra*) states that if the buyer fails to make the specification "the seller may . . . make the specification himself in accordance with the requirements of the buyer that may be known to him."

137.3   **(c) Quantity: Requirement and Output Contracts.**   Under Article 14(1) a proposal is sufficiently definite if (*inter alia*) it "expressly or implicitly fixes or makes provision for determining the *quantity*. . . ." Long-term contracts often call for the supply of a buyer's requirements or for the delivery of a seller's output; Article 14(1) should not be construed to nullify these important transactions on the ground that the quantity will not be fixed until the buyer's requirements or the seller's output become known.

     Under the Convention, as under domestic law, problems can arise if the quantity can be controlled freely by one party — by artificially increasing output when costs (or prices) drop, or by artificially increasing "requirements" when costs (or prices) rise.[7] Tools to cope with these problems are provided by the flexible principles of Article 8 governing contract interpretation (§§104–111 *supra*) and by the direction in Article 7(1) to interpret the Convention to promote "the observance of good faith in international trade."

(2) The Price

137.4   **(a) Scope of the Problem.**   In UNCITRAL and at the 1980 Vienna Conference this question arose: Do the parties have the power to make a binding sales contract that does not (Art. 14) "expressly or implicitly" fix or make "provision for determining" the price? As we shall see, the answer calls for close attention to both Articles 14 and 55 (§§137.5–.6, 325–325.3 *infra*).

     Usually sales contracts specify the price; long-term contracts may make elaborate provision for adjusting the initial price on the basis of

---

7. Weistart, 1973 Duke L.J. 599; *Farnsworth, Contracts* 528–529; (USA) UCC 2–306.

changes in cost.[8] Smaller transactions may make no specific reference to price but the least likely possibility is that the parties have no understanding concerning the price. A common situation in which the price is not expressly stated but (Art. 14) is "implicitly fixed" in the course of a series of communications may be illustrated as follows:

Example 14A. Seller distributed catalogues describing various types of goods and listing prices. Buyer sent Seller a telex requesting Seller to ship goods, designated by a model number in Seller's catalogue, to which the telex referred. Buyer's telex did not specify the price.

Buyer's order in response to Seller's catalogue did not close a binding contract. Under Article 14(1) Seller's catalogue was not addressed to "specific persons" and is not to be construed as an offer but as an invitation to submit offers. See §§135–136, *supra*. (The catalogue will probably state that the listed prices are subject to change; even in the absence of such a statement Seller may modify the price since the catalogue did not make a binding offer.) Buyer's order was, however, an offer that implicitly referred to the price stated in the catalogue.

Seller will usually respond to Buyer's order by an "Order Acknowledgement" that will state the price.[9] If the price is the same as that stated in Seller's catalogue a contract will be closed. If Seller's prices have changed Seller may phone or telex Buyer informing Buyer of a modification in the catalogue price and asking for confirmation of the order at the new price. If Buyer confirms the order, the price has then been fixed and the Order Acknowledgement closes a contract.

If Seller's catalogue prices have not changed Seller may immediately ship the goods and notify Buyer of the shipment by an invoice that states the catalogue price. Under Article 18(1) the seller clearly has accepted: the invoice constitutes a "statement made by . . . the offeree indicating assent to an offer," and (as discussed in §§163–164 *infra*) the shipment is "conduct of the offeree indicating assent" to the offer. Buyer's offer (Art. 14(2)) had "implicitly fixed" the price as that stated in the catalogue to which Buyer referred in its order.

Let us suppose that Seller had raised its prices from those in the catalogue to which Buyer referred but, in haste or carelessness, had shipped without securing Buyer's agreement to the new prices. This placed Seller at risk. If Buyer accepts the goods without knowledge of Seller's price change the parties are bound by contract at the lower price in Seller's catalogue: Buyer had reason to expect this price, and

---

8. See Kritzer Manual Ch. 4.

9. See the Prototype Export Transaction, §132.1 n.4, *supra*.

Seller's shipment without notification would reasonably be understood by Buyer as accepting Buyer's offer at the catalogue's price. Article 8(2), §108, Example 8B, *supra*. If Seller notified Buyer of the price change before Buyer accepted the goods ***Buyer would be aware that Seller did not intend to accept Buyer's offer to purchase at the lower price. Thus Seller's response would be a counter-offer at the higher price, and*** Buyer could either (1) reject the goods or (2) accept the goods at the modified price. If Buyer objects to the higher price he would normally phone or telex Seller and an agreement would be reached on the price. (Seller may find it difficult to redispose of the goods in Buyer's country and may be amenable to a compromise.)

Because of the importance of price to economic success, only rarely will the parties intend to enter into a binding contract without at least (Art. 14(1)) an "implicit" understanding on the price or a means "for determining" the price. Situations that approach the edge involve emergency orders for the manufacture of minor replacement parts or requests to rush a shipment of goods for which the seller has not listed a price. Even here, as the examples suggest, the buyer will seldom accept the goods before he receives an invoice or other notification of the seller's price. In other cases a method for determining the price will be established by trade usage or by a practice the parties have established (Art. 9, §§112–122, *supra*). Hence, rarely will it be necessary to face the question whether the Convention bars the parties from making a contract that neither "expressly" nor "implicitly fixes or *makes provision for determining* . . . the price." However, this question has generated discussion and raises intriguing questions of statutory interpretation and legal theory. It deserves our attention.

137.5   **(b) The Power of the Parties to Contract without Providing for the Price.**   The contested issue of theory can be exposed and tested in the setting of the following improbable case. (Improbable conduct is more useful to legal theory than to commerce.)

    Example 14B. Following negotiations, Seller and Buyer signed a "Contract of Sale" that called for Seller to manufacture and ship goods according to specifications and quantity stated in the agreement. The agreement did not fix a price and instead stated: "We intend to be bound by this agreement, and hereby derogate from any implication of Article 14(1) of the 1980 U.N. Convention that we have not made a binding contract in the absence of fixing or otherwise determining the price." Seller manufactured and delivered the goods which Buyer accepted and used. Thereafter, the parties were unable to agree on the price.

Seller seeks to recover for the goods and invokes Article 55 of the Convention:

> Where a contract has been validly concluded but does not expressly or implicitly fix or make provision for determining the price, the parties are considered, in the absence of any indication to the contrary, to have impliedly made reference to the price generally charged at the time of the conclusion of the contract for such goods sold under comparable circumstances in the trade concerned.

Buyer defends on the ground that the agreement did not "expressly or implicitly fix ... or make provision for determining the ... price" as required by Article 14, and therefore there was no contract.

Buyer's argument has to face, at the outset, the fact that Article 14 states that the issue is whether a "proposal" is "sufficiently definite and indicates an intention to be bound" to be "an *offer*." Here the parties did not exchange an "offer" and "acceptance"; instead they signed a "Contract of Sale" that stated that they intended to be bound by contract even though the price had not been fixed. ***Thus, arguably, Article 14 (including its language on fixing or making provision for determining the price) is inapplicable***. In addition (to lay bare the basic issue of validity) the parties in Example 14B expressly stated that they derogated (Art. 6) from any provision of the Convention that would deny effect to their intent. (This intent would normally be evidenced merely by executing a contract of sale.)

In the Introduction to Part II (§132.1 *supra*), we noted that the Convention's definitions of "offer" and "acceptance" are useful and necessary for deciding whether a contract was made by an exchange of communications. We found, however, that the Convention recognizes that contracts can be made without following the two-step offer-acceptance pattern: Article 18(3) provides that a contract may be concluded "by performing an act," and Article 8(3) provides that statements (including terms of agreements) are to be interpreted to include trade usages and the parties' practices and also are to be construed in the light of "any subsequent *conduct of the parties*." In the life of commerce, as in the above example, there is often no question as to whether a single communication should be construed as an "offer"; the parties' understanding that they have a contract will be disclosed by a series of communications, by their conduct (e.g., by delivering and accepting goods) or by executing a contract of sale.

Does Article 14 deal not only with whether a communication should be construed as an "offer" but also with the validity of a "Contract of Sale" that does not determine the price? This reading of Article 14 is difficult to sustain in the face of Article 4 which states that "except as otherwise *expressly* provided in this Convention, it is *not* concerned with: (a) *the validity of the contract or of any of its provisions. . . .*" Deference to the parties' agreement is also shown by Article 6: the parties may "derogate from or vary the effect of *any* of [the Convention's] provisions."[10] *It is particularly difficult to read Article 14 as containing a rule of validity applicable to contracts not concluded by offer-acceptance.* In any event, further light is shed by the legislative history of Article 55, *infra*.

137.6   **(c) Article 55 and the Two-Point Compromise.**   The question whether Article 14 denies validity to the parties' clearly expressed intent to be bound is important for all States that adopt the Convention without excluding Part II on Formation.[11] As we shall see in discussing Article 55 (§§324–325.3 *infra*), in developing this provision UNCITRAL in 1977 and the Diplomatic Conference in 1980 developed a two-part compromise between delegates that were opposed to and those that supported open-price contracts.

The Working Group draft that led to Article 55 provided: (1) "When a contract *has been concluded*" but does not make provision for the price, (2) the buyer must pay "the price generally charged *by the seller*" when the contract was concluded.[12]

(1) In reviewing the above draft UNCITRAL in 1977 changed the opening clause, quoted at (1), to read "If a contract has been *validly* concluded. . ." The formal statement of the decision by the Commission (sitting as a Committee of the Whole) stated (VIII YB 49 para. 340, *Docy. Hist.* 342): "The Committee decided to introduce an express statement into the article to make it clear that it only applied to agreements which were considered *valid by the applicable law*." The discussion that led to this decision made clear that "applicable law" meant (para. 328) "the applicable *national* law." Indeed, discussion related to the Convention used the phrase "applicable law" to refer to *domestic*

---

10. The one exception in Art. 6 to the principle of freedom of contract involves domestic requirements of form (such as a signed writing) that, under Arts. 12 and 96, may be preserved by a reservation obviating the no-formality rule of Art. 11.

11. As has been noted (§131, *supra*), Art. 92 permits a Contracting State to declare that it will not be bound by Part II or Part III. As of the time of writing no State has excluded Part III; the Scandinavian States have excluded Part II.

12. For the full text of the Working Group draft (then draft Art. 36), the amendment made by UNCITRAL (1977) and the understanding as to its meaning see VIII *Yearbook* 48–49, *Docy. Hist.*, 341–342.

law "applicable by virtue of the rules of private international law" (Art. 7(2)), in contrast to the uniform international rules set forth in the Convention.

(2) The second part of the compromise was made in 1980 at the Diplomatic Conference. Some delegates objected that the reference to the price charged by the *seller* gave an unfair advantage to the seller; to meet this objection the reference to the seller's price was replaced by "the price *generally* charged at the time of the conclusion of the contract." (These compromises are discussed further under Article 55, §§324–325.3, *infra*.)

As a result of these two compromises, in the formal final votes by the Plenary of the Conference, Article 14 (then draft Article 12) was adopted by 41 votes to none with 5 abstentions and Article 55 (then draft Article 51) was adopted by 40 votes to 3 with 5 abstentions.[13]

In view of this over-all compromise, including the concession to the *domestic* law of those States that make provision for the price an element of contract validity, it is quite impossible to conclude that Article 14 imposed such a rule of invalidity on all States that adopt Part II of the Convention.

A perfectly natural reading of Article 14(1) brings it into conformity with this history. The provision does not expressly state that a proposal lacking a price provision cannot be an offer: it merely asserts that a proposal is "sufficiently definite" (one of the requirements for an offer stated in the first sentence) if it (inter alia) "fixes or makes provision for determining . . . the price." There is no reason to derive from this statement a negative implication that a proposal lacking a price provision cannot be an offer. The second sentence of Article 14(1) is better understood as a "safe-harbor" rule — that is, a rule that a proposal meeting its requirements (including those relating to price) is conclusively to be deemed "sufficiently definite," although proposals not meeting all those requirements may still be "sufficiently definite." This safe-harbor approach, in fact, is quite clearly intended in the very similarly-drafted first sentence of Article 14(1). That sentence provides that a proposal is an offer if, inter alia, it is "addressed to one or more specific persons." Article 14(2), however, expressly states that a proposal "other than one addressed to one or more specific persons" is nevertheless an offer if that intent "is clearly indicated by the person making the proposal." Thus it is perfectly clear that the specific-addressee requirement in Article 14(1) does not have a negative

---

13. *O.R.* 205, 211, *Docy. Hist.* 740, 746.

implication, and is intended to state a safe-harbor rule: proposals meeting the specific-addressee requirement (along with the other requirements of the first sentence) are clearly offers, but those not meeting the specific-addressee requirement may nevertheless also be offers if the intent to make an offer "is clearly indicated." The price-provision requirement in the second sentence should be read the same way: a proposal that does not fix or make provision for determining the price should still be deemed an offer if the intent to make an offer is clear, as is the case in Example 14B.

Example 14B contains an express derogation from anything in Article 14 that would require the offer to include a price provision. Such derogation is permitted by Article 6 of the CISG. Even without an express derogation, a proposal that lacks a price provision but that clearly manifests an intent to be an offer could well be deemed to include an implied derogation to the same effect (see §76 supra). This offers an alternative path to the result advocated in the previous paragraph.[14]

Under one approach or another Article 14 should not be construed to block formation of a contract lacking a price term where the parties intend such a contract.[15] *This assumes that Article 55 will provide for the missing price. What the result would be if, on specific facts, Article 55 cannot do so — as was (somewhat surprisingly) found in an early CISG decision involving airplane engines*[16] *— is unclear, but unlikely to come up frequently.*

---

14. See Peter Schlechtriem, Art. 14 para. 2, *in* Schlechtriem & Schwenzer, *CISG Commentary* (2nd English ed. 2005) (describing the requirements stated in the second sentence of Art. 14(a) — contrary to the argument made in the previous paragraph — as "minimum elements" the absence of which will prevent a proposal from being an offer under Art. 14(1), but then noting that the parties can derogate from those minimum requirements pursuant to Art. 6 of the Convention).

15. For an opinion consistent with this approach see the decision of the Handelsgericht des Kantons St. Gallen, Switzerland, December 5, 1995, CLOUT case No. 330, English translation available at http://cisgw3.law.pace.edu/cases/951205s1.html. For other decisions addressing the treatment of offers or contracts lacking a price provision under the CISG see UNCITRAL Digest Art. 14 paras. 11–16.

16. See the decision of the Legfelsobb Bíróság, Hungary, September 25, 1992, CLOUT case No. 53 (United Technologies Int'l Inc. Pratt & Whitney Comm. Engine Bus. v. Magyar Légi Közlekedési Vállalat (Málev Hungarian Airlines)), English translation available at http://cisgw3.law.pace.edu/cases/920925h1.html.

137.7 **(1) Consequences of Invalidity for Lack of Provision for Price**

Finally, let us face some of the consequences of holding that the price provision of Article 14(1) invalidates transactions where the parties, by words or conduct, show their agreement to be bound despite their failure to provide for the price. The consequences can be serious when the seller manufactures or transports goods or when the buyer relies on expected supplies for resale or production; even more serious consequences can result when, in reliance on their agreement, goods are supplied, accepted and put into use.

Part III of the Convention (Arts. 25–88) is premised on the existence of a contract (Arts. 30, 53); denying validity to the agreement deprives the parties of all of the rights provided by the Convention. For example, the seller may not recover the price (Arts. 35, 62) or avoid the "contract" for breach and recover the goods for non-payment (Arts. 64(1), 81(2)). The buyer loses protection of rules on the required quality of the goods (Art. 35) and the right to recover the damages caused by defective goods (Arts. 45, 74). The ultimate irony is that in many situations (e.g., questions as to non-conformity and recovery of damages) the price of the goods is irrelevant.

137.8 **(a) Conclusion.**   Article 14(1) does not bar the parties from concluding a contract by express agreement or by conduct (e.g., by shipping, receiving and using goods) that shows their "intention . . . to be bound" (Art. 14(1)) despite their failure to fix or make provision for the price. The only rule of "validity" with respect to agreement on price results from the opening phrase of Article 55 which defers to applicable domestic law.[17]

---

17. But see Günter Hager, Art. 55 para. 5, *in* Schlechtriem & Schwenzer, *CISG Commentary* (2nd English ed. 2005). For a fuller development see Honnold, International Sales Law and the Open-Price contract, II *Barrera-Graf Festschrift* 915. See also *C-S Kommentar (1990)* Art. 14, pp. 128–136 (Schlechtriem); Art. 55, pp. 519–521 (Hager); Adami, Open-Price Contracts in CISG, 2 Int. Bus. L.J. 103 (1989) (parallel text English and French); Fortier, Le prix dans [CISG], 117 J. D. 1381 (1990) (French). See also references under Art. 55, *infra*, at §325.3 n. 5.

Article 15.
When Offer Becomes Effective; Prior Withdrawal

138   The special and narrow role of Article 15 may be illustrated by the following example:

Example 15A. On June 1 Seller mailed to Buyer a letter offering to sell Buyer specified goods at a stated price. The offer also stated: "This offer is binding and irrevocable until July 1." A letter from Seller to Buyer takes a week for delivery. On June 6, before Buyer received Seller's June 1 letter, Seller phoned Buyer and said, "Disregard the letter that I mailed to you on June 1. I have decided to withdraw the offer contained in the letter." On receipt of Seller's letter Buyer replied "I accept your June 1 offer."

The question whether the above parties are bound by contract is answered by the following provision.

Article 15[1]

(1) An offer becomes effective when it reaches the offeree.

(2) An offer, even if it is irrevocable, may be withdrawn if the withdrawal reaches the offeree before or at the same time as the offer.

In the above example, on June 6, the offer had not yet reached the offeree, and therefore was not yet "effective" under Article 15(1). The statement that the offer could not be revoked until July 1 would have become binding (Art. 16(2), *infra* at §139) when it reached the offeree. But the offer never became "effective" because of the withdrawal that reached the offeree in advance of the offer.[2]

The reason supporting Article 15 is that the enforcement of contracts is designed to protect expectations; none arose in this case before the offeror withdrew the offer. Article 22, *infra* §177, provides a parallel rule with respect to an acceptance: the offeree may withdraw the acceptance if the withdrawal "reaches the offeror before or at the same time as the acceptance would have become effective." The time when an offer, or a withdrawal of an offer, "reaches" the offeree is addressed in Article 24, §179 *infra*.

---

1. Article 15 is, in substance, the same as Art. 13 of the 1978 Draft Convention. *Cf.* ULF Art. 5(1).

2. As we shall see in connection with Arts. 16 and 18(2), if the offer had not been irrevocable, Seller could have "revoked" the offer by a communication that reached the Buyer after it received the offer but before acceptance.

Article 16.
Revocability of Offer

139   As we have seen, Article 15 empowers the offeror to "withdraw" an offer before it reaches the offeree. The present article deals with the power of the offeror to "revoke" an offer after it has reached the offeree and thereby has become "effective."

Article 16[1]

(1) Until a contract is concluded an offer may be revoked if the revocation reaches the offeree before he has dispatched an acceptance.
(2) However, an offer cannot be revoked:
(a) if it indicates, whether by stating a fixed time for acceptance or otherwise, that it is irrevocable; or
(b) if it was reasonable for the offeree to rely on the offer as being irrevocable and the offeree has acted in reliance on the offer.

This article must be viewed as a whole for the rule of revocability in paragraph (1) is deeply eroded by paragraph (2).

140 **A. Revocability Until Acceptance**

(1) The Common Law; "Consideration"

If Article 16 consisted only of paragraph (1) it would resemble the traditional common-law view that an offer may be revoked until it is accepted. Even if the offeror promises that the offeree will have a specified period for acceptance, under the traditional common-law approach this promise is not binding unless it is supported by "consideration" — a payment or some other act or thing given by the offeree in exchange for the promise to hold the offer open.[2] But the common law found a way

---

1. Article 16 of the Convention is based, with a drafting change in paragraph (1), on Art. 14 of the 1978 Draft Convention. *Cf.* ULF 5(2) and (3).
2. I *Schlesinger, Formation* 766–767 (Eng.), 768 (Aus., Can., & N.Z.), 747–760 (U.S.A. case law and statutory modification); Corbin §§42–44; *Farnsworth, Contracts* §3.17 (free revocability supported by the principle of "mutuality of obligation").

slightly to curtail this broad power to revoke — the famous "post-box" (or "mailbox" or "dispatch") rule. Where acceptance by mail is proper, the acceptance occurs and, more to the point, the offeror's power to revoke is cut off when the offeree posts his acceptance.[3] This common-law feature appears in the general rule of revocability of Article 16(1) — the revocation must reach the offeree "before he has *dispatched* an acceptance." *Although the Convention includes a rule stating when a communication "reaches" an addressee (see Art. 24, §179 infra), no provision directly addresses when a communication is "dispatched." In the case of electronic communications, the question may be governed by the United Nations Convention on the Use of Electronic Communications in International Contracts when it comes into force and is applicable. Article 10(1) of that Convention states the following rule: "The time of dispatch of an electronic com-munication is the time when it leaves an information system[4] under the control of the originator or of the party who sent it on behalf of the originator or, if the electronic communication has not left an infor-mation system under the control of the originator or of the party who sent it on behalf of the originator, the time the electronic communi-cation is received."[5]* Of course, the effectiveness of an offer ends if it is not duly accepted. See Article 18(2), §161 *infra.*

141 **B. Restriction on Revocability: Paragraph (2)**

The heart of Article 16 is paragraph (2). Cutting deep into the general rule of paragraph (1), paragraph (2) restricts the offeror's power to revoke on two alternative grounds: (1) a promise or other indication by the offeror that the offer is irrevocable or (2) acts by the offeree in reliance on the irrevocability of the offer.

---

3. I *Schlesinger, Formation* 158–159 (general report); II *id.* 1435–1443 (Eng., Aus., Can. & N.Z.). The most famous cases are Adams v. Lindsell, (1818) 1 B. & Ald. 681, 106 E.R. 250 and Dunlop v. Higgins, (1848) 1 H.L.C. 381, 9 E.R. 805. See *Corbin* §§78–81; *Restatement (Second) of Contracts* §63.

4. An "information system" is defined in Art. 4(f) of the Electronic Communications Con-vention as "a system for generating, sending, receiving, storing or otherwise processing data messages."

5. Article 10(2) of the Electronic Communications Convention addresses the time at which an electronic communication is "received."

142 **(1) Promise or Indication that the Offer is Irrevocable**

(a) Promise Not to Revoke.   Under the Convention, common-law doctrines on "consideration" are not available to nullify a promise that an offer will remain in effect.

Example 16A. On June 1 Seller delivered to Buyer an offer that included this statement: "I will hold this offer open until June 15." On June 2 Seller delivered to Buyer the following statement "I hereby revoke my offer of June 1." On June 14 Seller received a communication from Buyer stating that he accepted the offer of June 1.

Seller's attempt to revoke the offer was ineffective: under Article 16(2)(a) the offer could not be revoked before June 15 because it indicated it was irrevocable until that date. Buyer accepted within the period set by offer; the parties are bound by contract.

This result reflects the approach of various civil law systems.[6] In addition, under the (U.S.A.) Uniform Commercial Code an offer to sell goods may, under stated circumstances, be irrevocable even absent consideration for a promise of irrevocability.

> Section 2–205. Firm Offers
>   An offer by a merchant to buy or sell goods in a signed writing which by its terms gives assurance that it will be held open is not revocable, for lack of consideration, during the time stated or if no time is stated for a reasonable time, but in no event may such period of irrevocability exceed three months; but any such term of assurance on a form supplied by the offeree must be separately signed by the offeror.

The UCC's common-law background helps to explain the limitations on irrevocability in Section 2–205. Limiting irrevocability to an "offer by a merchant" does not substantially restrict the scope of UCC §2–205 compared to Article 16 of the Convention, in view of the mercantile nature of most international sales and the Convention's exclusion of consumer transactions (Arts. 2(a) and 5, *supra* at §§49, 71). More significant elements of UCC §2–205 are the requirement of a "signed writing"[7] (separately signed if the "assurance" that the offer will be held open is on a form supplied by the offeree) and the three-month

---

6. I *Schlesinger, Formation* 764–765 (Bulg., Hung., Cz., Yugo., and CMEA General Conditions), 769–770 (France), 782 (Ger., Sw., and Austria) 78, 79 (Poland), 862 (Italy); *Ont. L. Com.*, I *Sales* II (Quebec); Schmidt, The International Contract Law in the Context of Some of its Sources, 14 Am. J. Comp. L. 1, 10 (1965). Cigoj, International Sales: Formation of Contracts, 23 Neth. Int. L. Rev. 257, 278–281 (1976).

7. Nothing in CISG Art. 16(2) requires that an irrevocable offer be in writing. Under CISG Art. 11, *supra* at §126, contracts need not be in writing.

limitation on the effectiveness of a promise not to revoke. On the other hand, official recommendations in other common-law jurisdictions to revise the rules on the revocability of offers propose minimal formal requirements and are similar to Article 16(2) of the Convention.[8]

143   **(b) Implied "Indication" that Offer is Irrevocable.**   We turn to offers that do not state that they will be held open. Does the making of an offer, without more, assure the offeree of a period within which it may respond so that the offeror may not revoke the offer during that period?

Attempts to answer this question have had a troubled history. The Draft on Formation that was presented to the 1964 Hague Conference stated: "An offer . . . may not be revoked unless the offeror has reserved to himself the right of revocation in the offer."[9] This proposal was a center of controversy at the 1964 Conference. The upshot was a compromise (ULF Art. 5) that made revocability turn, in part, on : "good faith" and "fair dealing" — concepts that many UNCITRAL delegates concluded were too vague to be useful in this context. The revision of these rules on revocability was one of the more difficult tasks that UNCITRAL encountered in its work on formation of the sales contract.[10]

The most delicate issue was this: When the offer states a period within which the offeree must reply does it follow that the offer is irrevocable during this period? Support for an affirmative answer was based on civil code provisions that were interpreted to mean that if the offer must be accepted within a certain period it is irrevocable until the end of the

---

8. English Law Commission, Working Paper No. 60, Firm Offers, paras. 34–38 (1975): a firm offer for a specified period need not be in writing and would be effective for 6 years; the lack of consideration would be irrelevant. *Ont. L. Ref. Com.* I *Sale* 93–95: express statement that offer will be held open would be effective without a writing or time limit; Law Commission of India, Thirteenth Report (Contract Act) 77–78 (1958) discussed in I *Schlesinger, Formation* 784–786. Compare the Model Written Obligations Act, prepared for adoption by states, enforces promises not to revoke which in a signed writing but does not contain the other restrictions found in UCC 2–205. See also Sutton, Formation: Unity in International Sales of Goods, 16 U.W. Ont. L. Rev. 113, 134 (1977) (approval of Convention's approach from Australian perspective).

9. Art. 4(2). Art. 7(3) defined the period within which the offeree could accept. II *Records 1964 Conf.* 421–422, 426–427 (report of Special Commission). For caution as to implying irrevocability see Goldstajn, Formation of the Contract, *Unification Symposium 1964* 41, 52. *Cf.* Lagergren, *id.* 63 (compromise at 1964 Hague Conference).

10. *W/G 8* paras. 70–85, VIII *YB* 79–80, 97, *Docy. Hist.* 280–281; *W/G 9* paras. 189–196, IX *YB* 75; *Docy. Hist.*, 307; *UNCITRAL XI* Annex I paras. 117–139, IX *YB* 40–41; *Docy. Hist.* 374–375.

specified period.[11] In accordance with this view, the 1964 Hague Formation Convention (ULF Art. 5(2)) had provided that an offer may not be revoked if "the offer *states a fixed time for acceptance* or otherwise indicates that it is firm or irrevocable."

143.1 **(c) Effect of "Fixed Time for Acceptance."**   Some delegates urged that UNCITRAL should retain the above language of ULF Article 5(2) and contended that stating "a fixed time for acceptance" would be understood as a promise to hold the offer open. Others argued that in some settings the words would be understood merely to set a time limit beyond which an acceptance would be *too late* — the issue addressed in Article 18(2) by the provision that an "acceptance is not effective if the indication of assent does not reach the offeror within *the time he has fixed*" (§161, *infra*) rather than the issue (covered in Art. 16(2)) of whether the offeror *promised to hold the offer open* for a prescribed time. Those holding the latter view proposed that the rule on irrevocability be formed in general terms, i.e., the rule should state that an offer is irrevocable if it "indicates that it is irrevocable," but the rule should not specify the expression that would communicate this meaning.

The UNCITRAL Working Group, however, approved this language: ". . . an offer cannot be revoked: . . . (b) If the offer states a fixed time for acceptance" — a formulation that seemed to give decisive effect to a specified form of expression.[12] UNCITRAL in its 1978 review of the draft provisions on formation revised the Working Group draft to provide that an offer can not be revoked: "(a) If it indicates, whether by stating that a fixed time for acceptance or otherwise, that it is irrevocable." Some, but not all, delegates stated that this revision reflected the view that the ultimate test was the interpretation of the offer rather than the use of a specified expression.[13] At the Vienna Conference the "fixed time" and "general rule" proponents were unable to modify the language to clearly express their positions; the 1978 UNCITRAL draft became Article 16(2)(a) of the Convention.[14]

---

11. See report by K. Neumayer on German and Swiss law in I *Schlesinger, Formation* 780; Goldstajn, The Law of Sales in Yugoslavia, 14 *E. Eur.* 125, 152. (General Usages: offers without reference to time are binding for period adequate to allow acceptance, but not to exceed 8 days).

12. Sess. No. 8 (Jan. 1977), VIII *YB* 80, paras. 77–85, *Docy. Hist.*, 281; Sess. No. 9 (Sept. 1977), IX *YB* 75, paras. 189–196, *Docy. Hist.* 307.

13. IX *YB* 71, paras. 132–139, *Docy. Hist.*, 375.

14. *O.R.* 278–280, *Docy. Hist.*, 499–501.

It is not easy to assess the outcome of this dispute, which may well appear to be a tempest in a teapot.[15] It seems necessary to give effect to two decisions: (1) The 1978 UNCITRAL retreat from the Working Group draft and (2) the retention of the reference to a "fixed time for acceptance" in Article 16(2)(a). Both decisions can be accommodated by concluding that (1) the reference in an offer to a "fixed time for acceptance" creates a presumption of irrevocability until the stated date, but (2) the presumption can rebutted by showing that the offer in its full setting (Art. 8(3)) would be understood to refer to the automatic expiration of the offer (Art. 18(2)) rather than a promise not to revoke.[16] (The mandate of Art. 8(3) for interpretation of statements in their full setting is discussed at §§109–111, *supra*.)

An offeror who wishes to set a date for expiration of the offer and also to reserve the power to revoke the offer before that date would be well advised to make this meaning clear. The Convention, of course, respects the basic principle that the offeror is "master of its offer." See Article 6; *Kritzer Manual* Ch. 22.

143.2 **(d) The Meaning of Specified Words: International Drafting Technique.**   To the author (who did not take part in the controversy over Art. 16), the most interesting question is not the area of irrevocability but a general question about statutory drafting: Should a statute attempt to state the meaning of specified words or expressions used in private contracts? Statutory drafters may define the words *they* use but should not try to state the meaning of words and expressions used by *others*, especially in contracts made by private persons in a virtually infinite variety of settings.

Attempts in domestic statutes to define the expressions used in contracts have led to difficulties;[17] the problems are multiplied in an international statute prepared for enactment and use in numerous

15. As measured by reported decisions, Art. 16(2)(a) has generated no significant controversy in practice. See UNCITRAL Digest Art. 16 para. 2.

16. See Peter Schlechtriem, Art. 16 paras. 9 & 10, *in* Schlechtriem & Schwenzer, *CISG Commentary* (2nd English ed. 2005). Professor Schlechtriem suggests that the treatment of an offer's fixed time for acceptance in the domestic law of the offeror and the offeree is relevant, under the standards of Art. 8, in determining whether the presumption of irrevocability has been rebutted. *Id.* para. 10.

17. For example, the attempt in (U.S.A.) UCC §§2–319 *et seq.* to define the meaning of specified price-delivery terms such as "F.O.B.," "C.I.F." and the like has imposed static definitions on living terms that continued to evolve in meaning since the UCC was drafted. As a result, the statutorily-mandated definitions no longer reflect current usage, and may well

different languages and commercial settings. The only vessel in which one can hope to carry a uniform rule across multi-lingual terrain is by the description of a *thought* or an *idea* — not by a specified expression in a contract to which the statute attributes a particular meaning.

144   (2) Action in Reliance on the Offer

Let us now assume that the offeror made no statement that promised or indicated that the offer was irrevocable (Art. 16(2)(a)). Nevertheless, under paragraph 2(b) an offer cannot be revoked "if it was *reasonable for the offeree to rely* on the offer as being irrevocable and the offeree has *acted in reliance* on the offer." One application of this provision may be illustrated as follows:

Example 16B. On May 1 Builder asked Supplier to submit an offer for the sale to Builder of a specified quantity of bricks. Builder explained that he needed the offer to use in computing a bid on a contract to construct a building. Builder added that he must submit the bid by June 1 and that the bids would be opened and the contract awarded on June 15. On May 7 Supplier gave Builder an offer for the bricks, and Supplier used the offer in preparing his June 1 bid for the building contract. On June 10 Supplier notified Builder that he revoked his offer. On June 15 the bids were opened and Builder was awarded the contract. Builder thereupon informed Supplier that he accepted Supplier's offer.

In the above example, it was "reasonable for the offeree [Builder] to rely on the offer as being irrevocable" since Supplier when it made the offer knew that Builder would use it in compiling its bid. In addition, Builder "acted in reliance on the offer" in submitting a bid that led to a contract binding it to construct the building at an agreed price. Both requirements of paragraph (2)(b) are satisfied, and Supplier's attempt to revoke his offer is ineffective.[18]

---

distort the intentions of merchants using the terms — as a comparison between the UCC definitions and the definitions of the same terms in, for example, the current version of INCOTERMS shows. This problem caused the drafters of proposed amendments to UCC Art. 2 (amendments approved by the UCC's sponsoring organizations in 2003 but, at the time this is written, not yet enacted by any jurisdiction) to omit all definitions of price-delivery terms.

18. As we shall see, Art. 18(3) provides that "the offeree may indicate assent by performing an act, such as one relating to the dispatch of the goods or payment of the price . . . ." This language refers to acts which relate to the performance of the contract while Art. 16(2)(b) has wider scope. In Example 16B, Builder's use of Supplier's offer in computing Builder's bid was not part of the performance of a contract to buy from Supplier. Bordering on both

This approach has support in domestic law. As we have seen, some civil law legal systems hold offers to be irrevocable for the period needed for a response; other legal systems do not go so far but hold that reasonable reliance on the offer bars revocation or (in some cases) makes the offeror responsible in tort for damages.[19] In the United States the prevailing view is consistent with the Convention in barring revocation in cases like Example 16B.[20]

Example 16B provides only one illustration of situations where revocation of an offer may be ineffective because the offeree has reasonably relied on the offer. However, the legal effect of Article 16(2) is subject to an important limitation imposed by the Convention's rules on the time for acceptance. Regardless of the offeree's reliance, under Article 18(1), *infra* at §157, the making of a contract requires a "statement . . . or other conduct . . . indicating assent." And, under Article 18(2) there is no contract if the offeree's "indication of assent does not reach the offeror within the time he has fixed or, if no time is fixed, within a reasonable time . . ." (See Art. 18, *infra* at §164).

This limit on the time for acceptance imposed by Article 18(2) is especially significant in situations in which Article 16(2) does not limit the period of irrevocability — as in paragraph (2)(a) when an offer states that it is irrevocable "without stating a fixed time for acceptance" and in paragraph (2)(b) when "the offeree has acted in reliance on the offer."

This time limit is important to prevent the offeree from speculating at the offeror's expense. Some acts of reliance that may create irrevocability under paragraph (2)(b), such as proportions to perform that commit the offeree to the specific contract, create little danger of abuse. Other acts may be ambiguous, such as the purchase or assembly of goods or supplies that the seller might (or might not) need to fill an order by a buyer. In these cases, later events that make the contract more (or less) attractive may tempt the seller to claim that these steps were (or were not) taken in reliance on the buyer's order.

The mandate of Article 7(1) to interpret the Convention "to promote the observance of good faith in international trade" indicates the usefulness of two safeguards: (1) caution in basing irrevocability on ambiguous

---

Art. 16(2)(b) and Art. 18(3) is the beginning of the performance requested by the offeror. See Art. 18, *infra* at §§157, 163–164.

19. I *Schlesinger, Formation* 770, 776 (France; report by P. Bonassies).

20. See Restatement, Second of Contracts §87 and Illustration 6; *Farnsworth, Contracts* 183–186, §3.25 (earlier cases *contra*); Fuller & Perdue, The Reliance Interest in Contract Damages, 46 Yale L.J. 373, 410 (1937); I *Schlesinger, Formation* 747, 751–760 (report by I. Macneil). This aspect of contract law is not codified in the (U.S.A.) UCC.

conduct and (2) enforcement of the time limits for acceptance established by Article 18(2) (§164, *infra*). There are other similar situations calling for construction to prevent abuse and promote good faith; see, for example, Article 7 at §95 *supra* and Article 46 at §285 *infra*.[21]

145 **C. Responsibility in Tort for Reliance on Offer**

In some legal systems, if an offeror induces the offeree to incur expense in reliance on an offer and then withdraws the offer, the offeror may be liable in tort even though the withdrawal prevents the conclusion of a contract and thereby excludes the full battery of remedies for breach of contract.[22] Will such rules of domestic law apply, alongside the Convention, when the offeree suffers loss by reliance on an offer? One cannot envisage all of the circumstances in which this question may arise; hence, there will be no attempt to give a general answer, but the question does deserve attention because of its relationship to basic issues concerning the scope of the Convention.

146 **(1) Non-Contract Labels in Domestic Law**

In the Commentary to Articles 4 and 5 we examined some of the implications of the statement that the Convention "governs only the *formation of the contract*" of sale and the "rights and obligations of the seller and the buyer *arising from such a contract*." This question arose: Do domestic rules of "product liability," applicable when defective goods are supplied under a sales contract, co-exist with the Convention's rules that regulate breach of contract? In that context it was suggested that when the very facts that invoke rules of "product liability" invoke rules of the Convention, the domestic rules are supplanted by the Convention. In short, it would be wrong to bypass the uniform international rules by pinning a non-contract label to the very facts that are regulated by the Convention. (See *supra* §§71ff.) Are there situations in which this line of thought would bar recourse to domestic law that awards damages for wrongful revocation of an offer?

21. See Winship, 17 Int. Law. 1, 11 (1983).
22. Kessler and Fine, Culpa in Contahendo, Bargaining in Good Faith, and Freedom of Contract — A Comparative Study, 77 Harv. L. Rev. 407, 420–424 (1964); Farnsworth, Precontractual Liability and Preliminary Agreements, 87 Colum. L. Rev. 217 (1987); Summers, "Good Faith," 54 Va. L. Rev. 195, 220–227 (1968).

147   **(a) Operative Facts That Reach Beyond Contract. Domestic.** Domestic law would not be excluded whenever the offeror harms the offeree by wrongful conduct other than the making and revocation of the offer. For example, domestic remedies for fraudulent inducement to make a contract tract are not affected by the Convention.[23] (See Art. 4, *supra* at §65 and Art. 7, *supra* at §97.)

148   **(2) Wrongful Revocation that Aborts the Process of Contracting**

A more difficult question can best be examined against the following setting:

Example 16C. Buyer offered to purchase complex machinery from Seller, which Seller would manufacture according to designs supplied by Buyer. The offer included a stated price and stated that the offer would be held open for two months to enable Seller to determine whether he could make the machinery at that price. Seller immediately started the process of designing manufacturing procedures and computing costs of production. Two weeks later, when Seller had spent substantial sums in computing costs but had not completed this work, Buyer notified Seller that he could no longer use the machinery and withdrew the offer Seller thereupon stopped work on the cost estimates since it would be uneconomic to invest further funds in preparing to make machinery that Buyer would not accept and perhaps could not pay for.

149   **(a) Applicability of the Convention.** Has Seller a claim under the Convention? In Example 16C Buyer purported to revoke an offer that, under Article 16(2), "cannot be revoked." However, the only remedy explicitly stated in Part II of the Convention is to hold the offer open so that the offeree can accept and thereby complete a contract (Arts. 18 and 23). Examination of the remedies specified in Part III of the Convention indicates that they are applicable to breach of contract.[24] In Example 16C the offeror's (Buyer's) wrongful revocation made it impractical to conclude a contract since a decision as to acceptance

23. See Peter Schlechtriem, *Introduction to* Art. 14–24 para. 6b (ii) & (iii) and Art. 16 para. 13, *in* COMMENTARY ON THE UN CONVENTION ON THE INTERNATIONAL SALE OF GOODS (CISG) (Peter Schlechtriem & Ingeborg Schwenzer, eds. 2nd (English) ed. 2005).

24. See Arts. 71–77 and the official headings for the remedial provisions of Part III, Ch. II. Sec. III and Ch. III. Sec. 111. But *cf.* Arts. 45 & 61. As to questions of mitigation, see Art. 77, *infra* at §§417–419.

would require further expenditures and it would be hazardous and uneconomical to invest added funds that could be recouped only by a lawsuit.

150   **(b) Gap-filling.**   The above discussion suggests that a situation can arise where the Convention bars revocation but fails to provide an effective remedy. This invites our attention to Article 7(2), which provides that "questions concerning matters governed by this Convention which are not expressly settled in it are to be settled in conformity with the general principles on which it is based . . ." Does this authorize tribunals to develop a remedy under the Convention for the offeror's wrongful revocation?

The Convention — and only the Convention — controls the question whether the revocation of the offer is rightful.[25] The Convention provides one remedy for wrongful revocation — the offeree can accept the offer in spite of the revocation. But when special circumstances (as in Example 16C) make this remedy ineffective it would be reasonable for a tribunal to close the gap that is revealed by the above example. The need for a remedy addressed directly to the damages caused by a wrongful revocation is supported by domestic law and by studies directed to the reform of domestic law.[26] Responding to this need by filling a gap in the Convention could promote the declared goal of uniformity since solutions applying the Convention would be taken into account by other tribunals and a common *jurisprudence* would develop. (See the Commentary to Art. 7, *supra* at §96.)[27] Professor Schlechtriem disagrees with this approach, arguing that, in a situation like Example 16C, the only remedy available to the offeree is to accept the offer and treat the wrongful revocation as a repudiation of the contract, although he admits that

---

25. *Accord*, Peter Schlechtriem, *Introduction to* Art. 14–24 para. 6b (iii) and Art. 16 para. 13, *in* COMMENTARY ON THE UN CONVENTION ON THE INTERNATIONAL SALE OF GOODS (CISG) (Peter Schlechtriem & Ingeborg Schwenzer, eds. 2nd (English) ed. 2005).

26. See *Zweigert & Kötz II (1987)* 39: In French law an offeror has power to withdraw an offer before an agreed period but is liable in damages; Nicholas, French Law of Contract, 63–69. Proposals for reform: English Law Commission: Working Paper No. 60, Firm Offers, paras. 41–50 (1975) suggests that an offeree must elect between (a) a cause of action for wrongful revocation, and (b) treating the revocation as a nullity. *Cf. Ont. L. Ref. Com.* I *Sales* 95 (would not require election).

27. Filling this gap pursuant to Art. 7(2) would be consistent with the policy, underlying Arts. 71 and 72, *infra*, to protect a party threatened with a failure of counter-performance. In this instance, however, Arts. 71 and 72 are not directly applicable since they assume that a contract has been made.

this places the offeree "in a difficult position."[28] Requiring the offeree in Example 16C to conclude a contract in order to protect itself, however, may conflict with the principle underlying the mitigation of damages rule in Article 77.[29]

151   **(c) Remedy Supplied by Domestic Law.** Let us now assume that, contrary to the above suggestion, a tribunal declines to develop a remedy under Article 7(2) of the Convention. In this event, the tribunal should at least work from the premise that, by command of the Convention, the revocation of the offer was wrongful and draw on applicable domestic law for the remedy that is appropriate for this type of wrong.[30]

28. Peter Schlechtriem, Art. 16 para. 13, *in* COMMENTARY ON THE UN CONVENTION ON THE INTERNATIONAL SALE OF GOODS (CISG) (Peter Schlechtriem & Ingeborg Schwenzer, eds. 2nd (English) ed. 2005). Professor Bridge argues that an offeree in a situation like Example 16C has no remedy under the Convention unless it accepts the offer, although — unlike Professor Schlechtriem — Professor Bridge suggests that if such an offeree decides not to accept it would have recourse to rules of applicable domestic law that, in some cases, might afford a remedy. BRIDGE, INTERNATIONAL SALE OF GOODS para. 3.04.

29. Professor Bridge, for example, recognizes that an offeree "injured by the purported retraction of an irrevocable offer" may have to "run up more reliance costs to put itself in a position to accept the offer." BRIDGE, INTERNATIONAL SALE OF GOODS para. 3.04.

30. Professor Schlechtriem again disagrees with this approach, asserting that in this situation "the Convention leaves no room for remedies under domestic law" and that "claims for damages under domestic law arising in *culpa in contrahendo* or on the basis of the general law of tort or delict must be excluded." Peter Schlechtriem, Art. 16 para. 13, *in* COMMENTARY ON THE UN CONVENTION ON THE INTERNATIONAL SALE OF GOODS (CISG) (Peter Schlechtriem & Ingeborg Schwenzer, eds. 2nd (English) ed. 2005). Professor Schlechtriem argues, however, that domestic rules imposing liability for breaking off negotiations should be applied "in cases where the parties have not been moving towards a contract through corresponding offer and acceptance" because "the CISG does not govern the situation where an existing contracting procedure is broken off before the stage of 'offer' or 'acceptance' has been reached and it is unlikely that any general principle can be developed which could fill that gap." *Id.*, *Introduction to* Art. 14–24 para. 6 n. 36.

Article 17.
Rejection of Offer Followed by Acceptance

152　　The role of this brief article (quoted below) can be illustrated as follows:

Example 17A. On May 1 Seller delivered to Buyer an offer that stated: "I will hold this offer open until June 1." On May 7, Buyer delivered to Seller the following: "I cannot accept your offer since the price is too high," but on May 10 he delivered to Seller the following: "I hereby accept your offer of May 1." Seller immediately informed Buyer that this "acceptance" was not effective because of the earlier rejection; Buyer replied that this was not true because Seller had promised to hold the offer open.

This issue is settled by the following provision:

Article 17[1]

An offer, even if it is irrevocable, is terminated when a rejection reaches the offeror.

153　## A. Explicit Rejection

In the above example, Buyer's rejection of May 7 "terminated" the offer even though it would otherwise have been binding until June 1; there was no contract. In such cases, Article 17 avoids doubt that might arise from the rule of Article 16 that the offer was "irrevocable."[2] In addition, the rule that a rejection terminates an offer is supported by practical considerations. When an offer is rejected the offeror has no reason to expect that the offeree will change its mind; Article 17 enables the offeror to make plans promptly and make maximum use of its resources.

---

1. This article is the same as Art. 15 of the 1978 Draft Convention. There is no comparable provision in ULF; see n. 2, *infra*.

2. In 1964 a proposal that ULF should include a provision like Art. 17 was rejected by the UNIDROIT Commission: "This solution is so evident that it would seem superfluous to state it." II *Records 1964 Conf.* 473, 474.

154 (1) Prevailing Rules

The approach of Article 17 is widely supported in civil law systems, and probably in most common-law jurisdictions.[3] Decisions in the United States have held that one who has purchased an option for a specified term does not destroy the "option" by a rejection. However, most of these cases involve situations, like the rental of premises with an option to purchase, where substantial value has been given for the option and forfeiture or substantial loss would result from termination of the option. There is ground for scepticism that courts would extend this approach to an offer to sell or buy goods which becomes irrevocable merely on the basis of a statement that the offer is "firm." (See UCC 2–205 quoted under Art. 16, *supra* at §141.)[4] In contrast to these doubts, Article 17 is clear.

155 B. "Acceptance" that Modifies an Offer Followed by Unqualified Acceptance

An offeree can create difficult problems by a response that is not a clear-cut acceptance or rejection; the ambiguity may be a bargaining tool in the attempt to secure better terms while trying to hold the offer open. Whether an "acceptance" that includes modifications is an acceptance or a rejection is addressed by Article 19 and can best be considered under that article. However, the link between Articles 17 and 19 can be usefully illustrated at this point:

Example 17B. On May 1 Seller made the "firm" offer that was described in Example 17A. On May 7 the following message from Buyer reached Seller: "I accept your offer, as evidenced by my purchase order which is enclosed." The purchase order included a provision that

---

3. "In most, if not all the countries of the [European] Union, an offer lapses if it is rejected...." Principles of European Contract Law Art. 2:203, Note, at 168. Art. 2:203 of the Principles of European Contract Law states a rule substantively similar, if not identical, to CISG Art. 17. See also I *Schlesinger, Formation* 127 (general report). Civil law, II *id.* 1013 (various E. Eur. countries), 1018–1020 (France; renunciation of "option" must be unequivocal), 1022–1025 (Austria, Ger. & Sw.), 1035–1036 (Italy; rejection of option contract must be very clear), 1041 (Poland), 1043 (So. Af.). Common law: 1014–1015 (Eng., Aus., Can. & N.Z.), 1029 (India); *Farnsworth, Contracts* 174–175.

4. See MacNeil in II *Schlesinger, Formation* 1005–1008. *Cf.* Restatement, Second of Contracts §37. The UCC does not deal with this question; answers must be developed from relevant common-law principles which, in cases like Example 17A, may include estoppel.

the parties agreed to binding arbitration of any dispute arising under the contract; Seller's offer did not refer to arbitration. On May 10, Seller received a second message from Buyer which stated: "I hereby accept your May 1 offer without qualification." Seller did not reply to either message from Buyer. Seller claims no contract was concluded, and Seller has refused to ship Buyer the goods.

As we shall see more fully in examining Article 19, Buyer's May 7 communication, although it "purported to be an acceptance," probably was a "rejection" because of the additional material term. Under Article 17, this rejection terminated Seller's offer, and no contract was concluded. (For cases where the parties proceed with performance, see Art. 19 at §§170–170.4.)

156   ## C. Rejection Overtaken by Acceptance

Example 17C. On May 1 Seller made an offer as in Example 17A. On May 7 Buyer mailed a rejection but on May 8, before the letter reached Seller, Buyer phoned (or telexed) to Seller as follows: "Ignore my May 7 letter. I accept your offer." Seller contended that Buyer's letter of May 7 terminated the offer.

Article 17 states that an offer is terminated when a rejection "reaches" the offeror. Similarly, under Article 18(2), *infra* at §161, an acceptance becomes effective when the indication of assent "reaches" the offeror. In Example 17C the acceptance reached the offeror before the rejection, and a contract was concluded.[5] The time when a rejection or an acceptance "reaches" the offeror is addressed in Article 24, §179 *infra*.

5. The principle that a communication that is *en route* may be nullified by another communication that arrives first is also illustrated in Arts. 15(2) and 22. On "general principles" of the Convention, see Art. 7(2), *supra* at §85.

Article 18.
Acceptance: Time and Manner for Assent

157   The first four articles of Part II deal with the offer; we turn now to the acceptance. This initial article sets forth the criteria and also the time and manner for an acceptance.

Article 18[1]

(1) A statement made by or other conduct of the offeree indicating assent to an offer is an acceptance. Silence or inactivity does not in itself amount to acceptance.

(2) An acceptance of an offer becomes effective at the moment the indication of assent reaches the offeror. An acceptance is not effective if the indication of assent does not reach the offeror within the time he has fixed or, if no time is fixed, within a reasonable time, due account being taken of the circumstances of the transaction, including the rapidity of the means of communication employed by the offeror. An oral offer must be accepted immediately unless the circumstances indicate otherwise.

(3) However, if, by virtue of the offer or as a result of practices which the parties have established between themselves or of usage, the offeree may indicate assent by performing an act, such as one relating to the dispatch of the goods or payment of the price, without notice to the offeror, the acceptance is effective at the moment the act is performed, provided that the act is performed within the period of time laid down in the preceding paragraph.

158   A. Criteria for Acceptance

Under paragraph (1), an acceptance is effected by a statement or other conduct of the offeree "indicating assent." The words "indicating" and "assent" epitomize the two major problems of contract formation: (1) communication and (2) agreement. The present article concentrates on problems of communication; Article 19, *infra* at §165, addresses questions concerning assent.

---

1. Art. 18 of the Convention is the same as Art. 16 of the 1978 Draft Convention, except for a drafting change in paras. (1) and (2). *Cf.* ULF 2(2), 6 and 8.

Paragraphs (2) and (3) of Article 18 govern the time when an acceptance becomes "effective" — a concept that paragraph (2) uses in stating rules on whether an acceptance is too late to form a contract. The time when an acceptance becomes "effective" is also employed to decide whether an offeree may withdraw an "acceptance" after transmission (Art. 22, *infra* at §177) and to specify the time when a contract is concluded (Art. 23, *infra* at §178).

159 B. Indication of Assent; Communication

In connection with assent the Convention uses a delicate term — "indicating." A stronger word such as "stating" would not have been appropriate since assent may be shown not only by a "statement" but also by "other conduct." The mode of expression is unrestricted but communication of assent in some form is emphasized. Thus paragraph (1) states that "silence or inactivity," which generally does not communicate assent, normally does not in itself amount to acceptance; more clearly, paragraph (2) requires that the indication of assent "reach" the offeror. In §163 *infra* we shall consider the role of communication in situations governed by paragraph (3), which applies where the offeree is empowered to "indicate assent by performing an act . . . without notice to the offeror."

160 (1) Silence or Inactivity

Principles of fair dealing do not permit an offeror to impose on the offeree the duty to respond. Such is the predominant rule of domestic law.[2] The Convention's approach, embodied in Article 18(1), may be illustrated as follows:

Example 18A. On June 1 Seller sent Buyer an offer to sell a specified type and quantity of goods at a stated price, and added: "This is such an attractive offer that I shall assume that you accept unless I hear from you by June 15." Buyer did not respond. Seller shipped the goods on June 16.

---

2. Sutton, Formation of Contract: Unity in International Sales of Goods, 16 U. W. Ont. L. Rev. 113–121 (1977); Cigoj, International Sales: Formation of Contracts, 23 Neth. Int. L. Rev. 257, 267–268 (1976); Farnsworth, Formation of International Sales Contracts, 110 U. Pa. L. Rev. 305, 324 (1962); Houin, Sale of Goods in French Law, in *Comp. Sales (I.C.L.Q.)* 16, 22; *Corbin* §§72–75; Restatement, Second of Contracts §69. *Cf.* Laufer, Acceptance by Silence: A Critique, 7 Duke Bar Assn. J. 87 (1939).

By virtue of Article 18(1), no contract was formed and Buyer may reject the goods.[3] This provision states that silence or inactivity does not "in itself" amount to acceptance, and thus indicates that in special circumstances silence or inaction may constitute acceptance.[4] This possibility may be explored in the following setting:

Example 18B. On June 1 Buyer delivered the following to Seller: "Please rush price quotation for the following goods [specifying quantity and quality]. If you do not hear from me within three days after I receive your quotation, consider your offer as accepted." Seller delivered the quotation (which in these circumstances we will assume constitutes an offer) to Buyer on June 3; Buyer did not respond until June 10, when he objected to the prices that Seller had quoted.

In this case, Buyer's silence was an acceptance of Seller's offer. Unlike Example 18A, where the offeror tried to force the offeree to respond, the duty to respond was here assumed by the offeree — the one who failed to respond. The provision regarding silence in Article 18(1) is no barrier: Article 6 permits the parties to "derogate from or vary the effect" of any of the provisions of the Convention.[5] Buyer proposed that if Seller sent a quotation Buyer would be bound if he failed to reply within three days, and Seller sent the quotation with this understanding. Under Article 9 the parties are also contractually bound "by any usage to which they have agreed and by any practices which they have established between themselves." (Art. 9, *supra* at §114.) In Example 18A, an applicable usage or practice that no response was required could provide a basis for the making of a contract without an explicit response to the offer.[6]

Intriguing questions are presented by domestic rules on the effect of silence after receiving a letter "confirming" the terms of an "agreement" that had not been finalized. These domestic rules vary and present

---

3. See Peter Schlechtriem, Art. 18 para. 9, *in* Schlechtriem & Schwenzer, *CISG Commentary* (2nd English ed. 2005) (stating that offeror cannot insert a term in the offer stating that silence constitutes acceptance "as a way of binding the offeree if he fails to reply to the offer").

4. Peter Schlechtriem, Art. 18 para. 9, *in* Schlechtriem & Schwenzer, *CISG Commentary* (2nd English ed. 2005).

5. If one of the parties has its place of business in a State that, by a declaration under Art. 96, has reserved out of the Convention's rule dispensing with requirements as to written form (*cf.* Arts. 11 and 12), it would be necessary to consider which law is applicable to the contract and whether the form requirements of that law are satisfied by the written communications set forth in Example 18B. See Art. 12, *supra* at §128.

6. Decisions that deny as well as decisions that recognize acceptance by silence or inactivity under the CISG are cited and discussed in UNCITRAL Digest Art. 18 para. 7.

distinct problems of relationship to the Convention. To the extent that these rules create rebuttable presumptions regarding the actual practices of the parties or usages of the trade, questions of incompatibility with Article 18(1) are avoided by Article 9 which gives contractual effect to such practices and usages. (See §120.1 *supra*.) However, more serious problems are presented by rules that reach beyond Article 9 since they may invade and conflict with the Convention's rules on formation of the contract. Assume, for example, that in a transaction between parties in States A and B, only State B has a rule of law giving effect to silence after receipt of a letter of confirmation. In this setting application of the domestic rules of State B raises serious questions of conflict with Article 18 and the Convention's basic goal (Art. 7) to achieve uniformity in application.[7]

161   C. Time Limits for Acceptance

Paragraph (2) of Article 18 provides that acceptance is not effective unless and until the offeree's "indication of assent *reaches* the offeror" and that this communication must take effect within prescribed time limits.

In addition, Paragraph (2) indicates how long an offeree has to "indicate assent" to an offer. It states that an "oral" offer (when the parties speak face-to-face or over the telephone) "must be accepted *immediately* unless the circumstances indicate otherwise." (The most normal and decisive "circumstances" that indicates "otherwise" would be the offeror's consent to a later reply.[8]) In other cases, the offer must be accepted either within the time fixed by the offeror, or if the offeror has not fixed a time, within "a reasonable time" in the light of all the circumstances.[9] As has been suggested at §144, a delay that permits

---

7. See Esser, Commercial Letters of Confirmation, 18 Ga. J. Int. & Comp. L. 427 (1988). For further discussion of commercial letters of confirmation, see Peter Schlechtriem, *Introduction to* Arts. 14–24 para. 6, *in* Schlechtriem & Schwenzer, *CISG Commentary* (2nd English ed. 2005); Bonell/Ligouri, ULR (1997–3) 587–588 nn. 79–84.

8. An offer by a medium as instantaneous as telex is not "oral," both under the normal understanding of the word and pursuant to Art. 13: " 'writing' includes telegram and telex." However, under Art. 18(2) "the rapidity of the means of communication employed by the offeror" will bear on what is a "reasonable time" for reply.

9. For discussion of determining a "reasonable time" for acceptance under the CISG, see Peter Schlechtriem, Art. 18 para. 15, *in* Schlechtriem & Schwenzer, *CISG Commentary* (2nd English ed. 2005). For discussion of domestic law, see *Farnsworth, Contracts* 152–155,

the offeree to speculate at the offeror's expense may not be "reasonable," particularly in the light of the reference to "good faith" in Article 7(2) (see §95).

162 **(1) Delay or Loss in Transmission**

Work on Article 18 encountered two competing theories concerning the time when an acceptance becomes effective: the "dispatch" (or "post-box") theory and the "receipt" theory. We have met the "dispatch" theory in connection with attempts by the offeror to revoke his offer. (Art. 16 *supra* at §140.) In that setting the rule that an acceptance is effective when it is dispatched proved appropriate in limiting the offeror's power to revoke an offer. Once this specific situation was addressed in Article 16(1), it was possible to consider whether the "dispatch" or "receipt" approach is more appropriate for the problem presented by the delay or loss of a communication of acceptance sent by the offeree. This problem can be illustrated as follows:

Example 18C. On June 1 Seller mailed to Buyer the following letter: "I offer you, for your prompt acceptance, the following goods: (details as to quantity, price, etc.)." The mails between Seller and Buyer normally require a week for delivery and Seller's offer reached Buyer in due course on June 8. On June 9 Buyer mailed a letter to Seller accepting the offer. The letter was properly addressed and stamped but it was lost in the mails; Seller learned of the letter a month later when Buyer complained that the goods had not arrived.

Article 18(2) provides that an acceptance "is not effective if the indication of assent does not "reach" the offeror within the time he has fixed." (In Example 18C the offeror asked for "prompt acceptance.") Article 18(2) puts the risk of transmission on the offeree — the one who sent the message; in Example 18C, the acceptance was not "effective" within the time limit fixed by the offer. (The result would be the same if the offeree's reply, after a month's delay in the mails, had reached the offeror. However, under Art. 21(2), the offeror must notify the offeree that the offer has lapsed when the late acceptance shows that the period of transmission has been abnormal. See the Commentary to Art. 21, *infra* at §176.)

Under Article 18(2) the hazards of communicating an acceptance fall on the sender (the offeree) rather than the addressee (the offeror).

§3.19; Cigoj, *supra* n. 2 at 297; Sutton, *supra* n. 2 at 138; Restatement, Second of Contracts §41(1) and (2); *Corbin* §§35–36.

In determining which party should bear those risks the balance is about even, but the following considerations may tip the scale. When the transaction reaches the point of acceptance, delays or mishaps in communication become crucial, for acceptance creates a duty of performance, and failure to perform leads to disappointment and legal liability. The "receipt" principle calls for special care by the sender, and the sender has a greater opportunity to know whether the medium he uses is then subject to hazards or delays. At any rate, the "receipt" approach is widely followed in the civil law world, and many of the reasons that contributed to the common-law "dispatch" or "post-box" approach have been met by the Convention's rules (Art. 16) restricting revocation by the offeror.

163 D. Assent by Performing an Act

As has already been noted, Article 18(1) permits an offeree to accept by "conduct . . . indicating assent to an offer." What kind of conduct satisfies this criterion? The answer is a matter of interpretation, pursuant to the rules in Article 8 (which expressly address interpretation of "the conduct of a party"), in the circumstances of each case. Some more specific guidance is available. For example, Article 18(3) (discussed more fully below) mentions two categories of acts that can constitute acceptance — those "relating to the dispatch of the goods or payment of the price" — although (again) the circumstances of the individual case must always be considered.[10] Decisions applying the Convention and commentary on it provide further assistance.[11]

If Article 18(1) permits acceptance by conduct, what is the purpose of Article 18(3), which also addresses situations in which an offeree indicates assent "by performing an act"? Upon careful examination, it is clear that Article 18(3) is not about whether conduct can constitute acceptance — that is a matter governed by Article 18(1), despite some confusion on this score even by courts[12] — but rather is about the time when acceptance by conduct is effective. As we have seen, under

10. For example, a seller may ship ordered goods to a buyer, but make it clear to the buyer that the goods are not exactly what the buyer ordered (or that the seller will charge a higher price than the buyer asked) and that the buyer is free to refuse the goods if it does not agree.
11. For decisions on acceptance by conduct, see UNCITRAL Digest Art. 18 para. 6. For commentary on the kinds of acts that "indicate asset" to an offer, see Peter Schlechtriem, Art. 18 para. 7, *in* Schlechtriem & Schwenzer, *CISG Commentary* (2nd English ed. 2005).
12. See UNCITRAL Digest Art. 18 para. 10 and decisions cited in n. 25 thereto.

Article 18(2) an acceptance normally becomes effective (and thus, under Art. 23, concludes a contract) when the indication of assent "reaches the offeror." Article 18(3) creates an exception to this general rule: when it applies, Article 18(3) provides that an acceptance by conduct is effective at the moment the offeree performs the act indicating assent to the offer, even if at that time no indication of assent has yet reached the offeror.

Thus Article 18(3) is strictly a rule about the time when an acceptance by conduct is effective to conclude a contract. A crucial caveat, however, is in order: Article 18(3) does not apply simply because an offeree has indicated assent by performing an act. Two conditions must be satisfied to trigger the provision: (1) the offeree must have indicated assent to the offer by performing the act, and (2) the offeree must be authorized to so indicate assent without notice to the offeror. Article 18(3) further specifies that the authorization to accept without notifying the offeror must be "by virtue of the offer or as a result of practices the parties have established between themselves or of usage."[13] Since the "normal" rule in Article 18(2) is that notice must reach the offeror before an acceptance is effective, the exceptional situation where notice to the offeror is not needed for such purpose would have to be affirmatively established.[14] In summary, only a subset of acceptances-by-conduct are governed by Article 18(3): those where the offer, the parties' practices, or usages empower the offeree to indicate assent (by conduct) without notice to the offeror. Where this special condition is not met, an offeree's acceptance by conduct remains subject to the usual timing rule in Article 18(2), which requires an indication of assent to reach the offeror before the acceptance becomes effective.[15]

The application and effect of Article 18(3) can best be illustrated by starting with a relatively simple illustration:

Example 18D. On June 1 Buyer delivered to Seller the following: "Please rush shipment of the following goods: (description of the goods)." On June 2 Seller shipped the goods to Buyer via a third party carrier. The next morning (June 3), before Seller had notified Buyer that the

---

13. The reference in Art. 18(3) to "practices the parties have established between themselves" and to "usage" implicate Art. 9 of the Convention.

14. Although this commentary argues that burden of proof issues are generally outside the scope of the CISG (see §70.1 *supra*), presumably the burden of showing that notice to the offeror was not required would, in the procedures of most tribunals, be placed on the party claiming the benefit of the Art. 18(3) exception.

15. *Accord*, Peter Schlechtriem, Art. 18 para 7, *in* Schlechtriem & Schwenzer, *CISG Commentary* (2nd English ed. 2005).

goods were on the way, Buyer phoned Seller and said: "Do not ship the goods ordered June 1." Seller replied that it was too late to countermand the order since the goods had already been shipped. When the goods arrived on June 20, Buyer rejected them on the ground that there was no contract.

Under the Convention it seems clear that a contract was formed and the Buyer is liable to Seller for breach of contract. Buyer's instruction to "rush shipment" would invoke Article 18(3): "by virtue of the offer . . . the offeree may indicate assent by performing an act, such as one relating to the dispatch of the goods . . . , without notice to the offeror."[16] Thus Seller's acceptance became effective "at the moment the act [dispatching the goods] was performed," and the contract was concluded before Buyer attempted to revoke.

The same result follows from the rules on revocability in Article 16(2)(b): In view of the request for prompt shipment, "it was reasonable for the offeree to rely on the offer as being irrevocable and the offeree has acted in reliance on the offer" by shipping the goods; *as a result, the offer was irrevocable and Buyer's attempt to revoke ineffective. It can also be argued that, because Seller dispatched acceptance (by shipping the goods) before receiving Buyer's phone call, Buyer's attempt to revoke came too late under Article 16(1). Thus in a situation such as Example 18D, both Article 18(3) and Article 16 protect the offeree who has reasonably relied on a request contained in the offer from later attempts to revoke the offer.*

Other scenarios implicating Article 18(3), however, do not involve attempts to revoke an offer, and thus Article 16 would not solve the problems they raise. Consider the following:

Example 18D-1. Same facts as Example 18D, with the following additions: the offer authorized the seller to ship the goods via a third party carrier, and provided for delivery FCA Seller's Premises as per International Commercial Terms of the ICC (INCOTERMS) 2000. During the evening of June 2 (after the carrier had taken over

---

16. Domestic rules dealing with acceptance by an act: Cigoj, *supra* n. 2 at 288; Farnsworth, *supra* n. 2 at 324; Sutton, *supra* n. 2 at 137–139; Schmidt, *supra* n. 7 at 15–19; 1 *Schlesinger, Formation* 141–143 (general report), II *id.* 1203–1296 (individual reports). See ULF Art. 6(2): acceptance may consist of "dispatch of the goods or of the price . . . ."

The (U.S.A.) UCC (§2–206(1)(b)) states: "an order or other offer to buy goods for prompt or current shipment shall be construed as inviting acceptance either by a prompt promise to ship or *by the prompt or current shipment* of conforming or nonconforming goods . . . ." This rule on how the offer "shall be construed" provides less leeway for construction of the offer than Art. 18(3) but reaches the same result as the Convention in cases like Example 18D.

the goods but before Seller had communicated the fact of shipment to Buyer) the goods were destroyed in an accident. Buyer has refused to pay for the goods.

Under the FCA price-delivery term in the offer, risk would transfer to the Buyer when the goods were loaded on the vehicle or vessel provided by the carrier;[17] *thus Buyer should reasonably have expected to bear the risk at the time of the accident, even if it had not yet received word that the goods were en route, because its offer requested "rush shipment." If the timing rule of Article 18(2) applied, however, Buyer would point out that it had not yet received an indication of acceptance when the accident occurred; it would argue that it did not then bear the risk because no contract transferring risk had yet been concluded.*[18] *To permit Buyer to escape the obligation to pay in these circumstances would be unjust and contrary to proper commercial practices. The timing rule of Article 18(3), applicable here because of the "rush delivery" term in Buyer's offer, yields the proper result: it provides that a contract was concluded as soon as Seller performed the act indicating assent to the offer—that is, as soon as it delivered the goods to the carrier for shipment to Buyer. Because that contract included the FCA delivery term, Buyer would bear risk at the relevant time and thus, under Article 66, would remain obliged to pay for the goods despite their destruction.*

164   **(1) Communication of Acceptance by Action**

Example 18E. On June 1 Seller received a letter from Buyer dated May 28 requesting Seller to ship certain goods, at a price that was specified in Seller's catalogue. Seller did not reply to Buyer's offer but dispatched the goods on June 9. Normal delivery time was one week, and the goods arrived in Buyer's city in due course on June 16. On that date the carrier notified Buyer that the goods had arrived. When

---

17. See International Chamber of Commerce, *INCOTERMS 2000: ICC Official Rules for the Interpretation of Trade Terms* FCA §§A4 & B5 at 34, 37 (1999).

18. One might attempt to use the second sentence of Art. 68, dealing with transfer of risk when goods are sold in transit (see §§372 *et seq. infra*), to argue that Buyer bore the risk even if the contract of sale had not been concluded at the time the accident occurred. Art. 68 was not designed for circumstances like those in the example under discussion, however, and it would be difficult to manipulate it to achieve proper results here. For one thing, the main risk-transfer rule in the first sentence of Art. 68 actually reinforces Buyer's argument for escaping its obligations. Furthermore, if Seller already knew about the damage to the goods when a contract was eventually concluded, the final sentence of Art. 68 could cause problems. Thus Art. 18(3) provides a superior and more reliable solution.

the carrier notified Buyer that the goods had arrived, Buyer notified both Seller and the carrier that he would not accept the goods since Buyer was unaware that Seller had shipped the goods, and Buyer therefore had procured substitute goods.

Seller might attempt to invoke paragraph (3) of Article 18: By virtue of the offer, Seller could argue, it had "indicated assent by performing an act" (dispatching the goods) and thereby had closed a contract on June 9. Buyer might reply that, under Article 18(3), acceptance "is effective at the moment the act is performed" only if the offer has authorized not only "assent by performing an act" but also assent "*without notice* to the offeror." *Here, the request in Buyer's order that Seller "ship" the goods (unlike the instruction to "rush shipment" in Example 18D) arguably does not authorize acceptance without notice. Communication and notice are central to the Convention's system of contract formation — fostering communication and promoting cooperation between the parties have been identified as general principles on which the Convention is based*[19]*— which counsels care before concluding that the conditions triggering Article 18(3) are present. If Article 18(3) is not applicable, Seller's acceptance in Problem 18E would be governed by the first sentence of Article 18(2), and would not be effective until the indication of assent reached the offeror — presumably, when the goods arrived on June 16. If (as seems likely) this was beyond a "reasonable time," the acceptance was too late under the second sentence of Article 18(2).*

Alternatively, even if Article 18(3) applied in Example 18E and the acceptance was effective when Seller dispatched the goods, the acceptance may still have been too late. The final part of Article 18(3) requires the act indicating assent to be performed "within the period of time laid down in the preceding paragraph" — that is, Article 18(2). Because the offer in Example 18E did not fix a time for acceptance, the offeror's act of acceptance was due under the second sentence of Article 18(2) within "a reasonable time," but Article 18(2) requires a reasonable time to be determined with reference to how long it will take the offeror to receive notice of the acceptance. In other words, even if an emailed statement of acceptance that was sent and received on June 9 would have been timely in Example 18E, that does not mean shipment of the goods on that date, when the goods will not arrive (and

---

19. See the Commentary to Art. 7, *supra* §100; see also Peter Schlechtriem, Art. 7 para. 30 (citing the decision of the *Bundesgerichtshof*, Germany, October 31, 2001), *in* Schlechtriem & Schwenzer, *CISG Commentary* (2nd English ed. 2005).

Buyer will not learn of the shipment) for another week, is timely. Unless Buyer's decision in Example 18E to purchase substitute goods was unreasonably premature, it is highly likely that the Seller's act of acceptance came too late, and Seller should have sent earlier-arriving notice that the goods had been shipped in order to preserve its rights. This not only makes obvious common sense, but it is consistent with the focus of the second sentence of Article 18(2) on whether the offeror will receive notice of acceptance in timely fashion; nothing in Article 18(3) changes this focus. As stated in prior editions of this commentary, acceptance under Article 18(3) must "give[] the offeror the information he needs within the time he needs it." That clearly did not happen in Example 18E.

Suppose Buyer's offer in Example 18E had stated that Seller had "until the close of business on June 9 to accept." Under the second sentence of Article 18(2) Seller clearly could accept until June 9, and if Article 18(3) applies shipment within that deadline would conclude a contract. But setting a June 9 deadline to accept may strengthen the argument that Article 18(3) does not apply: construing this offer to authorize acceptance by shipment "without notice to the offeror" would mean that the offeror might not learn whether Seller had accepted until some three weeks after the offer was sent, which does not appear reasonable. If Article 18(3) does not apply, Seller's indication of assent to the offer would have had to reach Buyer by June 9 according to the first sentence of Article 18(1), and Seller's attempt to accept would be untimely.

Suppose Buyer's offer had not specified a deadline for acceptance, and Seller shipped the goods on June 3, the day after receiving the offer; but suppose also that transport of the goods to Buyer would normally take — and in this case actually did take — two weeks, so that the goods did not arrive until June 16, after Buyer had purchased substitute goods.[20] Unless notice of acceptance were required Buyer would not learn of Seller's acceptance until an extended period after the offer was made. This again suggests that construing the offer to dispense with such notice may not be reasonable, and thus application of Article 18(3) may not be justified. The fact that Seller dispatched the goods immediately after receiving the offer would, therefore, not suffice; an indication of Seller's assent would have to be received within a reasonable time in order to conclude a contract under Article 18(2).

20. With these changed facts the situation would correspond to the facts of Example 18E in prior editions of this commentary.

Seller (again) could have secured its rights by promptly notifying Buyer that it had shipped the goods (thus indicating asset to Buyer's offer), which would have prevented Buyer from entering into the redundant substitute purchase.

Even where Article 18(3) applies, an offeree who effectively accepts by conduct may be required to give the offeror appropriate and timely notice of such acceptance. The fact that under this provision an acceptance is effective at the moment an act (such as dispatching the goods) is performed does not preclude such an obligation,[21] and imposing such a requirement would promote the ideals of communication and cooperation that, as was noted above, inform the Convention. Professor Schlechtriem argues that an offeree whose acceptance by conduct is governed by Article 18(3) may have an obligation to give the offeror notice of such acceptance, but in his view such obligation only arises if the parties' contract expressly or impliedly so requires.[22] Construing the Convention to impose that duty is more of stretch, but it would also be a more consistent and useful expression of the Convention's values.

---

21. Compare the rule in U.S. domestic sales law, §2–206(2) of the Uniform Commercial Code, which provides: "If the beginning of a requested performance is a reasonable mode of acceptance, an offeror that is not notified of acceptance within a reasonable time may treat the offer as having lapsed before acceptance."

22. Peter Schlechtriem, Art. 18 para. 23, *in* Schlechtriem & Schwenzer, *CISG Commentary* (2nd English ed. 2005).

Article 19.
"Acceptance" With Modifications

165 ## A. The Commercial Setting

We now face the following situation: A reply to an offer purports to be an acceptance but states one or more provisions that add to or are inconsistent with provisions in the offer. Such "acceptances" are a common form of commercial life. High-speed, standardized production has been accompanied by measures to accelerate the placing and the acceptance of orders. Traditionally, the central tools in this process have been pre-printed Purchase or Sales Order and Acknowledgment of Order forms. The front of the form has blank lines and spaces where the seller or buyer states the description, quantity and price and other individualized aspects of the transaction; the front of the form also states that additional terms and conditions appear on the back of the form. Now substantially the same order process can be conducted electronically, for example, through emails that, in addition to specifying details of a particular transaction, state the standardized terms of the sender or attempt to incorporate those standard terms by a reference to, for example, a web site where the terms can be viewed.

Sellers' standard terms often include provisions that limit responsibility if supply or production difficulties are encountered, and limit liability for defects in the goods — particularly liability for consequential damages. Buyers' standard terms tend, of course, to emphasize different points. In routine transactions, the parties' communications are exchanged and the goods are supplied without attention to the divergent standard terms of the forms. A businessman who responded to a survey about the use of standard terms added the wry comment that business would come to a halt if sellers and buyers should "read the back-sides of the other"s forms.[1]

It is vital to focus on the precise and full situation from which each problem arises. Needless to say, no problem arises when O sends an offer to R whose reply rejects the offer. Difficulty arises only when R's reply is subject to ambiguity: The reply "purports to be an acceptance" but

---

1. Waddams, Research Paper No. II.1, summarized on *Ont. L. Ref. Com.*, I *Sale* 81 n. 25. This Research Paper reported that as many as 60% of the businesses that responded to a questionnaire had contacts with conflicts between sales and purchase forms. Additional data on the widespread use of such forms in Europe appears in van der Veiden, Uniform International Sales Law and the battle of the forms, in *Sauveplanne Festschrift* 233 (study of Dutch practices by F.A.J. Gras). See Symposium, Battle of the Forms, 4 Canad. Bus. L.J. 261 (1980); Rawlings, The Battle of the Forms, 42 Mod. L. Rev. 715 (1979).

adds one or more terms that add to or differ from the offer. To complete
the picture we need to know what, if anything, happens next. If O,
without undue delay, objects to the modifications in R's reply the answer
should be clear: There is no contract and will be none unless the parties
agree on the disputed terms.

As we have seen, difficulty results from the routine exchange of Order
and Acknowledgment forms without attention or objection to discrepancies between the terms printed on their forms.

In this setting the transaction usually moves ahead without controversy. Orders for standard goods are likely to be filled promptly before
either party has reason to regret the transaction. When the transaction
calls for delay in delivery, as in an order for the production of goods to
the buyer's specifications, changes in costs or price levels occasionally
may lead one of the parties to claim that it is not bound by contract.

Most problems, however, develop after delivery of the goods when the
buyer claims that defects in goods lead to dissatisfaction or claims by sub-
purchasers, or defects in production materials or machinery cause shut-
down costs or other consequential damages. In this setting the problem is
not "Was there a contract?" but "What were its terms?" A common
source of difficulty is a standard seller's provision limiting its responsibility to replacement or repair of defects; controversy can also develop
from a standard term requiring that disputes be resolved by arbitration.

It is fortunate that problems arising out of the "battle of the forms" do not
arise more frequently, for legal science has not yet found a satisfactory way
to decide what the parties have "agreed" when they have consummated a
transaction on the basis of the routine exchange of inconsistent forms or
electronic communications incorporating divergent standard terms.

166   **B. The Convention**

The Convention, of course, could not ignore this problem:

Article 19[2]

**(1) A reply to an offer which purports to be an acceptance but
contains additions, limitations or other modifications is a rejection
of the offer and constitutes a counter-offer.**

2. Article 19 of the Convention is the same as Art. 17 of the 1978 Draft Convention except for
the deletion, at the end of para. (3) of the following: "unless the offeree by virtue of the offer
or the particular circumstances of the case has reason to believe they are acceptable to the

(2) However, a reply to an offer which purports to be an acceptance but contains additional or different terms which do not materially alter the terms of the offer constitutes an acceptance, unless the offeror, without undue delay, objects orally to the discrepancy or dispatches a notice to that effect. If he does not so object, the terms of the contract are the terms of the offer with the modifications contained in the acceptance.

(3) Additional or different terms relating, among other things, to the price, payment, quality and quantity of the goods, place and time of delivery, extent of one party's liability to the other or the settlement of disputes are considered to alter the terms of the offer materially.

Paragraph (1) of Article 19 states the traditional and widely accepted rule that a reply which purports to accept an offer but which contains modifications "is a rejection of the offer and constitutes a counter-offer." Paragraphs (2) and (3) define a limited exception from the traditional rule. We shall need to consider the article as a whole.[3]

167 (1) The Offeror is Silent in the Face of a Modification

Example 19A. On June 1 Seller delivered to Buyer a Sales Order form that proposed the sale of $1,000 bags of No. 1 quality sugar on specified terms, including shipment on July 1. Printed provisions on the back of the Sales Order form included the statement: "The goods will be packaged in sound bags." On June 5 Buyer delivered to Seller a Purchase Order form that purported to accept Seller's offer. The back of the Purchase Order had printed terms that, in general, corresponded with those on Seller's form, but included the statement: "Shipment in new

---

offeror." A similar provision appears in the 1964 Hague Convention on Formation: ULF Art. 7. The draft transmitted to the 1964 Hague Conference had no comparable provision; ULF Art. 7 resulted from proposals by the ICC and Sweden. II *Records 1964 Conf.*, 421 (draft), 441 (ICC), 466 (Sweden). A careful review of the legislative history of Art. 19 of the Convention appears in Vergne, 33 Am. J. Comp. L. 233, 235–238 (1985) (high-lights difference in outlook between East and West).

3. The prevailing rules of domestic law are canvassed in von Mehren, The "Battle of the Forms," 38 Am. J. Comp. L. 265 (1990); Cigoj, International Sales: Formation of Contracts, 23 Neth. Int. L. Rev. 257, 291–295 (1976). On the binding effect, in German (F.R.G.) law, of silence after receipt of a commercial letter of confirmation, see von Mehren, *supra*, p. 290 n. 77; Esser, Commercial Letters of Confirmation, 18 Ga. J. Int. & Comp. L. 427 (1988). For discussion of the application of the CISG to commercial letters of confirmation, see §120.1 & §160 *supra*; Peter Schlechtriem, *Introduction to* Arts. 14–24 para. 4 and Art. 19 para. 4, *in* Schlechtriem & Schwenzer, *CISG Commentary* (2nd English ed. 2005).

packages or bags." Seller did not object to Buyer's Purchase Order and expected to ship the sugar on July 1 in new bags. On June 25 there was a sharp drop in the price of sugar Buyer consulted his lawyer to see whether he was legally bound. Comparison of the two forms revealed the divergency as to "new bags," and on June 27 Buyer cancelled the order on the ground that Seller had not accepted his "counter-offer" of June 5.

Under Article 19, the cancellation probably would not be effective. A tribunal could conclude that the "modification" did not "materially alter the terms of the offer" (Art. 19(2)): the different term in Buyer's response does not appear in the catalogue of material terms in Article 19(3), and does not otherwise appear to have a substantial effect on the transaction. Since the offeror (Seller) did not object to the "modification," the parties were bound by a contract consisting of "the terms of the offer with the modifications contained in the acceptance" — that is, shipment in new bags. Buyer would consequently be liable to Seller for breach of contract.[4]

The approach of Article 19 is probably inconsistent with traditional approaches still maintained in some legal systems.[5] However, there is evidence that tribunals have found ways in the past to defeat attempts to escape from contracts because of immaterial deviations between the offer and "acceptance" — by finding that the alleged deviation was not really inconsistent with the offer in the light of commercial practice or good faith, or was a request for modification of an agreement, or had been waived by the proposer or accepted in silence by the other party.[6]

---

4. For a survey of decisions applying Art. 19(2), see UNCITRAL Digest Art. 19 para. 4 & 5. Even if Buyer's divergent term requiring "new" bags were deemed material, so that its response would not conclude a contract but rather would operate as a counter-offer, its attempt to "cancel" the order might still be ineffective, and Seller might still have the opportunity to accept the counter-offer by, for example, shipping the goods). The cancellation notice would be an attempt to revoke the counter-offer, and it might fail if the offer was irrevocable under the rules of Art. 16(2) — that is, if the counter-offer indicated irrevocability by, for example, fixing a date for acceptance (e.g., stating a "respond by" or "ship by" date), or if Seller had reasonably relied on the irrevocability of the offer (e.g., by incurring costs preparing to fill the order).

5. For a survey of European jurisdictions whose domestic law takes this position, see Principles of European Contract Law art. 2:208, Note 3, at 180.

6. II *Schlesinger, Formation* 969–971 (Eng., Australian, Canadian & New Zealand), 974–976 (France), 978–984 (German, Austrian, Swiss.); Schlechtriem, The Battle of the Forms Under German Law, 23 Bus. Lawyer 655 (1968) (case law prior to German Standard Terms Act 1969, discussed at Art. 35, *infra* at §222); Vergne, 33 Am. J. Comp. L. 233 (1985); Murray, 8 J. Law & Comm. 11 (1988). For comparative study and analysis of 1964 Hague

In some countries, domestic law has formally adopted an approach similar to that in CISG Article 19.[7] This, combined with the influence of Article 19 itself, has led to suggestions that the Article 19 approach has become an international principle.[8]

168 (2) The Offeror Objects

Example 19B. On June 1 and June 5 Seller and Buyer exchanged Sales Order and Purchase Order forms like those in Example 19A. In this case (unlike Example 19A where there was no objection) on June 6 Seller wired Buyer: "Do not have adequate supply of sugar in new bags; can ship sugar in sound, secondhand bags." On June 7 Buyer replied: "Insist on new bags." On June 8 Seller wired "Cannot comply with your request." Buyer did not reply and Seller did not ship. By July 1 the price of sugar had advanced, and Buyer claims damages for breach of contract.

Under the Convention no contract was formed. Seller "without undue delay" objected to "the discrepancy," and thus Article 19(2) does not apply. Consequently, the answer is supplied by paragraph (1): Buyer's reply, because of the modification, was "a rejection of the offer"; the "counter-offer" was not accepted and no contract was formed.

169 (a) **What Modifications are "Material"?** The Convention provides a non-exclusive catalogue of "material" terms.[9] Under paragraph (3) the modifications that are considered to be "material" cover most of the aspects of the contract. As a result, most cases will probably fall under the traditional rule, stated in paragraph (1), that a reply with modifications "is a rejection of the offer and constitutes a

---

approach see Goldstajn, *Unification Symposium* 1964 52–54, Lagergren, *id.* 67–70; Honnold, *id.* 10–11.

7. See the European domestic law surveyed in Principles of European Contract Law art. 2:208, Note 2, at 179–180. Domestic sales law in the United States has also moved away from the traditional rule that an acceptance must mirror exactly the terms of the offer or it will be deemed a counter-offer, but the approach adopted in the [in]famous U.C.C. §2–207 differs substantially from that in Art. 19.

8. See UNIDROIT Principles 2004 Art. 2.1.11(2); Principles of European Contract Law art. 2:208(2) and Note 2 at 179–180.

9. The phrase "among other things" in Art. 19(3) shows that the list is not exclusive so that tribunals must consider whether provisions falling outside the list "alter the terms of the offer materially." This phrase shows that the test is not whether the different term deals with a *subject* that is "material" but whether it materially "alters the terms of the offer."

counter-offer."[10] It has been suggested that Article 19(3) merely sets up interpretative presumptions or guidelines in determining materiality, and that additional or different terms relating to the matters listed in the provision may be found immaterial based on the circumstances of the particular case.[11] *Indeed, the UNIDROIT Principles of International Commercial Contracts, which attempt to restate generally-accepted international contract principles (including those in the CISG), and the Principles of European Contract Law, which attempt to reflect contract principles common to European jurisdictions (including those of the CISG applicable in many of those jurisdictions), do not attempt to catalogue "material" terms à la Article 19(3), and both suggest that materiality must be determined on a case-by-case basis.*[12]

In some settings, usages or practices the parties have established between themselves (see Art. 9, supra at §112) might require an offeror to object to even "material" non-matching standardized terms in order to escape being bound by those terms should the parties proceed with the transaction.[13]

But the issue needs to be sharpened: The question is whether applicable usages and practices, in point of fact rather than legal theory, include the scrutiny of the clauses on the back of an acceptance form in a transaction like the one in question. Such a usage or practice would be more readily established where the transaction is large and does not call for rapid and routine handling. And even for a modest and routine order one might find that objection would be expected if the acceptance

---

10. For decisions on what terms are material under Art. 19, see UNCITRAL Digest Art. 19 paras. 3 & 5. For further discussion of the issue, see Peter Schlechtriem, Art. 19 paras. 8, 9 & 13, *in* Schlechtriem & Schwenzer, *CISG Commentary* (2nd English ed. 2005).

11. See Peter Schlechtriem, Art. 19 para. 8, *in* Schlechtriem & Schwenzer, *CISG Commentary* (2nd English ed. 2005) (arguing for "the possibility that even changes to those matters [listed in Art. 19(3)] in the declaration of acceptance may be considered immaterial on account of the particular circumstances of the case, the practices of the parties, preliminary negotiations, or usage . . . . In the author's opinion, Art. 19(3) does not therefore contain an irrebuttable presumption that the parties always intend to regard the matters listed as 'material'.); *Schlechtriem, 1986 Commentary* 55 n. 181; Secretariat Commentary, Art. 17 (later 19 No. 7 ('*normally* to be considered as material'); *Official Records* 24, *Documentary History* 414; decisions discussed in UNCITRAL Digest Art. 19 para. 3.

12. UNIDROIT Principles 2004 Art. 2.1.11 Official Comment 2 ("What amounts to a 'material' modification cannot be determined in the abstract but will depend on the circumstances of each case."); Principles of European Contract Law art. 2:208(2), Comment C, at 178–179.

13. As argued *infra* §170.3 and §170.4, the offeror should not normally be bound by those terms absent a usage or an established practice between the parties.

form was transmitted by a letter that stated: "We call your attention to the provision, on the back of the enclosed from, that provides for arbitration." If the recipient of such a letter proceeded with the transaction a tribunal might well conclude that he had agreed to the arbitration clause — but not to the other provisions of the form. See §100 and §160 *supra*, §170.3 and §170.4 *infra*, and Articles 39(1) and 48(2) on the duty to communicate needed information to the other party.

A term in a response may prove not to be an additional term,[14] or may be rendered immaterial by the fact that it states an obligation that would be an implied term of the contract because of practices established by the parties or by trade usage (Art. 9, §§133–122, *supra*).[15] Suppose that the parties' practices or trade usage imply an obligation to arbitrate disputes, and the response to an offer provides for arbitration under rules the parties had designated in a prior transaction. Article 19(3) states that terms relating to "settlement of disputes" are considered "material." However, an arbitration clause that reflects the parties' practices or an applicable trade usage should not make a material modifications in an offer that does not deal with dispute settlement. Thus, such a reply could close a contact if the offeror fails to object to this added term.

C. Contract Formation Based on Acts of Performance

170 (1) Scope of the Rules of Offer and Acceptance

The Introduction to Part II of the Convention (§132.1, *supra*) discussed the special and restricted scope of the Convention's provisions on whether a contract is formed when all that has happened is a communication by one party ("O") and a reply by the second party ("R"). As we have seen, these rules are necessary and useful in dealing with situations limited to an exchange of communications. In this setting we have met these problems: Is O's communication "sufficiently definite" and does it sufficiently indicate O's "intention to be bound" so that a contract is made if R replies "I accept"? (Art. 14, *supra* at §§134–137.) Does O have the right to withdraw or revoke an offer communicated to R? (Arts. 15 and 16,

---

14. See Peter Schlechtriem, Art. 19 para. 6, *in* Schlechtriem & Schwenzer, *CISG Commentary* (2nd English ed. 2005).

15. See Peter Schlechtriem, Art. 19 para. 8, *in* Schlechtriem & Schwenzer, *CISG Commentary* (2nd English ed. 2005); Farnsworth in *B-B Commentary*, §§2.2 and 2.8 (Illustration 3) pp. 178, 181;Van der Velden, in *Sauveplanne Frestschrift* 233, 237.

supra at §§138–143.) Who bears the risk of the delay or loss in the transmission of R's reply to O? (Art. 18, *supra* at §162.)

Under Article 19 we meet this problem: On receipt of an offer from O, a reply from R, although purporting to be an acceptance, deviates from the offer. In this setting the rules of Article 19 are strict: R's reply to O's offer will not close a contract if it contains a "material" deviation from the offer; an "immaterial" deviation will be fatal if O objects without undue delay. This strict approach is appropriate. Within the period between R's reply and the time allowed for O's objection substantial reliance interests rarely develop.[16] If a dispute develops at this threshold stage of a transaction the terms of an agreement can be settled more effectively by the parties than by the law. Thus, it would be fair to say that Article 19 follows a "traditional" approach. However, the important question is whether this approach is confined, as its terms suggest, to the effect of an "offer" and a "reply to an offer" or whether it extends to transactions where agreement is shown by the parties' conduct.

Serious problems do develop if the "offer"-"reply" provisions of Article 19 are extended more widely. Fortunately, the Convention does not deny commercial reality by suggesting that contracts can develop only from the exchange of communications. Under Article 18(1), "conduct of the offeree indicating assent to an offer is an acceptance." By Article 18, and by several other provisions noted below, the Convention gives legal effect to the fact that in sales transactions (as in other human affairs) actions can speak more loudly than words.[17]

170.1 (2) Conduct the Parties and Contract Formation

The introduction to Article 19 (*supra* at §165) stressed the importance of facing the full setting of the transaction. As a step towards analyzing more complex problems we may consider the following example.

---

16. When R reasonably relies on O's offer, R's reliance interest is protected by barring O's revocation of the offer. Art. 16(1)(b), quoted in n. 9, *infra*. See §144, *supra*.

17. Art. 16(1): An offer cannot be revoked if it indicates that it is irrevocable or if "(b) . . . the offeree has [reasonably] *acted in reliance* on the offer." Art. 8(1) 8(2): Interpretation based on "statements made by and *other conduct* of a party . . . ." Art. 9(1): Parties may be bound by "practices they have established . . . ." Art. 29(2): " . . . a party may be precluded *by his conduct*" from asserting a contract provision permitting only written modifications. Thus, the Convention is not subject to Llewellyn's reproach of the "promise for promise" emphasis in classical contract law as an approach that "binds eyes as ancient China [bound] a lady's little feet." 48 Yale L.J. 1, 32 (1938) quoted in Kelso, 21 Colum. J. Transn. L. 529, 533 n. 23 (1983).

Example 19C. On June 1 Buyer delivered to Seller a Purchase Order that offered to purchase specified production machinery. The Order, in addition to identifying the machinery, stated the price at $20,000, to be paid one month after receipt of the machinery, and called for shipment by August 1. The reverse side of the Order set forth the following terms: Clause #1: Seller will be responsible for damages resulting from defects in the machinery; Clause #2: Any dispute will be settled by arbitration.

On June 15 Seller delivered to Buyer an Order Acknowledgment stating that Seller would ship the machine ordered by Buyer by August 1 and that the price was $20,000 to be paid one month after receipt, as has been set forth in Buyer's Order. The reverse side of Seller's form included the following terms: Clause #1: Seller will replace or repair any defective part of the machinery but will not be responsible for shutdown costs or other consequential damages; Clause #2: An arbitration clause like the one in Buyer's Order.

Neither party mentioned the terms on the reverse of the other's forms. Seller shipped the goods on July 15 and they were received and put into use on August 1. However, Buyer failed to pay for the goods.

In response to Seller's demand for payment Buyer claimed: Seller's Acknowledgment included a provision (Clause #1, above) on the "extent of one party's liability to the other"; under Article 19(3) this was a "material alternation" of Clause #1 in Buyer's Order. Consequently, under Article 19(1), Seller's purported acceptance was a rejection of the offer and a "counter-offer." Since Buyer did not accept Seller's counter-offer there was no contract on which Seller could base an action for the price.

How would a tribunal react to Buyer's objections? In practice one could not avoid seeing the transaction in its full context: The exchange of Purchase and Acknowledgment forms followed by shipment and acceptance of the goods show that Seller and Buyer made a contract. The Order and Acknowledgment forms showed agreement on these basic terms: the description of the goods, the price, the time for shipment, and payment and the procedures for resolving disputes. As we have seen, this examination of the transaction as a whole is required by the Convention in Articles 18, 16, 8, and 9, and (as will be seen) by Article 29.

170.2   **(3) Problems Not Solved by the Contract Terms**

In the above Example the parties' communications agreed on the point at issue — the price for the goods that Buyer ordered and received. We now turn to a case where the communications fail to provide a solution for the problem that develops.

Example 19D. The facts are the same as in Example 19C except for the situation that led to difficulty: Shortly after Buyer placed the machinery in operation, defects in the machinery led to shutdown in Buyer's assembly plant with serious consequential damages. Seller offered to repair or replace the defective machinery pursuant to Clause #1 on the back of Seller's Acknowledgment. Buyer contended that, in addition, Seller must pay for shutdown and other consequential damages pursuant to Clause #1 on the back of Buyer's Order. Seller denied such liability on the basis of Clause #1 on its Acknowledgement.

Does Article 19 of the Convention answer the above problem? Immediately after the exchange of forms the answer was clear: Because of the material difference between the terms of Buyer's offer and Seller's reply, there was no contract; either party could refuse to perform.

This case, however, involves much more than the exchange of forms. For reasons developed in connection with Example 19C, above, it is clear from the parties' conduct — the exchange of an offer and a purported acceptance, followed by shipment and acceptance of the goods — that the parties made a contract. What rule governs the scope of Seller's responsibility for the defective goods?

170.3   (4) Conduct Showing Agreement: "Last Shot Theories"

One approach to a situation like Example 19D seeks a way to choose between the terms of the two conflicting communications. One application of this approach gives effect to the *last* form in the sequence on the ground that further performance indicates agreement to its terms.[18] (This is often called the "Last Shot" approach, invoking the metaphor that the parties have been engaged in a "Battle of the Forms" and the aphorism that battles are won by the side that "fires the last shot.")

Applying the "last shot" theory to Example 19D, Seller's reply purported to accept Buyer's offer but contained a material modification and therefore was "a rejection of the offer" and constituted a "counter-offer." Seller then shipped the goods to Buyer. Since no contract had yet formed, Buyer would have been free to reject the goods but, instead, accepted them. Acceptance of the goods, according to the "last shot" theory, was an acceptance of Seller's "counter-offer," and Buyer is bound by the provision in Seller's Sales Order that limited liability to repair or replacement of the defective goods.

18. Farnsworth in *B-B Commentary* 179–183.

Again, the precise facts become important. Suppose the Seller had sent its Order Acknowledgment with a covering letter that drew attention to Clause #1 on the back of the form and asked Buyer to reply before the agreed time for shipment if it objected.[19] In this setting Buyer's conduct in accepting the goods could be construed as assent.

However, when there is merely an exchange of communications with a conflict between incorporated standard terms, it is difficult to conclude that the Buyer gave (or was bound to give) closer attention to the Seller's terms than the Seller apparently gave to the terms of Buyer's offer. It is especially troubling to place this burden on one who received a reply that purported to be an acceptance and thereby created an ambiguity when it incorporated differing standard terms.

When both parties proceed with performance in the face of this ambiguity, if it were necessary to choose between competing terms, Article 8(2) would be relevant: statements or conduct of one party "are to be interpreted according to the understanding that a reasonable person of the same kind as the *other party* would have had in the same circumstances" — the generally accepted principle that doubt is to be resolved against the party who created the ambiguity. This approach also might discourage ambiguity by denying benefit to the party who created the ambiguity by sending an ambiguous "acceptance."[20] However, even this approach for choosing between conflicting forms seems artificial. (There may be a better way. See §170.4, *infra*.)

We can test the reality (as well as the practicality and fairness) of the "last shot" approach by the following case: Suppose that, before Seller shipped the goods, Buyer re-transmitted the terms of its original order, including Clause #1 material making Seller responsible for consequential damage caused by defective goods. Because Buyer's Clause #1 would materially alter the terms of Seller's counter-offer, Buyer's re-transmitted order would, under Article 19(1), constitute a counter-counter-offer. Under the "last shot" theory, Seller would deemed to have accepted the terms of Buyer's re-transmitted order when it thereafter shipped the goods. This would reverse the results in the problem, without justification from any real change in the parties' understanding of the situation. An approach that produces such arbitrary results is not

---

19. One leading seller will not ship until the buyer signs and returns the seller's form. See Murray, 4 Can. Bus. L.J. 290 (1980) (Item III of Panel Discussion). There are, of course, many ways to draw attention to a conflict in terms. See *Kritzer Manual* Ch. 20.
20. See §§107–108, *supra*.

consistent with commercial expectations or with standards of good faith and fair dealing.[21]

"Last shot" theories have been rightly criticized as casuistic and unfair.[22] They do not reflect international consensus that justifies importing them into the Convention.

170.4   (5) Gap-Filling by the Convention

Analysis of Example 19D led to the following conclusions: (1) Performance by the parties showed that they made a contract of sale; (2) The question that led to dispute was not resolved by contract.

If these conclusions are sound we are dealing with the commonest problem in commercial law: a contract fails to solve a problem that leads to dispute. Indeed, providing solutions to gaps left in contracts is the most basic function of laws applicable to commercial sales. For the gap in the contract in Example 19D, the Convention, of course, supplies an answer — a body of rules on remedies for breach (Arts. 45–52, 61–65) and especially the general rule on measurement of damages in Article 74.[23] The rule of Article 74 (and of many domestic systems) that a party in breach is liable for foreseeable consequential damages is not popular with sellers. Under Article 6 the parties can exclude or modify this and other provisions of the Convention but this must be done by agreement; fictitious theories for finding agreement should not suffice.

Thus where the parties exchange communications incorporating standard terms that do not coincide on at least one material point, and they then proceed with performance (i.e., the seller ships and the buyer accepts the goods), the parties are bound by a contract. The contract consists of the terms on which there is real agreement, including terms incorporated through usages and practices and terms common in substance in both parties' standard terms, but other standard terms of either party are not incorporated. Lacunae in the resulting agreement should be filled with the gap-filling provisions of the Convention.

---

21. Article 7(1) provides: "In the interpretation of this Convention, regard is to be had to the need to promote . . . the observance of good faith in international trade."

    See Van der Velden in *Sauveplanne Festschrift*, 233, 244 (German doctrine of *Treu and Glauben*), 245 (Dutch new Civil Code rejects "the later reference"), 248.

22. See Van der Velden, *supra*, 241–242, Murray, 39 Vand. L. Rev. 1307, 1369–1371 (1986); Shanker, 4 Can. Bus. L.J. 263, 271 (1980).

23. For issues not explicitly settled see Arts. 7(2) and 9, §§96–102, 112–122, *supra*.

There is support for such an approach in decisions applying the Convention and in commentary,[24] *and both the UNIDROIT Principles of International Commercial Contracts and the Principles of European Contract Law adopt similar views as a matter of international contract law.*[25] *There is, on the other hand, also considerable support for the "last shot" view.*[26] *Indeed, an extraordinary variety of approaches to the battle of the forms under the CISG has been suggested, including (for example) the idea that the matter is beyond the scope of the Convention and thus is governed by applicable domestic law.*[27]

This plethora of interpretations, often yielding contradictory results, poses an extremely serious threat to the fabric of the Convention. A U.S. trial court has even suggested that the Convention adopts an idiosyncratic U.S. domestic law approach to battle-of-the-forms issues — the so-called "rolling contract" theory[28] *— although nothing in the Convention provides explicit support for the approach and it contradicts authoritative case law; fortunately, this decision was overruled.*[29]

---

24. See decisions cited UNCITRAL Digest Art. 19 para. 6 n. 17. For commentary advocating a position similar to that advocated in the text see, for example, Peter Schlechtriem, Art. 19 paras. 19–20, *in* Schlechtriem & Schwenzer, *CISG Commentary* (2nd English ed. 2005).
25. UNIDROIT Principles 2004 Art. 2.1.22; Principles of European Contract Law Art. 2:209.
26. See decisions cited in UNCITRAL Digest Art. 19 para. 6 n. 18. For commentary supporting this view see, for example, Pilar Perales Viscasillas, *The "Battle of the Forms" under the 1980 United Nations Convention on Contracts for the International Sale of Goods and the UNIDROIT Principles of International Commercial Contracts*, 10 Pace Int'l L. Rev. 97, 147–148 & 151 (1998); John E. Murray, Jr., *The Definitive "Battle of the Forms": Chaos Revisited*, 20 J. L. & Com. 1, 41–42 (2000).
27. Different approaches to the issue are surveyed in Pilar Perales Viscasillas, The "Battle of the Forms" under the 1980 United Nations Convention on Contracts for the International Sale of Goods and the UNIDROIT Principles of International Commercial Contracts, 10 Pace Int'l L. Rev. 97, 136 ff. (1998).
28. Barbara Berry, S.A. v. Ken M. Spooner Farms, Inc., 2006 WL 1009299 (U.S.D.C.W.D. Wash.), available at http://cisgw3.law.pace.edu/cases/060413u1.html, *overruled by* 2007 WL 4039341 (U.S.C. App. 9th Cir.), available at http://cisgw3.law.pace.edu/cases/071108u1.html.
29. Barbara Berry, S.A. v. Ken M. Spooner Farms, Inc., 2007 WL 4039341 (U.S.C. App. 9th Cir.), available at http://cisgw3.law.pace.edu/cases/071108u1.html. Unfortunately, the appeals court did not specifically reject the lower court's application of the rolling contract theory under the Convention. For discussion of this issue, see Rob Schultz, *Rolling Contract Formation under the UN Convention on Contracts for the International Sale of Goods*, 35 Cornell Int'l L.J. 263 (2002), available at http://www.cisg.law.pace.edu/cisg/biblio/schultz.html.

The battle-of-the-forms issue appears to be one that particularly tempts interpreters to impose familiar domestic law approaches on the necessarily-flexible standards articulated in the Convention. Adopting non-uniform approaches to this issue is an extremely serious threat to the very purposes of the Convention because different theories produce vastly different results. If outcomes on such a critical matter come to depend on the tribunal before which the dispute is heard, the reason for having uniform international sales law is undermined, and the problems that the Convention was designed to address re-emerge.

This Commentary has argued for an approach that, it is argued, yields results superior to those of the "last shot" theory. Development of a consensus of interpretations around this view — as leading case law suggests may occur[30] *— would be the most desirable result. But Professor Perales has a made a strong argument that the last shot view is the most consistent with the Convention's drafting history,*[31] *and a uniform interpretation based on this view would be superior to entrenched inconsistent approaches.*

30. In both Austria and Germany the highest courts with jurisdiction in CISG cases appear to have adopted an approach similar to that advocated in the text. See Oberster Gerichtshof, Austria, December 14, 2004, English translation available at http://cisgw3.law.pace.edu/cases/041214a3.html (stating that, where parties have concluded a contract by performing after exchanging communications incorporating non-matching standard terms, "[o]nly mutually agreed terms are to have effect"); Bundesgerichtshof, Germany, January 9, 2002, English translation available at http://cisgw3.law.pace.edu/cases/020109g1.html (stating that, where parties have proceeded to perform, conflicting standard terms in communications they exchanged are excluded from the contract and the resulting gaps are filled by the Convention's provisions). For discussion of the latter decision, see Peter Schlechtriem, Art. 19 para. 21, *in* Schlechtriem & Schwenzer, *CISG Commentary* (2nd English ed. 2005); Pilar Perales Viscasillas, *Battle of the Forms and the Burden of Proof: An Analysis of BGH 9 January 2002*, 6 Vindobona J. Int'l Comm. L. & Arb. 217 (2002).

31. Pilar Perales Viscasillas, The "Battle of the Forms" under the 1980 United Nations Convention on Contracts for the International Sale of Goods and the UNIDROIT Principles of International Commercial Contracts, 10 Pace Int'l L. Rev. 97 (1998).

Article 20.
Interpretation of Offeror's Time Limits for Acceptance

171   Article 18(2) (*supra* at §161) provides that an acceptance is not effective "if the indication of assent does not reach the offeror within the time *he had fixed.* . . ." The offeror's statement fixing the time for acceptance may be ambiguous if it states a period of time (e.g., 15 days) for acceptance and does not specify when the period starts to run or does not deal with the effect of holidays.

Article 20[1]

(1) A period of time for acceptance fixed by the offeror in a telegram or a letter begins to run from the moment the telegram is handed in for dispatch or from the date shown on the letter or, if no such date is shown, from the date shown on the envelope. A period of time for acceptance fixed by the offeror by telephone, telex or other means of instantaneous communication, begins to run from the moment that the offer reaches the offeree.

(2) Official holidays or non-business days occurring during the period for acceptance are included in calculating the period. However, if a notice of acceptance cannot be delivered at the address of the offeror on the last day of the period because that day falls on an official holiday or a non-business day at the place of business of the offeror, the period is extended until the first business day which follows.

Article 20 is merely a guide to interpreting the offeror's statements. Under Article 18(2) the offeror may "fix" the time for acceptance: A statement such as "You may accept this offer within ten days after this offer *reaches you*" would override the interpretive rule of Article 20(1). The offeror's intention could be shown by less explicit language. Suppose that on June 1 Seller mails an offer to Buyer and states, "You will have five days to consider this offer." The mails between Seller and

---

1. Article 20 is based on Art. 18 of the 1978 Draft Convention, subject to drafting changes in para. (2). Paragraph (1) is similar to ULF 8(2). Paragraph (2) (the effect of holidays) was based on UNCITRAL Arbitration Rules (1976) Art. 2(2), VII *Yearbook* 22–27; *cf.* Convention on the Limitation Period in the International Sale of Goods (1974) Art. 29 (A/CONF. 63/15), V *YB* 213, 23 Am. J. Comp. L. 356 (1976).

Buyer normally take four or five days for delivery. It would be inconsistent with the expressed intention of the offer to start the five-day period on June 1. Article 20 thus plays the modest role of answering questions concerning the meaning of the offer when no answer is provided by the usual rules for interpreting the statements of a party. See Article 8, *supra* at §§106–111. *The second sentence of Article 20(1), under which the period for accepting an offer made by means of instantaneous communication begins to run from the moment the offer "reaches the offeree," of course implicates the rule of Article 24 governing the time when an offer "reaches" the addressee.*

Application of Article 20 to electronic communications has been the subject of several commentaries which have distinguished among different forms of electronic communications (e.g., email vs. instant messaging).[2] *As provided in CISG Article 90, questions such as when an electronic communication is "handed in for dispatch" or "received" under Article 20(1) may be subject to the United Nations Convention on the Use of Electronic Communications in International Contracts when it goes into force.*[3]

2. See Peter Schlechtriem, Art. 20 para. 3, *in* Schlechtriem & Schwenzer, *CISG Commentary* (2nd English ed. 2005); CISG Advisory Council, CISG-AC Opinion no. 1, Electronic Communications under CISG paras. 20.1 ff. (2003), available at http://www.cisg.law.pace.edu/cisg/CISG-AC-op1.html#art20-1.
3. See §10 of the Electronic Communications Convention, which addresses when (and where) electronic communications are received and dispatched. The text of the Electronic Communications Convention is available at http://www.uncitral.org/uncitral/en/uncitral_texts/electronic_commerce/2005Convention.html.

Article 21.
Late Acceptances: Response by Offeror

172   The present article, like Article 20, extends and elaborates the basic rule of Article 18(2) that an acceptance "is not effective if the indication of assent does not reach the offeror within the time he has fixed or, if no time is fixed, within a reasonable time. . . ." Under this rule the following two questions can arise. (1) The offeree's reply indicating assent "does not reach the offeror within the time he has fixed": When a late reply reaches the offeror can he make it "effective" by notifying the offeree? (2) A reply that normally would have arrived on time is subject to delays in transmission: Must the offeror notify the offeree that the offer has lapsed?

Answers to these questions may be found in the following article:

Article 21

(1) **A late acceptance is nevertheless effective as an acceptance if without delay the offeror orally so informs the offeree or dispatches a notice to that affect.**

(2) **If a letter or other writing containing a late acceptance shows that it has been sent in such circumstances that if its transmission had been normal it would have reached the offeror in due time, the late acceptance is effective as an acceptance unless, without delay, the offeror orally informs the offeree that he considers his offer as having lapsed or dispatches a notice to that effect.**

173   **A. Notice Giving Effectiveness to Late Acceptance**

The offeree's reply may fail to be effective as an acceptance either (1) because it was sent too late or (2) because of delays in transmission.

174   **(1) Tardy Dispatch**

Example 21A. On June 1 Seller mailed Buyer an offer that stated: "Your acceptance must reach me by June 30." Mail between Seller and Buyer normally takes 5 days. On June 29 Buyer mailed a letter expressing acceptance of the offer; the letter reached Seller in due course on July 4. On July 4 Seller sent the following email to Buyer: "Your June 29 letter was mailed too late to reach me by the June 30 limit set in my offer but I am treating it as an acceptance."

Although Buyer immediately objects to the closing of the contract, and even if the Buyer had dispatched a letter withdrawing the acceptance which arrived on July 5,[1] both parties are bound by contract. True, the market level or other conditions affecting Buyer's interest in the contract may have changed during the five-day period between June 29 and July 4 while Buyer's acceptance was in the mails. Nevertheless, Buyer bears the burden of such changes. Buyer chose a medium of communication that required five days for arrival, and failed to make use of this opportunity under Article 22, *infra* at §177, to overtake his letter by a withdrawal communicated by phone or wire. Note the appearance in Article 21(1) of the "dispatch" principle if the offeror gives non-oral notice that a late acceptance is effective: such notice, if properly dispatched, is effective even if it is delayed or lost.[2]

175 (2) Lateness Because of Transmission Delays

It may now be useful to examine Article 21 (1) when this provision is subject to stress. The following problem will not occur frequently but it may help us to explore the relationship between several provisions of the Convention.

---

1. A late "acceptance" (Example 21A) can be withdrawn until the offeror "dispatches" (Art. 21(1)) his notice that the offer is effective, whereas withdrawal of a timely acceptance must reach the offeror before or at the same time as the acceptance (Arts. 18(2) and 22). *Accord,* John E. Murray, Jr., *An Essay on the Formation of Contracts and Related Matters under the United Nations Convention on Contracts for the International Sale of Goods,* 8 J. L. & Com. 11, 33 (1988). Professor Schlechtriem argues that withdrawal of a late acceptance can be effective only if the withdrawal reaches the offeror before or at the same time as the late acceptance. See Peter Schlechtriem, Art. 21 para. 10, *in* Schlechtriem & Schwenzer, *CISG Commentary* (2nd English ed. 2005) (citing contrary authority in n. 34).

2. See Peter Schlechtriem, Art. 21 para. 7, in Schlechtriem & Schwenzer, CISG Commentary (2nd English ed. 2005); John E. Murray, Jr., An Essay on the Formation of Contracts and Related Matters under the United Nations Convention on Contracts for the International Sale of Goods, 8 J. L. & Com. 11, 33 (1988). Professor Schlechtriem argues, however, that Art. 21(1)'s use of the phrase "informs" in connection with oral communications means that such communications must "heard." See Peter Schlechtriem, Art. 21 para. 9, in Schlechtriem & Schwenzer, CISG Commentary (2nd English ed. 2005). As has been noted in several earlier connections, the time when an email or other electronic communication is "dispatched" (or received) may be subject to §10 of the United Nations Convention on the Use of Electronic Communications in International Contracts when it goes into force.

Example 21B. The facts are the same as in Example 21A, except that Buyer's reply was delayed in the mails and did not reach Seller until July 30. In mid-July the price-level for the goods in question had fallen sharply and Seller was glad to close a deal at the higher level reflected in his June offer. Consequently, on July 20 Seller wired Buyer, "In spite of late arrival of your June 29 letter I am treating it as an acceptance." Buyer objected on the ground that conditions had changed during the month while his letter was in the mails.

Article 21(1), read in isolation, suggests that Seller's wire would close a contract based on Buyer's reply, even though the reply otherwise would have lapsed because of its late arrival. In cases where the delay in transmission of the reply is not extreme, this view must be accepted in order to give effect to the policy expressed in paragraph (1). However, when the reply has been subject to extended delay and conditions have radically changed during this period, the scope of Article 21(1) may need to be considered in relation to other provisions of the Convention.

As we have seen, Article 21 provides an extension of the principle of Article 18(1) that an acceptance is made by a statement of other conduct that indicates "assent" to an offer — an assent that, under Article 18(2), is generally effective only when "the indication of assent *reaches* the offeror." Accord, Article 22, *infra*. In Example 21B, the sharp price-drop, during an extreme delay in the transmission of the offeree's reply, might support a finding that the offeree's June 29 letter, when read by the offeror on July 30, did not indicate to the offeror that the offeree still assented to the June 1 offer. Applying the interpretation standard of Article 8(2),[3] a "reasonable person" in Seller's position would likely not understand Buyer's response as indicating a continuing assent to the offer: under Article 8(3), the lengthy delay in the transmission of Buyer's reply and the changes in market conditions that occurred in the meantime must be given "due consideration" in determining the understanding of the reasonable person.[4] An analogy might be drawn to the English court's analysis in the famous case *Dickinson v. Dodds*,[5] in which an offeree attempted to accept after learning of actions by the offeror that were inconsistent with an intent to continue the offer (the

3. Given the unexpected delay in transmission and the unanticipated market changes, it is unlikely Buyer had an actual "subjective intent" concerning continuing assent in these circumstances, in which case the interpretation standard of Art. 8(1) could not be applied.
4. Buyer's failure to send a withdrawal of its reply when market conditions changed does not suggest a continuing intention to assent to Seller's offer, since Buyer was presumably not aware that transmission of its response had been delayed.
5. 2 Ch. D. 463 (1876).

offeror sold the subject matter of the offer to someone else): although the offeror had not even attempted to communicate a revocation of the offeror, the court held that the offeree had nevertheless lost the power to accept because "the plaintiff knew that [the offeror] was no longer minded to sell the property to him as plainly and clearly as if [the offeror] had told him in so many words, "I withdraw the offer." " The inference that Buyer in Problem 21B was "no longer minded" to assent to Seller's offer is only slightly less strong.

Article 18(2) states that (except in the unusual circumstance where Article 18(3) applies — see §§163–164) an acceptance "is not effective if the indication of assent does not reach the offeror" within the prescribed time limit. In that setting we noted (Art. 18 at §162) that this provision places transmission risks on the offeree. This proposition might suggest that in Example 21B the offeree bore the risk of the offeror's action. But the risk that Article 18(2) places on the offeree is the risk of *failing* to close a contract. A different and grave risk would result if, after a substantial change of circumstances over a substantial period of time, an offeror could elect to take up an "acceptance" that had lapsed because of delay in transmission. The period of such a delay could be indefinitely long; the period within which an acceptance must be received under Article 18(2), of course, is more circumscribed. And if an offeree *fails* to close a contract because of a delay in transmission (Art. 18(2)), the results do not lead to an unfair advantage to either party: there is no contract regardless of whether this favors the offeror or the offeree. But if the offeror is given a free choice under Article 21(1) to approve or disapprove an "acceptance" that has been substantially delayed in transmission while conditions radically change, the offeror will notify the offeree that he treats the reply as an effective acceptance only if the change in conditions makes the transaction more favorable to him — an unfair opportunity to speculate.[6] See also §§95, 144, and 285.

This opportunity to speculate in bad faith will be avoided in such extreme cases by construing Article 21(1) in relation to the basic rules of Article 18(1) and Article 8 that a statement is an acceptance only if it indicates "assent" to the offer in the light of the objective facts available to both parties.[7] This result would also respond to the rule of Article 7(1) that "in the interpretation of this Convention, regard is to be

---

6. Courts have strongly resisted attempts by one party to engage in speculation. See the discussion under Arts. 46 and 62, *infra*.

7. Professor Schlechtriem argues that, under Art. 21(1), an offeror can declare a late acceptance effective no matter how late it is: "[a]n acceptor [whose acceptance has arrived late]

had ... to the need to promote ... the observance of *good faith* in international trade." (See the discussion of Art. 7, *supra* at §94.)

176   **B. Obligation to Notify Offeree of Apparent Delay in Transmission of Acceptance**

We may now explore further the role of paragraph (2) of Article 21.

Example 21C. On June 1 Seller sent Buyer an offer like the one in Example 21B. Buyer's reply, which in this case was dated June 15, was delayed in transmission and reached Seller only on July 20. Seller did not respond to Buyer's acceptance; Buyer learned of the delay only on August 1 when he called Seller to ask why the goods had not arrived. Seller replied that he had ignored the Buyer's June 15 acceptance because it had not reached him by June 30, the date specified in the offer. Buyer claimed that he assumed that his July 15 letter had arrived in time to close the contract, and had expected to receive the goods.

Buyer's reply was dated June 15; the delay in the transmission was obvious. Consequently, under Article 21(2), the late reply was "effective as an acceptance." The parties are bound by contract and Seller will be responsible to Buyer for breach of contract.[8] *To prevent conclusion of a contract here, Seller would have had to dispatch[9] a notice (or orally inform Buyer) that he considered the offer as lapsed.*

---

must accept the risk that circumstances may have changed, e.g., because of falling prices, and that the acceptance has become disadvantageous to him, at least in a situation falling under Art. 21(1), where the lateness is attributable to him." Peter Schlechtriem, Art. 21 para. 4, *in* Schlechtriem & Schwenzer, *CISG Commentary* (2nd English ed. 2005). Where there has been a delay in transmitting an acceptance, on the other hand, Professor Schlechtriem invokes Art. 8(2) to argue that "considerably delayed declarations of acceptance contain an inherent limitation on the period of their validity and they lapse after the expiry of that period." *Id.* para. 23.

8. In common-law systems there has been no occasion to deal with this question since the "dispatch" (or "post-box") rule makes the acceptance effective when it is sent. See Art. 18, *supra* at §162. Many civil law codes, with "receipt" rules like Art. 18(2), have legislative provisions similar to Art. 21(2) of the Convention. Cigoj, International Sales: Formation of Contracts, 23 Neth. Int. L. Rev. 257, 302 (1976) quotes somewhat similar provisions from Germany (BGB 149), Switzerland (Code of Obligations 5(3)), the USSR (Civ. Code 67), Czechoslovakia (Int. Comm. Code 111), Hungary (Civ. Code 214) and Yugoslavia (G.U.T. 24).

9. As under Art. 21(1) (see §174 *supra*), the offeror's non-oral notice following receipt of a late acceptance under Art. 21(2) is effective if properly "dispatched," no matter when (or whether) it is received by the offeree. See Peter Schlechtriem, Art. 21 para. 20, *in* Schlechtriem & Schwenzer, *CISG Commentary* (2nd English ed. 2005).

In Example 21C, unlike in Example 21B, there is no suggestion of severe unforeseen changes in market conditions occurring during the time when transmission of Buyer's reply was delayed. Had there been such changes, the outcome might also change. If such changed market conditions made the transaction less attractive to Seller, it could protect itself by notifying Buyer that the offer had lapsed before acceptance arrived. If the changed market conditions favored Seller, we would face a situation similar to that in Problem 21B; and, as in that situation (see §175 supra), a proper interpretation of Buyer's reply and a policy to foreclose opportunities to speculate may lead to the conclusion that Buyer has not indicated assent to the Seller's offer given the changed situation, and thus no contract is concluded under Article 21(2) even if Seller does not respond to Buyer's delayed acceptance.

Professor Murray has pointed out that, in a situation like Example 21C, finding that a contract was concluded is not unfair to Buyer even if sharp, unanticipated market changes occurred during the time transmission of its acceptance was delayed:

> *If the offeree were not aware of the delay in transmission, presumably he assumed he was bound to a contract that has become undesirable because of market changes. In the latter case, it does not seem anymore harsh to hold the offeree to the contract than it does to hold any party to a contract that becomes undesirable because of market changes.*[10]

Thus, Professor Murray argues, the opportunity for speculation by the offeror here "does not appear to be at the expense of the offeree who . . . appears to assume that he was bound to the contract and would have been surprised to learn of the delay in transmission."[11]

Professor Murray's point is well taken; the problem with the potential for speculation created when an offeree's reply to an offer has been substantially delayed (without fault of the offeree) involves not so much unfairness to the offeree as encouragement of unjustified and undesirable behavior by the offeror. To allow an offeror to create a contract at a time when it knows the offeree almost certainly does not wish to assent to the offer violates the standards of Article 8. Of course had the delayed acceptance arrived in timely fashion a contract would have been concluded earlier, and the offeror would have been entitled

---

10. John E. Murray, Jr., An Essay on the Formation of Contracts and Related Matters under the United Nations Convention on Contracts for the International Sale of Goods, 8 J. L. & Com. 11, 36 (1988).

11. *Id.* at 38.

to the benefits of the subsequently-changed market conditions — but in that case, the offeror would also have borne the risk that the market could go in the other direction. A transaction in which this latter risk has been eliminated is one on much different terms from the one proposed in the original offer. Permitting the offeror to take advantage of a contract on such changed terms is not justified by the Convention's contract formation rules. Construing Article 21 to permit this result is not in keeping with the mandate of Article 7(1) to interpret the CISG in manner that has regard for the need to promote good faith in international trade.

Article 22.
Withdrawal of Acceptance

177   Under Article 15(2), an offer, even if it is irrevocable, may be withdrawn "if the withdrawal reaches the offeree before or at the same time
as the offer." The present article applies this approach to the acceptance:

Article 22[1]

**An acceptance may be withdrawn if the withdrawal reaches the
offeror before or at the same time as the acceptance would have
become effective.**

The time when acceptance becomes "effective," as specified in
Article 18(2), is "the moment the indication of assent *reaches the
offeror*," except where Article 18(3) applies, in which event an acceptance by conduct is effective at "the moment the act is performed" (see
§163 *supra*).

The discussion of Article 15 (*supra* at §138) applies to Article 22.
Indeed, these articles may constitute specific applications of a general
principle[2] that a party may withdraw or modify a communication by a
second communication that overtakes the first. (See the Commentary to
Article 7, *supra* at §96.) *Article 24 (discussed infra at §179) applies to
the question of when a withdrawal "reaches" an addressee. When the
United Nations Convention on the Use of Electronic Communications
in International Contracts goes into force, the time when an electronic
withdrawal of an acceptance is deemed to reach the offeror may, as
provided in CISG Article 90, be determined by that Convention.*[3]
    *Article 22, in combination with the rule of Article 16(1) cutting off
an offeror's power to revoke an offer upon dispatch of an acceptance,
could permit an offeree to speculate unfairly at the offeror's expense.*[4]

---

1. This article is the same as Art. 20 of the 1978 Draft Convention and is similar to ULF 10.
2. See Peter Schlechtriem, Art. 22 para. 1, *in* Schlechtriem & Schwenzer, *CISG Commentary*
(2nd English ed. 2005).
3. See §10 of the Electronic Communications Convention, which addresses when (and
where) electronic communications are received and dispatched. The text of the Electronic
Communications Convention is available at http://www.uncitral.org/uncitral/en/uncitral_
texts/ electronic_commerce/2005Convention.html.
4. John E. Murray, Jr., An Essay on the Formation of Contracts and Related Matters under the
United Nations Convention on Contracts for the International Sale of Goods, 8 J. L. & Com.

For example, a seller-offeree might mail an acceptance that prevents the buyer from thereafter revoking should market prices quickly fall; should market prices quickly rise, however, the offeree could overtake the dispatched acceptance with an emailed withdrawal of the acceptance. Professor Schlechtriem points out that similar possibilities exists under some domestic laws, but that this has not led to substantial abuse.[5] One hopes the same will prove true under the Convention for — unlike the potential for abusive speculation created by Article 21 (see §§175 & 176 supra) — it is difficult to construe the provisions of Articles 16(1) and 22 in a fashion that eliminates the problem. To date nothing in the record of decisions applying Article 22 suggests that the right to withdraw acceptance has been misused by offerees for speculative purposes.[6] An offeror could eliminate the potential for abuse by specifying that acceptance must occur by instantaneous means of communication — for example, telephone.

11, 28–29 (1988); authorities cited in Peter Schlechtriem, Art. 22 para. 6 n. 12, in Schlechtriem & Schwenzer, CISG Commentary (2nd English ed. 2005).

5. Peter Schlechtriem, Art. 22 para. 6, *in* Schlechtriem & Schwenzer, *CISG Commentary* (2nd English ed. 2005).

6. See UNCITRAL Digest Art. 22.

Article 23.
Effect of Acceptance; Time of Conclusion of Contract

178   Articles 18(2) and 18(3) (*supra* at §§161–164) in stating when an acceptance becomes "effective" implies that a contract is concluded at that time. This implication is made explicit by the present article.

Article 23[1]

A contract is concluded at the moment when an acceptance of an offer becomes effective in accordance with the provisions of this Convention.

Several articles of the Convention refer to conditions existing at the time of the conclusion of the contract. (See Arts. 42(1), 55, 68, 74, 79(1), 100(2)). Only rarely will it be important to determine the precise "moment" when the contract was concluded. One exception may be Article 68, *infra*, which provides that risk of loss of goods sold during transit passes to the buyer "from the time of the conclusion of the contract." It has been suggested that the time of the conclusion of the sales contract may be important in the application of domestic fiscal or regulatory laws; this, of course, is a question to be decided in the light of the language and purpose of the domestic legislation.[2] *Other issues that have arisen in connection with Article 23 include: the time a contract is concluded if it is subject to conditions;[3] and whether Article 23 can*

1. The present article is the same as Art. 21 of the 1978 Draft Convention. There is no comparable provision in ULF.

2. See Peter Schlechtriem, Art. 23 para. 2, *in* Schlechtriem & Schwenzer, *CISG Commentary* (2nd English ed. 2005); Canadian International Trade Tribunal, Canada, 6 October 2005 (Cherry Stix Ltd. v. President of the Canada Borders Services Agency), available at http://cisgw3.law.pace.edu/cases/051006c4.html (tribunal referred to CISG to help determine when a sale was concluded for purposes of the Canadian Customs Act and the Valuation for Duty Regulations). See also Schmidt, The International Contract Law in the Context of Some of Its Sources, 14 Am. J. Comp. L. 1, 29 (1965).

3. See UNCITRAL Digest Art. 23 para. 2; Peter Schlechtriem, Art. 23 paras. 3–5, *in* Schlechtriem & Schwenzer, *CISG Commentary* (2nd English ed. 2005).

be used to determine where a contract is concluded (an issue not expressly addressed in the Convention, but which can be important for choice-of-law questions).[4]

4. UNCITRAL Digest Art. 23 para. 3; Peter Schlechtriem, Art. 23 para. 7, *in* Schlechtriem & Schwenzer, *CISG Commentary* (2nd English ed. 2005).

Article 24.
When Communication "Reaches"
the Addressee

179   Part II of the Convention provides, in various settings, that a communication becomes effective when it "reaches" the other party. See
Article 15(1) (offer), Article 15(2) (withdrawal of offer), Article 16(1)
(revocation of offer), Article 17 (rejection), Article 18(2) (acceptance),
Article 20(1) (period for acceptance fixed by telephone, telex or other
means of instantaneous communication), Article 22 (withdrawal of
acceptance).

Practical problems of proof would arise if the applicability of these
provisions depended on evidence that a communication came to the
personal attention of the addressee. These problems are addressed in
the following provision.

Article 24[1]

**For the purposes of this Part of the Convention, an offer, decla-
ration of acceptance or any other indication of intention "reaches"
the addressee when it is made orally to him or delivered by any other
means to him personally, to his place of business or mailing address
or, if he does not have a place of business or mailing address, to his
habitual residence.**

Under Article 24, the communication "reaches" the addressee when it
is delivered "to his place of business or mailing address." This, of
course, requires "delivery" to an appropriate "place" — that is, within
the mailbox or mail slot, or by a transfer of possession to an authorized
person in the addressee's employ. Leaving a letter or telegram on the
door-step or in some other unattended place would not constitute "delivery" to the addressee's "place of business"; one relying on such a
communication would need to show that the letter or telegram reached

1. This article is substantially the same as Art. 22 of the 1978 Draft and is similar to ULF
12(1): "communicated" means "delivered at the address" of the relevant party.

the addressee or an authorized employee. The usefulness of Article 24 is indicated by the widespread use of the same approach.[2]

Article 27 (infra at §188) states a general rule, applicable to Part III of the Convention, that notices and other communications are effective when they are properly dispatched. However, for reasons discussed at §§189–190, this rule is subject to exceptions in Articles 47(2), 48(4), 63(2), 56(1) & (2), and 79(4) — provisions which make certain communications effective only when they are received. The definition in Article 24, supra, of when a communication "reaches" the addressee applies only to Part II, but there is no indication of a legislative intent to reject the approach of Article 24 in construing the above references to the "receipt" of communications. Indeed, the normal meaning of "receipt" is close to that expressed in Article 24; the widespread use of the approach of Article 24, indicated in note 2, seems to justify the use of this article by analogy.

Article 24 does not expressly address electronic communications. Arguably, however, the provision establishes a general principle which, pursuant to Article 7(2), governs the time when electronic communications reach the addressee.[3] This view precludes reference to domestic law on the issue, including national legislation based on the UNCITRAL Model Law on Electronic Commerce.[4] When the United Nations Convention on the Use of Electronic Communications in International Contracts goes into force, however, the time when electronics offers, acceptances, etc. . . . are received (or dispatched, which is relevant under certain provisions of the Convention[5])

2. II *Schlesinger, Formation* 1467–1471 (report by W. Lorenz on Austrian, German and Swiss law); Sutton, The Hague Conventions of 1964 and the Unification of the Law on International Sale of Goods, 7 U. Queensland L. J. 145 at n. 75–76 (1971). For the principle of the German Civil Code §130) that an acceptance or other declaration is effective when it reaches the addressee's "zone of control," see *Zweigert & Kotz II* (1987) 35; Schmidt, The International Contract Law in the Context of Some of its Sources, 14 Am. L. Comp. L. 1, 19–23 (1965) (implications of the foregoing *Zugangsprinzip* in various civil law systems).

3. See Peter Schlechtriem, Art. 24 paras. 1 & 2, *in* Schlechtriem & Schwenzer, *CISG Commentary* (2nd English ed. 2005).

4. Section 15 of the Model Law governs the time (and place) at which electronic communications are deemed to be received and dispatched.

5. See Arts 16(1) (to be effective, revocation of an offer must be received before acceptance is *"dispatched"*), Art. 19(2) (reply to an offer that contains immaterial additional or different terms will not constitute an acceptance if the offeror "objects orally to the discrepancy or *dispatches* a notice to that effect") and Art. 21(2) (an unexpectedly delayed late acceptance is nevertheless effective unless the offeror "informs the offeree that he considers the offer to have lapsed or *dispatches* a notice to that effect").

may, as provided in CISG Article 90, be determined by that Convention.[6]

Professor Schlechtriem discusses, in detail, application of Article 24 to a variety of factual scenarios and a number of communications technologies.[7]

---

6. See §10 of the Electronic Communications Convention, which addresses when (and where) electronic communications are received and dispatched. The text of the Electronic Communications Convention is available at http://www.uncitral.org/uncitral/en/uncitral_texts/electronic_commerce/2005Convention.html.

7. Peter Schlechtriem, Art. 24, *in* Schlechtriem & Schwenzer, *CISG Commentary* (2nd English ed. 2005).

Part III.

SALE OF GOODS

(Articles 25–88)

INTRODUCTION TO PART III OF THE CONVENTION

180   Part II of the Convention (Arts. 14–24, *supra*) addresses this question: Is there a contract? When the answer is Yes, Part III governs the rights and obligations of the seller and buyer.

Part III (the "Sales Part") has five chapters. Chapter I (Arts. 25–29) contains general provisions that are applicable throughout Part III of the Convention. Chapter II (Arts. 30–52) deals with the obligations of the seller: what the seller should do (Secs. I & II) and remedies for the seller's failure to perform its obligations (Sec. III). Chapter III (Arts. 53–65), paralleling the structure of Chapter II, states the obligations of the buyer: what the buyer should do (Secs. I and II) and remedies for breach (Sec. III). Chapter IV (Arts. 66–70) is devoted to risk of loss. Chapter V (Arts. 71–88) addresses anticipatory breach (Sec. I), damage-measurement and interest (Secs. II & III), excuse based on serious impediments ("exemptions") (Sec. IV), effects of avoidance (Sec. V), and duties to preserve goods that face loss or deterioration (Sec. VI).

CHAPTER I.

GENERAL PROVISIONS
(Articles 25–29)

Article 25.
Definition of "Fundamental Breach"

181 **A. Introduction**

The breach of a sales contract by one party gives the other party a right to recover damages, but we are here concerned with more specialized remedies — the buyer's right to reject goods and the seller's right to refuse to deliver. In domestic law these remedies may be called "rejection," "revocation of acceptance," "avoidance," "termination" or "cancellation." In the Convention (Arts. 49 & 64) a party's privilege not to perform the contract because of the other party's breach is called "avoidance of the contract."

In the Convention, as in domestic legal systems, "avoidance" is not available for every breach. As we shall see in examining Articles 49(1)(a) and 64(a)(a), *infra* at §§304, 354, a party may avoid the contract when the other party commits a "fundamental breach" — a term that is defined in the present article.

Article 25[1]

A breach of contract committed by one of the parties is fundamental if it results in such detriment to the other party as substantially to deprive him of what he is entitled to expect under the contract, unless the party in breach did not foresee and a reasonable person of the same kind in the same circumstances would not have foreseen such a result.

---

1. This article is based, with drafting changes, on Art. 23 of the 1978 Draft. *Cf.* ULIS 10, quoted *infra*.

181.1 (1) Domestic Usage: A "False Friend"

In English law the concept of "fundamental breach" was developed to deal with a very different problem than that addressed in CISG Article 50. The English doctrine focused on the effect of a contract provision restricting the buyer's rights when goods are defective. For a time English courts held that a "fundamental breach" of contract by the seller nullified such a contract provision. The rise and fall of this doctrine are described in *Benjamin* §§967–979, *cf.* §§982–1016. This doctrine was quite different in function and scope from "fundamental breach" in the Sales Convention. Domestic law was not employed in drafting Article 25; its provenance was the definition of "fundamental breach" in CISG. It would, of course, be a mistake to rely on this "false friend" from domestic law in construing the Convention. See, *accord*, Will in *B-B Commentary* 209.

181.2 (2) "Fundamental Breach" and Contract Avoidance

As we shall see (§186, *infra*), the Convention uses the term "fundamental breach" in various settings but it plays its most important roles in Articles 49(1)(a) and 64(1)(a) which state grounds on which the buyer or seller may "avoid" the contract and thereby become free from further contractual obligations — e.g. to receive and pay for the goods or to deliver them.

The diverse approaches to this problem in domestic law will be discussed more fully (§301) in connection with Article 49, which governs the circumstances in which the buyer may refuse to accept the goods when the seller's delivery is delayed or when the goods fail in some respect to conform to the contract. The correlative right of the seller to avoid the contract when the buyer fails to perform one or more of his contractual obligations is set forth in Article 64 and is discussed at §§353–356, *infra*.

"Avoidance" of the contract must be distinguished from a party's right to *suspend* performance under Article 71 (§§385–394, *infra*); suspension is a temporary (or at least not yet final) deferral of performance; avoidance definitively *terminates* the right and duty of both parties to proceed further with performance, subject to a claim for damages for breach of contract. See Articles 45(1)(b), 61(1)(b) and especially Article 81(1): "Avoidance of the contract releases both parties from their obligations under it, subject to any damages which may be due." Thus, in determining the grounds for "avoidance" the issue is not whether a party whose performance is defective in some minor respect will escape liability. Every breach, no matter how trivial, calls for compensation in damages (Art. 74, §§403–408, *infra*). Thus, a remedy by damages has a quality of justice lacking in avoidance since the cost to the one who pays and the benefit to the one who receives correspond to the harm caused by the breach.[2] In framing the scope of (e.g.) the buyer's right to avoid the contract the relevant questions are these: Which party is normally in the better position to redispose of goods? Will the buyer's retention of the goods jeopardize effective compensation for damages? Is there justification for reversing the contract's allocation between the parties of rises or declines in market price?

In developing the Convention there was no significant support for extending avoidance to include insubstantial deviations from the contract. Stricter avoidance (or "rejection") rules in some domestic laws failed to take account of the special circumstances of international trade, such as the fact that claims that the goods are defective often are made only after expensive transport to the buyer's place of business when avoidance for immaterial defects might needlessly lead to wasteful reshipment or redisposition of the goods in a foreign country. Moreover, the power to avoid the contract for immaterial defects in performance may tempt the seller (after a price rise) or the buyer (after a price decline) to avoid the contract and thus reverse the allocation of the effect of price changes which the contract contemplated.

Of course, these factors will not always be present and in many cases only avoidance will adequately protect the aggrieved party. *In applying the fundamental breach standard for avoidance, tribunals appear in general to have limited it to breaches that rip the fabric of the parties" contractual relationship. The German Bundesgerichtshof, for example, has labeled avoidance a remedy of "last resort," and has suggested that a lack of conformity in the goods will constitute a fundamental breach only if it prevents the buyer from putting the*

---

2. An early (1956) draft of the Hague (1964) uniform law for international sale provided that the buyer could avoid the contract with respect to goods that did not conform to the contract without regard to the degree of non-conformity (Art. 55). To reduce the harshness of this rule the definition of the seller's basic obligation to supply conforming goods provided (Art. 40) that no "deficiency in quantity" or "absence of any quality . . . shall be taken into consideration where it is not material to the interests of buyer. . . ." *Records, 1964 Conference*, Vol. II, pp. 13, 15. This lack of "proportionality," in which *no* compensation was provided for minor shortages of quantity or deviations as to quality but a drastic remedy was granted for the slightest deviation from this standard, was abandoned by the 1964 Conference; the approach of the 1964 Convention (ULIS 10, 43) is similar to that of the 1980 Convention.

goods to some "reasonable use," even one that the buyer had not originally contemplated.[3] In transactions where a party is concerned that Article 25 is too lax or too strict or that a tribunal might improperly apply the law, the contract can provide stricter (or looser) grounds for avoidance (Art. 6).

These pragmatic considerations are mentioned because the definition of "fundamental breach" in Article 25 had to be drafted in general terms and could not specify all the circumstances that may be relevant in determining whether a breach will "substantially" deprive a party "of what he is entitled to expect under the contract...." Some of these circumstances will be illustrated by concrete examples.

182 ### (3) "Fundamental Breach" in the 1964 Convention

ULIS (§10) contained the following definition of "fundamental breach":

> For the purposes of the present Law, a breach of contract shall be regarded as fundamental wherever the party in breach knew, or ought to have known, at the time of the conclusion of the contract, that a reasonable person in the same situation as the other party would not have entered into the contract if he had foreseen the breach and its effects.

This definition approached the question of the materiality of the breach by a hypothetical question put to the *party in breach* at the time of the conclusion of the contract: Would the party in breach have predicted that the other party would have "entered into the contract *if he had foreseen* the breach and its effects." Analysis of this provision in UNCITRAL made it clear that "fundamental breach" must be redefined in terms of the materiality of the breach.[4]

183 ### (4) Changes Made by 1980 Convention

The Convention's definition in Article 25 turns on the degree of the *detriment* resulting from the breach: Is it such "as *substantially* to deprive him of what he is *entitled* to expect under the contract?" This

---

3. Bundesgerichtshof, Germany, 3 April 1999, English translation available at http://cisgw3.law.pace.edu/cases/960403g1.html. For other decisions applying the fundamental breach standard, see UNCITRAL Digest Art. 25 paras. 5–11.

4. *Graveson, C & G.* 55–57, *Dölle. Kommentar* 49–58 (Huber); Honnold, ULIS: The Hague Convention of 1964, 30 Law & Cont. Prob. L.Q. 326, 344 (1965); Sutton, The Draft Convention on the International Sale of Goods, 4 Austral. Bus. L. Rev. 269, 285–288 (1976).

emphasis on "*detriment* to the other party" is more precise than expressions such as "substantial performance" of the contract. Temporal or physical deviations ("one day," ".001 millimeter") have no significance apart from the extent of the loss or detriment they cause to the other party.

The definition of "fundamental breach" in Article 25 has two elements: (1) The detriment to the aggrieved party, A, must "substantially" deprive A of what he is entitled to expect from the contract, and (2) since the detriment to A may be affected by a wide variety of circumstances peculiar to A, the relevant detriment is limited to what the party in breach, F, foresaw or should have foreseen.

Vantage-points for foreseeability. This second element is subject to an ambiguity that has generated a substantial literature: From what vantage point in time should F view the possibility of detriment to A? Is the detriment limited to what F foresaw (or could have foreseen) when the contract was made, or may it include detriment that F foresaw (or could have foreseen) at a later time? This issue may not arise often, but the possibility may be illustrated as follows:

Example 25A. S agreed to ship 100 bags of rice to B. B's order was on a printed form that specified "new bags." When B prepared to ship he had at hand sound, used bags that he believed were of the same quality as new bags and would be acceptable to B subject to a modest price allowance. However, before S bagged the rice B telexed to S, "Have obtained contract for resale of rice which emphasizes use of new bags. Although sound used bags would usually be acceptable subject to a price allowance, use of new bags for this shipment is very important." S replied, "Shipping in extra high quality used bags." B rejected the shipment and notified S that the contract was avoided because of the danger of rejection by the sub-purchaser.

On the assumption that at the time of contracting the seller could not have foreseen that the detriment to the buyer would be substantial, should the later information be taken into consideration?

The language of Article 25 does not answer this question. In setting forth the first of the two elements, as analyzed above, Article 25 refers to detriment that deprives the aggrieved party, A, of what A "is entitled to expect *under the contract*," but there is no reference to the time of the making of the contract in the second element that was based on the *detriment* that F, the party in breach, foresaw or could have foreseen.

In UNCITRAL and at the 1980 Conference some delegates proposed that this second element be amended to restrict consideration to those circumstances that the party in breach (F) could have foreseen when the contract was made. Both legislative bodies considered the issue and decided that this restriction should not be imposed. Extracts from this legislative history appear in a footnote.[5]

To return to Example 25A, we may conclude that the information the seller received subsequent to the contract but before shipment gave the seller reason to foresee that the breach of contract would "*substantially*" deprive the buyer of what he was entitled to expect under the contract, and that the buyer's avoidance was justified under Articles 25 and 49(1)(a). However, information that a party receives too late to affect performance seems outside the scope of Article 25, since the foreseeability principle presumably is designed to give F an opportunity to give special attention to minor details of performance the importance of which he could not otherwise have anticipated.[6]

Professor Schlechtriem has argued that detriment caused by a breach must be foreseeable at the time the contract was concluded in order to satisfy the requirements for a fundamental breach.[7] He notes that Article 25 defines fundamental breach in terms of the expectations created by the contract: thus, he asserts, determining whether a breach is fundamental is a matter of interpreting the parties contract; the foreseeability rule in Article 25, he reasons, is "a 'substitute' for the need to reach clear agreement in the contract on the importance of those matters, i.e,. it can make an appropriate interpretation of the contract possible."[8] The implication of this approach is that "the importance attached by a promise to a particular obligation, which

---

5. In UNCITRAL's final (1977) review of the "Sales" provisions, one delegate proposed to limit the time for foreseeability to "the conclusion of the contract." Under another view "it would be fairer to refer to the time at which the breach was committed." The decision was recorded as follows: "The Commission, after deliberation, did not consider it necessary to specify at what moment the party in breach should have foreseen or had reason to foresee the consequences of the breach." UNCITRAL, Report of Tenth (1977) Session, VIII *YB* 31 at 31, para. 90, *Docy. Hist.* 324. See, *accord, Secretariat Commentary*, Art. 23, §5, *O.R.* 26, *Docy. Hist.* 416. Finally, at the 1980 Diplomatic Conference one delegate (U.K.) proposed a similar amendment. Other delegates spoke in opposition to the proposal and no delegate spoke in support; as a result, the proposal was withdrawn. *O.R.* 99, *Docy. Hist.* 671 (text of proposal); First Committee deliberations, *O.R.* 302, *Docy. Hist.* 523.

6. See Will, in *B-B Commentary* 221, for opposing views. For a conclusion contrary to that suggested above see *Schlechtriem*, 1986 Commentary 60.

7. Peter Schlechtriem, Art. *25* para. 15, *in* Schlechtriem & Schwenzer, *CISG Commentary* (2nd English ed. 2005). There is some support for this position in case law. See UNCITRAL Digest Art. 25 para. 4.

8. Peter Schlechtriem, Art. *25* para. 15, *in* Schlechtriem & Schwenzer, *CISG Commentary* (2nd English ed. 2005).

has been shown otherwise than by express agreement, must nevertheless be fixed by the time the contract is concluded."[9]

In the current editor's view, this approach misconstrues the purposes of Article 25 and its foreseeability rule, and as a result misinterprets the provision. Before the question of fundamental breach arises there must, first of all, be a breach — a violation by one party of its obligations under the contract. The existence of such obligations is, of course, determined as of the time of the conclusion of the contract. The focus of Article 25 is different — it addresses whether the breach would justify avoidance, or whether non-avoidance remedies for the breach should suffice. Professor Schlechtriem's approach appears to lose sight of this distinction — to some degree it seems to confuse the question of the existence of a breach with the question whether such breach is fundamental.

Returning again to Example 25A, the seller has violated its contractual obligations — obligations based on the reasonable expectations of the parties as established at the time the contract was concluded — by shipping the rice in used bags. When it committed that violation the seller knew that its breach would cause substantial harm to the buyer. It makes no sense to say that the contractual relationship has not been damaged in a way that justifies avoidance just because the seller was not aware how important that would be to the buyer when the seller originally promised to ship the rice in new bags.

Avoidance of contract does not subject the breaching party to special liability beyond expectation remedies: the foreseeability requirement in Article 25 thus does not focus on determining the financial risk assumed by the breaching party. The purpose of the Article 25 foreseeability rule — identifying those breaches that truly disrupt the parties' contractual relations — is much different than the function of the rule in Article 74 limiting recoverable damages to losses foreseeable "at the time of the conclusion of the contract."

Of course permitting avoidance in Example 25A might cause the seller to lose a favorable exchange, but that hardly seems unfair given that it breached in a fashion that, to its knowledge, would cause the buyer substantial damage. Indeed, not permitting avoidance here would leave the innocent buyer in an untenable position: if at the time the contract was concluded it was not foreseeable that the buyer would resell the rice in a contract requiring new bags, then the foreseeability requirement in Article 74 might preclude damages for the

9. *Id.*

buyer's losses. In that case, denying the right to avoid would leave the buyer without recourse. Why should the buyer not be allowed to rely on the seller's express promise to ship in new bags, and at least avoid the contract and have the opportunity to use other suppliers to fulfill its customers' needs, when the seller — who knows full well the impact its breach will have when it commits it — fails to keep its promise?

Burden of proof. The second element in Article 25, as analyzed above, has generated discussion of yet another refinement: Who has the burden of providing whether the detriment to the aggrieved party, A, was or was not foreseen or foreseeable by the other party, F?[10] *It was argued earlier (supra §70.1) that, in general, burden of proof matters are beyond the scope of the Convention, but the issue of foreseeability posed by Article 25 may be one of the rare exceptions.* Any doubt from the text of Article 25 (or from practical considerations of allocating burdens of proof) concerning who has the burden with respect to the foreseeability element is removed by the legislative history: In UNCITRAL's 1977 review of the Working Group "Sales" draft, attention was drawn to the following language: "A breach . . . is fundamental . . ." *if* it results in substantial detriment *and* the party in breach foresaw or had reason to foresee such a result. The view was suggested that under this language "the burden of proof would be on the innocent party and this could not be the proper solution." To meet this objection the Commission, without objection, replaced the above language by the "unless . . ." clause that appears in Article 25.[11]

---

10. Professor Schlechtriem discusses the burden of proof under Art. 25 at length. See Peter Schlechtriem, Art. *25* para. 16, *in* Schlechtriem & Schwenzer, *CISG Commentary* (2nd English ed. 2005).

11. VIII *YB* 31, para. 89, *Docy. Hist.* 324. For fuller review of the discussion see Michida, 27 Am. J. Comp. L. 279, 285 (1979) and Will, *B-B Commentary*, 216, para. 2.2.1. In many legal systems, decisive effect as to burden of proof may be given to the syntax of the sentence. In other systems where syntax is given less weight the same interpretation should be given to this language of Art. 25, for the legislative history shows that allocation of burden of proof was the premise for the amendment that produced the final language of the article. Moreover, in these systems the same result can be reached on pragmatic principles of proof-allocation since the party in breach is in a better position to prove what he could have foreseen. Thus, the travaux préparatoires indicate that Art. 25 was drafted to deal with the burden of proof issue indirectly, through applicable (probably domestic) non-Convention law, thus tending to confirm that burden of proof issues are, generally, beyond the scope of the CISG.

184　**B. "Fundamental Breach" in Specific Situations**

(1) The Effect of an Offer to Cure

To help preserve transactions from technical mishaps, the Convention includes important provisions permitting the seller to "cure" a nonconforming delivery by replacing or repairing defective goods. See Article 37 (cure until date for delivery — §244) and Article 48 (cure after the date for delivery — §292). The relationship between these provisions and "fundamental breach" can be illustrated as follows.

Example 25B. On June 1, the date for delivery specified in the contract, Seller delivered to Buyer a large and expensive machine. On June 15, when Buyer put the machine into operation, one essential part of the machine did not function with the result that the machine did not operate. Buyer notified Seller who offered immediately to replace the defective part. Although the brief period required for making this replacement did not interfere with Buyer's plans for using the machine, Buyer did not permit Seller to replace the defective part. Claiming that a defect that prevented the machine from operating was a "fundamental breach" under Article 25, Buyer declared that the contract was avoided (Art. 49(1)(a)) and stated that the seller must remove the machine and refund the price (Art. 81).

Buyer was correct in stating that, without the replacement of the defective part, the seller's breach might be "fundamental" (depending on, *e.g.*, whether a proper replacement part was readily available from another source) and that avoidance might be justified. On the other hand, a rapid replacement of the defective part, even after the agreed date of delivery, would prevent any "substantial" detriment to the buyer; on this assumption, the breach would not be "fundamental" and the contract could not be avoided. As we shall see, Article 48 authorized Seller to replace the defective part under the circumstances described in Example 25B. The question whether the breach was "fundamental" for the purpose of avoidance must be answered in the light of the effect of a rightful offer to cure, for otherwise Seller's exercise of this right would be futile. When the applicable provisions (Arts. 25, 48, 49) are construed together. Buyer's attempt to avoid the contract should be ineffective.[12]

---

12. At UNCITRAL's 1977 review of the Draft Convention on Sales, there was discussion of whether the definition of fundamental breach (now Art. 25) should be amended to make clear that the definition called for consideration of "all the circumstances, including a reasonable

185   **(2) Refund and Price Adjustment**

Other situations call for evaluating the substantiality of the breach in the light of all of the facts. This point may be illustrated by comparing the two following cases:

Example 25C. A contract between Seller and Buyer called for the delivery of 1,000 bags of No. 1 quality sugar; the price was $20,000 ($20 per bag). On delivery, inspection showed that the sugar in 970 bags complied with the contract but that the sugar in 30 of the bags was so defective that it could not be used. Other sugar was available in Buyer's market. When the defect in the delivery was discovered, Seller offered not to charge for the 30 bags. (In a documentary transaction, this could be effected by Seller's drawing a draft for $19,400 instead of $20,000.)

Example 25D. The facts are the same as in Example 25C, except that Seller refused to permit the delivery of any sugar except for the full price of $20,000.

These examples suggest that the question of how "substantially" a party has been deprived of "what he is entitled to expect under the contract" (Art. 25) cannot be answered simply by looking at the goods. In Example 25C, buyer has been deprived of very little; the tender of the goods accompanied by the price adjustment would probably not constitute a "fundamental breach." In Example 25D, the tender of the same goods, without the price adjustment, should constitute a "fundamental breach." Recovery of money paid for the defective goods, at the very least, would involve the delays, expenses and uncertainties of pressing a claim. If Seller is far from Buyer and is of questionable financial responsibility, the test of "fundamental breach" in Article 25 is even more clearly established. The relevance of this approach is recognized by Article 48(1), *infra* at §293, by providing that the seller may not remedy (e.g., repair) a failure of performance if there is "*uncertainty of reimbursement* by the seller of expenses advanced by the buyer."[13]

---

offer to cure." The Commission decided that such an amendment was "unnecessary" and "superfluous." *UNCITRAL X* Annex I, paras. 93–95, VIII *YB* 31–32, *Docy. Hist.* 324–325. Michida, Cancellation of Contract, *AJCL UNCITRAL Symposium* 286–288 (1979). *See also* Art. 41, *infra* at §266.

13. Commercial practice and contractual patterns dealing with such problems were examined in Honnold, Buyer's Right of Rejection, — A Study In the Impact of Codification Upon a Commercial Problem, 97 U. Pa. L. Rev. 457, 468–472 (1949).

186   **(3) "Fundamental Breach" in Context**

There are other significant applications of Article 25 but these can be best be explored in connection with the articles that use "fundamental breach" as a basis for avoidance of the contract — Article 49 (avoidance by buyer) and Article 64 (avoidance by the seller). (Avoidance under the Convention is compared with the approach of various systems of domestic law in the Commentary to Art. 49, *infra* at §301.) "Fundamental breach" is also used to deal with avoidance in special situations: in Article 51(2) on avoidance of an entire contract based on defective performance of a part of the contract, in Article 72 on anticipatory breach, and in Article 73 on deliveries by installments. This concept is also used in Article 46(2) to limit the remedy of specific performance: the buyer "may require delivery" of goods to substitute for nonconforming goods "only if the lack of conformity constitutes a fundamental breach of contract." Avoidance for fundamental breach can also affect risk of loss — e.g. the responsibility for casualty during transit. See Article 70, §§379–383, *infra*. All that is feasible at this stage is to provide background for the examination of these several provisions.

Article 26.
Notice of Avoidance

187   The discussion of Article 25 referred to the right of either party to avoid the contract in the circumstances defined in Articles 49, 51, 64, 72, and 73. Article 26, applicable to all of the provisions on avoidance, marks one of the significant advances of the 1980 Convention over the 1964 Hague Convention.

Article 26[1]

A declaration of avoidance of the contract is effective only if made by notice to the other party.

187.1   A. Departure from ULIS; Need for Notification

At various points ULIS provided a remedy called *ipso facto* avoidance; this type of avoidance (unlike a second type of avoidance which required a "declaration") occurred automatically; the party who relied on this remedy need not have notified the other (ULIS 25, 26(1)). Consequently, a party might be led to perform in ignorance of the other party's decision to refuse the performance.

At the 1964 Hague Conference attempts were made to eliminate *ipso facto* avoidance but this concept was such an integral part of the structure of the draft that the necessary changes were not feasible.[2]

In the UNCITRAL proceedings, it was possible to remove the complex and elusive doctrine of *ipso facto* avoidance; the result was the above simple rule of Article 26.[3] Requiring that notice be given of a remedy as drastic as avoidance is strongly supported by domestic law. See (U.S.A.) UCC 2–602(1) (notice of rejection), 2–608(2) (notice of revocation of acceptance); *Treitel, Remedies (Int. Enc.)* §148

---

1. This article is the same as Art. 24 of the 1978 Draft Convention. As is explained more fully *infra*, ULIS had no comparable notice requirement.
2. *II Records, 1964 Conference* 236; Honnold, ULIS: The Hague Convention of 1964, 30 Law & Cont. Pr. L.Q. 326, 348 (1965).
3. For the studies and discussion on which this decision was based see *Rep. S-G. "Ipso Facto* Avoidance in ULIS." III *YB* 41–46, *Docy. Hist.* 83–88; *W/G/I* paras. 92–104, I *YB* 184–185, *Docy. Hist.* 22–23.

(requirement in French law of a formal notice — *sommation* — even when the contract states that it shall terminate by operation of law).

A careful student of the 1964 Sales Convention has noted that *ipso facto* avoidance was useful to prevent a party from claiming specific performance after a price rise and thereby speculate at the other party's expense.[4] Such conduct is clearly intolerable, but *ipso facto* avoidance proved to be an awkward and overbroad remedy; resources in the 1980 Convention for dealing with the problem of taking advantage of market changes after a delay are explored elsewhere in this Commentary. See Article 7, *supra* at §95, Article 28, *infra* at §193, Article 46, *infra* at §285, Article 77, *infra* at §416.

187.2   B. The Notice: Content, Transmission

What must a notice say to constitute an effective "declaration of avoidance" under Article 26? As we shall see, under Article 39(1), §§254–259, a buyer who wishes "to rely on a lack of conformity of the goods" must "give notice to the seller specifying the lack of conformity." A notice specifying a "lack of conformity" in accordance with Article 39 would not, without more, constitute a "declaration of avoidance" under Article 26. A buyer who specifies non-conformity (Art. 39) may, and often does, choose to retain the goods and claim a reduction in the price or other damages to compensate for the deficiency. Avoidance of the contract is a different and much more drastic remedy.[5] In the setting of the tender or delivery of defective goods "avoidance of the contract" by the buyer means that the buyer will not accept or keep the goods, and that the seller has the responsibility to take over their disposition.[6] A buyer's declaration of *avoidance*, to be effective under Article 26, need not use the term "avoidance,"[7] but it must inform the

---

4. Hellner, Ipso Facto Avoidance, in *Weitnauer Festgabe* 85. *See also* Rainer Hornung, Art. 26 para. 14, *in* Schlechtriem & Schwenzer, *CISG Commentary* (2nd English ed. 2005).

5. *See* §§437–444 *infra*. *See also* Rainer Hornung, Art. 26 para. 4, *in* Schlechtriem & Schwenzer, *CISG Commentary* (2nd English ed. 2005).

6. General rules on the effects of avoidance are set forth in Arts. 81–84, §§439–444, *infra*. For the situation where rejected goods face rapid deterioration or spoilage, a buyer who has avoided the contract may have the responsibility to take reasonable measures to prevent loss. See Arts. 86–88, §§455–457, *infra*.

7. See UNCITRAL Digest Art. 26 para. 5.

seller that the buyer will not accept or keep the goods.[8] Conversely, a seller's declaration of avoidance must inform the buyer that the seller will not deliver the goods or, if the goods have been delivered, that the seller demands their return. See Article 81(2) and 84, §§439–444, 450–452, *infra*.

The notice required by Article 26 is effective if it is properly "dispatched" pursuant to Article 27. As we shall see, the principle underlying this rule and its exceptions is that transmission risks should fall on the party in breach rather than on an aggrieved party who, in this setting, is exercising a right to avoid the contract.[9]

Article 26 does not require that the notice be given in writing or in any other particular form,[10] but to avoid dispute a prompt written confirmation of an oral declaration seems advisable.[11] A number of States, however, have made declarations under Article 96 rejecting provisions of CISG that allowed effective notification in form other than writing — e.g. Articles 11, 12, 96.

Whether a buyer can withdraw notice of avoidance once it has been given, and then pursue one or more of the remedies available when a contract has not been avoided, should depend on the particular facts of the situation and the general principles of the Convention, including the promotion of good faith in international transaction and the protection of a party (even a breaching party) if it has reasonably relied on the declaration of avoidance.[12]

8. *See* Landgericht Frankfurt, Germany, 16 September 1991, CLOUT case No. 6 available online at http://cisgw3.law.pace.edu/cases/910916g1.html. For cases exploring whether an aggrieved party had declared avoidance with sufficient clarity see UNCITRAL Digest Art. 26 para. 5. *See also* Rainer Hornung, Art. 26 para. 10, *in* Schlechtriem & Schwenzer, *CISG Commentary* (2nd English ed. 2005). Limits on the time for avoidance are set in Arts. 49(2) (avoidance by buyer) and 64(2) (avoidance by seller). See §§306–308, 355–356, *infra*. A buyer who fails to give the notice "specifying the nature of the lack of conformity" required by Art. 39(1) may "lose the right to rely" on the lack of conformity, and thereby lose the right to avoid the contract for non-conformity of the goods. See §§259–261, *infra*.
9. See §190, *infra*; UNCITRAL, Tenth Session (1977), VIII *YB* 32, para. 98–99, 101, *Docy. Hist.* 325.
10. *See* UNCITRAL Digest Art. 26 para. 3; Rainer Hornung, Art. 26 para. 8, *in* Schlechtriem & Schwenzer, *CISG Commentary* (2nd English ed. 2005).
11. For unsuccessful attempts to require that the notice be in writing see UNCITRAL, Eighth Session (1977), VIII *YB* 32, para. 102, *Docy. Hist.* 325; Date-Bah, *B-B Commentary* 224, para. 3.1.
12. *See* Peter Schlechtriem, Art. 27 para. 14 and Markus Müller-Chen, Art. 45 para. 16, *in* Schlechtriem & Schwenzer, *CISG Commentary* (2nd English ed. 2005).

Article 27.
Delay or Error in Communications

188   Under Article 26, *supra*, avoidance of a contract is effected "by notice" and in other settings communications have important consequences. E.g., Articles 39(1) (notice of lack of conformity) and 43 (notice of right or claim of third party). The present article addresses the problems that arise when a notice is sent but, because of a mishap in transmission, is delayed, garbled or lost.

Article 27[1]

Unless otherwise expressly provided in this Part of the Convention, if any notice, request or other communication is given or made by a party in accordance with this Part and by means appropriate in the circumstances, a delay or error in the transmission of the communication or its failure to arrive does not deprive that party of the right to rely on the communication.

189   ## A. Reasons for the "Dispatch" Principle

In examining the Convention's rules in Part II (Formation of the Contract) we saw that an offeree's acceptance was not effective unless it "reached" the offeror within the specified time; this rule placed the risks of transmission on the sender. See Article 18, *supra* at §161. The examination of the rules on acceptance in Article 18 indicated that it was a close question whether acceptance should be effective on "dispatch" or on "receipt." Article 27, with which we are now concerned, applies only to the communication of notices made in accordance with Part III, which applies if an international sales contract has been concluded, since they present problems that are different from communications involved in contract formation (Part II). For instance, a mishap transmitting a buyer's notice that the goods were defective (Art. 39) could, under

---

1. This article is substantially the same as Art. 25 of the 1978 Draft. ULIS had no general rule on this point. *But see* Art. 39(3) ("dispatch" rule for notice of non-conformity of goods). The provision that became Art. 27 was added during UNCITRAL's 1977 review of the Draft Convention on Sales. *UNCITRAL X* Annex I paras. 104–114, VIII *YB* 32–33, *Docy. Hist.* 325–326. *See also* VI *YB* 96 (Report of Secretary-General) paras. 74–75, *Docy. Hist.* 221.

the "receipt" approach, deprive the innocent party of "the right to rely" on the lack of conformity, and the buyer would have to pay the seller the full price for defective goods. In this and in similar situations it seemed advisable to provide that the appropriate dispatch of a communication satisfied the notice requirement.

As Professor Schlechtriem has noted (*1986 Commentary* 61), ULIS 14 and ULF 12(2) provided that communications shall be made "by the means *usual* in the circumstances," while Article 27 substitutes "appropriate" for "usual" — a change that gives the sender a somewhat wider choice of media. *Professor Schlechtriem argues that the dispatch principle of Article 27 does not apply to oral communication, so that, e.g., a declaration on the telephone that is rendered unintelligible by technical problems is not effective.*[2]

Professor Schlechtriem also argues, despite some contrary opinion, that a communication governed by Article 27 is effective at the time it is dispatched[3] *(although he also asserts that, to be timely, such a communication must be dispatched early enough to arrive within the period required by the Convention*[4]*). As was noted in connection with Article 16 (see supra §140), the CISG does not expressly address the time at which a communication is deemed dispatched. When the United Nations Convention on the Use of Electronic Communications in International Contracts*[5] *goes into force, the time an email or other type of electronic communication is "dispatched" maybe governed by Article 10(1) of that Convention.*

190 (1) Exceptions Where "Receipt" is Required

This general rule making notices effective on dispatch is subject to specific exceptions in Articles 47(2), 48(4), 63(2), 65(1) & (2) and 79(4). Nearly all of these provisions involve a communication by a party who is in breach of contract; the "receipt" principle was used so

---

2. Peter Schlechtriem, Art. 27 para. 5, *in* Schlechtriem & Schwenzer, *CISG Commentary* (2nd English ed. 2005); *Schlechtriem, 1986 Commentary* 61). *See also* UNCITRAL Digest Art. 27 para. 6.
3. Peter Schlechtriem, Art. 27 para. 13, *in* Schlechtriem & Schwenzer, *CISG Commentary* (2nd English ed. 2005).
4. *Id.* para. 11.
5. Available at http://www.uncitral.org/uncitral/en/uncitral_texts/electronic_commerce/ 2005 Convention.html.

that a mishap in transmission would not add to the burdens of the aggrieved party.[6]

Domestic rules on the effect of a mishap in communication are not uniform and often are unclear, but there is support for the approach of Article 27 of the Convention.[7]

6. See First Committee Deliberations, *O.R.* 303, *Docy. Hist.* 524. Article 24 may be helpful, by analogy, in determining whether a notice has been "received." See §179, *supra.*

7. (U.S.A.) UCC 2–607(3)(a) requires the buyer to "notify" the seller of breach or "be barred from any remedy." Under UCC 1–201(26) one "notifies" another "*by taking such steps* as may be reasonably required to inform the other in ordinary course whether or not such other actually comes to know of it." Exceptions from this rule are made by stating duties that arise on "receipt" of a notification — *e.g.*, §2–616. *Schlechtriem, 1986 Commentary* 61, notes that the "receipt" principle is more widely applicable in German law.

Article 28.
Requiring Performance and the Rules of the Forum

191   **A. Introduction**

Article 28 brings to the foreground the basic distinction between (I) the *obligation* (or *duty*) that one party (D) owes to the other party (C) and (II) the *remedy* given to C for D's breach. The Convention is built around this distinction. The *seller's obligations* to the buyer are set forth in Chapter II Sections I & II (Arts. 31–44); *remedies* given the buyer for the seller's breach of its obligations appear in Section III (Arts. 45–52). Following the same structure, the *buyer's obligations* to the seller are set forth in Chapter III, Sections I & II (Arts. 53–60); *remedies* given the seller for the buyer's breach of its obligations appear in Section II (Arts. 61–65). Supplemental rules on remedies applicable to both parties are stated in Chapter V (Arts. 71–84).

Examination of the above provisions will show that here, as elsewhere in the law, stating D's duties to C is simpler than stating C's remedies when D fails to perform. In most situations there is only one right way for D to perform its contract; on the other hand, D's deviations from the contract can occur in a wide variety of circumstances, causing different degrees of harm to C, and therefore call for alternative remedial provisions: avoidance of the contract (Arts. 25, 49, 64, 72), damages (Arts. 50, 74–78), and judicial "requirement" of performance (Arts. 28, 46, 62), a type of remedy that in "common law" may be implemented by a judicial decree ordering "specific" performance.

The scope of the remedy "requiring" (specific) performance was one of the most stubborn issues encountered in the preparation of the uniform rules. Article 28 — a compromise that was developed in 1964 at the Hague — relaxes general rules on coerced performance that appear later in the Convention; before examining the compromise we need to look quickly at the general rules which Article 28 modifies. (Art. 28 is quoted *infra* at §194.)

192   **B. The Convention's Basic Rules on Requiring Performance**

(1) The Premise: Enforced Performance

The Convention's system of remedies includes general rules that a party in breach may be compelled to perform its obligations. When the seller deviates from any of his contractual duties (Art. 45(1)), "the buyer may *require performance* by the seller of his obligations" (Art. 46(1)). Similarly, when the buyer fails to perform any of his obligations, "the seller may *require* the buyer to pay the price, take delivery or perform his other obligations. . . ." (Art. 62).

The Convention does not specify the measures that courts shall employ to enforce remedies. Remedial provisions that establish claims for damages (e.g. Arts. 74–78) do not specify measures for (e.g.) the seizure and sale of the defendant's assets to satisfy a money judgment. Similarly, the Convention does not specify what measures courts shall employ to "require" the performance of the contract. All such matters, without detailed discussion, are necessarily left to the general procedures of the *forum*.

In framing the Convention, Article 28 was accepted as a legacy from the 1964 Hague Sales Convention (Art. VII(1), ULIS 16). In preparing the 1964 Convention, without discussing the extent and means whereby various civil law procedural systems coerced performance, deference to procedural rules of the *forum* was usually regarded as a concession to the special procedural approach of legal systems based on English law.[1] However, comparative law studies have shown that on this point the supposed contrast between common law and civil law and the homogeneity of "civil law" procedures are not as great as had been supposed.

It is true that systems that stem from English law have special restrictions and procedures that other systems do not share. Competition between the "common-law" courts and the separate Courts of Chancery (or "Equity") led to a compromise whereby the "Equity" courts would

---

1. For the 1964 background see *Records 1964 Conf.*, Vol. II, 27, 33 (Comm. Rep. on 1956 Draft); Rabel, The Draft of a Uniform Law (ULIS) in UNIFICATION OF LAW 57, 63 (1948); Honnold, Uniform Law for International Sales, 107 U. Pa. L. Rev. 209, 327–328 (1959).

For the 1980 Convention see WG 2d Sess. (1970), II *YB* 61–62, *Docy. Hist.* 67; WG 6th Sess. (1975), VI *YB* 54, *Docy. Hist.* 245; Sec. Comm., *O.R.* 27, *Docy. Hist.* 417; 1st Cee, *O.R.* 304, *Docy. Hist.* 525–526 (comment by delegate of Greece that draft Art. 26, (CISC 28) would be useful in a civil law setting).

not intervene unless the remedy "at law" was not adequate.[2] The "Equity" courts, drawing on their ecclesiastical background, issued their decisions in the form of "decrees" ordering a defendant to do (or to refrain from doing) specified acts; to enforce these decrees the court could commit a recalcitrant defendant to prison for "contempt of court" until he obeyed the court's decree.

Other legal systems did not inherit these procedures for enforcement or the restrictions on "requiring" (specific) performance. However, comparative studies show that there are significant differences among civil law approaches to enforcing contractual promises. Thus, in some civil law systems "requiring" performance in some situations means that substitute performance will be purchased at the expense of the debtor — a remedy that to common-law eyes resembles an action concretely to fix the defendant's damages.[3]

As we shall see, the divergent domestic approaches to requiring performance raise important questions concerning the application of Article 28 of the Convention.

193   (2) Exceptions and Restrictions

Article 46(1), in providing that the buyer "may require performance by the seller of his obligations," immediately provides exceptions from this general rule: When goods have been delivered that do not conform with the contract, the buyer "may require delivery of substitute goods *only if the lack of conformity constitutes a fundamental breach of contract*" (Art. 46(2)), and may require the seller to repair the goods "unless this is unreasonable, having regard to all the circumstances" (Art. 46(3)). On the other hand, the rule of Article 62 that the seller may "require" the buyer to perform his obligations does not include any exceptions; it is unclear that the seller's right (Art. 62) to "*require*

---

2. See F. Maitland, *Equity* 1–10 (1909) reprinted in J. Honnold, The Life of the Law 30–37 (1964).

3. Compare UCC 2–706 (resale by seller fixing damages) and UCC 2–706 (damages fixed by buyer's purchase of substitute goods) with comparable provisions in CISG 75.

For requiring performance in various legal systems see *Treitel, Remedies (Int. Enc.)* §9; *Treitel Remedies (1988)* Ch. III, 43–74. *See also Zweigert & Kotz II (1987)*, Ch. 12, Part II, p. 163–169. Under German procedure (§887 CCP), where an act need not be performed by the defendant personally the court may authorize a third party to perform the act at the expense of the debtor (*vertretbar*); *Zweigert & Kötz, id.*, p. 165: "French law generally admits the issuance of judgments for performance in kind but enforces them in a very grudging manner." But see *id.* 165–169: the *astreinte* (daily monetary penalties).

the buyer to pay the price" calls for remedial measures that are different from the enforcement of money judgments such as the right "to *claim* damages" (Arts. 45(1)(b), 61(1)(b)). See the discussion of Article 62, §345 *infra*. The relationship between Article 28 and the specific rules on requiring performance in Articles 46(2) and (3) is discussed at §285.1, *infra*.

Exceptions applicable to both parties do result indirectly from rules in Articles 85, 86, and 88 that, in some circumstances, place the burden of disposing of unwanted goods on the party who is in a better position to perform this function — even when this lightens the duties of a party in breach. For example, when "the buyer is in delay in taking delivery" the seller may be required not only to take steps "to preserve" the goods (Art. 85) but also, if the goods "are subject to rapid deterioration or their preservation would involve unreasonable expense," the seller "must take reasonable measures to sell them" (Art. 88(2)). In practical effect, these provisions limit the power of the seller under Article 62 to "require the buyer to pay the price," for the significant feature of the remedy of price recovery (as contrasted with damages) is to force the buyer to take possession of the goods.

The power to compel performance may also be curtailed by Article 77 which states that "a party who relies on a breach of contract must take such measures as are reasonable in the circumstances to mitigate the loss. . . ." In examining this provision, *infra* at §416, we shall need to consider questions such as these: If a buyer notifies the seller that he cannot use the goods he has ordered may the seller thereafter lay out labor and materials in manufacturing goods to the buyer's specifications or incur heavy expenses by shipping the goods to the buyer? If not, the seller's remedy must be damages rather than an action for the full price.

Finally, if a party may choose to compel performance after a change in the market he may be in a position to speculate at the defendant's expense. This abuse may be controlled by application of the above requirement of mitigation, construed (as Art. 7(1) requires) in order to promote the "observance of good faith in international trade."[4]

---

4. See Art. 7, *supra* at §95, Art. 46, *infra* at §279, Art. 77, *infra* at §416. *Zweigert & Kötz II (1978)* 162–163 (rules of German law controlling such abuses).

193.1   (3) Functional Consequences of "Requiring Performance"

In many settings "requiring" performance involves more than procedure; important functional and practical consequences are at stake.

When a buyer has *received* the goods and fails to pay for them there will usually be little or no practical difference between "requiring" the buyer to pay the price (Art. 62) and awarding the seller damages for breach (Arts. 61(b), 74, 78). However, when the buyer has *not* received the goods, requiring the buyer to pay the full price (see §193 *supra*) in effect compels the buyer to continue with the transaction. Sometimes such coerced performance involves heavy costs for the buyer without corresponding gains to the seller.

Example 28A. Seller, a Stockholm furniture manufacturer, and Buyer, a furniture distributor in Buenos Aires, made a contract for Seller to ship 500 of its standard coffee-tables to Buyer. Before Seller shipped, Buyer learned that customers in Buyer's area did not care for these items. Buyer telexed these facts to Seller, requested cancellation of the shipment, and offered to compensate Seller for any loss on the transaction. Seller replied, "Shipping as ordered. Require you to pay the agreed price."

As we shall note (§199, *infra*). Seller's reaction seems abnormal. Seller, the manufacturer, is regularly engaged in selling this item in large quantities and can resell the item more efficiently than Buyer. Moreover, continuing with the transaction requires substantial costs in shipping the goods to an area where they are not wanted. Unnecessary waste may also result from forcing the consummation of a transaction (as contrasted with payment of damages) when a seller encounters production difficulties that fall short of exemption under Article 79, §§423–435, *infra, cf. force majeure*. In this and similar situations the substantial transportation costs common in international sales can augment the waste involved in forcing the completion of an unwanted transaction.[5]

---

5. See Lando in *B-B Commentary* 234–238. Farnsworth, Damages and Specific Relief, *AJCL UNCITRAL Symposium*, 247, 250–251, makes a broader argument for limiting specific performance based on the economic efficiency of the parties" freedom to reallocate their resources; R. Posner, Economic Analysis of Law, 105, 117 (3d ed. 1986). *Contra*, Kastely, The Right to Require Performance in International Sales, 63 Wash. L. Rev. 607, 630–633 (1988); Schwartz, The Case for Specific Performance, 89 Yale L.J. 271 (1979); Friedmann, The Efficient Breach Fallacy, 18 J. Leg. Stud. 1 (1989).

194 ## C. General Concession to the Domestic Law: Article 28

Even with the restrictions just mentioned, the Convention grants specific performance on a wider scale than does the common law, which works from the premise that performance will be compelled only when damages do not provide an adequate remedy. (See *infra* at §196.) In response to the differences among domestic approaches to "requiring" performance, the Convention includes the following:

Article 28[6]

If, in accordance with the provisions of this Convention, one party is entitled to require performance of any obligation by the other party, a court is not bound to enter a judgement for specific performance unless the court would do so under its own law in respect of similar contracts of sale not governed by this Convention.

195 ## (1) Law of the Forum or Proper Law of the Contract

Under Article 28, rules of domestic law on requiring performance can prevail over the rules of the Convention.[7] In multistate transactions, which jurisdiction will supply the applicable rule?

Questions that fall outside the scope of the Convention normally would be governed by the domestic rules of the jurisdiction that is selected by principles of private international law. See, e.g., Articles 4 and 7(2), *supra* at §§61 and 85. However, Article 28 refers the court to "its *own* law in respect of similar contracts of sale not governed by this Convention." Does this language invoke the domestic law of the

---

6. Article 28 is the same as Art. 26 of the 1978 Draft, with a small but significant change: "could" was changed to "would." With this change, Art. 28 corresponds to the 1964 Hague Convention on Sales. See Art. VII(1) of the Convention and Art. 16 of the annexed uniform law (ULIS). Provisions in ULIS 25 and 61(2) that further restricted specific performance do not appear in the 1980 Convention. See Arts. 46 and 62, *infra* at §§279 and 345.

7. Indeed, although Art. 6 does not expressly except Art. 28 from the parties" power to "derogate from or vary the effect of" any CISG provision, it is likely that the parties do not have the power to eliminate or modify Art. 28 by agreement: Art. 28 is directed to fora hearing disputes rather than to the rights or obligations of the parties. *See* Markus Müller-Chen, Art. 28 para. 24, *in* Schlechtriem & Schwenzer, *CISG Commentary* (2nd English ed. 2005).

forum on requiring performance or does it call for the rules applicable under rules of private international law?[8]

The question may be illustrated as follows: When a domestic sale in State A is litigated in State F, assume that the *forum* in State F would consider that a request for specific performance was a matter of "substance" to be decided in accordance with the proper law of the contract — the law of State A. Bearing in mind this rule of State F, suppose that State F provides the forum for an international sale between parties in States A and F, both of which have adhered to the Convention. If the plaintiff demands specific performance, does Article 28 refer to the *whole* law of State F, including its rules of private international law that might invoke the rules on specific performance of State A? The diplomatic conference of 1980 did not focus its attention on the question but an answer can be found in the legislative history of the comparable provision in the 1964 Hague Convention.[9]

Article 28 of the 1980 Convention was based on substantially identical provisions in the 1964 Sales Convention. The 1964 Convention was clearly understood to invoke the rules on specific performance of the *forum*. The 1956 Draft, on which this action at the 1964 Conference was based, provided (Art. 27) that the buyer's right to specific performance depended on whether this was "possible and permitted by the *municipal* law of the Court *in which the action is brought.*" Article 72 used similar language with respect to price recovery by the seller. The Special Commission that prepared this draft, in responding to comments by governments, emphasized that the draft referred to *lex fori* — the rules in force in the country "where performance is sought." The virtual identity on this point of the 1964 and 1980 Conventions indicates that the reference in Article 28 to what the court "would do . . . under its *own* law" refers, as indeed the language suggests, to the domestic rules of the *forum*.[10]

---

8. Rules of private intentional law have varied as to whether the right to specific performance should be regarded as "substance" or "procedure." *Cf.* Restatement, Second of Conflict of Laws §§130, 131 (1969); *Dicey & Morris* 1175–78 (1980 10th ed.).

9. At the 1980 Conference one representative remarked that the court's "own law" under Art. 28 included the rules of private international law. The Conference was not debating this issue; little weight can be given to the fact there was no reply to this comment. See Art. 7, *supra* at §91.

10. II *Records 1964 Conf.* 11,18 (Secs. 27 and 72 of the 1956 Draft), 179 (Comments by the Commission that prepared the draft). *Accord*, Markus Müller-Chen, Art. 28 para. 9, *in* Schlechtriem & Schwenzer, *CISG Commentary* (2nd English ed. 2005); Zweigert & Drobnig, 29 *Rabels Z* 146, 165 ULIA. On the legislative history, Riese, 29 *id.* 1, 28–29. For

Article 28 states that a court *"is not bound* to enter a judgment for specific performance unless the court would do so under its own law." The phrase "is not bound" indicates that a court that would not "require" performance under its own law is free either to "require" performance or to apply other remedies provided by the Convention such as awarding damages under Article 74, §§403–408, *infra*.[11] Professor Kastely suggests (n.5, *supra*, 639–640) that such a court may "require performance" to effectuate the reasonable expectations of the foreign party (Arts. 6, 8) or to promote uniformity in the application of the Convention. (*Cf.* §233 *supra*). Response to these suggestions, although not required by the Convention, would be consistent with the view that domestic law should be sensitive to the special needs of international transactions.[12]

As we shall see more fully in connection with Article 46, *infra*, Article 28 permits deviation only from rules of the Convention that *"require* performance of any obligation of the other party" and does not affect the Convention's *restrictions* on specific performance.[13] See §193 *supra*, and §§282–285, *infra*.

196 **(2) Domestic Rules on Specific Performance**

The most that can be done here is to provide a brief introduction to some of the domestic rules on specific performance; references to more thorough studies can be found in the notes.

198 **(a) The (U.S.A.) Uniform Commercial Code.**   *Buyer's Action to Compel Delivery.* The UCC (unlike the Sale of Goods Act (SGA), *supra*) does not restrict specific performance to contracts that call for "specific or ascertained" goods. UCC 2–716 addresses two remedies for the recovery of goods: (1) Specific performance, which may lead to a coercive decree enforceable by punishment for contempt and (2) Replevin (in some jurisdictions called "detinue" or "claim and

---

additional reasons for reference to the domestic law of the forum and not to its choice of law rules see Kastely, 63 Wash. L. Rev. 607, 637–638 (1988).

11. *Accord*, Markus Müller-Chen, Art. 28 para. 22, *in* Schlechtriem & Schwenzer, *CISG Commentary* (2nd English ed. 2005).

12. *See id.* para. 23; C. Schmitthoff, Selected Essays on International Trade Law 25–29, and *passim* (1988).

13. *Accord*, Markus Müller-Chen, Art. 28 para. 11, *in* Schlechtriem & Schwenzer, *CISG Commentary* (2nd English ed. 2005).

delivery") which authorizes a sheriff to seize the goods and deliver them to the plaintiff:

> Section 2–716. *Buyer's Right to Specific Performance or Replevin.*
> (1) Specific performance may be decreed where the goods are unique or in other proper circumstances.
> (2) The decree for specific performance may include such terms and conditions as to payment of the price, damages, or other relief as the court may deem just.
> (3) The buyer has a right of replevin for goods identified to the contract if after reasonable effort he is unable to effect cover for such goods or the circumstances reasonably indicate that such effort will be unavailing or if the goods have been shipped under reservation and satisfaction of the security interest in them has been made or tendered.[14]

Neither remedy is automatically available for breach of contract but the right to decree specific performance in "proper circumstances" is sufficiently flexible to permit courts to grant this remedy in cases of need. Whether specific performance should be available as a matter of course recently has become a subject for debate. The most significant argument for limiting the remedy is that this permits a party who is in breach of contract to escape from overly-rigid advance planning and to reallocate resources for maximum productivity.[15]

Seller's Action to Recover the Price. As has been mentioned, seller's recovery of the full price for goods the buyer has not received, in effect, compels full performance of the contract. The UCC (§2–709) of course calls for the recovery of the full price when the buyer has "accepted" the goods. However, the Code's restrained approach to this remedy is illustrated by the provision of UCC 2–709(1)(b) that the seller may recover the price "of goods identified to the contract if the seller is unable after reasonable effort to resell them at a reasonable price or the circumstances reasonably indicate that such effort will be unavailing."[16]

---

14. In 2003 the organizations that produce and sponsor the Uniform Commercial Code approved significant revisions in the model law. The revision of §2–716(1) does not change the existing text, but adds a clause stating that in non-consumer contracts specific performance can be ordered if the parties have agreed to that remedy. The 2003 revisions to the UCC are not effective unless enacted by individual states or territories, and to date no jurisdiction has adopted the revisions.

15. Farnsworth, Damages and Specific Relief, 27 Am. J. Comp. L. 247 (1979). *Contra*, Kastely, note 5, *supra*; Schwartz, The Case for Specific Performance, 89 Yale L.J. 271 (1979). *Atiyah, Freedom of Contract* 111, 131 refers to the uneconomic effect at early common law of powerful enforcement of future "estates" in land.

16. UCC 2–709 authorizes price recovery in other limited circumstances. See *White & Summers* §§7–3 — 7–5.

UCC 2–716 and 2–709 will be applicable when a party to a sale governed by the Convention sues in court in the United States to compel delivery of the goods or to recover the full price for goods the buyer has not received.

199 **(b) Civil Law Systems.** Articles 46 and 62 of the Convention provide that each party may "require performance" by the other. These broad rules reflected the delegates" understanding of the remedies provided by some civil law systems.[17] It is not feasible to probe the extent to which these general rules accurately reflect the actual operation of those systems;[18] it must suffice to refer to studies that suggest that the concession to the common law provided by Article 28 of the Convention may also permit civil law tribunals to continue a nuanced and realistic approach of their domestic law on the extent to which courts will "require performance" of contracts.[19]

In view of the uncertainties inherent in this delicate compromise, it is fortunate that attempts to compel performance play a minor role in the life of commerce. Legal action to coerce performance takes time even

17. The right to require performance is said to be an axiom of the German legal system. *Sweigert & Kötz II* (1987) 159. The German Civil Code in the very first article of the provisions on obligations (§241) seems to reflect such an axiom: "The effect of an obligation is that a creditor is entitled to claim performance from the debtor." Zweigert in *Comp, Sales* (I.C.L.Q.) 1.5. For a survey of the right to compel performance of non-monetary obligations in European civil law systems, see Principles of European Contract Law Art. 9:102 Comment B and Notes 1 & 3.

18. "[C]omparative research of the laws and especially commercial practices demonstrate that even in the Civil Law countries the principle of [specific] performance must be limited." Principles of European Contract Law, Comment B to Art. 9:102 at 395. Limits on the availability of specific performance are incorporated in Arts. 9:101(2) and 9:102(2) of the European Contract Law Principles. Compare Art. 7.2.2 (a)-(e) of the UNIDROIT Principles 2004 (limiting the availability of specific performance for non-monetary obligations). See also the discussion of limitations on the availability of specific performance in Civil Law jurisdictions in Principles of European Contract Law Art. 9:101 Note 3, at 393–394, & Art. 9:102 Note 3, at 400–401.

19. *See* Markus Müller-Chen, Art. 28 paras. 12, 16 & 18, *in* Schlechtriem & Schwenzer, *CISG Commentary* (2nd English ed. 2005). For further discussion of the remedy of compelled performance (and limitations thereon) in non-Common Law systems, see *Treitel, Remedies (Int. Enc.)* §§10, 12–14, 18; *Treitel, Remedies* 51 *et seq.*; Dawson, Specific Performance in France and Germany, 57 Mich. L. Rev. 495, 523–525 (France), 530 (Germany) 1959; Von Mehren, A Comparative View of the Remedies Available to a Party Aggrieved by Non-performance of a Contractual Obligation in Festschrift für Pan J. Zepos, 434, 444, 450, 457 (Athens: Katsikalis, 1973); Hellner, The Draft of a New Swedish Sale of Goods Act, 22 *Scan. Stud.* 55, 66 (1978) (buyer may not require specific performance that would impose sacrifices which are disproportionate to the buyer's interest in obtaining performance).

when the breach is admitted. However, the defendant often will be able to present evidence and argument to justify non-performance by alleging a breach by the plaintiff or impediments that provide an excuse. (See Art. 79, *infra*.) During the protracted course of litigation the buyer's commercial needs for the goods are not met; and a seller who insists on compelling acceptance of goods must hold the goods until the buyer can be compelled to pay the full price. Usually it is more efficient for an aggrieved buyer promptly to purchase substitute goods or for an aggrieved seller to resell rejected goods; in this manner productive activity can continue while an aggrieved party pursues a claim for damages. In both the common law and civil law worlds, the parties are more interested in efficiency than in legal theory. In civil law settings (as at common law) remedies to coerce performance are seldom employed even in domestic commerce. *Based upon available decisions, the same appears to be true under the CISG: apparently aggrieved buyers seldom invoke their right to compel performance under Article 46*[20] *and aggrieved seller's seldom invoke their right to compel a buyer to take delivery under Article 62.*[21] *As a result, Article 28 has seldom been invoked in available case law, and appears to have had little or no impact.*[22]

One might be tempted to dismiss this area as a non-problem except for the (possibly remote) possibility that in a setting of commercial ill-will a party might be tempted to demand a remedy that is wasteful to the other party as a negotiating weapon to exact a settlement out of proportion to the loss resulting from the breach. See Article 7(1) ("good faith") §§94–95, *supra*.

199.1 (3) Conclusion

Article 28, properly understood in the setting of domestic procedural systems, can mitigate the appearance of rigidity of the Convention's general rules on "requiring performance." Certainly it would be wrong to assume that there are only two rules: (1) Rigid rules of the civil law world, embodied in Articles 46(1) and 62, that call for coerced performance; (2) A more flexible approach under Article 28 applicable only to actions before "common-law" courts. The flexibility permitted under Article 28 is not confined to the procedural approach of one legal

---

20. *See* UNCITRAL Digest Art. 46 para. 4.
21. *See* UNCITRAL Digest Art. 62 para. 2.
22. *See* UNCITRAL Digest Art. 28 para. 3.

system. As Professor Treitel has shown, remedial law in many legal systems is less rigid than the "require performance" rule of the Convention.[23] In sum, domestic rules mitigating the harshness and the dangers of abuse from demands for coerced performance are available in any *forum* where the Convention is in force.[24]

---

23. *See Treitel, Remedies (1988)* Ch. III, 47 *et seq. See also supra* n.20.

24. Although Art. 28 only expressly refers to a "court," it probably also is applicable to arbitral tribunals. *See* Markus Müller-Chen, Art. 28 para. 8, *in* Schlechtriem & Schwenzer, *CISG Commentary* (2nd English ed. 2005).

Article 29.
Modification of Contract; Requirement of a Writing

200   **Agreements of Modification.** Article 29 addresses questions that arise when the parties agree to modify their contract. Will the agreement be effective although nothing additional is given to satisfy common-law requirements with respect to "consideration?" Some contracts provide that modifications must be in writing: Will these agreements nullify modifications that are made orally?

Article 29[1]

(1) **A contract may be modified or terminated by the mere agreement of the parties.**

(2) **A contract in writing which contains a provision requiring any modification or termination by agreement to be in writing may not be otherwise modified or terminated by agreement. However, a party may be precluded by his conduct from asserting such a provision to the extent that the other party has relied on that conduct.**

201   A. Modification or Termination by "Mere Agreement"

Paragraph (1) is addressed to a problem presented by the traditional common-law doctrine of "consideration." When an agreement to modify a contract merely increases or reduces the obligations of one of the parties, the agreement may be ineffective since it is not supported by "consideration" — i.e., by an act or promise given in exchange for the new promise. This restriction on the parties" ability to adapt their

---

1. This article is substantially the same as Art. 27 of the 1978 Draft. The 1964 Hague Conventions had no comparable provisions. The article was initially included in the Formation Draft. For the evolution of the provision, see *W/G 8* paras. 36–47 and Appendix I — Proposed Art. 3A; VIII *YB* 76–77, 95, *Docy. Hist.* 277–278, 290; *W/G 9* paras. 138–153 (Art. 3A revised as Art. 13 and later as Art. 18), IX *YB* 72, *Docy. Hist.* 304; *UNCITRAL XI* para. 28 and Annex 1 paras. 187–194 (summary of deliberations) IX *YB*, 45, *Docy. Hist.* 379; *Com. I* (Art. 27); *SR. 13*, paras. 53–74. *O.R.* 305–306, *Docy. Hist.* 526–527.

transaction to new circumstances has generated pressure for modifications of the traditional rule.[2]

The (U.S.A.) Uniform Commercial Code swept aside this common-law rule by this brief statement (§2–209(1)): "An agreement modifying a contract within this Article needs no consideration to be binding." Article 29(1) of the Convention achieves the same result by stating that a contract may be modified or terminated *"by the mere agreement"* of the parties.[3] "Agreement" need not be explicit but may be based on conduct (Art. 18(3), §§163–164, *supra*), or on practices established by the parties or usage of trade (Art. 9, §§112–122, *supra*).

202 B. Contract Restrictions on Modification

The fact that the sales contract is in writing does not bar oral modification. Articles 11, 29(2).[4] However, contracts sometimes provide that they may be modified only in writing. Article 29(2) gives effect to these No-Oral-Modification ("NOM") clauses, sometimes described as private "statutes of frauds." What is the effect of a contract term that requires formalities for modification other than a "writing?" Suppose the initial contract permits modification only by a writing "signed by the parties" or requires the "approval in writing by the managing director."[5] Under Article 6, the parties may "vary the effect of *any*" of the Convention's provisions; thus the parties, by a written agreement, may broaden the scope of Article 29, e.g., by requiring that written modifications be signed.[6]

2. English Law Revision Commission, Sixth Interim Report (Statute of Frauds and the Doctrine of Consideration) (Cmd. 5449) Recs. 3, 4 and 8; *Ont. L. Ref. Com.*, *I Sale* 96–102. Civil law systems impose no comparable restriction. *Zweigert & Kötz II* (1987) 71–82.

3. Domestic rules requiring a writing or other formality may be applicable to the agreement if one of the parties has its place of business in a Contracting State that has made a declaration under Art. 96. See the Commentary to Art. 12, *supra* at §129.

4. *See* UNCITRAL Digest Art. 29 para. 5.

5. The Convention's few rules with respect to a "writing" do not require signatures or other formalities. Under Art. 13 " "writing" " includes telegram and telex." See Art. 21(2) (letter or other "writing" containing a late acceptance).

6. *Accord*, Peter Schlechtriem, Art. 29 para. 7, *in* Schlechtriem & Schwenzer, *CISG Commentary* (2nd English ed. 2005). The requirement of Art. 29(2) that restrictions on modification must be contained in a "contract in writing" would *a fortiori* apply to the more elaborate contractual restrictions mentioned in the text. On the effect of a Contracting State's declaration under Art. 96, see note 3, *supra* at §201, and the Commentary to Art. 12, *supra* at §128.

204   **(1) Conduct Precluding Reliance on Formal Requirement**

The role of the second sentence of Article 29(2) may be illustrated as follows:

Example 29A, A written contract called for Seller to manufacture 10,000 units of a product according to specifications that were supplied by Buyer and set forth in the contract. The contract provided: "This contract may only be modified by a writing signed by the parties." Before Seller started production, the parties by telephone agreed on a change in the specifications. Seller produced 2,000 units in accordance with the new specifications; Buyer refused to accept these units on the ground that they did not conform to the specifications in the written contract.

Because of the contract provision, under Article 29(2) the oral agreement to the change in specifications, by itself, was ineffective to modify the contract. However, Buyer's oral agreement could be held to constitute "conduct" that would preclude him from invoking the contract clause "to the extent that the other party has relied on that conduct"; Seller's production of the 2,000 units in accordance with the oral agreement could constitute such reliance. However, Buyer is precluded only "to the extent" of the reliance; he should be able to insist on the original specifications for further production.[7]

Under this view, Article 29(2) reliance may be based on "conduct," such as a statement by one party that it would accept a shipment made a week later than the date specified in the contract, followed by a shipment made in accordance with this assurance.

It may be argued that a "no-oral-modification" clause means: "This contract may be modified only by written agreement, and may not be modified by an oral agreement or other conduct regardless of reliance thereon." This construction of a "no-oral-modification clause," or an express contract provision in the terms just quoted, raises a difficult question on the relationship between Article 29(2) (last sentence) and Article 6 (§§74–77, *supra*). Article 6 states: "The parties may . . . derogate from or vary the effect of any of [the Convention's] provisions."

---

7. *Secretariat Commentary* Art. 27, para. 9, *O.R.* 28, *Docy. Hist.* 418. Comparable provisions in UCC 2–209(4) and (5) are stated in terms of "waiver" — the voluntary relinquishment of a known right. See *White & Summers* §1–5. Under UCC 2–209(5) a party may "retract the waiver by reasonable notification . . . . . . that strict performance will be required, unless the retraction would be unjust in view of a material change of position in reliance on the waiver." The second sentence of Art. 29(2) of the Convention is less elaborate but seems to reach similar results. *Cf.* the doctrine of promissory estoppel.

Under one view Article 6 would authorize the parties to override the "reliance" provision of Article 29(2). However, the "reliance" provision addresses a specific problem of *abuse* of a "no-modification" clause rather than the general effectiveness of the clause. Consequently, it may be suggested that Article 6 should not be construed to authorize contracting to nullify the narrow protection against abuse of contracting in Article 29(2).[8] In further support is the mandate of Article 7(1) that, in interpreting the Convention, "regard is to be had to ... the need to promote ... *the observance of good faith* in international trade."

If, contrary to this suggestion, the protective rule of Article 29(2) may be nullified by contract, the party prejudiced by such a contract term may invoke applicable domestic rules on "unconscionability," "good faith" or other rules invalidating such contract provisions.[9] As we have seen, domestic rules on the validity of contract terms are preserved by Article 4(a). See §§64–67, *supra*.[10]

204.1   ## C. The Convention and Common-law "Consideration"

Common lawyers who have never met a problem of "consideration" in practice will still recall that at classical common law a promise might not be enforceable unless the promisee gave something in exchange: a promise or an act — possibly only a peppercorn. Does the Convention abolish the common-law doctrine of "consideration"? This question, sometimes posed by concerned jurists,[11] is reminiscent of questions concocted by clever, mischievous students to test their professor's mettle. The question is interesting but calls for a slightly narrower focus: Can a problem of common-law "consideration" arise within the area governed by the Convention? Perhaps the doctrine's principal

8. *See* Robert A. Hillman, Art. 29(2) *of the United Nations Convention on Contracts for the International Sale of Goods: A New Effort at Clarifying the Legal Effect of "No Oral Modification" Clauses*, 21 Cornell Int'l L. J. 449, 462 (1988). *Contra*, Peter Schlechtriem, Art. 29 para. 10A, *in* Schlechtriem & Schwenzer, *CISG Commentary* (2nd English ed. 2005).

9. *See* Peter Schlechtriem, Art. 29 para. 10A, *in* Schlechtriem & Schwenzer, *CISG Commentary* (2nd English ed. 2005).

10. Domestic law may also be available under Art. 4(1) to deal with contract modifications obtained by economic duress such as threats to suspend performance unless the other party accedes to unreasonable demands for contract modification.

11. *See* Harry M. Flechtner, *More U.S. Decisions on the U.N. Sales Convention: Scope, Parol Evidence, "Validity," and Reduction of Price Under* Art. 50, 14 J.L. & Com. 153, 166–69 (1995).

significance has been to deny enforcement to promises to make a gift —
a type of open-handedness that does not plague commercial practice.
The doctrine has, however, had an impact on issues more likely to arise
in practice. Those issues are discussed below.

204.2   (1) Formation of the Contract (Part II of the Convention)

As we have seen, problems of "consideration" can arise when an
offeror, without receiving anything in exchange, promises not to revoke
the offer (§140 *supra*). However, Article 16(2) of the Convention provides that such an offer "cannot be revoked" (§§139–142 *supra*).

Our clever student, however, may exclaim: "Haven't you overlooked
Article 4 which states that "except as otherwise expressly provided in
this Convention, it is not concerned with (a) the *validity* of the contract"?
Our contract law states that consideration is necessary for *validity*.
Hence our rules on consideration are in force in spite of the Convention." *The Convention, however, expressly provides in Article 16(2)(a)
that an "indication" of irrevocability makes an offer irrevocable, with
no requirement that consideration be given in exchange. Thus even if
domestic consideration doctrine is deemed a matter of "validity," the
issue of whether consideration is required for an undertaking to
refrain from revoking an offer is, as provided in Article 4, pre-empted
by the express provisions of the Convention, much as domestic requirements concerning the form of a valid sales contract are preempted by
the informality rule of Article 11.[12]*

204.3   (2) Rights under the Contract (Part III of the Convention)

The rules of Article 29 permitting modification of the contract by
"mere agreement," as we have seen, also collide with traditional
common-law rules on "consideration" (§201 *supra*). Here, too,
domestic consideration requirements, even if deemed a matter of validity, must yield to the express (and uniform) rule of the Convention, as
provided in Article 4. There are a few other provisions of the Convention
that might be regarded as involving a readjustment of the parties'' agreement. See Articles 47(2) and 63(2) (effect of a notice fixing an additional
period for performance). Article 48(2) (effect of a request that a buyer

---

12. Such domestic form requirements are preempted unless, of course, an Art. 96 reservation
comes into play. See the Commentary on Art. 12 *infra*.

make known whether it will accept delayed performance), Article 65(1) (effect of a request to make specifications). If any of these provisions should collide with domestic rules on "consideration" the domestic rule is superseded by the uniform international rule permitting readjustment of the contract by "mere agreement."

204.4   ## (3) Conclusion Regarding "Consideration" and the Convention

It is difficult to envisage cases in which common-law rules on "consideration" would come into play within the area governed by the Convention but are not pre-empted by the Convention's express provisions. In Part II (Formation), except for promises not to revoke an offer expressly governed by Article 16(2)(a), the formation of sales agreements does not present a problem of "consideration" since each party's promise is made in exchange for the other party's promise or (in rare instances) performance.

In Part III (obligations under the Contract) it is difficult to think of a promise made after the initial making of the contract that is not made binding either by Article 29 ("A contract may be modified or terminated by *mere agreement*") or by one of the above-mentioned provisions facilitating readjustment of the parties" obligations.

Beyond the situations covered in Articles 16(2)(a) and 29(1), where the Convention expressly addresses the matter (and thus would pre-empt domestic consideration doctrine), should consideration requirements be deemed to raise questions of "validity" and thus continue to apply in transactions governed by the CISG? A U.S. case tends to confirm that the issue is likely to be one of primarily, perhaps even purely, academic interest. In Geneva Pharmaceuticals Technology Corp. v. Barr Laboratories, Inc.[13] *one party challenged whether a contract governed by the Convention was unenforceable because it was not supported by consideration. The court treated the consideration requirement of applicable U.S. domestic law as a matter of validity beyond the scope of (and thus not displaced by) the Convention, but*

---

13. 201 F. Supp. 2d 236 (U.S. District Court for the Southern District of New York, 10 May 2002). The case is discussed in Petra Butler, *The Doctrines of Parol Evidence Rule and Consideration—A Deterrence to the Common Law Lawyer?* (paper presented at the UNCITRAL-Singapore International Arbitration Centre Conference, "Celebrating Success: 25 Years United Nations Convention on Contracts for the International Sale of Goods," Singapore, 22–23 September 2005), available at http://www.cisg.law.pace.edu/cisg/biblio/butler4.html#44.

held that consideration (as defined by New Jersey law) had been suf-
ficiently alleged.[14] *Thus the result was unaffected by the application of*
domestic consideration requirements.

Of course it remains possible that imposition of consideration
requirements where they are not preempted by express rules of the
CISG might impact the outcome of future cases. Thus the question
whether consideration is a doctrine of "validity" may yet arise in
practice. Consideration requirements may indeed fit some of the defi-
nitions of "validity" that have been put forward (see supra §64).[15] On
the other hand, on each occasion when this question came to the fore
(Arts. 16, 29) the Convention rejected "consideration" as a barrier to
enforcing the agreement. This policy consequently might be deemed to
quality as one of the "general principles" on which the Convention is
based and therefore to be given effect under Article 7(2) (§§96–102
supra). More importantly, the legal systems in much of the world
have no doctrine comparable to common-law "consideration." See
Zweigert v. Kötz II (1987), supra n.2. Perhaps subjecting international
sales governed by the Convention to this arcane doctrine would be
inconsistent with the mandate of Article 7(1) (§§85–87 *supra*) to interpret the Convention with regard "to its *international* character and the
need to promote *uniformity in its application*."

---

14. 201 F. Supp. 2d at 282–84.

15. The *Geneva Pharmaceuticals* court in fact found that consideration was a validity doctrine under Professor Hartnell's definition. 201 F. Supp. 2d at 282–83.

CHAPTER II.

OBLIGATIONS OF THE SELLER
(Articles 30–52)

INTRODUCTION TO CHAPTER II

205   Chapter II opens with a brief statement giving the essence of the seller's obligations (Art. 30). The remaining articles of the Chapter are grouped in three sections. Two sections define the seller's most important duties: The time and place for delivering the goods (Sec. I, Arts. 31–34) and the quality of the goods and their freedom from third-party claims (Sec. II, Arts. 34–44). The final section sets forth the basic remedies that are given to the buyer when the seller fails to perform its duties under the contract (Sec. III, Arts. 45–52).

    These remedies for breach by the seller and comparable remedies in Chapter III for breach by the buyer (Arts. 61–65) are supplemented in Chapter V by remedial provisions applicable to both parties (Arts. 71–84).

Article 30.
Summary of Seller's Obligations

206   Article 30 introduces the reader to the scope of Chapter II and draws attention to the principal topics dealt with in the Chapter and the order of their presentation. (Chapter III — Obligations of the Buyer — has a similar chapeau (Art. 53).)

Article 30[1]

The seller must deliver the goods, hand over any documents relating to them and transfer the property in the goods, as required by the contract and this Convention.

This introductory article is significant for its explicit statement of the central and unitary role that the Convention gives to the contract. The issue of a fragmented versus a unitary approach to the contract was introduced in the Overview (Ch. 2, *supra* at §24), and will be explored further under Article 31 at §207 and in connection with the Convention's remedial system. (See the Introduction to Sec. III of this Chapter *infra* at §272; Art. 44 *infra* at §255.) The relation between the Contract and the Convention has been examined in the Overview (Ch. 1, *supra* at §2) and in the Commentary to Article 6, *supra* at §75.[2]

The fact that the Convention applies fully to sales of goods to be consummated by the delivery of documents is made explicit here in Article 30. See also Article 34, §§217–219, *infra*.

---

1. This article is substantially the same as Art. 28 of the 1978 Draft and is similar to ULIS 18.
2. Discussions of the obligations of the seller: Commentary on Arts. 30–52 in Schlechtriem & Schwenzer, *CISG Commentary* (2nd English ed. 2005); Schlechtriem, *Parker Colloq.* Ch. 6, 1984; Ghestin, Les obligations du vendeur selon [CISG], 1 I. B. L.J. 5 (1988) (parallel texts, English and French). See also *Rep. S-G*, "Obligations of the Seller," Annex II, paras. 69–71, IV *YB* 45–46, *Docy. Hist.* 122–123 and the Commentary to Arts. 45 and 61; *infra* at §275 and §344.

SECTION I.

DELIVERY OF THE GOODS AND HANDING OVER OF DOCUMENTS
(Articles 31–34)

Article 31.
Place for Delivery

207   When the contract (interpreted in the light of practices and usages) does not state where the seller should deliver the goods, the question is answered by the present article.

The place for delivery, in addition to determining the duties of the parties, in several jurisdictions may also provide a basis for jurisdiction: E.g., Article 5(1) of the Brussels Convention (European Convention on Jurisdiction and Enforcement of Judgments in Civil and Commercial Matters, Sept. 27, 1968)[1] and Article 5(1) of the Lugano Convention (European Communities — European Free Trade Association: Convention on Jurisdiction and Enforcement of Judgments in Civil and Commercial Matters, Sept. 16, 1988[2]). Professor Schlechtriem's Commentary provides extended discussion of the jurisdictional impact of Article 31.[3]

---

1. 1998 O.J. (C 27) 1. The Brussels Convention has now been largely (but not completely) superseded by the Brussels I Regulation, Council Regulation 44/2001 of 22 December 2000 on Jurisdiction and the Recognition and Enforcement of Judgments in Civil and Commercial Matters, 2001 O.J. (L 012) 1. The extent to which Art. 31 is relevant to jurisdiction under the Brussels I Regulation is a matter of controversy. *Compare* Ulrich Huber & Corinne Widmer, Art. 31 Paras. 12, 88, 93–99, *in* Schlechtriem & Schwenzer, *CISG Commentary* (2nd English ed. 2005), *with* Ronald A. Brand, *CISG Article 31: When Substantive Law Rules Affect Jurisdictional Results*, 25 J.L. & Com. 181, 187–190 (2005–06).

2. 1988 O.J. (L 319) 9.

3. See Ulrich Huber & Corinne Widmer, Art. 31 paras. 12, 87–99, *in* Schlechtriem & Schwenzer, *CISG Commentary* (2nd English ed. 2005). For decisions employing Art. 31 for jurisdictional purposes, see UNCITRAL Digest Art. 31 para. 2.

Article 31[4]

If the seller is not bound to deliver the goods at any other particular place, his obligation to deliver consists:

(a) if the contract of sale involves carriage of the goods — in handing the goods over to the first carrier for transmission to the buyer.

(b) if, in cases not within the preceding subparagraph, the contract relates to specific goods, or unidentified goods to be drawn from a specific stock or to be manufactured or produced, and at the time of the conclusion of the contract the parties knew that the goods were at, or were to be manufactured or produced at, a particular place — in placing the goods at the buyer's disposal at that place;

(c) in other cases — in placing the goods at the buyer's disposal at the place where the seller had his place of business at the time of the conclusion of the contract.

208 ## A. Place for Delivery in Specific Settings

(1) Contracts Involving Carriage

All sales involve movement of goods, at the very least by the buyer's removal of the goods he has purchased. Article 31(a), however, is applicable only to contracts that involve "carriage." This refers to transport by a "carrier" to which the seller "hands the goods over" for "transmission to the buyer." This language shows that "carrier" does not include transport facilities, such as delivery trucks, operated by the parties.[5]

Normally the contract will refer to the use of a carrier; in other cases the distance that separates the parties and their practices will often show that the contract involves the use of a "carrier."[6] In these transactions, paragraph (a) applies and the seller completes its contractual obligation

---

4. Art. 31 is substantially the same as Art. 29 of the 1978 Draft, *O.R.* 8, *Docy. Hist.* 385. *Cf.* ULIS 23. The Convention's rejection of the approach of ULIS 19 is considered *infra* at §210. See, in general, Schlechtriem, Com. (1998) 221–251 (Huber).

5. See Ulrich Huber & Corinne Widmer, Art. 31 paras. 15, 21–23, *in* Schlechtriem & Schwenzer, *CISG Commentary* (2nd English ed. 2005); UNCITRAL Digest Art. 31 para. 6.

6. *Compare* Ulrich Huber & Corinne Widmer, Art. 31 paras. 17–18, *in* Schlechtriem & Schwenzer, *CISG Commentary* (2nd English ed. 2005) and UNCITRAL Digest Art. 31 para. 5.

with respect to delivery by "handing the goods over to the first carrier for transmission to the buyer."

As we shall see (*infra* at §210), the question whether a party has complied with its contractual obligation is distinct from the allocation of loss from fire, theft or other casualty. However, when the seller dispatches the goods by carrier the rules on contract performance correspond closely to the Convention's rules on risk of loss. Thus, Article 67(1) provides: "If the contract of sale involves carriage of the goods and the seller is not bound to hand them over at a particular place, the risk passes to the buyer when the goods are *handed over to the first carrier for transmission to the buyer....*"

These rules reflect mercantile practice. As we shall see in greater detail in the commentary to the rules on risk of loss in Chapter IV (Arts. 66–77, *infra* at §§360–419), even when the seller undertakes to pay the freight costs to destination under "C.I.F." and "C. & F." ("CFR") terms, it has long been settled that the seller both completes his delivery duties and transfers risk to the buyer when the goods are (at the latest) loaded on the carrier. And the 2000 version of INCOTERMS reflects modern transport practices by providing that even though the seller undertakes to bear transport costs under a term "Carriage Paid to..." ("CPT"), the seller completes its duties as to delivery (and transfers risk to the buyer) when the seller delivers the goods "to the first carrier." A similar approach is reflected in the definition of the important term — "Free Carrier ... (named place)" ("FCA").[7]

Practical considerations underlie these rules. Damage in transit usually is discovered only when the goods arrive and are unpacked; at this point the buyer (especially in international shipments) is in a better position than the seller to salvage the goods and to file a claim against the carrier or the insurer.[8] The provision that the seller's responsibility is not discharged until the goods have been "delivered" to the carrier (as contrasted with leaving the goods on an unattended dock pending arrival of the carrier) means that the seller remains responsible until the carrier has taken possession of the goods and thereby has assumed some responsibility for them.[9]

---

7. For discussion of decisions involving the use of *Incoterms* in transactions governed by the CISG see UNCITRAL Digest Art. 31 para. 3.

8. See John O. Honnold, *A Uniform Law for International Sales*, 107 U. Pa. L. Rev. 299, 322–323 (1959).

9. See United Nations Convention on Carriage of Goods by Sea, 1978 (the Hamburg Rules) Art. 4. The United States COGSA implementation of the 1924 Brussels Convention (46 U.S.C. §1311) preserves the wider scope of the Harter Act of 1893 (46 U.S.C. §190) and thus

These basic rules are also embodied in the Uniform Commercial Code. Under UCC 2–509(1):

(1) Where the contract requires or authorizes the seller to ship the goods by carrier

(a) if it does not require him to deliver them at a particular destination, the risk of loss passes to the buyer when the goods are duly delivered to the carrier even though the shipment is under reservation (Section 2–505)...

209 **(2) Sales Not Involving Carriage**

Paragraphs (b) and (c) of Article 31 apply to a small minority of international sales — sales that do not "involve carriage" and where "the seller is not bound to deliver the goods at any particular place." These provisions are most likely to apply when the seller and buyer are relatively near each other and the buyer operates trucks that can conveniently come to (b) where the goods are or (c) to the seller's place of business. When the contract calls for the buyer to come for the goods, the seller completes its contractual duties with respect to delivery by "placing the goods at the buyer's disposal."[10]

210 **B. "Délivrance" in ULIS and the Contractual Approach**

Article 31 of the Convention marks a change from the approach of ULIS that, at first glance, seems merely a change in theory but, in fact, affects the clarity and workability of the two versions.

In ULIS the concept of *"délivrance"* dominated the draft's approach to several problems, including risk of loss and the time for payment of the price. This approach could have been successful in some of these settings if the draft had used a simple definition of "delivery" — the

---

is closer to the 1978 Hamburg Rules than to the narrow scope of the 1924 Brussels Convention.

10. As was noted *supra* at §208, the fact that the seller has complied with its contractual obligations does not necessarily mean that risk of loss passes to the buyer. Under Art. 69, when the contract does not involve carriage, risk passes to the buyer only when he "takes over" the goods or "commits a breach of contract by failing to take delivery." This rule becomes important when the contract (e.g.) provides: "Buyer shall remove the goods within thirty days following notification by the seller that the goods are at the buyer's disposal." See the Commentary to Art. 69, *infra* at §373. *Cf.* (U.S.A.) UCC 2–308(b).

handing over of the goods. Instead, under ULIS 19(1) *délivrance* "consists in the handing over of goods which conform with the contract."[11] This was a very plausible approach to the question whether the seller had performed his contractual duties but it complicated the drafting in other settings, such as risk of loss, and made this central concept so abstract (in French, *délivrance* as contrasted with *remise*) that no appropriate term could be found in English and in various other languages. ULIS was drafted in French. When, at a late stage, an English text was prepared, there was no escape from rendering *délivrance* as "delivery," although this led to the curious result that if the goods had a defect they were never "delivered" to the buyer while he used or even consumed the goods. More important, the use of *délivrance* produced untoward consequences with respect to risk of loss and payment of the price. Efforts to correct this problem were made at the 1964 conference but *délivrance* was such an integral part of the draft's structure that repairs were not feasible.[12]

In UNCITRAL it was possible to deal with this problem. The Working Group at an early stage decided that the problems of risk and payment of the price should be disentangled from *délivrance*, and should be handled as separate problems.[13] In addition, the provisions on Obligations of the Seller with which we are now concerned (Art. 31 and succeeding articles in the present Chapter) are stated in terms of whether the seller had performed his "obligation" with respect to delivery. The seller fails to perform his obligations if he *tenders* non-conforming goods; with regard to this contractual issue it does not matter whether the buyer rejects the goods (no "handing over" or "delivery") or whether the buyer takes possession of and uses the goods, subject to a damage claim to compensate for the breach.

---

11. See *Tunc, Commentary,* I. *Records, 1964 Conf.* 356 at §371 (Col. 2). The use of *délivrance* was designed to avoid difficulties with the civil law concept of "guarantee." *Ibid.*

12. II *Records 1964 Conf.* 236; Honnold, *A Uniform Law for International Sales,* 107 U. Pa. L. Rev. 317–320 (1959) and Honnold, *ULIS: The Hague Convention 1964,* 30 Law & Cont. Pr. L.Q. 326 at 350 (1965). For criticism of ULIS and approval of the UNCITRAL approach see Huber, 43 *Rabels Z* 413, 451 (1979); Tallon in *Rechtsvergleichung* 753, 757–759 (unfortunate) departure from simpler physical (*material*) text of early French law); Lando, *B-B Commentary* 245–246. Similar difficulties resulted from the abstract concept of property in the (U.K.) Sale of Goods Act (1893) and the (U.S.A.) Uniform Sales Act (1906). For similar problems in Continental Law see *Zweigert & Kötz II (1987),* 3–7 (German law: "juristic act"), 8 (French law: "object").

13. *Rep. S-G,* "Delivery in ULIS," III *YB* 31–41, *Docy. Hist.* 73–82; *W/G 4,* paras. 16–21, IV *YB* 62–63, *Docy. Hist.* 140–141; *Rep. S-G,* "Obligations of the seller," paras. 6–14, IV *YB* 37–38. *Rep. S-G,* "Pending Questions," para. 82, VI *YB* 97, *Docy. Hist.* 114–115, 222.

Thus, the Convention has no provision like that of ULIS 19(1): "Delivery *consists* in. . . ." The contractual approach of the Convention is typified by the introduction to Article 31: the seller's "*obligation* to deliver consists" in performing specified acts, regardless of whether "delivery" takes place. The same contractual approach is used in Chapter III — *Obligations of the Buyer*. E.g., Article 60 ("[t]he buyer's *obligation* to take delivery consists . . .").

The point deserves emphasis. Assume that the contract calls for the seller to place the goods at the buyer's disposition at the seller's plant by May 1 for removal by the buyer by the end of the month. If the seller on May 1 places the goods at buyer's disposition Article 31 provides that the seller has fulfilled his "*obligation* to deliver" the goods. This provision does not state (and for the purposes of the Convention does not need to state) that the seller has "*delivered*" the goods, nor does Article 31 determine when the risk of loss passes to the buyer, for this issue is governed by the rules on risk of loss in Chapter IV. As we shall see at §374 (Examples 69A and 69B), Article 69 provides that in the above situation risk of loss rests on the seller until the buyer "takes over" the goods; the result is different if the buyer "commits a breach of contract by failing to take delivery." E.g., if the buyer fails, as agreed, to come for the goods by May 30 risk passes to the buyer on June 1.

In short, Article 31 and the other provisions in this Chapter deal with the *contractual obligations* of the parties; problems such as allocation of risk are dealt with by provisions addressed directly to those problems.

211 C. The Role of General Rules on Place and Time

Article 31, in addressing the question whether the seller has performed his contractual duties with respect to delivery, plays a modest role. In most cases, questions as to "place" and "time" will merge into a single issue: Did the goods get to the agreed place on time? Article 33, *infra* at §216, is concerned with the time for delivery. But in most situations the combined place-time question will be answered by the contract, either in specific terms or by the meaning supplied by the circumstances mentioned in Article 8(3), by the parties" practices (Art. 9(1) or by commercial usage (Art. 9(2)).[14]

---

14. On the artificial nature of the distinction between place and time see the Intro. to Ch. II, Sec. III, *infra* at §274. *Cf. Treitel, Remedies (Int. Enc.)* §75. In a few situations, the place for delivery (set by the contract or, failing guidance from the contract, by Art. 31) will be

Export Licenses and Taxes. The rules on the place for delivery can also be useful, when the contract is silent, in allocating responsibility for matters such as export licenses and export taxes. For example, assume that the contract provides that the seller will place the goods at the buyer's disposal at the seller's place of business. Under Article 31(b) the seller fulfills his obligation to deliver at his own factory or warehouse; the buyer has the responsibility to remove the goods and to make any arrangements for exportation. INCOTERMS (2000) reflects a similar approach: Under a sale "EXW" (*Ex Works*) "[t]he buyer must obtain at his own risk and expense any export or import license or other official authorization and carry out, where applicable, all customs formalities for the export of the goods."[15] On the other hand, the seller must bear these costs when the contract requires the seller to deliver the goods in the buyer's country under the term "DDP" (delivered duty paid).[16]

When the contract calls for the seller to dispatch the goods by carrier, Article 31(a), allocating responsibility for export licenses and taxes is less clear-cut. Modern transport procedures call for expedited carriage as soon as the carrier receives the goods; these procedures have led to practices placing the responsibility for export clearances on the seller. Thus, INCOTERMS (2000) provides that under the modern term "FCA (Free Carrier (. . . named place))," even when the designated point is inland, "A2. The seller must obtain at his own risk and expense any export license or other official authorization and carry out, where applicable, all customs formalities necessary for the export of the goods." The same result follows under the term "CPT (Carriage Paid to . . .)" and also under the traditional terms "C&F" (now abbreviated "CFR"), "CIF," "FAS," "FOB." and "CFR (Cost and Freight (. . . named port of destination)").

---

relevant in measuring damages for breach. See Art. 76(2), *infra* at §409. The Convention's approach is supported in Barrera-Graf, Comparative Study §3(b), *Barrera-Graf Colloquium.*
15. See UNCITRAL Digest Art. 31 para. 11 and decisions cited in n.21.
16. Where the delivery point is at the water's edge in the buyer's country under the term "DEQ" (delivered *Ex Quay*), *Incoterms (2000)* provides that the seller has responsibility for any export license or tax, but the buyer is responsible for import formalities and costs. A similar division of responsibility applies under the terms "DAF" (delivered at frontier) and "DES" (delivered *Ex Ship*).

It is best if the parties deal specifically in the contract with the question of responsibility for export licenses and export taxes.[17] When the contract is silent, modern practices governing export sales often indicate that the seller's responsibility to dispatch goods to a foreign destination calls for him to deal with these matters.

17. One way to clarify the issue is for the contract to refer to *Incoterms* and use one of the trade terms defined therein.

Article 32.
Shipping Arrangements

212   As we have just seen, in international sales the seller usually completes his obligations with respect to delivery of the goods by "handing over the goods to the first carrier for transmission to the buyer." Article 31, *supra* at §208. Any provision of the agreement (including usage and any practice between the parties) is decisive; to the extent that there is no agreement with respect to shipping arrangements, Article 32 applies.

Article 32[1]

(1) If the seller, in accordance with the contract or this Convention, hands the goods over to a carrier and if the goods are not clearly identified to the contract by markings on the goods, by shipping documents or otherwise, the seller must give the buyer notice of the consignment specifying the goods.

(2) If the seller is bound to arrange for carriage of the goods, he must make such contracts as are necessary for carriage to the place fixed by means of transportation appropriate in the circumstances and according to the usual terms for such transportation.

(3) If the seller is not bound to effect insurance in respect of the carriage of the goods, he must, at the buyer's request, provide him with all available information necessary to enable him to effect such insurance.

213   ## A. Identification of the Shipment

The specific goods (e.g., specific bags of sugar) that will be supplied are usually not identified when the contract is made; the seller may supply any goods that conform to the agreed qualities and characteristics. In these situations it is sometimes said that the contract calls for "generic" goods or that the goods are "unascertained" or "unidentified."

---

1. Art. 32 is the same as Art. 30 of the 1978 Draft except for drafting changes in paragraph (1). Paragraph (1) is based on ULIS 19(3); paragraphs (2) and (3) are based on ULIS 54(1) and (2). See, in general, Schlechtriem, Com. (1998) 252–260 (Huber).

At some stage in the performance of each sales contract, specific goods will be designated or "identified" as those which are provided pursuant to that contract. As we shall see in examining the rules on risk in Chapter IV (Arts. 67(2) and 69(3)), casualty loss will generally not fall on the buyer until (at the very least) the goods have been "identified" to the buyer's contract. *When goods transported by carrier have not otherwise been identified to the contract, the notice required by Article 31(1) may result in such identification.*[2]

Article 32(1) creates an obligation on the part of a seller who ships goods to provide the buyer with information that he needs. Often the contract (especially when the seller is to be paid on presentation of documents specified in a letter of credit) provides that the seller will arrange for insurance, and will transfer a policy or certificate of insurance to the buyer (or to the buyer's bank) when payment is made. Occasionally, however, the buyer will need to take out insurance on goods in transit; even if the buyer has general coverage under a "blanket" policy, it is important to be clear as to which goods are in transit to him.

Identification for this purpose, and for the purpose of passing risk, usually is effected by naming the buyer in the documents issued by the carrier — the consignment note or bill or lading; where possession of the shipping document controls the delivery of the goods (e.g., the shipping document is an "order" or "negotiable" bill of lading) the document will normally give the buyer's name as the person the carrier is to notify concerning arrival of the shipment. Even if the shipping document does not connect the buyer and the goods, this may be done by identifying marks on the goods. If the goods are not clearly identified in one of these ways, under Article 32(1) "the seller must give the buyer notice of the consignment specifying the goods."[3]

What are the consequences of failure by the seller to give such a timely notice of the consignment? If the goods are lost or damaged before the goods are identified to the contract, the consequences can be serious by virtue of the rules on risk of loss in Chapter IV.[4] The

2. Article 67(2) mentions identification to the contract "by markings on the goods, by shipping documents, **by notice given to the buyer** or otherwise" (emphasis added). See also Ulrich Huber & Corinne Widmer, Art. 32 para. 8, *in* Schlechtriem & Schwenzer, *CISG Commentary* (2nd English ed. 2005).

3. *Cf. Dölle, Kommentar* (Huber) Art. 19 at 122, p. 184; *Meriens & Rehbinder* Art. 19 at 14, p. 150.

4. See Arts. 67(2) and 69(3), discussed *infra* at §363 and §373. See also Ulrich Huber & Corinne Widmer, Art. 32 paras. 8 & 10, *in* Schlechtriem & Schwenzer, *CISG Commentary* (2nd English ed. 2005).

seller's failure to comply with the identification or notice provisions of the contract or of Article 32(1) will, of course, constitute a breach of contract. The remedies for the breach depend on its seriousness. In any event, the seller will be liable to the buyer for damages that result (Arts. 45 and 74)[5]; if the seller's breach is "fundamental" (Art. 25, *supra*), the buyer may be able to "avoid the contract" (Art. 49) — i.e., he may reject the goods.[6]

214 B. Transportation Arrangements

Paragraph (2) applies whenever "the seller is bound to arrange for carriage of the goods." The contract may call for the seller to make shipping arrangements even though, under the contract, the buyer bears the risk of increase in freight rates or of the unavailability of shipping space. Article 32(2) merely articulates the seller's duty to make appropriate "arrangements" — arrangements for the type and means of transport and the terms of the contract with the carrier. *Unless the parties" agreement is more specific, Article 32(2) permits the seller to choose the arrangements for carriage, provided they meet the standards of Article 32(2).*[7] As was noted with respect to paragraph (1), above, a seller's failure to perform the duties imposed by Article 32 is a breach of contract; the remedy depends on the seriousness of the breach.[8] Unless the contract or usage (Art. 9) provides otherwise, the seller's duty to "arrange" for shipping does not make the seller liable if space or facilities for carriage are unavailable.

5. See Ulrich Huber & Corinne Widmer, Art. 32 para. 11, *in* Schlechtriem & Schwenzer, *CISG Commentary* (2nd English ed. 2005).
6. See Ulrich Huber & Corinne Widmer, Art. 32 para. 12, *in* Schlechtriem & Schwenzer, *CISG Commentary* (2nd English ed. 2005).The statement that the seller "must" give notice is the form of expression used throughout the Convention for expressing a contractual duty. Saying that a party "must" (F. *doit*; Sp. *debera*) do a specified act carries no implication as to the importance of the obligation or the seriousness of failure to perform this duty. The phrase in Art. 32(1). — "in accordance with the contract or this Convention" — also seems to have no special significance, for the seller's duty to identify or notify would not be lightened by his failure to perform some other act "in accordance with" his contractual duties.
7. See Bezirksgericht der Saane, Switzerland, 20 February 1997, CLOUT case No. 261, English translation available at http://cisgw3.law.pace.edu/cases/970220s1.html (holding that under applicable domestic law the buyer bore the burden of proving that the parties had agreed to transport the goods by truck, and that buyer failed to carry the burden).
8. Art. 32(2) is similar to the rules of domestic law: (U.S.A.) UCC 2–504(a); (U.K.) SGA (1893) 32(2) (first sentence).

215 C. Information Necessary for Insurance

Paragraph (3) articulates a duty of cooperation that, in most cases, probably could be established as an aspect of applicable usages or practices. *Cf.* (U.S.A.) UCC 2–311 (Options and Cooperation Respecting Performance); UCC 2–319(1)(c) and (3) (buyer's duty to give needed instructions to seller); (U.K.) SGA (1893) 32(3).[9]

9. Other examples of the duty to cooperate by providing needed information are collected in the commentary to Art. 7(2), *supra* at §100.

Article 33.
Time for Delivery

Article 33[1]

216   **The seller must deliver the goods:**
   (a) if a date is fixed by or determinable from the contract, on that date;
   (b) if a period of time is fixed by or determinable from the con-tract, at any time within that period unless circumstances indicate that the buyer is to choose a date; or
   (c) in any other case, within a reasonable time after the conclu-sion of the contract.

The statement in paragraph (a) that the seller must act in conformity with the contract reinforces the general rules of Articles 6 and 30, *supra* at §§74 and 206. Most articles of the Convention do not reiterate the parties'' obligation to comply with the contract, but in a few places where detailed provision is made for points that are usually covered by contract (as in Art. 33) it seemed advisable to underscore the dominant role of the contract. (Compare Arts. 34, 35(1), 41.) The number of these references was minimized to avoid giving the impres-sion that the contract controls only when it is specifically invoked.[2]

Subparagraph (b) applies when contracts provide a *period* within which delivery shall occur but do not state whether the seller or the buyer has the choice as to the precise time within the period. The pre-sumption that the seller may choose the date reflects the seller's more complex duties — procurement or production, packaging and other arrangements for delivery. For decisions on the choice of a delivery date when the contract provides for delivery within a period of time, see UNCITRAL Digest Article 33 para. 6. We have just seen illustra-tions in Article 32 of shipping arrangements that may need to be made by the seller.[3]

1. Art. 33 is substantially the same as Art. 31 of the 1978 Draft. Subparagraphs (a), (b) and (c) are based (respectively) on ULIS 20, 21 and 22.
2. A similar concern is reflected in (U.S.A.) UCC 1–102(4): "The presence in certain provisions of this Act of the words "unless otherwise agreed" or words of similar import does not imply that the effect of other provisions may not be varied by agreement...."
3. *Accord,* Lando in *B-B Commentary* 261; *Incoterms* (2000): the trade terms generally (at A4) authorize the seller to deliver "within the agreed period").

The "reasonable time" rule of subparagraph (c), which applies when neither a particular date nor a period of time for delivery is "fixed by or determinable from" the contract, is similar to rules of domestic law.[4]

The buyer's duty to take delivery is governed by Articles 53 and 60, discussed in §§322, 34–43, *infra*.

---

4. For decisions on what constitutes a "reasonable time," see UNCITRAL Digest Art. 33 para. 7. For further discussion of the "reasonable time" issue, see Ulrich Huber & Corinne Widmer, Art. 33 paras. 16–17, *in* Schlechtriem & Schwenzer, *CISG Commentary* (2nd English ed. 2005).

Article 34.
Documents Relating to the Goods

217 ## A. The Commercial Setting

When the seller lacks sufficient knowledge of the buyer to justify a delivery on credit, an exchange of goods for the price can be efficiently arranged by the use of a document that controls delivery of the goods, such as a negotiable or "order" bill of lading. See Article 58, *infra* at §333. Such documentary exchanges are accepted by standard statements of trade practice and by domestic law.[1] Even when the seller delivers on credit, the contract (including practices or usage) may require the delivery of additional documents such as an insurance policy and invoices.

218 ## B. The Convention

The above commercial practices provide the setting for the following provision:

Article 34[2]

If the seller is bound to hand over documents relating to the goods, he must hand them over at the time and place and in the form required by the contract. If the seller has handed over documents before that time, he may, up to that time, cure any lack of conformity in the documents, if the exercise of this right does not cause the buyer

---

1. See *Incoterms* (2000), *e.g.* CFR, CIF, CPT, CIP *et al.*, description of documents at A8; GAFTA Contract No. 30 (Grain in Bulk) 13 ("Payment . . . in exchange for Shipping Documents') 14 (listing of Shipping Documents); (U.S.A.) UCC 2–310(b): "if the seller is authorized to send the goods he may ship them under reservation and may tender the documents of title." *Cf.* UCC 2–505, 2–507(2); Swedish Sales Act 14–15, 71(2).

2. The first sentence of Art. 34 is the same as Art. 32 of the 1978 Draft, *cf.* ULIS 50. The second and third sentences were added at the 1980 Diplomatic Conference in the deliberations on draft Art. 35 that became Art. 37. *O.R.* 309–340, 426 (Report of Drafting Committee transferring proposal from draft Art. 35 (Art. 37) to draft article (Art. 34), *Docy. Hist.* 530–531, 647.

unreasonable inconvenience or unreasonable expense. However, the buyer retains any right to claim damages as provided for in this Convention.

219   (1) A Drafting Problem: Documents and Goods

In the preparation of ULIS and in UNCITRAL this question arose: When the law refers to the delivery or handing over of "goods," should the law also refer to delivery effected by "documents of title?" It was found this would have called for many references to delivery by documents; the first sentence of the present article was included to provide a simpler and less cluttered text. This sentence merely states that the seller must perform the contract — a statement that would have been unnecessary but for the drafting problem arising from references to delivery of "goods."[3]

220   (2) Cure of Non-Conforming Documents

The second and third sentences of Article 34 were added at the 1980 Diplomatic Conference to make clear that the seller's right to "cure" a defective delivery of goods extended to the delivery of documents.[4] As we shall see (Art. 37, *infra* at §244), a seller who has made a defective delivery before the date of delivery may deliver a "missing part" or "make up any deficiency in the quantity of the goods" or "deliver goods in replacement" or "remedy" (repair) the lack of conformity. This language dealt so specifically with the special problems of "goods" that it seemed hazardous to rely on the assumption that references to delivery of "goods" extended to "documents." The second and third

---

3. *Rep. S-G*, IV *YB* 39–40, *Docy. Hist.* 116–117; 4th W/G, VI *YB* 64, 70, *Docy. Hist.* 142, 148. See Ulrich Huber & Corinne Widmer, Art. 34 para. 1, *in* Schlechtriem & Schwenzer, *CISG Commentary* (2nd English ed. 2005). For decisions on when the contract requires the seller to hand over documents and which documents are covered by Art. 34, see UNCITRAL Digest Art. 34 paras. 3–5.

4. For discussion of what constitutes a non-conforming document, see Ulrich Huber & Corinne Widmer, Art. 34 para. 8, *in* Schlechtriem & Schwenzer, *CISG Commentary* (2nd English ed. 2005); UNCITRAL Digest Art. 34 para. 7. For discussion of curing non-conforming documents, see Ulrich Huber & Corinne Widmer, Art. 34 para. 10, *in* Schlechtriem & Schwenzer, *CISG Commentary* (2nd English ed. 2005).

sentences of Article 34 were modeled closely on the "cure" provisions of Article 37. The discussion of Article 37, *infra* at §244, will be generally applicable to the provisions of Article 34 with respect to "cure" of defects in documents.[5] Cure of documents after the date for delivery is considered at Article 48, §295, *infra*.

5. At the Diplomatic Conference an amendment to expand the "cure" provisions now in Art. 37 was adopted and referred to the Drafting Committee. *SR.14*, paras. 49–72, *O.R.* 309–310, 426, *Docy. Hist.* 530–531, 647.

SECTION II.

CONFORMITY OF THE GOODS AND THIRD-PARTY CLAIMS
(Articles 35–44)

221 **INTRODUCTION TO SECTION II**

Articles 35 and 36 define the seller's obligations with respect to the quality of the goods. The next four articles (37–40) describe procedures that apply when goods are non-conforming — the seller's privilege to cure defects in the goods (Art. 37) and the buyer's obligation to examine the goods and notify the seller of non-conformity (Arts. 38–40). Articles 41 and 42 define the rights of the buyer when the goods are subject to third-party claims — of ownership (Art. 41) and of rights based on patents, trademarks or other types of intellectual property (Art. 42); Article 43 requires the buyer to notify the seller of these claims. The concluding article (Art. 44) gives grounds for granting partial relief from the usual consequences of a failure to notify the seller as required by Articles 39(1) or 43.

Article 35.
Conformity of the Goods

222 A. The Role of Rules about Quality

Most sales controversies grow out of disputes over whether the goods conform to the contract. In many cases these disputes present only a question of fact: What was the condition of the goods? Disputes over quality, however, cannot always be resolved simply by measuring the goods against the specific terms of the contract. When an order is routine and calls for speedy shipment the parties may not even attempt to articulate the expectations that are associated with transactions in such goods. Even a carefully prepared contract will often fail to express the most basic expectations — that a machine will operate or that a steel girder will be structurally sound — because the parties assume that these points are so obvious that they "go without saying." (Compare the implied obligation that the seller will deliver goods that "are free from any right or claim of a third-party," Art. 41, §§262–266, *infra*.) Consequently, courts and codifiers have had to try to describe, in general terms, those understandings that would have been written into the contract if the parties had drafted a contract provision to deal specifically with the question that led to dispute.[1]

Domestic legal systems address this problem in various ways. In United States law, the seller's obligations as to quality are referred to as "warranties," and are dealt with under three headings: (1) "express warranties," (UCC 2–313); (2) an implied warranty of merchantable quality (UCC 2–314); and (3) an implied warranty of fitness for a particular purpose (UCC 2–315). The (U.K.) Sale of Goods Act (1893), in general, leaves the parties" express statements to the general law of contracts but in Sec. 14 establishes implied "conditions" and

---

1. Developments of the past century have not advanced beyond (and indeed have only obscured) the insight of L. J. Brett in Randall v. Newson, 2 Q.B. 102 (C.A. 1877): "The governing principle ... is that the thing offered or delivered under a contract of purchase and sale must answer the description of it which is contained in words in the contract, or which would be so contained if the contract were accurately drawn out." A similar approach to interpretation was suggested by Jeremy Bentham in A General View of a Complete Code of Laws, 3 Works of Jeremy Bentham, 157, 191 (Bowring ed. 1843). See also Rebel, *The Nature of the Warranty of Quantity*, 24 Tul. L. Rev. 273 (1950); Schlechtriem, in *Parker Colloq.* §6.03 p. 620 (approving the above basic principle stated by L.J. Brett, as quoted in the first edition).

"warranties" of quality and fitness.[2] Other legal systems use different concepts. Codes based on the French pattern tend to deal with questions of quality with a light touch that is directed to the distinction between latent defects (*vices cachés*) and apparent defects (*vices apparents*). This brief approach has been supplemented by other doctrines such as *erreur*; students of the civil law report that the result is complex and unclear.[3]

223 ## B. The Convention

Article 35 presents a unified approach[4] to the seller's contractual obligations with respect to the goods:

Article 35[5]

(1) The seller must deliver goods which are of the quantity, quality and description required by the contract and which are contained or packaged in the manner required by the contract.

(2) Except where the parties have agreed otherwise, the goods do not conform with the contract unless they:

(a) are fit for the purposes for which goods of the same description would ordinarily be used;

---

2. *Atiyah* 103–153, *Benjamin* §§755–853, (U.K.) SGA (1893) 13, 15 (in many cases applies to express contractual provisions).

3. For an illuminating comparison of French, German and common-law approaches in relation to CISG see Tallon in *Rechtsvergleichung* 753, 754–757 (French); Nicholas, Fault and Liability, *Freiburg Colloq.* 283 (1987). See also Ghestin, Les Obligations du Vendeur selon [CISG], Int. Bus. L.J. No. 1, 1988, 5, 8–9, 26, Kahn, La Convention de la Haye, 17 Revue Tri. de Dr. Comm. 689, 712 (1964); *Québec Civ. Code, Rev'n, Sales* 50–55; Durnford, *What is an Apparent Defect In Sale?*, 10 McGill L.J. 60, 341 (1964); Tallon, *Erreur sur la Substance at Guarantee des Vices, Mélanges Hamel* 435 (Paris: Dalloz, 1961); Rabel, at 271, 283, 286: "utter confusion" in various legal systems; need for a "sound theory." *But cf.* Field, *The Law of Latent Defects in Quebec*, 2 Can. Bus. L.J. 209 (1976).

4. See Ingeborg Schwenzer, Art. 35 para. 4, *in* Schlechtriem & Schwenzer, *CISG Commentary* (2nd English ed. 2005): "Article 35 is based on a uniform concept of "lack of conformity." That concept includes not only differences in quality, but also differences in quantity, delivery of an *aliud*, and defects in packaging. In so doing, the CISG differs materially from most domestic laws on liability for defective goods, which often make subtle distinctions."

5. Art. 35 closely follows Art. 33 of the 1978 Draft Convention. In paragraph (2)(d), the concluding phrase ("or, where . . .") was added at the Diplomatic Conference and there were minor drafting changes. *O.R.* 308–309, 315–318, 103–105, *Docy. Hist.* 529–530, 536–539, 675–677. *Cf.* ULIS 33 and 36 and *Rep. S-G*, "Obligations of the Seller," paras. 58–61, IV *YB* 44, *Docy. Hist.* 121.

(b) are fit for any particular purpose expressly or impliedly made known to the seller at the time of the conclusion of the contract, except where the circumstances show that the buyer did not rely, or that it was unreasonable for him to rely, on the seller's skill and judgment;

(c) possess the qualities of goods which the seller has held out to the buyer as a sample or model;

(d) are contained or packaged in the manner usual for such goods or, where there is no such manner, in a manner adequate to preserve and protect the goods.

(3) The seller is not liable under subparagraphs (a) to (d) of the preceding paragraph for any lack of conformity of the goods if at the time of the conclusion of the contract the buyer knew or could not have been unaware of such lack of conformity.

224   (1) Quality Required by the Contract: Paragraph (1)

Paragraph (1) emphasizes a point that could go without saying: the parties must comply with their contract. (See the discussion of Art. 33(a), *supra* at §216; and Arts. 6 and 30, *supra* at §274 and §206.)[6] The Sales Article of the (U.S.A.) Uniform Commercial Code also emphasizes the importance of the contract. Section 2–313 (Express Warranties by Affirmation, Promise, Description, Sample) carried forward a provision, drafted by Professor Williston for the Uniform Sales Act (1906), that was designed to nullify decisions that had hesitated to give contractual effect to the seller's "representations" and "affirmations" (as contrasted with "promises") and also to overturn decisions that had insisted on evidence that the seller "intended to be bound" by statements concerning the quality of the goods.[7]

The technical distinctions in these early cases have been softened by more recent case law.[8] In any event, these distinctions are not useful in deciding what quality is "required by the contract" under Article 35(1).

---

6. Some sales laws do not articulate this point. E.g., (U.K.) SGA (1983).

7. Uniform Sales Act §12; S. Williston, *What Constitutes an Express Warranty In the Law of Sales*, 21 Harv. L. Rev. 555 (1908); 1 *Williston, Sales* §§194–201. Under UCC 2–313, an "express warranty" may be based on an "affirmation of fact" as well as a "promise" and does not require that the seller use "formal words such as "warrant" or "guarantee" or that the seller "have a specific intention to make a warranty." "

8. Savage v. Blakney, [1970] 119 C.L.R. 435 (H. Ct. of Australia); Howard Marine v. Ogden, [1978] Q.B. 574. See *Benjamin* §§755–851. *Cf.* New Zealand Contractual Remedies Act 1979.

As we shall see, Article 35(2)(a) gives effect to the expectations latent in any "description" of the goods. And the basic rules on contract interpretation in Article 8 do not draw any technical distinction between different types of "statements" and emphasize the "understanding" that statements produce in a reasonable person. (See Art. 8, *supra* at §105 and §109.)[9]

225　**(2) Presumed Implications from the Contract: Paragraph (2)**

(a) Description and Ordinary Purposes.

Paragraph (2)(a) embodies the clearest ideas that have been developed for defining the seller's responsibility for quality. These ideas are both subtle and fundamental. Commercial law does not impose standards of quality: it accommodates sales of cars for scrap as well as sales of new cars for resale to consumers. Often, detailed specifications in the contract will resolve any question as to quality but in routine transactions the parties would think it needless and a bit absurd to say things that "go without saying." In these situations interpretation of the contract, calls for finding the full meaning of the contract description in the light of the expectations that have developed for such sales.

The Convention builds on these assumptions and goes a step further. Things are bought for use — raw materials are bought for processing; machinery is bought for use in production; commodities are bought for resale and use. Legislators could not develop detailed, technical specifications for such goods; hence, paragraph (2)(a) asks whether the goods "are fit for the *purposes* for which goods of the same description would *ordinarily* be used." (Fitness for a *particular* purpose is dealt with in paragraph (2)(b).)

---

9. For the evolution of Art. 35 see WG 3d (1972), III *YB* 86–87, *Docy. Hist.* 103–104; *Rep. S-G*, IV *YB* 43–46, *Docy. Hist.* 120–123, WG 4th (1973), VI *YB* 64–65, *Docy. Hist.* 142–143; UNCITRAL (1977)), VIII *YB* 36–37, *Docy. Hist.* 329–330, *O.R.* 308, 315–318, 103–105, 207–208, *Docy. Hist.* 529, 536–539, 675–677, 742–743.

　　Art. 35(2)(a), in referring to the expectations implicit in a "description" of the goods, fortunately avoids the phrase "*sale* of goods *by* description," which, in early cases, generated litigation over whether the phrase embraced "sales" of specific goods and goods the buyer has seen. (U.K.) SGA (1893) 13(1); *Benjamin* §§760, 780–781; Feltham, *The Sale by Description of Specific Goods*, (1969) J. Bus. L. 16. On the difficulties produced in other legal systems by distinctions based on whether the goods were "specific" see Rabel, at 275–278.

The basic standard in paragraph (2)(a) is similar to the warranty of "merchantable quality" developed in early English case law incorporated in the Sale of Goods Act (1893). However, the meaning of "merchantable quality" was left to case law. The basic ideas developed by the cases were used by the (U.S.A.) Uniform Commercial Code in defining "merchantable quality." Under Section 2–314(2), "goods to be merchantable" must "(a) pass without objection in the trade under the contract *description*" and "(c) are fit for the *ordinary* purposes for which *such* goods are used."[10] ***Debate has arisen over whether the standard in CISG Article 35(2)(a) requires goods of "average" quality, or whether something less — e.g., "marketable" quality — suffices.[11] Deciding between such abstract and necessarily imprecise verbal formulations standards may prove neither helpful nor necessary for deciding real cases. If, as argued above (§222), Article 35(2)(a) is a tool for determining the meaning of the parties' agreement, the question is one of the parties' expectations concerning the "fitness" of the goods for normal applications, taking into consideration (as per Article 8(3)) "all relevant circumstances of the case." This standard is also, obviously, vague and will not yield mechanically-easy answers, but it at least maintains the relevant focus and avoids unhelpful distractions.[12]***

10. A definition of "merchantable quality" was added to the (U.K.) SGA (1893) 62(1A) by the Supply of Goods (Implied Terms) Act 1973. The background for this amendment appears in (English) Law Commission Report No. 24, Scottish Law Commission, Report No. 12, Exemption Clauses in Contracts, First Report: Amendments to the Sale of Goods Act 1893, para. 43 (1969). The Ontario Law Reform Commission discussed the concept of "merchantable quality" and proposed a definition based on the U.K. Act. *Ont. L. Ref. Com., I Sales* 210–220. *Cf.* German (F.R.G.) Civil Code 459. On the relevance of fitness for ordinary purpose in the G.D.R. Code of International Commercial Contracts see Enderlein in *Dubrovnik Lectures* 157.

11. The debate is discussed (with citation of many authorities) in Ingeborg Schwenzer, Art. 35 para. 15, *in* Schlechtriem & Schwenzer, *CISG Commentary* (2nd English ed. 2005). See also Bundesgerichtshof, Germany, 8 March 1995, CLOUT case No. 123, English translation available at http://cisgw3.law.pace.edu/cases/950308g3.html.

12. Professor Schwenzer points out in her commentary on Art. 35 that the "reasonable quality" standard adopted in a Dutch arbitration — which rejected the debate between the "average quality" and "marketable quality" standards, with their domestic law entanglements — may comport best with Art. 35(2)(a). Ingeborg Schwenzer, Art. 35 para. 15, *in* Schlechtriem & Schwenzer, *CISG Commentary* (2nd English ed. 2005) (discussing Netherlands Arbitration Institute, 15 October 2002, CLOUT case No. 720, English text available at http:// cisgw3.law.pace.edu cases/021015n1.html). Provided "reasonable quality" is determined by reference to the parties" agreement/reasonable expectations, Professor Schwenzer's point is well taken.

Some have felt that it is necessary to give a general answer to the following question: Does subparagraph (2)(a) refer to the understanding of the contract description of the goods that prevails at the seller's place of business or at the place where the buyer intends to use the goods? Writers have disagreed over the choice between these two places.[13]

It should not be necessary to answer this question if one accepts the view, suggested above (§222), that the role of Article 35(2) is to aid in *construing the agreement of the parties*. The question is this: What was the parties' understanding of the contract provision describing the goods? More precisely (in the language of Article 35(2)) what was their understanding of the "purposes for which goods of the same *description* would ordinarily be used?" Since the problem concerns fitness for the "ordinary" use of goods described in the contract, serious misunderstandings should be infrequent; in domestic law disputes under this test usually arise out of a question of fact: Were the goods subject to defects that were abnormal for goods sold under the description?

If the parties do have different understandings of the connotations of the agreed description, the problem needs to be resolved pursuant to the Convention's rules for interpreting sales contracts. These rules are set forth in Article 8, §§104–111, supplemented by the practices of the parties and trade usages Article 9, §§112–222. Under these rules the relevant facts are: Which party drafted the description? (This may be either the seller or buyer.) What, under Article 8(2), would be "the understanding that a reasonable person of the same kind as the other party would have had in the same circumstances?" To ascertain this understanding Article 8(3) directs attention to all relevant circumstances including "the negotiations, any practices which the parties have established between themselves, usages and any subsequent conduct of the parties."

In sum, under the Convention problems of contract interpretation are to be solved on the basis of the *facts of each transaction* and not under a general legal rule specifying that the seller's (or buyer's) region controls the parties' understanding. *This approach can be used to deal with an issue that has justifiably garnered much attention: does Article 35(2) require a seller to supply goods that meet public law standards of the buyer's jurisdiction?*

The German Bundesgerichtshof (BGH) confronted the issue in a relatively early (and much commented-upon) decision involving a

13. See Ingeborg Schwenzer, Art. 35 para. 16 and authorities cited nn.52 & 53, *in* Schlechtriem & Schwenzer, *CISG Commentary* (2nd English ed. 2005).

Swiss seller's delivery of mussels with cadmium levels that exceeded government recommendations in the buyer's state (Germany).[14] The BGH held that, generally, neither Article 35(2)(a) nor 35(2)(b) required the seller to supply goods meeting regulations in the buyer's jurisdiction, reasoning that the buyer was more likely to be familiar with such regulations and under Article 35(1) could demand an express contractual requirement that the goods comply with them. Compliance was required under Article 35(2), the court stated, only where the seller's own jurisdiction imposed the same standards; the buyer had brought the regulations to the seller's attention; or the seller knew or should have been aware of the standards because of "special circumstances." The BGH suggested that such "special circumstances" might exist if the seller maintained a branch in the buyer's state, had a long-term business relationship with the buyer, or regularly exported to or promoted its products in the buyer's jurisdiction.

The BGH decision, which has been praised for bringing a sophisticated international perspective to the issue,[15] has been followed outside Germany,[16] including by a U.S. federal district court reviewing an arbitration ruling that had employed the BGH approach.[17] On the other hand, Professor Schlechtriem criticized its approach, although not its result. He argued that Article 35(2)(b) (and not 35(2)(a)) governs whether a seller is under an implied obligation to ship goods that comply with regulations of the buyer's jurisdiction, and that (in contrast to the BGH approach) "[i]f the seller knows where the goods are intended to be used, then he will usually be expected to have taken the

---

14. Bundesgerichtshof, Germany, 8 March 1995, CLOUT case No. 123, English translation available at http://cisgw3.law.pace.edu/cases/950308g3.html.

15. See Peter Schlechtriem, *Uniform Sales Law in the Decisions of the Bundesgerichtshof*, English translation by Todd J. Fox available at http://cisgw3.law.pace.edu/cisg/biblio/schlechtriem3.html; Harry M. Flechtner, *Funky Mussels, a Stolen Car, and Decrepit Used Shoes: Non-Conforming Goods and Notice Thereof under the United Nations Sales Convention ('CISG')*, 26 B.U. Int'l L. J. 1 (2008), available in the Social Sciences Research Network (SSRN) as University of Pittsburgh Legal Studies Research Paper No. 2008–16.

16. *E.g.*, Oberster Gerichtshof, Austria, 13 April 2000, CLOUT case No. 426, English translation available at http://cisgw3.law.pace.edu/cases/000413a3.html.

17. Medical Marketing Int'al Inc. v. Internazionale Medico Scientifica, S.r.l., 1999 WL 311945 (Fed. Dist. Ct. E. D. La., 17 May 1999, available at http://cisgw3.law.pace.edu/cases/ 990517u1.html). The court affirmed the ruling of an arbitration panel that, pursuant to Art. 35(2), the contract between an Italian seller and a U.S. buyer for medical equipment required goods that met U.S. safety regulations because the situation fit within the "special circumstances" exception articulated by the BGH in the mussels case.

factors that influence the possibility of their use in that country into consideration."[18]

Who is right in this debate? Certainly the approach of the BGH in the mussels case focuses on factors that should be considered in determining whether a seller who has not expressly promised to do so is obligated to deliver goods that meet regulations in the buyer's state. But Professor Schlechtriem's critique also identifies considerations that are relevant to that determination.

The limitation of both approaches is that they attempt to erect rule-like formulations that are independent of an inquiry into the proper interpretation of the parties' agreement. Why should we begin with a presumption that the seller is not responsible for complying with the regulations in the buyer's jurisdiction, as the BGH advocates, rather than approaching the question with an open mind free to assess the implications of "all relevant circumstances of the case" as mandated by Article 8(3)? For example, the fact that the buyer is likely to be more familiar with the requirements of its own jurisdiction is certainly relevant, but suppose those requirements are very well known internationally?[19]

And why should the issue be relegated strictly to Article 35(2)(b), as Professor Schlechtriem advocates? The standard in Article 35(2)(a) is a flexible one, geared to the ordinary purposes of goods of the "same description." The concept of the contractual description of the goods is an extremely pliable one. Is the relevant "description" of the goods in the mussels case simply "mussels for human consumption" or is it "mussels for consumption in Germany"? If the parties included a clause disclaiming any seller obligations under Article 35(2)(b) (but not mentioning 35(2)(a)), should that by itself establish that the seller need not meet regulations of the buyer's jurisdiction? A better

---

18. Peter Schlechtriem, *Uniform Sales Law in the Decisions of the Bundesgerichtshof*, English translation by Todd J. Fox available at http://cisgw3.law.pace.edu/cisg/biblio/schlechtriem3.html. See also the account in Ingeborg Schwenzer, Art. 35 paras. 17a & 20, *in* Schlechtriem & Schwenzer, *CISG Commentary* (2nd English ed. 2005). Professor Schlechtriem noted that, where it was unreasonable for the buyer to rely on the seller to deliver goods that complied with certain buyer-jurisdiction regulations (for instance, when the applicability of those regulations was uncertain, as in the mussels case), the seller would be protected by the requirements of Art. 35(2)(b)). *Id.*

19. Professor Schlechtriem suggests the several examples: voltage requirements for appliances to be used in the United States and restrictions on the sale or consumption of certain meats in particular countries based on religious considerations. Peter Schlechtriem, *Uniform Sales Law in the Decisions of the Bundesgerichtshof*, English translation by Todd J. Fox available at http://cisgw3.law.pace.edu/cisg/biblio/schlechtriem3.html.

approach is to consider such a clause in resolving the issue, but also to consider whether the seller's preserved obligation to deliver goods fit for "ordinary purposes" as provided in Article 35(2)(a) encompasses a reasonable expectation that the goods would comply with regulations of the buyer's state.

The formulations of Article 35(2) are tools available to decision makers for the delicate and demanding task of determining the parties' agreement concerning the quality of goods the seller was obliged to deliver. Keeping that understanding in mind helps maintain those tools in proper working order.

226   **(b) Fitness for Particular Purpose.**   The role of Article 35(2)(b) may be illustrated as follows:

Example 35A. Buyer wrote as follows to Seller, a manufacturer of drills. "Please ship me a set of drills [giving sizes] for drilling holes in plates of carbon steel." Seller shipped the Buyer a set of drills that were of the size designated by Buyer. The drills were satisfactory for drilling holes in ordinary steel, but were not sufficiently hard for carbon steel.

Relationship to Contract. In this example, as in most (perhaps all) of the sales that fall within paragraph (2)(b), it would be possible to conclude that the shipment of the drills created an "understanding" (Art. 8(2) & 8(3)) that the drills would meet the standards specified in Buyer's order; conformity of the goods with this understanding would be required by Article 35(1) although Seller had said nothing about whether the drills would cut through carbon steel. Thus, paragraph (2)(b) of Article 35 may not have been necessary, but may help to reduce uncertainty over whether a seller may be responsible for an understanding to which he was a party but which he did not articulate.

Reliance on Seller's Skill and Judgment. The structure of paragraph (2)(b) may lead tribunals to conclude that the buyer makes a *prima facie* case by showing that the seller knew of the buyer's particular purpose at the time of the conclusion of the contract and that the goods were unfit for that purpose; the seller then has the burden to show that "the buyer did not rely, or that it was unreasonable for him to rely, on the seller's skill and judgment."[20] The indication in Article 35(2)(b) that the seller bears the burden of proving that the buyer did not rely on the seller's skills and judgment (or that the buyer did not rely "reasonably") represents one of the rare occasions where the Convention itself, rather than

---

20. The (U.K.) SGA (1893) 14(3), as amended and renumbered by the Supply of Goods (Implied Terms) Act (1973), is similar in substance and structure to Art. 35(2)(b).

applicable domestic law, appears to govern the allocation of responsibility for proof. See §70.1 *supra.*

In Example 35A, Seller would find it difficult to disprove reliance by Buyer. Seller, the manufacturer of the drills, would know more about their cutting qualities than Buyer, and Buyer relied on the Seller to select a drill that would cut through carbon steel, or inform Buyer that Seller had no such drill. Indeed, the crux of Article 35(2)(b) is the buyer's known reliance on the seller to select and furnish a commodity that will satisfy a stated purpose.[21]

Where it has been expressly or impliedly made known to the seller that the goods will be resold or used in a particular country (e.g., the country where the buyer is located), does Article 35(2)(b) require that the goods comply with special regulations in that country? That issue explored is explored in §225 *supra.*

227   **(c) Goods Held Out as Sample or Model.**   Where the seller has "held out" goods to the buyer "*as a sample or model*" he has created an "understanding" (Art. 8) that the goods would conform to the sample or model. Thus, paragraph (2)(c) of Article 35, even more clearly than paragraph (2)(b), articulates contractual understandings that are given effect by paragraph (1). Such is the approach of Section 2–313(1)(c) of the (U.S.A.) Uniform Commercial Code: "Any sample or model which is made part of the basis of the bargain creates an *express* warranty that the whole of the goods shall conform to the sample or model." See also the (U.K.) Sale of Goods Act Sec. 15. All of these provisions are of modest value to a tribunal that is equipped to give full effect to the contract made by the parties.[22]

228   **(d) Packaging.**   On occasion advocates for sellers have gone so far as to argue that implied obligations ("warranties") with respect to the quality of "goods" do not extend to the container or package. Whether the packaging is part of the goods is a false issue; the relevant question is whether the seller's contractual duty extends to packaging. This question is answered by Article 35(2)(d): The goods shall be "contained or packaged in a manner *usual for such goods. . . .*" The reference to what is "usual" gives effect to reasonable expectations, and is consistent with

21. For further discussion of facts relevant to the reliance element of Art. 35(2)(b) see Ingeborg Schwenzer, Art. 35 para. 23, *in* Schlechtriem & Schwenzer, *CISG Commentary* (2nd English ed. 2005).
22. *White & Summers* §9–6; *Benjamin* §§838–844.

the approach of Article 35(2)(a) (ordinary use) and the Convention's general rules for interpretation of the contract. See Articles 8(3) and 9(2), *supra* at §104 and §112.

The corresponding provision of the 1978 Draft Convention did not include the concluding clause: "or, where there is no such manner, in a manner adequate to preserve and protect the goods." At the Diplomatic Conference it was suggested that the Draft failed to deal with contracts for new types of commodity for which no "usual" manner of packaging had yet developed; language was added to assure that in such cases packaging should be "adequate." In considering this proposal it was noted that this new language should not be construed to require packaging where packaging was not usual (e.g., new cars; bulk shipments of coal or ore). Nor was it contemplated that packaging must be able to withstand unprecedented shocks and hazards; what is required is the degree of protection that is usual for goods of comparable fragility.[23]

229 (3) Buyer's Knowledge of Condition of Goods at the Time of Contracting

(a) The Scope and Role of Paragraph (3).

The case that will fall most clearly within paragraph (3) is the sale of a specific, "identified" object (e.g., a secondhand lathe) that the buyer inspects and then agrees to purchase. Paragraph (3) provides that in such cases the seller is not liable under the implied obligations of paragraph (2) for those facts of which "the buyer knew or could not have been unaware." Paragraph (3) does not affect the obligations "required by the contract" under paragraph (1).[24] *Its purpose is to fine-tune the rules in Article 35(2) to ensure that they operate as intended — as tools for determining the true agreement of the parties relating to the quality of goods (see §222 supra).*

"*Could not have been unaware.*" Paragraph (3) is applicable when the buyer "could not have been unaware" of the condition of the goods when he made the contract. Is this different from knowledge?

---

23. *Com 1; SR.15*, paras. 72–89, *O.R.* 316–317, *Docy. Hist.* 537–538. See (U.S.A.) UCC 2–314(2)(e): To satisfy the implied warranty of merchantable quality the goods must be "adequately contained, packaged and labelled as the agreement may require."

24. When the buyer agrees to purchase goods in conformity with a sample and later objects to a condition that was apparent from the sample, the seller may be able to show that the parties impliedly agreed on the quality exhibited by the sample. *Accord*, Bianca in *B-B Commentary* §2.9.1, p. 279.

The Convention differentiates among: (A) facts that a party "knows" or of which he is "aware"; (B) facts of which a party "could not have been unaware"; and (C) facts that a party knew or "ought to have known."[25]

The facts one *"ought* to have known" include those facts that would be disclosed by an investigation or inquiry that the party should make. But an obligation based on facts of which one "could not have been unaware" does not impose a duty to investigate — these are the facts that are before the eyes of one who can see.[26] This expression is used at various places in the Conventions slightly to lighten the burden of proving that facts that were before the eyes reached the mind. However, since a tribunal would normally draw this inference, there is little practical difference between the provisions that refer to facts that a party "knows" and provisions that refer to facts of which a party "could not have been unaware."[27] This choice of language significantly narrows the impact of paragraph (3) on the buyer's protection afforded by paragraph (2).

230 **(b)** *Disclaimers.* **The seller's obligations under Article 35 are subject to the parties' right, specified in Article 6, to derogate from or vary the effect of provisions of the Convention. Article 35(2) emphasizes this by declaring that the (implied) obligations described therein apply "[e]xcept where the parties have agreed otherwise."**[28]

U.S. domestic sales law (Article 2 of the Uniform Commercial Code) treats the matter of eliminating or limiting a seller's obligations

---

25. Examples of these three forms of expression: (A) "knows" or is "aware" — Arts. 43(2), 49(2), 64(2)(a); (B) "could not have been unaware" — Arts. 35(3), 40, 42(1), 42(2); (C) knew or "ought to have known" — Arts. 38(3), 39(1), 43(1), 49(2)(b)(i), 64(2)(b)(i), 68, 79(4). ULIS 36, which corresponds to Art. 35(3), similarly uses the expression "knew or could not have been unaware."

26. For further discussion of this point see Ingeborg Schwenzer, Art. 35 para. 35, *in* Schlechtriem & Schwenzer, *CISG Commentary* (2nd English ed. 2005).

27. *Accord*, ULIS 36. Compare with Art. 35(3); (U.K.) SGA (1893) 14(2)(b) ("defects which that examination ought to reveal"); (U.S.A.) UCC 2–316(3)(b) ("defects which an examination ought in the circumstances to have revealed"). Field, *supra* note 3, examines (212–215) the buyer's obligation under Quebec law to inspect goods when he relies on a "latent" defect, and (224) discusses proposals to lighten that burden.

28. Article 35(1) does not express this limitation because the subpart is stated in terms of what the parties have agreed. It would be redundant and confusing to declare that, "unless otherwise agreed," the seller must deliver goods "of the quantity, quality and description required by the contract" because, if the parties had agreed otherwise, the contract would not require goods of that quantity, quality or description. *But* see Ingeborg Schwenzer, Art. 35 para. 41, *in* Schlechtriem & Schwenzer, *CISG Commentary* (2nd English ed. 2005).

concerning the required quality of the goods under the rubric "disclaimer of warranty."[29] A U.S. court, apparently conditioned by the elaborate and highly particularized rules on this subject in U.S. domestic law, failed to recognize that the Convention deals with the subject through the simple, general declaration in Article 35(2) that the parties can derogate from the seller's implied quality obligations merely by "agree[ing] otherwise": the U.S. court declared that "Article 35...does not discuss disclaimers."[30] That, of course, is false—the Convention permits a "disclaimer" of any of the quality obligations in Article 35(2) by a simple agreement between the parties to that effect. Of course such an agreement must be determined under the rules of the Convention, including, e.g., the rules of interpretation in Article 8 (see §230.1 infra) and the contract formation rules in Part II.

The "validity" of such a disclaimer, furthermore, is beyond the scope of the Convention (Article 4(a)). That means that it is subject to the rules of applicable domestic law relating to matters such as fraud, duress, unconscionability, etc.[31] See §§64–68 supra.

This does not mean, however, that the particular verbal formulas or writing requirements specified in the U.C.C. for disclaiming the implied warranty of merchantability and the implied warranty of fitness for particular purpose[32] apply to "disclaimers" of the seller's obligations under Article 35(2)(a) or (b). The U.C.C. disclaimer requirements were designed specifically for the U.C.C. warranty provisions, and were not intended to apply to quality-obligation rules in other laws.[33] Thus an agreement relieving a seller of the obligations stated in CISG Article 35(2)(a) is not a "disclaimer of the implied warranty of merchantability" within the meaning of U.C.C. 2–316,

---

29. As is appropriate in an *international* sales law, the Convention avoids the term "warranty," which is associated with Common-law systems.

30. Supermicro Computer Inc. v. Digitechnnic, S.A., 145 F. Supp. 2d 1147, 1151 (U.S. Dist. Ct. N.D. Cal. 30 Jan. 2001), available at http://cisgw3.law.pace.edu/cases/010130u1.html.

31. See Ingeborg Schwenzer, Art. 35 para. 42, *in* Schlechtriem & Schwenzer, *CISG Commentary* (2nd English ed. 2005).

32. E.g., U.C.C. 2–316(2): "[T]o exclude or modify the implied warranty of merchantability or any part of it the language must mention merchantability and in case of a writing must be conspicuous, and to exclude or modify any implied warranty of fitness the exclusion must be by a writing and conspicuous."

33. For example, the fact that the UCC disclaimer rules apply in consumer transactions means they take into account considerations irrelevant under the Convention, which is inapplicable to consumer sales. See Art. 2(a), discussed at §50 *supra*.

nor should an agreement derogating from Article 35(2)(b) be treated as a disclaimer of the implied warranty of fitness for particular purpose under U.S. domestic law. The validity of such agreements is not subject to the requirements of U.C.C. 2–316(2) or (3).

230.1 Effect of the Convention's Rules on Interpretation

In some situations the Convention's rules on contract interpretation may limit the impact of standard clauses artfully designed to make unexpected inroads on the rights of the other party, such as the rights granted by Article 35. Article 8(2) provides that statements (including contract terms) "are to be interpreted according to the understanding that a reasonable person of the same kind as the *other party* would have had in the same circumstances." (See the Commentary to Article 8, *supra* at §106.) Let us assume that a seller's reply to an order for machinery states the following standard term: "The seller shall not be subject to any obligations with respect to conformity other than those specifically stated herein"; a rapid and routine sales transaction is concluded which, under the contract formation rules of the Convention, incorporates this term. Article 8(2) would invite tribunals to consider whether a reasonable person in the position of the buyer would have understood that, unless the contract expressly provides otherwise, it would have no recourse if (e.g.,) the machine will not operate or in other ways falls far short of the usual standards for such goods.

Of course, each contract must be construed with close attention (in the language of Article 8(3)) "to all relevant circumstances of the case"; these circumstances would include the extent to which terms were negotiated and adapted to the particular transaction, as contrasted with a set of self-serving standard terms incorporated by one party in a fashion that is unlikely to draw the other's attention during a rapid an routine transaction.

231   *Conflicting Quality Obligations. The various quality obligations expressed in Article 35(2)(a)–(d) are intended to be cumulative — that is, unless otherwise agreed the seller must comply with all obligations that are applicable. Occasionally an obligation under one subpart of Article 35(2) may conflict with an obligation under another subpart or even, apparently, with the express requirements of the contract (Article 35(1)). For example, to be made suitable for a particular purpose that the buyer make known to the seller (see Article 35(2)(b)) goods may be necessarily rendered unfit for one or more ordinary purposes (see Article 35(2)(a)).*

In dealing with such situations it is again important to remember that, as described in §222 supra, the rules of Article 35(2) are ultimately tools to determine the proper construction of the parties' agreement. A reasonable construction of that agreement generally should not require the seller to provide goods with an impossible combination of qualities — at least not where the buyer knew or should have known of such impossibility. Where a true conflict between quality obligations apparently exists, it may necessary to identify which quality obligations under Article 35 represent the parties' true agreement.

U.S. domestic sales law has developed rules for dealing with such conflicting quality obligations (U.C.C. 2–317, dealing with "Cumulation and Conflict of Warranties"). These rules are based not on the legal features of the U.S. sales regime but on insights into the presumed (rebuttably) intention of the parties, and thus they might be consulted for guidance without violating the "internationality" and "uniformity" mandates.[34] Those rules suggest, for example, that an obligation to provide goods suitable for a particular purpose under Article 35(2)(b) is likely to have had precedence in the parties' intentions over a conflicting obligation to provide goods suitable for ordinary purposes (Article 35(2)(a)) — although the facts of the particular transaction must always be consulted.

238   **(c) Domestic Rules Based on Innocent Misrepresentation as to Quality; "Mistake"**   We now meet another significant question concerning the boundary-line between domestic rules and the uniform law of the Convention. Under Article 5, §§72–73 *supra*, we met this question in relation to domestic rules, such as "product liability," that apply to the same facts as those governed by the Convention but under a label such as "tort" rather than "contract." The commentary to Article 4, *supra* at §64, noted that domestic remedies for international fraud would remain in full force but that further attention would be given to domestic remedies for innocent but erroneous statements regarding the quality of the goods.

It is not feasible to describe the various rules of domestic law that might be encountered under headings such as "rescission for innocent

---

34. Indeed, commentators from outside the U.S. (and outside the Common-law systems) have adopted approaches that are consistent with the rules in U.C.C. 2–317. See Ingeborg Schwenzer, Art. 35 para. 25, *in* Schlechtriem & Schwenzer, *CISG Commentary* (2nd English ed. 2005).

misrepresentation" or "mistake" (*erreur*). Instead, our discussion will address a concrete factual situation in which such domestic remedies might arguably be applicable.

Example 35B. Seller made the following offer: "I have purchased a cargo of 200 bales of No. 1 quality Manilla hemp now en route from Singapore to Liverpool. I offer you this cargo ex ship Liverpool, at £100 per bale." Buyer accepted this offer and paid the agreed price. When the hemp arrived in Liverpool it was discovered that, prior to the shipment from Singapore and prior to the sale to Seller, the hemp had been so seriously damaged by water that it graded No. 6 rather than No. 1 and was unfit for the purposes for which Manilla hemp was normally used.[35] *Seller did not know and could not have known of the poor condition of the hemp.*

Assume that the sale was subject to the Convention but that under domestic law, selected by conflicts rules, the buyer's only remedy is to rescind the contract for innocent misrepresentation or for "mistake" (*erreur*).[36]

240 (1) The Issue Posed by the Convention

One should not hastily decide to apply a dividing line like that suggested by the above domestic statutes to international sales governed by the Convention.[37] It is true that one of the objectives of these domestic statutes was to provide uniform law, and that this is the dominant purpose of the Convention. But each of these domestic laws was prepared with an eye to domestic rules that were familiar to the domestic parties and their advisors.

The unifying role of the Convention is more dominant and more difficult; as we have seen in various settings, this role would be crippled

---

35. Students of English law may recognize a resemblance between this example and Jones v. Just, [1868] L.R. 3 Q.B. 197.

36. Tallon, Erreur sur la substance et garantie des vices dans la vente mobilière, *Hamel Festschrift* (1961) 435; Hoff, *Error in the Formation of Contracts in Louisiana: A Comparative Analysis*, 53 Tul. L. Rev. 329 (1979) at 351–358 (error in *substantia*); B. Nicholas, *An Introduction to Roman Law* 178 (1962); Lawson, *Error in Substantia*, 62 Law Q. Rev. 79 (1936). This writer does not suggest that these legal systems give only limited relief in Example 35B, which is used for analysis.

37. The (U.K.) SGA does not deal fully with the seller's promises. Contrast (U.S.A.) UCC 2–313. Nevertheless three seems to be doubt as to whether common-law rules on "mistake" may supplement the SGA on points where the statutory rules supply an answer. See *Atiyah* 154–159; *Benjamin* §§204–205.

by domestic rules that govern the same situations and issues as those governed by the Convention.[38] To cope with this problem it is necessary to ask a pointed question: Does the Convention address the situation presented by Example 35B?

In Example 35B, the seller made an innocent but important misstatement that the hemp was "No. 1 quality." This statement must be regarded as part of his contract with the buyer for reasons discussed *supra* at §224. In addition, this statement was a "description" which, under Article 35(1) and (2)(a), is given legal effect as part of the seller's contract. Indeed, such statements are indistinguishable from the other aspects of the seller's obligation as to quality specified in Article 35.

When (as in Example 35B) the goods do not conform to the contract, the Convention provides a full battery of powerful remedies prepared specifically for international sales. See Articles 45–50, §§272–313, *infra*. Hence the buyer's rights resulting from innocent misrepresentation of the type presented in Example 35B should be derived only from the Convention.[39] Of course, other types of representations by the seller (such as his identity and similar statements by the buyer) may not be addressed by the Convention; in this event the line of analysis suggested above may call for the application of domestic law. The important point is to focus on whether the Convention addresses the situation in question; if so, the uniform international rules should not be displaced merely because of the labels attached to various doctrines of domestic law.[40]

38. *E.g.*, Art. 5, *supra* at §71 ("Product liability"); Art. 7 at §99 (gap-filling); Art. 16 at §146 (domestic remedies for revocation); Art. 35 at §230 (domestic rules on warranty disclaimers).

39. *Accord*, Ingeborg Schwenzer, Art. 35 paras. 45–46, *in* Schlechtriem & Schwenzer, *CISG Commentary* (2nd English ed. 2005); Tallon in *Rechtsvergleichung* 753, 755 at n.6, 759 (confusion in French law between *garantie* and *erreur*; overcome in CISG).

40. See *accord*, Heiz, Validity of Contracts under CISG and Swiss Contract Law, 20 Vanderbilt J. Tr. L. 639 (1987) for a brilliant analysis of decisions on mistake under Swiss law in relation to CISG. At 649–651 Heiz discusses the legislative history of the decision by the UNCITRAL Working Group not to include rules on validity and mistake. See WG 9th Sess., IX *YB* 65–66, *Docy. Hist.* 297–298.

Article 36.
Damage to Goods: Effect on Conformity

241   Goods arrive in poor condition because of damage in transit. Does it follow that they fail to conform to the contract? Paragraph (1) of Article 36 sets forth a general rule; paragraph (2) deals with modifications of that rule that result from breach of the seller's obligations.

Article 36[1]

(1) The seller is liable in accordance with the contract and this Convention for any lack of conformity which exists at the time when the risk passes to the buyer, even though the lack of conformity becomes apparent only after that time.

(2) The seller is also liable for any lack of conformity which occurs after the time indicated in the preceding paragraph and which is due to a breach of any of his obligations, including a breach of any guarantee that for a period of time the goods will remain fit for their ordinary purpose or for some particular purpose or will retain specified qualities or characteristics.

242 **A. Conformity as of Time When Risk Passes**

The general rule set forth in Paragraph (1) may be illustrated as follows:

Example 36A. A contract called for Seller (located in Seattle) to ship No. 1 quality white wheat flour to Buyer, "FOB Seattle as per INCOTERMS (2000)." The FOB term places the risk of loss on Buyer after the goods pass the ship's rail (see §B5 of INCOTERMS (2000) description of "FOB.")[2] Seller shipped flour that conformed with the contract but during the shipment the flour was damaged by water so that when it reached Buyer (located in Bombay) the quality was "No. 4"

---

1. This article follows Art. 34 of the 1978 Draft, subject to drafting changes in paragraph (2); *O.R.* 105, 312–315, *Docy. Hist.* 533–536, 677. Paragraph (1) carries forward ULIS 35(1) (first sentence). The converse of Art. 36(1) is (perhaps unnecessarily) stated in Chap. IV on Risk of Loss, Art. 66, §§360–361, *infra*: the buyer is responsible for the price of the goods although they have been lost or damaged after risk of loss passed to the buyer.

2. Even if the contract contained no term allocating risk of loss, risk while the goods were in transit would rest on the buyer under Art. 67(1).

rather than "No. 1." Buyer claimed that the goods did not conform to the quality required by the contract.

By virtue of Article 36(1), Seller complied with the contract since the goods conformed to the contract when risk passed to the Buyer. On the other hand, if the contract had placed transit risks on Seller (e.g., "*Ex Ship* Bombay") as per INCOTERMS (2000), Buyer's claim based on non-conformity of the goods would have been correct.[3]

Provisions similar to Article 36(1) appear in some Continental statutes; under common-law formulations the result is the same as a necessary implication of the rules on risk of loss.[4]

The language of paragraph (1), making the seller responsible "even though the lack of conformity becomes apparent only after" the time when risk passes, would protect the buyer when a latent defect appears at a later date, including a failure to comply with the requirement of Article 35(2)(a) that the goods be "fit for the purposes for which goods of the same description would ordinarily be used." This interpretation is supported by the action at the 1980 Conference to delete from paragraph (2) of draft Article 34 (which became CISG Article 36(2)) a reference to "any *express* guarantee that the goods will remain fit for their ordinary purpose" (emphasis added); this change gave effect to expectations of durability implied under Article 35(2) of the Convention.[5] Stale claims may, however, be barred by the buyer's failure to meet the notice requirements of Article 39 (see, in particular, Art. 39(2)), or by applicable rules on limitation or prescription of actions. The UNCITRAL Convention on the Limitation Period in the International Sale of Goods is introduced at §§254.2 and 261.1, *infra. **Deterioration occurring while the goods are in transit, after risk has shifted to the buyer, may be due to the seller's failure to comply with Article 35(2)(d), requiring the goods to be "contained or packaged in the manner***

---

3. *Rep. S-G*, "Obligations of the Seller," para. 65, IV *YB* 36, 45, *Docy. Hist.* 113, 122. *Cf. Rep. S-G*, "Pending Questions," paras. 94–96, VI *YB* 88, 98 99, *Docy. Hist.* 213, 223–224. For decisions applying Art. 36(1), see UNCITRAL Digest Art. 36 paras. 1–5. On the meaning of the trade terms, *Rep. S-G*, "Pending Questions," paras. 94–96, *Docy. Hist.* 223–224. For possible exemption of seller from damages (as contrasted with reduction of the price) if the loss or damage of the goods resulted from *force majeure* met by an independent carrier see Art. 79(2) §433, *infra*.

4. See Ingeborg Schwenzer, Art. 36 para. 2, *in* Schlechtriem & Schwenzer, *CISG Commentary* (2nd English ed. 2005). The same rule results by inference from (U.S.A.) UCC 2–509, 2–510 and 2–725(2). *Cf.* UCC 2–301, 2–312(1)(b).

5. *O.R.* 105 (C.6, proposal of Greece), 312–315 (paras. 30–31), *Docy. Hist.* 677 (text of proposal), 533–536.

usual for such goods or, where there is no such manner, in a manner adequate to preserve and protect the goods." In such cases, the lack of conformity (the violation of Article 35(2)(d)) generally would already exist at the time risk passed to the buyer.[6]

243 ## B. Effect of Contractual Guarantee

Paragraph (2) reflects the fact that some warranties include undertakings that extend after delivery. Examples include a contract to service the goods for a designated period, or a guarantee that the goods will perform for a specified period—e.g., two years, 10,000 miles, or the like. *As noted in §242 supra, the drafting history of Article 36 demonstrates that the "guarantees" to which it refers may include implied obligations under Article 35(2); for example, goods that wear out too quickly may violate the Article 35(2)(a) requirement that they be fit for ordinary purposes.*[7] Under some warranties, the buyer would not be required to prove that there was a non-conformity when risk passed (e.g., on shipment of the goods or delivery to the buyer). However, the effect of paragraph (2) depends on the contract. One would not expect to find a guarantee that protects a buyer from his failure to maintain and protect the goods; thus, in substance, the guaranty applies only when a failure of performance results from a defect in materials or workmanship. Compare Article 80, *infra* at §436 (failure of performance by one party caused by the other party's act or omission).

A special provision on express guarantees might not have been necessary in view of the general rule of the Convention giving effect to the agreement of the parties. Article 36(2) underscores the importance of the contract and may avoid doubt concerning the seller's responsibility under the Convention when the seller's failure properly to service the goods causes damage or deterioration.[8]

---

6. See Compromex Arbitration Tribunal, Mexico, 29 April 1996, English translation available at http://cisgw3.law.pace.edu/cases/960429m1.html; Ingeborg Schwenzer, Art. 36 para. 4, *in* Schlechtriem & Schwenzer, *CISG Commentary* (2nd English ed. 2005).

7. See Ingeborg Schwenzer, Art. 36 para. 8, *in* Schlechtriem & Schwenzer, *CISG Commentary* (2nd English ed. 2005).

8. For decisions applying Art. 36(2), see UNCITRAL Digest Art. 36 paras. 1 & 6.

Article 37.
Right to Cure Up to the Date for Delivery

244   Destruction of contract rights involves hardship and economic waste. Suppose that the seller has manufactured a complex machine to meet the buyer's special requirements and there is a minor or correctable defect in the goods: May the buyer "avoid" the contract? In the Commentary to Article 25, *supra* at §181, we saw that in most situations "avoidance of the contract" (Arts. 49, 51, 64) must be based on a "fundamental breach," which likely does not exist in such a case. Avoidance may also be prevented by curing a defect in performance. The Convention has two provisions that address cure of a delivery of non-conforming goods. Article 37 permits cure until the date for delivery; Article 48, *infra* at §292, in limited circumstances authorizes cure after the date for delivery. *The seller's right to cure under these provisions must be distinguished from the buyer's right under Article 46 to require the seller to replace or repair non-conforming goods (see §§283–284 infra).*[1] *Cure under Articles 37 or 48 is the right of a breaching seller to rectify its own breach, thereby minimizing the impact of the breach on the parties' contractual relationship and limiting the seller's exposure from the breach. The remedial rights granted by Article 46, in contrast, belong to an aggrieved buyer and are designed to protect the buyer's interest in proper performance of the contract.*

Article 37[2]

If the seller has delivered goods before the date for delivery, he may, up to that date, deliver any missing part or make up any deficiency in the quantity of the goods delivered, or deliver goods in replacement of any non-conforming goods delivered or remedy any lack of conformity in the goods delivered, provided that the exercise of this right does not cause the buyer unreasonable inconvenience or unreasonable expense. However, the buyer retains any right to claim damages as provided for in this Convention.

---

1. See UNCITRAL Digest Art. 37 para. 1.
2. This article is the same as Art. 35 of the 1978 Draft and, in substance, is the same as ULIS 37. See WG III *YB* 81, *S-G*, IV *YB* 46, WG VI *YB* 65–66, *Docy. Hist.* 98, 123, 143–144; UNCITRAL (1977) VIII *YB* 38–39, *Docy. Hist.* 331–332, *O.R.*, 33–34, 309–340, 105–106, 159, 208, *Docy. Hist.* 423–424, 530–531, 677–678, 718, 743.

245 **A. Types of Non-Conformity Subject to Cure**

(1) Non-conformity of Documents and Goods

As we have seen, Article 34, §220, in language similar to Article 37, gives the seller the right to cure any lack of conformity in documents.[3]

Article 37 applies to various types of non-conformity in the goods. For example, the seller may supply missing goods, including a missing part of a machine. Non-conformity of the goods may be cured by "replacement" or by "remedying" the lack of conformity by repairing a defective part. None of these measures is available when cure would "cause the buyer unreasonable inconvenience or unreasonable expense." For example, the buyer should be able to reject a proposal to repair a machine in its place in the buyer's assembly line when that would seriously interfere with assembly operations; in these circumstances only a prompt replacement of the machine might be permitted.[4] Of course, when the buyer has immediately reshipped a delivery that was only slightly early, cure under Article 37 would usually be impractical; however, under these circumstances it may be possible to cure pursuant to Article 48, §292 *infra*.

"Date for Delivery." Contracts often provide a period (e.g., "during June") within which the seller may deliver. Suppose the seller delivers on June 10: Does Article 37 permit cure (e.g.) on June 20 if (as Article 37 requires) this "does not cause the buyer unreasonable inconvenience or unreasonable expense?" The answer should be Yes: In Article 37 "date for delivery" refers to the date after which delivery becomes a breach of contract — in this case, June 30. The more strict rules of Article 48 governing cure "even *after* the date for delivery," with liability for damages, refer to cure after (e.g.) June 30.[5] There must, of course, be no gap in the periods covered by these two interlocking provisions.

---

3. For background to the provision in Art. 34 for curing lack of conformity in documents, see Ingeborg Schwenzer, Art. 37 para. 1, *in* Schlechtriem & Schwenzer, *CISG Commentary* (2nd English ed. 2005).

4. For further discussion of when cure would subject a buyer to "unreasonable inconvenience or unreasonable expense," see Ingeborg Schwenzer, Art. 37 paras. 13 & 14, *in* Schlechtriem & Schwenzer, *CISG Commentary* (2nd English ed. 2005).

5. *Accord*, Ingeborg Schwenzer, Art. 37 para. 5, *in* Schlechtriem & Schwenzer, *CISG Commentary* (2nd English ed. 2005).

245.1 ## (2) Cure in Analogous Situations: Third-party Claims

There are situations in addition to those specified in Articles 34, 37 or 48 in which cure may be useful. In connection with Article 41, §226 *infra*, attention is drawn to the awkward problems that may arise in an international sale when a third-party claims an ownership interest in the goods. Similar problems may arise under Article 42, §§267–270 *infra*, from a third-party claim based on intellectual property such as a patent, copyright or trademark. When the buyer notifies the seller of the claim (Art. 43(a)) the seller may be able promptly to solve the problem by satisfying an outstanding lien or other security interest, by settling with a patent or trademark claimant, or by obtaining an injunction against pressing a groundless claim.

There is no indication that providing for cure of defective documents (Art. 34) and non-conforming goods (Arts. 37 and 48) was intended to foreclose the seller's opportunity to use this efficient remedy in analogous situations. If such a gap had been suggested during the legislative process it is unlikely that the framers would have chosen either to (1) reject the possibility of cure or (2) remit the problem to the vagaries of domestic law. See the provision in Article 7(2) for settling matters "in conformity with the general principles on which [the Convention] is based . . . ," §§96–102, *supra*.[6] This approach is supported not only by the provision for cure in Articles 34, 37 and 48, but also by the emphasis in the Convention's remedial provisions on avoiding the waste that results from needless destruction of the contract. See Artcle 25, §§181–186: definition of "fundamental breach"; Articles 49 and 64, §§301–308, 353–356: avoidance of contract by buyer and seller; Article 77, §§416–419; mitigation of damages; and Chapter VI, Preservation of the goods, Articles 85–88, §§453–457.

246 # B. Effect of Cure on Avoidance

(1) Avoidance for Fundamental Breach

The above-mentioned provision concerning unreasonable inconvenience or expense is the only restriction on the seller's right

---

6. *Accord*, Ingeborg Schwenzer, Art. 37 para. 6, *in* Schlechtriem & Schwenzer, *CISG Commentary* (2nd English ed. 2005); Enderlein, Rights and Obligations of the Seller, *Dubrovnik Lectures* 133, 164–165.

to cure defects before the date for delivery. The right to cure extends to serious deficiencies or defects that (in the absence of cure) would constitute a "fundamental breach." Consequently, unless it is clear that the seller will not cure, the buyer may not effectively avoid the contract until the date for delivery has passed.[7] (This question will be explored more fully in connection with Article 48 in the more complex situation in which the buyer, after the date for delivery, notifies the buyer of avoidance. See §296, *infra*.)

247   (2) The Slightly Imperfect "Cure"

Does the right to "deliver goods in replacement of any non-conforming goods" depend on perfect conformity of the second delivery? This question may arise in any of the various types of cure envisaged by Article 37; the basic issue may be illustrated as follows:

Example 37A. A contract called for the delivery by June 1 of 100 bags of No. 1 white, granulated sugar. On May 15 Seller delivered to Buyer, a sugar dealer, 100 bags of sugar that had been so contaminated by mildew that it could not be resold. Buyer immediately notified Seller; on May 25 Seller tendered to Buyer a second delivery of 100 bags in exchange for the 100 bags delivered 10 days earlier. In the second delivery, 99 bags complied fully with the contract; one bag graded No. 2 and could be resold by Buyer but at a 15% discount. Buyer refused to accept any of the sugar tendered on May 25 on the ground that it did not comply perfectly with the contract.

On the assumption that the non-conformity of the one bag was not a "fundamental" breach Buyer could not have rejected the entire shipment ("avoided the contract" under Art. 49) if this had been the initial tender. See Article 51(2) §317, *infra*. On the other hand, if the May 25 delivery could have been rejected (the contract "avoided") as an initial tender there would be no doubt as to Buyer's right to reject such goods when delivered as a "cure."

The language of Article 37 and its legislative history do not clearly answer the question whether the cure must be perfect. However, the

---

7. Under Art. 52(1) the buyer need not take delivery prior to the contract date. *Cf.* Art. 86(2). The seller's right to cure pursuant to Art. 37 also restricts avoidance under Art. 72 for anticipatory breach, since Art. 72 provides for avoidance only when "it is clear" that a party will commit a fundamental breach. This restriction would be satisfied by a refusal to cure; on the effect of a seller's failure to respond to a buyer's inquiry as to whether he would cure see Art. 7, *supra* at §85. See also Art. 48, *infra* at §296.

sweeping language of the Article allowing the seller to remedy "any" deficiency or lack of conformity unless this causes "unreasonable" inconvenience or expense, and the last sentence of the Article preserving the buyer's right to claim damages, indicate that perfection with respect to the second tender may not be required.

Any inconvenience in receiving the May 15 delivery and in exchanging that shipment for the May 20 delivery and any burden of disposing of (or rejecting) the one bag of No. 2 sugar will be relevant in determining whether the cure will "cause the buyer unreasonable inconvenience or unreasonable expense." But if this restriction does not apply, it seems that Article 37 empowers Seller to make the second delivery described in Example 37A.[8] *If one attempt at cure does not succeed or does not fully solve the problem (as in Example 37A), the seller may be able to try again (e.g., replacing the one remaining non-conforming bag of sugar)[9] although multiple attempts to cure are more likely to cause the buyer "unreasonable inconvenience or unreasonable expense."*[10] Of course Buyer has the right to recover damages for any expense in permitting cure (e.g., making a second exchange in Example 37A) and for any non-conformity remaining after the seller's cure.[11]

---

8. *But cf.* Bianca in *B-B Commentary* §2.6, p. 293. For discussion of the consequences of a buyer's refusal to accept cure see Ingeborg Schwenzer, Art. 37 para. 17, *in* Schlechtriem & Schwenzer, *CISG Commentary* (2nd English ed. 2005).

9. Multiple attempts to cure, of course, have to occur by the contractual delivery date in order to come under Art. 37. If the seller initially attempts to cure under Art. 37 before the delivery date, and then attempts a subsequent cure after the delivery date, the second attempt would have to meet the more stringent requirements imposed by Art. 48.

10. See Ingeborg Schwenzer, Art. 37 para. 11, *in* Schlechtriem & Schwenzer, *CISG Commentary* (2nd English ed. 2005).

11. For other examples of damage to the buyer suffered despite cure by the seller see Ingeborg Schwenzer, Art. 37 para. 16, *in* Schlechtriem & Schwenzer, *CISG Commentary* (2nd English ed. 2005). The significance of an offer by the seller to make a price adjustment to compensate for the buyer's damages is discussed under Art. 25, *supra* at §185.

Article 38.
Time for Examining the Goods

249 **A. Significance of the Time for Examination**

Article 38 provides rules on how soon the buyer "must examine" the goods. These rules are given legal effect by other provisions: Article 39(1) cuts off the buyer's rights if it fails to notify the seller of a non-conformity within a reasonable time after the buyer "ought to have discovered" it.[1] (*Cf.* Art. 44, *infra* at §254.) Under Article 49(2)(b) the buyer loses its right to avoid the contract a reasonable time after it "knew or *ought to have known* of the breach."[2] Under these provisions Article 38 is important in fixing the time when the buyer ought to have discovered the defect. *There is no independent remedy or sanction for a buyer's non-compliance with Article 38 beyond the possibility that a failure to timely discover a lack of conformity may cause the buyer to miss the deadlines imposed by Article 39 and 49(2)(b).*[3]

The rules of Article 38, like (almost) all other provisions of the Convention, can be excluded or derogated from or have their effects varied by the agreement of the parties (see Article 7).[4]

---

1. See UNCITRAL Digest Art. 38 para. 2; Ingeborg Schwenzer, Art. 38 para. 3, *in* Schlechtriem & Schwenzer, *CISG Commentary* (2nd English ed. 2005).

2. See Ingeborg Schwenzer, Art. 38 para. 3, *in* Schlechtriem & Schwenzer, *CISG Commentary* (2nd English ed. 2005).

3. See Ingeborg Schwenzer, Art. 38 para. 5 and authorities cited therein, *in* Schlechtriem & Schwenzer, *CISG Commentary* (2nd English ed. 2005); Harry M. Flechtner, *Funky Mussels, a Stolen Car, and Decrepit Used Shoes: Non-Conforming Goods and Notice Thereof under the United Nations Sales Convention ("CISG")*, 26 B.U. Int'l L.J. 1 (2008), draft available online in SSRN as University of Pittsburgh Legal Studies Research Paper No. 2008–16, http://ssrn.com/abstract=1144182. *But* see Landgericht Frankfurt, Germany, 11 April 2005, English translation available at http://cisgw3.law.pace.edu/cases/050411g1.html (the "used shoes" case), commented on and criticized in §252 *infra* and in Flechtner, *Funky Mussels, supra.*

4. For decisions on excluding or derogating from Art. 38 see UNCITRAL Digest Art. 38 paras. 6–7 & 18. For further discussion of the topic see Ingeborg Schwenzer, Art. 38 paras. 28–31, *in* Schlechtriem & Schwenzer, *CISG Commentary* (2nd English ed. 2005).

Article 38[5]

(1) The buyer must examine the goods, or cause them to be examined, within as short a period as is practicable in the circumstances.

(2) If the contract involves carriage of the goods, examination may be deferred until after the goods have arrived at their destination.

(3) If the goods are redirected in transit or redispatched by the buyer without a reasonable opportunity for examination by him and at the time of the conclusion of the contract the seller knew or ought to have known of the possibility of such redirection or redispatch, examination may be deferred until after the goods have arrived at the new destination.

250 **B. Legislative Background: ULIS**

The 1964 Hague Convention on Sales (ULIS 38) stated rules on the time for examination that proved to be too rigid. Their most serious flaw was the requirement that the buyer must examine the goods at the place of "destination" unless the goods were redispatched "*without* transshipment." When a buyer purchases goods in sealed cans or cartons for resale in chain transactions employing containerized transport and, in general, whenever efficient distribution calls for rapid transshipment of large quantities of goods, there would be no practical opportunity to inspect the goods (as ULIS required) at the initial terminal. As a result, the buyer's time for giving notice of defects could expire and the buyer could be deprived of its rights before it had a fair opportunity to discover the defect. Efforts were made at the 1964 Hague Conference to correct the problem but to no avail. In the UNCITRAL proceedings it was possible to make the rules on examination of goods more flexible and consistent with current commercial practices.[6]

---

5. This article is the same as Art. 36 of the 1978 Draft, except for the addition in paragraph (3) of references to "redirection" of goods in transit. *Cf.* ULIS 38, discussed *infra* at §250.

6. II *Records 1964 Conf.* 306; Honnold, ULIS: The Hague Convention of 1964, 30 Law & Contemp. Pr. 326, 346–347 (1965). *Accord,* Ingeborg Schwenzer, Art. 38 paras. 1–2, *in* Schlechtriem & Schwenzer, *CISG Commentary* (2nd English ed. 2005). Bianca in *B-B Commentary* 295. The UNCITRAL proceedings: I *YB* 185–186, *Docy. Hist.* 23–24; *Rep. S-G,* IV *YB* 47, *Docy. Hist.* 124.

251   C. Time for Examination under Article 38

(1) Redispatch and Examination of Goods Transported by Carrier

The heart of the change made in preparing the 1980 Convention was to delay the time for inspection (and the running of the time for notice) if the goods are "redirected in transit" or "redispatched," as provided in Article 38(3). In such cases, examination can be deferred during the time consumed in transportation following the redirection or redispatch, provided the seller knew (or ought to have known) of this possibility.[7] *Otherwise, if the contract involves "carriage of the goods" (i.e., transport by a third-party carrier, as opposed to transport using the buyer's or seller's own vehicles), examination is due under Article 38(2), "after the goods arrive at their destination." This means examination is due after they arrive at the place to which they are to be carried to the buyer pursuant to the contract, regardless of whether technical "delivery," e.g., for risk of loss purposes, takes place earlier in the transport (as under an F.O.B. contract).*[8]

252   (2) Examination that is "Practicable In the Circumstances"

All of Article 38 is subject to the standard set forth in paragraph (1): The examination must be made "within as short a period as is practicable in the circumstances." This standard was designed to stress the importance of timely inspection, a necessary step towards the timely notification of defects required by Article 39, *infra*. Timely notice may be needed to enable the seller to take samples or take other steps to preserve evidence of the condition of the goods. In some cases timely notice may enable the seller to cure defects (Arts. 37, 48) or make a price allowance or other adjustment to meet the buyer's complaint. See also §255, *infra*.

The phrase "as short a period as is practicable in the circumstances" embodies nuanced responses to the interests of both parties.[9] ULIS 38(1) stated that the buyer "shall examine the goods ... *promptly*" — a

---

7. For decisions on Art. 38(3) see UNCITRAL Digest Art. 38 para. 19.

8. For decisions on Art. 38(2) see UNCITRAL Digest Art. 38 para. 20.

9. For decisions on the time limits for examination see UNCITRAL Digest Art. 38 paras. 11–15. For discussion of the issue see Ingeborg Schwenzer, Art. 38 paras. 15–26, *in* Schlechtriem & Schwenzer, *CISG Commentary* (2nd English ed. 2005).

standard that might not permit consideration of circumstances that would require delay. (See §250, *supra*, and the legislative history referred to below and in §250 *supra*.) On the other hand, it was concluded that the need for inspection called for greater urgency than was suggested by the "reasonable" time standard established in many other provisions. See Articles 33(c), 39(1), 43(1), 47(1), 48(2), 49(2), 63(1), 64(2)(b), 65, 75, 79(4), 88(1). Where extreme urgency is required and is feasible the Convention calls for "immediate" action: Under Article 71(1) a party suspending performance "must *immediately*" give notice of the suspension. ***Given the extraordinary variety of goods involved in international trade, and the great diversity in methods of examination they require***,[10] setting a rigid time limit for inspection (6 days, 2 weeks) is, of course, impractical; the most that a law can do is to call for action "within as *short* a period as is *practical in the circumstances*."[11]

Local standards. Another step towards flexibility was the omission of ULIS 38(4) which stated that, in the absence of agreement, methods of examination were governed "by the law or usage of *the place where the examination is to be effected*." This provision was omitted because of concern that it might invoke practices designed for local transactions in contrast to practices and usages applicable to international trade. See Article 9, §§112–122, *supra*: "usage ... in *international* trade."[12]

Example 38A. A sales contract called for the delivery to Buyer of 500 gallon cans of chlorine in sealed metal containers; when the seal is broken the chlorine must be used promptly or it will evaporate. On June 1 a shipment under this contract was delivered to Buyer. Buyer stored the containers in his warehouse without counting the number of cans or testing the contents. On September 1 Buyer notified Seller that he had just opened the containers to use the chlorine in his chemical processes, and found that there were only 400 containers, and that 200 contained chlorine that did not meet the contract specifications.

10. For methods of examination under Art. 38 see UNCITRAL Digest Art. 38 paras. 9–10; Ingeborg Schwenzer, Art. 38 paras. 10–14, *in* Schlechtriem & Schwenzer, *CISG Commentary* (2nd English ed. 2005).

11. *Accord*, Ingeborg Schwenzer, Art. 38 para. 15, *in* Schlechtriem & Schwenzer, *CISG Commentary* (2nd English ed. 2005).

12. See Ingeborg Schwenzer, Art. 38 para. 1, *in* Schlechtriem & Schwenzer, *CISG Commentary* (2nd English ed. 2005). *Compare Schlechtriem, 1986 Commentary* 69, citing Huber, 43 *Rabels Z* 413 at 482 (regretting deletion of ULIS 38(4) with *Bianca, B-B Commentary* §2.3, pp. 297–298 (approving deletion).

In these circumstances, one might well conclude that Buyer failed to check the *number* of cans within the required period but that the *contents* were examined as soon as "was practicable in the circumstances."[13]

The general standard of practicability set forth in paragraph (1) remains applicable under paragraph (2) when the contract involves carriage of the goods. The fact that in such transactions the risk of loss normally shifts to the buyer under Article 67(1) "when the goods are handed over to the first carrier" (§§363–367 *infra*) is irrelevant; in the absence of agreement to the contrary (Art. 6), Article 38(2) defers the examination "until after the goods have arrived at their destination." The basic rule of "practicality" in Article 38(1), the language of Article 38(2) and the legislative history all reject rules that turn on risk in transit and technical concepts such as an "agency" status of the carrier.[14]

A 2005 decision[15] *involving a sale of used shoes vividly demonstrates how <u>not</u> to apply Article 38. The German seller had represented the shoes to be of quality class one ("very good condition") and quality class two ("good quality"). Although the buyer was located in Kampala, Uganda, the contract called for delivery "FOB Mombassa, Kenya." The goods arrived in Mombassa and, after the buyer paid the final installment of the purchase price, the seller transferred the bill of lading on May 24. The buyer then had the goods shipped on to Uganda, where it examined them for the first time on June 16. It discovered serious non-conformities: the shoes were "defective and unusable,"*

---

13. This discussion does not address the issue that arises under Art. 39, *infra* at §254: Was the delay of three months in notifying the seller more than a "reasonable time" after Buyer "ought to have discovered" the non-conformity as to quantity (Art. 35(1))? Even if more than a "reasonable time" expired, Art. 44, *infra* at §254, permits the buyer to "reduce the price . . . or claim damages, except for loss of profit, if he has a reasonable excuse" for failure to give the required notice. The buyer's *duty* to examine imposed by Art. 38 must, of course, be sharply distinguished from the buyer's *privilege* to examine the goods before it pays (Art. 58).

14. For the legislative history see WG 1 *YB* 185–186, 197; *S-G* IV *YB* 47; WG VI *YB* 66, 76; *S-G* VI *YB* 99, 112–113; WG VI 55, *Docy. Hist.* 23–24, 35, 124, 144, 154, 224, 237–238, 246. UNCITRAL; VIII *YB* 39–40, *Docy. Hist.* 332–333; *S-G Commy. O.R.* 34, *Docy. Hist.* 424 (risk of loss irrelevant) DIPL. CONF.: *1st Comm. O.R.* 320, 427, 106–107, *Docy. Hist.* 541, 648, 678–679; *Plenary, O.R.* 208, *Docy. Hist.* 743.

15. Landgericht Frankfurt, Germany, 11 April 2005, CLOUT case No. 775, English translation available at http://cisgw3.law.pace.edu/cases/050411g1.html. The editor of the current edition previously commented on this decision. See Harry M. Flechtner, *Funky Mussels, a Stolen Car, and Decrepit Used Shoes: Non-Conforming Goods and Notice Thereof under the United Nations Sales Convention ("CISG")*, 26 B.U. Int'l L.J. 1 (2008), draft available online in SSRN as University of Pittsburgh Legal Studies Research Paper No. 2008-21, http://ssrn.com/abstract=1144182.

and the shipment included "in-line skates and shoe trees." Indeed, the Uganda National Bureau of Standards declared the shoes "unfit for usage" because of "bad and unhygienic condition"; it refused to permit their importation, and recommended they be destroyed "at the parties' cost." On June 17 — the day after discovering the condition of the goods — the buyer notified the seller of the lack of conformity. The buyer eventually sued to recover the purchase price it had paid, along with damages and interest.

The court held that the condition of the shoes fundamentally breached the contract, but that the buyer could not rely on the shoes' lack of conformity because its notice to the seller came too late under Article 39(1) (infra §§255–59). It so held even though the notice was given slightly over three weeks from the time the buyer received the bill of lading — a time frame often found acceptable for non-perishable goods. The basis for the court's decision was that the buyer's examination of the goods was untimely under Article 38. The court held that, since the contract specified FOB Mombassa, the buyer should have examined them in Mombassa on or shortly after May 24, rather than waiting until the goods reached Uganda.

The buyer pointed out that examining the goods in Kenya would have entailed considerable extra expense, including incurring Kenyan import duties. It also noted that Article 38(3) provides that examination of goods that are "redispatched" can be deferred until their arrival at the new destination (here, Uganda), provided the buyer did not have a "reasonable opportunity for examination" at their original destination. The court, however, found that the buyer had failed to show that it did not have a reasonable opportunity to inspect the goods in Kenya,[16] relying primarily on the buyer's agreement to the "FOB Mombassa" term. The court declared,

> *the inconvenience of a flight from Uganda to Kenya cannot be an argument against the Seller, as the Buyer itself has chosen Mombassa as the goods' destination. It was free to agree upon a different destination with the Seller.... The argument that paying the [Kenyan] customs duties would have been unreasonable, cannot be followed ....[I]t would have been possible for the Buyer to agree upon Kampala, Uganda and not Mombassa, Kenya as the destination of the goods.*

16. The court also questioned whether the buyer had established another requirement for the application of Art. 38(3) — that "at the time of the conclusion of the contract the seller knew or ought to have known of the possibility of such . . . redispatch." The court stated that "[t]he fact that the Buyer has its place of business in Uganda is insofar insufficient," but it did not finally resolve this question, relying instead on the buyer's supposed failure to show lack of a reasonable opportunity to examine the goods in Mombassa.

The court's reasoning seriously distorts the meaning of Article 38 and undermines the provision's intended purposes. It renders Article 38(3) virtually a dead letter by holding that, if a buyer agreed to a delivery point for the goods for risk of loss purposes (e.g., through a price-delivery term like FOB), then the buyer is deemed to have a reasonable opportunity to examine the goods at that place, no matter how many difficulties such an examination presents: the agreement to a delivery point, in the court's view, renders the difficulties irrelevant as a matter of law. Of course a buyer <u>always</u> agrees (either expressly or by silence) to a delivery point for the goods, so under the court's approach examination could never be delayed because of transshipment, and Article 38(3) might as well not exist. Even if the approach were limited to express agreements on the place of delivery (which, of course, are very common), nothing in the history of Article 38(3) suggests that an agreement on a delivery point means that the obstacles to examining at that place should be ignored. The court's approach simply contradicts the purpose of Article 38(3).

Indeed, even if Article 38(3) were inapplicable the buyer's decision to delay examining the goods until they arrived in Uganda was arguably proper. Under Article 38(2), if the contract involves carriage of the goods (as did this contract), "examination may be deferred until after the goods have arrived at their destination." As noted above, this provision was specifically designed to relieve the buyer of the burden of examining the goods where delivery occurs for risk of loss purposes: "destination" in this provision is not defined by, e.g., technical delivery under a price-delivery term, but rather by the actual destination of the goods where buyer will take physical possession.[17] Given the buyer's location and lack of facilities in Kenya, the parties likely contemplated from the inception of the transaction that the goods would be shipped on to Uganda. Thus under Article 38(2) the buyer could, arguably, defer examination until the shoes arrived in Uganda,[18] and it was not required (as the court asserts) to examine them as soon as they showed up in Mombassa.

The court's approach in the used shoes case also ignores the language in Article 38(1) stating that examination is not due until it is "practicable in the circumstances." The court appears to assume that,

---

17. See Ingeborg Schwenzer, Art. 38 paras. 21–22, *in* Schlechtriem & Schwenzer, *CISG Commentary* (2nd English ed. 2005).

18. A significant unexpected delay in shipment from Kenya to Uganda might have raised issues, but that did not occur in the case.

if the buyer has agreed to a delivery point (as it always, at least impli-edly, does) the buyer <u>*must*</u> *examine the goods at that place no matter how inconvenient or expensive. There is simply no justification for this refusal to recognize the terms of Article 38.*

In short, under the misguided approach adopted by the used shoes court a provision intended, as noted above, to "reject rules that turn on risk in transit and technical concepts" becomes the apotheosis of tech-nical rules focused on risk of loss.

Even if the court's conclusion that the buyer's examination was too late under Article 38 had been correct, the consequences the court imposes would still be erroneous. The buyer notified the seller of the lack of conformity on June 17, less than four weeks after the goods, by the court's own analysis, became available for examination on May 24. Even if the buyer had examined the goods in Kenya as soon as they were available to inspect, notice on June 17 would arguably have been within a "reasonable time" as required by Article 39(1).[19] *The court, however, reasons simply that "[t]he examination of the goods, and consequently the notice was . . . too late." In other words, the court holds that if a buyer examines too late it will lose its rights with regard to non-conformities that a timely examination would have revealed, even if the buyer expedites notice so that it arrives within the time mandated by Article 39(1). In these circumstances, of course, the seller has suffered nothing from the late examination; it has received notice within the prescribed time, and the buyer's late examination simply has no impact on the seller. The court in the used shoes case, nevertheless, is inexplicably driven to punish the buyer for what the court sees as late examination — and to punish the buyer very severely.*

The court in effect chooses to impose the same sanction for late examination as is imposed for late notice under Article 39 — a complete loss of rights with respect to non-conformities. It does so without support in the text of Article 38 or its drafting history, and even though the Article 39 sanction was extremely controversial at the 1980 diplomatic conference; indeed, concern, particularly by develop-ing countries, over the "draconian" punishment imposed for late notice under Article 39 threatened the entire CISG project; the threat was averted only by the addition of a provision (Article 44) designed to

19. See Harry M. Flechtner, *Funky Mussels, a Stolen Car, and Decrepit Used Shoes: Non-Conforming Goods and Notice Thereof under the United Nations Sales Convention ('CISG'),* 26 B.U. Int'l L.J. 1 (2008), draft available online in SSRN as University of Pittsburgh Legal Studies Research Paper No. 2008–21, http://ssrn.com/abstract=1144182.

soften the punishment.[20] *The used shoes court nevertheless chooses to extend this controversial remedy to the late examination situation without even attempting to justify the maneuver. As Professor Schwenzer points out,*[21] *and as noted above (§249 supra), the only sanction for a buyer's untimely examination of the goods is the possibility that late discovery of non-conformities will lead to late notice thereof under Article 39 — but the buyer's notice in the used shoes case arguably was timely even if you assume the buyer should have examined in the goods in Kenya.*

The consequence of the court's mishandling of Article 38 was a gross injustice. The buyer ended up paying full price for goods that were not just substantially non-conforming, but that were so far below the standards to which the seller agreed that the goods had to be destroyed for hygienic reasons (probably at the buyer's own expense!). The court imposed this result even though the buyer examined the goods in a fashion that only the most misguided interpretation of Article 38 found lacking, and even though the buyer still managed to give arguably-timely notice of non-conformities. The editor of the current edition has previously labeled the analysis in the used shoes case a perverse tour de force, and this characterization still seems correct.

The used shoes case teaches how important it is to keep in mind the purposes and background of Article 38, and its place within the overall scheme of the Convention. The seller is entitled to timely notice of a claimed lack of conformity in delivered goods. The buyer's examination of the goods plays a crucial role in meeting the obligation to give notice. Article 38 exists to rebut the argument that the time for giving notice does not begin to run until a lack of conformity reveals itself during the buyer's use or resale of the goods: the buyer is under an obligation, before it begins using or reselling the goods, to examine them, and to do so "within as short a period as is practicable in the

---

20. See §§254.1 and 261 *infra*; Harry M. Flechtner, *Funky Mussels, a Stolen Car, and Decrepit Used Shoes: Non-Conforming Goods and Notice Thereof under the United Nations Sales Convention ("CISG"),* 26 B.U. Int'l L.J. 1 (2008), draft available online in SSRN as University of Pittsburgh Legal Studies Research Paper No. 2008–21, http://ssrn.com/abstract=1144182; Harry M. Flechtner, "Buyer's obligation to give notice of lack of conformity," *The Draft UNCITRAL Digest and Beyond: Cases, Analysis and Unresolved Issues in the U.N. Sales Convention* 377 at 378–79 (Franco Ferrari, Harry Flechtner and Ronald A. Brand eds., 2004). The used shoes court also manages to misconstrue Art. 44, but this will be addressed below in the discussion of Art. 44 (*infra* §261).

21. See Ingeborg Schwenzer, Art. 38 para. 5, Art. 39 paras. 2 & 20, and Art. 44 para. 2, *in* Schlechtriem & Schwenzer, *CISG Commentary* (2nd English ed. 2005).

circumstances." As a result, the time for giving notice of non-conformities that should have been discovered during such an examination begins to run from the time the examination should have occurred.

Examination is not due, however, until it is truly practicable in the circumstances. Article 38 was designed to correct the inflexibility of the ULIS and its over-reliance on technical delivery terms. The Convention's rule was crafted to insure that the buyer is not unreasonably burdened by its obligation to examine. Examination is a means to a secondary goal of the Convention — to ensure the seller receives timely notice of lack of conformities. The meaning and purposes of the Convention are distorted when Article 38 is applied in a fashion that undermines one of the Convention's primary goals — to ensure that seller delivers goods of the quality required by the contract — in circumstances where the seller has suffered little or no prejudice from the timing of the buyer's examination.

252.1 Article 38 and Latent Defects

Article 39(1) requires the buyer to notify the seller of a claimed lack of conformity within a reasonable time after the buyer "discovered it or ought to have discovered it." The Article 38 obligation to examine the goods "within as short a period as is practicable in the circumstances" means that the time when the buyer "ought to have discovered" a lack of conformity that would be revealed by an initial examination begins to run from the time that examination was (or should have been) conducted. Suppose, however, the non-conformity consists of a latent defect — i.e., a problem not reasonably discoverable until the goods have been put into use or otherwise after the passage of time. It is clear that the buyer's reasonable time for giving Article 39(1) notice in such a case begins later, since the buyer "ought to have discovered" the lack of conformity later. But does Article 38 play a role in determining when the buyer "ought to have discovered" a latent lack of conformity? Or is that a matter beyond the scope of Article 38, governed simply by Article 39(1) itself?

The answer depends on how one conceives of the examination required by Article 38. Is it a discrete event that is completed "within as short a period as is practicable" after delivery?[22] Or is it a continuous process of looking for non-conformities — one that begins

---

22. Of course, even if conceived of as a discrete post-delivery event the Art. 38 examination may require not a single inspection or test but a series, depending on the nature of the goods

shortly after delivery but that keeps going until the buyer can no longer make a claim based on a newly-discovered lack of conformity (e.g., after the 2-year period for giving notice specified in Article 39(2))? If the latter is the case, determining whether a buyer gave timely notice of a latent lack of conformity involves analysis of whether the buyer properly met its continuing Article 38 obligation to examine the goods. Under the former approach, however, Article 38 has no relevance to latent non-conformities that the buyer reasonably does not discover during the discrete post-delivery examination process; determining whether the buyer gave the seller timely notice thereof is simply a matter of determining when the buyer "ought to have discovered" the latent non-conformity under Article 39(1).

There is authority for both approaches.[23] To the editor of the current edition, treating examination as a discreet event that is completed within a relatively short time after delivery, and that thus has no bearing on when a buyer "ought to have discovered" later-appearing latent defects, seems more consistent with the phrasing of Article 38, with the Convention's general approach to the post-delivery period, and with common sense.[24] After all, there comes a point when, psychologically, delivered goods become the buyer's, and when charging the buyer with an obligation to continuously scrutinize them for defects is unrealistic.[25]

To date the difference between the approaches has had little or no practical impact: authorities that invoke the buyer's Article 38 obligation when analyzing for timely notice of latent defects seem to do so largely to ensure that, once indications of a latent defect have appeared, the buyer is reasonably diligent in following the matter up; such diligence, however, is equally relevant to the general Article 39(1) inquiry into when the buyer <u>ought</u> to have discovered a latent defect. In the future, however, applying Article 38 in the latent defect situation may prove a source of confusion.

---

and other circumstances of the transaction. For decisions on the method of examination required by Art. 38 see UNCITRAL Digest Art. 38 paras. 9–10.

23. See UNCITRAL Digest Art. 38 para. 16.

24. These views are developed more fully in Harry M. Flechtner, "Buyer's obligation to give notice of lack of conformity," *The Draft UNCITRAL Digest and Beyond: Cases, Analysis and Unresolved Issues in the U.N. Sales Convention* 377 at 389–91 (Franco Ferrari, Harry Flechtner and Ronald A. Brand eds., 2004).

25. *Accord,* Ingeborg Schwenzer, Art. 39 para. 20, *in* Schlechtriem & Schwenzer, *CISG Commentary* (2nd English ed. 2005).

Article 39.
Notice of Lack of Conformity

Article 40.
Seller's Knowledge of Non-Conformity

Article 44.
Excuse for Failure to Notify

254 **A. Introduction: Notice Requirements in Two Settings**

We now face a complex problem of organization and presentation. Perhaps a brief preview will help.

The Convention requires buyers to notify sellers of breach of contract in two different settings: (1) Articles 39, 40, and 44 establish (and limit) buyers" obligation to notify sellers of lack of conformity of *goods*: (2) Article 43 requires buyers to notify sellers of *third-party claims* to the goods. (For buyers" protection against such claims see Articles 41 and 42, *infra*.)

In preparing the Convention attention (and policy conflicts) centered on the first type of notification — lack of conformity of the goods. Articles 39, 40 and 44 dealing with this question are so interrelated that they need to be examined as a group. However, one of these three provisions — Article 44, granting a limited "excuse" for failing to notify — also applies to notification of the second type: *third-party claims*.

In presenting these interlocking provisions we shall first examine Articles 39, 40 and 44 requiring buyers to give notice of *non-conformity in the goods*.

254.1 **(1) The Package of Three Related Articles**

The Commentary on Article 38, *supra* at §249, showed that the period within which the buyer must examine the goods is closely related to the buyer's obligation to notify the seller of non-conformity — an obligation that is governed by Articles 39, 40 and 44. Article 39 states general rules on the time for notification and the consequences of failure to comply with this requirement. Articles 40 and 44 contain special exceptions from the general rules of Article 39.

These three articles embody a delicate compromise of views that were vigorously pressed during the UNCITRAL proceedings and at the 1980 Diplomatic Conference. Indeed, this is one of the few points where perceptions of differing regional and economic interests came to the fore. Representatives of several industrial States, primarily of the Continent of Europe, stressed the importance of maintaining the strict notice requirements embodied in their domestic rules. This position was opposed primarily by representatives of developing States. This opposition reflected fears that defects in heavy machinery might appear long after the machinery is delivered and put into use and that purchasers might be unaware of the drastic effects of delay in giving notice. The evolution of provisions designed to reconcile these views will be described *infra* at §§256–261.

254.2   **(a) Notice Requirements and Limitations for Legal Proceedings**   We need to distinguish two types of rules that relate to delay: (1) Rules, like Articles 39, 40 and 44, requiring timely *notice* to the other party, and (2) Rules setting time limits for *bringing legal action*. Rules of the second type are not included in the Sales Convention[1] and are the subject of a closely-related Convention on the Limitation Period in the International Sale of Goods (1974 and 1980 Protocol of amendment). The Limitation Convention will be introduced at §261.1, *infra*.

Following are the three articles (Arts. 39, 40, 44) of the first type — rules requiring *notice* to the other party of lack of conformity of the goods.

Article 39

(1) The buyer loses the right to rely on a lack of conformity of the goods if he does not give notice to the seller specifying the nature of the lack of conformity within a reasonable time after he has discovered it or ought to have discovered it.

(2) In any event, the buyer loses the right to rely on a lack of conformity of the goods if he does not give the seller notice thereof at the latest within a period of two years from the date on which the goods were actually handed over to the buyer, unless this time-limit is inconsistent with a contractual period of guarantee.

---

1. See Ingeborg Schwenzer, Art. 39 para. 28, *in* Schlechtriem & Schwenzer, *CISG Commentary* (2nd English ed. 2005); UNCITRAL Digest Art. 39 para. 24.

Article 40

The seller is not entitled to rely on the provisions of article 38 and 39 if the lack of conformity relates to facts of which he knew or could not have been unaware and which he did not disclose to the buyer.

Article 44[2]

Notwithstanding the provisions of paragraph (1) of article 39 and paragraph (1) of article 43, the buyer may reduce the price in accordance with article 50 or claim damages, except for loss of profit, if he has a reasonable excuse for his failure to give the required notice.

255 ## B. Seller's Need for Notice; Domestic Rules

Let us assume that the buyer receives goods and, without objection, retains the goods and uses or resells them, but later declines to pay or claims damages on the ground that the goods were defective. If the seller learns of the claim after the goods have been used or after a period during which the goods could have deteriorated, it will be difficult to ascertain whether the buyer's claim is just. The seller's responsibility was to provide goods that conformed to the contract when the risk of loss passed to the buyer (Art. 36(1), *supra*— normally when the seller shipped or when the buyer received the goods. Art. 66–70, *infra* at §§360–383). If the buyer notifies the seller promptly, the seller can inspect and test the goods to ascertain whether a claim is justified. Moreover, when the inspection shows that the goods are defective, the seller may be able

---

2. Arts. 39 and 40 of the Convention are the same as Arts. 37 and 38 of the 1978 Draft and are similar to ULIS 39 and 40. Art. 44 was added during the 1980 Diplomatic Conference. The legislative history of Art. 39 is extensive and deserves noting: WG: 1 *YB* 181, 202, *Docy. Hist.* 19, 40; *S-G* 1 *YB* 195, *Docy. Hist.* 33; WG: III *YB* 81, 87, *Docy. Hist.* 98, 104; *S-G* IV *YB* 47–49, *Docy. Hist.* 124–126; WG: VI *YB* 66–67, 76, V *YB* 54, *Docy. Hist.* 144–145, 154, 200; *S-G* VI *YB* 99–101, *Docy. Hist.* 224–226; WG: VI *YB* 55, *Docy. Hist.* 246. UNCITRAL: VIII *YB* 25–26, 40, *Docy. Hist.* 318–319, 333. *DIPL. CONF.*: *O.R.* 77, 34–35 (*Sec. Comm'y*), 320–324, 427, 107–108, 159, 208, *Docy. Hist.* 398, 424, 425, 541–545, 648, 679–680, 718, 743.

Art. 40 did not attract significant discussion.

Art. 44 emerged only at the Diplomatic Conference: *O.R.* 108, 323, 427, 159, 170, 208, *Docy. Hist.* 680, 544, 648, 718, 728, 743.

to exercise its right to cure the defect (Art. 37, *supra* at §244; Art. 48, *infra* at §292).[3]

256 C. The Occasion, Time and Contents of Notice

(1) "Lack of Conformity"

The buyer must notify the seller of "lack of conformity." The area embraced by this concept is defined in Article 35, and includes quantity, quality, description and packaging.[4]

Do these notice requirements apply to defects in documents, such as a misdescription in a bill of lading, inspection certificate or invoice? Article 39 refers to a lack of conformity "of the goods." However, the Convention is drafted on the assumption that goods will often be delivered by way of documents; in such deliveries supplying the correct documents is part of the seller's obligation to deliver the goods. (See Art. 34, *supra* at §217.) Moreover, the provision in Article 34 allowing the seller to cure a defect in documents would be of little value unless the seller is notified of the defect.[5]

---

3. For further discussion of the purposes for requiring notice of lack of conformity see Ingeborg Schwenzer, Art. 38 para. 4, *in* Schlechtriem & Schwenzer, *CISG Commentary* (2nd English ed. 2005); UNCITRAL Digest Art. 39 para. 10. The notice requirements of Arts. 39, 40 and 44 have special significance when the buyer retains or resells the goods. If the buyer wishes to reject the goods ("avoid the contract"), the special rules applicable to avoidance require that avoidance (and notice thereof) occur within a "reasonable time" (Arts. 26 & 49(2)), which is generally measured from the time the buyer "knew or ought to have known of the breach." For discussion of the relationship between the "reasonable time" for giving notice of lack of conformity under Art. 39 and the "reasonable time" for giving notice of avoidance under Art. 49(2), see §257 *infra*.

Some of the domestic rules requiring notice of defects were mentioned under Art. 38, *supra* at §249; others will be noted in connection with specific aspects of the present group of three articles. As we shall see, Arts. 39, 40 and 44 are an amalgam and do not reproduce the provisions of any single legal system. For further discussion of notice requirements under domestic law see Ingeborg Schwenzer, Art. 39 para. 4.

4. For decisions on what constitutes a lack of conformity for purposes of Art. 39 see UNCITRAL Digest Art. 39 para. 2.

5. Problems of prolonged delay in notification can seldom arise with respect to defects in documents, for when the buyer receives the goods from the carrier the documents will usually become irrelevant. When the buyer rejects the seller's tender because of defects in documents the rules on "avoidance" (Arts. 26, 49(2)) require the buyer to notify the seller within a "reasonable time." See note 2, *supra*.

(a) Specificity.   Article 39(1) states that the buyer must give notice *"specifying the nature* of the lack of conformity." Questions as to what the notice must say should be answered with regard for the functions served by the notice. As was noted at §255, the principal functions are to give the seller an opportunity to obtain and preserve evidence of the condition of the goods and to cure the deficiency (Arts. 37 and 48). See the Secretariat Commentary on draft Article 37 (para. 4), *O.R.* 35, *Docy. Hist.* 425. A notice that said no more than "goods defective" usually would not give the seller all the information the seller needs for the above purposes and (as Art. 39(1) requires) would not specify *"the nature* of the lack of conformity." Some early decisions were overly demanding in the level of detail they required for effective Article 39 notice; the trend in recent cases, however, is more favorable.[6]

The notice requirement should not operate as a trap for unwary or naïve buyers. Notice is a matter of communication between the parties; a seller who wants to know more than is contained in the buyer's initial notice can be expected to inquire, particularly in an age of electronic communications. The consequences if Article 39 is deemed unsatisfied, furthermore, are extreme: the buyer will generally lose all rights with respect to an (alleged) breach by the seller of the crucial obligation to deliver conforming goods (see §259 *infra*). Tribunals should not be quick to impose this severe sanction absent indicators that the seller was substantially prejudiced by inadequacies in the buyer's notice.[7]

256.1   **(b) Delivery of "Different" Goods (Aliud).**   Suppose that in a contract calling for cans of soybean oil the buyer discovers that the cans contain mineral oil or fish oil or some other liquid quite different from that specified in the contract. Does Article 39 require the buyer to notify the seller of "a *lack of conformity* of the goods?"

This question would only occur to one whose domestic law draws a distinction between "non-conforming" goods and "different" goods (sometimes called an *"aliud"*). The Convention does not draw this distinction. As has been noted, §§222–223, *supra,* Article 35 deals with the question of non-conformity in broad terms: The issue is whether the

---

6. See Ingeborg Schwenzer, Art. 39 paras. 6–10, *in* Schlechtriem & Schwenzer, *CISG Commentary* (2nd English ed. 2005); UNCITRAL Digest Art. 39 paras. 11–14; Harry M. Flechtner, *Buyer's obligation to give notice of lack of conformity* (Arts. 38, 39, 40 and 44), *in* The Draft UNCITRAL Digest and Beyond: Cases, Analysis and Unresolved Issues in the U.N. Sales Convention 377, 379–85 (Franco Ferrari, Harry Flechtner & Ronald A Brand eds., 2004).

7. Compare the discussion of the buyer's Art. 38 obligation to examine goods, §252 *supra.*

seller's delivery conforms to the contract. Article 35(1) states: "The seller must deliver goods which are of the *quantity*, quality and *description* required by the *contract*. . . ."

In short, the delivery of goods that are totally different from the "description required by the contract" is a breach of Article 35 on conformity of the goods and invokes the requirement of Article 39 that the buyer notify the seller of "a lack of *conformity* of the goods" as a foundation for the remedies afforded the buyer (Arts. 45–52) for breach of contract.[8]

257   (2) Time

(a) "Reasonable Time."   Article 39(1) requires that notice be given "within a reasonable time after [the buyer] has discovered [a lack of conformity] or ought to have discovered it." Article 38, in fixing the time when the buyer must inspect the goods, is useful in determining when the buyer "ought to" discover a non-conformity. Of course, the buyer is bound only to discover those defects that a normal examination would reveal. (See Art. 38 and Example 38A, *supra* at §252.) Thus, examination at the point of destination would normally show the number of containers and the apparent condition of goods that are open to inspection, but the contents of sealed containers and the inner workings of machinery may not be discoverable until later.[9] The determination of the "reasonable period" for notice following the time when the buyer discovers (or ought to have discovered) the non-conformity would be influenced by a wide range of factors. Considerations indicating the need for speed include the perishable and/or seasonable nature of the goods, the need for impartial sampling or testing, and the possibility of cure by the seller.[10]

---

8. *Accord*, Ingeborg Schwenzer, Art. 35 para. 10 and Art. 39 para. 8, *in* Schlechtriem & Schwenzer, *CISG Commentary* (2nd English ed. 2005); Bundesgerichtshof, Germany, 3 April 1996, CLOUT case No. 171, English translation available at http://cisgw3.law.pace.edu/cases/960403g1.html.

9. For discussion of the point at which the "reasonable time" for giving Art. 39(1) notice commences, see Ingeborg Schwenzer, Art. 39 paras. 19–21, *in* Schlechtriem & Schwenzer, *CISG Commentary* (2nd English ed. 2005); UNCITRAL Digest Art. 39 paras. 16–19.

10. For discussion of the factors to consider in determining a "reasonable time" for giving Art. 39(1) notice, see Ingeborg Schwenzer, Art. 39 para. 16, *in* Schlechtriem & Schwenzer, *CISG Commentary* (2nd English ed. 2005); UNCITRAL Digest Art. 39 para. 21. Analysis of factors bearing on the need for speedy notice under comparable domestic rules may be useful in applying the Convention. See *White & Summers* §11–10.

Some assert that the remedy the buyer intends to invoke for breach should influence the calculation of the "reasonable time" for notice under Article 39(1). It is argued that a buyer who intends to "reject" non-conforming goods (by avoiding the contract or demanding a delivery of substitute goods from the seller) should have less time to give Article 39 notice than a buyer who plans to keep the goods and seek other remedies (recovery of damages under Article 74 or reduction of the price under Article 50) because, in the former case the seller must have time to make arrangements to deal with the rejected goods.[11] This approach "puts the cart before the horse," as the saying goes. Once the buyer has discovered a lack of conformity it can give notice thereof, but it will often require additional time to decide among the various remedial options the Convention makes available. At any rate that order of proceeding — first Article 39 notice, followed later by choice of the desired remedy — is contemplated by Articles 46(2) (the buyer's right to demand substitute goods from the seller) and 46(3) (the buyer's right to demand that the seller repair goods): both provisions state that a request for the remedies must be made "in conjunction with notice given under Article 39 or within a reasonable time thereafter" (emphasis added). How can a remedy that has not even been chosen at the time Article 39 notice is given influence the time for giving the notice?

Of course in those cases where the buyer has determined the desired remedy by the time it gives notice, that choice might be considered in determining the Article 39(1) "reasonable time." Issues raised by the choice of a particular remedy, however, are best considered when determining the availability of that remedy, not when judging whether notice was timely under Article 39(1). For example, Article 49(2)(b) provides that a buyer who wishes to avoid the contract because of the goods' lack of conformity must do so "within a reasonable time." The seller's need, after avoidance, to deal with rejected goods can be far more appropriately and logically considered in connection with Article 49(2) than under Article 39(1). A finding that avoidance was late under Article 49(2) leaves other potential remedies available to the buyer, whereas a finding that the buyer's Article 39 notice was too late precludes all remedies; the latter makes little sense if the problem is only with avoidance.

For example, suppose a buyer gives Article 39 notice at a time when it intends to avoid the contract, but then it changes its mind and decides

---

11. See Ingeborg Schwenzer, Art. 39 para. 16, *in* Schlechtriem & Schwenzer, *CISG Commentary* (2nd English ed. 2005).

to retain the goods and seek damages for the lack of conformity. Does the remedy (subjectively) intended at the time of notice determine the "reasonable time," or does it depend on the remedy ultimately chosen? Suppose the buyer gave notice of avoidance at the same time it gave Article 39 notice, and the Article 39 notice was too late if the avoidance remedy is considered in determining a "reasonable time." Is the buyer now precluded from seeking to reduce the price under Article 50 even if the Article 39 notice would be timely in light of that remedy? Clearly, resolving these issues in light of the time limits for avoidance under Article 49(2), rather in connection with the time for notice under Article 39(1), is the correct approach. Considering the remedy chosen by the buyer in determining the reasonable time under Article 39(1) is confusing and unworkable. The remedy selected by the buyer should be irrelevant to the time for notice under Article 39(1).

257.1   "Reasonable Time" Presumptions

A number of decisions and commentaries have suggested imposing a specific period as the standard Article 39(1) "reasonable time," then adjusting the period in the particular case based on its specific facts (e.g., the period might be shortened if goods were perishable).[12] In essence, this approach establishes a presumed reasonable time that will determine whether a buyer's notice of lack of conformity was timely, unless a party proves that the presumed period should be lengthened or shortened. The suggested presumptive periods have varied considerably; some have suggested less than a week.[13] The Austrian Oberster Gerichtshof has indicated that notice given beyond 14 days following delivery would be presumed too late unless special circumstances were shown.[14] Professor Schwenzer has suggested a

---

12. See the decisions surveyed in UNCITRAL Digest Art. 39 para. 20; Ingeborg Schwenzer, Art. 39 para. 17 and authorities surveyed therein, *in* Schlechtriem & Schwenzer, *CISG Commentary* (2nd English ed. 2005).

13. See Ingeborg Schwenzer, Art. 39 para. 17, *in* Schlechtriem & Schwenzer, *CISG Commentary* (2nd English ed. 2005); UNCITRAL Digest Art. 39 para. 20.

14. Oberster Gerichtshof, Austria, 15 October 1998, CLOUT case No. 240, English translation available at http://cisgw3.law.pace.edu/cases/981015a3.html; Oberster Gerichtshof, Austria, 27 August 1999, CLOUT case No. 423, English translation available at http://cisgw3.law.pace.edu/cases/990827a3.html; Oberster Gerichtshof, Austria, 14 January 2002, CLOUT case No. 541, English translation available at http://cisgw3.law.pace.edu/cases/020114a3.html. This approach demonstrates that sometimes (but not always) the time for the buyer's examination of the goods under Art. 38 is included in the period. It

one-month period (sometime referred to as the "noble month") "as a rough average."[15] *This suggestion counteracts some of the extremely short suggested presumptive notice periods, and it seeks to provide an internationally-oriented compromise between those (mainly Germanic) authorities that, perhaps influenced by short notice periods in domestic law, have been quite strict in allotting time for notice, and authorities that reflect more forgiving domestic law traditions.*

Professor Schwenzer's "noble month" approach has undoubtedly had a positive influence, and reflects a genuine international impulse. In the view of the editor of the current edition, however, the very idea of a presumptive "reasonable time" period in Article 39 departs from the intention of the drafters. They could easily have included a presumptive period in Article 39(1), and the process of negotiating the Convention's text would have been the proper milieu for arriving at an internationally-acceptable compromise. The drafters, however, eschewed reference to any specific period and chose a radically flexible standard — a "reasonable time" — designed to vary with the facts of each situation. Instituting a presumptive "reasonable time" for Article 39(1) notice invades the function of the Convention's drafters and the sovereign prerogatives of the Contracting States.[16]

The German Bundesgerichtshof, after initially signaling agreement with the "noble month" approach, has more recently stated: "The circumstances of each individual case are decisive in measuring the time period, so that a schematic fixing of the time for the notice of defect is impossible."[17] *The editor of the current edition of this treatise has proposed a test for determining whether a buyer's notice is within a "reasonable time" under Article 39(1) that differs for each particular case and is incompatible with a presumptive period. The test asks whether the seller suffered substantial prejudice from the buyer's*

---

is sometimes not clear whether a proposed presumptive period encompasses both the time for Art. 39(1) notice and the time for Art. 38 examination. As Professor Schwenzer notes, it is important to distinguish the two periods. See Ingeborg Schwenzer, Art. 39 paras. 15, *in* Schlechtriem & Schwenzer, *CISG Commentary* (2nd English ed. 2005).

15. Ingeborg Schwenzer, Art. 39 para. 17, *in* Schlechtriem & Schwenzer, *CISG Commentary* (2nd English ed. 2005).

16. See Harry M. Flechtner, *Funky Mussels, a Stolen Car, and Decrepit Used Shoes: Non-Conforming Goods and Notice Thereof under the United Nations Sales Convention ("CISG"),* 26 B.U. Int'l L.J. 1 (2008), draft available online in SSRN as University of Pittsburgh Legal Studies Research Paper No. 2008–16, http://ssrn.com/abstract=1144182.

17. Bundesgerichtshof, Germany, 11 January 2006, English translation available at http://cisgw3.law.pace.edu/cases/060111g1.html.

delay in giving notice.[18] *Such a test sacrifices the predictability of the presumptive period, but it appears more in keeping with the approach adopted by the Convention's drafters. It also preserves the important function of Article 39 notice in the Convention's architecture, while ensuring that the notice requirement does not exceed its proper role as a secondary or derivative obligation intended to advance rather than interfere with the Convention's primary goals; those goals are to require the seller to deliver goods of the quality and in the manner required by the contract, and to obligate the buyer to pay therefor as agreed.*

257.2 (3) Form of Notice

Neither the express terms of Article 39 nor decisions interpreting it have imposed particular requirements as to the form of notice that will satisfy Article 39.[19] *Written notice has of course, been found sufficient, as has oral (e.g., telephonic) notice — although the latter may (naturally) raise evidentiary issues.*[20] *The parties, of course, can agree to require a particular form of notice.*[21]

257.3 Derogation, Waiver and Estoppel

As provided in Article 6, the parties can agree to derogate from or alter the operation of the Article 39 notice requirement.[22] *Even absent an agreement a seller can, after delivering (allegedly) non-conforming goods, waive or forfeit its right to object to the buyer's failure to comply with Article 39 notice requirements.*[23] *For example, a seller was found to have waived its right to object to late notice under Article 39 where the seller stated it would take the goods back if the buyer's complaints*

---

18. See Harry M. Flechtner, *Buyer's obligation to give notice of lack of conformity* (Arts. 38, 39, 40 and 44), *in* Draft UNCITRAL Digest and Beyond, *supra* note 37, at 377, 387–88.

19. See Ingeborg Schwenzer, Art. 39 para. 11, *in* Schlechtriem & Schwenzer, *CISG Commentary* (2nd English ed. 2005); UNCITRAL Digest Art. 39 para. 5.

20. See decisions cited in UNCITRAL Digest Art. 39 para. 5.

21. See Ingeborg Schwenzer, Art. 39 para. 12, *in* Schlechtriem & Schwenzer, *CISG Commentary* (2nd English ed. 2005); UNCITRAL Digest Art. 39 para. 5.

22. See Ingeborg Schwenzer, Art. 39 paras. 34, 35, *in* Schlechtriem & Schwenzer, *CISG Commentary* (2nd English ed. 2005); UNCITRAL Digest Art. 39 para. 7.

23. See Ingeborg Schwenzer, Art. 39 paras. 33, 33a, *in* Schlechtriem & Schwenzer, *CISG Commentary* (2nd English ed. 2005); UNCITRAL Digest Art. 39 para. 8.

about defects were confirmed.[24] *No such waiver occurred, however, where the seller accepted return of the goods in order to examine them, even though the seller gave the buyer a provisional credit for the price.*[25] *Estoppel theory has also been employed to block a seller from invoking its rights under Article 39 where the buyer relied on the seller's representations that it would not object to the timeliness of the buyer's notice.*[26]

258 **(b) The Two-Year Limit.** Some legal systems simply require notice within a "reasonable time" and do not specify an outer time-limit. (See (U.S.A.) UCC 2–607(3), Article 38, *supra* at §253.) Others specify cut-off periods of one year or less. ULIS 49(1) set a cut-off limit of one year. The two-year period in paragraph (2) Article 39 was part of an overall compromise.

Paragraph (2) opens with the phrase "in any event"; the notice must be given within the two-year period even though a defect is discovered subsequent to that period, and even though a later notice would satisfy the general standards of Article 39(1) and Article 44.[27]

The exception at the end of paragraph (2), for cases where the two-year limit "is inconsistent with a contractual period of guarantee," meets a problem that could arise, in rare instances, when the contract guarantees performance for a period of two years or longer. (See Art. 36(2), *supra* at §243.) Suppose that a contract guarantees performance for a period of two years, and the goods break down at the very end of the two-year period. In this situation the two-year cut-off could be "inconsistent with [the] contractual period of guarantee" so that a later notice would be effective.[28]

The cut-off period of paragraph (2) starts to run only when the goods are "actually handed over to the buyer." This emphatic reference to the physical act of *actually* handing over the goods to the buyer was

---

24. *Bundesgerichtshof*, Germany, 25 June 1997, CLOUT case No. 235, English translation available at http://cisgw3.law.pace.edu/cases/970625g2.html.

25. *Oberlandesgericht* Düsseldorf, Germany, 12 March 1993, CLOUT case No. 310, English translation available at http://cisgw3.law.pace.edu/cases/930312g1.html.

26. Internationales Schiedsgericht der Bundeskammer der gewerblichen Wirtschaft (case No. SCH-4318), Austria, 15 June 1994, CLOUT case No. 94, English translation available at http://cisgw3.law.pace.edu/cases/940615a4.html.

27. For discussion of Art. 39(2) generally, see Ingeborg Schwenzer, Art. 39 paras. 22–25, *in* Schlechtriem & Schwenzer, *CISG Commentary* (2nd English ed. 2005).

28. See Ingeborg Schwenzer, Art. 39 paras. 26–27, *in* Schlechtriem & Schwenzer, *CISG Commentary* (2nd English ed. 2005).

designed to prevent transit-time from eating into the two-year period, regardless of whether the buyer bore the risk of loss during carriage.[29] The 1964 Convention on the Limitation Period in the International Sale of Goods similarly provides (Art. 10(2)) that the 4-year limitation period for a claim arising from lack of conformity commences when the goods "are actually handed over to, or their tender refused by the buyer." This language was also selected to avoid shortening the period while goods are in transit.[30]

259 ## D. Consequence of Failure to Give Notice

(1) The Basic Rule of Article 39

Article 39 states that if the buyer fails to notify the seller within the prescribed period he "loses the right to rely" on the non-conformity. This language, standing alone (but see Art. 44, §261 *infra*), bars the full range of remedies: a claim for damages (Art. 45(1)(b) and 74–77), requiring performance by the seller (Art. 46), avoidance of the contract (Art. 49) and reduction of the price (Art. 50). Under this language a seller's action to recover the price would not be subject to a set-off or counterclaim based on a defect which the buyer knew or ought to have discovered if the buyer fails to notify the seller within the periods stated in Article 39.[31] However this rigorous rule is subject to exceptions, to which we now turn.

---

29. See Ingeborg Schwenzer, Art. 39 para. 24, *in* Schlechtriem & Schwenzer, *CISG Commentary* (2nd English ed. 2005). Proposals at the Diplomatic Conference to make the period start on "delivery" were defeated. *Com. I O.R.* 349, paras. 54–65. *O.R.* 107–108, *Docy. Hist.* 570, 679–680. On the ambiguities of the concept of "delivery" see Art. 31, *supra* at §210.
30. See the Secretariat Commentary on the Limitation Convention (A/CONF. 63/17), Art. 10, paras. 3–5, p. 27, X *YB* 145, 156. For discussion of the distinction between the Art. 39(2) cut-off period for notice and limitation or prescription periods for bringing legal actions, see *infra* §261.1.
31. See Ingeborg Schwenzer, Art. 39 para. 30, *in* Schlechtriem & Schwenzer, *CISG Commentary* (2nd English ed. 2005); UNCITRAL Digest Art. 39 para. 3. Domestic rules may also strip a buyer of remedies for failure to notify the seller of claimed non-conformities in delivered goods. See UCC 2–607(3)(a) (barring the buyer from "any remedy" if it does not notify the seller within a "reasonable time" of claimed non-conformities in goods that the buyer has accepted). Under proposed revisions to UCC Art. 2, the buyer would lose its remedies only if the seller could establish that it suffered "prejudice" from the lack of proper notice; at the time this is written, no jurisdiction has enacted the revisions.

260   **(2) Exceptions**

(a) Knowledge of Seller: Article 40.   Article 40, quoted *supra* at
§254, relieves the buyer of these notice requirements when a lack of
conformity relates to facts of which the seller "knew or could not have
been unaware." Such a rule appears in ULIS (Art. 38) and, even though
it departs from the approach in the domestic law of some states,[32] calls
for little comment.[33] *A small number of observations may, however, be
useful.*

*Unlike the "excuse" rule in Article 44 (discussed in the next
section), Article 40 relieves the buyer of the consequences of a failure
to comply not only with Article 39(1), but also Article 39(2).*

*Article 40 does not specify the time at which the seller must have
known (or could not have been aware) of the lack of conformity. As
Professor Schwenzer has persuasively argued,[34] this issue is best
resolved by referring to the purpose of Article 40. The provision is
designed to prevent unnecessary punishment of a buyer for failing
to meet its Article 39 notice obligations where the seller does not
need (and is not prejudiced by the lack of) such notice. Thus Article
40 should be triggered if the seller knew or could not have been
unaware of a lack of conformity by the end of the period for timely
notice[35] (i.e., a "reasonable time" with respect to notice under Article
39(1); "two years from the date the goods were actually handed over to
the buyer" for notice under Article 39(2)).*

*Article 40 provides that it does not apply if the seller disclosed the
lack of conformity to the buyer. It appears odd indeed that the seller's
disclosure of information concerning a lack of conformity reinstates*

---

32. See Ingeborg Schwenzer, Art. 40 para. 2, *in* Schlechtriem & Schwenzer, *CISG Commentary* (2nd English ed. 2005).

33. The phrase "could not have been unaware" is discussed under Art. 35, *supra* at §229. See also Ingeborg Schwenzer, Art. 40 para. 4, *in* Schlechtriem & Schwenzer, *CISG Commentary* (2nd English ed. 2005); UNCITRAL Digest Art. 40 paras. 4, 6–7. The notice required by Art. 43(1) (which applies when the buyer claims a breach arising from a right or claim of a third party) is not applicable when the seller *knew* of the fact in question. See Art. 43(2), *infra* at §271. When the seller *knew* of a non-conformity in the goods, domestic rules governing fraud may be applicable. See Ingeborg Schwenzer, Art. 40 para. 10, *in* Schlechtriem & Schwenzer, *CISG Commentary* (2nd English ed. 2005).

34. See Ingeborg Schwenzer, Art. 40 para. 8, *in* Schlechtriem & Schwenzer, *CISG Commentary* (2nd English ed. 2005).

35. *But* see contrary authorities cited in Ingeborg Schwenzer, Art. 40 para. 8 n.17, *in* Schlechtriem & Schwenzer, *CISG Commentary* (2nd English ed. 2005); UNCITRAL Digest Art. 40 para. 8.

the buyer's obligation to (re-) inform the seller of that same information. Unless carefully and very narrowly construed, this exception could undermine the sensible purposes behind Article 40, and become a trap for unwary buyers that have not been advised by legal counsel schooled in legal technicalities. One of the last things that would occur to a reasonable buyer to whom the seller has disclosed a lack of conformity is to notify the seller of what the seller already knows. A narrow construction of the disclosure exception is required by the mandate in Article 7(1) to interpret the Convention with regard "to the need to promote . . . the observance of good faith in international trade." Professor Schwenzer has suggested that the exception applies only when the seller has merely suggested the possibility that the goods might lack conformity, and notice by the buyer is needed to clarify that the goods delivered were in fact non-conforming; if the seller has clearly stated that the goods do not conform, however, Article 40 continues to protect the buyer. This construction confines the exception to a suitably narrow scope. Perhaps the exception could also apply where disclosure followed by the buyer's acceptance of the goods creates genuine ambiguity about whether the buyer objects to the lack of conformity. This situation should rarely arise: it is quite unlikely that a buyer's willingness to take delivery of goods that it knows have a substantial non-conformity would actually lead the seller to think that the buyer had no objection. But in those rare cases where the ambiguity arises — probably confined to situations where the disclosed non-conformities are quite minor — requiring the buyer to give notice that it deems the goods non-conforming serves a purpose.[36]

Nothing in Article 6 excepts Article 40 from the rule that the parties can agree to "derogate from or vary the effect of any of its provisions." Yet it will be extremely rare that an informed buyer will agree to a provision stripping it of its rights unless it notifies the seller of a lack of conformity of which the seller is already aware. Such an agreement may even violate domestic validity principles that enshrine public policy.[37] *Thus it has been suggested Article 40 is beyond the parties' autonomy, and that its provisions are applicable even when the parties*

36. It has been held that the U.S. domestic sales law requirement that a buyer notify the seller of a claimed breach (UCC 2–607(2)) applies even when the seller is aware of the breach if the notice is needed to clarify that the buyer will seek legal recourse and to open the way to settlement negotiations.

37. See Ingeborg Schwenzer, Art. 40 para. 11, *in* Schlechtriem & Schwenzer, *CISG Commentary* (2nd English ed. 2005).

have fashioned their own contractual regime for giving notice of lack of conformity.[38]

261 **(b) Excuse for Failure to Notify: Article 44.** There was no provision like Article 44 in the 1978 Draft Convention that was submitted to the Diplomatic Conference. Efforts to relax the notice requirements of Article 39 had failed by narrow margins and it seemed that the question had been resolved. Thereafter, informal discussions revealed that some developing countries were seriously dissatisfied by this result; representatives of industrial countries that had strongly resisted relaxation of the notice requirements proposed that the issue be reopened so that a compromise solution could be developed. This led to the addition of Article 44, quoted *supra* at §254.[39]

Article 44 relieves the buyer of some of the consequences of failing to give notice within a "reasonable time" under Article 39(1) when the buyer "has a *reasonable excuse* for failing to give the required notice." It is important to note that this excuse is limited to failure to comply with *paragraph (1)* of Article 39 and does not affect the two-year cut-off period of Article 39(2). Contrast Article 40, discussed in §260 *supra*.

The "reasonable excuse" for a failure to give notice in conformity with Article 39(1) needs to be understood and applied in the light of its legislative history. At the Diplomatic Conference several representatives, primarily from developing States, objected that consequences imposed by Article 39(1) were too drastic: The provision that "the buyer loses the right to rely on a lack of conformity of the goods" means (*inter alia*) that one could be required to pay the full price for defective goods. Concern was also expressed that it would be especially difficult to ascertain defects in complex industrial machinery typical of

---

38. See *id.*; Stockholm Chamber of Commerce Arbitration Award, Sweden, 5 June 1998, CLOUT case No. 237, English text available at http://cisgw3.law.pace.edu/cases/980605s5.html.

39. The move for a compromise was led by Sweden and Finland. These two were joined by Ghana, Kenya, Nigeria, and Pakistan in developing a joint compromise proposal. This was drafted as a third paragraph of Art. 39, but became a separate article (Art. 44) so that it could also apply to the notice requirements in Art. 43(1). *O.R.* 108, 323, *Docy. Hist.* 680, 544; see also §254 n.1, *supra*. For a further account of the history of Art. 44, see Harry M. Flechtner, *Buyer's obligation to give notice of lack of conformity (Articles 38, 39, 40 and 44), in* The Draft UNCITRAL Digest and Beyond: Cases, Analysis and Unresolved Issues in the U.N. Sales Convention 377, 378 (Franco Ferrari, Harry Flechtner & Ronald A Brand eds., 2004). As has been noted (§154, *supra*) "excuse" under Art. 44 also applies to Art. 43, *infra*. See Date-Bah, Problems of Developing Countries, in *Potsdam Colloq.* 39 *et seq.*, and Date-Bah in 11 Rev. Ghanaian Law 50 (1979).

imports to developing areas, and that their importers might be unaware of the Convention's notice requirement and the drastic consequences of failure to comply.

Against this background the use of the expression "reasonable *excuse*" indicates the applicability of more individualized considerations than would otherwise be relevant under Article 39(1).[40] Thus, Article 44 might countenance difficulties encountered by the individual importer, or at least by importers of the region, that might not be relevant under the more objective standard of Article 39(1).[41]

The "excuse" provisions of Article 44 do not preserve all of the buyer's remedies — only reduction of the price (Art. 50) and recovery of damages other than loss of profit (Art. 74). Consequently, a buyer who fails to give notice within a "reasonable time" (Art. 39(1)) may not require performance (Art. 46), avoid the contract (Arts. 49 and 73; *cf.* Arts. 75–76) or rely on the non-conformity as a basis for delaying the passage of risk of loss (Art. 70).[42]

In his 1986 Commentary on the Convention Professor Schlechtriem raises interesting questions concerning problems that may arise when a buyer qualifies for the limited "excuse" provided by Article 44.[43] Suppose that the seller would have been able to cure the lack of conformity (Arts. 37, 48) and thereby avoid damages if the buyer had notified the seller of the non-conformity within the "reasonable time" required by Article 39(1). Under these circumstances may the seller invoke Article 77 calling for measures to mitigate loss (§§416–419) *infra*) and thereby reduce the buyer's claim for damages? ***By itself, late notice excused under Article 44 should not trigger a reduction in damages under Article 77. If the notice was late because the buyer failed to comply with its Article 38 obligation to examine the goods "within as short a period as is practicable in the circumstances," however, Professor***

---

40. See Ingeborg Schwenzer, Art. 44 paras. 4–5, *in* Schlechtriem & Schwenzer, *CISG Commentary* (2nd English ed. 2005); UNCITRAL Digest Art. 44 paras. 3 & 6.

41. See Ingeborg Schwenzer, Art. 44 para. 7, *in* Schlechtriem & Schwenzer, *CISG Commentary* (2nd English ed. 2005). Courts in the United States have given consideration to the problems of the buyer in question in applying a notice provision (UCC 2–607(3)(a)) similar to Art. 39(1), even in the absence of an "excuse" provision like Art. 44. *White & Summers* §11–10 nn. 2 & 10.

42. See Ingeborg Schwenzer, Art. 44 para. 10, *in* Schlechtriem & Schwenzer, *CISG Commentary* (2nd English ed. 2005); UNCITRAL Digest Art. 44 para. 1. Barring the buyer from avoiding the contract when he fails to give notice within a "reasonable time" is important to prevent the buyer from speculating — *e.g.*, by invoking the breach and avoiding the contract after a drop in the market. *SR.16*, para. 57. *O.R.* 322, *Docy. Hist.* 543.

43. *Schlechtriem, 1986 Commentary* 71 and n.271.

Schlechtriem suggests a different result: he argues that "the failure to examine the goods . . . is not excusable on the basis of Article 44:" He also suggests that, despite Article 44, a seller might be able to reduce the buyer's damage claim or the amount of a price reduction by invoking Article 80, which provides that a party cannot "rely" on a breach to the extent it itself caused the breach. Finally, he suggests that excuse under Article 44 may not preclude a seller from claiming damages arising from the buyer's failure to meet its obligations to examine goods or give timely notice.

This writer sees force in the suggestion concerning mitigation of avoidable damages based on Article 77,[44] *although there is no reason to distinguish notice that is late because of a failure of timely examination: it is now settled that the Article 44 excuse is available to buyers who failed to meet their Article 38 obligation to examine goods.*[45] *But the suggestion that a seller can use Article 80 to limit (or even escape from) exposure to the remedies expressly preserved for a buyer under Article 44, or can claim damages for a buyer's late examination or notice despite the excuse provided by Article 44, is not supportable. Professor Schwenzer has advanced detailed and persuasive arguments against these positions.*[46] *The overarching reason to reject them is that they would undermine the hard-fought excuse provided by Article 44, and widen perceived divisions between developing and developed countries that uniform international sales law must bridge.*

A decision involving an Ugandan buyer's purchase of wholesale quantities of used shoes from a German seller[47] — *a decision already discussed (critically) in connection with Article 38 (see supra §252) — is a case study in how Article 44 should not be applied. The contract called for delivery "FOB Mombassa, Kenya." When the goods arrived*

---

44. See Ingeborg Schwenzer, Art. 44 paras. 11–14, *in* Schlechtriem & Schwenzer, *CISG Commentary* (2nd English ed. 2005).

45. See Ingeborg Schwenzer, Art. 44 para. 5a, *in* Schlechtriem & Schwenzer, *CISG Commentary* (2nd English ed. 2005); UNCITRAL Digest Art. 44 para. 2.

46. See Ingeborg Schwenzer, Art. 44 paras. 15–16, *in* Schlechtriem & Schwenzer, *CISG Commentary* (2nd English ed. 2005).

47. Landgericht Frankfurt, Germany, 11 April 2005, CLOUT case No. 775, English translation available at http://cisgw3.law.pace.edu/cases/050411g1.html. The editor of the current edition previously commented on this decision. See Harry M. Flechtner, *Funky Mussels, a Stolen Car, and Decrepit Used Shoes: Non-Conforming Goods and Notice Thereof under the United Nations Sales Convention* ("CISG"), 26 B.U. Int'l L.J. 1 (2008), draft available online in SSRN as University of Pittsburgh Legal Studies Research Paper No. 2008–21, http://ssrn.com/abstract=1144182.

in Mombassa the buyer transshipped them to their ultimate destination in Uganda. Almost immediately upon their arrival in Uganda several weeks later, the buyer examined the shoes and discovered that they were substantially below the quality standards stated in the contract — so much so, in fact, that Ugandan authorities refused to permit their importation and indicated the shoes should be destroyed for hygienic reasons. The court hearing the buyer's claim for a refund, however, ruled (improperly, as noted in the discussion in §252 supra) that the buyer should have examined the goods in Mombassa, and that its reasonable time to give notice under Article 39(1) began to run from that point. As a result, the court found that the buyer's notice that the goods were not conforming, which it gave the seller the day after discovering the shoes' condition upon their arrival in Uganda, came too late. The buyer, the court held, had forfeited all its rights with regard to the shoes (appallingly) substandard condition.

The buyer argued, however, that it had a "reasonable excuse" for giving late notice, and thus that it should at least be able to reduce the price for the goods — one of the remedies preserved under Article 44.[48] *The buyer noted that examining the goods in Mombassa would not only have required the considerable added expense of traveling to or arranging for examination at that port, but that such examination would also have triggered Kenyan customs duties; thus its decision to wait the relatively short time until the goods reached Uganda was "reasonable."*[49] *These are the very kind of special challenges facing traders from developing countries which inspired Article 44, and the situation was exactly the kind for which Article 44 was designed — a buyer from a developing country whose notice may have been delayed because of the special challenges it faced, and because of the relative lack of financial resources to deal with those challenges. The court in the used shoes case, however, was dismissive: "The Buyer also cannot reduce the price. The lack of a timely notice of non-conformity has not been supported by an acceptable excuse by the Buyer (Art. 44*

---

48. As noted above, the excuse provided by Art. 44 applies whether the buyer's failure to comply with the notice obligations of Art. 39(1) is caused by delay in giving notice, or delay in examining the goods.

49. As noted in the earlier discussion of this case (§252 *supra*), the buyer invoked the same facts to argue that, pursuant to Art. 38(3), it did not have "a reasonable opportunity for examination" of the goods until they arrived in Uganda.

CISG)."[50] This conclusory rejection ignores — indeed, it **seems** *to purposefully reject — the purposes of Article 44. With any luck, the decision will remain a curious outlier that, except as an object lesson in poor interpretation, has no influence on the interpretation of Article 44.*

The "excuse" provision of Article 44 was drafted hastily at a late stage of the Diplomatic Conference and consequently is not well integrated with the notice provisions developed in UNCITRAL, but the problems it poses for sellers can easily be overstated. The sanction imposed by Article 39(1) that the "buyer loses the right to rely on a lack of conformity of the goods" is severe and significant sanctions are preserved against even a buyer who qualifies for "excuse" under Article 44. Consequently buyers are not likely to refrain from making a prompt complaint when they receive defective goods.[51] In any event, an undue delay in asserting a defect will continue to militate against the credibility of the claim. Moreover, despite stern rules like Article 39(1), contracts often include precise rules on timely notification of defects; as we have seen (Art. 6, §74–81, *supra*) the Convention does not interfere with the parties" freedom to make their own rules.[52] *Even when parties have exercised that freedom, however, Article 44's tempering influence on strict notice requirements appears sensible, and the provision has been applied where the buyer failed to meet a deadline imposed in the contract.[53]*

50. Landgericht Frankfurt, Germany, 11 April 2005, CLOUT case No. 775, English translation available at http://cisgw3.law.pace.edu/cases/050411g1.html.

51. Under the many sales laws that follow the (U.K.) Sale of Goods Act a failure to give timely notice may bar the buyer from rejecting the goods but does not foreclose a claim for damages. The USA Uniform Sales Act (1906), however, deviated from the UK model by inserting a provision (§49) that was similar to CISG 39(1); this rule was preserved in UCC 2–607(3)(a). Under proposed revisions to Art. 2 of the UCC, however, §2–607(3)(a) would be amended to provide that a buyer who fails to give timely notice of breach loses its remedies only if the lack of notice caused the seller "prejudice." (Although the proposed revisions were approved the UCC's sponsoring organizations in 2003, at the time this is written no jurisdiction has yet enacted them.) For an intensive study of "cut-off" rules in their historical and comparative context see J. Reitz, 36 Am. J. Comp. L. 437 (1988) (Part I: CISG), 37 *id.* 247 (1989) (Part II).

52. Contract clauses containing unreasonably short notice periods may be held invalid under domestic law. See Art. 4(a), §64 *supra*.

53. Tribunal of International Commercial Arbitration at the Russian Federation Chamber of Commerce and Industry, Russia, 24 January 2000, CLOUT case No. 474, English translation available at http://cisgw3.law.pace.edu/cases/000124r1.html.

261.1   **E. Time Limits for Legal Proceedings — Statutes of "Limitation" or "Prescription"**

Distinct from timing rules related to notice requirements are limits on the time for instituting legal proceedings.[54] Such domestic rules on "Limitation" or "Prescription" vary widely on the length of time limits for legal action and also on whether these limits are rules of "procedure" or of "substantive" law — a difference in theory that leads to divergent rules of private international law. These difficulties led to an early decision by UNCITRAL to prepare uniform rules that were finalized in the Convention on the Limitation Period in the International Sale of Goods (New York, 1974).[55] The Convention entered into force on August 1, 1988 and (as of this writing) has been adopted by twenty-eight States.[56]

The 1974 Convention sets a general limitation period of four years (Art. 8) from "the date on which the claim accrues" (Art. 9–1). A claim for lack of conformity of goods accrues when "the goods are actually handed over to, or their tender is refused by, the buyer" (Art. 10–2).

The Limitation Convention (Art. 1–1) does "not affect" time limits for giving notice, such as those imposed by CISG 39 or 43, *supra*. Consequently, a buyer who fails to comply with these requirements for giving notice will have lost "the right to rely" on the provisions of CISG 35, 41 or 42 relating to defects in the goods or third-party claims even though the limitation period for instituting legal action has not expired. Conversely, a buyer who has promptly notified the seller may be barred from instituting judicial or arbitral proceedings after expiration of the four-year period provided by the 1974 Limitation Convention.

54. See Ingeborg Schwenzer, Art. 39 para. 28, *in* Schlechtriem & Schwenzer, *CISG Commentary* (2nd English ed. 2005); UNCITRAL Digest Art. 39 para. 24.

55. United Nations Conference on Prescription (Limitation) in the International Sale of Goods, Official Records (U.N. Doc. A/CONF. 63/16; UN Pubn. E. 74.V.8). See Smit, Convention on the Limitation Period: UNCITRAL's First Born, 23 Am. J. Comp. L. 337 (1975) (text of the Convention at 356); Knapp, 19 J. World Tr. L. 343 (1985); Sono, 35 La. L. Rev. 1127 (1975); Hill, 25 Texas Int. L.J. 1 (1990). Landfermann, 39 *Rabels Z* 253 (1975), Giardina, 1975 *Riv. Dir. Int. Pr. & Proc.* 465; Secretariat Commentary on the 1974 Convention, *UNCITRAL YB* Vol. 10, pp. 145–173.

56. The Limitations Convention has been adopted by the following States: Argentina, Belarus, Belgium, Bosnia & Herzogovina, Burundi, Cuba, Czech Republic, Dominican Republic, Egypt, Ghana, Guinea, Hungary, Liberia, Mexico, Moldova, Montenegro, Norway, Paraguay, Poland, Romania, Serbia, Slovakia, Slovenia, Uganda, Ukraine, USA, Uruguay, Zambia.

Jurisdictions that have not adopted the Limitation Convention and whose domestic limitations period for claims of lack of conformity is less than two years struggle to reconcile their prescription rules with the two-year notice period provided in Article 39(2). These jurisdictions have adopted a variety of solutions.[57] The situation illustrates the advantages of the Limitation Convention as a component of a uniform international sales law regime.

---

57. For a full discussion of this issue see Ingeborg Schwenzer, Art. 39 para. 29, *in* Schlechtriem & Schwenzer, *CISG Commentary* (2nd English ed. 2005). See also UNCITRAL Digest Art. 39 para. 24.

Article 41.
Third-Party Claims to Goods

262   **A. Scope of the Article: Buyer's Rights Against Seller**

One of the limits on the scope of the Convention is set by Article 4: "... this Convention ... is not concerned with ... (b) the effect which the contract may have on the property in the goods sold." Suppose that a third person claims to own goods that B purchased from S: The question whether the buyer is protected, as a *bona fide* purchaser, against that third-party claim is not governed by the Convention but is left to applicable domestic law.[1]

The Convention addresses this question: When the seller supplies goods that are subject to a third-party claim, what are the rights of the buyer *against the seller?* This question is treated in Article 41; related questions that arise when a third-party claim is "based on industrial property or other intellectual property" (e.g., a patent or copyright) are dealt with in Article 42, *infra* at §267.

Article 41[2]

The seller must deliver goods which are free from any right or claim of a third-party, unless the buyer agreed to take the goods subject to that right or claim. However, if such right or claim is based on industrial property or other intellectual property, the seller's obligation is governed by Article 42.

Under this article (as under Art. 35, §223 *supra*) the seller "must deliver" goods that meet the prescribed standard; the seller's knowledge of the defect is irrelevant. (Contrast Art. 42, §269 *infra*.)[3] The buyer's

---

1. See Ingeborg Schwenzer, Art. 41 para. 2, *in* Schlechtriem & Schwenzer, *CISG Commentary* (2nd English ed. 2005).

2. This article is substantially the same as Art. 39(1) of the 1978 Draft. *Cf. ULIS 52*, which was sharply criticized by the WG, III *YB* 90, *Docy. Hist.* 107, and by the *S-G*, IV *YB* 50–51, *Docy. Hist.* 127–128. Language like the first sentence of Art. 41 was approved at VI *YB* 72–73, *Docy. Hist.* 150–151. UNCITRAL: VIII *YB* 4–41, *Docy. Hist.* 333–334. DIPL. *CONF.*: *O.R.* 35–36, 324–328, 109–110, 159, 208, *Docy. Hist.* 425–426, 545–549, 681–683, 718, 743.

3. See Ingeborg Schwenzer, Art. 41 paras. 15–16, *in* Schlechtriem & Schwenzer, *CISG Commentary* (2nd English ed. 2005).

obligation to notify the seller of a third-party right or claim under Articles 41 and 42 is dealt with in Articles 43 and 44, *infra*.

264 ## B. The Contested Third-Party Claim

Example 41A. After Buyer received goods from Seller, Claimant brought an action to recover the goods from Buyer. Claimant asserted that it owned the goods, and Seller had never been the owner; hence under applicable law, Claimant argued, Seller could not transfer the property in the goods to the Buyer.[4] Buyer immediately informed Seller of the claim; Seller replied that Claimant's assertions were false. Claimant, however, brought legal proceedings to recover the goods. Buyer successfully defended the action but suffered losses of $5,000 because the litigation prevented the prompt use of the goods. In addition, Buyer had to pay $1,000 in legal fees which were not recoverable from Claimant. Has Buyer any redress against Seller?

266 ## (1) The Convention

The Convention provides that the seller has an obligation to deliver goods that are free from "any right *or claim* of a third-party." If Claimant had prevailed in its action and had recovered the goods from the Buyer, clearly Seller would have violated this obligation.[5] The language of Article 41 should also protect the normal expectation of a buyer that he is not purchasing a lawsuit.[6] In international sales, the third-party claim is likely to involve the domestic rule of the State where the seller

---

4. Similar problems would arise if Claimant asserted that it held a property interest in the goods to secure a $10,000 debt that Seller owed to Claimant. See Ingeborg Schwenzer, Art. 41 para. 4, *in* Schlechtriem & Schwenzer, *CISG Commentary* (2nd English ed. 2005).
5. See Ingeborg Schwenzer, Art. 41 paras. 3–7, *in* Schlechtriem & Schwenzer, *CISG Commentary* (2nd English ed. 2005).
6. See Ingeborg Schwenzer, Art. 41 paras. 3, 9–14, *in* Schlechtriem & Schwenzer, *CISG Commentary* (2nd English ed. 2005). For decisions on what constitutes a breach of Art. 41, see UNCITRAL Digest Art. 41 para. 2. For drafting history, see *Secretariat Commentary* Art. 39, para. 3, *O.R.* 36, *Docy. Hist.* 426, *but cf.* III *YB* 90, *Docy. Hist.* 107, para. 135 (claim meant *valid* claim); *contra* VI *YB* 73, *Docy. Hist.* 151. The reference in Art. 41 to "right or claim" is rendered, in the French version, as "*droit ou prétention*" and, in the Spanish, as "*derechos o pretensiones*." The requirement that the seller "*deliver* goods which *are* free . . ." could be read to exclude claims that are asserted subsequent to delivery; on the other hand, this language could be understood to refer to claims that relate to ownership as of the time of delivery.

has its place of business; it would often be difficult and costly for the buyer to evaluate and contest such a claim.

A third-party claim contested by the seller can present awkward problems but they can be minimized by careful handling. Article 43(1), *infra* at §271, requires the buyer to notify the seller of a third-party claim "within a reasonable time."[7] When the claim is petty, such as an encumbrance to secure a small debt owed by the seller, one could expect the seller quickly to remove the encumbrance. When the claim is frivolous, such as one based on an encumbrance for a debt that has been paid but not discharged in the public records, the seller could often immediately secure clarification of the record. When the defense of the claim calls for substantial litigation and the buyer desires to keep the goods, effective protection for the buyer would require the seller to take over the defense of the action.

The seller would be obliged to reimburse the buyer for any expense or loss caused by the claim.[8] But if the seller quickly and effectively resolves the problem, the seller's breach may not be "fundamental" (Art. 25, *supra* at §181) and the buyer could not avoid the contract (Art. 49(1)(a), *infra* at §301). But a third-party claim might well involve such detriment to the buyer that would authorize avoidance, and the threat of this drastic remedy should stimulate the seller to take effective action.[9] The seller's obligation to take over defense of the claim will be explored further in connection with Article 42, §270.1 *infra*.

7. The notice requirement of Art. 39(1), *supra* at §254, is confined to "lack of conformity of the goods."

8. Under Art. 45(1), *infra* at §275, the buyer may "claim damages as provided in Arts. 74–77" when "the seller fails to perform any of his obligations under the contract or this Convention." Art. 74, *infra* at §403, drafted in general terms, would include "loss" resulting from a breach under Art. 41. See *Dölle, Kommentar,* Art. 52 at 17–18, p. 334.

9. Article 37, *supra* at §244, empowers the seller, up to the date for delivery, to cure specified problems; the problems so specified, if read narrowly, might not extend to the removal of third-party claims. However, §245.1 *supra*, suggests that cure under Art. 37 should be extended by analogy to third-party claims. In any event, Art. 48(1) states that the seller may "even after the date for delivery, remedy at his own expense *any failure to perform his obligations . . .*" — subject to restrictions that need not apply to third-party claims. In any event, as was suggested under Art. 25, *supra* at §184, whether a breach is fundamental must be considered in the light of all the relevant facts, including the seller's offer promptly and effectively to solve the problem. (Under ULIS 52(1) a buyer could not avoid the contract pending the seller's response to a request to free the goods from the claim or to supply substitute goods.)

266 ## C. "Nullity" of the Contract under Domestic Law

Suppose under domestic law the sale of goods that the seller does not own is "void" and the buyer has different remedies than those provided by the Convention.[10] The CISG (Art. 4, §64 *supra*) states that "except as otherwise expressly provided in this Convention," it "is not concerned with (a) the *validity* of the contract...." Does it follow that, in an international sale otherwise subject to the Convention, a rule of domestic law that the sale is "void" will displace the rights given the buyer by Article 41 and the rules of the Convention that implement this provision?[11]

Examples of the Convention's rules in the area include: the buyer's obligation to notify the seller, Articles 43 and 44 (§§261, 271); the buyer's right under Article 46 (§§279–285) "to require performance by the seller of his obligations . . ." including its obligation under Article 41 to "deliver goods which are free from any right or claim of a third party" (e.g., by removing the defect in title or delivering substitute goods); the buyer's right under Article 45(1)(b), when the seller breaches any of his obligations, to "claim damages as provided in articles 74 to 77" — including the right under Article 74 to recover "the loss, including loss of profit, suffered as a consequence of the breach."

In light of this carefully-designed system for dealing with claims of ownership by a third-party, the suggestion for displacing the provisions of the Convention should be rejected. As we have seen in connection with Articles 4 and 5 (§§66, 72–73), *supra*), giving effect to the labels that are attached to domestic rules could undermine the rules of the Convention which Contracting States have engaged to apply in lieu of the diverse rules of domestic law. The purport of Article 4(a) is to prevent the Convention from *authorizing* transactions and contract provisions that domestic law *prohibits*. Here the Convention and domestic law have the same objective: to provide a remedy when the seller fails to transfer ownership to the buyer; however, the Convention provides a battery of remedies that are appropriate for international commercial

---

10. *Cf.* Civil Code of France Art. 1599: "The sale of the thing of another is void; it may give rise to damages when the buyer did not know that the thing belonged to another."

11. This question, of course, could arise only if, in the absence of the Convention, the above rule of domestic law would be applicable pursuant to rules of private international law.

transactions and, more particularly, are designed to achieve uniformity in international trade.[12]

The legal issue, of course, is the proper interpretation of the *Convention*. When Article 4(a) is read in the context of the Convention as a whole the statement in Article 4(a) that (except where otherwise expressly provided) the Convention "is *not concerned* with (a) the validity of the contract" cannot be read to mean that the Convention is not concerned with problems (like the seller's lack of title) that the Convention *does* directly address in Article 41.[13]

266.1   **Consent to Take Goods Subject to a Claim; Derogation**

The first sentence of Article 41 states that the seller is relieved of the obligation to deliver goods free of a third-party's right or claim if "the buyer agreed to take the goods subject to that right or claim." As Professor Schwenzer has noted, although such an agreement need not be express, it requires more than mere knowledge of the claim by the buyer.[14] It would be at least somewhat unusual for a buyer knowingly to agree to pay for goods that are subject to a third-party right or claim, particularly one that could strip the buyer of all rights to the goods. Thus, this exception to the seller's obligations under Article 41 must be applied carefully to avoid undermining what is usually the buyer's most fundamental expectation in a contract for sale — that it will, at the least, receive clear ownership of the goods.

The "agreement" exception in the first sentence of Article 41 focuses on the buyer's consent to take the goods subject to a specific claim or claims. When it applies, the seller remains liable to the buyer for third-party claims other than the one (or ones) to which the buyer consented. Under Article 6, the parties can also agree to exclude the seller's

---

12. Supporting this conclusion see Ingeborg Schwenzer, Art. 41 paras. 22–23, *in* Schlechtriem & Schwenzer, *CISG Commentary* (2nd English ed. 2005); Schlechtriem, 1986 Commentary 73 at n. 280.

13. The above principles apply to sales of goods that the seller owns but which are subject to an outstanding pledge or other security interest (a problem also governed by Art. 41) and to sales subject to Art. 42, §§267–270 *infra*, in which the seller transfers title to goods that are subject to an outstanding patent, trademark or copyright.

14. Ingeborg Schwenzer, Art. 41 para. 17, *in* Schlechtriem & Schwenzer, *CISG Commentary* (2nd English ed. 2005).

Article 41 obligations entirely, so that the seller would not be liable for any third-party claims.[15]

It would be quite unusual for a buyer to pay for goods while giving the seller blanket immunity should the buyer lose them to any third-party claimant. Thus the realistic construction of the parties' intent required by Article 8 again mandates care in finding an effective agreement to derogate from Article 41.[16]

Such an agreement, furthermore, remains subject to rules of validity in applicable non-CISG law, as provided in Article 4.[17] *Section 2–312 of the (U.S.) UCC provides that the "warranty of title"—the UCC equivalent of CISG Article 41—is excluded only by "specific language or by circumstances which give the buyer reason to know that the person selling does not claim title in himself or that he is purporting to sell only such right or title as he or a third person may have." These requirements have been quite strictly construed by the courts. Thus even contract language that expressly disclaimed the "warranty of title" has been held insufficient because it was "couched in negative terminology, expressing what the seller will not be liable for rather than what the buyer is or is not receiving."*[18]

It was argued earlier that the rules for disclaiming warranties of quality in §2–316 of the UCC should not apply in transactions governed by the Convention (see §230 supra). The same should presumably be true for the warranty of title disclaimer rules in UCC §2–312(2). There is a possibility, however, that the UCC rules on disclaiming the warranty of title (and equivalent provisions in other domestic laws) will be applied, as rules of validity, to attempts to derogate from Article 41 of the CISG. The disclaimer rules in UCC §2–316 which address warranties of quality are distinguishable: they are geared to the specific terminology and warranty system in the UCC, and thus were never intended to be applied under the CISG. The rules on disclaiming the warranty of title in UCC §2–312(2), in contrast, express a general principle—the expectation that the buyer will receive unencumbered

---

15. Under Art. 6 the parties can also, of course, agree merely to modify or limit the seller's obligations under Art. 41.

16. The Convention thus, ironically, provides twice for the parties'' power to derogate from Art. 41 — once in Art. 41 itself, and once in Art. 6 — even though (in the view of the editor of the current edition) this provision is one of the less-likely candidates for an actual agreement to derogate.

17. See Ingeborg Schwenzer, Art. 41 para. 19a, *in* Schlechtriem & Schwenzer, *CISG Commentary* (2nd English ed. 2005).

18. Sunseri v. RKO Stanley Warner Theatres, Inc. 374 A.2d 1342, 1344 (Pa. Super. 1977).

ownership of sold goods is so basic that the seller's obligation in that regard can only be excluded by a particularly specific and clear agreement.

That general principle, however, need not be imported into the CISG: under the rules of the Convention itself it can and should inform all analysis of attempts to exclude or substantially limit the seller's Article 41 obligations. An approach grounded on that general principle, which expresses a realistic view of the parties' likely intentions, is mandated by the Convention's rules on interpretation in Article 8. The Convention must be applied so that an agreement to derogate from the fundamental obligations stated in Article 41 is found only when such an unusual arrangement is clearly established. Only such an approach will ease the temptation to turn to non-uniform domestic law as a way of preventing what is, except in unusual cases, an injustice — requiring the buyer to pay in full for goods for which it does not receive good title.

Article 42.
Third-Party Claims Based on a Patent
or Other Intellectual Property

267 ## A. Infringement Claims in Multi-State Settings

In international trade, claims based on patents, copyrights and trademarks can generate problems of considerable complexity. *Article 42 of the Convention (set out infra at §269) attempts to address the intersection of these matters with sales law. The provision was drafted, however, before the "information age" and the "digital revolution" (as well as the legal responses to them) increased exponentially the complexity and importance of such issues.* The examination of Article 42 may be aided by first considering the following illustration:

Example 42A. Seller is located in State S and Buyer in State B. After Buyer purchased goods from Seller, Claimant notified Buyer that use or resale of the goods would infringe Claimant's patent rights.

In international trade the problem is complicated by the variety of geographical (and legal) settings in which claims based on industrial or other intellectual property may arise. Distinct problems arise in the four settings that follow:

(1) Buyer proposes to use or resell the goods in Seller's State (State S) and the infringement claim arises under a patent registered in that State.

(2) Buyer proposes to use or resell the goods in its State (State B) and the infringement claim is asserted under a patent registered in that State.

(3) Buyer proposes to use or resell the goods in a third State (State T) and the infringement claim is asserted under a patent registered in that State.

These situations involve an infringement claim based on a patent registered in the state of use or resale. Note that the patent on which Claimant relies may have been registered initially in some other State, but the patent may be recognized by the State of use or resale as a result of streamlined registration procedures provided for by treaty.[1]

---

1. See Ingeborg Schwenzer, Art. 42 para. 13, *in* Schlechtriem & Schwenzer, *CISG Commentary* (2nd English ed. 2005). For treaties providing for such streamlined procedures for registering intellectual property rights in multiple states, see, *e.g.*, International Convention for the Protection of Industrial Property, Paris 1883, and Lisbon Revision of 1958, 13 U.S.T. & D.I.A. T.I.A.S. No. 4931; Patent Cooperation Treaty of June 19, 1970, text (as currently amended) available in the website of the World Intellectual Property Organization

268   **B. Evolution of Article 42**

(1) The 1964 Sales Convention: ULIS

The 1964 Sales Convention (ULIS) did not expressly address these questions. Article 52 of ULIS (placed in a section entitled "Transfer of Property") gave the buyer protection where "the goods are subject to a right or claim of a third person." Although this language would appear to apply to a "right or claim" based on patents or other types of intellectual property and has been so construed,[2] the preparatory papers and Professor Tunc's commentary discuss this provision in terms of third-party *ownership* claims. In short, the 1964 uniform law did not clearly face problems of considerable importance and difficulty. Certainly the drafters of ULIS did not consider the problems that could arise (as in paragraph (3), *supra* at §267) if the buyer takes the goods to a third State (State T) and encounters difficulties under a patent registered only in that State.

269   ## (2) Legislative Process in UNCITRAL[3]

These problems were confronted at a late stage in UNCITRAL's work. In 1976 the Working Group tentatively excluded from the Convention problems arising from "rights or claims which relate to industrial or intellectual property or the like."[4] The Comments and proposals that were submitted to UNCITRAL's tenth session (1977) called for further attention to the problem[5] and a special working group was appointed to deal with the problem. A consensus developed that the ULIS approach was not adequate and that the problem was too

---

("WIPO") at http://www.wipo.int/pct/en/texts/articles/ atoc.htm; Madrid Agreement Concerning the International Registration of Marks of April 14, 1891, text (as currently amended) available in the website of WIPO at http://www.wipo.int/ madrid/en/legal_-texts/trtdocs_wo015.html.

2. See Ingeborg Schwenzer, Art. 42 para. 1, *in* Schlechtriem & Schwenzer, *CISG Commentary* (2nd English ed. 2005).

3. Compare Professor Schwenzer's account of the evolution of Art. 42 in Ingeborg Schwenzer, Art. 42 para. 2, *in* Schlechtriem & Schwenzer, *CISG Commentary* (2nd English ed. 2005).

4. *W/G 7*, Annex I (Art. 7(2)), VII *YB* 90.

5. *Rep. S-G*, "Analysis of Comments by Governments," Art. 7, paras. 4–7, VIII *YB* 147. These comments are reproduced in VIII *YB* 110 (Australia), 115 (Finland), 116 (F.R.G.), 120 (Norway), 130 (U.S.S.R.).

important to be left to diverse national rules and to the uncertainties of private international law.[6] A draft prepared during UNCITRAL's tenth session led to the following provision of the Convention:

Article 42[7]

(1) The seller must deliver goods which are free from any right or claim of a third party based on industrial property or other intellectual property, of which at the time of the conclusion of the contract the seller knew or could not have been unaware, provided that the right or claim is based on industrial property or other intellectual property:

> **(a) under the law of the State where the goods will be resold or otherwise used, if it was contemplated by the parties at the time of the conclusion of the contract that the goods would be resold or otherwise used in that State; or**

> **(b) in any other case, under the law of the State where the buyer has his place of business.**

(2) The obligation of the seller under the preceding paragraph does not extend to cases where:

> **(a) at the time of the conclusion of the contract the buyer knew or could not have been unaware of the right or claim; or**

> **(b) the right or claim results from the seller's compliance with technical drawings, designs, formulae or other such specifications furnished by the buyer.**

270   C. Responsibility of Seller

Article 42 attempts to protect a buyer's expectations in purchasing goods from being undermined by claims that the goods infringe another's intellectual property rights.[8] Article 42, like Article 41

---

6. *UNCITRAL X*, paras. 210–229, VII *YB* 40–41, *Docy. Hist.* 333–334. See also the Summary Records of this session of UNCITRAL, A/CN.9(X)/C.1, *SR.11*, paras. 32–33 (appointment of working group) and *SR.29, 30* and *32*.

7. Art. 42 is substantially the same as paragraphs (1) and (2) of Art. 40 of the 1978 Draft. The substance of paragraph (3) of the 1978 Draft, dealing with notice to the seller, became Art. 43(1), *infra*. For action at the Diplomatic Conference see *O.R.* 9, 36–37, 324–328, 427, 109–111, 159, 208, *Docy. Hist.* 386, 426–427, 398–399, 545–549, 648, 681–683, 718, 743.

8. For discussion of the kind of third-party claims covered by the phrase "industrial property or other intellectual property" in Art. 42 see Ingeborg Schwenzer, Art. 42 paras. 4–5, *in* Schlechtriem & Schwenzer, *CISG Commentary* (2nd English ed. 2005). For a broad

(§§264–266, *supra*), provides that the buyer is entitled to receive goods that "are free from any right or *claim* of a third-party." It thus protects the buyer from both rightful and contested claims.[9]

270.1   (1) Limitations on Seller's Obligations: Knowledge

The seller's responsibility is limited by this general rule: Under Article 42(1) the buyer is protected with respect to only those rights or claims of which "the seller knew or could not have been unaware" when the contract was concluded.[10] The seller's responsibility for defects in the goods under Article 35 (§§223–225 *supra*) and for third-party claims to the property under Article 41 (§262 *supra*) is subject to no comparable restriction: Under these articles the seller's lack of knowledge of the defect in the goods or of the third-party claim is irrelevant.

The phrase "could not have been unaware" in Article 42 seems to set a standard close to actual knowledge, in contrast to the phrase "ought to have known," which can imply a duty to inquire. (See the fuller discussion of these standards at §229, *supra*.) On the other hand, a duty of inquiry under Article 42 is suggested in the Secretariat Commentary, which states that the Seller is responsible for knowledge "of a patent application or grant which has been published in the country in question."[11] *Professor Schwenzer, who argues for such a (limited) duty of inquiry, notes that "if such a duty [to investigate at least registered intellectual property rights] is denied, liability for third*

---

definition of "intellectual property" see The Convention Establishing the World Intellectual Property Organization (1967), Art. 2(viii). See also R. Gadbaw & T. Richards, *Intellectual Property Rights* (1988); Ladas, *Patents, Trademarks and Related Rights, National and International Protection* (1975).

9. See Oberster Gerichtshof, Austria, 12 September 2006, CLOUT case No. 753, English translation available at http://cisgw3.law.pace.edu/cases/060912a3.html; Ingeborg Schwenzer, Art. 42 para. 6, *in* Schlechtriem & Schwenzer, *CISG Commentary* (2nd English ed. 2005).

10. This restriction on the seller's responsibility is criticized in Huber, 43 *Rabels Z* 413, 503 (1979). Under (U.S.A.) UCC 2–312(3) a merchant seller "warrants that the goods shall be delivered free of any rightful claim of any third person by way of infringement or the like": whether the seller knows of the claim is irrelevant.

11. Secretariat Commentary, comments on draft Art. 40 at para. 6, O.R. 37, *Docy. Hist.* 427. Perhaps this conclusion is based on a rule of "constructive knowledge" imposed by the statute or treaty. Compare *Schlechtriem, 1986 Commentary* 74: seller "must inform himself," but citing Huber for a much lighter standard. See also O.R. 78 (draft Art. 40 at §5), *Docy. Hist.* 399.

party intellectual property rights would be reduced to such an extent that it would cease to be of any practical importance."[12] *If (as seems proper) such a duty to investigate is found to exist, technical advances in searching for registered intellectual property rights, such as online patent searches, may have expanded the information of which a seller "could not have been unaware" while at the same time reducing at least some concerns over the burden such a duty imposes.*

270.2 Limitations on the Seller's Obligations: Locale of Claim

The protection that Article 42 affords to buyers is also restricted since the seller is only responsible for rights or claims that are based on the law of specified places.[13] Under paragraph (1)(a), if the parties contemplated that the goods would be resold or otherwise used in a specified State the seller may be responsible only for a right or claim asserted under the law of that State. If the transaction did not contemplate where the resale or other use would occur, under paragraph (1)(b) the seller may be responsible only for a right or claim asserted under the law of the State where buyer has its place of business. In the unusual (but possible) situation in which the parties contemplate that a foreign buyer will resell or otherwise use the goods in the seller's State, limiting the seller's responsibility to claims of which "the seller *knew or could not be unaware*" seems surprising and, in view of the unusual nature of the case, may have been unintended.

International agreements in the intellectual property realm may *de facto* have expanded the seller's obligations *qua* the locale of third-party intellectual property claims. The European Patent Convention,[14] for example, creates a single procedure for acquiring a bundle of national patents from European jurisdictions. This increases the likelihood that a patent recognized under the law of one European State will also be recognized under the laws of another.

---

12. Ingeborg Schwenzer, Art. 42 para. 14, *in* Schlechtriem & Schwenzer, *CISG Commentary* (2nd English ed. 2005).

13. For further discussion of this territorial limitation, see Ingeborg Schwenzer, Art. 42 paras. 10–13, *in* Schlechtriem & Schwenzer, *CISG Commentary* (2nd English ed. 2005).

14. Convention on the Grant of European Patents of 5 October 1973, text (as currently amended) available through the website of the European Patent Office, http://www.epo.org/about-us/publications/procedure/convention.html (pdf version of text available at http://documents.epo.org/projects/babylon/eponet.nsf/0/b8be2484d06e90dec1257258003c8a3c/$FILE/epc_2006_e-bookmarks.pdf).

270.3 Limitations on the Seller's Obligations: Article 42(2)

Paragraph (2) adds further restrictions on the seller's Article 42 obligations. Subparagraph (2)(a), denying protection to a buyer "who knew or could not have been unaware of the right or claim," is similar to Article 35(3), *supra* at §222.[15] Sub-paragraph (2)(b), relieving the seller of responsibility where the buyer furnishes the specifications, is of limited scope. Where a third-party asserts an infringement claim based on specifications dictated by the buyer, of course, the buyer rather than the seller should be responsible. Indeed, the seller can complain if it must incur liability and/or expenses as a result. Under U.S. domestic sales law, which contains a restriction similar to Article 42(2)(b), the seller would have a damages claim against the buyer for such losses.[16] No such claim is expressly provided for in Article 42(2)(b), but it has been argued that one can be implied.[17]

270.4 Buyer's Remedies

Litigation problems in connection with contested ownership claims (Art. 41) were considered *supra* at §266. Similar problems are generated by third-party claims based on patents or other types of intellectual property. As has been noted (§266, *supra*), when the buyer does not find it desirable or practicable to escape from the difficulty by avoiding the contract, the only effective protection for the buyer will be for the seller to take over the responsibility and expense of resisting the claim. The seller may voluntarily do this because of its interest in the further salability of its product. If the seller should fail to respond the buyer will need to consider the resources provided by the remedial provisions of the Convention and by domestic procedural law.

---

15. For further discussion of Art. 42(2)(a), see Oberster Gerichtshof, Austria, 12 September 2006, CLOUT case No. 753, English translation available at http://cisgw3.law.pace.edu/cases/060912a3.html (account of judgment of court of first instance); Cour d'appel de Colmar, 13 November 2002, CLOUT case No. 491, English translation available at http://cisgw3.law.pace.edu/cases/021113f1.html; Cour de Cassation, France, 19 March 2002, CLOUT case No. 479, English translation available at http://cisgw3.law.pace.edu/cases/020319f1.html; Ingeborg Schwenzer, Art. 42 paras. 16–18, *in* Schlechtriem & Schwenzer, *CISG Commentary* (2nd English ed. 2005).

16. UCC §2–312(3) provides, "a buyer who furnishes specifications to the seller must hold the seller harmless against any such claim which arises out of compliance with the specifications."

17. See Ingeborg Schwenzer, Art. 42 paras. 22–23, *in* Schlechtriem & Schwenzer, *CISG Commentary* (2nd English ed. 2005).

A strong premise for effective legal action is provided by CISG 46(1): "The buyer *may require performance* by the seller of his obligations. . . ." As was noted earlier (§266, *supra*), vindication of the buyer's right to protection from third-party claims may require defense of the claim by the seller. The buyer would hope that the seller has sufficient commercial contacts with the State of the *forum* in which the third-party claim is brought so that this *forum* has jurisdiction to require the seller to defend the action. If jurisdiction may not be based on such contacts the buyer will wish to explore whether the *forum* has rules like those developed by common-law courts to deal with similar problems presented by the large number of separate jurisdictions in the United States.[18] This common-law procedure was broadened and codified by the Uniform Commercial Code, Section 2–607:

> (5) Where the buyer is sued for breach of a warranty or other obligation for which his seller is answerable over
> (a) he may give his seller written notice of the litigation. If the notice states that the seller may come in and defend and that if the seller does not do so he will be bound in any action against him by his buyer by any determination of fact common to the two litigations, then unless the seller after seasonable receipt of the notice does not come in and defend he is so bound.
> (b) if the claim is one for infringement or the like (subsection (3) of Section 2–312) the original seller may demand in writing that his buyer turn over to him control of the litigation including settlement or else be barred from any remedy over and if he also agrees to bear all expense and to satisfy any adverse judgment, then unless the buyer after seasonable receipt of the demand does turn over control the buyer is so barred.

270.5 Contractual Derogation and Modification

A statutory provision of reasonable length, particularly one drafted before the flowering of the revolution in information technology, can scarcely deal adequately with claims based on the various types of industrial or intellectual property in all of the legal settings that may arise in an international sale. In important transactions in which third-party claims are possible, the buyer should insist on contract provisions that clearly state the protection that the seller provides in the case of third-party claims (for the limitations on this protection see §270,

18. These rules, called "vouching in the warrantor" were developed at an early day to cope with jurisdictional problems arising from the liability of prior parties to a negotiable (money) instrument, such as the liability of the maker of a note to an endorser who was sued by a holder of the instrument. See *White & Summers* §9–12 at note 12, citing S. Williston, Contracts §980 (ed. 1964).

supra), including the responsibility to defend (or "hold the buyer harmless" from) such claims. *Article 42, drafted during the 1970's, may not adequately reflect the role that intellectual property plays in modern commerce. A buyer understandably objects to paying the full price for goods that, because of intellectual property issues, it cannot use or resell as desired. A seller, equally plausibly, fears responsibility for knowing of intellectual property rights everywhere the goods could end up. The parties are the best judge of whether, and how, the terms of Article 42 should be adjusted to reflect a proper balance between these competing interests.*

Article 43.
Notice of Third-Party Claim

271   Article 39 required the buyer to notify the seller of "a lack of conformity of the goods." (See Arts. 39, 40 and 44, *supra* at §256.) Under
Article 43 the buyer must also notify the seller of third-party claims for
which the seller may be responsible under Articles 41 and 42, *supra.*

Article 43[1]

**(1) The buyer loses the right to rely on the provisions of article 41
or article 42 if he does not give notice to the seller specifying the
nature of the right or claim of the third party within a reasonable
time after he has become aware or ought to have become aware of
the right or claim.**

**(2) The seller is not entitled to rely on the provisions of the pre-
ceding paragraph is he knew of the right or claim of the third party
and the nature of it.**

The notice requirement under paragraph (1) is comparable to the
"reasonable time" notice requirement in Article 39(1).[2] *It is thus
sensible to look to the interpretation of Article 39(1), which has
been applied in many decisions, for guidance in interpreting the rel-
atively-rarely invoked Article 43.*[3] Article 43 contains nothing comparable to the two-year limit for notice set in Article 39(2).

*The Article 43(1) "reasonable time" standard, like the one in Article
39(1) (see §257.1, supra), has sometimes been applied with unnecessary (and counter-productive) strictness.*[4] *This is quite unfortunate*

---

1. Paragraph (1) of this article is based on Arts. 39(2) and 40(3) of the 1978 Draft Convention.
Cf. ULIS 52(1), summarized under Art. 41, *supra* at §266 n. 9.

2. See Ingeborg Schwenzer, Art. 43 paras. 2–3 & 5, *in* Schlechtriem & Schwenzer, *CISG
Commentary* (2nd English ed. 2005).

3. See UNCITRAL Digest Art. 43 para. 2; Harry M. Flechtner, *Funky Mussels, a Stolen Car,
and Decrepit Used Shoes: Non-Conforming Goods and Notice Thereof under the United
Nations Sales Convention ("CISG"),* 26 B.U. Int'l L.J. 1 (2008), draft available online in
SSRN as University of Pittsburgh Legal Studies Research Paper No. 2008–16, http://
ssrn.com/abstract= 1144182.

4. See Harry M. Flechtner, *Funky Mussels, a Stolen Car, and Decrepit Used Shoes: Non-
Conforming Goods and Notice Thereof under the United Nations Sales Convention
("CISG"),* 26 B.U. Int'l L.J. 1 (2008), draft available online in SSRN as University of
Pittsburgh Legal Studies Research Paper No. 2008–16, http://ssrn.com/abstract=1144182

because failure to comply with Article 43(1) carries the same severe sanction for the buyer as failure to meet the notice obligations imposed by Article 39 — loss of "the right to rely on" the seller's breach for which notice should have been given. In other words, a buyer who fails to give the notice required by Article 43 loses all remedies for a seller's breach of its obligations under Articles 41 or 42.[5] If the buyer has a "reasonable excuse" for failing to satisfy the Article 43 notice requirement, however, Article 44 preserves some (but not all) of the buyer's remedies. [Article 44, "Excuse for Failure to Notify," is discussed with Articles 39 and 40, *supra* §261 *et. seq.*).]

Paragraph (2) dispenses with the notice requirement if the seller "knew" of the right or claim. This corresponds to Article 40, except that the present article omits the phrase "or could not have been unaware and which he did not disclose to the buyer." *Thus it is clear that only the seller's actual knowledge of a claim will trigger this exception from the notice requirement[6] — a standard that presents evidentiary challenges to a buyer seeking to invoke Article 43(2). The evident purpose of the exception is to dispense with the Article 43(1) notice requirement where the seller does not need such notice; knowledge that the seller acquires by the end of the "reasonable time" for the buyer to give notice should, therefore, trigger the exception.[7]* Article 43(2) needs to be considered in relation to Article 41, which denies protection to a buyer who "agreed to take the goods subject to" a third-party claim of ownership, and also Article 42(2)(a) which denies protection with respect to third-party claims based on intellectual property where the buyer "knew or could not have been unaware of the right or claim."

(critiquing the decision of the Bundesgerichtshof, Germany, 11 January 2006, English translation available at http:// cisgw3.law.pace.edu/cases/060111g1.html).

5. See Ingeborg Schwenzer, Art. 43 para. 8, *in* Schlechtriem & Schwenzer, *CISG Commentary* (2nd English ed. 2005).

6. See Ingeborg Schwenzer, Art. 43 paras. 9–10, *in* Schlechtriem & Schwenzer, *CISG Commentary* (2nd English ed. 2005).

7. See Ingeborg Schwenzer, Art. 43 para. 11, *in* Schlechtriem & Schwenzer, *CISG Commentary* (2nd English ed. 2005).

SECTION III.

REMEDIES FOR BREACH OF CONTRACT BY THE SELLER
(Articles 45–52)

INTRODUCTION TO SECTION III

272 **A. A Bird's Eye View of the Section**

The first two sections of Chapter II (Arts. 30–44) defined the seller's duties; this section (Arts. 45–52) sets forth remedies given the buyer when the seller fails to perform those duties.

Section III opens (Art. 45) with a general overview of the remedial system and indicates the relationship of different remedies to each other. Article 46 states the buyer's right to compel performance by the seller.

Three articles (Arts. 47–49) address the buyer's right to "avoid" the contract, a concept that includes the rejection of goods. Article 47 empowers the buyer to fix an additional final period for the seller's delivery of the goods — a step that clarifies the buyer's right to avoid the contract for delay in delivery. Article 48 empowers the seller to "cure" defects in performance and thus forestall avoidance of the contract. Article 49 states the grounds on which the buyer may avoid the contract.

The section closes with three articles dealing with special situations — buyer's right to reduce the price (Art. 50), the applicability of remedies to only part of the goods (Art. 51) and deliveries that are early or excessive in quantity (Art. 52).

273 **B. Relationship to Other Parts of the Convention**

Section III of the present chapter provides remedies that apply only to breach by the seller; Section III of Chapter III (Arts. 60–65) provides comparable remedies for breach by the buyer. These two sections are supplemented by remedial provision in Chapter V that apply to both parties — e.g., anticipatory breach (Sec. I), the measurement of damages, and interest (Secs. II and III), "exemption" from damages (Sec. IV) and the effects of avoidance of the contract (Sec. V).

274 C. The Remedial System of ULIS: Criticism and Reform

Among the features of the 1964 Sales Convention (ULIS) that stood in the way of widespread adoption were length and complexity — problems that resulted primarily from fragmenting the rules on remedies for breach. For example, performance by the seller was divided into five categories and a separate remedial system was provided for each. This approach was designed to make the remedial system clear but the distinctions between the five categories of performance were so artificial that the system produced ambiguity, complexity and unnecessary length.

Some of the delegates to the 1964 Hague Conference (including the present writer) were concerned lest the complexity of the rules on remedies would stand in the way of adoption of the 1964 Convention but it was not feasible to recast the basic structure of the law during the three-week diplomatic conference.[1]

UNCITRAL was able to deal with this question. A report of the Secretary-General analyzed the problems that resulted from this fragmentation and proposed a plan for a unified remedial system which the Working Group implemented — a step that simplified the law and reduced its length by one-fourth.[2] In addition, a unified remedial system strengthened the Convention's unitary approach centering on the contract. (See the Overview, Ch. 2, *supra* at §24.)

---

1. Honnold, ULIS: The Hague Convention of 1964, 30 Law & Contemp. Pr. 326 at 342–343 (1965). Specific instances of the fragmentation and duplication of ULIS's provisions dealing with remedies of ULIS appear in the comments on Arts. 46 and 47, *infra* at §§279–291. On the fragmentation of remedies in German law see *Zweigert & Kotz II (1987)* 179–186. Unification of remedies was recommended in Rabel, A Specimen of Comparative Law: The Main Remedies for the Seller's Breach of Warranty, 22 Rev. Jur. Univ. Puerto Rico 167, 191 (1953).

2. *Rep. S-G* "Obligation of the Seller," paras. 27 *et seq.*, 162–177, IV YB 40–60, *Docy. Hist.* 117–137; *W/G 4*, paras. 79–149, IV YB 67–73, *Docy. Hist.* 145–152; *Rep. S-G* "Pending Questions with respect to the Revised ULIS," paras. 83–85, VI YB 97, *Docy. Hist.* 222. On the increased clarity resulting from UNCITRAL's revision of the system of remedies see Huber, 43 *Rabels Z* 413, 518 (1979).

Article 45.
A Round-up of Remedies Available to Buyer

275   Article 45 sums up the remedies granted to the buyer in various parts of the Convention and indicates the relationship between them. Article 61 is a parallel provision focusing on the remedies available to an aggrieved seller.

Article 45[1]

(1) If the seller fails to perform any of his obligations under the contract or this Convention, the buyer may:
(a) exercise the rights provided in articles 46 to 52;
(b) claim damages as provided in articles 74 to 77.
(2) The buyer is not deprived of any right he may have to claim damages by exercising his right to other remedies.
(3) No period of grace may be granted to the seller by a court or arbitral tribunal when the buyer resorts to a remedy for breach of contract.

276 A. The Range of Remedies

Paragraph (1)(a) of Article 45 draws attention to the buyer's remedies that appear in this Section of the Convention. Paragraph (1)(b) makes available to an aggrieved buyer the rules on damages (applicable to both parties) that appear in Chapter V.[2]

Paragraph 1 serves as a useful index to the Convention's remedial provisions but it does a bit more. The opening language: "If the seller *fails to perform any of his obligations under the contract and this Convention, the buyer may . . .*" has legal bite. Some of the cited articles do not expressly state that they are available for breach; Articles 74–77 state how damages are to be measured but do not expressly state that damages

---

1. This article is the same as Art. 41 of the 1978 Draft. The corresponding provisions of ULIS are scattered among Arts. 24, 41, 51. 52 and 55; see the Introduction of Section III, *supra* at §272.
2. See Markus Müller-Chen, Art. 45 para. 1, *in* Schlechtriem & Schwenzer, *CISG Commentary* (2nd English ed. 2005); UNCITRAL Digest Art. 45 paras. 1, 6 & 8.

are to be awarded. Article 45 also emphasizes the unitary approach and strength of the remedies for breach of contract. (See Arts. 30 and 31, *supra* at §206 and §210.)

This approach is emphasized by paragraph (1)(b), which announces a principle that is more important than may be evident at first sight: the buyer may "claim damages" if the seller "fails to perform any of his obligations under the contract or this Convention." By this language the Convention rejects the view that one who fails to perform his contract is not responsible in damages unless he has been negligent[3] — an approach with an uneasy history in domestic law. Some legal systems that have espoused this doctrine have seen the principle become eroded and unclear. Other legal systems reject the "negligence" principle. In preparing uniform rules for international trade it was important to make a clear choice among these divergent approaches; that choice is expressed in the above-quoted language of Article 45(1)(b).[4]

277   B. Cumulation v. "Election" of Remedies

(1) Loss of the Right to Recover Damages

In domestic law the question whether recourse to one remedy excludes others has also been haunted by confusion. Case law and statutory rules in the common-law world at an early stage denied the buyer compensation for damages if it rescinded the contract — e.g., by requiring the seller to take back defective goods. This approach may have been useful to defeat "rescission" (or rejection) based on trivial grounds. But when the seller's breach was serious, the buyer had to choose between forfeiting the right to damages or bearing the burden of disposing of seriously defective goods — a choice that in some cases pressed towards the rejection of goods which the buyer could salvage more efficiently

---

3. See Markus Müller-Chen, Art. 45 paras. 5 & 8, *in* Schlechtriem & Schwenzer, *CISG Commentary* (2nd English ed. 2005); UNCITRAL Digest Art. 45 para. 7.

4. Rabel, A Specimen of Comparative Law: The Main Remedies for the Seller's Breach of Warranty, 22 Revista Jur. Univ. of RR. 167, 180–188 (1953): The confusions and exceptions inherent in the "fault" principle prevented its use in unification since "straight-lined rules are necessary to a uniform law"; see also 1952 writing by Rabel (in German) cited by Will in *B-B Commentary* 330; Zweigert, Aspects of the German Law of Sale, in *Comp. Sales (I.C.L.Q.)* 1, 3–4 (damage liability without fault, although inconsistent with German law, is more appropriate for international trade); Houin, Sale of Goods in French Law, *id.* 16, 26.

than a distant seller. The early rules imposing such choices have been eroded or abandoned.[5]

The Convention's approach is stated in paragraph (2) of Article 45: "The buyer is not deprived of any right he may have to claim damages by exercising his right to other remedies." Thus, a buyer who requires the seller to perform (Art. 46) may also recover damages (Art. 74) for the loss resulting from the delay or other deficiency in the seller's performance.[6] Similarly, a buyer who avoids the contract (Art. 49) and thus rejects delivered goods (Art. 81) may also claim damages (Art. 74) for "the loss suffered as a consequence of the breach."[7]

278   C. Grace Period Granted by Tribunal

Article 45(3) (and a parallel provision in Article 61(3)) bars recourse to tribunals for a "period of grace" for performance. Judicial intervention to provide a "period of grace," available in some jurisdictions,[8] was rejected as impractical for international trade.[9] In the Convention protection against destruction of the contract on insubstantial grounds is provided by the opportunity to "cure" defects (Arts. 34, 37, 48) and by rules governing avoidance of the contract (Arts. 49, 64). See also Article 51 (avoidance as to the non-conforming part of a delivery).

5. For developments in English law see Art. 81, *infra* at n. 2. The choice imposed by the (U.S.A.) Uniform Sales Act (1906) §69 was overturned by UCC 2–711(1). The conflicting interests and commercial practices are discussed in Honnold, *Buyer's Right of Rejection, A Study in the Impact of Codification Upon a Commercial Problem*, 97 U. Pa. L. Rev. 457 (1947). For conflicts among European legal systems see Will, in *B-B Commentary* 331.
6. See Markus Müller-Chen, Art. 45 paras. 25–28, *in* Schlechtriem & Schwenzer, *CISG Commentary* (2nd English ed. 2005); UNCITRAL Digest Art. 45 para. 10. For a detailed discussion of when a buyer can change its choice of a remedy, see Markus Müller-Chen, Art. 45 paras. 14–21, *in* Schlechtriem & Schwenzer, *CISG Commentary* (2nd English ed. 2005).
7. This general rule preserving the right to damages on avoidance is reinforced by the rules on damage measurement in Arts. 75 and 76. The seller's right to damages is protected by Art. 61(2), which parallels Art. 45(2). On the other hand, the right to compel performance (Arts. 46, 62) and to avoid the contract (Arts. 49, 64) may be lost by action that is inconsistent with these special remedies. See Arts. 46(1) and 62, *infra* (specific performance) and Arts. 48(2), 49(2), 63(2) and 64(2), *infra* (avoidance).
8. On French rules allowing a *délai de grâce*, see *Treitel, Remedies (Int. Enc.)* §§147–148; *Treitel, Remedies (1988)* 323, 331–332 (other legal systems); *Zweigert & Kotz II (1987)* 187. For rejection of this procedure even in legal systems that are influenced by French law see Will, in *B-B Commentary* 332.
9. See Markus Müller-Chen, Art. 45 para. 29, *in* Schlechtriem & Schwenzer, *CISG Commentary* (2nd English ed. 2005).

Article 46.
Buyer's Right to Compel Performance

279　　As we have seen (Art. 28, *supra* at §196), domestic legal systems follow varying practices concerning "requiring performance" (in common-law parlance, "specific performance"). The result has been a series of delicate adjustments and compromises. We have already seen a concession to domestic practice in Article 28 which carves out an exception from the right to "require performance" that is given to the buyer in Article 46 and to the seller in Article 62. The general rule on the buyer's right to require performance is as follows:

Article 46[1]

(1) The buyer may require performance by the seller of his obligations unless the buyer has resorted to a remedy which is inconsistent with this requirement.

(2) If the goods do not conform with the contract, the buyer may require delivery of substitute goods only if the lack of conformity constitutes a fundamental breach of contract and a request for substitute goods is made either in conjunction with notice given under article 39 or within a reasonable time thereafter.

(3) If the goods do not conform with the contract, the buyer may require the seller to remedy the lack of conformity by repair, unless this is unreasonable having regard to all the circumstances. A request for repair must be made either in conjunction with notice given under article 39 or within a reasonable time thereafter.

---

1. Paragraphs (1) and (2) of Art. 46 are the same as Art. 42 of the 1978 Draft. Paragraph (3) was added at the Diplomatic Conference. ULIS gave the buyer broad grounds to require performance by the seller in Arts. 24(1)(a) (date and place of delivery), 26(1) and 27(1) (date of delivery); 30(1) and 31 (place for delivery); 41(1)(a) (non-conformity of goods); 42 (remedying defects, delivering goods or missing parts); 55(2) (other obligations). However, Art. 25 of ULIS barred specific performance by the buyer when "it is a conformity with usage and reasonably possible for the buyer to purchase goods to replace those to which the contract relates" and Art. 61(2) similarly restricted the seller's recovery of the price. In addition, ULIS 16 and Art. VII(1) of the 1964 Convention (like Art. 28 of the 1980 Convention) deferred to rules of the forum that limited the remedy of specific performance.

280　A. The General Rule for "Requiring" Performance

Paragraph (1) of Article 46 lays down the general rule that the buyer may "*require* performance" by the seller; the seller's package of remedies (Ch. III, Sec. III) has a parallel rule (Art. 62) that the seller may "*require* the buyer to pay the price." Both articles reflect the principle, embedded in civil law theory, that an aggrieved party may "require" the other party specifically to perform its contractual obligations.[2]

The rule of paragraph (1) that the buyer may require the seller to perform its "obligations" may be invoked in a wide variety of circumstances. The most common example is when the seller fails to procure or produce the goods or to deliver them at the place (Art. 31) or date (Art. 33) provided by the contract. In addition, subject to restrictions stated in Article 46(1) & (2) (§§283–284 *infra*), a buyer may require the seller to deliver goods that are in conformity with the contract (Art. 35). Under Article 46(1) the seller may also require the seller to perform its obligations under Articles 41 and 42 to deliver goods free from any right or claim of a third party; we have considered (§270.1 *supra*) the use of Article 46 to require the seller to remove such claims or to defend them on behalf of the buyer. It is not possible to itemize all of the applications of Article 46 (or of the seller's parallel remedy under Article 62) since these provisions apply generally to the parties" "obligations" under the Convention and the contract (Arts. 6, 30, 53).

281　B. The Concession to the Rules of the Forum: Article 28

Article 28, *supra* at §194, states that even though the Convention's general rules provide that a "party is entitled to require performance," a court "is not bound to enter a judgment for specific performance unless the court would do so under its own law in respect of similar contracts of sale not governed by this Convention." As was noted under Article 28 (§§191, 195, *supra*), this concession to the procedures of the *forum* was granted by ULIS (1964) in response to the objection that common-law systems compelled ("specific") performance only when alternative remedies (e.g., damages) were not adequate. Comparative research

---

2. See Principles of European Contract Law art. 9:102 Comment B and Note 1. Dawson, *Specific Performance in France and Germany*, 57 Mich. L. Rev. 495 (1959); *Treitel, Remedies (Int. Enc.)* §9; *Treitel, Remedies (1988)* Ch. III; *Benjamin* §§1415–1421; Farnsworth, Damages and Specific Relief, *AJCL UNCITRAL Symposium* 247.

also revealed that some civil law systems would not always compel performance by the coercive measures, such as imprisonment for contempt, that may be available in "common-law" systems; as a consequence flexibility based on Article 28 is not confined to common-law jurisdictions.[3]

281.1   **(a) Requiring Performance by the Seller at Common Law.**
"Common-law" restrictions on requiring (specific) performances of sellers" obligations are sometimes exaggerated. It is true that common-law courts will not ordinarily compel a seller to deliver goods that the buyer can readily acquire; common examples are standard raw materials — wheat, cotton or the like. In these cases the courts usually find that the buyer's only loss is the added cost of purchasing the goods — a loss that can readily be ascertained and compensated by awarding damages. However, if substitute goods cannot readily be obtained because of shortages or their unique character the buyer's loss may not be readily measured or compensated by a damage award.[4] Other examples include a seller's repudiation of a long-term contract; in this and similar situations the buyer's loss may be difficult to ascertain. In these and many other situations where damages do not fully compensate the buyer one may expect a favorable response to an action to require ("specific") performance in common-law jurisdictions.[5]

It is easy to exaggerate the differences between civil law and common-law attitudes towards compelled performance as a remedy. Even in civil law jurisdictions the right to require performance is subject to restrictions that in practice significantly narrow the differences between the common law and civil law approaches.[6] *The drafters of the Principles of European Contract Law have declared: "The basic*

3. See Principles of European Contract Law art. 9:102 Comment B and Note 3(a).

4. UCC Art. 2–716(1), for example, provides that a buyer can obtain an order of specific performance "where the goods are unique or in other proper circumstances." Official Comment 2 to this provision states, "inability to cover" is strong evidence of "other proper circumstances."

5. The above examples only suggest judicial responses in jurisdictions with which the writer is familiar. See also D. Dobbs, Remedies §12.18, pp. 884–886 (1973); *White & Summers* §6–6; *Farnsworth, Contracts* 827–831; *Benjamin* §§1417–1421. As was noted *supra* at §270.1, on requiring the seller to take steps to remove or defend third-party claims to the goods, the inadequacy of damages could be expected to invoke specific relief in a common-law jurisdiction. There are fewer situations in which a common-law court would find that coercing a buyer to accept and pay for the goods would be justified by the inadequacy of a money judgment. See Art. 62, §§345–349 *infra*.

6. See Principles of European Contract Law art. 9:102 Comment B and Note 3.

differences between common law and civil law [with regard to specific performance] are of theoretical rather than practical importance." That assertion is supported by the small number of cases in which aggrieved buyers have sought to compel a seller to perform under Article 46,[7] and the miniscule number in which domestic law restrictions on specific performance have been invoked via Article 28 (see supra §199). Indeed, the editor of the current edition has been unable to locate a single decision in which a buyer has sought to compel performance under Article 46 and been denied by a court on the basis of domestic rules invoked via Article 28.[8]

The international specific performance rules found in the UNIDROIT Principles of International Commercial Contracts (Article 7.2.2) and the Principles of European Contract Law (Article 9:102), which incorporate consideration of both the common law and the civil law approaches, would seldom produce different results than under U.S. domestic law (U.C.C. §2–716(1)). The editor of the current edition has suggested that U.S. courts should promote the cause of uniform international sales law by following the rule of the UNIDROIT Principles in exercising the discretion granted in Article 28 to deny specific performance.[9] Experience has show that, for practical

---

7. "Despite its importance, the right to require performance has not been the subject of much case law. In practice other remedies — in particular the right to claim damages — are preferred." UNCITRAL Digest Art. 46 para. 4.

8. Two reported arbitral awards have denied a buyer's request for specific performance. In one, the tribunal refused the remedy by invoking the specific performance rule in the UNIDROIT Principles of International Commercial Contracts (Art. 7.2.2) rather than domestic law. International Arbitration Court of the Chamber of Commerce and Industry of the Russian Federation, 30 January 2007, English abstract available in UNILEX at http://www.unilex.info/case.cfm?pid=1&do=case&id=1333&step=Abstract. In the other decision it does not appear that Art. 28 of the Convention was involved. Arbitration Tribunal of the Zurich Chamber of Commerce, Switzerland, 31 May 1996, English text available at http://cisgw3.law.pace.edu/cases/960531s1.html. See also the commentary on this case in Nayiri Boghossian, *A Comparative Study of Specific Performance Provisions in the United Nations Convention on Contracts for the International Sale of Goods*, in Pace Review of the Convention on Contracts for the International Sale of Goods 3, 71 (1999), available at http://cisgw3.law.pace.edu/cisg/biblio/boghossian.html. In the one reported U.S. decision where the buyer sought specific performance under Art. 46, the court found that the buyer would have been entitled to the remedy under U.S. domestic law, and thus that Art. 28 did not justify denying the award. Magellan Int'l Corp. v. Salzgitter Handel, GmbH, 76 Fed. Supp. 2d 919 (U.S. Dist. Ct. N. Dist Ill., 7 December 1999), available at http://cisgw3.law.pace.edu/cases/991207u1.html.

9. Harry M. Flechtner, *The CISG's Impact on International Unification Efforts: The UNIDROIT Principles of International Commercial Contracts and the Principles of*

reasons, generally an aggrieved buyer pursues specific performance (as opposed to a monetary remedy) only in those relatively rare cases where it would be deemed appropriate and available under both civil and common-law approaches (see the discussion of Article 28 at §199 supra).

282 ## C. Limits on Compelling Performance Under Article 46

(1) Resort to Inconsistent Remedies

Paragraph (1) of Article 46 withdraws the right to compel performance when "the buyer has resorted to a remedy that is inconsistent with this requirement." For example, the buyer loses the right to compel delivery when the buyer takes the position that it will not accept the goods — e.g., by declaring the contract avoided (Art. 49(1)).[10] The basic inconsistency between these remedies is made explicit in Article 81, *infra* at §439: Avoidance "releases both parties from their obligations under [the contract] subject to any damages that may be due." *Claiming price reduction for delivery of non-conforming goods (Article 50) is also inconsistent with requiring performance under Article 46.*[11]

282.1 **(a) Inconsistency: Form and Substance.** Inconsistency between avoidance and requiring performance is evident when the buyer declares the contract avoided (e.g., "I avoid: Don't ship the goods") and later demands performance: "Ship the goods." Indeed, the rule of Article 46(1) that a buyer may not "require performance" if it "has resorted to a remedy that is inconsistent with this requirement" serves a policy that is deeper than the logic (or esthetics) of inconsistency — the likelihood of reliance on the buyer's declaration by stopping production, reselling the goods, or canceling the reservation of shipping space. *Such considerations should affect whether a buyer can withdraw a declaration of avoidance of contract (see §187.2 supra).*

In examining the Convention's rules on risk of loss (Article 70, §382.1, *infra*) it may be relevant to consider whether a buyer who has

---

European Contract Law, in The 1980 Uniform Sales Law: Old Issues Revisited in the Light of Recent Experiences 169, 196 (Franco Ferrari ed., 2003).

10. See UNCITRAL Digest Art. 46 para. 9.

11. See UNCITRAL Digest Art. 46 para. 7.

received seriously defective goods may *concurrently*: (A) under Article 49(1)(a) declare the contract avoided ("I avoid: Take back the goods") *and also* (B) under Article 46(2) require the seller to deliver substitute goods. Whether the remedies are inconsistent calls for comparing their impact in specific situations. Both call for the buyer to return the goods. Article 82(1) (§§445–448, *infra*) provides: "(1) The buyer loses the right to *declare the contract avoided* or to require the seller *to deliver substitute goods*" if the buyer can not return the goods. The remedies are consistent in other respects such as requirements of notification (Arts. 46(2), 49(2)(b)) and recovery of damages (Arts. 45, 74, 81(1)).

Example 46A. Seller delivered goods that were seriously defective — i.e., a "fundamental breach" under Article 25. Buyer telexed, "Rejecting shipment for the following serious defects [specifying them]. Demand prompt delivery in conformity with the contract." Seller replied, "Your rejection of the goods avoided the contract which (CISG 81) releases both of us from our obligations under the contract."

Seller's point based on Article 81 ("avoidance . . . releases both parties from their obligations . . .") is, of course, in error for it fails to note that Article 46(2) makes a special and narrow exception from the general rule on avoidance in Article 81; both provisions must be given effect whereas Seller's argument would nullify Article 46(2).

Could Seller have invoked the above rule on avoidance in Article 81 if Buyer had telexed: "*Avoid* contract for the following serious defects . . . Demand prompt delivery . . . (etc.)." The ill-advised use of words referring to "avoidance" should not prejudice the buyer: Under Article 46(2) the buyer was entitled to refuse the goods for fundamental breach and demand substitute goods; the buyer's position was clear in spite of the improper language. (The above example may help to expose the snares concealed in the phrase "avoidance of the contract." The implications of the "avoidance" remedy are articulated in Articles 47–49, 51, 72, 73, 81 and 82.)

In sum, a declaration of "avoidance" and a demand and for substitute goods may not violate Article 46(1)'s prohibition of "inconsistent" remedies when they are expressed concurrently; indeed, a buyer's reference to "avoidance" in connection with a demand under Article 46(2) for substitute goods is redundant since it repeats one aspect of the buyer's rights under Article 46(2) — the buyer's right to require the seller to take back the defective goods. On the other hand, inconsistency may arise if the buyer simply declares that the contract is avoided under Article 49(1) or 46(2).

It is not feasible here to explore questions of inconsistency of remedies in the various settings in which they may arise. This discussion is designed to suggest that applying the rule prohibiting inconsistent remedies calls for attention to their impact in specific situations.

283 **(2) Compelling Delivery of Substitute Goods**

Paragraph (2) of Article 46 governs the scope of specific performance when the seller tenders goods that do not conform to the contract. When the non-conformity is minor, compelling a second delivery may impose burdens that are out of proportion to the buyer's needs;[12] hence this remedy is available "only if the lack of conformity constitutes a fundamental breach of contract...."[13] *It has been suggested that, if generic goods are to be delivered where they are located or at a place of business of the seller pursuant to Articles 31(b) or (c), a buyer may refuse delivery, treat the situation as a case of "nondelivery," and require replacements if the tendered goods are discovered to be non-conforming before the buyer accepts delivery, even if the lack of conformity does not constitute a fundamental breach.[14] That position amounts to a limited "perfect tender" rule and is without support in the text of Article 46(2): this provision makes no distinction between sales of generic and non-generic goods, nor based on the place of delivery or the time a lack of conformity is discovered; most importantly, the provision indicates no exception to the requirement that substitute goods can be required only where there is a nonconformity that is a fundamental breach.*

Example 46B. A contract called for a shipment of 100X-type machines. Seller shipped the 100 machines but inspection on arrival showed that 10 were defective. This defect was so serious that if all of the machines had been subject to this defect there would have been a "fundamental breach" of the contract, and Buyer could have rejected the entire shipment (Arts. 25 and 49(1)(a), §304 infra). However, the

---

12. See Markus Müller-Chen, Art. 46 paras. 24–25, *in* Schlechtriem & Schwenzer, *CISG Commentary* (2nd English ed. 2005).

13. "Fundamental breach" is discussed at Art. 25, *supra* at §181. The reasons for restricting paragraph (2) to fundamental breach were brought out at the Diplomatic Conference in resisting proposals to eliminate this restriction. *O.R.* 337, *Docy. Hist.* 558.

14. See Ulrich Huber & Corinne Widmer, Art. 31 para. 66, and Markus Müller-Chen, Art. 46 para. 19 & Art. 49 para. 17, *in* Schlechtriem & Schwenzer, *CISG Commentary* (2nd English ed. 2005), *in* Schlechtriem & Schwenzer, *CISG Commentary* (2nd English ed. 2005). See also the discussion of avoidance of the contract in this situation in §304 *supra*.

defect in the ten machines did not interfere with Buyer's use or market-ing of the other 90 machines. Under Article 46(2) may Buyer, by appro-priate notice, require Seller to deliver (a) ten conforming machines to substitute for the defective ones or (b) a new shipment of one hundred conforming machines?

As we shall see, Article 51 addresses this question (§§316–317 *infra*). Article 51(1) states that "if only part of the goods delivered is in con-formity with the contract, Articles 46 to 50 apply in respect of the *part . . .* which does not conform." Thus, the answer to the first question is Yes: By virtue of Articles 46(2) and 51(1) Buyer may require Seller to substitute ten conforming machines for the defective units. Under Article 51(2) (§317 *infra*) the answer to the second question is probably No: If it is feasible to deal separately with the conforming and non-conforming units and the defects in the ten machines are not a "fundamental breach" of the entire contract, Buyer may not require Seller to deliver an entirely new shipment.[15]

284 (3) Repair

Under paragraph (3) the buyer's right to "require the seller to remedy the lack of conformity by repair" is slightly stronger than the buyer's right under paragraph (2) to require "delivery of substitute goods." Requiring the delivery of substitute goods — a new shipment of a raw commodity or the substitution of a new machine — might involve trans-portation costs that would be unreasonably onerous when the non-conformity is insubstantial. Repair of the goods — which might merely involve a mechanical adjustment or replacing a defective part — usually is more efficient; the buyer may require the seller to "repair" even when the breach is not fundamental. However, repair may not be required when this remedy would be "unreasonable having regard to all the circumstances." Some minor repairs can be made more readily by the buyer, particularly when the seller's facilities for repair are in a distant country.[16] The statutory language was designed to encourage a reason-able and flexible approach to such cases.[17]

---

15. See Harry M. Flechtner, *Remedies Under the International Sale of Goods Convention: The Perspective From Article 2 of the U.C.C.*, 8 J.L. & Com. 53, 86–87 (1988).
16. See UNCITRAL Digest Art. 46 para. 18.
17. *O.R.* 332–333, *Docy. Hist.* 553–554.

285   D. Limits Set by Other Parts of the Convention

The discussion of Article 28, *supra* at §193, mentioned other provisions of the Convention that, in some situations, would restrict actions to compel performance. The Convention's rules on the obligation to preserve and dispose of goods (Arts. 85, 86, 88(2)), and on the duty to mitigate loss (Art. 77) in some settings may bar specific performance; the reasons will be examined in the commentaries to these articles. As was mentioned in discussing the "good faith" principle of Article 7, *supra* at §95, that principle may call for a restrained interpretation of the Convention's provisions on compelling performance when a party seeks this remedy only after a delay that permits him to speculate at the expense of the other party — as when a buyer seeks to compel delivery (rather than damages) only after a sharp rise in the market, or when a seller seeks to require specific performance (rather than damages) only after a market collapse.[18]

285.1   (1) Special Rules on Requiring Performance and Domestic Law (Article 28)

As we have seen. Article 46(2) provides that in specified circumstances the buyer may require the seller to deliver "substitute goods" (§183, *supra*) and Article 46(3) specifies the circumstances in which the buyer may require the seller to "repair" defective goods (§184, *supra*). Do domestic rules of the *forum* accepted by Article 28 supersede those of Article 46(2) or (3)?[19]

The problem needs to be broken apart. Suppose that a buyer, invoking the law of the *forum*, seeks to require a seller to deliver substitute goods even though the lack of conformity is not a fundamental breach as required by Article 46(2). Or suppose that a buyer, invoking the law of the *forum*, seeks to require the seller to repair the goods even though, pursuant to Article 46(3), under "all the circumstances" requiring the

---

18. Even civil law systems that strongly support specific performance do not permit this remedy to be abused by excessive delay. See *Treitel, Remedies (Int. Enc.)* §150, *Treitel, Remedies (1988)* 49. See also Principles of European Contract Law art. 9:102(3). *But* see *id.* Note 4 (attributing limitations on the right to claim performance because of the aggrieved party's delay to the common law).

19. Since Art. 46(2) and (3) would require a seller to take action to redress a breach of the seller's obligation to deliver conforming goods, these remedies fall within Art. 28 as remedies "to require performance of any obligation of the other party...." *Accord*, Kastely, *Right to Require Performance*, 63 Wash. L. Rev. 607, 635–636 (1988).

seller to repair "is unreasonable." In these cases the buyer's attempt to invoke domestic law is untenable: Article 28 applies only when the buyer "*is entitled* to performance" in "*accordance with the provisions of this Convention.*" A less technical but more substantial reason is that the international community decided that it would be appropriate to require substitute delivery and repair only under the conditions specified in Article 46(2) and (3).

Now let us suppose that domestic law of the forum would *not* require the seller to deliver substitute goods or repair non-conforming goods in cases where the conditions specified in Article 46(2) and (3) were *satisfied*. Does Article 28 authorize the court to apply its domestic rules in place of those of the Convention?

Article 28, standing alone, seems to say that domestic law will prevail[20] but this conclusion would overlook the specificity and nuanced character of the rules of Article 46(2) and (3) governing these precise situations. In the absence of evidence that UNCITRAL and the Diplomatic Conference faced this problem and evidenced a decision to give an unqualified reading to Article 28, Articles 46(2) and (3) should be regarded as *lex specialis* qualifying the general provisions of Article 28. Indeed, it seems out of keeping with the spirit of fairness that was characteristic of UNCITRAL and the Diplomatic Conference to conclude that, in facing these specific cases, the law-makers would decide to restrict the grounds for relief in some jurisdictions without requiring liberalization of the grounds in others.[21]

286 **E. Evaluation**

It would be easy to over-estimate the importance of the Convention's rules on "requiring" performance. Buyers seldom need to coerce sellers to replace or repair defective goods as provided in Articles 46(2) and (3). Replacement and repair are opportunities sought by sellers — to preserve good will, reduce damage liability and avoid the drastic remedy of avoidance of the contract. In the infrequent instances where sellers

---

20. See Harry M. Flechtner, *Remedies Under the International Sale of Goods Convention: The Perspective From Article 2 of the U.C.C.*, 8 J.L. & Com. 53, 60 n. 32 (1988).
21. See Kastley, note 7, *supra*, 635–636: The language of Art. 28 that "a court is not *bound*" to give specific relief indicates that courts "have discretion to vary from domestic law in order to give effect to the international character of the contract and the need for uniformity...."

are unwilling to perform, coercing performance is seldom so speedy and effective as purchasing substitute goods (see §199 *supra*).[22] The delays inherent in obtaining coerced performance usually render this remedy impractical even for domestic transactions and are magnified when the parties are far apart. Active participants in commerce and their legal advisors who are familiar with the practical problems of coercing action usually choose to supply their needs elsewhere and proceed with business — subject to compensation for damages after the cumbersome processes of litigation have taken their course. *This is confirmed by the dearth of reported cases in which aggrieved buyers have invoked their rights under Article 46.*[23]

It is true that meager returns can be expected from a damage claim against a seller who faces financial failure or is in the course of liquidation or reorganization. Theoretically, the buyer's position would be improved by forcing the seller to perform the contract. However, the recovery of penalties, like damages, would be subject to similar difficulties of collection. Can this problem be solved by harsher penalties such as committing the seller to prison for contempt of court? Domestic rules on bankruptcy and creditors'' rights may well bar the draconian allocation of the scarce resources of a failing debtor to a single creditor. And such domestic rules would not be supplanted by the Convention's rules on "requiring performance": The rights of third parties are at stake while the Convention's rules are confined to "the rights and obligations of the seller and the buyer" (see Art. 4, *supra* at §70).[24]

---

22. See also UNCITRAL Digest Art. 46 para. 4.

23. See UNCITRAL Digest Art. 46 para. 4.

24. The United States Bankruptcy Reform Act of 1978, 11 U.S.C. §365 empowers the trustee in bankruptcy to "reject any executory contract." The defendant's inability to satisfy a judgment for damages is a basis for enjoining his commission of a tort but not for specific enforcement of a contract when the plaintiff would gain an unfair advantage over the other creditors. See Walsh, Equity 318–321 (1930); *Restatement, Second of Contracts* §360 Comment d, §365 Comment b.

Article 47.
Buyer's Notice Fixing Additional Final Period for Performance

287   **A. Relationship to Rules on Avoidance of Contract**

As we shall see more fully in examining Article 49, *infra* at §301, that article provides two grounds for avoiding the contract — (1) when the seller commits a "fundamental breach of contract" (Art. 25, *supra* at §181) and (2) when the seller fails to deliver the goods "within the additional period of time fixed by the buyer in accordance with paragraph (1) of Article 47...." The provision for fixing an additional final period for delivery is as follows:

Article 47[1]

(1) **The buyer may fix an additional period of time of reasonable length for performance by the seller of his obligations.**
(2) **Unless the buyer has received notice from the seller that he will not perform within the period so fixed, the buyer may not, during that period, resort to any remedy for breach of contract. However, the buyer is not deprived thereby of any right he may have to claim damages for delay in performance.**

288   **B. Notice as a Step Toward Avoidance**

(1) Restriction to Non-Delivery

Article 47(1), read in isolation, seems to empower the buyer to fix an additional final period for the seller to perform any of its obligations. However, the only teeth for the provision are those provided by Article 49(1)(b): "(b) in case of *non-delivery*, if the seller *does not deliver the goods*..." within the time fixed by the buyer under Article 47, the buyer

---

1. Article 47 is the same as Art. 43 of the 1978 Draft Convention. *Cf.* ULIS 27(2), 31(2), 44(2), 45, 51.

may declare the contract avoided. The notice-avoidance procedure thus applies only to non-delivery.[2]

In UNCITRAL and at the Diplomatic Conference proposals were made to extend the notice-avoidance procedure to cases where the seller delivers goods that fail to conform to the contract. UNCITRAL rejected these proposals on the ground that the notice-avoidance procedure could be abused to convert a trivial breach into a ground for avoidance. For instance, a buyer who wishes to escape from his contractual obligations — e.g., after a price-collapse — might notify the seller that it has a specified time to correct specified minor defects in the goods although the distance separating the parties makes it impractical for the seller to comply with the notice. This understanding of the decisions taken by UNCITRAL was confirmed at the Diplomatic Conference by the rejection of proposals to broaden the scope of notice-avoidance to include non-conformity; in addition, to avoid any possible misunderstanding, the Diplomatic Conference added the words "in case of *non-delivery*" at the beginning of the notice-avoidance provision in Article 49(1)(b).[3]

289 ## (2) Content of the Notice

What type of notice will provide a basis for avoidance of the contract?
Example 47A. A contract called for Seller to manufacture and deliver a complex stamping machine to Buyer by June 1. Seller was late in making delivery and on June 2 Buyer wired Seller: "We are anxious to receive machine. Hope very much that it can arrive by July 1." Seller delivered the machine on July 3, but Buyer refused the machine and declared that the contract was avoided for failure to comply with the

---

2. See Markus Müller-Chen, Art. 47 para. 1, *in* Schlechtriem & Schwenzer, *CISG Commentary* (2nd English ed. 2005); UNCITRAL Digest Art. 47 paras. 1 & 3. The Art. 47 notice followed by avoidance under Art. 49(I)(b) can be used with respect to a failure to deliver only a part of the goods. See Art. 51, *infra* at §314. (Under Art. 51(2) avoidance of the *entire* contract based on delivery of only a *part* may only be based on "fundamental breach.")
3. WG: VI *YB* 69–71, 77, *Docy. Hist.* 147–148, 155; UNCITRAL: VIII *YB* 46, *Docy. Hist.* 339; DIP. CONF.: *O.R.* 9–10, 78–79, 41 (para. 8), 354–56, 427, 116–17, 160; *Docy. Hist.* 386–87, 399–340, 431 (para. 8), 575–77, 648, 688–89, 719. This decision rejected the contrary approach embodied in ULIS 44(2). Some domestic legal systems have developed the concept that the delivery of goods basically different from those required under the contract was a delivery of a "something else" — *aliud* — and hence equivalent to complete non-delivery. This concept has proved difficult to apply. Fortunately, delivery of totally different goods is a delivery of non-conforming goods (Art. 35) and, of course, is a fundamental breach empowering the buyer to avoid the contract under Art. 49(1)(a), §304, *infra*. See also §256.1, *supra* (rejection of *aliud* concept).

July 1 delivery date set forth in its wire of June 2. Buyer was not prepared to show that the delay in delivery from June 1 to July 3 constituted a "fundamental breach" (Art. 25) and relied solely on the notice-avoidance rules of Articles 47(1) and 49(1)(b).

A notice like that sent by Buyer on June 2 should not be held to "fix an additional period of time . . . for performance," and should not provide the basis of avoidance under Article 49(1)(b). Such a notice gives no warning that a deadline has been "fixed."[4] Indeed, a communication that invites performance without making clear that a final deadline has been set could mislead the seller into an attempt at substantial performance. Although it need not use the term "avoid" (see §18.2 *supra*), an effective notice under Article 47(1) should make clear that the additional period sets a fixed and final limit on the date for delivery: E.g., "The last date when we can accept delivery will be July 1."[5]

Suppose that the buyer sends the seller the following ominous notice: "Your delivery is late. We shall be forced to reject the goods and avoid the contract if they do not arrive promptly." This notice does not comply with Article 47(1) since it does not "fix" a "period."[6] The consequences of the notice-avoidance remedy are serious; unless the buyer sends a notice of the clarity required by Article 47(1) avoidance must be based on fundamental breach.[7]

The notice under Article 47(1) must fix an additional period "of reasonable length."[8] The Convention uses flexible language; different periods of time could be "reasonable." Within this leeway the choice is given to the buyer—the innocent party who faces breach by the seller. Indeed, respect must be given to the buyer's discretion in setting the "reasonable" period if the notice-avoidance procedure is to serve its

---

4. See Markus Müller-Chen, Art. 47 para. 5, *in* Schlechtriem & Schwenzer, *CISG Commentary* (2nd English ed. 2005).

5. *Quebec Civ. Code Revn., Obligations*: A notice putting a debtor "in default" need not indicate "the right [the creditor] intends to exercise" (Art. 247, pp. 320–321), but if the creditor "wishes to avail himself of *resolution*" he "must *so advise* his debtor." See also German (F.R.G.) Civil Code 326, quoted *infra* at §290.

6. See Oberlandesgericht Düsseldorf, Germany, 24 April 1997, CLOUT case No. 275, English translation available at http://cisgw3.law.pace.edu/cases/970424g1.html; Markus Müller-Chen, Art. 47 para. 4, *in* Schlechtriem & Schwenzer, *CISG Commentary* (2nd English ed. 2005).

7. *Secretariat Commentary* Art. 43, para. 7, *O.R.* 39, *Docy. Hist.* 429; VIII *YB* 44, *Docy. Hist.* 337.

8. For analysis of factors bearing on the reasonableness of the time see *Dölle, Kommentar* (Huber), Art. 26 at 34, p. 235. See Markus Müller-Chen, Art. 47 para. 16, *in* Schlechtriem & Schwenzer, *CISG Commentary* (2nd English ed. 2005); UNCITRAL Digest Art. 47 para. 5. On respect for decisions of the aggrieved party *cf. Farnsworth, Contracts* §12.12, p. 867.

purpose — reducing uncertainty concerning the right to avoid the contract. (The risk of delay or loss of the notice is discussed under Article 63 at §352 n.2, *infra*.)

In determining whether the period the buyer fixes is "reasonable" the dominant consideration is the buyer's need for delivery of the goods without further delay. (Impediments that prevent or delay performance are dealt with in Article 79, *infra* §§423, 435: temporary impediment.) On the other hand, since the seller's failure to comply with the period fixed by the buyer empowers the buyer to avoid the contract (Art. 49(1)(a), §305 *infra*), the reasonableness of this period should be considered in the light of the basic policy decision, embodied in Articles 25, 49 and 64, that contracts should not be avoided on insubstantial grounds.

290 ## C. The Role of Notice-Avoidance: Analogies in Domestic Law

Domestic legal systems have not developed clear or uniform rules on whether a delay in performance empowers the other party to reject performance. (The issue is expressed in many different ways — rescission, repudiation, cancellation, avoidance.) Sometimes the rule is put in terms of whether time is "of the essence." The (U.K.) Sale of Goods Act states that unless a different intention appears, the time of payment is not "of the essence"; as concerns delay in delivery: "Whether any other stipulation as to time is of the essence of the contract or not depends on the terms of the contract."[9]

The notice-avoidance approach of Articles 47 and 49(1)(b) of the Convention was inspired by a provision of German law that, on default by one party:

> the other party may give him a reasonable period within which to perform his part with a declaration that he will refuse to accept the performance after the expiration of the period.

If performance is not made in due time, the person who gave the above notice (often termed a *Nachfrist*) may "withdraw from the contract."[10]

---

9. (U.K.) SGA (1893) 10 (1). For the case law see *Benjamin* §588; *Atiyah* 88. The (U.S.A.) UCC is discussed under Art. 49, *infra* at §301.

10. German (F.R.G.) Civil Code 326. *Treitel, Remedies (Int. Enc.)* §§149–151, on which the present discussion relies, helpfully discusses the above provision and similar provisions in other legal systems — see also *Treitel, Remedies (1988)* Ch. IX, pp. 318–410; *Zweigert &*

Other aspects of the German *Nachfrist* were not employed in the Convention. As has been noted, under the Convention when the seller commits a breach that is fundamental the buyer may declare the contract avoided (Art. 49(1)(b)) without giving the seller an "additional period of time of reasonable length," although several earlier decisions appear confused on this point.[11] However, the opportunity by advance notice to clarify the situation for both parties has received widespread international approval; the basic utility of this legal tool was never seriously questioned in the UNCITRAL proceeding or at the Diplomatic Conference.

291   ## D. Obligation to Accept Requested Performance

Paragraph (2) of Article 47 reflects a principle that might have "gone without saying": A party may not refuse performance that he has invited.[12] *Specifically, paragraph (2) provides that, if a buyer fixes a Nachfrist period, the buyer may not resort to a remedy for breach during that period, unless the seller declares it will not perform within the period.*[13] The other party can be expected to rely on the invitation; domestic law would bind a party to accept the requested performance by doctrines such as waiver, estoppel or election. Paragraph (2) avoids the uncertainties of recourse to domestic law.[14] (In addition, paragraph (2) may provide an instance of a "general principle" that, by virtue of Art. 7, could be applicable in other similar situations. See *supra* at §96.)

Paragraph (2) also provides that the buyer's demand that the seller perform within a fixed period does not relieve the seller of responsibility for damage resulting from the late performance, including damages resulting from delay during the "additional period" fixed in the notice. This result is consistent with the general rule of Article 45(2), *supra* at §275, that preserves the buyer's right to recover damages when (for

---

Kotz (1987) 187–188; *Treitel, Remedies (1988)* 327–334, 338–339 (*Nachfrist* notice under CISG). The (U.S.A.) UCC does not explicitly establish an additional time notice comparable to *Nachfrist*, but the official Comments to UCC 2–309 commend the use of such notices to add certainty to the relationship between the parties. (Comments 3 and 5.)

11. See UNCITRAL Digest Art. 47 para. 4 and cases cited in n.5 therein.

12. See Markus Müller-Chen, Art. 47 para. 3, *in* Schlechtriem & Schwenzer, *CISG Commentary* (2nd English ed. 2005); UNCITRAL Digest Art. 47 para. 8.

13. See Markus Müller-Chen, Art. 47 paras. 14 & 17, *in* Schlechtriem & Schwenzer, *CISG Commentary* (2nd English ed. 2005).

14. See UNCITRAL Digest Art. 47 para. 2.

example) he compels performance under Article 46. (The scope of the "election" principle was discussed under Article 45 *supra* at §277.) Thus, a notice under Article 47(1) can foreclose an argument that the buyer has agreed to a modification of the contract or has waived or otherwise forfeited a claim for damages resulting from late delivery.

These modest consequences based solely on Article 47 apply generally to a notice fixing an additional period for the seller's performance "of his obligations." On the other hand, the more serious consequence of *avoidance* under Article 49(1)(b) based on an Article 47 notice is restricted to cases of "non-delivery" (see §§288, 305).

Article 48.
Cure After Date for Delivery; Requests for Clarification

292 **A. Tools for Cooperation**

A sales transaction may be regarded (at the extremes) either as a duel fought with deadly weapons or as a relationship calling for cooperation and accommodation. The latter, of course, is the attitude of persons engaged in commerce; this approach is reflected in several provisions of the Convention.

293 **(1) The Convention**

Two articles deal with the cure of defective performance. Article 37, *supra* at §245, gives the seller the right to cure defective performance up to the date for delivery; the present Article gives the seller a more restricted right to cure defects in performance after the date for delivery.

Article 48[1]

(1) Subject to article 49, the seller may, even after the date for delivery, remedy at his own expense any failure to perform his obligations, if he can do so without unreasonable delay and without causing the buyer unreasonable inconvenience or uncertainty of reimbursement by the seller of expenses advanced by the buyer.[2] **However, the buyer retains any right to claim damages as provided for in this Convention.**

---

1. Article 48 was based on Art. 44 of the 1978 Draft. Paragraph (1) was redrafted at the Diplomatic Conference by deleting an opening phrase, "Unless the buyer has declared the contract avoided ..." and by deleting (after "obligations") the phrase, "if he can do so without such delays as will amount to a fundamental breach of contract." ULIS 44(1) contains a similar provision permitting cure "after the date fixed for the delivery of the goods."

2. For discussion of the requirement that cure be affected "without unreasonable delay and without causing the buyer unreasonable inconvenience or uncertainty of reimbursement by the seller of expenses advanced by the buyer," see Markus Müller-Chen, Art. 48 paras. 9–12, *in* Schlechtriem & Schwenzer, *CISG Commentary* (2nd English ed. 2005); UNCITRAL Digest Art. 48 para. 3.

(2) If the seller requests the buyer to make known whether he will accept performance and the buyer does not comply with the request within a reasonable time, the seller may perform within the time indicated in his request. The buyer may not, during that period of time, resort to any remedy which is inconsistent with performance by the seller.

(3) A notice by the seller that he will perform within a specified period of time is assumed to include a request, under the preceding paragraph, that the buyer make known his decision.

(4) A request or notice by the seller under paragraph (2) or (3) of this article is not effective unless received by the buyer.

295   B. Cure and Delay in Delivery

Paragraph (1) provides that "even after the date for delivery" the seller may remedy "*any* failure to perform his obligations." This language is broad enough to include a defect in documents (*cf.* Art. 34, §220, *supra*)[3] and any other breach by the seller. Applying Article 48(1) to a delay in delivery, however, is problematic. If the seller tenders delivery either (a) after a delay that constitutes a fundamental breach or (b) after the expiration of a period fixed by the buyer under Article 47 (*supra* at §287) the buyer may "declare the contract avoided" under Article 49(1), *infra* at §303. Time that has passed cannot be recalled; "remedy" is intrinsically impossible. On the other hand, if the seller's delay in delivery does not fall under either (a) or (b), above, the buyer must accept the delivery; there is no need for "cure" to obligate the buyer to take delivery, and there is no way to prevent damage that the buyer has already suffered from the delay.

In sum, paragraph (1) addresses the seller's right to remedy defects or deficiencies in performance that has been tendered — e.g., by substituting conforming goods for defective goods or by repairing (or replacing) a defective component part. (As we shall see, paragraphs (2)–(4) are not so limited and apply to a seller's inquiry as to whether the buyer will accept a late delivery. See *infra* at §297.)

---

3. *Accord*, Markus Müller-Chen, Art. 48 paras. 3 & 5, *in* Schlechtriem & Schwenzer, *CISG Commentary* (2nd English ed. 2005).

296   **C. Cure and Avoidance for Fundamental Breach**

The relationship between cure and remedies based on "fundamental breach" has already been introduced in connection with the definition of "fundamental breach." (See Article 25, *supra* at §184.) The issue is important and merits attention in the present setting; the following illustration will recall Example 25A, *supra* at §184.

Example 48A. Seller delivered a machine to Buyer. When Buyer tested the machine a defect in one of the component parts prevented the machine from operating. Only Seller had replacement parts for the machine. Buyer notified Seller that the machine had failed to operate. Seller offered immediately to replace the defective part but Buyer refused this offer and declared that the contract was avoided. The time required for replacing the defective part was not important to Buyer; his contention was that the machine had failed to function and that this constituted a fundamental breach of the sales contract (Art. 25) empowering him to avoid the contract (Art. 49(1)(a)).

In the 1978 Draft Convention, the provision allowing a seller to cure after the date for delivery (Art. 44(1) which became Art. 48(1) in the Convention) opened with these words: "Unless the buyer has declared the contract avoided in accordance with article 45 [now article 49]. . . ." At the Diplomatic Conference several delegates expressed their concern that, in situations like Example 48A, this "Unless" clause might be construed to authorize avoidance of the contract that would frustrate the seller's right to cure. There was widespread agreement that whether a breach is fundamental should be decided in the light of the seller's offer to cure (Art. 25, *supra* at §184) and that the buyer's right to avoid the contract (Art. 49(1)) should not nullify the seller's right to cure (Art. 48(1)). However, it was difficult to find language that would clearly express the proper relationship between avoidance and cure. Finally, the Conference adopted a joint proposal prepared by delegates who had been anxious to protect the seller's right to cure. Under this proposal, the "Unless . . ." clause of the 1978 Draft was deleted and replaced by the present cross-reference to Article 49.[4]

In cases like Example 48A, the seller's right to cure could not have been frustrated even under the 1978 version that included the "Unless"

---

4. The initial proposals: *Com. I* Art. 44, paras. 3(i) & (iii); the group proposal, *id.* para. 6, Alt. II (para. (1)). Discussion and action: *SR.20*, paras. 37–76; *SR.22* paras. 5–21 *O.R.* 114–115, 341–343, 351, *Docy. Hist.* 686–687, 562–564, 572. See also *Sec. Commy. O.R.* 41–42, *Docy. Hist.* 431–432 (paras. 6, 17).

clause; any other result would have nullified the Convention's narrow and specific provision authorizing cure.[5]

The amendment to Article 48(1) leaves little room for doubt. The seller's right to cure should also be protected if, in cases like Example 48A, where cure is feasible, the buyer hastily declares the contract avoided before the seller has an opportunity to cure the defect. As was noted under Article 25, *supra* at §181, whether a breach is "fundamental" should be decided in the light of *all* of the circumstances. In cases like Example 48A, where cure is feasible and where an offer of cure can be expected, one cannot conclude that the breach is "fundamental" until one knows the answer to this question: Will the seller cure?[6]

Professor Will in an incisive analysis of this problem (*B-B Commentary* 349–352) rightly emphasizes the buyer's need for a prompt and clear answer to the above question: "Will the seller cure?" Will suggests (p. 351) that the buyer should not be required to delay avoidance of the contract unless the answer to the above question is "Yes" based on the buyer's "actual knowledge (good experience with the seller, and *ad hoc* commitment, the underlying conditions of sale). . . ." Fortunately, the parties can avoid doubt by communicating with each other.[7]

The first step normally must be taken by the buyer since the defect usually comes to light during inspection or testing at the end of transport. Let us suppose that, in a case like Example 48A, on June 1, shortly after arrival of the goods, Buyer emailed: "Machine does not operate apparently because of a defect in Part X. Will you remedy the defect? Must have machine in working order by June 20 or will be forced to avoid

---

5. Avoidance under Art. 49(1) is applicable to a wide range of circumstances other than cure, whereas the cure provisions of Art. 48(1) could be frustrated by an unqualified application of Art. 49(1). In such situations, a general provision yields to the specific. The same result follows from the conclusion that an offer to cure prevents the breach from being "fundamental." See Art. 25, *supra* at §181. See the discussions in UNCITRAL (1977), VIII *YB* 31 para. 94, *Docy. Hist.* 324. Also supporting the view that the right to cure limits avoidance: Huber, 43 *Rabels Z* 413, 489–491; *Mertens & Rehbinder* Art. 37 at 2, p. 18. See also GDR Int. Comm. Contracts Act. 1976, §281, Enderlein, 3 Dr. et Pr. Comm. Int. 123, 136 (1977). *Cf. Schlechtriem, 1986 Commentary* 78. *But see* Will, *B-B Commentary* 348: The cross-reference to Art. 49 in Art. 48(1) is "enigmatic" and leaves the relationship to avoidance "open to interpretation."

6. *Accord*, Markus Müller-Chen, Art. 48 paras. 14–15, *in* Schlechtriem & Schwenzer, *CISG Commentary* (2nd English ed. 2005); UNCITRAL Digest Art. 48 paras. 2 & 5, and Art. 49 para. 12.

7. *Accord*, Markus Müller-Chen, Art. 48 para. 16, *in* Schlechtriem & Schwenzer, *CISG Commentary* (2nd English ed. 2005).

contract and obtain machine elsewhere. Need to know by June 10 what you plan to do with respect to arrival of your engineer and plans for repair."

Such a message would respond to the parties" normal commercial interests to maintain a productive business relationship. In addition, the message lays the foundation for protecting Buyer's legal rights if (contrary to normal practice) Seller should fail to cooperate: (1) The message satisfies the buyer's obligation under Article 39 to notify the seller of the lack of conformity. (2) Since the seller has the "*obligation*" to supply the buyer with goods that conform to the contract (Art. 35), the message constitutes a *Nachfrist* notice under Article 47 fixing "an additional time of reasonable length for performance by the seller of his *obligations*"; until the seller refuses or the fixed time expires the time does not run on the period within which the buyer may take further steps such as avoidance for fundamental breach (Art. 49(2)(b)(ii)). (3) This advanced stage of the relationship between the parties, with the buyer in possession of defective goods shipped by the seller, leads to the conclusion that the seller also has the "obligation" to respond to the buyer's request for early information regarding the seller's plans concerning cure. (See §100 *supra*, on the "general principle" (Art. 7(2)) to communicate information needed by the other party derived (e.g.) from Arts. 19(2), 21(2), 26, 39(1) and, in a closely-related setting. Arts. 47(2) and 48(2).) On this assumption the buyer's request for early (June 10) information about the seller's plans may also be supported by the notice-avoidance provisions of Articles 47(1) and 49(1)(b).

The buyer's inquiry need not follow the style or approach of the above example. Moreover, in normal business relationships the Convention's sanctions for failing to reply to the buyer's inquiry will be irrelevant: When cure of a defect is feasible the seller will be anxious to effect the cure to preserve good business relationships and also to minimize the loss resulting from avoidance of the contract. The point of the above example is to suggest that the buyer need not be consumed by doubt over whether the seller will cure the defect; a simple inquiry will provide the answer.

296.1   **(1) Cure and the Buyer's Other Remedies**

The previous section explored the relationship between the seller's right to cure under Article 48 and the buyer's right to avoid under Article 49 — an issue expressly (although not clearly) addressed in the opening phrase of Article 48(1). What is the relationship between the right to cure and a buyer's other remedies under the Convention?

Article 50 specifies that the buyer does not have the right to reduce the price for non-conforming goods "if the seller remedies any failure to perform his obligations in accordance with article 37 or article 48 or if the buyer refuses to accept performance by the seller in accordance with those articles." The effect of Article 48(1) on the buyer's right to other remedies, such as the right to claim repair of or substitutes for non-conforming goods under Article 46(2) & (3), or the right to claim damages under Article 74, is not expressly specified in the Convention.

It has been argued that the negative implication of the first clause of Article 48(1) is that, unlike the right to avoid, the buyer's right to other remedies is subordinate to the seller's right to cure.[8] As a general matter this see ms correct: otherwise, the seller's right to cure might be defeated by a buyer's hasty invocation of other remedies.

Treating this implied relationship as an inflexible legal rule, however, may not be the best approach, or the most in keeping with the intentions of the drafters. It has been suggested, for example, that a buyer may not itself correct defects in the goods, and then seek damages for the costs of repair, without first affording the seller an opportunity to cure under Article 48.[9] A buyer faced with a non-conformity that it can readily correct, however, is likely — understandably — to simply correct it. Indeed, that action may be required to mitigate the buyer's damages pursuant to Article 77.

Punishing buyers by denying damages for such an apparently reasonable response would violate the mandate of Article 7(1) to interpret the Convention in a fashion that promotes good faith in international trade. Perhaps the best answer is to look to the remedy for the buyer's failure to afford the seller an opportunity to cure. If it can be shown that the seller could have cured the defect at lower cost than buyer's repair,[10] the seller should be entitled to reduce the buyer's damages by that amount. Otherwise, the buyer's response appears at most to have been harmless (or, perhaps, beneficial-to-seller) error, and should not

---

8. Markus Müller-Chen, Art. 48 paras. 19–21, *in* Schlechtriem & Schwenzer, *CISG Commentary* (2nd English ed. 2005).

9. See Markus Müller-Chen, Art. 48 para. 21, *in* Schlechtriem & Schwenzer, *CISG Commentary* (2nd English ed. 2005).

10. This commentary argues that burden of proof questions are generally not governed by the Convention (see §70.1 *supra*). Under most domestic burden of proof systems, presumably, the burden would be on a breaching seller to prove that, because of its right to cure, buyer was not entitled to damages to cover the costs of correcting a lack of conformity.

prejudice the buyer. The point is to interpret and apply the various remedy-related provisions of the Convention in a fashion that supports reasonable and good faith behavior both by those who have suffered a breach, and those who have breach but strive to respond properly.

297   D. Requests for Clarification

As was suggested *supra* at §292, a modern sale involves a relationship that may require cooperation. This calls for open lines of communication between the parties so that each knows what to expect from the other. In business practice this is taken for granted; paragraphs (2)–(4) of Article 48 give legal effect to this expectation. We shall first examine the operation of paragraphs (2)–(4) on a proposal to cure a failure of performance under paragraph (1), and then consider the applicability of paragraphs (2)–(4) in other situations.

298   (1) Proposal to Cure by Repair

Example 48B. The facts are like those in Example 48A: Seller delivered a machine to Buyer; Buyer notified Seller that it failed to operate. Seller thereupon emailed Buyer, "My mechanics will arrive within one week to put the machine in operation." Buyer did not reply. At the time stated in Seller's message his mechanics arrived to repair the machine but Buyer refused to admit them on the ground that the machine was too defective for repair.

Buyer acted wrongfully in refusing to permit the mechanics to make the repair. Seller's notice complied with Article 48(2) and (3). The notice did not expressly request Buyer "to make known whether he will accept performance" (Art. 48(2)) but, by virtue of paragraph (3), the seller's notice "that he will perform" is assumed to include a request "that the buyer make known his decision." Consequently, "the seller may perform within the time indicated in his request."

We must assume that paragraph (2) of this article does not merely duplicate paragraph (1). Hence, the rule of paragraph (2) that when the buyer fails to respond "the seller may perform within the time indicated in his request" is not confined to the circumstances for cure stated in paragraph (1). For example, if the seller's request proposes to cure the defect within two weeks, the buyer who fails to respond may not contend that cure within the two-week period is barred as an "unreasonable delay" under paragraph (1). Here, again, the Convention gives effect to the parties" duty to communicate — in this setting to prevent avoidable expense. See §§100, 292, and 296, *supra*.

299 (2) Proposal to Make a Late Delivery

As was noted at §295, the provision on cure in paragraph (1) extends to "*any* failure" by a seller to perform its obligations — language that literally includes a late delivery, although it is difficult to envisage a way to "remedy" a delay that has occurred. This difficulty, however, does not extend to the provisions on communications in paragraphs (2)–(4).

Example 48C. The contract for the sale of a machine called for delivery to Buyer on June 1. Seller fell behind schedule and on May 31 he sent Buyer the following message: "Regret cannot deliver machine until June 10. Will you accept delivery on that date?" Buyer did not respond; Seller delivered the machine on June 10. Buyer refused to accept the delivery and declared the contract avoided on the ground that the delay in delivery constituted a fundamental breach.

Seller's inquiry of May 31 was authorized by Article 48(2): the wire requested Buyer to "make known" whether he would "accept performance." Seller needed this information before laying out the funds necessary to complete the machine and transport it to Buyer. Buyer had a duty to respond; as a result of his failure "the seller *may perform* within the time indicated in his request." In short, Buyer lost any right he might have had to avoid the contract because of the delay specified in Seller's communication of May 31. (Of course, Seller is liable for any damages. Art.48(1).)[11]

300 (3) Failure to Receive the Notice

Article 27 laid down the general rule that a party discharges its duty to notify by dispatching a notice "by means appropriate in the circumstances"; under this rule the risks of delay or non-transmission fall on the addressee. Paragraph (4) reverses this rule for communications under paragraphs (2) and (3). Here the one giving the notice is in breach of contract; a seller who has deviated from the contract may not impose on the buyer a duty to respond to an inquiry that he did not receive. (See

---

11. At the Diplomatic Conference the brief discussion of paragraphs (2)–(4) indicated that these provisions could have wider scope than cure under paragraph (1). Thus, a proposal to make a separate article of paras. (2)–(4) was considered merely a matter of drafting and was referred to Drafting Committee. *SR.22*, paras. 17, 43. *O.R.* 352, 352, *Docy. Hist.* 573, 574.

Art. 27, *supra* at §190.) On the other hand, if the aggrieved buyer dispatches an objection to the proposed cure and the message fails to arrive, Article 27 provides that such a failure of transmission "does not deprive [the buyer] of the right to rely on the communication." In sum, the exception to the general "dispatch" rule carved out by Article 48(4) applies only to the request by the seller — the party who is in breach of contract.[12]

12. See *Secretariat Commentary* Art. 44, para. 15 *O.R.* 41, *Docy. Hist.* 431.

Article 49.
Buyer's Right to Avoid the Contract

301 **A. The Problem of Avoidance in Domestic Law**

When does a breach of contract by one party release the other party from its contractual obligations? Attempts to answer this question have produced rules of domestic law of unusual technicality and uncertainty.

The common law initially found it difficult to release a party (Party A) from its promise because of breach by the other party (B), unless the promises of the two parties were linked by some verbal formula such as: "A promises *in exchange* for B's delivery of first-quality hemp, to pay . . ." Late in the eighteenth century this technical approach was relaxed by the judicial creation of rules that performance by B could be an implied "condition" of A's duty of performance; under some of the case law, whether B's breach released A depended on questions of degree such as the seriousness of the breach.[1] The Ontario Law Reform Commission proposed that the question whether the buyer had the right to reject should be answered in terms of one general standard: Was the seller's breach "substantial?"[2] The (U.S.A.) Uniform Commercial Code created a somewhat different set of distinctions. In an earlier study, this writer found these provisions to be casuistic and unresponsive to commercial practice and the significant interests of the parties.[3]

---

1. An important contribution to this development was made by Lord Mansfield in Kingston v. Preston, 99 Eng. Rep. 437 (K.B. 1773). See 8 Holdsworth, *History of English Law* 70–88 (2d ed. 1973); Corbin, *Conditions in the Law of Contract*, 28 Yale L.J. 739 (1919), reprinted in Selected Essays in the Law of Contracts 871 (1939); Patterson, *Constructive Conditions in Contracts*, 42 Colum. L. Rev. 903 (1942).

2. *Ont. L. Ref. Com. II Sales* 444–461. This report notes that a similar recommendation was made by Law Reform Commission, New South Wales, Working Paper on Sales of Goods (1975) para. 13.17. *Cf.* (U.K.) SGA (1979) §11(3) (Whether a stipulation is a "condition" depends "on the construction of the contract"); §11(4) (modified rule on effect of acceptance; reference to passage of property deleted); §13 ("by description"); §30(1) & (2) (deviations as to quantity).

3. Honnold, *Buyer's Right of Rejection—A Study in the Impact of Codification on a Commercial Problem*, 97 U. Pa. L. Rev. 457 (1949). See also Priest, *Breach and Remedy for the Tender of Non-conforming Goods under the UCC: An Economic Approach*, 91 Harv. L. Rev. 960 (1978) (includes economic analysis of UCC decisions).

302 B. The Convention's Rules on Avoidance for Breach

We have encountered the Convention's rules on avoidance of the contract in connection with several provisions — the definition of "fundamental breach" (Art. 25); the rule that a declaration of avoidance is effective "only if made by notice to the other party" (Art. 26), an approach that rejected the ULIS system of *ipso facto* avoidance (§187 *et seq.*, *supra*); the right of the seller to cure defects in performance (Arts. 37 and 48); and the buyer's power to fix an additional final period for performance (the *Nachfrist* notice, Art. 47). All of these provisions relate to the following general basic rules on avoidance of the contract:

Article 49

(1) The buyer may declare the contract avoided:

(a) if the failure by the seller to perform any of his obligations under the contract or this Convention amounts to a fundamental breach of contract; or

(b) in case of non-delivery, if the seller does not deliver the goods within the additional period of time fixed by the buyer in accordance with paragraph (1) of article 47 or declares that he will not deliver within the period so fixed.

(2) However, in cases where the seller has delivered the goods, the buyer loses the right to declare the contract avoided unless he does so:

(a) in respect of late delivery, within a reasonable time after he has become aware that delivery has been made;

(b) in respect of any breach other than late delivery, within a reasonable time:

(i)   after he knew or ought to have known of the breach;

(ii) after the expiration of any additional period of time fixed by the buyer in accordance with paragraph (1) of article 47, or after the seller has declared that he will not perform his obligations within such an additional period; or

(iii) after the expiration of any additional period of time indicated by the seller in accordance with paragraph (2) of article 48, or after the buyer has declared that he will not accept performance.

303　**(1) Grounds for Avoidance**

Paragraph (1) of Article 49 states two grounds on which buyers may avoid the contract; (a) when a failure by the seller to perform "any of his obligations" amounts to a "fundamental breach of contract"; and (b) "in case of non-delivery, if the seller does not deliver the goods" within an additional period of time fixed by a *Nachfrist* notice under Article 47.

The aggrieved party need not apply to a court for relief from the obligation of the contract. Avoidance is effected by a "declaration" which (Art. 26) is made "by notice to the other party." Of course, the attempt to avoid must be authorized by the Convention.[4] The essential point is that the transfer of responsibility is not delayed pending litigation — a process that could be particularly awkward in international transactions.

304　**(a) Avoidance for Fundamental Breach of Contract.**　The Convention applies one general rule to non-performance by the seller of "any of his obligations": The buyer may avoid the contract if the seller's breach is "fundamental." The application of this rule was explored in discussing the Convention's definition of "fundamental breach" (Art. 25, *supra* at §183).[5]

In brief, a breach of contract by one party (A) is "fundamental" if it results in such "detriment" to the other party (B) as to "substantially" deprive B of what B is entitled to expect under the contract. The framing of this text was based on the conclusion that international contracts usually are of a complexity and importance to the parties that avoidance should not be available for trivial departures that may readily be redressed by other remedies.

The rejection of trivial grounds for avoidance necessarily led to a test that is based on degree. Application of this test requires attention to the aggrieved party's need for this remedy in the light of all the facts. Situations that were discussed under the definition in Article 25 included the

---

4. For discussion of the effect of a buyer's unjustified declaration of avoidance, see Markus Müller-Chen, Art. 49 paras. 44–48, *in* Schlechtriem & Schwenzer, *CISG Commentary* (2nd English ed. 2005). In U.S. domestic sales law (Art. 2 of the U.C.C.) a buyer can "effectively" (albeit "wrongfully") reject tendered goods even without proper grounds for such rejection.
5. See Rabel, The Hague Conference on the Unification of Sales Law, 1 Am. J. Comp. L. 58, 65 (1952).

effect of an offer to cure (§184, *supra*) and the adequacy and assured availability of an adjustment of the price or other compensation (§185). *If a buyer discovers that goods are non-conforming while they are still in the possession of the seller before being transported, it has been suggested that the buyer may "reject" the goods and avoid the contract, even if the non-conformity does not constitute a fundamental breach, unless the seller corrects the defect.[6] This is closely related to the suggestion that a buyer can require replacement goods in this situation despite the provisions of Article 46(2) conditioning the right to substitute goods on the existence of a fundamental breach. See §283 infra. The argument that a fundamental breach is not necessary to avoidance in these circumstances must also be rejected: it amounts to a (limited) "perfect tender rule," is without support in the text of Article 49(1), and would undermine the principle that international sales contracts should be preserved except in the face of serious breaches.*

304.1   **(i) Avoidance as to Part of the Goods.**   The buyer's remedy of avoidance is made more flexible by Article 51, §§314–317, *infra*. Article 51(1) states that if "the seller delivers only a part of the goods" or if only "a part of the goods" conforms to the contract, "articles 46 to 50" (note the inclusion of Article 49) "apply in respect of the *part* which is *missing* or which *does not conform*." See §§314–316 *infra*.

  Example 49A. In a contract for 1,000 computers 980 conformed with the contract but 20 were seriously defective. The defects of the 20 did not suggest that similar problems might develop with the other computers. Arrangements for payment, the circumstances of use or resale, and other factors with respect to the buyer's needs did not require that all 1,000 computers be handled as a unit; as a consequence we may assume that the defects in the 20 did not constitute a fundamental breach of the contract as a whole (Arts. 25, 51(2)).

  Under these circumstances Buyer may avoid as to the 20 defective computers (Art. 51(1)) and, of course, also recover damages (Arts 45, 74–76, 81(1)). Article 51 opens up other remedies. For example, on these facts the breach with respect to the defective computers was "fundamental"; under Article 46(2) the buyer "may require delivery

---

6. See Markus Müller-Chen, Art. 49 para. 17, *in* Schlechtriem & Schwenzer, *CISG Commentary* (2nd English ed. 2005), *in* Schlechtriem & Schwenzer, *CISG Commentary* (2nd English ed. 2005).

of substitute goods" to replace the defective computers. (For discussion of avoidance (Art. 49) in connection with requiring delivery of substitute goods (Art. 46(2)), see §282.1 *supra*.)

305   **(b) Non-delivery within Time Fixed by Nachfrist Notice.**
This second ground for avoidance has been examined in the setting of Article 47(1), which authorizes the buyer to "fix an additional period of time of reasonable length for the performance by the seller of his obligations" (§287). This *"Nachfrist"* notice provides a basis for avoidance without proof that delay beyond the "additional period" fixed in the notice constitutes a "fundamental breach." The point that deserves emphasis here is that the seller's failure to comply with this notice is a basis for avoidance only when the seller has failed to deliver the goods. This point was reemphasized at the diplomatic conference by adding at the outset of Article 49(1)(b) the words "in case of non-delivery."

When a buyer sets an additional final period "of reasonable length" this (in common-law parlance) makes this period of time "of the essence." Of course, if the circumstances make any delay in delivery a fundamental breach (as when prices for the goods are subject to sharp fluctuations) the buyer may avoid the contract under paragraph (1)(a) without giving additional time to the seller. The reasons for limiting avoidance under paragraph (1)(b) to late delivery were explained in the debates at the Diplomatic Conference.[7] These debates showed adherence to UNCITRAL's decision that the special circumstances of international trade (the importance of the typical contract and the waste resulting from reshipment and redisposition after shipment abroad) called for limiting avoidance of the contract to substantial breach. See also Article 51, *infra*, and Example 46B, §283, *supra*.

As noted above (see §304 supra), it has been argued that a buyer can "reject" non-conforming goods while they are still in the possession of the seller before they have been transported (e.g., where a buyer is to take delivery at the seller's place of business and discovers the lack of conformity before taking over the goods) even if the lack of conformity does not constitute a fundamental breach. This argument is based on the position that the situation is a case of "non-delivery" rather than

---

7. *O.R.* 354–356, *Docy. Hist.* 575–577. See also UNCITRAL (1977) VII *YB* 46, *Docy. Hist.* 339.

delivery of non-conforming goods. For this reason, it has also been suggested that the buyer can establish grounds for avoidance in these circumstances by setting a Nachfrist deadline pursuant to Article 47; if the seller fails to deliver conforming goods by the deadline, it is argued, the buyer has the right to avoid pursuant to Article 49(1)(b).[8] This argument should be rejected: nothing in the text of Article 49 (or the rest of the Convention) suggests that a seller's tender of non-conforming goods in the circumstances at issue should be treated as a case of "non-delivery"; the argument, furthermore, would muddy the Convention's clear distinction between a failure to deliver and a delivery of non-conforming goods, and undermine the fundamental breach standard for avoiding a contract on the basis of non-conformities in the goods. Compare §283 and §305 supra.

306   ## (2) Limits on Time for Avoidance

(a) Reasons for Limiting the Time; Domestic Law.   Avoidance of the contract has important practical consequences with respect to responsibility for the care and redisposition of the goods. Assume that a buyer learns that the goods have arrived at their destination in a nearby seaport or rail siding and proposes to avoid the contract: If the buyer delays its declaration of avoidance, demurrage and warehouse costs will accrue, the goods will be subject to unnecessary risks of damage or loss, and the market price may fall. In the alternative, assume that the buyer receives the goods and proposes to avoid the contract because of non-conformity of the goods (Arts. 35, 49(1)(a)). A delay in the buyer's declaration of avoidance will delay the seller's opportunity to repair or redispose of the goods and will enhance expense and risk.

Because of these problems, domestic law limits the time within which the buyer may avoid the contract. Under the (U.S.A.) Uniform Commercial Code (§2–602(1)) rejection of goods must take place "within a *reasonable time* after their delivery or tender" and is "ineffective unless the buyer *seasonably* notifies the seller." Similarly, under UCC 2–608(2) "revocation of acceptance must occur with a *reasonable time* after the buyer discovers or should have discovered the ground for it."

---

8. See Markus Müller-Chen, Art. 49 para. 17, *in* Schlechtriem & Schwenzer, *CISG Commentary* (2nd English ed. 2005), *in* Schlechtriem & Schwenzer, *CISG Commentary* (2nd English ed. 2005).

307 **(b) The Convention's Rule on Time**

(i) Non-Delivery and Late Delivery. Under Article 49(2) the time for avoidance begins to run only when "the seller *has delivered* the goods." A buyer who is awaiting a delayed delivery need not try to estimate when the delay is sufficient to constitute a "fundamental breach" and thereupon notify the seller that the contract is avoided.[9] The buyer may await delivery; after the buyer "has become aware that delivery has been made" he may decide to keep the goods or (if the delay is a fundamental breach or if the seller has failed to comply with a *Nachfrist* notice under Article 47(1)) the buyer may reject the goods by a declaration of avoidance, provided that avoidance occurs "within a reasonable time after [the buyer] has become aware that delivery has been made."[10]

The fact that the buyer *may* defer avoidance for late delivery until after delivery (Art. 49(2)(a)) does not, of course, prevent a waiting buyer from avoiding more promptly. When the delay constitutes a fundamental breach the buyer may thereupon declare the contract avoided (Art. 49(1)(a)). If the buyer is uncertain as to whether the breach is fundamental, or if the buyer wishes to give the seller a last chance to deliver, the buyer may give the seller a *Nachfrist* notice under Article 47(1); if the seller fails to deliver within the reasonable additional period set in the buyer's notice the buyer may thereupon declare avoidance under Article 49(1)(b) (§305, *supra*).

A seller who finds that his delivery will be late may need to know whether to lay out funds for packing and shipping. Uncertainty over whether the buyer will accept usually can be removed by communications between the parties. And any danger that the buyer would refuse to clarify his position until the goods have arrived is met by Article 48(2)–(3), *supra* at §292, which gives the buyer a duty to reply to a request that he "make known whether he will accept performance" within a specified time; if the buyer fails to respond "the seller may perform within the time indicated in the request."

---

9. See Markus Müller-Chen, Art. 49 para. 27, *in* Schlechtriem & Schwenzer, *CISG Commentary* (2nd English ed. 2005).

10. For discussion of the "reasonable time" for declaring avoidance in a case of late delivery, see Markus Müller-Chen, Art. 49 para. 29, *in* Schlechtriem & Schwenzer, *CISG Commentary* (2nd English ed. 2005).

308   **(ii) Delivery of Non-Conforming Goods.**   Paragraph (2)(b) of
Article 49 applies "in respect of any breach other than late delivery" —
typically the arrival of goods that fail to conform to the contract. The
basic rule is that avoidance must occur "within a reasonable time (i)
after [the buyer] knew or *ought* to have known of the breach." The time
when the buyer *ought* to know of the breach would be influenced by
Article 38, *supra* at §249, which governs the period within which the
buyer "must examine the goods."[11] The length of a "reasonable time"
for declaring an avoidance is necessarily determined by a wide variety of
circumstances such as whether the goods are perishable or are subject to
price fluctuations.[12]

The remainder of Article 49, perhaps unnecessarily, spells out the
effect of certain important communications between the parties. For
example, let us assume that a buyer, pursuant to Article 47(1), informs
the seller that the goods are defective but that within one-month
the seller may cure the defect by replacement or repair. Article
49(2)(b)(ii) provides that the buyer's time for declaring avoidance
does not start to run until the one-month period expires. Paragraph
(2)(b)(iii) gives similar effect to a seller's request under Article 48(2)
that the buyer "make known" whether he will accept a cure of a defect in
the goods.[13]

It has been suggested that the Nachfrist procedure can be employed
after the expiration of a "reasonable time" for avoidance under
Article 49(2)(b)(i) in order to extend the time available for avoidance
via Article 49(2)(b)ii), and that Nachfrist can be used multiple times
for the purpose of extending the time for avoidance where the buyer
has received non-conforming goods.[14] *Such suggestions should be*

11. For discussion of the "reasonable time" for declaring avoidance in a case of late delivery,
see Markus Müller-Chen, Art. 49 para. 29, *in* Schlechtriem & Schwenzer, *CISG Commentary*
(2nd English ed. 2005).

12. See Markus Müller-Chen, Art. 49 paras. 32 & 35, *in* Schlechtriem & Schwenzer, *CISG*
Commentary (2nd English ed. 2005). For decisions on what constitutes a "reasonable time"
for avoidance following delivery of non-conforming goods see UNCITRAL Digest Art. 49
para. 16.

13. As we saw in examining Art. 47(1), *supra* at §288, avoidance may be based on failure to
comply with a *Nachfrist* notice only in cases of non-delivery. When non-conforming goods
are delivered (as in the case just put in the text) the buyer's notice inviting cure empowers the
seller to make the requested cure and extends the buyer's *time* for avoidance but does not
establish a *basis* for avoidance; in this setting avoidance must be based on fundamental
breach (Arts. 25, 49(1)(a)).

14. See Markus Müller-Chen, Art. 49 paras. 22, 36–38, 40 & 42, *in* Schlechtriem &
Schwenzer, *CISG Commentary* (2nd English ed. 2005).

rejected. They are based on a flawed understanding of the purpose of the Nachfrist procedure, and they would undermine the purposes of the time limits in Article 49(2)(b). A buyer that fails to avoid the contract within a reasonable time after he knew or ought to have known of the lack of conformity, or within a reasonable time after the seller has failed to cure the non-conformity after one Nachfrist period, should keep the goods and look to damages or price reduction for redress. That result is proper: after a certain time, returning non-conforming goods becomes a wasteful, overly complex exercise. There comes a point where a buyer that has held on to goods despite opportunities to avoid the contract must simply "own" the goods and expect only financial compensation for their lack of conformity.

308.1   **(ii) Effect of Seller's Knowledge of Defect.**   Interesting questions arise concerning the extent to which the Convention's requirements that a buyer notify the seller (e.g.) of defects in the goods apply to the buyer's right to avoid the contract.

As we have seen, notice requirements are imposed in two settings. (1) Article 39(1) provides that the buyer "loses the right to rely on a *lack of conformity* of the goods" if the buyer does not give the seller notice of the lack of conformity within a specified period. See the combined discussion of Articles 39, 40 and 44, §§254–261, *supra*. (2) In a different setting, Article 43(1) provides that the buyer "loses the right to rely on the provisions of Article 41 or 42" protecting the buyer against *third-party claims* if the buyer fails to give the seller notice of the claim within a specified period (§271, *supra*). Both of these drastic rules nullifying the buyer's substantive rights are subject to exceptions, one of which is that a seller may not rely on these provisions if the seller knew of the defect of which the buyer was otherwise required to give notice.[15]

Suppose that a seller knows of the defect of which the buyer would otherwise be required to give notice: Does the seller's knowledge excuse the buyer from the provisions of Article 49(2) that the buyer "loses the right to declare the contract avoided" unless the buyer avoids the contract within "a reasonable time"? Professor Will, in his excellent analysis of Article 49, suggested that the seller's knowledge of the non-conformity or the third-party claim removes the time limits with respect to avoidance of the contract. Although the exemptions based on the seller's knowledge (Articles 40 and 43(2)) refer only to the requirement that the buyer notify the seller of the *non-conformity* (as contrasted with

---

15. See Arts. 40 and 43(2).

the decision to *avoid* the contract), it was suggested that it would be "absurd" to permit such a seller to invoke the limits on *avoidance* stated in Article 49(2), *supra*.[16]

The present writer has some hesitation about this conclusion. The problem is complex and may not arise often. However, the question may be worth discussing to explore the differences between the two distinct remedies — damages and avoidance. As was noted (§255 *supra*) the seller needs to know of a claim of defects in the goods so he can take samples or inspect the goods to ascertain the facts before the evidence is lost; the seller also needs prompt notice of a claim in order to exercise his rights to cure the defect (Arts. 37, 48). However, Articles 40 and 43(2) recognize that it would be monstrous to apply these drastic sanctions (loss of all substantive rights) because a buyer fails to give the seller *facts* that the seller *already knew*.

Requiring a buyer to communicate its decision to *avoid the contract* within "a reasonable time" is based on different reasons than requiring *notice of defects*. As has been noted (§306, *supra*), undue delay in declaring avoidance of the goods creates risks of needless cost and risk with respect to the care and return of the goods and, when the goods are subject to market fluctuations, may give the buyer a chance to speculate at the seller's risk. Unless the "reasonable time" limit of Article 49(2) is preserved a buyer presumably could delay a decision on avoidance for the full limits of the period of limitation (prescription) which, under some domestic system can be a decade or more and under the 1974 U.N. Convention on the Limitation Period in the International Sale of Goods is four years.

The rules on notice of defects differ from the rules on time for avoidance (Art. 49(2) in yet another respect; a buyer who waits beyond a "reasonable time" in declaring avoidance is not deprived of other remedies, such as the right to damages (Arts. 45(2), 81(1); a buyer who fails to give the required notice of defects, unless excused (Arts. 40,43(2), 44), *loses all substantive and procedural rights*. The Convention recognizes this difference: Article 44 provides that a buyer who has "a reasonable excuse for failing to give" the notice of defects required by Articles 39(1) and 43(1) can still reduce the price (Art. 50) or claim damages (Art. 74); Article 44 does not extend this excuse to restrictions on avoidance of the contract.

---

16. Will, *B-B Commentary* 366. In this discussion Professor Will refers only to the Art. 43(2) exemption from notice of *third-party claims*; his comments, however, seem to apply also to the Art. 40 exemption with respect to notice of *non-conformity of the goods*.

In sum, it seems difficult to conclude that the seller's knowledge of a defect in the goods removes the "reasonable time" limit on avoidance set forth in Article 49(2).

308.2 (3) Avoidance Against Party Exempt from Damages

Article 49 bases the right to avoid the contract on a failure by the other party "to *perform*" its "obligations under the contract"; avoidance does not depend on liability to *pay damages* for breach. As we shall see, Article 79 in specified circumstances (*cf. force majeure*) provides that a party is exempt from *damages* for "failure to perform" its obligations and adds (paragraph (5)): "Nothing in this article prevents either party from exercising any right *other than to claim damages* under this Convention." In other words, exempting a party from damages does not prejudice the other party's right to avoid the contract. The underlying reason is compelling: a buyer is not required to pay for goods the seller can not deliver. Indeed, when Article 79 exempts a party from damages for failure to perform, the appropriate remedy is usually avoidance of the contract. See §423 *infra*.

Article 50.
Reduction of the Price

309   *Where a buyer has received delivery of non-conforming goods,*
Article 50 makes available a remedy of a type and approach likely
to be unfamiliar to those with a common-law background. This article
has a special role in determining how much the buyer owes the seller for
non-conforming goods when unusual circumstances relieve the seller of
liability for "damages."

Article 50[1]

If the goods do not conform with the contract and whether or not
the price has already been paid, the buyer may reduce the price in
the same proportion as the value that the goods actually delivered
had at the time of delivery bears to the value that conforming goods
would have had at that time. However, if the seller remedies any
failure to perform his obligations in accordance with article 37 or
article 48 or if the buyer refuses to accept performance by the seller
in accordance with those articles, the buyer may not reduce the
price.

310   A. The Special Role of "Price-Reduction"

The issues presented by Article 50 are subtle and complex; examples
may help.

*Example 50A. On April 1 Seller contracted to sell a $100,000 cargo of
No. 1 quality Edam cheese to Buyer, a food processor, with delivery by
June 1 "Ex Ship" at a port in Buyer's country. (Under this delivery term,
transit risks were assumed by Seller.) Seller dispatched cheese that
conformed to the contract,* **but it arranged for carriage on a ship not
equipped for proper storage of the cheese. As a result, when the ship
arrived at the designated port shortly before June 1** *the cheese was
moldy and graded at only No. 4 quality but the cheese could be used,*

---

1. Article 50 resulted from the redrafting, at the Diplomatic Conference, of Art. 46 of the
1978 Draft. *Cf.* ULIS 46. For action in UNCITRAL see III *YB* 89, IV *YB* 56–57, 60, VI *YB* 71,
77, VIII *YB* 46; *Docy. Hist.* 106, 133–134, 137, 149, 155, 339. For action at the Diplomatic
Conference see *O.R.* 42–43, 357–361, *Docy. Hist.* 432–438, 578–582. See *generally* Will,
B-B Commentary 368–376; Schlechtriem, Com. (1998) 437–448 (Huber).

with trimming and other treatment. The price level for No. 1 Edam cheese was the same on August 1 as when the contract was made; the moldy cheese was worth $20,000, one-fifth of the contract price of $100,000. Buyer needed the cheese for its food processing and elected to keep the cheese; preparing the moldly cheese for processing required additional time and expense, and led to a shutdown of Buyer's processing plant, with a loss of $15,000.

The delivery of No. 4 quality cheese when the contract specified No. 1 quality is a breach by Seller—a delivery of goods that do not conform to the contract. In the circumstances of Example 50A, Seller would be liable in damages under Article 74 for the difference in value between the cheese called for by the contract and the cheese actually delivered. Provided the plant-shut down and Buyer's increased expenses were, at the time the contract was concluded, fore see able consequences of delivering non-conforming cheese, and provided those losses could not have been avoided by reasonable actions in mitigation as provided in Article 77, Buyer could also recover $15,000 in consequential damages under Article 74. Because Seller has delivered goods that do not conform to the contract, however, Buyer could invoke reduction of the price under Article 50. If Buyer does so, how much will the price be reduced and what effect will the price reduction have on Buyer's damage claims?

311 (1) Seller's Exemption from "Damages"

Example 50B. Same facts as Example 50A, except Seller shipped the cheese on a properly-equipped ship, and the time of dispatch and other shipping arrangements would have led, under normal conditions, to timely and safe arrival of the shipment. However, unexpected hostilities led to the interning of the ship for two months during its transit through a canal. Normal refrigeration facilities on the ship could not cope with the hot climate in the canal area; when the ship finally arrived on August 1 the cheese was (as in Example 50A) moldy and graded at No. 4 quality. **As in Example 50A, however, Buyer elected to keep the cheese, with the same consequences as specified in the earlier Example.**

Article 79, *infra* at §424, provides that a party is excused from liability for "damages" when his failure to perform is "due to an impediment beyond his control." (Under domestic law the grounds for exemption may be referred to as "impossibility," "*force majeure*" "Act of God.") In the circumstances described in Example 50B, we may assume that the unexpected hostilities constituted an "impediment" that excused Seller from "damages." (See §433 n.17.) Buyer could have avoided the contract (Arts. 25, 49(1), 79(5)) but he elected to accept the cheese. The goods, however, did not "conform with the contract." Although Buyer may not recover "damages," he may nevertheless invoke the non-damages remedy in Article 50. How much must he pay?

312 **(2) The Price-Reduction Formula**

In both Example 50A and Example 50B Buyer may, under Article 50, "reduce the price in the same proportion as the value that the goods actually delivered had at the time of the delivery bears to the value that conforming goods would have had at that time." The No. 4 quality cheese delivered to Buyer had one-fifth the value of conforming goods. Buyer must pay Seller only one-fifth of the price — i.e., $20,000.[2]

The above formula is more significant when the price-level changes between the making of the contract and the delivery of the goods. Suppose that the price for all grades of this type of cheese doubled between April and August. Consequently, the No. 4 cheese would have sold for $40,000 and No. 1 cheese for $200,000. Under Article 50 Buyer may reduce "the price" ($100,000) by the prescribed "proportion." Since the No. 4 quality cheese that was delivered was worth one-fifth of the value "that conforming goods would have had at that time," Buyer must pay Seller one-fifth of the "price" of $100,000 or $20,000.

Paying only $20,000 for cheese that was worth $40,000 might seem to give Buyer a windfall. However, this advantage to Buyer reflects a portion of the protection that performance would have provided. Buyer should have received cheese that had increased in value to $200,000 but would have paid $100,000. For reasons noted *supra* at §311, in Example 50B the impediment that prevented performance by Seller exempts it from paying damages; thus in that example Buyer must bear its shutdown expenses and other consequential damages.

---

2. For elaboration on the formula employed in Art. 50 see Markus Müller-Chen, Art. 50 para. 8, *in* Schlechtriem & Schwenzer, *CISG Commentary* (2nd English ed. 2005). The editor of the current edition of this Commentary has described the Art. 50 formula as "a two-step process: first, divide the value of the non-conforming goods at the time of delivery (*not* the time of contracting) by the higher value that conforming goods would have had at that time; next, take the result (a fraction) and multiply it by the original contract price. The result is the reduced price authorized by Art. 50." John E. Murray, Jr. and Harry M. Flechtner, *Sales, Leases and Electronic Commerce: Problems and Materials on National and International Transactions* 465 (2nd ed. 2003).

These examples illustrate the narrow scope of Article 50. The price-reduction formula applies only when the buyer accepts and retains non-conforming goods. It plays a particularly important role when the seller is not liable in damages for the non-conformity. That combination of circumstances, however, is rare. A supervening "impediment" (*force majeure*) usually prevents the production or delivery of the goods; and in the rare case where the "impediment" causes serious non-conformity of goods that reach their destination, the buyer is not likely to accept the defective goods.

Suppose that by August 1, the market price for all grades of Edam cheese, instead of rising, had dropped to one-half; on August 1, Grade No. 4 sold for $10,000 and Grade No. 1 sold for $50,000. If Buyer accepts the cheese, under Article 50 he may reduce the price "in the same proportion as the value that the goods actually delivered had at the time of delivery [$10,000] bears to the value that conforming goods would have had at that time [$50,000]." This proportion — one-fifth — would once again call for the Buyer to pay Seller $20,000 for the moldy cheese. However, in this case Buyer would probably avoid the contract (reject the moldy cheese) if he could obtain substitute cheese at the low market level prevailing on August 1.

Except where Article 79 exempts the seller from liability for damages as in Example 50B, buyers who accept defective goods may have a choice between two remedies — price reduction under Article 50 and a claim for damages under Article 74, *infra* at §403. It is difficult at this point to compare results under Articles 50 and 74. In brief, if buyer suffers "no consequential" damages (such as shutdown losses), the allowance for defects in the goods will normally be the same under Articles 50 and 74 when (as in Example 50A) there is no change in the market level.

When the price-level rises, a buyer normally will claim damages under Article 74, since this approach protects his contractual "expectation interest." Thus, if the market price for No. 1 Edam cheese had risen to $200,000 at the time of delivery and No. 4 cheese was then worth $40,000 the right to damages under Article 74 protects the buyer's right to receive that value. Since Buyer received cheese worth only $40,000, a claim for damages might amount to $160,000 — a much more favorable result than the price reduction of $80,000 to $20,000 allowed by Article 50.

The situation is quite different when the price-level falls. As has been noted, in such cases the buyer would seldom accept the goods and hence could not use the price-reduction formula of Article 50. However, if he should accept the goods, price reduction under Article 50, in some situations, would provide more compensation for the non-conformity than would damages under Article 74. As we have seen, if at the date of delivery the market price for No. 1 Edam cheese had fallen to $50,000 and the price for No. 4 grade cheese was $10,000, the buyer could reduce the price under Article 50 from $100,000 to $20,000, a reduction of $80,000. Under Article 74, the difference between the value of conforming goods at the low price-level ($50,000) and the value of the goods received ($10,000) would give buyer a damage claim of $40,000, which is less favorable than the price reduction allowed by Article 50.

Suppose, however, the buyer has also suffered "consequential" loss (such as a plant shutdown). Article 45(a) and (b) does indicate that "rights provided in articles 46 to 52" (note the inclusion of article 50) do not bar damages under Article 74. On this basis the buyer could claim both price reduction and consequential losses — e.g., delays in production because of defects in the goods.[3] In any event, Article 45 should not be construed to permit double recovery based on the reduced value of the goods.[4]

Difficult problems can arise in integrating price reduction under Article 50 with the general rule on damage measurement in Article 74, §§403–408, *infra*. Suppose that a buyer notifies the seller of price reduction under Article 50 and later seeks to prove a more generous measure of the loss available under Article 74. (See Example 50B and the favorable protection under Article 74 for the buyer's "expectation interest" when the market price rises between the making of the contract and delivery of the goods.) The Convention does not seem to deal with this question of election of remedies. Perhaps the buyer should be held to have elected the price-reduction formula of Article 50 only if this had been part of an agreement to settle damages or if the seller had changed its position relying on the seller's notification.[5]

3. See Markus Müller-Chen, Art. 50 para. 18, *in* Schlechtriem & Schwenzer, *CISG Commentary* (2nd English ed. 2005); UNCITRAL Digest Art. 50 para. 7; Nicholas, 105 L.Q. Rev. 201, 226 (1989).

4. See Markus Müller-Chen, Art. 50 para. 18, *in* Schlechtriem & Schwenzer, *CISG Commentary* (2nd English ed. 2005); UNCITRAL Digest Art. 50 para. 7.

5. See Markus Müller-Chen, Art. 50 para. 5, *in* Schlechtriem & Schwenzer, *CISG Commentary* (2nd English ed. 2005).

313 B. Genesis and Evolution of "Price Reduction"

One can only appreciate Article 50 when it is seen in historical perspective — as a vestige of an important tool designed to cope with a traditional civil law doctrine (eroded but not abandoned) that a seller is liable for "damages" caused by defective goods only when he is guilty of fault or fraud. However, at an early stage in the development of the civil law it was decided that even though the seller was not liable for the buyer's damages it would be unjust for the seller to receive the full price for defective goods; such is said to be the basis in Roman law for the buyer's right to reduce the price to the degree of the deficiency — the *actio quanti minoris*.[6]

The traditional role of this special price-reduction mechanism was removed by the Convention's adoption of a unitary contractual approach, and its rejection of the idea that liability for damages should be conditioned on fault. Under Article 45(1), *supra*, "If the seller fails to perform *any of his obligations* under the contract or this Convention, the buyer may . . . (b) *claim damages* as provided in Articles 74 to 77." Common-law observers saw little reason to retain this venerable legal tool. The lack of such a provision in their statutes had not led to difficulties; in rare cases like Example 50B, where *force majeure* relieves the seller from damages for the delivery of defective goods, the question of how much the buyer should pay if it retains the defective goods could be handled under domestic rules providing for restitution to avoid unjust enrichment (*cf.* Art. 81(2), *infra* at §439). Ernst Rabel, writing in 1952, doubted the current utility of the *actio quanti minoris*, but in the Hague and UNCITRAL proceedings most representatives from civil law systems insisted on retaining this feature of their legal heritage.[7] And a common lawyer must concede that Article 50, by providing a solution

---

6. See Markus Müller-Chen, Art. 50 para. 1, *in* Schlechtriem & Schwenzer, *CISG Commentary* (2nd English ed. 2005); *Treitel, Remedies (Int. Enc.)* §67; *Treitel, Remedies (1988)* 107–109; Honoré, The History of the Aedilitian Actions From Roman to Roman-Dutch Law in Daube, Studies in the Roman Law of Sale 132 (1959); German (F.R.G.) Civil Code 462, 472 (reduction "in the proportion which at the time of the sale, the value of the thing in a condition free from defect would have borne to the actual value"); Swedish Sales Act 42, 43 (buyer may claim "such reduction in the price as is proportionate to the defect").

7. Rabel, A Specimen of Comparative Law: The Main Remedies for the Seller's Breach of Warranty, 22 Rev. Jur. Univ. Puerto Rico 167, 191 (1953). The proposed revision of the Quebec Civil Code omits a special "price-reduction" formula. *Quebec Civ. Code Revn., Sales* 62–63: Proposed Art. 37: "Damages for non-fulfilment may be claimed by way of reduction of price, or otherwise." The Comment explains: "Under this article, an action *quanti minoris* does not differ from an action for damages."

for cases like the above examples, will avoid the uncertainty and disunity of recourse to domestic rules on restitution.

In the 1978 Draft, as in ULIS 46, the formula for price reduction was based on the ratio between the value of non-conforming and of conforming goods "at the time of the *conclusion of the contract.*" At the Diplomatic Conference the reference-point was changed to the time for *delivery.* This change avoided constructing a theoretical value for defective goods that might not exist at the time of the contract.[8]

The work in UNCITRAL on "price reduction" was complicated by a failure to appreciate the traditional role of this legal tool.[9] Until 1976 the draft lacked the phrase "whether or not the price has already been paid"; until this lack was corrected in 1976, the provision that "the buyer may reduce the price" was understood by some to be addressed to the amount that the buyer should remit to the seller as a result of set-off.[10]

The final sentence of Article 50, in denying price-reduction to a buyer who refuses to allow the seller to exercise his right to cure, underscores the pervasive significance of the duty to mitigate damages. (See the discussion of "general principles" under Art. 7, *supra* at §101 and Art. 77, *infra* at §418.)[11]

313.1 C. Field of Application

(1) Possible Application beyond Non-Conformity of Goods

Article 50 states that price reduction is available when the "goods do not conform with the contract" — an area which the Convention

---

8. *Com. I* Art. 46, *SR.23*, paras. 23–41, *O.R.* 357–358, *Docy. Hist.* 578–579. See Markus Müller-Chen, Art. 50 paras. 9–11, *in* Schlechtriem & Schwenzer, CISG Commentary (2nd English ed. 2005).

9. Delay by some (including the present writer) in grasping the special role of the civil law doctrine of "price-reduction" contributed to difficulty in preparing ULIS and in the UNCITRAL proceedings. An interesting account of this background is given by Bergsten & Miller, The Remedy of Reduction of Price, *AJCL UNCITRAL Symposium* 255. The structure of the Convention helps to clarify the most important role of Art. 50. Art. 45(1), in introducing the system of remedies, distinguishes between the buyer's privilege to "(a) exercise the rights provided in Arts. 46–52" (requiring performance, avoidance, price reduction) and the buyer's privilege to "(b) claim *damages* as provided in Arts. 74–77."

10. See Bergsten & Miller, *The Remedy of Reduction of Price*, AJCL UNCITRAL Symposium 255.

11. See also Markus Müller-Chen, Art. 50 para. 7, *in* Schlechtriem & Schwenzer, *CISG Commentary* (2nd English ed. 2005).

distinguishes from other types of breach such as the place and time for delivery of goods and documents (Arts. 31–34), existence of third-party claims (Art. 41, 42) and other obligations imposed by contract (Art. 30).[12] Nevertheless, questions have been raised as to whether price reduction under Article 50 (as contrasted with the rules governing "damages" in Article 74, §§403–408, *infra*) applies to other types of non-performance such as delay, delivery at the wrong place, defects in documents and the like.[13] At the Diplomatic Conference Norway proposed an amendment that the right of price reduction should apply when the goods are subject to third-party rights or claims. The proposal attracted conflicting views; Norway withdrew the proposal.[14] On the other hand. Article 44, a compromise developed late in the Diplomatic Conference to meet objections to the notice requirements of Article 39(1) (conformity of goods), includes references to the notice requirements of Article 43(1), and adds that these requirements do not prejudice the buyer's rights to various remedies, including Article 50.[15] However, nothing in the legislative history indicated that Article 44 was understood to amend Article 50. Indeed, the debate that led to the failure of the Norwegian proposal (note 8 *supra*) recognized the difficulty of applying the price-reduction formula of Article 50 outside of its stated sphere — claims of non-conformity. Nor is there need to stretch Article 50 beyond its stated scope. As we shall see, Article 74's general provisions on the measurement of damages provide a flexible measure of the buyer's loss in diverse circumstances (§§404–408, *infra*) and in most situations are

---

12. See Markus Müller-Chen, Art. 50 para. 2, *in* Schlechtriem & Schwenzer, *CISG Commentary* (2nd English ed. 2005). The heading approved by the Diplomatic Conference for Section II (Arts. 35–44) is "Conformity of the Goods *and* Third-party Claims." Different notice requirements are established for claims of "lack of conformity of the goods" (Arts. 39, 40) and claims that the goods are subject to a "right or claim of a third-party" (Arts. 41, 42).

13. See UNCITRAL Digest Art. 50 para. 2.

14. The provision on price reduction was then draft Art. 46. The proposal: *O.R.* 118, *Docy. Hist.* 690; the discussion: *O.R.* 360–361, *Docy. Hist.* 581–582. The Norwegian sponsor said he withdrew the proposal "on the understanding that it would be up to the courts to decide whether and to what extent" the price reduction provision would apply to third-party claims. No weight should be given to such a statement by an individual delegate in the absence of evidence that the Conference agreed to such an "understanding." See Lord Diplock's properly skeptical response to such an "understanding" at §91 *supra*. For helpful discussion see Will in *B-B Commentary* 375–376; *Schlechtriem, 1986 Commentary* 79.

15. The significance of this provision was noted by Will, *B-B Commentary* 375–376.

more appropriate than the formula stated in Article 50.[16] (Recourse to Article 50 is, of course, optional.)

313.2 (2) Misapprehensions regarding Article 50

Language in earlier versions of Article 50 ("the buyer *may declare* the price to be reduced") might have been construed to give special weight to the buyer's declaration. (Contrast the *Nachfrist* notice under Article 47, §289 *supra*.) To prevent this interpretation the Diplomatic Conference deleted the above language.[17]

May a buyer who receives non-conforming goods reduce payment of the price only by virtue of Article 50? Does the buyer have a similar right under Articles 45(1)(b) and 74? The answer depends on rules such as set-off and counterclaim. Under procedural systems with which this writer is familiar a buyer with a damage claim based on non-conformity of the goods will have an opportunity to establish that claim as a set-off or counterclaim to an action for the price; payment and settlement practices reflect this legal right.[18]

---

16. *Cf.* Markus Müller-Chen, Art. 50 para. 2, *in* Schlechtriem & Schwenzer, *CISG Commentary* (2nd English ed. 2005).

17. The text of the U.K. proposal: *O.R.* 118, *Docy. Hist.* 690; the deliberations: *O.R.* 359–360, *Docy. Hist.* 580–581. See para. 61 — the buyer's action was "subject to the jurisdiction of courts." It has nevertheless been asserted that price reduction under Art. 50 requires "a declaration that does not have to satisfy any formal requirements." Markus Müller-Chen, Art. 50 para. 4, *in* Schlechtriem & Schwenzer, *CISG Commentary* (2nd English ed. 2005).

18. The U.N. Convention on the Limitation Period in the International Sale of Goods (1974: A/CONF. 63/14) Art. 25(2) gives protection to the right of set-off "(a) if both claims relate to the same contract or to several contracts concluded in the course of the same transaction." See (U.S.A.) Federal Rules of Civil Procedure, Rules 12 and 13; (U.S.A.) UCC 2–717; "The buyer on notifying the seller of his intention to do so may deduct all or any part of the damages resulting from any breach of the contract from any party of the price still due under the contract."

Article 51.
Non-conformity of Part of the Goods

314   The problems addressed by Article 51 can be exposed by a simple illustration:

Example 51A. A sales contract calls for the delivery of 100 bales of cotton. On delivery, 10 of the 100 bales prove to be so seriously defective that they cannot be used.

There are two distinct problems: (1) May the buyer reject the 10 defective bales and accept the rest? (In legal language — May the buyer "avoid the contract" as to only some units?) (2) May the buyer reject the delivery of 100 ("avoid" the entire contract) when only 10 units are defective? (Similar problems arise when the seller delivers only 90 bales instead of 100.)

Article 51[1]

(1) If the seller delivers only a part of the goods or if only a part of the goods delivered is in conformity with the contract, articles 46 to 50 apply in respect of the part which is missing or which does not conform.

(2) The buyer may declare the contract avoided in its entirety only if the failure to make delivery completely or in conformity with the contract amounts to a fundamental breach of the contract.

Paragraph (1) of Article 51 addresses the first question that was stated under Example 51A: May the buyer reject only the defective goods? Paragraph (2) addresses the second question: May the buyer reject all of the goods when only a part of the goods are defective? It may help to apply these provisions in the light of the reasons for Article 51.

315 A. Rules About "Goods" v. "Avoidance" of Contract

Attempts to answer the two problems posed by Example 51A have been encumbered by using overly-abstract concepts such as "rescission" or "avoidance" of the contract. Merchants ordinarily do not

---

1. This article is the same as Art. 47 of the 1978 Draft Convention and Art. 45 of the ULIS. See *generally* Flechtner, *Pittsburgh Symposium* 86–88.

think in terms of *avoiding a contract*; they think about what they may do with particular *goods*. It is no compliment to legal science to discover that the merchants" mode of thought is more precise. The concept of "avoidance" is misleading: "avoidance" does not destroy the contract: for example, the party whose breach leads to "avoidance" remains contractually liable to compensate the aggrieved party for its loss, and contractual provisions designed to deal with an alleged breach (e.g., liquidated damages clauses, arbitration provisions) remain in force. (See Art. 81(1), *infra* at §441–443.)

In most parts of the Convention the necessity to draft in terms that could be translated and understood in different linguistic and legal settings produced down-to-earth language that was clearer than that of the traditional domestic codes; here tradition was too strong to permit a fresh start. Article 49, *supra* at §302, provides that a buyer who encounters serious non-performance "may declare *the contract* avoided." When the seller's breach involves only part of the goods this broad rule has to be refined; this is done in Article 51.

316 (1) Remedies Applicable to a Non-conforming Part

The first question raised by Example 51A is this: What may Buyer do with respect to the 10 defective bales? Article 51(1) provides that the battery of remedies set forth in Articles 46 to 50 may be applied to the "part" of the delivery that fails to conform to the contract. *In other words, the non-conforming portion of the delivery can be treated, for purposes of Buyer's remedies, as if it were the subject of a separate contract. This applies, however, only to units of a delivery that are, from a commercial standpoint, independent and separate from each other, and not to component or constituent parts of a larger commercial unit.*[2] *The bales of cotton in Example 51A constitute (apparently) independent units, and they can thus be dealt with separately from the rest of the delivery for purposes of Buyer's remedies. In the sale of an automobile, however, a defective part could not generally be dealt with separately from the rest of the car.*[3]

Consequently, Article 51(1) gives Buyer these options — he may (i) require the seller to deliver substitute goods (Art. 46(2)), or (ii) "avoid

2. See Markus Müller-Chen, Art. 51 para. 2, *in* Schlechtriem & Schwenzer, *CISG Commentary* (2nd English ed. 2005); UNCITRAL Digest Art. 51 para. 2.
3. See Markus Müller-Chen, Art. 51 para. 2, *in* Schlechtriem & Schwenzer, *CISG Commentary* (2nd English ed. 2005).

the contract" (i.e., reject) with respect to the 10 defective units (Art. 49(1)(a)), or (iii) accept the defective goods and reduce their price (Art. 50) or claim damages (Art. 74). Article 51(1) also assures Seller of the right to cure under Article 48 (§§292–300, *supra*) with respect to the 10 defective bales.

Assume that in this contract for 100 bales Seller delivered only 90 bales, all of which conformed to the contract. If Buyer fixes "an additional period of time of reasonable length" for delivery of the 10 bales (Art. 47(1)) and Seller fails to comply with this demand, or if any delay in delivering the missing bales constitutes a fundamental breach. Buyer may "declare the contract avoided" with respect to the 10 missing bales (Art. 49(1)(a) & (b)); in other words, Buyer's duty to accept the missing units, should seller thereafter tender them, has come to an end.[4]

317   (2) Avoidance as to the Entire Contract

One of the purposes of paragraph (2) of Article 51 is to make clear that paragraph (1) does not force the buyer to sort out the non-conforming goods for separate handling. The buyer may "avoid" (reject) as to the entire delivery if the breach as to part causes detriment that is so substantial as to constitute a "fundamental breach" of the contract as a whole. The definition of "fundamental breach" in Article 25, *supra* at §181, calls for close examination of the facts of the case in relation to the policies served by avoidance. One factor of special significance with respect to avoidance of the entire contract because of a partially non-conforming delivery is whether the non-conformity of some of the goods interferes with the use or salability of the remainder.[5]

Subsection (2) makes an additional point in stating that avoidance of the entire contract may "only" be based on fundamental breach. Let us suppose that in Example 51A, above, only 90 bales were delivered, the buyer makes a *Nachfrist* demand that the seller deliver missing units within a fixed additional period (Art. 47(1), *supra* at §287), and the seller fails to comply. As we saw at §316, the seller's failure to comply with the notice empowers the buyer to avoid as to the missing units; the buyer

---

4. Under (U.S.A.) UCC 2–601 (c) and 2–608(1) remedies may be applied to commercial units that fail to conform.

5. (U.S.A.) UCC 2–601 (c) provides that on a defective delivery the buyer may "accept any commercial unit or units and reject the rest." "Commercial unit" is defined (2–105(6)) as a unit the "division of which materially impairs its character or value on the market or in use." This concept serves to bar rejection of part of such a unit, and also to permit rejection of an entire unit when part is defective. See §316 *supra*.

need not show that the breach was fundamental (Art. 49(1)(b)). However, the buyer may not base avoidance of the entire contract on the failure to comply with the *Nachfrist* notice; under Article 51(2), the buyer must show that the breach was fundamental as to the entire contract (Arts. 49(1)(a), 51(2)).[6]

As the editor of the current edition has argued elsewhere,[7] the approach of Article 51(2) appears flawed. Of course it makes sense to prevent a buyer from using the Nachfrist procedure to elevate a failure to receive an insubstantial portion of a delivery into grounds for avoiding the entire contract. Thus if Seller in Example 51A delivered 90 of the 100 cotton bales called for by the contract, Buyer should not be permitted to avoid the entire contract merely because Seller does not deliver the 10 missing bales by a Nachrist deadline set by Buyer. Suppose, however, Seller had delivered only five of the required 100 bales. Must Buyer wait until it is sure that the delay in delivering the missing 95 bales constitutes a fundamental breach before avoiding the entire contract, even if it cannot make proper use of only five bales? Isn't the purpose of the Nachfrist procedure to relieve a buyer awaiting delivery of the burden of making this difficult call? Should a seller be able to deprive the buyer of its right to use the Nachfrist procedure to create grounds for avoiding the entire contract simply by delivering an insignificant portion of the goods (e.g., one bale of cotton in Example 51A)?

The answer, of course, would be to allow a buyer to use Nachfrist to establish grounds for avoiding the entire contract where the seller has failed to deliver a material portion of the goods — a portion that, if it were never delivered, would constitute a fundamental breach of the entire contract. That might be a superior rule, but it appears to contradict the terms of Article 51(2): perhaps because they did not consider this situation,[8] the drafters apparently intended categorically to deny use of Nachfrist to avoid the entire contract in a partial delivery situation. The desirable result can nevertheless probably be achieved without violating the terms of Article 51(2). A buyer awaiting a material portion of a delivery can set a Nachfrist deadline for receiving the missing goods, even if the process does not directly create grounds for avoiding the entire contract under Article 51(2). If the seller fails

---

6. *Accord,* Flechtner in *Pittsburgh Symposium* 53, 72–73. The approach of Art. 51 is applied to installment contracts in Art. 73, *infra* at §399. *But cf.* §400 n.3.

7. Flechtner in *Pittsburgh Symposium* 53, 88.

8. Flechtner in *Pittsburgh Symposium* 53, 71–73.

to meet the deadline, that fact — along with the buyer's good faith conduct in granting the seller extra time to deliver[9] — should be taken into account in determining whether the seller's delay constitutes a fundamental breach of the entire contract.

To sum up with respect to Buyer's right to avoid the entire contract in the face of Seller's tender of a partially non-conforming delivery: Under Article 51(2) Buyer may "declare the contract avoided in its entirety" (all 100 bales) only if the breach was "fundamental" with respect to the contract *as a whole*. Factors that bear on this issue include: (1) A timely offer by Seller to "cure" (Arts. 37, 48) by replacing the 10 defective bales; (2) The feasibility of separate action with respect to the 10 defective bales; (3) If separate avoidance of the 10 bales is not feasible, does acceptance of the entire shipment and redisposition of the 10 defective bales (subject to a claim for damages for the deficiency) (Art. 25) "substantially ... deprive [the buyer] of what he is entitled to expect under the contract ..." ? As has been noted under Article 25, at §185, *supra*, Buyer probably needs the remedy of total avoidance if Seller refuses delivery except in exchange for payment of the full price; Buyer's need for avoidance would be reduced if Seller offers to reduce the sum Buyer must pay upon delivery by an amount adequate to compensate Buyer for the reduced value of the 10 bales and any other loss (Art. 74) resulting from the breach of contract.

9. Even where it does not create grounds for avoidance, the *Nachfrist* procedure imposes costs on an aggrieved buyer who employs it: the buyer loses the right to pursue any remedies for breach until either the *Nachfrist* deadline has passed or the seller declares that it will not meet the deadline. Art. 47(2).

Article 52.
Early Delivery; Excess Quantity

318   Paragraph (1) of this article deals with a situation that seldom causes serious difficulty — the enthusiastic seller who delivers too soon; paragraph (2) addresses the more complex consequences of delivering an excess quantity.

Article 52[1]

(1) If the seller delivers the goods before the date fixed, the buyer may take delivery or refuse to take delivery.

(2) If the seller delivers a quantity of goods greater than that provided for in the contract, the buyer may take delivery or refuse to take delivery of the excess quantity. If the buyer takes delivery of all or part of the excess quantity, he must pay for it at the contract rate.

319 **A. Early Delivery**

Applying paragraph (1) may call for interpretation of the contract. If the contract calls for delivery "not later than June 1," a delivery on May 20 would not necessarily occur "before the date fixed." The option given the buyer to "refuse to take delivery" would apply only if the date of delivery was inconsistent with the contract, as where the contract permitted delivery "between May 25 and June 1."[2]

The buyer's option to refuse or accept an early delivery need not be based on a showing of inconvenience or "fundamental breach" (Art. 25). However, the buyer could gain little by an unreasonable refusal to take an early delivery. *And the buyer may have good reason to reject an early delivery. For example, if the contract requires payment upon delivery, the buyer may not yet have the requisite funds available.*[3]

1. This article is the same as Art. 48 of the 1978 Draft. Paragraph (1) is similar to ULIS 29 except for deletion of a provision that a seller who accepts "may reserve" the right to claim damages. Paragraph (2) is similar to ULIS 47.
2. See Markus Müller-Chen, Art. 52 para. 1, *in* Schlechtriem & Schwenzer, *CISG Commentary* (2nd English ed. 2005); UNCITRAL Digest Art. 52 para. 2.
3. For the obligation to pay upon acceptance of an early delivery if the contract requires payment upon delivery, see UNCITRAL Digest Art. 52 para. 3. For a different view of how

The option that Article 52(1) gives the buyer is not avoidance of the contract, but the right to refuse the early delivery; the buyer remains obligated to take goods that the seller properly retenders at a date authorized by the contract. (Similarly, under Article 37 the seller may cure defects in delivery "up to" the date for delivery.)[4]

320 B. Excess Quantity

When the market falls after the making of the contract, the seller may be tempted to take advantage of the high contract price and deliver a larger quantity than the contract specified; if the buyer "takes delivery of all or part of the excess quantity, he must pay for it at the *contract rate*"[5] (Art. 52(2)), unless the parties agree otherwise (Art. 6). Under paragraph (2) the buyer may alternatively "refuse to take delivery *of the excess quantity.*" Questions of interpretation may arise if the seller's tender does not give the buyer the opportunity to accept the quantity specified in the contract and refuse the rest.

Example 52A. A contract called for the shipment of 1,000 bags of sugar at $50 per bag, a total of $50,000. Seller shipped an excess quantity, 1,200 bags. All of the sugar was shipped under a single negotiable bill of lading. Seller (through a correspondent bank) tendered his bill of lading in exchange for payment of a sight draft for $60,000 — the price for 1,200 bags.

Under these circumstances the seller's demand for cash outlay of more than that called for by the contract would probably be a

---

this situation should be addressed, see Markus Müller-Chen, Art. 52 para. 4, *in* Schlechtriem & Schwenzer, *CISG Commentary* (2nd English ed. 2005).

4. *Accord*, Markus Müller-Chen, Art. 52 para. 3, *in* Schlechtriem & Schwenzer, *CISG Commentary* (2nd English ed. 2005). Although the buyer is privileged to refuse an early delivery, if the seller is not present and other conditions specified by Art. 86(2) are met, the buyer may be obliged to take possession of the goods on behalf of the seller. See Ch. V, Sec. VI, Preservation of the Goods, and Art. 86, *infra* at §455; Markus Müller-Chen, Art. 52 para. 3, *in* Schlechtriem & Schwenzer, *CISG Commentary* (2nd English ed. 2005). For conflicting views on whether the rejection of an early delivery must be reasonable see Will, *B-B Commentary* 380; Markus Müller-Chen, Art. 52 para. 3, *in* Schlechtriem & Schwenzer, *CISG Commentary* (2nd English ed. 2005). On buyer's possible claim for storage expenses for early delivery see Will, *B-B Commentary* 381; Markus Müller-Chen, Art. 52 paras. 4–5, *in* Schlechtriem & Schwenzer, *CISG Commentary* (2nd English ed. 2005).

5. See UNCITRAL Digest Art. 52 para. 5; Oberlandesgericht Rostock, Germany, 25 September 2002, English translation available at http://cisgw3.law.pace.edu/cases/020925g1.html.

"fundamental breach." Payment of $60,000 followed by a rejection of the 200 excess bags and a claim for the refund of 10,000 may subject the buyer to hazards with respect to the seller's financial responsibility and the burdens and delays of litigation. See Article 25, *supra* at §181.[6] On the other hand, the buyer may decide to accept the overshipment when the excess in quantity is trivial, and may be obliged to do so if that is consistent with the contract, including practices established by the contract, including parties or usage (Art. 9).[7] If in example 52A Seller's sight draft had only required payment of the original contract price ($50,000), Buyer might be obliged to authorize payment, take possession of the delivery, and then separate the excess goods that it wishes to return to Seller. *Whenever a buyer is in possession of delivered goods that it intends to "reject," Article 86(1) requires the buyer to take reasonable steps to preserve them, although the buyer is entitled to reimbursement for its expenses* (see Articles 86(1), 87 and 88).[8]

Of course, parties who are acting in good faith can normally make an arrangement that would meet the needs of both. The seller could wire authorization for reduction in the draft or for delivery to an intermediary (e.g., a sugar dealer at the point of destination) who, after satisfying the bank's interest in the draft, could take delivery of the shipment and permit the buyer to take the agreed quantity in exchange for the appropriate payment. A seller's refusal to make a reasonable arrangement would give the buyer reason for concern about a prompt refund and would be an added reason supporting rejection of the entire shipment.

If the buyer does decide to take excess goods, applying the apparently-simple rules of Article 52(2) can involve challenges. Suppose a buyer agrees to buy goods at seller's standard (list) price for the quantity called for by the contract, but the seller tenders an excess quantity that, under the seller's standard pricing practices, would qualify for a volume discount. If the buyer decides to accept the overshipment, what is the "contract rate" at which the buyer must pay for the excess goods? Is it simply the per-unit price determined by dividing the full contract price by the quantity of goods called for in the contract? Or should it include the seller's volume discount, on the footing that the

---

6. See *Sec. Commy.* on draft Art. 48, para. 9, *O.R.* 44, *Docy. Hist.* 434. *Cf.* Markus Müller-Chen, Art. 52 para. 8, *in* Schlechtriem & Schwenzer, *CISG Commentary* (2nd English ed. 2005).

7. See UNCITRAL Digest Art. 52 para. 5.

8. See Markus Müller-Chen, Art. 52 para. 9, *in* Schlechtriem & Schwenzer, *CISG Commentary* (2nd English ed. 2005).

parties impliedly adopted the seller's standard pricing rates? At the time this is written such thorny questions have not been raised in reported decisions — probably because over-delivery by the seller is not a common occurrence, and can usually be worked through on a consensual basis by parties operating in good faith. Given the ambiguity of the phrase "contract rate," a buyer that has received an over-delivery should be cautious in taking the extra goods without a documented understanding with the seller concerning the price for the extra goods.

CHAPTER III.

OBLIGATIONS OF THE BUYER
(Articles 53–65)

321 **INTRODUCTION TO CHAPTER III**

The structure of Chapter III is similar to that of the preceding chapter on Obligations of the Seller. Two sections state the buyer's duties: to pay the price (Sec. I, Arts. 53–59) and to take delivery (Sec. II, Art. 60). The final section defines the remedies that are available to the seller when the buyer fails to perform these duties (Sec. III, Arts. 61–65). These remedies given the seller (like those given the buyer (Arts. 45–52) in Chapter II) are supplemented by general rules on remedies in Chapter V (Arts. 71–88).

The buyer's obligations are as vital as those of the seller but are less complex; Chapter III is shorter than Chapter II but poses some unique and challenging problems.[1]

---

1. See *generally* Tallon, *Parker Colloq.* Ch. 7; Sevón, *Dubrovnik Lectures* ch. 6.; Maskow, *B-B Commentary* Ch. 3; Niggerman, 1 Int. Bus. L.J. 27 (1988).

Article 53.
Summary of Buyer's Obligations

322   Chapter II opened with a brief summary of the seller's obligations. The present chapter opens with a similar summary of the buyer's obligations.

Article 53

The buyer must pay the price for the goods and take delivery of them as required by the contract and this Convention.

Article 53, like Article 30, emphasizes the role of the contract in defining the parties' obligations — a point that was discussed under Article 30 at §206 and need not be repeated here. *Article 53, along with Article 30, has been invoked to define the obligations that create a sale of goods subject to the CISG.*[1]

---

1. See UNCITRAL Digest Art. 53 para. 1.

SECTION I.

PAYMENT OF THE PRICE
(Articles 54–59)

Article 54.
Enabling Steps

323   The Convention at many points responds to the fact that consummating an international sale calls for cooperation; each party must take steps that are related to corresponding steps by the other.[1] The present article reflects the importance of preliminary steps by the buyer that are necessary for timely payment of the price, such as arranging for the issuance of a letter of credit and applying for governmental authorization to transmit funds to the seller.

Article 54[2]

The buyer's obligation to pay the price includes taking such steps and complying with such formalities as may be required under the contract or any laws and regulations to enable payment to be made.

The above steps are a part of the buyer's "obligation to pay the price." This language is important. Under Article 63(1), *infra* at §350, the seller "may fix an additional period of time of reasonable length for performance by the buyer of *his obligations*" — the seller's corollary of the buyer's *Nachfrist* notice (Art. 47(1), *supra* at §288). Under Article 64(1)(b), *infra* at §353, if the buyer does not "perform his obligation to pay the price" within the additional period fixed by the seller's notice the seller may declare the contract avoided. Consequently, if the seller gives the buyer an appropriate notice providing a final additional period for taking one of the required steps for price payment such as obtaining

---

1. *E.g.*, Arts. 19(2), 21(2), 32(2) & (3), 48(2), 58(3), 60(a), 65, 71, 73(2), 79(4), and 85–88. It may add a bit of romance to commercial law to suggest that the parties' inter-related steps resemble old-fashioned ballroom dancing.

2. This article is the same as Art. 50 of the 1978 Draft Convention. ULIS 69 is similar but somewhat more detailed.

the issuance of a letter of credit by a specified date (Art. 54),[3] avoidance by the seller need not be based on proof that the buyer's failure to comply is a "fundamental breach" (Arts. 25 and 64(1)(a)).

In addition, the failure to take one of the required steps "to enable payment to be made" (Art. 54) itself constitutes a breach of contract (Arts. 53 and 54). If the seller can show that this breach is "fundamental" he may declare the contract avoided (Arts. 25 and 64(1)(a)) without first giving a *Nachfrist-notice* fixing "an additional period of time."[4]

The fact that Article 54 incorporates steps necessary to affect payment into the buyer's payment obligation means that robust remedies are available to a seller if the buyer neglects those steps. Of course in proper circumstances the Convention provides relief when a future breach is merely threatened. Article 71, *infra* at §385, authorizes a party under some circumstances to suspend performance if "it becomes apparent that the other party *will not* perform a substantial part of his obligations." This authorization applies even when the other party has not yet committed a breach of contract; although, naturally, the grounds for suspension are circumscribed. (See the discussion under Art. 71, *infra* at §385.) Under Article 71, "a serious deficiency" in the buyer's "ability to perform" — e.g., its ability to pay the price — may, in some circumstances, authorize the seller to "suspend" his own performance. Because the buyer's failure to take one of the steps required by Article 54 constitutes *a present breach*, not just a threat of a future breach, the seller need not rely on the "suspension" provisions of Article 71; it may employ the remedies provided for breach of contract — the *Nachrist*-avoidance remedy (Arts. 63(1) and 64(1)(b)) and avoidance for fundamental breach (Arts. 25 and 64(1)(a)).[5] These remedies respond to the expenses a seller may need to incur in preparation for delivery (e.g., producing, procuring or packing the goods) — expenses that, as a practical matter, the seller may not be able to recoup or recover when the buyer is derelict in making arrangements for payment.

3. See UNCITRAL Digest Art. 54 para. 3.
4. *Accord*, Huber, 43 *Rabels Z* 413, 511 (1979). *Cf.* Hellner, *Dubrovnik Lectures* 352–353.
5. See Günter Hager, Art. 54 para. 7, *in* Schlechtriem & Schwenzer, *CISG Commentary* (2nd English ed. 2005); UNCITRAL Digest Art. 54 para. 2.

Article 55.
Open-Price Contracts

324 ## A. Interplay of Rules on Formation and on Price-Determination

We have already considered open-price contracts in examining the criteria for an offer stated in Article 14; there we met conflicting views over whether the parties may make a contract without determining the price. At the Diplomatic Conference, the final decisions on this issue involved both Article 14 and Article 55. For this reason, both Articles were considered in detail in connection with Article 14, *supra* at §§134–137.6; that discussion is a necessary part of the present examination of Article 55.

The relevant provisions are as follows:

Article 14

(1) A proposal for concluding a contract addressed to one or more specific persons constitutes an offer if it is sufficiently definite and indicates the intention of the offeror to be bound in case of acceptance. A proposal is sufficiently definite if it indicates the goods and expressly or implicitly fixes or makes provision for determining the quantity and the price.

[The full text of Article 14, including paragraph (2), is set forth *supra* under Article 14 at §133.]

Article 55[1]

Where a contract has been validly concluded but does not expressly or implicitly fix or make provision for determining the price, the parties are considered, in the absence of any indication to the contrary, to have impliedly made reference to the price generally charged at the time of the conclusion of the contract for such goods sold under comparable circumstances in the trade concerned.

---

1. *Cf.* ULIS 57. Art. 51 of the 1978 Draft Convention was substantially revised at the Diplomatic Conference. The legislative history of these changes is examined at notes 2–4 *infra*.

325 **B. Proposals and Agreements that do not State the Price**

In examining the relationship between Articles 14(1) and 55 we need to recall the central points of the discussion of Article 14(1), at §§132.1, 133 and 137.4, *supra*. That discussion is summarized under headings (1) and (2), which follow.

325.1 **(1) Evidence of Formation Limited to Two Communications**

The Introduction to Part II — Formation (§132.1 *supra*) noted that the Convention's rules on "offer" and "acceptance" are addressed to situations in which the only relevant facts are two communications: one that may (or may not) be an "offer" and a reply that may (or may not) be an "acceptance." While situations with this limited setting are not typical of contract-formation in international trade the offer-acceptance rules are useful; serious problems develop only if one leaps to the conclusion that no contract is formed if an "offer" and "acceptance" cannot be isolated from a flow of communications that mature into agreement, or if the parties' decision to make a contract becomes clear only as a result of conduct such as the shipment of goods and their acceptance.

The discussion (§170 *supra*) of Article 19 had to face a similar issue: Delivery and acceptance of goods often follow the exchange of forms that include material inconsistencies; after the transaction has been consummated the question is not *"Was* there a contract?" but *"What* were its *terms?"* On the other hand, when the only basis for finding a contract is the exchange of communications, the rules on contract-formation are (and should be) strict. The following example provides one of many possible illustrations.

Example 55A. On June 1, Buyer emailed Seller, "Can you ship me 1,000 bales of No. 1 Cotton?" Seller emailed a reply, "Accept your offer. Cotton at $110 per bale will be shipped July 1." Buyer responded, "My email was only an inquiry: Cannot agree to your terms." Seller answered, "Accepted your offer and will hold you to the contract."

Unless Buyer's June 1 email impliedly incorporated the $110 price mentioned in Seller's reply (e.g., by reference to Seller's listed prices through a course of dealing or trade usage, as in Example 14A in §137.4 *supra*),[2] the parties are not bound by contract. Under Article 14(1)

---

2. Günter Hager, Art. 55 para. 7, *in* Schlechtriem & Schwenzer, *CISG Commentary* (2nd English ed. 2005); Oberlandesgericht München, Germany, 19 October 2006, English translation available at http://cisgw3.law.pace.edu/cases/061019g1.html.

Buyer's "proposal" may not be construed as an "offer": it was not "sufficiently definite" because it did not "expressly or implicitly" fix or make "provision for determining . . . the price."

The reasons for this strict rule for construing proposals were explored in discussing Article 14 and Example 14A, §137.4 *supra*.

325.2   (2) Article 14(1) as Rule of Contract Validity

Is the provision on price in Article 14(1) a rule for the construction of "proposals" or is it a rule of validity that nullifies an agreement in which the parties show that they intend to be bound? Reasons for the former conclusion were developed in discussing Article 14 at §137.5, *supra*. This question of validity *under Article 14* (unlike the question of validity *under domestic law* to be discussed next) is of great importance; at stake is the freedom to contract in all international sales governed by Part II of the Convention; also at stake is the applicability of the uniform substantive rules of Part III. The dimensions of the problem were explored in greater detail under Article 14 at §§137.5–137.6.

325.3   (3) Article 55 and Domestic Rules on "Validity"

We turn now from Article 14 to Article 55 (quoted at §324) and, more particularly, to the opening phrase: "When a contract has been *validly* concluded . . ."

This language emerged during UNCITRAL's 1977 review of the Working Group's "Sales" Draft (VIII *YB* 48–49, *Docy. Hist.* 341–342) and responded to concerns of some delegates that the Convention should not disturb the rule of their domestic law that provision for the price in an agreement was a requisite for a valid contract.[3]

---

3. The concern to preserve this rule of domestic law was expressed at different stages of the legislative proceedings. VI *YB* 73 (para. 153), 74, IV *YB* 32, IV *YB* 113 (para. 38) 57, VIII *YB* 48–49; *O.R.* 363–367, 392–393; *Docy. Hist.* 151, 152, 209, 238, 341–342, 584–588, 613–614. The Commission's decision to add the opening phrase to what became Art. 55 (then draft Art. 37) was as follows (Report of Tenth Session, 1977, A/32/17, Annex I): The Commission sitting as the Committee of the Whole "decided to introduce an express statement into the article to make it clear that it applied to agreements which were considered *valid by the applicable law*." (Emphasis added). VII *YB* 49, *Docy. Hist.* 342, (paras. 329, 340). On the meaning of "applicable law" see the discussion under Art. 14 at §137.6, *supra*. See *Docy. Hist.* 341 para. 328 (applicable *national* law).

This concern was aggravated by the fact that the draft then provided that, in the absence of agreement, the buyer must pay "the price generally charged *by the seller*," a provision that could be abused by the seller.[4] This view persisted and, at the Diplomatic Conference the reference to "the price charged by the *seller*" was replaced by "the price *generally* charged."[5]

A second aspect of this 1977 review was the addition of the reference to "validity" to the opening phrase of Article 55. The legislative history shows that this amendment was designed to restrict the scope of the article "to agreements that were *valid by the applicable* law"[6] — i.e., domestic law applicable under rules of private international law. See Article 14, *supra*, at §137.6.[7]

This departure from uniformity is unfortunate but is of acceptable proportions. The rule requiring a price term for "validity" is rejected by the (U.K.) Sale of Goods Act (the pattern for most of the common-law world), by the (U.S.A.) Uniform Commercial Code, and also by many code systems that on this point do not follow French law.[8] The practical consequence of the Convention's concession to domestic law is that, in making agreements with parties with places of business in States that retain the strict "validity" rule, the parties must exercise no less (and no more) care than formerly to comply with this feature of domestic law. (The serious consequences, including total loss of protection under the Convention, were analyzed under Article 14, *supra*, at §137.7.)

As we have seen, some domestic "validity" rules responded to concern that, in the absence of a contract provision, the seller would set the price. In view of the deletion of the reference in the UNCITRAL draft to "the price generally charged by the *seller...*" in favor of the

---

4. The language pointing to the seller's price was inherited from ULIS (1964) Art. 57. For discussion in UNCITRAL, see VI *YB* 73 (para. 152), 74, IV *YB* 33; *Docy. Hist.* 151 (para. 152), 152, 210. Decisions in France that seem to reflect this view are discussed in Tallon, *Parker Colloq.* at 7–11 & 7–12. See also Fortier, Le prix dans la Convention de Vienne, 117 J. D.I. 381 (1990).

5. *O.R.* 392–393, *Docy. Hist.* 613–614.

6. See the discussion of the travaux préparatoires in note 3 *supra*.

7. *But* see Günter Hager, Art. 55 para. 5, *in* Schlechtriem & Schwenzer, *CISG Commentary* (2nd English ed. 2005).

8. (U.K.) SGA (2); (U.S.A.) UCC 2–305. See Murray, "Open Price" in a Worldwide Setting, Comm. L.J. 491, 496–499 (Nov. 1984); Niggeman, Buyer's Obligations, Int. Bus. L.J. No. 1, 1988, 27, 31–33; Sevón, *Dubrovnik Lectures* 209.

reference in Article 55 to "the price *generally* charged,"[9] some domestic systems may wish to consider whether their traditional rule has become unnecessary for international trade.[10]

Some delegates from Eastern European countries with planned economies also noted that a contract that did not state the price would be inconsistent with the formality of their foreign trade agreements. (This outlook had also generated objections to Article 11 which rejected domestic formal requirements; to meet this concern Articles 12 and 96 authorized reservations to Article 11. The "validity" exception in Article 55 seems functionally similar to the provision allowing a reservation to Article 11.) In any event, formal foreign trade agreements are not likely to fail to provide for the price, and will avoid the question posed by Articles 14 and 55.[11]

325.4 Methodology for Calculating the Price

Where Article 55 applies, the price for the goods if presumed to be "the price generally charged at the time of the conclusion of the contract for such goods sold under comparable circumstances in the trade concerned."[12] If the parties intend to conclude a contract even though they have not expressly or implicitly provided for the price, their intention should be honored if at all possible. An early decision finding that no price for the goods could be determined pursuant to Article 55[13] appears to violate this principle. The court in that case could have used any of a number of tools provided by the Convention to effectuate the intent of the parties. For example, Article 76(2) may suggest a general principle that, where the price mandated by Article 55 cannot be

---

9. 1978 UNCITRAL draft, Art. 51, *O.R.* 10, *Docy. Hist.* 387.

10. See, e.g., Fortier, *supra* note 4 at 387–388.

11. The discussion of Art. 29, §§204.2–204.3, *supra*, suggested that the common-law rule requiring "consideration" for the modification of a contract may not be preserved by the provision of Art. 4(a) that the Convention "is not concerned with: (a) the validity of the contract . . . " The reason, in brief, was that Art. 4(a) could not mean that the Convention was not "concerned" with issues on which it framed a rule—in that setting the rule of Art. 29 that a contract could be modified by "mere agreement of the parties." This principle, of course, does not apply to specific concessions to domestic law such as the opening phrase of Art. 55 and the provisions of Arts. 12 and 96 allowing reservations excluding Art. 11.

12. For further discussion of the method for determining the price under Art. 55, see Günter Hager, Art. 55 paras. 8–9, *in* Schlechtriem & Schwenzer, *CISG Commentary* (2nd English ed. 2005).

13. Legfelsobb Bíróság (Supreme Court), Hungary, 25 September 1992, English translation available at http://cisgw3.law.pace.edu/cases/920925h1.html.

proven directly, proof of a "reasonable substitute" price may suffice. Frustrating the parties' intent to enter into an otherwise valid contract merely because the fact-finder is not equal to the task of determining the proper price pursuant to Article 55[14] is an extraordinarily undesirable — and generally avoidable — result.

---

14. See §137.5 *supra*; Günter Hager, Art. 55 paras. 8–9, *in* Schlechtriem & Schwenzer, *CISG Commentary* (2nd English ed. 2005).

Article 56.
Net Weight

Article 56[1]

328   **If the price is fixed according to the weight of the goods, in case of doubt it is to be determined by the net weight.**

This Article, inherited from ULIS, is unimportant, but on occasion may be useful to help determine the price in the absence of evidence as to an express agreement concerning the use of gross or net weight in determining price, or as to the practices of the parties or usage of trade on this issue (Art. 9). The statement that the rule applies only "in case of doubt" emphasizes its subordinate role.[2]

---

1. This article is the same as Art. 52 of the 1978 Draft and ULIS 58.
2. *Cf.* German (F.R.G.) Commercial Code 380(1), Israeli Sales Law 20(b).

Article 57.
Place of Payment

329   This is the first of three articles addressed to the manner of payment. The modalities for payment include *place* (the present Article) and *time* (Arts. 58 & 59).

330   A. Significance of Place for Payment

It is sometimes impossible to export funds without a license; without such a license, payment may be of little value to a seller from a different country. By the same token, buyers in "soft currency" countries may find it difficult to pay in "hard currency" countries. The parties will usually be keenly aware of this problem so that the contract will specify the place for payment and the currency of payment; the Convention, of course, gives effect to the parties' agreement, which includes the practices they have established (Arts. 6, 9(1)). When the contract fails to provide an answer the present article fills the gap.

331   B. The Convention; Policy Considerations

Article 57[1]

(1) If the buyer is not bound to pay the price at any other particular place, he must pay it to the seller:
    (a) at the seller's place of business; or
    (b) if the payment is to be made against the handing over of the goods or of documents, at the place where the handing over takes place.
(2) The seller must bear any increase in the expenses incidental to payment which is caused by a change in his place of business subsequent to the conclusion of the contract.

---

1. Article 57 is the same as Art. 53 of the 1978 Draft and is substantially the same as ULIS 59. See V *YB* 81–83 (*S-G*), 31–32, VIII *YB* 49, *O.R.* 79 (proposals), 45–46 (Sec. Comm.), 368–369, 112; *Docy. Hist.* 160–162, 177–178, 342, 400, 435–36, 589–590, 694.

Paragraph (1)(a) points to the "seller's place of business,"[2] a choice that responds to the fact that in some circumstances payment at the buyer's place of business would be of little value to the seller. The buyer is entitled to goods that are usable (Art. 35(2)(a)); the present Article gives the seller similar protection with respect to the price.[3] The rule that, when the parties have not agreed otherwise, the buyer must pay at the seller's place of business is consistent with standard contract practices applicable to international trade.[4]

Under Article 57, the only exception from the norm calling for payment at the seller's place of business is that of subparagraph (1)(b). This exception applies only "if the payment *is to be made* against the handing over of the goods or of documents." If, pursuant to the contract, the seller ships the goods to the buyer and in the buyer's country tenders documents controlling the goods, this contractual arrangement overrides the general rule of paragraph (1)(a) that the buyer must pay "at the seller's place of business."[5]

Article 58 of the Convention, in defining the time for payment, provides in paragraph (2) that "the seller may dispatch the goods on terms whereby the goods, or documents controlling their disposition, will not be handed over to the buyer except against payment of the price." As we shall see, this provision permits but does not require the seller to arrange

---

2. If the seller has two places of business or has no place of business, the reference point is supplied by Art. 10, §§42, 123, *supra. Accord*, Günter Hager, Art. 57 para. 2, *in* Schlechtriem & Schwenzer, *CISG Commentary* (2nd English ed. 2005).

3. Comparable policies are reflected in the general rule that unless the seller has agreed to extend credit, the buyer must pay at the time he receives control of the goods. See Art. 58(1), *infra* at §335; Brand, *Pittsburgh Symposium* (1988) 170–186.

4. See Günter Hager, Art. 57 para. 4, *in* Schlechtriem & Schwenzer, *CISG Commentary* (2nd English ed. 2005). See also *General Conditions (ECE) Dry and Dried Fruit (1979)* 39(c): "Unless otherwise agreed, the place of payment shall be that where the seller has his principal place of business . . . " (Other ECE contracts in the series and *General Conditions (ECE) Plant and Machinery* state that payment shall be as "agreed by the parties'): The Asian-African Legal Consultative Committee (AALCC), Standard Form of F.O.B. Contract, Part VII at 3–5, indicates payment in the seller's country by calling for payment by a "*confirmed* . . . letter of credit" in exchange for a bill of lading. See Art. 58, *infra* at §337.

Domestic law; *Fridman* 283 at n.33 & 34; German (F.R.G.) Civil Code 270(1): "In case of doubt the debtor shall remit money at his own risk and expense to the residence of the creditor." (U.S.A.) UCC 2–310(a) and Swedish Sales Act 15 seem to respond to domestic conditions by calling for dispatch of the goods with payment for the goods at the point of receipt (destination).

5. *Accord*, Maskow, *B-B Commentary* 413. For detailed discussion of Art. 57(1)(b), see Günter Hager, Art. 57 paras. 12–24, *in* Schlechtriem & Schwenzer, *CISG Commentary* (2nd English ed. 2005).

for the payment only after arrival of the goods. See Article 58, *infra* at §§336–337.

331.1   (1) Delivery and Payment Procedures

Whether a transport document (bill of lading, waybill or the like) controls disposition of the goods depends on its terms: Does the carrier contract to deliver to the seller, to the order of the seller or to the buyer (§336 *infra*)? Similar principles govern delivery of goods by handing over a warehouse receipt or similar document evidencing possession by a third party.

When the contract does not specify the place (or other arrangements) for payment, the seller's expectations will usually be indicated by the invoice that the seller sends to the buyer at the time the seller ships the goods; in many cases the buyer's subsequent communications or conduct will show its assent to this term (Arts. 8(3), 18, 29). If there is no indication of the buyer's assent the invoice will *authorize* the buyer to pay in accordance with the terms of the invoice but will not *require* the buyer to pay in a manner inconsistent with the contract or the provisions of the Convention.[6]

When payment is to be made by a letter of credit the contract may (and the letter of credit almost certainly will) refer to the I.C.C. Uniform Customs and Practice for Documentary Credits.[7]

332   (2) The Convention and Jurisdiction for Suit

Article 57(1) has been used in Europe for jurisdictional purposes. For example, under Article 5(1) of the Brussels Convention[8] and Article 5(1) of the Lugano Convention,[9] which grant jurisdiction to the courts of the place of performance of an obligation, Article 57(1)(a) calling for payment at the seller's place of business has been deemed to confer

---

6. See Sevón, *Dubrovnik Lectures* 212.

7. See Maskow, *B-B Commentary* 416–418; *Schmitthoff's Essays* 449–467. Note: UNCITRAL Model Law on International Credit Transfers (1992) and UNCITRAL Model Law on Electric Commerce (1996). *Cf.* (U.S.A.) Uniform Commercial Code, Art. 4A, Funds Transfers (1989).

8. European Convention on Jurisdiction and Enforcement of Judgments in Civil and Commercial Matters, Sept. 27, 1968, 1998 O.J. (C 27) 1.

9. European Communities — European Free Trade Association: Convention on Jurisdiction and Enforcement of Judgments in Civil and Commercial Matters, Sept. 16, 1988, 1988 O.J. (L 319) 9.

jurisdiction on the courts of the seller's State in actions to recover the price.[10] This approach was employed even though the results were not necessarily practical or desirable.[11]

CISG Article 4 states that (apart from formation of the contract) the Convention "governs only . . . the rights and obligations of the seller and the buyer" under the sales contract. This language hardly supports the extension of the Convention to procedural and jurisdictional matters, and the legislative history gives no indication that the Convention was designed to deal with these issues.[12]

In some Contracting States (such as the United States), furthermore, there is no necessary connection between the place for payment and the place for suit. Thus using Article 57 for jurisdictional purposes subjects the Convention's rules to interpretational pressures and considerations that may be inconsistent with Article 7(1), which calls for interpreting the Convention from an international perspective and in a manner that promotes "uniformity in its application."

Under the Brussels I Regulation,[13] which contains the current jurisdictional rules for most of the European Union, CISG Article 57 no longer determines the place where suit to recover payment may be brought, provided the place of delivery of goods is in a Member State of the European Union (other than Denmark).[14]

---

10. See Günter Hager, Art. 57 paras. 10 & 11a, *in* Schlechtriem & Schwenzer, *CISG Commentary* (2nd English ed. 2005); UNCITRAL Digest Art. 57 para. 4.

11. See Günter Hager, Art. 57 para. 11, *in* Schlechtriem & Schwenzer, *CISG Commentary* (2nd English ed. 2005); Huber, 43 Rabels Z 413, 512 (1979).

12. *O.R.* 368–369, *Docy. Hist.* 589–590.

13. Council Regulation 44/2001 of 22 December 2000 on Jurisdiction and the Recognition and Enforcement of Judgments in Civil and Commercial Matters, 2001 O.J. (L 012) 1.

14. See Günter Hager, Art. 57 para. 11a, *in* Schlechtriem & Schwenzer, *CISG Commentary* (2nd English ed. 2005); UNCITRAL Digest Art. 57 para. 5.

Article 58.
Time for Payment; Inspection of the Goods

333 A. Questions Concerning Payment

Article 58 addressees these questions:[1] When must the buyer pay for the goods?[2] Must he pay before he receives the goods?[3] Is the seller obliged to surrender the goods before he is paid?[4] How may the goods be exchanged for the price when (as is usual in international sales) the contract calls for carriage of the goods? May the seller require the buyer to pay before the buyer has an opportunity to examine the goods?

Procedures for payment are of concern to the parties and usually are dealt with in the contract; Article 58 provides answers only when the contract is silent (Art. 6).[5] As we shall see, Article 58 is designed to minimize risks for both parties — risk to the seller from delivery before payment and risk to the buyer from payment for defective goods. *The time for payment of the price as determined under Article 58 has also been used to establish the point from which interest on the unpaid price accrues under Article 78.*[6]

334 B. The Convention

Article 58[7]

(1) If the buyer is not bound to pay the price at any other specific time, he must pay it when the seller places either the goods or documents controlling their disposition at the buyer's disposal in accordance with

---

1. See Günter Hager, Art. 58 para. 2, *in* Schlechtriem & Schwenzer, *CISG Commentary* (2nd English ed. 2005).
2. See UNCITRAL Digest Art. 58 paras. 1 & 5.
3. See UNCITRAL Digest Art. 58 para. 3.
4. See UNCITRAL Digest Art. 58 para. 2.
5. See UNCITRAL Digest Art. 58 paras. 4 & 5.
6. See UNCITRAL Digest Art. 58 para. 1.
7. Article. 58 is substantially the same as Art. 54 of the 1978 Draft Convention; the "If" clause at the beginning of para. (1) was added to conform to the language of Art. 57(1), *supra* at §329. Article 58 is similar to ULIS 71 and 72. There was little difficulty with developing this article. For the evolution from ULIS see V *YB* 81–83 (*S-G*), *Docy. Hist.* 160–162; *O.R.* 46–47 (Sec. Comm.), 369–370; *Docy. Hist.* 436–437, 590–591.

the contract and this Convention. The seller may make such payment a condition for handing over the goods or documents.

(2) If the contract involves carriage of the goods, the seller may dispatch the goods on terms whereby the goods, or documents controlling their disposition, will not be handed over to the buyer except against payment of the price.

(3) The buyer is not bound to pay the price until he has had an opportunity to examine the goods, unless the procedures for delivery or payment agreed upon by the parties are inconsistent with his having such an opportunity.

335 (1) Exchange of Goods for Price

Paragraph (1) makes two points: (i) The buyer is not obliged to pay the price until the seller places the goods at the buyer's disposition; (ii) The seller is not obliged to hand over the goods until the buyer pays the price. In short, goods are to be exchanged for the price.[8]

336 (2) Contracts Involving Carriage

Paragraph (2) of Article 58 builds on the principle, stated in paragraph (1), that when the contract is silent there is to be a concurrent exchange of goods for the price.[9] When (as in most international sales) the contract calls for carriage of the goods, paragraph (2) authorizes the seller to deliver the goods to the carrier in exchange for a document "controlling [the] disposition" of the goods — usually a bill of lading providing that the goods will only be delivered in exchange for the surrender of the document.[10] Alternatively, under streamlined delivery systems, the carrier (e.g., an air carrier) may collect the price when the buyer receives the goods.[11]

---

8. See Günter Hager, Art. 58 paras. 3–10, *in* Schlechtriem & Schwenzer, *CISG Commentary* (2nd English ed. 2005); UNCITRAL Digest Art. 58 para. 6. *Compare* (U.K.) SGA (1893) 28: "...delivery of the goods and payment of the price are concurrent conditions..." (unchanged in SGA (1979) 28; (U.S.A.) UCC 2–310(a), 2–507(1); Swedish Sales Act (1905) 124; Israeli Sales Law 23; Mexican Commercial Code 380.

9. See UNCITRAL Digest Art. 58 para. 7.

10. *Incoterms* (2000) CIF, CPT and CIP call for the seller to provide the "usual transport document" that *may* be a "negotiable bill of lading" by "an equivalent electronic data interchange (EDI) message." See Rule A8 under each of these terms. Compare (U.S.A.) UCC 2–310(b) (seller may ship "under reservation").

11. See UNCITRAL Digest Art. 58 paras. 5, 7, 8 & 9.

337 **(a) The Place for the Documentary Exchange.** Exchanging the goods for the price brings two provisions into confluence: (i) The present Article dealing with the *time* for payment and (ii) Article 57, *supra* at §329, on the *place* for payment. Under Article 57(1), unless the contract provides otherwise, the buyer must pay the price "(a) at the seller's place of business; or (b) if the payment is to be made against the handing over of the goods or of documents, at the place where the handing over takes place." The contract will usually state the place for the documentary exchange; when the contract is silent we face a question of interpretation that will require us to bring into focus several provisions of the Convention.

Example 58A. Seller in State A and Buyer in State B contracted for Seller to ship specified goods to Buyer. The contract said nothing about the place or other conditions for payment. Where and under what circumstances should Seller surrender the goods and Buyer pay the price?

It may help to recall the following points: (1) Seller may require the buyer to pay at the seller's place of business (Art. 57(1)(a)); (2) Seller may not require Buyer to pay the price before he receives the goods (Art. 58(1)); (3) Buyer may not require surrender of the goods prior to payment (Art. 58(1)); (4) Seller may ship the goods and hold a shipping document that controls delivery of the goods until the buyer pays the price (Art. 58(2); *cf.* (Art. 57(1)(b)).

Certainly Seller may elect to tender the documents for payment where Buyer has his place of business. Buyer would not object: The time for payment would be delayed; payment in Buyer's country would be more convenient and would minimize problems with exchange controls. Moreover, it would be easier for Buyer to inspect the goods before it pays.

Such an arrangement is common where the seller and the buyer are located in the same State and the cost of shipment is not unusually high.[12] But when the seller delivers in another State following extended and expensive transport the seller runs substantial risk. If the buyer fails to pay, it may be difficult for the seller to redispose of the goods; if payment is made, currency restrictions may block removal of the funds. These considerations have led to the common arrangement in which the seller will not deliver the goods to the carrier until the buyer has arranged for the issuance (or confirmation) of a letter of credit by a bank that is

---

12. See (U.S.A.) UCC 2–310(a): "payment is due at the time and place at which the buyer is to receive the goods even though the place of shipment is the place of delivery"; Swedish Sales Act 15.

near the seller; the seller is then assured of payment by a local bank when the seller presents the documents specified in the letter of credit.[13]

In Example 58A, may Seller require Buyer to arrange for the issuance (or confirmation) of a letter of credit by a bank near Seller, so that the documentary exchange may take place at that point? The Convention does not refer to the use of letters of credit. However, as we have seen, Article 57(1)(a) provides that the buyer must pay the price to the seller "at the seller's place of business." Arranging for a documentary exchange in the seller's locale would usually be the cheapest and safest way for the buyer to exchange funds for the goods in the vicinity of the seller's place of business (Art. 57(1)(a)). However, special arrangements may be necessary when it is important for the buyer to examine the goods before he pays; these will be considered under (3), below.

338   **(3) Examination Before Payment**

(a) The Place for the Examination.   Paragraph (3) states the general rule that the buyer "is not bound to pay the price until he has had an opportunity to examine the goods." When the transaction calls for the buyer to send for the goods (*cf.* a sale "ex works") or when the seller delivers the goods in its own trucks, inspection before payment may be quite feasible.[14] When the seller dispatches the goods by carrier and provides for a documentary exchange at destination, the seller may delay the presentation of the documents until after the goods arrived and are unloaded, and may instruct the carrier to allow the buyer to inspect the goods before the buyer has received the bill of lading.[15] However, for reasons that have been outlined above at §337, it may be risky for the seller to defer the time for payment until the goods reach the buyer. The Convention does not require the seller to run these risks. Article 57(1)(a), *supra*, regulates the place for payment, and states that the buyer must pay the price to the seller "(a) at the seller's place of business."[16]

---

13. Sevón, *Dubrovnik Lectures* 216–217. See *id.*, for the possible abuse by the buyer of inspection after goods have arrived after extensive international carriage.

14. See Günter Hager, Art. 58 para. 11, *in* Schlechtriem & Schwenzer, *CISG Commentary* (2nd English ed. 2005).

15. See Günter Hager, Art. 58 para. 12, *in* Schlechtriem & Schwenzer, *CISG Commentary* (2nd English ed. 2005).

16. The *Hague Sales Convention* (1964) was to the same effect. Under ULIS 72(1), where the contract involves carriage "the seller may either *postpone dispatch of the goods until he receives payment* or proceed to dispatch them on terms that reserve to himself the right of disposal of the goods during transit."

When the seller and the buyer are far from each other, distance enhances the practical problems of exchanging goods for price. The seller faces greater hazards if the buyer fails to pay after the goods arrive, while the buyer faces added inconvenience if he must inspect the goods before they are shipped.[17] Is the inconvenience to the buyer so great that it denies him the "opportunity to examine the goods" before payment? If so, it might be argued that Article 58(3), in allowing the buyer to defer payment until it has an opportunity to inspect the goods, modifies the basic rule on the place for payment stated in Article 57(1)(a). However, a buyer who is concerned that the seller might ship defective goods can usually arrange for a commercial inspection agency to act on its behalf in inspecting the goods before they are loaded on the carrier — a step that normally is less onerous than for the seller to redispose of goods that the buyer has wrongfully rejected after they have arrived in his country. These polices have been recognized and reconciled by arrangements that the documents the seller must tender for payment by letter of credit shall include a certificate of quality by an independent inspection agency.[18] As an alternative, the buyer could reasonably demand the opportunity, personally or through an agent, to inspect the goods before they are shipped.[19]

In short, it is possible to satisfy the standards of Article 58 for a mutually safe exchange of the goods and the price in a manner that is consistent with the rule of Article 57(1)(a) on the place for payment.

339 **(b) Agreed Procedures Inconsistent with Inspection.** Under Article 58(3) the buyer has no right to examine the goods before he pays when "the procedures for delivery or payment agreed upon by the parties are inconsistent with his having such an opportunity."

Example 58B. A contract called for Seller to ship goods to Buyer on June 1 on the "S.S. North Star" which (as the parties knew) was scheduled to dock at Buyer's city on or about July 15. The contract further

17. These problems do not loom large in the numerous cases where the parties have confidence in each other, but rules of law should be designed to minimize hazards when confidence has been misplaced. Although sellers frequently deliver on credit, they need not do so unless the contract so provides (Art. 58(1)).
18. See Günter Hager, Art. 58 para. 12, *in* Schlechtriem & Schwenzer, *CISG Commentary* (2nd English ed. 2005); Goldstajin, The Contract of Goods Inspection, 14 Am. J. Comp. L. 383 (1965).
19. See Günter Hager, Art. 58 para. 7, *in* Schlechtriem & Schwenzer, *CISG Commentary* (2nd English ed. 2005).

*provided that on June 10 Seller would present a sight draft, with accom-
panying bill of lading, to Buyer for the full price.*

These agreed terms are inconsistent with inspection before
payment.[20] The crucial question is the provision in the contract. If the
contract has no such provision bearing on the time for payment. Seller's
presentation of the documents for payment while the goods were at sea
would be inconsistent with Buyer's right of inspection conferred by Art.
58(3). If the Seller insisted on such "blind" payment, Buyer could reject
the tender and avoid the contract. (See Art. 25, *supra* at §185.)

339.1   **(c) Inspection Rules.**   One must not confuse two very different
rules on inspection of the goods. Article 38 (§§249–253, *supra*) establishes a *duty* to inspect: "(1) The buyer *must* examine the goods...
within as short a period as is practicable..." — a preface to Article 39
whereby a buyer may lose the right to rely on lack of conformity of the
goods by failure to notify the seller within a "reasonable time." (The
seller's need for notice that prompted this requirement is discussed
at §255, *supra*.) In sharp contrast, Article 58(3) gives the buyer a
privilege to inspect before payment — a privilege that the buyer may
forego without violating any obligation to the seller. True, the extent
of any opportunity to inspect is relevant to the time for notifying the
seller pursuant to Article 39 but inspecting in connection with payment
may not provide adequate opportunity to discover defects in the goods
(Arts. 38, 39).[21]

339.2   **(d) Step-by-Step Performance.**   The concurrent exchange of the
goods for the price (the central theme of Article 58) can best be illustrated in the setting of a typical international sale involving payment by
letter of credit.

The numerous steps in the making and performance of such a transaction have been summarized elsewhere (§132.1 *supra*). For simplicity
let us consider only these four steps: (1) Following preliminary correspondence the seller transmits to the buyer a *pro forma* invoice that, *inter
alia*, describes the goods, the quantity, the price and the date when the
goods will be available for shipment. (2) The buyer, through its local
bank ("Firstbank") arranges for the issuance of a letter of credit for the
price and its confirmation by a bank near the seller ("Secondbank").

20. See Günter Hager, Art. 58 para. 12, *in* Schlechtriem & Schwenzer, *CISG Commentary*
(2nd English ed. 2005); UNCITRAL Digest Art. 58 para. 9.
21. See Maskow, *B-B Commentary* 425.

(3) The seller ships the goods to the buyer and obtains various documents including a policy of insurance and a bill of lading that calls for delivery of the goods to the "order of Secondbank." (4) The seller present documents, including the invoice, policy of insurance and bill of lading, to Secondbank and receives the price.

One will note that these steps need to be taken separately and in the above sequence. Step (1) must precede Step (2) since the letter of credit needs to be written in terms of the description of the transaction provided by the *pro forma* invoice. Step (2) must precede Step (3) since the seller needs assurance of payment by the letter of credit before shipping the goods to a foreign destination. Step (3) must precede Step (4) since the seller needs the documents that result from shipment (e.g., the bill of lading) to comply with the conditions for payment prescribed in the letter of credit. In sum, a transaction designed for the exchange of the goods and the price calls for a series of separate steps; the concurrent exchange occurs only at Step (4). (In some transactions additional preliminary steps are required.)

As one turns from the facts of the transaction to legal analysis one notes that at each step a party's duties do not arise until the other party has taken the preceding step. This results simply from the interpretation of the agreement in the light of basic commercial facts; legal rules are available (Arts. 57, 58, 71, 72, 80) but in this concrete setting they speak less eloquently than the internal logic of the parties' plans for delivery and payment.[22] Indeed, as we have seen in connection with Article 14, 19 and 55 (§§137.4, 170, 325.1 *supra*), in routine transactions that lack a formal "Contract of Sale" the parties may not be bound by contract until the final step when goods are exchanged for the price. However, if the parties are bound by contract and one fails to proceed with the agreed steps for performance the other party has a wide range of remedies — to require performance (Arts. 46, 62), avoid the contract (Arts. 47, 49, 63, 64) and claim damages (Arts. 45(1), 61(1), 74–77) — remedies that are examined more fully elsewhere in this book.

---

22. If legal rules on the above point are needed, the Convention's basic goal of uniformity (Art. 7) requires that they be derived from the above-cited remedial provisions rather than the diverse common-law doctrines concerning "conditions" or civil law doctrines such as *exceptio non adimpleti contractus. Cf.* Maskow, *supra*, 429.

Article 59.
Payment Due Without Request

Article 59[1]

340   **The buyer must pay the price on the date fixed by or determinable from the contract and this Convention without the need for any request or compliance with any formality on the part of the seller.**

This provision was inherited from ULIS 60, which was designed to overturn the rule of some Continental legal systems that a party may not recover damages for delay unless he has given an advance warning or protest directed at delay.[2] The purpose of Article 59 is to eliminate unnecessary formalities or delays in payment when the date for payment is "fixed by or determinable from" the contract and the Convention. *When this prerequisite is met, the rule of Article 59 means, for example, that interest on the unpaid price begins to accrue under Article 78 of the Convention (infra at §420 et. seq.) without a formal demand for payment by the seller.*[3] Implicit in the language of Article 59 is the policy that liability for delay in performance should arise only when the date for performance is fixed or determinable. As we shall see, the Convention's general rules on the obligations of the parties are consistent with this policy.

Article 59 may be applied without difficulty when the seller has delivered the goods on credit; in this case the price will be due on a fixed date and should be remitted by the buyer on that date "without the need for any request or the compliance with any formality on the part of the seller." Normally a delay in payment will not result in damages other than an obligation to pay interest on any "sum that is in *arrears.*" See Article 78, *infra* at §420. In any event, in connection with the delivery the seller will normally send the buyer an invoice that would be understood as a request for payment.[4]

---

1. This article, except for minor redrafting, is the same as Art. 55 of the 1978 Draft, and is closely patterned on ULIS 60.

2. *Treitel, Remedies* (Int. Enc.) §75: France (*mise en demeure*); Germany (*Mahnung*); *Treitel, Remedies (1988)* 129–130, 132; *Nicholas, French Law of Contract* 232–234.

3. See Günter Hager, Art. 59 para. 2, *in* Schlechtriem & Schwenzer, *CISG Commentary* (2nd English ed. 2005); UNCITRAL Digest Art. 59 para. 1.

4. See Günter Hager, Art. 59 para. 2, *in* Schlechtriem & Schwenzer, *CISG Commentary* (2nd English ed. 2005).

In documentary exchanges, the statement in Article 59 that the buyer must pay without "any request" calls for interpreting Article 58, *supra* at §333. Article 58(1) states that the buyer must pay the price when the seller places the goods "at the buyer's disposal." Before the seller can place the goods at the buyer's "disposal" he must complete a series of operations that may include procurement or production of the goods, packaging (Art. 35(2)(d)) and arrangements for carriage (Art. 32) and documentation (Art. 58). The contract normally allows the seller to complete these operations within a specified period or prior to a specified date. Only the seller knows when all these steps have been completed; this requires the seller to take the lead. Consequently, the seller does not place the goods "at the buyer's disposal" (Art. 58(1)) until it informs the buyer that the goods are ready. At this point, the buyer will know that it has the next move, and that its duty to pay the price has matured. At this point Article 59 makes it clear that the buyer must pay without any "request or . . . formality."[5]

In a helpful analysis of Article 59, Professor Tallon supports interpreting the Convention so that liability for delay in performance will not arise until the date for performing is fixed or determinable.[6] Tallon also raises this interesting point: Article 59 rejects domestic formal demands for payment of the price whereas the French Civil Code, Article 1139, requires a formal demand (*mise en demeure*) for every kind of obligation. Does this suggest that the Convention preserves such domestic formal requirements for all obligations other than payment of the price?

It seems difficult to reconcile such domestic formalities with Articles 30, 33 and 45 (obligations of the seller) and 53 and 61 (obligations of the buyer). Each set of provisions states that the party "must" perform the duties "required by the contract and this Convention" (Arts. 30, 53), and adds that when a party "fails to perform any of his obligations under the contract or this Convention" the other party "may exercise" the full battery of remedies that the Convention provides for breach (Arts. 45, 61). There is no indication in the legislative history that Article 59 on payment of the price carried a negative implication that domestic formalities in other settings could postpone the obligations and remedies established by the Convention in Articles 30, 53, 45 and 61. (*Cf.* Arts. 45(3) and 61(3) barring application for a "period of grace".) The draft that became Article 59 attracted little attention in UNCITRAL and the Diplomatic Conference: discussion was limited, on one hand, to

---

5. *Accord*, Huber, 43 *Rabels* Z 413, 515 (1979).
6. Tallon, *Parker Colloq.* 7–14, §7.03(b).

suggestions that the provision was unnecessary and, on the other, to comments that it was found in ULIS and might be "useful."[7] *Indeed, it can be argued that the rule of Article 59 dispensing with a formal demand for performance when the time therefore is fixed or determinable from the contract or the Convention represents a general principle of the Convention within the meaning of Article 7(2), and thus is applicable to obligations even if not expressly stated.*[8]

In sum, Article 59 embodies two principles: (1) Domestic formalities such as *mise en demeure* may not interfere with obligations and remedies established by the Convention. (2) liability for delay must be based on failure to comply with a date or performance that is fixed or determinable. Both principles can be implemented through proper interpretation of the contract and the Convention without subjecting international sales to domestic formalities.

7. See V *YB* 31, IV *YB* 34, VIII *YB* 50, *O.R.* 47, 370–371; *Docy. Hist.* 177, 211, 343, 437, 591–592. ULIS included a provision (Art. 20) rejecting formalities as a prelude to the seller's obligation to deliver where "the parties have agreed upon a date for delivery or where such date is fixed by usage . . . " — a provision similar to ULIS 60 on which CISG 59 was based. Language based on ULIS 20 disappeared in the general consolidation and streamlining of ULIS's remedial system; there was no indication that the omission was designed to reestablish domestic formalities. See IV *YB* 40, 51–60, V *YB* 83–84, VI *YB* 67–72; *Docy. Hist.* 117, 128–137, 162–163, 143–150. It is probable that ULIS 20 was considered unnecessary in view of CISG 33 which includes detailed provisions for determining the time when the "seller must deliver the goods."

8. See UNCITRAL Digest Art. 59 para. 2.

SECTION II.

TAKING DELIVERY
(Article 60)

Article 60.
Buyer's Obligation to Take Delivery

341   Article 53, in opening this chapter on the obligations of the buyer
(§322), stated that the buyer must "take delivery" of the goods.

Article 60[1]

The buyer's obligation to take delivery consists:
(a) in doing all the acts which could reasonably be expected of him
in order to enable the seller to make delivery; and
(b) in taking over the goods.

341.1   A. Supplying and Receiving Goods: Correlative Contractual Obligations

As we have seen (§210 *supra*) many of the rules of ULIS (1964) turned
on an artificial concept (*délivrance*) which defied adequate translation
and, because of its complexity, led to unintended and impractical consequences. At an early session UNCITRAL decided to replace this
approach with rules that addressed the parties' contractual obligations
with respect to the specific problem at hand. For example, Article 31
(§§207–211 *supra*) speaks of the seller's "*obligation* to deliver" and
one will note that Article 60 similarly speaks of the buyer's "*obligation*
to take delivery." We can now examine the application of this contractual
approach to the commercial process of supplying and receiving goods.

   Sales contracts normally call upon the seller to take the initiative in
procuring or manufacturing goods and in placing them at the buyer's
disposition (§340 *supra*). Usually the contract states what the seller
should do to make the goods available to the buyer; if not, Article 31

---

1. This Article is the same as Art. 56 of the 1978 Draft. *Cf.* ULIS 65.

in three detailed paragraphs fills the gaps. The brevity of Article 60 results from the fact that the buyer's obligation to take the goods does not arise until the seller makes the goods available.

Under Article 58 (§339.1 *supra*) we examined contractual arrangements for documentary transfers in which the seller performs its "obligation to deliver" (Art. 31) concurrently with the buyer's obligation to "take delivery." However, in other settings the parties' contractual duties arise at different times. When "the contract of sale involves carriage of the goods," Article 31(a) states that the seller's "obligation to deliver consists . . . in handing the goods over to the first carrier"; in this setting the buyer's "obligation to take delivery" cannot arise until after the goods reach their destination.[2] When the contract does not call for transport the seller's obligation consists (Art. 31(b)) in "placing the goods at the buyer's disposal" at specified places; however, the buyer's obligation to "take over" the goods (Art. 60(A)) need not be performed until the expiration of an agreed or reasonable time to collect the goods (*cf.* Art. 33).[3] Similarly, in these situations risk of loss does not pass to the buyer until (Art. 69(1), §§373–377, *infra*) the buyer actually "takes over" the goods or, at the latest, "from the time the goods are placed at his disposal and he commits a breach of contract by failing to take delivery."

In short, the Convention does not attempt to define an abstract concept of "delivery" (*délivrance*). Instead, Article 60 asks this question: Has the buyer broken his *contractual obligation* to "take over" the goods?

If the answer is Yes, the legal consequences of breach of this and other obligations of the buyer are set forth in Section II (Arts. 61–65; §§344–357, *infra*).

342   B. Cooperation With the Seller

Paragraph (a) provides yet another instance of the Convention's recognition of the importance of cooperation in carrying out the interlocking steps of an international sales transaction.[4] Action by the buyer that

---

2. *Accord*, Günter Hager, Art. 60 para. 2a, *in* Schlechtriem & Schwenzer, *CISG Commentary* (2nd English ed. 2005).

3. *Accord*, Günter Hager, Art. 60 para. 2a, *in* Schlechtriem & Schwenzer, *CISG Commentary* (2nd English ed. 2005).

4. See the discussion under Art. 54 *supra*, and Arts. 19(2), 21(2), 32, 48(2), 58(3), 60(a), 65, 71, 73(2), 79(4) and 85–88. These many instances suggest that providing needed cooperation

"could reasonably be expected . . . to enable the seller to make delivery" might include designation of the precise place to which the seller should send the goods, having personnel on hand to receive the goods, making the arrangements for carriage required under trade terms such as INCOTERMS (2000) "F.O.B." (B-3) and "Free Carrier" ("FCA") (B-3), and other aspects of cooperation that are too detailed for listing in the Convention.[5]

Article 60(a)'s statement that the above "enabling" steps are part of the buyer's "obligation to take delivery" broadens the seller's right under Article 64(1)(b) to avoid the contract. The interlocking relationship between these provisions can be seen clearly in the setting of Article 64, *infra* at §§353–356. For now it must suffice to note that if the seller gives the buyer a *Nachfrist* notice (Art. 63(1)) that fixes an additional reasonable period for performing the "enabling" steps described in Article 60(a) and the buyer fails to comply, the seller may avoid the contract based on the buyer's failure timely to perform this aspect of the buyer's "obligation to take delivery." The significant point is that, because the seller can avoid the contract under Article 64(1)(b), the seller need not show that the buyer's breach was "fundamental" (Art. 25) as would be required under Article 64(1)(a).[6]

343 C. Taking Delivery

The seller's primary interest is to receive the price for the goods (Arts. 54–59 *supra*) but the buyer's obligation to take delivery, expressed in Article 60(b), is not without significance. When the seller makes the contract with the carrier (Art. 32(2)) the seller will be interested in the buyer's prompt removal of the goods from the carrier's possession, for the seller may be liable to the carrier for freight and demurrage if the buyer fails to pay.

Delay in taking over the goods may also have significant consequences when the goods are lost or damaged during the period of

---

is one of the "general principles on which [the Convention] is based." See Art. 7(2), *supra* at §100.

5. For further discussion of actions that Article 60 might require see Günter Hager, Art. 60 para. 2, *in* Schlechtriem & Schwenzer, *CISG Commentary* (2nd English ed. 2005); UNCITRAL Digest Art. 60 para. 2.

6. Article 54 (§323, *supra*) similarly provides that the buyer's obligation "to pay the price" includes steps to "*enable* payment to be made," with similar broadening of the seller's right, following a *Nachfrist* notice, to avoid the contract under Art. 64(1)(b).

delay. See Ch. IV, Articles 66–70, *infra*. When the contract does not involve carriage, risk normally passes to the buyer when he "takes over the goods," but the risk may shift when the buyer "commits a breach of contract by *failing to take delivery*" (see Art. 69(1), §374 *supra*). Under Article 60, the buyer's failure to perform its obligations with respect to "taking over the goods" is a breach of contract and thus invokes the above rule making this buyer responsible for casualty to the goods; it also may provide a ground for the seller to avoid the contract (Arts. 63 & 64 §§350, 353, *infra*). However, the buyer's liability for casualty to the goods may be reduced by the seller's responsibility under Article 85 (§454 *infra*) to take reasonable steps to preserve the goods and, under some circumstances, to sell them for the buyer's account (Art. 88(2) §457 *infra*).

SECTION III.

Article 61.
Remedies Available to Seller

344   Section III (Arts. 61–65), stating the seller's remedies for breach by the buyer, follows the same pattern as Section III of the preceding chapter (Arts. 45–52). Both sets of rules are supplemented in Chapter V (Arts. 71–82) by remedial provisions applicable to both parties.

The present section opens with an article that sums up the remedial system available to aggrieved sellers and indicates the relationship among the various remedies. (*Cf.* Art. 45, *supra* at §275.)

Article 61[1]

(1) If the buyer fails to perform any of his obligations under the contract or this Convention, the seller may:
(a) exercise the rights provided in Articles 62 to 65;
(b) claim damages as provided in Articles 74 to 77.
(2) The seller is not deprived of any right he may have to claim damages by exercising his right to other remedies.
(3) No period of grace may be granted to the buyer by a court or arbitral tribunal when the seller resorts to a remedy for breach of contract.

The analysis of Article 45 — the comparable provision in the preceding chapter which catalogues buyers' remedies — is applicable here. *For example, Articles 45 and 61 both make it clear that an aggrieved party's entitlement to damages (or any other Convention remedy) is not conditioned on a showing that the breaching party was at fault;*[2]

---

1. This article is the same as Art. 57 of the 1978 Draft Convention. In ULIS, comparable provisions appear at Arts. 61, 64, 66, 68 and 70.
2. See Günter Hager, Art. 61 para. 2, *in* Schlechtriem & Schwenzer, *CISG Commentary* (2nd English ed. 2005); UNCITRAL Digest Art. 61 para. 2.

and Article 61(1)(b) provides the basis for the aggrieved seller's claim to damages,[3] *just as Article 45(1)(b) performs that function for aggrieved buyers. See §276 supra.* It should suffice to refer to the discussion under Article 45, supra at §277, of the extent to which an aggrieved seller's choice of one remedy excludes others.

3. See Günter Hager, Art. 61 para. 3, *in* Schlechtriem & Schwenzer, *CISG Commentary* (2nd English ed. 2005); UNCITRAL Digest Art. 61 para. 1.

Article 62.
Seller's Right to Compel Performance

345   A. Factual Settings

The buyer's duty (or "obligation") to pay the price was defined in Articles 53 to 59. This duty may, of course, be broken after the buyer receives the goods but the more difficult questions concern the seller's remedy to force the buyer to take the goods and pay the price when the buyer has refused to proceed with the contract.

Article 62[1]

The seller may require the buyer to pay the price, take delivery or perform his other obligations, unless the seller has resorted to a remedy which is inconsistent with this requirement.

Article 62 states that the seller "may *require* the buyer to pay the price [and] take delivery." This remedy given to the seller is similar to the buyer's remedy under Article 46 to "*require* performance by the seller." Much of the discussion under Article 46 (§§279–286 *supra*) will be relevant here although the commercial settings are different.

When the buyer has received and retains the goods, enforcing the buyer's obligation to pay the price does not create the practical problems that arise from attempts to force an unwilling party to deliver goods.[2] When the buyer has accepted the goods the seller's legal remedy to recover the price normally resembles an action to collect a debt. In addition, in some legal systems (other than common law) the failure by a buyer to pay may give the seller the right to recover the goods. Under the Convention this remedy is granted, if the seller avoids the contract, by Article 81(2) (§444 *infra*) but may be ineffective when the rights of the buyer's creditors intervene.[3]

---

1. This article is the same as Art. 58 of the 1978 Draft. *Cf.* ULIS 61 and 62 (payment of price), 70(2) (taking delivery and other obligations of buyer).

2. See UNCITRAL Digest Art. 62 para. 2. Avoidance of the contract by either party releases the buyer from its obligation to pay the price (Art. 81, §440, *infra*).

3. CISG 4 (§70, *supra*) limits the Convention's rules to the "rights and obligations of the seller and buyer." Whether the seller's rights to reclaim the goods under Art. 81(1) would prevail over creditors depends on the rights of such a claimant against third persons under domestic law. See Flechtner, *Pittsburgh Symposium* 67.

When a buyer refuses to receive the goods the seller's action under Article 62 to require the buyer "to pay the price" and "take delivery" resembles a buyer's action under Article 46 to require the seller to deliver goods, but has this difference of substance: a seller proceeding under Article 62 is not seeking possession of a commodity (raw materials, machinery) that the seller needs in its current operations. Nonetheless, both Articles 46 and 62 embody remedies to "require" performance, and hence both are subject to the concession to domestic law provided by Article 28 (§§191–199). The impact of Article 28 will be considered at §348 *infra*.

346 B. Domestic Rules

The (U.S.A.) Uniform Commercial Code states:

Section 2–709 Action for the Price
(1) When the buyer fails to pay the price as it becomes due the seller may recover, together with any incidental damages under the next section, the price
   (a)   of goods accepted or of conforming goods lost or damaged within a commercially reasonable time after risk of their loss has passed to the buyer; and
   (b)   of goods identified to the contract if the seller is unable after reasonable effort to resell them at a reasonable price or the circumstances reasonably indicate that such effort will be unavailing.[4]

The most common situation qualifying for an action for the price falls under UCC 2–709(1)(a): the buyer has "accepted" the goods, usually after their receipt and inspection (UCC 2–606). Price recovery in this setting is of the first type just mentioned (§345) — a remedy that resembles the collection of a debt rather than a remedy that compels the consummation of a transaction including receipt of the goods.

This second type of remedy is provided by UCC 2–709(1)(b) when the seller is "unable after reasonable efforts to resell [the goods] at a reasonable price..." — a rule that reflects the principle that it is usually more efficient for a seller in possession of the goods to resell the goods and claim damages for any resulting loss than to use the processes of the law to force goods on an unwilling buyer. However, the second type of

---

Under (U.S.A.) U.C.C. in domestic transactions a seller's right to reclaim (absent fraudulent acquisition) must rest on a written security agreement signed by the debtor; effectiveness against creditors depends, in most situations, on public filing. UCC 9–203(1), 9–302.
4. The 2003 revisions to UCC Art. 2 — which were approved by the (non-legislative) organizations that sponsor the model law but at the time this is written have not been enacted in any jurisdiction — would make no changes to §2–709(1).

action for the price would be available, for example, when the seller has manufactured goods to the buyer's special specifications or, especially in international sales, when a buyer wrongfully rejects goods after their arrival at a distant port where the seller lacks facilities for sale.[5]

In transactions governed by the UCC, the seller may also have recourse to the "principles of law and *equity*" (UCC 1–103); this latter body of remedial law authorizes an equity decree for specific performance when recovery of damages (the usual remedy "at law") is not adequate. Assume that a buyer repudiates a long-term contract for purchase of the seller's output or for supplying the buyer's requirements; in these settings a claim for damages may not provide an adequate remedy because of difficulty in assessing the seller's loss in future months or years.[6] One will note that the grounds for compelling an unwilling buyer to receive and pay for goods under U.S. domestic law are not as broad as the grounds under UCC 2–716 to compel an unwilling seller to deliver the goods[7] — a difference that reflects a judgment that a buyer's need to obtain goods not readily obtainable elsewhere is greater than a seller's need to force goods on an unwilling buyer.

As was noted under Articles 28 and 46, *supra*, in civil law legal theory one may "require" the performance of obligations. However, as Professor Treitel observes, courts seldom physically coerce the performance of obligations, and the principle that performance may be "required" is subject to exceptions that in practice "are far more important than the general rule"; indeed, when a buyer refuses to accept goods held by the seller, the "enforcement" of the buyer's obligation to pay the price may consist of the resale of the goods for the buyer's account, supplemented by an action to recover any deficiency — action that hardly "requires" the buyer to "take delivery" and "pay the price."[8] Under Article 75 of the Convention, if the seller avoids the contract (as he may and normally would do when the buyer refuses to accept and pay for the

---

5. The seller's problems of redisposition at a distant port and the possibility of abuse by the buyer of the seller's awkward situation are discussed in Sevón, *Dubrovnik Lectures* 203, 216–217. See *Atiyah* 370. The above examples are only illustrative.

6. See Schwartz, The Case for Specific Performance, 89 Yale L.J. 271, 276 (1979); Kastely, The Right to Require Performance, 63 Wash. L. Rev. 607, 615 (1988); D. Dobbs, Remedies 885 n.7 (1973).

7. See the discussion of CISG Art. 46 at §§279–286, *supra*.

8. *Treitel, Remedies (Int. Enc.)* §§10–29; *Treitel, Remedies (1988)*, Ch. III; *Zweigert & Kötz II (1987)* 157–169; Dawson, Specific Performance in France and Germany, 57 Mich. L. Rev. 495 (1959); *Hager* 141–169.

goods) the seller may resell the goods and "recover the difference between the contract price and the price in the substitute transaction" plus additional damages he has suffered. A similar remedy is provided in (U.S.A.) UCC 2–706 as a means for measuring the seller's damages and not as a device to "require" the buyer to pay the price.

347 **C. Compulsory Price Payment Under the Convention**

When the buyer has received and accepted the goods, Article 62 of the Convention will apply with full force: "The seller may require the buyer to pay the price . . ."[9] But — as discussed in the Sections that follow — when the seller is in possession of the goods, other provisions of the Convention may bear on the question whether the seller may force the buyer to "take delivery" and "pay the price."[10]

348 **(1) Applicability of Limits of Domestic Law: Article 28**

Under Article 28 (§§192–199 *supra*) a court "is not bound to enter a judgment for specific performance unless the court would do so under its own law." At §281 we examined the impact of Article 28 on the buyer's right under Article 46 to "require performance by the seller"; we now face the impact of Article 28 on Article 62.

Article 28, above, is written in terms of whether a court is "bound to enter a judgment of *specific performance*."

Legal systems that stem from English law do not normally refer to an action to recover the full price from the buyer as "specific performance"; this terminology is normally reserved for orders that resemble the decrees that were traditionally issued by courts of equity — decrees that could be enforced by various penalties, including imprisonment for "contempt of court." Requiring a seller to deliver goods (Art. 46) would be described as requiring "specific performance."[11]

---

9. See UNCITRAL Digest Art. 62 para. 2.
10. See UNCITRAL Digest Art. 62 paras. 2–3.
11. At "common law," in the narrow sense that excludes law made by the separate courts of equity, recovery of the price would be sought in an action of "debt." This action was restricted to recovery of the price for things of value *received* by the defendant — more technically, where the defendant had received a *quid pro quo*. The defendant received the *quid pro quo* when he received the goods — and also when he received "property" in goods that still were in the possession of the seller.

Nevertheless, an action by a seller to recover the price from a buyer that has not accepted the goods is an action for "specific performance" for purposes of Article 28. When the buyer has not received or accepted the goods and does not wish to receive or accept them, recovering the full price is functionally the equivalent of compelling the buyer to consummate the transaction; this is the approach of the Convention. As was noted above, the statement in Art. 62 that the seller "may *require* the buyer to pay the price [and] take delivery" parallels the statement in Article 46 that the buyer may *"require* performance by the seller." Both remedies are subject to the concession to domestic law set forth in Article 28: although, under provisions of the Convention, "one party is entitled to *require performance"* by the other, the restrictions on this remedy under the domestic law of the *forum* will apply. See the discussion of Art. 28 at §§194–195.

The point is important: When a seller seeks to force an unwilling buyer to receive goods by an action under Art. 62 to "require the buyer to pay the price," the limitations on this remedy under the domestic law of the *forum* may be decisive. And, as careful students of the civil law have shown, these limitations are not confined to the common law. As has just been noted, jurists of common-law persuasion do not think of an action to recover the price as comparable to an action to require delivery of the goods. But one cannot be tied to local terminology in construing the Convention. See Article 7, *supra* at §87. The significance of the parallel language of Articles 46 and 62, just mentioned, is confirmed by the Convention's structure and its legislative history, discussed in a note.[12] In all legal systems an action under Article 62 to "require the

---

12. Article 28, invoking the remedial restrictions of the domestic law of the forum is placed in Part I, Chapter I — General Provisions; if it applied only to requiring performance by the *seller* it would have been placed in Chapter II, Obligations of the Seller, under Section III on the Remedies of the Buyer. This point is confirmed by the drafting history. The concession to the common law was initially incorporated into both of the two parallel remedies to "require performance" — the buyer's recovery of the goods and the seller's recovery of the price. Later, to avoid duplication, these parallel provisions were consolidated into one provision in Chapter I: General Provisions. *W/G 5* para. 50 and Annex I, (text of Art. 42 (buyer's remedy) and Art. 71 (seller's remedy), V *YB* 34, 56, *Docy. Hist.* 180, 202. The reference in Art. 28 to "a judgment for specific performance" should not be limited in common-law contexts to an equity decree since the Convention must be given the same functional effect in its various linguistic and legal settings. (In the French version the above language of Art. 28 is rendered "ordonner l''exécution en nature" and in Spanish "ordenar el cumplimento especifico.") Limiting this phrase to an equity decree in actions by the buyer would exclude actions such as detinue and replevin, and in common-law settings would have little meaning in actions by the seller, although this provision was designed primarily as a concession to the common law.

buyer to pay the price" is subject to the concession to the domestic rules of the forum provided by Article 28.[13]

349   ## (2) Other Limiting Provisions

The discussion of Article 28, *supra* at §193, and Article 46, *supra* at §285, referred to other provisions of the Convention that restrict coercion of performance. Two of these, Articles 85 and 88 (§§454, 457 *infra*) have special relevance if a seller, who is in possession of goods, should seek to hold the goods indefinitely at the buyer's risk and expense.[14] Under Article 85, "If the buyer is in delay in taking delivery" (which would include delay after a refusal to accept the goods) a seller who has possession or control of the goods "must take such steps as are reasonable in the circumstances to preserve them." This leads to an important provision in Article 88(2): when such goods "are subject to loss or rapid deterioration or their preservation would involve unreasonable expense" the seller "must take reasonable measures to *sell them.*" It would seem that even when "deterioration" would not be "rapid," prolonged retention would inevitably involve "loss" through wasteful storage costs.

For reasons suggested in discussing the buyer's remedy to "require performance." Article 46, *supra* at §286, sellers will not frequently seek to use the broad language of Article 62 to force goods on an unwilling buyer. Compelling payment calls for holding the goods until the processes of the law finally force the buyer to accept and pay for the goods. Mounting storage costs and dangers of obsolescence and loss make this a risky remedy. Only in legal theory are legal "rights" fully realized; when litigation to force the buyer to accept and pay finally reaches its end (and litigation may be particularly protracted in an international setting) the seller may find that the reluctant buyer is in bankruptcy and the seller has only obsolete goods on his hands. In most cases, sellers can be expected promptly to reduce the amount at risk by reselling the goods (Art. 75); when loss results the seller may, of course, recover

---

For strong support of this view see Kastely, The Right to Require Performance, 63 Wash. L. Rev. 607, 634 (1988).

13. *Accord*, Günter Hager, Art. 62 paras. 8–12, *in* Schlechtriem & Schwenzer, *CISG Commentary* (2nd English ed. 2005); UNCITRAL Digest Art. 62 para. 3.

14. See Günter Hager, Art. 62 para. 15, *in* Schlechtriem & Schwenzer, *CISG Commentary* (2nd English ed. 2005).

damages (Arts. 74, 76, 78, *infra*). *The paucity of reported cases in which sellers have invoked Article 62 to force goods on an unwilling seller — in contrast to cases in which sellers have invoked Article 62 to collect the price for goods the buyer has accepted — tends to confirm this point.*[15]

15. See UNCITRAL Digest Art. 62 para. 2.

Article 63.
Seller's Notice Fixing Additional Final Period for Performance

350   This article gives the seller the same remedial tool that Article 47 gives the buyer — the power to "fix an additional period of time of reasonable length for performance." If the buyer fails to perform certain basic obligations within this additional period, Article 64(1)(b), *infra* at §353, provides that the seller may declare the contract avoided without proving that the buyer's breach was "fundamental."[1]

Article 63[2]

(1) The seller may fix an additional period of time of reasonable length for performance by the buyer of his obligations.

(2) Unless the seller has received notice from the buyer that he will not perform within the period so fixed, the seller may not, during that period, resort to any remedy for breach of contract. However, the seller is not deprived thereby of any right he may have to claim damages for delay in performance.

351   A. Notice as a Basis for Avoidance

In examining Articles 47 and 49(1)(b) we saw that the buyer's *Nachfrist* notice provide a basis for avoidance only in a limited area — failure by the seller to deliver the goods. Similarly, the seller's *Nachfrist-notice* under Article 63 provides a basis for avoidance under Article 64(1)(b) only when the buyer fails, within the specified period, to perform his obligation to "*pay the price or take delivery* of the goods."[3] Article 54 states that the buyer's "obligation to pay the price" includes enabling steps required by the contract; thus, failure to establish a letter of credit may provide the basis for a *Nachfrist* notice under the present article (§323 *supra*).[4] In any event, the notice-avoidance remedy applies only to the most important of the buyer's obligations; his failure in other areas

---

1. See Günter Hager, Art. 63 para. 2, *in* Schlechtriem & Schwenzer, *CISG Commentary* (2nd English ed. 2005).
2. This article is the same as Art. 59 of the 1978 Draft. *Cf.* ULIS 62(2), 66(2).
3. See UNCITRAL Digest Art. 63 para. 3.
4. For decisions on this point, see UNCITRAL Digest Art. 63 para. 3.

(such as specifying features of the goods, Art. 65) constitutes a breach of contract but the seller may avoid the contract only if the breach is fundamental (Arts. 25, 64(1)(a)).

The discussion of the seller's *Nachfrist-notice* (Art. 47, *supra* at §289) concluded that the notice can serve as a basis for avoidance only if it states that the other party has an additional and *final* period for performance,[5] and that the reasonableness of the period should be decided in conformity with the Convention's general policy against the avoidance of contracts on insubstantial grounds.[6] That discussion is equally applicable here.[7]

352   B. Obligation to Accept the Performance Invited in the Notice

Paragraph (1) states that the seller may fix an additional period for the buyer's performance "of his obligations"; the notice may be given with respect to defaults that do not invoke the notice-avoidance remedy of Article 64(1)(b). In this larger area the notice has the consequences that are stated in paragraph (2) — the seller is obliged to accept the performance it has invited but is not deprived of the right to claim damages for delay, including delay during the "additional period" fixed in the notice.[8] (See the discussion under Art. 47(2), *supra* at §291.)

5. *Compare* Günter Hager, Art. 63 para. 3, *in* Schlechtriem & Schwenzer, *CISG Commentary* (2nd English ed. 2005).

6. For decisions on what constitutes an additional period "of reasonable length," see UNCITRAL Digest Art. 63 para. 2. For further discussion of this issue, see Günter Hager, Art. 63 paras. 3 & 3a, *in* Schlechtriem & Schwenzer, *CISG Commentary* (2nd English ed. 2005).

7. Knapp in *B-B Commentary* 460 §2.8 suggests that the seller's *Nachfrist* notice does not become effective until it reaches the buyer. Art. 27 states that "unless otherwise expressly provided" in the Convention, a communication that is dispatched by appropriate means is effective in spite of "delay or error" in transmission. Knapp suggests that the above rule should not apply because of "the purpose of this notice." However the Convention provides "express' exceptions from Art. 27 in several situations, but not here. Moreover, most of these exceptions deprive a party in breach of the benefit of the dispatch rule, while the one who sends the *Nachfrist* notice is a party aggrieved by the other party's delay. See §190, *supra*. *Compare* Günter Hager, Art. 63 para. 3, *in* Schlechtriem & Schwenzer, *CISG Commentary* (2nd English ed. 2005).

8. See Günter Hager, Art. 63 paras. 2 & 4, *in* Schlechtriem & Schwenzer, *CISG Commentary* (2nd English ed. 2005); Knapp in *B-B Commentary* 459 §2.5. The seller's time for avoiding the contract does not run while he is waiting for a response to his notice. See Art. 64(2)(b)(ii), *infra*, and the discussion of the comparable provision in Art. 49(2)(b)(ii), §308, *supra*.

Article 64.
Seller's Right to Avoid the Contract

353 ## A. The Significance of Avoidance

Avoidance by the seller is usually based on delay by the buyer in paying the price. The seller normally may delay handing over the goods until the buyer pays (Arts. 58(1), 71) but avoidance has more far-reaching consequences—a seller who avoids the contract need not ever deliver the goods. Article 49, *supra* at §302, defined the buyer's right to avoid the contract; the present Article on the seller's right to avoidance is a mirror image of Article 49.[1]

Article 64

(1) The seller may declare the contract avoided:

(a) if the failure by the buyer to perform any of his obligations under the contract or this Convention amounts to a fundamental breach of contract; or

(b) if the buyer does not, within the additional period of time fixed by the seller in accordance with paragraph (1) of article 63, perform his obligation to pay the price or take delivery of the goods, or if he declares that he will not do so within the period so fixed.

(2) However, in cases where the buyer has paid the price, the seller loses the right to declare the contract avoided unless he does so:

(a) in respect of late performance by the buyer, before the seller has become aware that performance has been rendered; or

(b) in respect of any breach other than late performance by the buyer, within a reasonable time:

(i)   after the seller knew or ought to have known of the breach; or

(ii)   after the expiration of any additional period of time fixed by the seller in accordance with paragraph (1) of Article 63, or after the buyer has declared that he will not perform his obligations within such an additional period.

---

1. The effects of avoidance are dealt with in Ch. V, Sec. V (Arts. 81–84). Under Art. 81(1), one who avoids a contract retains his right to damages (Arts. 74–76) but loses the right to compel performance (Arts. 46, 62).

354 B. Means and Grounds for Avoidance

Avoidance by the seller, like avoidance by the buyer (Art. 49), is made by a "declaration" which (Art. 26) "is effective only if made by notice to the other party." If the notice is dispatched by "means appropriate to the circumstances" the notice is effective in spite of "delay or error" in transmission (Art. 27, §§188–190, *supra*).

Paragraph (1) of Article 64 (like Art. 49(1)) states two alternative grounds for seller's avoidance: (a) Fundamental breach of contract by the buyer; and (b) Failure by the buyer "to pay the price or take delivery" within an additional final period fixed by the seller under Article 63(1) — the *Nachfrist* notice. The first ground for avoidance was explored in connection with the definition of "fundamental breach" (Art. 25 at §184).[2] The second ground, based on a *Nachfrist* notice, was introduced under Article 63, but one point bears emphasis: failure to comply with the *Nachfrist* notice provides a basis for avoidance only when the notice calls for performance of the buyer's basic obligations "to pay the price or to take delivery of the goods" (Art. 64(1)(b)). However, the buyer's "obligation to pay the price" includes the required steps "to enable payment to be made" (Art. 54, *supra* at §323); for example, the notice-avoidance remedy (Arts. 63(1), 64(1)(b)) may be employed if the buyer fails to comply with his obligation to establish a letter of credit (see *supra* at §351).[3]

As we have seen, avoidance by the buyer based on the seller's failure to comply with a *Nachfrist* notice (as contrasted with establishing "fundamental breach" under Art. 49(1)(a)) is limited to "non-delivery" (Art. 49(1)(b)). See *supra* at §305. A buyer's avoidance based on a *Nachfrist*-notice is restricted to the seller's failure to perform its basic obligation to deliver the goods, to avoid erosion of the general principle that contracts should not be destroyed on trivial grounds. See §288, *supra*.[4]

A problem of consistency with this principle is presented by Article 64(1)(b), whereby, the *seller* may avoid the contract based on a buyer's failure to comply with a *Nachfrist* notice "to pay the price *or take delivery* of the goods." Avoidance based on a failure to comply with

---

2. See also Günter Hager, Art. *64* paras. 4–7, *in* Schlechtriem & Schwenzer, *CISG Commentary* (2nd English ed. 2005); UNCITRAL Digest Art. 64 paras. 3–6.

3. See also Günter Hager, Art. 64 para. 8, *in* Schlechtriem & Schwenzer, *CISG Commentary* (2nd English ed. 2005); UNCITRAL Digest Art. 64 para. 8.

4. For application of this principle to avoidance by an aggrieved seller, see Case No. 9887 of the Court of Arbitration of the International Chamber of Commerce, August 1999, English text available at http://cisgw3.law.pace.edu/cases/999887i1.html.

a *Nachfrist* notice to pay the price (or to pay the price *and* take delivery) would be consistent with the approach of Article 49(1)(b); the problem of consistency arises when the buyer has paid the price, if avoidance could be based solely on failure to comply with a notice to take delivery within a fixed period.

A seller who has been paid is not likely to want to avoid the contract, even if the buyer is late in taking delivery, since a seller who avoids the contract must repay the price (Art. 81(2)). Moreover, a buyer who has paid for the goods will generally make every effort to take delivery within an additional period that has been fixed by the seller. However, it is conceivable that a sharp increase in the value of the goods might tempt a seller to try to escape from the contract by sending the buyer a *Nachfrist-notice* fixing a short, final period for taking delivery.

The Convention is not without resources to deal with this problem. Article 63(1) (like Article 47(1)) requires that the *Nachfrist-notice* fix "an additional period of time of *reasonable length*...." As was suggested at §351, *supra*, the reasonableness of the period set in the notice should be decided in conformity with the Convention's general policy against the avoidance of the contract on insubstantial grounds. A seller who has received the price would seldom face irreparable loss from the buyer's delay in taking delivery. The buyer would be responsible for the seller's expenses, such as storage, and the seller (Art. 85, §454, *infra*) "is entitled to retain [the goods] until he has been reimbursed his reasonable expenses by the buyer." Moreover, in situations where there is danger of abuse, the requirement that the period fixed by the seller be of "reasonable length" (Art. 63(1)) should be construed (Art. 7(1)) "to promote... the observance of *good faith* in international trade." See §§94–95 *supra*.

355   **C. Limits on Time for Avoidance**

Paragraph (2) sets time limits for avoidance. Practical considerations that bar excessive delay by the buyer in avoiding the contract were considered under Article 49, *supra* at §306; some of these considerations apply to late avoidance by the seller.

356   **(1) Buyer has Paid the Price**

The time limits set by paragraph (2) apply only to avoidance by the seller "in cases where the buyer has paid the price." Getting paid is usually the seller's principal concern; after the buyer has paid a seller would rarely seek (or have adequate grounds) to avoid the contract. At §354 we considered the narrow circumstances in which a *Nachfrist- notice* calling on the buyer to take delivery might provide a basis for avoidance. Conceivably, avoidance for fundamental breach might be based on the buyer's unexcused failure to obtain an import license or by a failure to comply with obligations to establish a distributorship and develop a program for promoting sale of the goods. In any event, a seller who has been paid and who seeks to avoid the contract must comply with the strict time limits of paragraph (2).[5]

356.1 (2) Buyer has not Paid the Price

Article 64 does not state a time limit for avoidance when the buyer has *not* paid the price. This may seem anomalous unless one considers the awkward position of the seller as he waits for the buyer to pay. If a time limit on avoidance is running, the seller is in danger of declaring avoidance either (a) too early — on the ground that the delay is not yet a "fundamental" breach or that an additional *Nachfrist* period set by the seller is not of "reasonable length" or (b) too late — on the ground that he waited too long after that indefinite point was reached. Article 64(2) relieves the aggrieved seller of such hazardous navigation between Scylla and Charybdis.[6]

If the buyer has not received the goods and the price is due only in exchange for delivery (Art. 58(1)), the seller may choose to take advantage of the opportunity that Article 64(2) affords for delaying a decision about avoidance while the buyer solves its "cash-flow" problem; while the seller delays this decision the buyer, of course, has the right to pay for and receive the goods.

If the seller wishes to avoid the contract and is in doubt over whether the buyer's delay constitutes a "fundamental breach" (Arts. 25,

---

5. The opening phrase of para. (2)(b) — "in respect of *any breach other than late perfor- mance* by the buyer" is awkwardly drafted. The context shows that para. (2)(b) was designed to deal with situations not covered by para. (2)(a): "*late performance* by the buyer." Para. (2)(b) might have been expressed more clearly by replacing the italicized words with "any obligation that the buyer has failed to perform" or "any other failure to performance." See the Secretariat Commentary on draft Art. 60(2)(b), at para. 10. *O.R.* 50, *Docy. Hist.* 440. See also Günter Hager, Art. 64 paras. 12–15, *in* Schlechtriem & Schwenzer, *CISG Commentary* (2nd English ed. 2005).

6. Similar considerations underlie the rule of Art. 49(2) that the buyer's time for avoidance does not begin to run until the seller "has delivered" the goods. See Art. 49, *supra* at §308.

64(1)(a)), the seller can clarify the situation by giving the buyer a *Nachfrist* notice (Art. 63(1)) prior to declaring avoidance (Art. 64(1)(b)).

If the buyer has received the goods and fails to pay the price when it is due, the seller would be well advised to avoid the contract only under unusual circumstances. Avoidance will nullify the seller's right to recover the price (Art. 81(1)). True, Article 81(2) states that the seller "may claim restitution from the [buyer] of whatever [the seller] has supplied..." However, when the buyer fails to pay this seller, other creditors may have levied execution on the goods; whether the seller's right under Article 81(2) to reclaim the goods from the buyer is effective against third persons will be determined by domestic law. See Article 4(a), §70, *supra* and Article 81(2), §444, *infra*.[7] Moreover, the goods may have been used or damaged, and their value may deteriorate during the period required for reclamation.

A seller who has not avoided the contract may exercise legal remedies to collect the full price (Art. 62) plus damages and interest for delay (Arts. 74 and 84, §§403–404, 420–422, *infra*). In addition, since the goods have been received (and presumably accepted) by the buyer, the common-law restrictions on "specific performance" do not apply (Art. 28; Art. 62, §§347–349, *supra*).

Additional provisions on avoidance, applicable to both buyer and seller, appear in Articles 72 (anticipatory breach), 73 (delivery by installments) and 81–82 (effects of avoidance).

---

7. See also Flechtner, *Pittsburgh Symposium* 67.

Article 65.
Seller's Notice Supplying Missing Specifications

357   The present article deals with a special type of "gap" in the contract — specifications for the goods which the buyer fails to supply. *Because of the specialized nature and narrow focus of this rule, it has seldom been invoked in litigation.*[1]

Article 65[2]

357   **(1) If under the contract the buyer is to specify the form, measurement or other features of the goods and he fails to make such specification either on the date agreed upon or within a reasonable time after receipt of a request from the seller, the seller may, without prejudice to any other rights he may have, make the specification himself in accordance with the requirements of the buyer that may be known to him.**

     (2) If the seller makes the specification himself, he must inform the buyer of the details thereof and must fix a reasonable time within which the buyer may make a different specification. If, after receipt of such a communication, the buyer fails to do so within the time so fixed, the specification made by the seller is binding.

Article 65 was designed to prevent a buyer from escaping from its obligations by refusing to supply missing specifications.[3] Supplying the missing specification by the procedure provided in Article 65 forestalls the contention that the contract is too vague for the measurement of damages (Art. 74)[4] and permits the seller to establish the amount of damages by reselling the goods (Art. 75). When the contract states a fixed price, rather than a "cost-plus" or similar formula, the parties

---

1. See UNCITRAL Digest Art. 65.
2. This article is substantially the same as Art. 61 of the 1978 Draft: "within the time so fixed" was inserted in para. (2) at the Diplomatic Conference. *SR. 26*, paras. 34–39, *O.R.* 374, *Docy. Hist.* 595. *Cf.* ULIS 67.
3. *SR. 26* paras. 7–11 *O.R.* 372, *Docy. Hist.* 593. *Cf.* Art. 14: "A proposal is sufficiently definite if it *indicates the goods . . .*" See *Dölle, Kommentar* (von Caemmerer) Art. 67 at 9, p. 394 (the provision for supplying missing specifications bars any contention that the contract is void because of incompleteness or vagueness).
4. See Günter Hager, Art. 65 para. 2, *in* Schlechtriem & Schwenzer, *CISG Commentary* (2nd English ed. 2005).

probably would not intend that the buyer's specifications should substantially affect the cost. Similarly, the parties probably would not intend that the seller could have wide discretion to decide the characteristics of the buyer's goods. Consequently, references in the contract and in Article 65 to "the form, measurements or other features of the goods" should be construed with sufficient strictness to avoid these problems.

Article 65 can readily be applied where the contract calls for the selection of goods that the seller has in stock, or even for the manufacture of goods to buyer's specifications where such goods are readily resalable. More difficult problems may arise when the contract calls for the manufacture of goods to specifications that are so unique that they cannot be resold and the buyer notifies the seller that it can no longer use the goods. If the seller thereafter supplies specifications and manufactures goods that have no substantial value, the seller's action to recover damages or the full contract price may collide with the rules on mitigation of loss in Article 77, *infra* at §416.[5] (One who engages in such wasteful production faces commercial and legal hazards that are so serious that extreme cases are unlikely to arise.)

When the buyer fails to supply the missing information the seller "may" but need not act for the buyer.[6] The refusal by the buyer to comply with this requirement of the contract would seem, *at least in some circumstances,*[7] sufficiently serious to authorize the seller to avoid the contract (Arts. 25, 64(1)(a)).[8] The seller also may recover damages which could include "loss of profit" (Art. 74) such as the contribution to the seller's overhead costs that would have resulted from performance. See §415 *infra*.

---

5. *Contra*, Günter Hager, Art. 65 paras. 4 & 7a, *in* Schlechtriem & Schwenzer, *CISG Commentary* (2nd English ed. 2005).

6. See UNCITRAL Digest Art. 65 para. 2.

7. See Günter Hager, Art. 65 paras. 1 & 8, *in* Schlechtriem & Schwenzer, *CISG Commentary* (2nd English ed. 2005).

8. A contrary view by Knapp, *B-B Commentary* 478 §2.6, seems to overlook avoidance under Art. 64(1)(a). Moreover, the broad statement in Art. 60(a) that the "buyer's obligation to take delivery" includes acts to enable the seller to make delivery, §342, *supra*, may authorize the seller to give the buyer a *Nachfrist* notice (Art. 63(1)) fixing an additional period for supplying the specifications; if the buyer fails to comply the seller may be able to avoid the contract under Art. 64(1)(b) without proving that the buyer had committed a "fundamental" breach of contract (Art. 25). See Günter Hager, Art. 65 para. 8, *in* Schlechtriem & Schwenzer, *CISG Commentary* (2nd English ed. 2005).

CHAPTER IV.

PASSING OF RISK
(Articles 66–70)

INTRODUCTION TO CHAPTER IV

358   Casualty to the goods (e.g., theft or fire) may occur in various settings — while the seller holds the goods before delivering them to a
carrier or to the buyer, while the goods are in transit, while the buyer
is examining the goods, while the buyer holds the goods after rejecting
them. Usually the loss will be covered by insurance. Allocating the risk
of loss between seller and buyer should reflect considerations such as
these: Which party is in a better position to evaluate the loss and press a
claim against the insurer and to salvage or dispose of damaged goods?
Who can insure the good at the least cost? Who is more likely to carry
insurance under standard commercial practice? What rules on risk will
minimize litigation over negligence in the care and custody of the
goods?

359   **A. The 1964 and 1980 Conventions**

     ULIS approached the problem of risk in a manner that in general took
account of the above considerations of policy and was consistent with
modern sales law. However, as we have seen (Art. 31, *supra* at §210), the
rules on risk (and other issues) were complicated by the role given to the
concept of *délivrance*. In the UNCITRAL proceedings the concept of
délivrance was abandoned; instead, the Convention speaks of physical
acts of transfer of possession — the "handing over" of the goods to a
carrier or to the buyer.[1]

---

1. *Reps. S-G* III *YB* 31–40, V *YB* 89–94, VI *YB* 108–110, *Docy. Hist.* 73–82, 168–173,
233–235. *WK. GR*: V *YB* 47–50, 60 (revised text), *Docy. Hist.* 193–196, 206 (revised
text). *UNCITRAL*: VII *YB* 62–65, *Docy. Hist.* 355–357. *S-G* (Draft Arts. 78–82): *O.R.*
63–66, *Docy. Hist.* 453–456. See Sevón, *Lausanne Colloq.* 191, 192–193. *Cf.* Huber, 43
Rabels Z 413, 451, 458 (1979) (approves change in approach); Neumayer in *von Caemmerer
Festschrift* (1978) 955, 959.

The most important provisions in this chapter (Arts. 66–70) are in Articles 67, 69 and 70. Article 67 applies when the contract involves carriage of goods; Article 69 applies when the buyer is to come for the goods *or the seller itself is to transport the goods to their destination.* Article 70 deals with the effect of serious breach by the seller. Article 68 deals with a specialized and troublesome situation — the sale of goods while they are in transit.

359.1 Risk Following Avoidance of Contract or Buyer's Refusal of Delivery

Complex risk of loss issues arise where one party has breached the contract. Some of these situations are expressly addressed in the risk of loss rules of Chapter IV. See Article 69(1) and 70, §§374, 379–383 infra. Concerning others, however, the Convention is silent. For example, suppose goods are delivered and risk of loss passes to the buyer, but the buyer discovers a serious lack of conformity and properly avoids the contract. The buyer in that case must make restitution of the goods to the seller. Responsibility for damage that occurred while the goods were in the hands of the buyer but before the buyer avoided the contract is discussed below in connection with Article 70. Suppose, however, the goods are damaged after the buyer avoids the contract, while they are being transported back to the seller (e.g., on a carrier). Who is responsible for the damage? This and related questions concerning responsibility for damage that occurs when the goods are being returned to the seller or when the buyer refuses delivery are discussed more generally below (see §§448.1A & 448.1B infra).

One aspect of this issue, however, requires discussion here. The highest court of Austria, the Oberster Gerichtshof, has held that a seller bore the risk while non-conforming goods were being returned after the parties had agreed to avoid the contract.[2] As one basis for its decision, the court suggested that the risk of returning goods to a breaching seller should be allocated in a way that is the mirror image of the allocation of transit risk under the parties" contract. Thus because the parties had contracted, for delivery "ex works," so that the buyer bore the risk while the goods were being transported to it, the court ruled that the seller should bear transit risk when the goods were returned.

2. Oberster Gerichtshof, Austria, 29 June 1999, English translation available at http://cisgw3.law.pace.edu/cases/990629a3.html.

This reasoning — although not the result it produced in this case[3] — makes little sense as a rule for allocating risk when goods are being returned following a buyer's justifiable avoidance of contract. Suppose the parties" contract had provided for delivery of the goods "DDP (Delivered Duty Paid)," so that the seller bore transit risk when the goods were originally delivered to the buyer. Should this mean that buyer must bear the risk in transporting non-conforming goods back to the seller, despite the fact that — as stated by the Oberster Gerichtshof itself — the seller "caused these risks with his breach of contract?" The aggrieved buyer bargained not to bear transit risk under the contract, and presumably paid a premium for that term. It seems perverse to use that as a reason for imposing the risk of returning non-conforming goods on the buyer.

As argued below (see §448.1A infra), where a buyer properly avoids the contract the risk of returning the goods should be borne by the breaching seller: a buyer should not be liable for damage occurring during such return unless the damage was caused by the buyer's fault. This approach is supported not only by Article 82(2) (the provision cited by the Austrian court) but also by the rules regulating the obligations imposed on the buyer by Articles 86–88 to preserve goods after avoidance of contract.

The Oberster Gerichtshof's "implied-mirror-image-delivery-term" approach, under which an aggrieved buyer's responsibility for damage occurring during return of the goods following proper avoidance of the contract varies with the risk provisions of the original contract, may have been influenced by European rules giving jurisdiction over contract claims to courts where an obligation is to be performed.[4] If so, it illustrates the pernicious impact that jurisdictional considerations arising out of non-uniform law can have on the Convention. (Compare the discussion in §332 supra.) The fact that correct rules for dealing with risk when goods are being returned to a breaching seller could lead to undesirable or unpredictable results under regional jurisdictional rules is not, under Article 7(2), a valid consideration in interpreting the Convention. Contracting States not subject to the regional procedural rules should not be punished to overcome problems in non-uniform law.

---

3. As discussed in §448.1A *infra*, the result in the case — the breaching seller was held responsible for damage to the non-conforming goods that occurred while they were being returned — appears proper.

4. See UNCITRAL Digest Art. 81 para. 7; Rainer Hornung, Art. 81 paras. 17–18, *in* Schlechtriem & Schwenzer, *CISG Commentary* (2nd English ed. 2005).

Article 66.
Loss or Damage After Risk Has Passed to Buyer

360   Article 36(1), *supra* at §241, laid down the basic and possibly self-evident principle that questions concerning conformity of the goods to the contract are determined as of the time when risk passes to the buyer; deterioration prior to that time is the responsibility of the seller. Article 66 is a corollary of that proposition.

Article 66[1]

Loss of or damage to the goods after the risk has passed to the buyer does not discharge him from his obligation to pay the price, unless the loss or damage is due to an act or omission of the seller.

361   ## A. Destruction of the Goods and the Duty to Pay

Example 66A. A contract called for Seller to send 10 bales of No. 1 quality cotton to Buyer; the terms were F.O.B. Seller's city. Buyer agreed to pay in exchange for shipping documents that were to be presented after arrival of the goods. The F.O.B. term (alternatively, the Convention's rules on risk — Art. 67(1)) placed transit risks on Buyer. Seller loaded the 10 bales of No. 1 quality but during carriage the cotton was so charred by fire as to be worthless. Buyer exercised his right to inspect the goods before payment (Art. 58(3)) and refused to pay for the goods because they were not "No. 1" quality as required by the contract.

Article 36(1), *supra* at §241, answers Buyer's contention that the goods were not "No. 1" quality: the goods did conform to the contract when the risk of loss passed to Buyer. Article 66 states, in effect, that the damage or destruction of the goods after risk passed to Buyer does not

---

1. This article is the same as Art. 78 of the 1978 Draft, and is substantially the same as ULIS 96. At the Diplomatic Conference the rules on risk of loss in the 1978 Draft (Arts. 78–82) were moved from the very end of the sales provisions to this earlier position between Chapters III and V; this change was designed to emphasize the close relation between risk of loss and the obligation of the parties to perform their contract (Chs. II and III), as contrasted with the remedies for non-performance (Ch. V); *O.R.* 401–402, *Docy. Hist.* 622–623.

relieve Buyer of his obligation to pay the price.[2] *In Example 66A Buyer bore risk while the goods were in transit regardless of who had title to the goods at that time, and regardless of who was responsible for making arrangements to ship or insure the goods.*[3]

A buyer who is asked to pay for goods that have been destroyed (Example 66A) may well feel that something has gone terribly wrong and wonder whether the Convention's general provision on excuse (Art. 79 §423, *infra*) might apply. These are two answers to the buyer's query about relief based on general principles of exemption (excuse).

The first is that any general rule on excuse is excluded by the specific rule of Article 66. This article deals narrowly and solely with the effect of "loss of . . . the goods" after risk has passed to the buyer, and provides that when this occurs the buyer must pay the price. At first glance the result may seem harsh but the result responds to pragmatic considerations. It is feasible and customary for transit loss to be covered by insurance. Moreover, loss or damage is usually discovered at the end of the carriage; the buyer usually is in a better position than the seller to assess the damage, make a claim against the insurer and salvage the usable goods.[4] A second and equally compelling answer calls for examination of the Convention's provision on exemption (or excuse) in Article 79, §§423–435, *infra*. In brief, Article 79 provides exemption only when performance is prevented by an "impediment beyond [the party's] control"; no impediment prevents payment of the price. A more substantive answer is that exemption does not apply when a party could "have avoided or overcome [the impediment] or its consequences"; it is possible (and customary) for a party bearing transit risk to "overcome" the "consequences" by insurance.

2. The general rule of Art. 58(1) that the buyer "is not bound to pay the price" until the seller places the goods at the buyer's disposal is subject to the more specific provision of Art. 66 on risk of loss. Of course the contract can reverse the Convention's rules on risk (Art. 6). See UNCITRAL Digest Art. 66 Intro to Chapter IV paras. 6 & 8–9. A term calling for payment in exchange for documents or goods, however, would normally be intended to deal with the time and manner of payment rather than risk.

3. See UNCITRAL Digest Art. 67 para. 1 and decisions cited therein.

4. Similar principles apply to claims against the carrier. However, when carriage is by sea the narrow and limited responsibility of ocean carriers under the Hague Rules (1924) makes insurance especially important. *But cf.* The U.N. Convention on the Carriage of Goods by Sea ('Hamburg Rules," 1978) *ACL UNCITRAL Symposium* 353–448 (text of Convention at 421); W. Tetley, Marine Cargo Claims (2d ed. 1987).

362   **B. Damage Due to Seller's Act or Omission**

Under the last clause of Article 66, even after risk has passed to the buyer the seller is responsible for loss or damage that is due to its "act of omission."

Example 66B. A contract called for Seller to ship 5,000 pounds of No. 1 quality rice in new hemp bags "F.O.B. Seller's City." The contract term (alternatively, the Convention's rules on risk—Art. 67(1)) placed transit risk on Buyer. Seller shipped 100 bags of No. 1 quality rice but one of the bags was old and so weak that it broke open during transit and the rice was lost.

Did the fact that the seller broke its contract by failing to pack all of the rice in new bags prevent transit risk from passing to the buyer? As we shall see, under Article 70, *infra* at §380, the answer is No if we assume (as seems plausible) that the use of one second-hand bag did not constitute a "fundamental breach of contract."[5] (This point becomes especially important when casualty to the goods results from a cause unrelated to a defect in the goods. See *infra* at §380.)

We may now return to Example 66B. Although risk of casualty to the goods had passed to Buyer, Article 66 makes Seller responsible for the loss of the bag of rice that resulted from Seller's breach of contract.[6] Consider a similar example suggested by another source: Seller loads fruit or other perishable goods that conform with the contract. Seller, however, is in breach of contract by delaying the shipment; because of the delay the goods deteriorate.[7] Under these circumstances, as in Example 66A, Seller is responsible for the loss during transit that results from the breach of contract.[8]

One may ask: What rules or standards decide what "acts or omissions" will make the seller responsible for loss or damage after risk has passed to the buyer?[9] Example 66B presented no difficulty for the damage resulted from the seller's breach of contract. This example also illustrated the linkage between "act" and "omission": It would be difficult to decide whether the loss of the rice resulted from an "act" (shipment in an old, weak bag) or an "omission" (failure to ship in new bags). The linking of these two concepts and the nebulous

5. See *also* Nicholas, *B-B Commentary* §1.2.
6. *Cf.* (U.K.) SGA (1893 & 1979) 20(2): *Atiyah* 250.
7. Nicholas, *B-B Commentary* §1.2:
8. See UNCITRAL Digest Art. 66 para. 4.
9. See Sevón, *Lausanne Colloq.* 196–197 and notes 13–16.

dimensions of "omission" show that the seller's liability must be derived from the violation of some binding standard.

To avoid the vagaries and inappropriateness for international trade of scraps of domestic law (Art. 7(1)), the primary standard for the parties" obligations should be (Arts. 30 & 53) the requirements established by "the contract and this Convention," including (Art. 9) the parties" practices and trade usage. However, UNCITRAL in 1977 rejected a proposal to amend Article 66 (then draft Art. 64) to limit the "act or omission" to a breach of contract.[10] This decision not to restrict the scope of Article 66 seems wise since the seller, by a wrongful seizure of the goods or abuse of legal process, might cause damage to the goods under circumstances that might not constitute a breach of contract.[11] The standard established by the phrase "act or omission" is considered more fully in connection with the use of this phrase in Article 82, §448 *infra*.

10. VIII *YB* 63, para. 531, *Docy. Hist.* 356. See also Sevón, *supra*, at 196; Nicholas, *B-B Commentary* §2.2.

11. See Günter Hager, Art. 66 paras. 6–7, *in* Schlechtriem & Schwenzer, *CISG Commentary* (2nd English ed. 2005).

Article 67.
Risk When the Contract Involves Carriage

363 ## A. Risk and the Contract

Nearly all international sales call for carriage of the goods but the type of transport reflects varying geographical settings, types of goods and needs of the parties. In recent decades transport arrangements have been profoundly influenced by the "container revolution" which, in turn, has encouraged multimodal transport in which the container is sealed at an inland point and carried to (or near) the buyer by a series of different modes of transport such as truck, rail, and ship. However, the parties to even an international sale sometimes can use simple one-stage transport by trucks operated by the seller, the buyer or an independent carrier. Bulk goods (e.g., grain, ores, oil) often move from port to port in ships chartered by one of the parties. Before or after an international carriage local transport often will be needed to take the goods from the seller's warehouse to a rail terminal or to an ocean carrier's warehouse or dock and may also be needed when the goods reach a point near the buyer. This local transport may be handled by the trucks of the seller or buyer or by transport agencies engaged by or affiliated with one of the parties.

No statute can adequately define when risk passes in all these circumstances, any more than a statute can define the characteristics and quality of the goods. Fortunately, the parties to an international sale usually appreciate this fact and provide in the contract for the point at which risk passes.[1] This may be done by an explicit provision on risk, or by referring (e.g.) to *Incoterms* and its definition of a specified trade term.[2] As we have seen (Art. 6, §§74–76, *supra*), contract provisions prevail over rules of the Convention.[3]

---

1. See Günter Hager, Art. 67 para. 2, *in* Schlechtriem & Schwenzer, *CISG Commentary* (2nd English ed. 2005); UNCITRAL Digest Art. 67 para. 3.

2. See UNCITRAL Digest Art. 67 paras. 3 & 6.

3. The grounds on which a standard trade term may be used in interpreting the contract were discussed under Art. 9 at §115. The reasons why the Convention did not attempt to define commercial terms are discussed in Honnold, ULIS: The Hague Convention of 1964, 30 Law & Cont. Pr. L.Q. 326, 339–341 (1965).

364   ## B. The Convention and Transit Risk

The Convention's general rule on risk in transit is stated in Article 67; in brief, when the goods are handed over to the carrier risk passes to the buyer.

Article 67[4]

(1) If the contract of sale involves carriage of the goods and the seller is not bound to hand them over at a particular place, the risk passes to the buyer when the goods are handed over to the first carrier for transmission to the buyer in accordance with the contract of sale. If the seller is bound to hand the goods over to a carrier at a particular place, the risk does not pass to the buyer until the goods are handed over to the carrier at that place. The fact that the seller is authorized to retain documents controlling the disposition of the goods does not affect the passage of the risk.

(2) Nevertheless, the risk does not pass to the buyer until the goods are clearly identified to the contract, whether by markings on the goods, by shipping documents, by notice given to the buyer or otherwise.

Article 67 and Article 69 (§§373–378, *infra*) need to be read together since situations not governed by Article 67 will, in most cases, fall automatically into Article 69.[5] One will note that Article 67 states that it applies only "[i]f the contract of sale involves carriage of the goods" — language identical to that found in Article 31(a)[6] — and provides rules on the transfer of risk only for cases where the seller "hands over" goods to a "carrier." *As discussed above in connection with Article 31 (§§208–209 supra), "carriage" refers to arrangements involving use of a third party's transport facilities — e.g., a trucking service, railroad or maritime shipping provider — rather that trucks or other transport vehicles of the parties themselves.*[7] Contractual

---

4. Article 67 of the Convention is based on Art. 79 of the 1978 Draft, but with significant redrafting in both paragraphs. The basic rule on passage of risk in para. (1) of Art. 67 is similar to the result under ULIS 19(2) and 97(1); para. (2) is similar to ULIS 19(3).

5. Article 69 applies to "cases not within Arts. 67 and 68." Article 68, §§372 *infra*, deals with a special situation that, for purposes of orientation, can be put to one side.

6. See UNCITRAL Digest Art. 67 para. 4.

7. *Accord*, Günter Hager, Art. 67 para. 5, *in* Schlechtriem & Schwenzer, *CISG Commentary* (2nd English ed. 2005).

arrangements that are *not* governed by Article 67 and therefore *are* governed by Article 69 include: (1) The buyer is to come for the goods (Article 67(1) does not apply since the seller does not hand over the goods to a "carrier" but to the buyer); (2) the seller, instead of "handing over" the goods to a "carrier," transports the goods to the buyer in the seller's own vehicles (see §369.1, *infra*).[8] The point at which risk passes in these cases is discussed in connection with Article 69, §§373–378, *infra*.

365   (1) The Basic Rule: Underlying Considerations

Article 67 reflects the dominant approach of domestic law and commercial practice to risk of loss during carriage.[9]

366   **(a) Domestic Law.**   The approach to transit risk in the Convention is similar to that of the (USA) Uniform Commercial Code:

> *Section 2–509. Risk of Loss in the Absence of Breach*
> (1) Where the contract requires or authorizes the seller to ship the goods by carrier
> (a) if it does not require him to deliver them at a particular destination, the risk of loss passes to the buyer when the goods are duly delivered to the carrier even though the shipment is under reservation (Section 2–505)....

Other rules of domestic law also operate from the baseline that, unless the parties agree to the contrary, transit risks fall on the buyer.

367   **(b) Commercial Practice.**   There are practical considerations that support these norms. As has been noted (§361, *supra*), damage during carriage usually is discovered only when the goods reach the buyer. In international transactions the seller is likely to be far from the damaged goods; the buyer is in a better position to assess the damage and to make a claim against the carrier or the insurer. In many transactions, before the seller ships the buyer will arrange for the issuance (or confirmation) of a letter of credit by a bank near the seller. The seller, in exchange for the payment, will surrender a negotiable bill of lading and an insurance policy which the bank will forward to the buyer. The buyer will have

---

8. See Günter Hager, Art. 67 para. 3, *in* Schlechtriem & Schwenzer, *CISG Commentary* (2nd English ed. 2005); UNCITRAL Digest Art. 67 para. 10.

9. See Günter Hager, Art. 67 para. 3, *in* Schlechtriem & Schwenzer, *CISG Commentary* (2nd English ed. 2005).

these documents in hand when he examines the goods and discovers the damage — facts that make it particularly efficient for the buyer to deal with the damage claim.[10]

Standard trade definitions respond to these considerations. Under the traditional "C.I.F." term, although the seller is responsible for the cost of carriage to the stated destination the buyer bears transit risks. Similarly, under the *Incoterms* (2000) definitions of "CPT," "Carriage Paid to . . . (named place of destination)," and "CIP," "Carriage and Insurance paid to . . . (named place of destination)" — a quotation that also responds to modern transport practices such as containerization, and is expected to be used in place of the older quotations — the buyer must bear all risks of the goods from the time they have been delivered to the first carrier" (A4, B5).

368　(2) Response to Current Practices

368.1　(a) Loading "On Board" or Delivery to Carrier.　Under

some of the older trade terms (F.O.B., C & F, CIF) risk passes only when the goods are put "on board" or "pass the ship's rail"; on the other hand, as we have just seen, modern trade definitions make risk pass when the goods are delivered into the "custody" or "charge" of the carrier. Article 67 follows the more recent practice in providing that risk passes when the goods are *"handed over"* to the carrier.[11] When the carrier is in a position to accept custody prior to loading it is difficult to determine whether damage discovered at destination occurred before, during or after loading. In some cases, as when the seller has facilities for dockside loading (e.g., grains or other bulk commodities) the seller will not "hand over" the goods to the carrier until they enter the ship's hold; when the seller delivers the goods to an intermediary at the port or to a port authority it will be especially important for the contract to specify the point at which risk passes.

368.2　(b) "Hi-tech" Goods and Contract Drafting.　The practical

considerations that led to the general rules placing transit risk on the

---

10. See Roth, The Passing of Risk, *AJCL UNCITRAL Symposium* 291 at 296; Honnold, *supra* note 3, at 338. Contra, von Hoffman, *Dubrovnik Lectures* 287.

11. See Günter Hager, Art. 67 para. 3, *in* Schlechtriem & Schwenzer, *CISG Commentary* (2nd English ed. 2005); Ramberg, Incoterms 1980, *Transnational Law: Bielefeld Colloq.* 137, 147 (unsuitability of the "ship's rail'); Honnold, Uniform Law and Uniform Trade Terms, *id.* 161, 165.

buyer are strongest in sales of goods that the buyer can salvage or repair. Only the parties are in a position to decide whether these prevailing rules of domestic law on which Article 67 is based are appropriate for their contract: all that is feasible here is to raise a *caveat* as to whether the Convention's norm is appropriate for high-technology equipment that only the seller can repair or adjust. In such cases the parties may wish to consider whether it would be efficient to provide that, after arrival of the equipment, the parties will supervise a test run for a specified period and the seller will have the responsibility to see that the equipment is in working order.[12] Fortunately, the Convention (Art. 6) gives the parties a free hand for fine-tuning to meet their needs.

369 (3) Other Applications of Article 67(1)

As was noted briefly at §374, Article 67(1) provides for transfer of risk only when the seller "hands over" the goods to a "carrier." We can now deal with the application of Article 67(1) to specific situations.

369.1 (a) Use of Seller's own Transport. Does Article 67(1) apply when in the sales contract the seller engages to transport the goods to the buyer in the seller's own trucks or other transport vehicles? In some contracts this intent will be expressed by language such as "We are quoting you a delivered price and engage to deliver the goods to your place of business in our own transport vehicles." When the seller agrees to deliver the goods but an understanding as to risk is not made clear by the contract, including the parties" practices or trade usage, the issue in terms of Article 67(1) is this: "When the seller loads the goods in its own trucks does the seller "hand over" the goods to a "carrier"?"

The answer is No. "Hand over" is used deliberately here and at many places in the Convention to denote a transfer of possession. This does not

---

12. See Ramberg, *supra* note 11, at 140. Contractual arrangements can take many forms, including bank guarantees for payment (or repayment) based on the results of the test run. See Horn, *Transnational Law: Bielefeld Colloq.* 275. The present writer in *Parker Colloq.* Ch. 8, at 8–4 to 8–8 discussed some of the considerations that influenced UNCITRAL's choice among (1) following the prevailing rule of domestic law and of 1964 ULIS; (2) reversing the prevailing rules and (3) Attempting to carve out an exception for "high-technology" or some other category of goods. Alternative (3) had to be rejected to meet the requirements of clarity in drafting while alternative (2), overturning the prevailing pattern of domestic law, would have led to difficulties in many lines of trade and might have jeopardized worldwide adoption.

occur when the seller employs its own means of transport.[13] *And as noted above (see §§208 & 364 supra), the term "carrier" refers to a third party that transports the goods, and not to transport facilities of the parties themselves.*

There are practical reasons for holding risk on the seller when it is also the transporter, for damage at this stage is likely to generate a claim that the seller failed to exercise due care; litigation and related transaction costs are reduced by the Convention's rule that the seller does not perform its contractual obligation to deliver conforming goods (Arts. 31(a), 35, 36(1)) until the seller has completed its own duties with respect to the goods. Moreover, when the seller engages to deliver the goods in its own transport facilities the price will normally reflect the cost of transportation, including the cost of insuring the vehicles and their contents — a risk that can be underwritten most efficiently for the operator of the vehicles.

In sum: When the seller engages to deliver the goods in its own transport facilities, Article 67(1) does not apply and transit risk remains on the seller. Consequently, transfer of risk is governed by Article 69. As we shall see, under Article 69(2) risk passes when (in brief) "the goods are placed at [the buyer's] disposal" at the place where the buyer "is bound to take over the goods" (§377, *infra*).

369.2   **(b) Transport by Successive Carriers.**   We now face problems of risk in two specialized situations.

(i) Transport to a "Particular Place" Named in the Contract.

The first sentence of Article 67(1) commences as follows: "If the contract of sale involves carriage of the goods and the seller *is not bound to hand them over to a particular place . . .*" This exception to the scope of the first sentence leads into the second sentence: "If the seller *is bound to hand the goods over to a carrier at a particular place*, the risk does not pass to the buyer until the goods are *handed over to the carrier at that place.*" What situations are governed by these provisions?

Example 67A. A contract between Seller, located in the inland French city of Lyon, and Buyer, of New York City, states: "Seller will deliver the goods to the North Star Line in Marseille." The goods are damaged

---

13. See Günter Hager, Art. 67 para. 5, *in* Schlechtriem & Schwenzer, *CISG Commentary* (2nd English ed. 2005); Nicholas, *B-B Commentary 490*, §2.2; *Finnish Sales Act (1987)* Secs. 7, 13.

during transport to Marseille either (a) in Seller's own trucks or (b) in the trucks of a transport company engaged by Seller.

In either case Seller is responsible for transit damage between Lyon and Marseille; under the second sentence of Article 67(1) risk does not pass "until the goods are handed over to the carrier" at the "particular place" designated in the contract.[14] True, in alternative (b), this result is inconsistent with the general principle of Article 67 that the buyer bears transport risks. However on this point (as so often) the statute reflects a judgment as to the probable intent of the contract term designating a "particular place" for handing over the goods.[15] If a contrary intent as to risk had been expressed in the contract that, of course, would govern. Indeed, if a modular container is to be packed and sealed in Lyon the seller would be well advised to propose a contract provision stating that risk passes to the buyer in Lyon when the container is sealed: *"splitting" the transit risk — i.e., making the seller responsible for damage during a portion of the transport and the buyer responsible for damage during the remainder — is generally unwise as it invites costly litigation over exactly when and how damage occurred;[16] it is particularly wasteful and unnecessary in the case of multimodal transport.*

(ii) Transshipment. Example 67A illustrated a contract in which (Art. 67(1), second sentence) "the seller is bound to hand the goods over to a carrier *at a particular place*" and the seller engaged a carrier to take the goods to the designated place. It is important to distinguish this case from contracts that do not designate a "particular place" when two carriers are used to carry the goods from the seller to the buyer.

Example 67B. A contract between Seller in Savannah (on the southeast coast of the U.SA.) called for shipment to Buyer in Le Havre (on the north coast of France). The contract failed to designate the point for transfer of risk, or designate the route for shipment. (This

---

14. See Günter Hager, Art. 67 paras. 6–7, *in* Schlechtriem & Schwenzer, *CISG Commentary* (2nd English ed. 2005).

15. The language of Art. 67(1) under discussion and its application to Example 67A are consistent with *Incoterms 1990*: FREE CARRIER . . . (named place). See Ramberg, *supra* note 11, at 145 and 409 (definition of term). Language in the first edition of this work could be construed to suggest a different conclusion. Professor Nicholas, *B-B Commentary* 491–492, clearly analyzed the problem and cited legislative history that supports his view and that suggested above in connection with Example 67A. See VIII *YB* 63, *Docy. Hist.* 356, *Sec. Commy.* (draft Art. 79), *O.R.* 64, *Docy. Hist.* 454 (paras. 6–7).

16. See Günter Hager, Art. 67 paras. 4–6, *in* Schlechtriem & Schwenzer, *CISG Commentary* (2nd English ed. 2005).

omission is abnormal but could occur; when shipping arrangements are left open, under Article 32(2), §214 supra, the seller "must make such contracts as are necessary for carriage to the place fixed by means of transportation appropriate in the circumstances . . ." Seller found that no carrier operated between Savannah and Le Havre and, following standard practice, arranged for transport by Carrier A from Savannah to New York, and for Carrier A to deliver the goods to Carrier B for carriage to Le Havre. Inspection in Le Havre showed that the goods had been damaged in transit.

In this case risk of loss passed to the buyer when the goods (Art. 67(1), first sentence) were "handed over to the *first* carrier for transmission to the buyer . . ." The exception to this rule that controlled Example 67A does not apply since the seller was not "bound" to "hand over" the goods to a carrier at any place other than at the seller's port city of Savannah. The result is driven home by the statement in the first sentence that risk passes when the goods are handed over to the "*first* carrier." The Convention thus rejects the view that in sales requiring two carriers risk does not pass until the goods are delivered to the second carrier. As noted earlier in this discussion, such splitting of transit risks is inconsistent with modern practices for multimodal transport and presents practical problems of determining where the damage occurred.[17] The parties may, by agreement, split transit risks but this is not encouraged by the Convention.

369.3   **(c) Minor Deviations and Risk.**   The first sentence of Article 67(1) closes with the phrase, "for transmission to the buyer *in accordance with the contract of sale.*" Suppose that the goods or the arrangements for shipment deviate from the contract in some minor respect: Does this make risk of loss remain on the seller? The answer is controlled by Article 70, §§379–383, *infra*, which provides that the rules on risk in Articles 67, 68 and 69 yield to the remedies given "the buyer on account of *fundamental breach*" — in short, the rules on risk are not overturned by minor deviations that do not satisfy the standards of Article 25. The phrase in Article 67(1) "for transmission to the buyer in accordance with the contract of sale" consequently imposes the condition that the contract authorized the seller *to ship.* The buyer, of

---

17. See Günter Hager, Art. 67 paras. 4–6 & 11, *in* Schlechtriem & Schwenzer, *CISG Commentary* (2nd English ed. 2005); U.N. Convention on International Multimodal Transport of Goods (Geneva, 24 May 1980). See Mankabady, Int. Contract L. & Fin. Rev. V. 2, 233 (1981).

course, may recover for the loss that results from the seller's deviation from the contract: Articles 45(1) and 74; see also Article 66 and Example 66B, §362 *supra*.

370 **(4) Retention of Documents Controlling Disposal of the Goods**

Paragraph (1) closes with this important provision: "The fact that the seller is authorized to retain documents controlling disposition of the goods does not affect the passage of the risk." This rule is useful to avoid unintended upset of the basic rule on risk and is consistent with commercial practice.[18] In arranging for a documentary transfer the parties are concerned with payment of the price rather than damage in transit. Moreover, the contract may call for payment in exchange for documents at a time when the goods are on the way — on a truck or railcar, or on a ship in mid-ocean. In many situations (e.g., water seepage, shifting of cargo) it would be impossible to determine when the damage occurred; a rule that makes risk pass when the documents are handed over is difficult to apply.[19]

371 **(5) Identification of Goods to the Contract**

Paragraph (2) states that risk does not pass to the buyer "until the goods are clearly identified to the contract." The concluding language "whether by markings on the goods, by shipping documents, by notice given to the buyer or otherwise" shows that a wide range of acts will suffice to provide the necessary identification. The goods are usually identified with a specified buyer even when the carrier issues a negotiable bill of lading made out to the order of the seller; in such a bill of lading the buyer or his bank or other agent is usually identified as the party to be "notified" on arrival of the goods.[20] In any event, the invoice or correspondence will usually link the shipment with the buyer. The identification requirement is designed to prevent a seller from claiming falsely, after goods have suffered casualty, that these were the goods

18. See Günter Hager, Art. 67 para. 8, *in* Schlechtriem & Schwenzer, *CISG Commentary* (2nd English ed. 2005); (U.S.A.) Uniform Commercial Code §2–509(1)(a) (risk passes to the buyer when the goods are delivered to the carrier "even though the shipment is under reservation (Section 2–505)").

19. For the reasons underlying CISG 67(1), see *S-G Rep.* III *YB* 34–35, *Docy. Hist.* 76–77.

20. See Günter Hager, Art. 67 para. 9, *in* Schlechtriem & Schwenzer, *CISG Commentary* (2nd English ed. 2005).

purchased by the buyer. Any identification that would forestall this abuse should be sufficient under paragraph (2).[21]

The question may arise: Is notification to the buyer necessary for "identification?" The range of alternative means for identification listed in the above language of paragraph (2), and the closing phrase "by *notice* given to the buyer or *otherwise*" shows that notice is only one means of identifying goods to the contract. This is fortunate since it may not be practical to notify the buyer of the shipment until after the goods are on their way. A common cause of transit damage is seepage of water into the cargo hold; in many cases it would be difficult to establish whether damage occurred before or after the giving of notice. Even if there is no indication in the shipping documents and no markings on the goods, the place stated for off-delivery and the relationship between the type and quantity of the goods and the contract description will usually leave no doubt of their "identification" to this contract under Article 67(2).[22]

(a) Undivided shares of fungible goods. In discussing the scope of the Convention (Art. 2 at §56.3, *supra*) we saw that the Convention applies to an important type of transaction — contracts for the sale of fungible goods (e.g., grade #2 heating oil) in terms of quantities or shares of the contents of an identified "bulk" — e.g., the tanker North Star sailing June 1; oil tank #17. Can these contracts satisfy the "identification" requirement of Article 67(2)? *Cf.* Article 69(3), §378, *infra*.

When the "bulk" is not identified the answer is No. The first step in solving risk problems requires one to answer the question: Risk in *what*? This question, however, can be answered when the parties agree on a sale to Buyer A of one-half of the No. 2 heating oil loaded on the tanker North Star and the sale of the other half to Party B. (Such a contract would normally state the price per unit (e.g., barrel) and the approximate total

---

21. See UNCITRAL Digest Art. 67 para. 13. Stricter rules for identification in Art. 79 of the Draft Convention were relaxed by an amendment approved at the Diplomatic Conference. *O.R.* 402, *Docy. Hist.* 623. In ULIS 19(3) a somewhat similar rule was drafted in terms of "appropriation" to the contract. This concept was alien to many legal systems and carried "property" overtones; to avoid these problems the concept of "identification" was used in CISG 32(1) and 67(2). See *S-G Rep.*, V *YB* 92, *Docy. Hist.* 171, para. 84.

22. See Günter Hager, Art. 67 paras. 9–10, *in* Schlechtriem & Schwenzer, *CISG Commentary* (2nd English ed. 2005). Art. 32(1) on "notice of the consignment" relates to seller's contractual duties; breach of these duties can lead to a damage claim (Arts. 45(1), 74). However, failure to comply with each contractual duty specified in Arts. 30–44 does not shift the risk of loss. See Art. 70, §§379–383, *infra*.

quantity.) If the contract provides that risk in transit falls equally on Buyer A and Buyer B, nothing in the Convention invalidates the agreement.[23] Because of the complications inherent in such arrangements the requirement of Article 67 that the goods be "clearly identified" indicates that the buyers should not be held to have agreed to loss sharing in an identified bulk unless this result is clearly indicated by the contract.

23. The loss may be allocated in various ways: (1) The quantity the seller must deliver may be defined in terms of "outturn" meaning that the seller would bear the loss at sea; (2) The buyers would pay for the quantity loaded and would share (subject to insurance coverage) the loss during transit. See *generally Benjamin* §§119, 1546–1557, *Atiyah* 25–26, 321–322 (resistance to part ownership).

Article 68.
Sale of Goods During Transit

372   This article addresses a special type of transaction that may be illustrated as follows:

Example 68A. Middleman, in the U.K., owned a cargo of 1,000 bales of No. 1 long-staple cotton that had been shipped from India on June 1 for arrival in the U.K. on July 1. On June 15, Middleman informed Buyer that the cotton was en route and the parties agreed on a contract for the sale of the cotton to Buyer. Inspection of the goods on arrival showed that, during the ocean passage, the cotton had been damaged by seawater. Who bears this risk?

Article 67(1) does not apply since the goods were not handed over to the carrier "for transmission to the buyer."[1] The problem calls for a special provision:

Article 68

The risk in respect of goods sold in transit passes to the buyer from the time of the conclusion of the contract. However, if the circumstances so indicate, the risk is assumed by the buyer from the time the goods were handed over to the carrier who issued the documents embodying the contract of carriage. Nevertheless, if at the time of the conclusion of the contract of sale the seller knew or ought to have known that the goods had been lost or damaged and did not disclose this to the buyer, the loss or damage is at the risk of the seller.

372.1   ## A. Debate and Compromise

The 1978 UNCITRAL draft (draft Art. 80) had no provision like the first sentence of Article 68: under the 1978 draft "the risk is assumed by the buyer *from the time the goods were handed over* to the carrier..." (like the second sentence of Art. 68), followed by a provision on the effect of seller's knowledge (like the third sentence of the present draft).[2]

---

1. See Günter Hager, Art. 67 para. 2, *in* Schlechtriem & Schwenzer, *CISG Commentary* (2nd English ed. 2005); UNCITRAL Digest Art. 67 para. 3.
2. For development of the draft in UNCITRAL see V *YB* 48–49, 60, VIII *YB* 63, *Docy. Hist.* 194–195, 206, 356. See also the Secretariat Commentary on the UNCITRAL draft, *O.R.* 65, *Docy. Hist.* 455.

In the First Committee of the 1980 Conference some delegates objected to the retroactive assumption of risk by the buyer; some stressed that this was unfair to buyers in developing countries and inconsistent with a recommendation by the Asian-African Legal Consultative Committee. Other delegates noted that the UNCITRAL draft was based on commercial practice that had been designed to avoid controversy over the time when transit damage occurred; the First Committee approved an amendment to clarify the draft and approved the provision.[3] However, on review by the Conference Plenary the article did not receive the two-thirds majority that, at this stage, was required for approval, and the Plenary voted to reconsider the article. A group representing divergent views then developed a draft that received the necessary majority. The compromise provision added the first sentence making risk pass "from the time of the conclusion of the contract," and retained the next two sentences (in substance the UNCITRAL draft) for application when "the circumstances so indicate" — a provision that, as we shall see, has special application when the contract of sale calls for the transfer to the buyer of the policy of cargo insurance.[4]

372.2 B. "Circumstances" Invoking the Original Rule

As has been noted, the UNCITRAL draft making risk pass "from the time the goods were *handed over to the carrier*" was designed to avoid controversy over the time when transit loss occurred. This problem is less serious when damage results from an identifiable event — a fire, a storm at sea, a train wreck or a truck collision, but is difficult when damage results from water seepage, overheating or the like.[5]

The parties can avoid this problem by an express agreement that risk passes either at the beginning or the end of the transit (Art. 6). In addition, Article 68 refers to "circumstances" that "indicate" that "the risk is assumed from the time the goods are handed over to the carrier."

3. *O.R.* 403–406, *Docy. Hist.* 624–627. The First Committee deleted a confusing reference to documents controlling the goods. *O.R.* 404, *Docy. Hist.* 625.

4. Initial action by the Conference Plenary *O.R.* 21–215, *Docy. Hist.* 748–750. Final action by the Plenary: *O.R.* 215–218, 22–222, *Docy. Hist.* 750–753, 755–756 (the vote — 26–12 with 9 abstentions). Similar to CISG 68: *Finnish Sales Act (1987)* Sec. 15.

5. See Günter Hager, Art. 67 para. 2, *in* Schlechtriem & Schwenzer, *CISG Commentary* (2nd English ed. 2005); UNCITRAL Digest Art. 68 para. 3. For case law on this problem, see *Benjamin* §1696–1697 (risk *as from* shipment). See also 22 Colum. J. Transn. L. 575, 589.

Suppose that in Example 68A the parties consummated the sale by transferring to the buyer the standard package of documents covering the shipment, including a policy of insurance payable (e.g.) "to the order of the Assured," and endorsed by Middleman (the assured) to Buyer. The endorsement would make Buyer the only person who could claim under the policy and would clearly evidence an intent to transfer to Buyer the total risk of the voyage. This conclusion is aided by the fact that Article 68 refers to "circumstances" that "indicate" that the buyer assumed the risk; express agreement is not required. It would be difficult to find clearer indicative circumstances than taking over the seller's policy of insurance.[6]

Of course, the opportunity to press a claim under an insurance policy is not the equivalent of the receipt of sound goods. If the seller knew (or ought to have known) that the goods had been damaged he should have communicated this fact to the Buyer so the Buyer could decide whether to buy into such a situation. Under the last sentence of Article 68 if the seller fails to disclose the loss or damage "the loss or damage is at the risk of the seller."

Does this mean that the seller bears only the loss or damage it failed to disclose? This reading probably would have been required under UNCITRAL draft, which referred to "*such* loss or damage";[7] at the Conference this phrase was cha51ged to "*the* loss or damage" which leaves the meaning open to interpretation. Nicholas, on the basis of a careful review of suggestive but inconclusive legislative history, concludes that when the seller fails to disclose loss or damage that had occurred before the making of the contract the seller would be liable not only for the loss or damage that the seller knew or should have known but also for all the damage that had occurred when the contract was made and for all subsequent damage "which is causally connected with the original damage." Nicholas noted that this interpretation "has the advantage

---

6. For further discussion of circumstances indicating that risk for goods sold in transit should pass to the buyer from the time the goods were handed over to the carrier see Günter Hager, Art. 68 para. 4, *in* Schlechtriem & Schwenzer, *CISG Commentary* (2nd English ed. 2005); von Hoffman, *Dubrovnik Lectures* 294. At the time this is written there appear to be no CISG decisions addressing when the second sentence of Art. 68 should apply. See UNCITRAL Digest Art. 68 and the decisions cited at "UNCITRAL Digest cases plus added cases - Art. 68" on the CISG website maintained by the Pace University Institute for International Commercial Law at http://www.cisg.law.pace.edu/cisg/text/digest-cases-68.html.

7. See Roth, The Passing of Risk, *AJCL Symposium* 291, 298, commenting on the awkward consequences of splitting transit loss between the parties.

of avoiding a splitting of the transit risks, with the attendant difficulties of proof . . ."[8]

The present writer warmly supports this approach in so far as it supports holding transit loss on the seller[9] but is doubtful about the basis and advisability of a "causally connected" limitation. As has been suggested, under the final version of Article 68 the provision concerning the effect of seller's knowledge relates only to the second sentence in which retroactive passing of risk depends on "circumstances" indicating that result—usually the transfer to the buyer of the shipping documents, including a policy of cargo insurance.[10] Under these circumstances dividing the loss involves complications in sharing responsibility for salvage and in sharing claims under one policy of insurance. When a seller knows of the loss and does not disclose this to the buyer the seller's conduct constitutes (or closely approximates) fraud; non-disclosure when the seller "ought to have known" of the loss is a serious breach of the seller obligations. Conduct of this character should not inflict on the buyer the complications of loss sharing.

Under the Convention's system of remedies the seller, at the very least, has committed a serious breach which, apart from the rules on risk, should empower the buyer (Arts. 25, 49(1)(a)) to avoid the contract—i.e., return of the goods (or bill of lading) and insurance policy to the seller in exchange for any part of the price the buyer has paid. See Article 70 §§379–382, *infra*, preserving the buyer's remedies for fundamental breach. (In practice this strong remedy could assist the buyer in negotiating an appropriate settlement with the seller.)

---

8. Nicholas, *B-B Commentary* §2.3, pp. 499–500, citing (*O.R.* 220–221, *Docy. Hist.* 755–756) the rejection in Plenary of a proposal to change "*the* loss or damage" to "*that* loss or damage, to conform to the UNCITRAL language "*such* loss or damage." The reason for the rejection was unclear; one point was that the change to "the loss," presumably made by the Drafting Committee, had changed the meaning of the UNCITRAL text; on the other hand, the French version was the equivalent of "*the* loss or damage."

9. Compare and contrast Günter Hager, Art. 68 para. 5, *in* Schlechtriem & Schwenzer, *CISG Commentary* (2nd English ed. 2005).

10. As Nicholas, *id.*, §2.4, p. 500 demonstrates, the third sentence on the seller's failure of disclosure relates only to the second sentence on retroactive passing of risk. As we have seen, these two sentences were linked together in preparing the UNCITRAL draft. Moreover, as Nicholas points out, damage prior to shipment presents a problem of conformity of the goods (Arts. 35, 36(1), 66) rather than risk of loss.

372.3   Discrepancies in the Text of the Russian Version of Article 68

It appears that the version of Article 68 in one of the six official U.N.-language texts of the CISG — the Russian version — reflects the language of the 1978 UNCITRAL draft of the Convention rather than the final version approved at the 1980 Vienna diplomatic conference[11]*: in other words, the Russian version omits the first sentence of Article 68, which states the general rule (subject to the exception in the second sentence) that risk with respect to goods sold in transit passes from the time of the conclusion of the contract. Under the Russian version, risk for goods sold in transit generally passes as provided in the second sentence of Article 68 — retroactively at the time the goods were handed over to the carrier.*

This, obviously, creates problems: the Witness Clause at the end of the official text of the Convention — as ratified by all Contracting States — states that the official text of the Convention constitutes "a single original, of which the Arabic, Chinese, English, French Russian and Spanish texts are equally authentic." The issue of discrepancies among the various official language versions of the Convention is not, of course, confined to Article 68,[12] *but the discrepancy in the Russian version with respect to this article is likely one of the more dramatic.*

It has been suggested that discrepancies among the official texts should be resolved pursuant to Article 33(4) of the Vienna Convention on the Law of Treaties, including consultation of the Convention's travaux préparatoires, but that the English and "occasionally" the French texts should be "given precedence, because drafting was carried out almost exclusively in those languages."[13] *Under this approach, the discrepancy in the Russian text could presumably be set aside and the text of Article 68 as reflected in the other language*

---

11. See Albert H. Kritzer, "Editorial Remarks" to the decision of the Federal Arbitration Court for the Northwestern Circuit, Russian Federation, 3 June 2003, available at http://cisgw3.law.pace.edu/cases/030603r1.html.

12. See Harry M. Flechtner, The Several Texts of the CISG in a Decentralized System: Observations on Translations, Reservations and Other Challenges to the Uniformity Principle in Art. 7(1), 17 J. L. & Com. 187, 189–193 (1998).

13. Peter Schlechtriem, *Witness Clause* para. 4, *in* Schlechtriem & Schwenzer, *CISG Commentary* (2nd English ed. 2005).

versions followed; indeed, UNCITRAL may be in the process of "correcting" the Russian version of Article 68.[14]

Given the relatively minor importance of Article 68, and the fact that the error in the Russian text appears clear-cut, the discrepancy in this case may not cause much difficulty. But it is also possible that Contracting States whose decision to ratify the Convention was based primarily on the Russian text may be unpleasantly surprised to discover that they are bound to a notably different treaty text, particular when the version they relied upon is an official and "equally authentic" version.[15]

Of course such discrepancies must be resolved if the Convention is to fulfill its fundamental purpose, declared in its Preamble, of providing "uniform rules which govern contracts for the international sale of goods" (emphasis added). A Contracting State dissatisfied with the result of resolving discrepancies among the different language versions of the Convention can always withdraw from the Convention — although that would be an extreme and highly counterproductive outcome that, it is devoutly to be hoped, will never occur, and certainly should not result from the problems with the text of Article 68.

14. Albert H. Kritzer, "Editorial Remarks" to the decision of the Federal Arbitration Court for the Northwestern Circuit, Russian Federation, 3 June 2003, available at http://cisgw3. law.pace.edu/cases/030603r1.html.

15. See Harry M. Flechtner, The Several Texts of the CISG in a Decentralized System: Observations on Translations, Reservations and Other Challenges to the Uniformity Principle in Art. 7(1), 17 J. L. & Com. 187, 207–208 (1998).

Article 69.
General Residual Rules on Risk

373　　This article governs "cases not within Articles 67 and 68." In view of this approach to defining the scope of Article 69 we need to recall that Article 67 governs contracts in which the seller hands the goods over to a "carrier" for transmission to the buyer and that Article 68 governs contracts in which goods are sold while in the possession of a "carrier." Article 69 applies to contracts not covered by the foregoing provisions.

Article 69[1]

(1) In cases not within articles 67 and 68, the risk passes to the buyer when he takes over the goods or, if he does not do so in due time, from the time when the goods are placed at his disposal and he commits a breach of contract by failing to take delivery.

(2) However, if the buyer is bound to take over the goods at a place other than a place of business of the seller, the risk passes when delivery is due and the buyer is aware of the fact that the goods are placed at his disposal at that place.

(3) If the contract relates to goods not then identified, the goods are considered not to be placed at the disposal of the buyer until they are clearly identified to the contract.

Paragraph (1) of Article 69 applies when the contract calls for the buyer to come for the goods at the seller's place of business, often called a sale "ex works."[2] (This scope for paragraph (1) results from the fact that paragraph (2) carves out an exception from paragraph (1) for cases where "the buyer is bound to take over the goals at a place *other than* a place of business of the seller.")

Paragraph (2) of Article 69 governs all other transactions *not* within Articles 67, 68 or paragraph (1) of Article 69 — in other words Article 69(2) applies when the contract does *not* call for the seller to hand the

---

1. Article 69 is the same as Art. 81 of the 1978 Draft. As to Art. 69(1) see ULIS 19(1), 97(1) and 98(1); as to Art. 69(3), see ULIS 98(2).

2. *Accord*, Günter Hager, Art. 69 para. 2, *in* Schlechtriem & Schwenzer, *CISG Commentary* (2nd English ed. 2005); *but see* Oberlandesgericht Köln, Germany, 9 July 1997, CLOUT case No. 283, English translation available at http://cisgw3.law.pace.edu/cases/970709g3. html (indicating that the term "list price ex works" was, on the particular facts of the case, consistent with application of Art. 67(1) rather than Art. 69(1)).

goods over to a "carrier" for transmission to the buyer (Art. 67), the goods were not sold while they were already in transit by carrier (Art. 68), and the buyer is *not* to take over the goods at the seller's place of business (Art. 69(1)). Happily, at long last we can now speak affirmatively of types of transactions that *do* fall, by default, into paragraph (2) of Article 69: (1) Contracts that call for the seller to deliver the goods to the buyer in (e.g.) the seller's own transport vehicles, or by carriage for which the seller is responsible, e.g., delivery to the buyer "DAF (Delivery at Frontier) as per Incoterms (2000)." (2) Contracts that call for the buyer to take over the goods "at a place other than a place of business of the seller" — e.g., goods in storage at a public warehouse.[3]

374 ## A. Taking Over Goods at Seller's Place of Business (Art. 69(1))

As we have just seen, by a tortuous process of exclusion paragraph (1) applies only when the buyer is bound to take over the goods at seller's place of business. The scope and effect of paragraph (1) can be shown by two examples:

Example 69A. A contract called for Seller to produce and pack goods and hold them at his place of business for Buyer by May 1; the contract stated that Buyer would take the goods away, by his own transport, at any time during the month of May. On May 1, Seller had the goods packed and ready for delivery. On May 10 the goods were destroyed by a fire in Seller's warehouse.

Since the contract permitted the buyer to take the goods at any time during May, Buyer had not committed a "breach of contract by failing to take delivery." In such cases, under paragraph (1) risk passes to the buyer "when he takes over the goods." In Example 69A, Seller was still in possession of the goods at the time of the fire and bears the risk of loss.

Example 69B. The facts are the same as in Example 69A except that Buyer failed to take the goods during May, and the fire destroyed the goods on June 2.

---

3. See Günter Hager, Art. 69 para. 6, *in* Schlechtriem & Schwenzer, *CISG Commentary* (2nd English ed. 2005); UNCITRAL Digest Art. 69 para. 6; Court of Arbitration of the ICC International Chamber of Commerce, Case No. 7197, 1992, CLOUT case No. 104, English abstract available in Unilex database at http://www.unilex.info/case.cfm?pid=1& do=case&id=37&step=Abstract.

Here Buyer bears the risk since his breach of contract in failing to take the goods during May left the goods with Seller at the time of the fire.[4] There is no indication that Seller notified Buyer that the goods were ready for delivery. In this case a notice should not be necessary since the contract provided that Seller would have the goods ready by May 1 and Seller did so. Buyer had no reason to suppose that Seller had not complied with the contract.

Assume that the contract merely stated, "Buyer will remove the goods within thirty days after they are ready for delivery." On these facts the goods would not be at Buyer's "disposal" until Seller notifies Buyer that the goods are ready; otherwise Buyer would need to make daily inquiries to discover where things stood. (The discussion of gap-filling under Art. 7(2) suggested (§100 *supra*) that one of the Convention's "general principles" was a duty to communicate information needed by the other party. Compare Article 69(2), providing that risk passes when the buyer is aware of the fact that the goods are placed at his disposal.

375   (1) Policies Affecting Risk; Insurance

Policies relevant to the allocation of risk were mentioned in the introduction to this chapter, *supra* at §358. The Convention responds to the view that the risk of casualty (in the absence of breach of contract or an applicable agreement) should be allocated to the party who is in the better position to care for the goods and to cover the risk by insurance.[5] In Example 69A, the seller, pursuant to the agreement, had possession and control of the goods. If the seller asks the buyer to pay for goods that burned while they were held by the seller, the buyer is likely to claim that the loss was a result of the seller's failure to exercise due care; settling or litigating such claims involve expense and uncertainty for both parties.[6] Moreover, cost-efficient insurance rating calls for information as to the conditions of storage — e.g., whether the building is made of metal or wood and whether it is equipped with an automatic sprinkler. Consequently, it is customary to carry insurance for "building and contents"; the policy usually covers goods that await delivery following a contract

---

4. See Günter Hager, Art. 69 paras. 4–5, *in* Schlechtriem & Schwenzer, *CISG Commentary* (2nd English ed. 2005).

5. See Günter Hager, Art. 69 para. 1, *in* Schlechtriem & Schwenzer, *CISG Commentary* (2nd English ed. 2005).

6. See Günter Hager, Art. 69 para. 1, *in* Schlechtriem & Schwenzer, *CISG Commentary* (2nd English ed. 2005).

of sale since the seller cannot be sure he will be paid, particularly if the goods are destroyed.[7]

376 (2) Domestic Law

These policies on the allocation of risk are reflected in the (U.S.A.) Uniform Commercial Code. In non-shipment cases like Example 69A, when the seller is a merchant (as in that Example) risk passes to the buyer "on his receipt of the goods" (UCC 2–509(3)); the result is the same as that of the Convention. When the buyer is in breach, as in Example 69B, the UCC gives weight to both the breach and to the availability of insurance: "the seller may to the extent of the deficiency in his effective insurance coverage treat the risk of loss as resting on the buyer for a commercially reasonable period" (UCC 2–510(3)).

The Convention's approach to the problem of risk is more direct and clear-cut than those domestic rules that, unless modified by case law on international trade, invoke concepts such as "property" and "appropriation."[8]

377 B. Taking Over Other Than at Seller's Place of Business (Art. 69(2))

Paragraph (2) states a separate rule on risk when "the buyer is bound to take over the goods at a place *other than* a place of business of the seller." No such provision appeared in ULIS; the Commission's discussion of this provision was directed particularly to the sale of goods held at a public warehouse and reflected the possibility that the buyer might leave the goods in the warehouse for a substantial period after the goods were made available.[9]

Under paragraph (1) risk passes to the buyer when he "takes over the goods." Under paragraph (2) risk passes at an earlier point — "when delivery is due and the buyer is aware of the fact that the goods are placed at his disposal" at the designated place.

---

7. See *Rep. S-G*, V *YB* 90–93, *Docy. Hist.* 169–172; Roth, *AJCL UNCITRAL Symposium* 291, 299–300; Honnold, A Uniform Law for International Sales, 107 U. Pa. L. Rev. 319 (1959); *Honnold, Sales* 167–169 (includes extracts from standard policies of insurance).

8. See Atiyah 246–251; Benjamin §394 et seq.; Ont. L. Ref. Com., I Sales 265–269.

9. *UNCITRAL X*, Annex I, paras. 550–552, VIII *YB* 64, *Docy. Hist.* 357. See Günter Hager, Art. 69 para. 1, *in* Schlechtriem & Schwenzer, *CISG Commentary* (2nd English ed. 2005).

Example 69C. A sales contract involved goods known by both parties to be held in a warehouse operated by a third person. When Seller deposited the goods in the warehouse Seller received a warehouse receipt stating that the goods would be released to Seller or to any person who held a delivery order executed by Seller. On May 1, at the time of the contract, Seller gave Buyer a delivery order directing the warehouseman to deliver the goods to Buyer.[10] *On May 2 a fire in the warehouse destroyed the goods.*

Under Article 69(2), risk passed to Buyer on May 1, since delivery was then due and the buyer knew that the goods were at his disposal.[11]

Paragraph (2) also applies when the seller, or a carrier *that is fulfilling the seller's delivery obligations (e.g., under a "D" (delivered) price-delivery term as defined in Incoterms)*,[12] makes the goods available to the buyer at the end of transit or at the buyer's place of business. For example, in a quotation *"Ex Ship* Buyer's port," risk passes when the goods are placed at the buyer's disposal, even though the "free time" for taking over the goods has not expired. Under paragraph (2), unlike paragraph (1), the goods are not at the seller's place of business and the practical considerations involving insurance practices, mentioned above, do not apply fully; there is no reason for risk to remain on the seller.[13] This result is consistent with commercial practice embodied in *Incoterms* (2000): Under a sale "Delivered Ex Ship" risk passes to the buyer when the goods are placed "at the disposal of the buyer" (A4, A5, B5). Similarly, under (U.S.A.) Uniform Commercial Code 2–509(1)(b), when the contract requires the seller "to deliver [the goods] at a particular destination" risk passes "when the goods are there duly *so tendered as to enable the buyer to take delivery.*"

10. In the alternative, we may assume that Seller delivered to Buyer a negotiable ("order") warehouse receipt the possession of which controlled delivery of the goods. If the warehouse receipt is not negotiable or does not contain a statement like that mentioned in Example 69C, the question whether the goods have been placed at the buyer's "disposal" (Art. 69(2)) may depend on (1) domestic law governing the warehouse's obligation to deliver to a subpurchaser or (2) an understanding between the seller and buyer that the seller would authorize delivery on buyer's request.

11. See Günter Hager, Art. 69 para. 7, *in* Schlechtriem & Schwenzer, *CISG Commentary* (2nd English ed. 2005).

12. See Court of Arbitration of the ICC International Chamber of Commerce, Case No. 7197, 1992, CLOUT case No. 104, English abstract available in Unilex database at http://www.unilex.info/case.cfm?pid=1&do=case&id=37&step=Abstract.

13. See Günter Hager, Art. 69 para. 6, *in* Schlechtriem & Schwenzer, *CISG Commentary* (2nd English ed. 2005).

378 **(1) Identification**

Paragraph (3) requires that goods be "clearly identified to the contract" before risk can pass to the buyer. A similar provision in Article 67(3) was discussed at §371. The question of "identification" in sales of shares of an identified bulk (e.g., grain in a specified warehouse, oil in an identified tank) was discussed in connection with Article 67(2) at §371, *supra*.[14] See also §56.3, *supra* (applicability of the Convention to such sales).

---

14. See Günter Hager, Art. 69 para. 8, *in* Schlechtriem & Schwenzer, *CISG Commentary* (2nd English ed. 2005).

Article 70.
Risk When Seller is in Breach

379   In Article 69(1) we saw that when the *buyer* "commits a breach of contract by failing to take delivery" this breach may transfer risk to the buyer. Article 70 addresses the question whether a breach of contract by the *seller* (e.g., by dispatching non-conforming goods) will prevent the risk from passing to the buyer.

Article 70[1]

If the seller has committed a fundamental breach of contract, Articles 67, 68 and 69 do not impair the remedies available to the buyer on account of the breach.

380   ## A. Effect of Non-Conformity of Goods on Risk in Transit

Article 70 applies only when "the seller has committed a fundamental breach of contract" *(although it has also been argued — sensibly — that it applies if a seller fails to deliver goods within a reasonable additional time fixed by the buyer as provided in Art. 47).*[2] To see the significance of this provision we need to consider the effect of breach that is not "fundamental."

Example 70A. Seller and Buyer made a contract calling for Seller to ship to Buyer 1,000 bags of No. 1 quality soybeans. The contract did not require Seller to bear the risk during transit. (Hence, under the general rule of Art. 67(1), supra at §363, risk would pass to Buyer "when the goods are handed over to the first carrier for transmission to the buyer.") Seller shipped 1,000 bags of soybeans; 999 bags conformed to the contract but one bag was graded "No. 2" rather than "No. 1." (Let us assume that this non-conformity was not a "fundamental breach" under Article 25. On this assumption, Buyer could not avoid the contract under Article 49(1)(a)). However, during the shipment to Buyer, 500 bags of beans were ruined by seawater. May Buyer claim damages (or reduce the price) because of the failure of the 500 bags to

---

1. Article 70 is substantially the same as Article 82 of the 1978 Draft. *Cf.* ULIS 7(2).

2. See Günter Hager, Art. 70 para. 3, *in* Schlechtriem & Schwenzer, *CISG Commentary* (2nd English ed. 2005).

grade No. 1 at arrival? May Buyer reject the shipment ("avoid the contract") on the ground that the 500 worthless bags constituted a "fundamental breach?"

In this case Article 70 is inapplicable because (by hypothesis) the breach with respect to the one bag was not "fundamental." It follows that the general rule on risk in transit (Art. 67(1), *supra* at §363) governs the case, and transit risk passed to Buyer. Under Article 36(1), *supra* at §241, the seller is only responsible for a "lack of conformity which exists at the time when risk passes to the buyer." Consequently, Seller is not responsible for the poor quality of the 500 bags that resulted from the casualty in transit.[3] Of course, Seller is responsible in damages for the bag that graded No. 2 rather than No. 1, and Buyer may reduce the price pursuant to Article 50; since (by hypothesis) this deviation was not a "fundamental breach," however, Buyer may not avoid the contract (i.e., reject the shipment).

381 ## (1) Fundamental Breach and Risk in Transit

Example 70B. This case is like Example 70A except that the beans shipped by Seller were seriously defective: 600 bags were worthless for any purpose other than cattle feed. (We may assume that this constituted a "fundamental breach" of the contract as a whole.) Of the 400 bags that conformed to the contract on shipment, 150 were seriously damaged in transit by seawater. May Buyer claim damages (or reduce the price) based on the failure of this part of the shipment to grade No. 1? May Buyer reject all the goods ("avoid the contract") because of the fundamental breach at the time of delivery to the carrier? Or would the Buyer be barred from "avoidance" on the ground that, under the contract, loss in transit was his responsibility, and he cannot return the goods in substantially the same condition as when they were shipped? (Cf. Art. 82(2)(a), infra at §445.)

Again we start with the basic rule of Article 67(1) that, apart from breach, risk of loss would pass to the Buyer when the goods were handed over to the carrier. But here the serious non-conformity of the 600 bags constituted a "fundamental breach" of the contract as a whole; Buyer may avoid the contract under Article. 49(1)(a).

Do other provisions create barriers to avoidance? We may assume that the buyer notified the seller of avoidance promptly after the arrival of the

---

3. See Günter Hager, Art. 70 para. 5a, *in* Schlechtriem & Schwenzer, *CISG Commentary* (2nd English ed. 2005).

goods and thereby complied with Article 49(2)(b). As we shall see, Article 82, *infra* at §445, establishes an additional barrier to avoidance: Under paragraph (1) A Buyer loses his "right to declare the contract avoided . . . if it is impossible for him to make restitution of the goods substantially in the condition *in which he received them.*" However, Buyer had not "received" the goods when they were damaged during transit. *Cf.* Articles. 21 & 60(b). In any event, the requirement of Article 82(1) that the goods be returned in the same condition as when received is subject to an exception in paragraph (2)(a) when the change in the condition of the goods was "*not* due to [the buyer's] act or omission." In our case, the change in condition of the goods was not due to an "act or omission" of the buyer but resulted from a transit casualty.[4]

In short, when a serious breach of contract by the seller gives the buyer the right to reject goods ("avoid the contract"), this right is not lost because of damage to the goods during transit.[5] *Successful avoidance relieves the buyer of its obligation to pay the price for the damaged goods (Article 81(1), §440.1 infra) and entitles the buyer to recover of payments already made (Article 81(2)). Thus as a result of the buyer's avoidance, the breaching seller ends up with the damaged goods without a right to collect the price: in effect, the seller has the risk for the damage.[6] (For discussion of responsibility for damage to goods that occurs after a buyer's rejection of the goods, see §§448.1A infra.)*

This same result protecting the buyer's right to reject is embodied in the (U.S.A.) Uniform Commercial Code:

> *Section 2–510. Effect of Breach on Risk of Loss*
> (1) Where a tender or delivery of goods *so fails to conform to the contract as to give a right of rejection* the risk of their loss remains on the seller until cure or acceptance. . . .

Under this language, a trivial breach that does not give a right of rejection ("avoidance") — as in Example 70A — does not overturn the risk provisions of the contract or the general statutory rules on risk. But when — as in Example 70B — the breach is so serious "as to give a right of rejection" ("avoidance") the defective delivery to the carrier

---

4. See Günter Hager, Art. 70 para. 2, *in* Schlechtriem & Schwenzer, *CISG Commentary* (2nd English ed. 2005).

5. See *Rep. S-G,* "Issues Presented by Chapters IV to VI of ULIS," paras. 89–105. V *YB* 93–94, *Docy. Hist.* 172–173. Huber, 43 *Rabels Z* 413, 457 (1979).

6. See Günter Hager, Art. 69 para. 2, 4 & 6, *in* Schlechtriem & Schwenzer, *CISG Commentary* (2nd English ed. 2005).

is not effective to transfer transit risks to the buyer, and his right to reject because of the breach is preserved.[7]

(a) Partial avoidance. In Example 70B Buyer, if it chooses, need not avoid (reject) with respect to the entire shipment. Article 51(1), §304 *supra*, provides that if "only a part of the goods" conforms to the contract "Articles 46 to 50 apply in respect of the part . . . which does not conform." Consequently, Buyer may effect a partial avoidance limited to the 600 bags that were seriously defective when they were shipped, and keep the 250 bags that arrived in good condition as well as the 150 bags that were seriously damaged during transit.

One might argue that although the language of Article 51 seems to limit partial avoidance to the goods that were defective when shipped (see also Arts. 36(1) and 66), its overall purpose is to give an option to an aggrieved party to limit avoidance of the contract: When a buyer has the power to avoid the contract as a whole the theory that "the whole includes its parts" suggests that the buyer, instead of exercising its right to avoid as to the entire shipment of 1,000 bags, can elect to avoid as to the 750 bags damaged during transit and keep only the 250 that arrived in good condition. The seller is not in a worse position than if the buyer had avoided as to the 1,000 bags; indeed, both parties probably are in a better position since the buyer can use the 250 good bags and the seller will be paid for them, so that the seller's burden of redisposition, to this extent, will be lightened. It is difficult to predict a tribunal's reaction to laying such a heavy hand on the language of Article 51; counsel for the buyer might be well advised to inform the seller of the buyer's right to avoid the contract as a whole and suggest that it would be to the advantage of both parties to agree on a less drastic course.

382 **(b) Damages Based on Transit Casualty.** We return to Example 70B — the shipment of seriously defective soybeans that were subject to damage in transit. Of the 1,000 bags, 600 were defective when the seller delivered the goods to the carrier. Of the remaining 400 bags, 150 were damaged in transit and 250 arrived in good condition. Let us assume that the buyer needed the soybeans and accepted the shipment, but immediately notified the seller of the poor condition of the goods (Art. 39). May the buyer recover damages not only for the 600

---

7. For the background of this provision see the writer's analysis and proposal in I Report of the New York Law Revision Commission: Study of the Uniform Commercial Code 494–495 (1955).

bags that were defective at the time of shipment but also for the poor condition of the 150 bags that resulted from damage in transit? (For the sake of completeness we here face a problem that will seldom arise. When the goods are subject to two serious difficulties — non-conformity at shipment that is "fundamental" plus damage in transit — the buyer would often exercise its right to avoid the contract.)

A buyer who accepts the goods probably may recover damages from the seller only for the non-conformity at the time of shipment; for the damage in transit the buyer must look to the carrier or the insurer. Article 70 merely provides that the seller's fundamental breach does not *"impair the remedies* available to the buyer on account of the breach." This language (unlike U.C.C. 2–510(1), quoted *supra*) does not directly modify the Convention's rules on passage of risk. Risk in this case passed to the buyer (Art. 67(1)) "when the goods were handed over to the first carrier"; Article 70 says merely that when the seller has committed a fundamental breach, the articles on risk of loss (Arts. 67, 68 and 69) do "not impair the remedies available to the buyer on account of the breach." Prior to the transit damage the buyer had the right to avoid the contract. Article 70 preserves the buyer's right of *avoidance* with relief from the obligation to pay the price — a remedy that the buyer, surprisingly, did not invoke. When a buyer chooses to accept a shipment that is doubly defective (seriously defective at shipment and damaged further during transit) it is difficult to conclude that Article 70 enlarges the buyer's *damage* claim to include the damage that resulted after risk passed to the buyer.[8]

The result that flows from a literal reading of Article 70 may be unfortunate in encouraging the buyer to reject ("avoid") rather than to salvage the shipment and claim damages. However, as we noted above, the buyer will rarely choose to take responsibility for the goods when they are so seriously defective. If the buyer does choose to accept the goods, his responsibility for transit casualty may be justified since a buyer in possession of the goods at the end of an international shipment is usually in a better position than the seller to claim for transit damage against the carrier and insurer.[9]

8. *Accord*, Günter Hager, Art. 70 para. 2, *in* Schlechtriem & Schwenzer, *CISG Commentary* (2nd English ed. 2005).

9. At the Diplomatic Conference the author proposed an amendment under which risk in transit would remain with the seller when the goods are so defective as to constitute a fundamental breach. The proposal was rejected; it is not clear whether this action was based on the substance of the proposal or on problems of implementation or drafting. *O.R.* 408, 128 (text of proposal), *Docy. Hist.* 629, 700. See §91 *supra*.

382.1   **(c) Requiring Delivery of Substitute Goods.**   When the seller
commits a fundamental breach Article 70 preserves not only the buyer's
right to avoid but also the right (Art. 46(2)) to require the delivery of
substitute goods.

*Example 70C. Seller contracted to ship 100 machines to Buyer. As in
the preceding examples, under Article 67(1) risk passed to the buyer
when the seller handed over the goods to the carrier. On arrival of the
goods, inspection showed that in all the machines a vital component
"X" was defective at shipment. (Let us assume that this defect was a
fundamental breach.) In addition, seawater had seriously damaged
another component — component "Y" — in 30 of the machines. Only
Seller made this type of machine and Buyer wanted to receive the
machines despite the delay that would result from a second shipment.
May Buyer require Seller to "deliver substitute goods" pursuant to
Article 46(2) for all 100 of the machines in spite of the transit damage
to 30 that occurred after risk passed to Buyer?*

The answer is Yes.[10] As we saw from Example 70B, Article 70 provides that "when the seller has committed a fundamental breach of
contract" the Convention's rules on risk (Arts. 67, 68, and 69) "do
not impair *the remedies* available to the buyer on account of the breach."
Avoidance calls for return of the goods to the seller which, in effect,
transfers the loss from transit damage back to the seller. The same is true
when a buyer exercises its right under Article 46(2) in the event of
fundamental breach to "require delivery of substitute goods." See
Article 46 at §283, *supra*, and Article 82(1) §446, *infra* (both avoidance
and requiring substitute goods calls for return of the defective goods).

The above example gives us an opportunity to bring into focus a wider
range of principles dealing with risk of loss and remedies. If component
"X" constituted only part of the machine and was readily replaceable,
the defect in this component might not constitute a "fundamental
breach" (Arts. 25 & 49(1)(a)); in that case, Buyer could not make transit
risk fall on Seller by avoidance (Art. 70). In this situation, in normal
commercial practice Seller would offer to replace component "X."
(Sellers may have this right under the "cure" provisions of Articles
37 and 48; if, contrary to normal practice, Seller does not offer to repair
Buyer probably could require this repair under Article 46(3).) If the
defect in component "X" was not a "fundamental breach, Buyer
would bear the cost of repairing the transit damage to component

---

10. *Accord*, Günter Hager, Art. 70 para. 2, *in* Schlechtriem & Schwenzer, *CISG Commentary*
(2nd English ed. 2005).

"Y." However, Seller might well agree to bear this cost as part of a settlement of Buyer's claim based on the defect in component "X." (Seller might feel that a generous settlement, following a defective shipment, would help to maintain, or restore, good commercial relations with Buyer.)

383　## B. Casualty to Non-Conforming Goods After Receipt by Buyer

Example 70D. On June 1 Seller handed over goods to Buyer. Buyer's inspection on June 2 disclosed that the goods were not in conformity with the contract. On June 3 a fire in Buyer's warehouse damaged the goods. Buyer did not declare the contract avoided but claimed damages from Seller for the non-conformity at the time of delivery and also for the damage resulting from the fire.

Buyer, of course, may recover damages for the non-conformity at the time of delivery, but he has no claim for the damage to the goods resulting from the fire. Under Article 69, risk passed to Buyer when he "took over" the goods. Where the buyer does not declare the contract avoided, the risk of loss passes to him when he takes over the goods regardless of the seriousness of the non-conformity.

Example 70E. The facts are the same as in Example 70D, except that the non-conformity was so substantial as to constitute a "fundamental breach" and on June 4 Buyer declared the contract avoided.

The result here is like that in Example 70C, above, and Buyer may avoid the contract even though the goods returned to the seller will be subject to two types of defect: (i) the initial serious non-conformity; and (ii) the damage caused by the fire. Article 70 provides that if the seller commits a fundamental breach of contract, Articles 67, 68 and 69 [on transfer of risk] *"do not impair* the remedies available to the buyer on account of the breach." One of these remedies, when the goods are seriously defective, is avoidance of the contract (Arts. 25 and 49(1)(a)). This result is consistent with Article 82(2)(a), discussed *supra*, at §381. See the further discussion of Art. 82, *infra* at §445.

Problems of policy are presented if the seller must bear the risk of loss while the buyer holds goods in his possession for extended periods of time.[11] But under Article 49(2), "where the seller has delivered the

---

11. See the discussion under Art. 69, *supra* at §375, on policy reasons for placing casualty risk on the possessor. Of course, if the non-conformity of the goods caused the loss (*e.g.*

goods, the buyer loses the right to declare the contract avoided unless he does so: ... (b) ... within a reasonable time: (i) after he knew or ought to have known of the breach."[12] Because of practical problems that result from divorcing risk from possession, the "reasonable" period should not be long.[13]

For discussion of responsibility for damage to goods that occurs after a buyer has avoided the contract or otherwise rejected the goods, see §§448.1A infra.

---

defective wiring in a machine caused a fire that damaged the machine) this loss must be borne by the seller. (See Art. 74, *infra* at §403.)

12. *Accord*, Günter Hager, Art. 70 paras. 6 & 8, *in* Schlechtriem & Schwenzer, *CISG Commentary* (2nd English ed. 2005). Avoidance is not barred by Art. 82 for reasons developed in connection with Example 70C, *supra* at §381.

13. For criticism of the 1978 Draft with respect to risk of loss during cure and periods allowed for inspection, see Roth, The Passing of Risk, *AJCL UNCITRAL Symposium* 291, 303.

CHAPTER V.

PROVISIONS COMMON TO THE OBLIGATIONS OF THE SELLER AND OF THE BUYER
(Articles 71–88)

INTRODUCTION TO CHAPTER V

384 Remedies specially applicable to breach of contract by the seller were provided in Chapter II (Arts. 45–52) and corresponding remedies for breach by the buyer were set forth in Chapter III (Arts. 61–65). The present chapter addresses remedial problems that may be faced by either party.

Section I, Anticipatory Breach and Installment Contracts (Arts. 71–73), is concerned primarily with protection against impending breach. A party who faces this problem may, in some circumstances, suspend performance (Art. 71) or avoid the contract (Art. 72). Article 73, in large part, deals with similar problems that arise in contracts for the delivery of goods by installments.

Section II (Arts. 74–77) provides rules for measuring damages. Section III consists of a brief provision (Art. 78) concerning interest on sums in arrears. Section IV, Exemptions (Arts. 79–80), confronts the difficult question of excuse from liability when performance is prevented by an impediment (e.g., *force majeure*). Section V, Effects of Avoidance (Arts. 81–84), includes provisions on the restitution of benefits received under a contract that has been avoided. Section VI, Preservation of the Goods (Arts. 85–88), is designed to prevent the waste or deterioration of goods that have been rejected.

SECTION I.

ANTICIPATORY BREACH AND INSTALMENT CONTRACTS
(Articles 71–73)

Article 71.
Suspension of Performance

385 **A. Introduction**

This article and the next address problems like these: (1) A seller has agreed to deliver goods on credit but, prior to the time for delivery, the buyer becomes insolvent or otherwise has manifested an inability to pay for the goods. (2) A buyer has agreed to pay before receiving the goods but, prior to the time for payment, the seller's insolvency or some other circumstance makes it apparent that the seller will not deliver the goods.

Articles 71 and 72 afford protection for the party who is threatened with a failure of performance by the other party. Article 71 provides that, in some circumstances, a party facing such a threat may suspend its own performance. Article 72 provides that, in more extreme circumstances, a party facing such a threat may put a permanent end to the contract (i.e., avoid it).

Article 71[1]

(1) A party may suspend the performance of his obligations if, after the conclusion of the contract, it becomes apparent that the other party will not perform a substantial part of his obligations as a result of:
  (a) a serious deficiency in his ability to perform or in his creditworthiness; or
  (b) his conduct in preparing to perform or in performing the contract.
(2) If the seller has already dispatched the goods before the grounds described in the preceding paragraph become evident, he may prevent the handing over of the goods to the buyer even though

---

1. Article 71 is based on Art. 62 of the 1978 Draft Convention; para. (1) was significantly modified at the Diplomatic Conference. See *infra* at §388. *Cf.* ULIS 73.

the buyer holds a document which entitles him to obtain them. The present paragraph relates only to the rights in the goods as between the buyer and the seller.

(3) A party suspending performance, whether before or after dispatch of the goods, must immediately give notice of the suspension to the other party and must continue with performance if the other party provides adequate assurance of his performance.

Paragraph (1) applies to a threat of non-performance by either party. Paragraph (2) applies to a specialized situation of concern to sellers — a threat of non-payment by the buyer that becomes apparent while goods are in transit.

Paragraph (3) governs a suspending party's obligation to give the other party notice of suspension and to resume performance upon receipt of adequate assurances that the other side will perform.

386   B. Suspension of Performance Under Paragraph (1)

(1) Types of Performance Subject to Suspension

In limited circumstances (examined *infra* at §387), paragraph (1) authorizes a party to suspend the performance of obligations such as delivery of the goods (Arts. 31–34) or payment of the price (Arts. 54–59). Article 71(1) also has a broader reach. For instance, the contract may require the seller to procure or manufacture goods described in the contract; when it is apparent that the buyer will not be able to accept delivery and pay for the goods, the seller may suspend procurement or production. Similarly, when it appears that the seller will not be able to deliver the goods, the buyer may suspend required steps leading toward payment, such as the establishment of a letter of credit (Art. 54).[2]

The contract and the Convention may require a variety of preliminary steps leading to final performance. See, for example, Article 32 (shipping arrangements), Article 34 (handing over of documents), Article 54 (required steps such as establishing a letter of credit), Article 65 (supplying specifications for goods). Failure to take these steps may constitute a breach of contract, not merely a portent of a future breach; in some cases the breach may justify avoidance because it was sufficiently

---

2. See Rainer Hornung, Art. 71 paras. 6 & 19, *in* Schlechtriem & Schwenzer, *CISG Commentary* (2nd English ed. 2005).

serious (Arts. 49(1)(a), 64(1)(a)) or was the subject of a *Nachfrist* notice (Arts. 49(1)(b), 64(1)(b); see §323, *supra*). However, if the aggrieved party is hopeful of obtaining performance or if grounds for avoidance are not clear, the aggrieved party will prefer a less drastic approach such as suspension of its own performance.

Article 71 does not authorize a seller who has suspended its performance to dispose of goods held for the buyer, nor does it authorize a suspending buyer to purchase goods to replace those to be supplied by the seller; under Article 75, *infra*, these remedies apply only when the contract is avoided.[3] The point is significant since *avoidance* of the contract by one party because of prospective failure of performance by the other (Art. 72, *infra* at §395) is subject to standards that are more strict than the standards that Article 71 applies to *suspension* of performance.[4]

387   **(2) Grounds for Suspension**

Grounds for suspension provided by the 1978 Draft Convention were revised by the Diplomatic Conference. The revised language presents delicate problems of interpretation; a review of the legislative history seems advisable.

388   **(a) Legislative History of Article 71(1): The "Becomes Apparent" Standard.** The 1978 Draft Convention, (Art. 62(1)) suggested that suspension could not be based on facts existing at the time of contracting that indicated the inability by one party to perform even though these facts were not known by the other party. The Diplomatic Conference revised this language to state that suspension could be based on pre-existing facts that *became apparent* only after contracting.[5]

---

3. See Rainer Hornung, Art. 71 para. 23, *in* Schlechtriem & Schwenzer, *CISG Commentary* (2nd English ed. 2005).

4. See UNCITRAL Digest Art. 71 para. 2.

5. *O.R.* 374–376, *Docy. Hist.* 595–597. See Rainer Hornung, Art. 71 paras. 13–14, *in* Schlechtriem & Schwenzer, *CISG Commentary* (2nd English ed. 2005). In addition, see *id.* para. 16 and *Schlechtriem, 1986 Commentary* 92–93, for the perceptive observation that this change has the important consequence of excluding domestic rules granting avoidance (inter alia) based on mistake about capacity to perform. Schlechtriem also suggests (*Cornell Symposium* at 474 n. 23) that Art. 71 excludes domestic remedies for innocent or negligent misstatement as to ability to perform, such as an inaccurate financial statement supplied by one party on which the other party relies in entering into the contract. This latter

The more important change in the 1978 Draft narrowed the grounds for suspension. This draft authorized suspension of performance by a party who has "good *grounds to conclude* that the other party will not perform a substantial part of his obligations." At the Diplomatic Conference the representative of Egypt, Professor Mohsen Chafik, criticized this language on the ground that it gave excessive effect to the subjective view of one party. To meet this problem Professor Chafik proposed that provisions of the article on *suspension* (then Art. 62, now Art. 71) and the following article on *avoidance* for anticipatory breach (then Art. 63, now Art. 72) should be combined. Under this proposal, if it "becomes apparent that one of the parties [Party A] will commit a fundamental breach of contract," the other party [Party B] may give notice that he intends to suspend performance if Party A fails "to provide adequate assurances . . . of properly performing his obligations"; if Party A does not provide this assurance, Party B "may declare the contract avoided." This restriction of the right to suspend performance received substantial support on the ground that it was important for the protection of developing countries but, on an equally divided vote, failed to be adopted. Concern lest this decision might impede adherence to the Convention led to the appointment of an *ad hoc* working group of ten countries to develop a compromise solution. A revised text developed by this group became Article 71 of the Convention.[6]

When a party proposes to suspend performance what degree of certainty is required by the phrase "it becomes *apparent* that the other party will not perform a substantial part of his obligations?" Certainly the new language meets the objection that the 1978 Draft authorized suspension

---

suggestion may be questioned since the Convention does not address this factual situation. Contrast the discussion at §§239–240, *supra*, on the exclusion of domestic remedies for innocent misstatements of quality, which is addressed by Art. 35 of the Convention. Moreover, Art. 71 allows only *suspension* of performance and is subject to a stricter standard (*inability* to perform) than domestic law may provide for a contract obtained by a misstatement of fact. On the availability of domestic remedies for fraud see §65, *supra*.

6. For the evolution of Art. 71 see *O.R.* 129–130, *Docy. Hist.* 701–702 (Art. 62) para. 10 (text of proposal by Egypt), para. 12 (rejection of proposal), para. 14 (proposal of working group), paras. 15–17 (oral amendments and adoption by the First Committee of Art. 62, now Art. 71). For the discussion see *O.R.* 419–420, *Docy. Hist.* 640–641 (statement by Professor Chafik) and *O.R.* 420–422, *Docy. Hist.* 641–643 (final action by First Committee). The compromise developed by the working group included the addition of paragraphs (2) and (3) to Art. 72, *infra* at §395; these new paragraphs also drew on ideas in the above proposal by Professor Chafik. See generally Strub, CISG: Anticipatory Repudiation Provisions and Developing Countries, 38 Int. & Comp. L.Q. 475 (1989).

based on mere subjective fear.[7] Does Article 71(1) restrict suspension to cases where there is objective certainty that the other party will not perform?

This latter construction is subject to two objections. In the first place, the conference rejected the proposal to assimilate suspension under Article 71 with avoidance of the contract under Article 72, and took pains to preserve different language authorizing these different remedies. Suspension under Article 71 is permitted when "it becomes *apparent*" that a party will not "perform a substantial part of his obligations"; avoidance under Article 72 is authorized only when "it is *clear*" that a party will commit a fundamental breach of contract.[8] *This differing language means that greater certainty of future breach is required in order to justify final avoidance of the contract under Article 72 than is required for the less radical remedy of suspension under Article 71.*[9]

A second objection derives from Article 71(3). As we shall see (*infra* at §§391–392) a party suspending performance must notify the other party of the suspension "and must continue with performance if the other party *provides adequate assurance of his performance.*" Thus, circumstances that make it "apparent" that the other party will not perform need not establish a certainty of non-performance since the initial appearance may be modified by clarification of the situation or by the removal of the initial barriers to performance.[10]

In sum, under Article 71(1) subjective fear will not justify suspension; there must be objective grounds showing substantial probability of non-performance.

---

7. See Rainer Hornung, Art. 71 para. 17, *in* Schlechtriem & Schwenzer, *CISG Commentary* (2nd English ed. 2005).

8. See also the other official language versions: in French "il *apparait*" (Art. 71) v. "il est *manifeste*" (Art. 72); in Spanish "*manifiesto*" (Art. 71) v. "*patente*" (Art. 72). The intent to distinguish between these terms is shown by *O.R.* 432, *Docy. Hist.* 653, paras. 104–106 and *O.R.* 432–433, *Docy. Hist.* 653–654, paras. 3–21. Cohn suggests that "appears" and "evident" in ULIS 73(1) & (2) indicate that the circumstances must be generally known in business circles. 23 Int. & Comp. L.Q. 520, 526 (1974).

9. See Rainer Hornung, Art. 71 para. 17 and Art. 72 para. 12, *in* Schlechtriem & Schwenzer, *CISG Commentary* (2nd English ed. 2005); UNCITRAL Digest Art. 72 para. 2; Flechtner, *Pittsburgh Symposium* 93.

10. *Accord*, Rainer Hornung, Art. 71 para. 17, *in* Schlechtriem & Schwenzer, *CISG Commentary* (2nd English ed. 2005); *Schlechtriem, 1986 Commentary* 93 n.383a (citing first edition). Art. 72, *infra* at §395, under some circumstances, requires advance notification and an opportunity to provide adequate assurances of performance. Thus, breach may not eventuate even when "it is clear" that a party will commit a fundamental breach of contract.

388.1   **(b) Seriousness of the Threatened Breach: "A Substantial Part" of a Party's Obligations.**   Article 71 permits suspension only if there is a threat "that the other party will not perform a substantial part of his obligations." Clearly this precludes suspension where the threatened breach would be a minor matter,[11] but the standard is — necessarily — vague and the result of its application could be difficult to predict. One question is whether the "substantial part" standard in Article 71 is equivalent to requiring a threat of a "fundamental breach" as defined in Article 25. There is strong authority for concluding that the two standards are not the same, that the "substantial part" standard in Article 71 would be satisfied by something less than a threat of a fundamental breach.[12] This result is supported by the fact that the very next provision of the Convention (Article 72) expressly requires a threat of a "fundamental breach," and by the fact that Article 71 (or at least the English version thereof) chose a different phrase. These reasons were sufficient to convince the editor of the current edition that the two standards differ.[13] Later examination of the official French text of Article 71, however, raised questions about this conclusion[14] — another example of the challenges presented by differences among the six official language versions of the Conventions (see §372.3 supra for further discussion of this issue).

388.2   **(c) Required Grounds for the Threatened Breach: Article 71(a) and (b).**   Article 71(1)(a) and (b) limit the origins or basis of a threatened breach that will justify avoidance: the breach must result either from "a serious deficiency" in the other party's "ability to perform" or "creditworthiness," or from the other side's "conduct in preparing to perform or in performing the contract." The evident purpose of this limitation is to ensure that there are objective grounds for the

---

11. See Rainer Hornung, Art. 71 para. 8, *in* Schlechtriem & Schwenzer, *CISG Commentary* (2nd English ed. 2005) ("breach of an ancillary obligation is insufficient"). For examples of threatened breaches that courts have found did and did not justify avoidance, see UNCITRAL Digest Art. 71 paras. 6–8.

12. See, e.g., Rainer Hornung, Art. 71 para. 8 and authorities cited therein, *in* Schlechtriem & Schwenzer, *CISG Commentary* (2nd English ed. 2005); UNCITRAL Digest Art. 71 para. 5 and Art. 72 ¶ 2.

13. See Flechtner, Pittsburgh Symposium 93–94.

14. See Harry M. Flechtner, The Several Texts of the CISG in a Decentralized System: Observations on the Uniformity Principle in Art. 7(1) of the U.N. Sales Convention, 17 J.L. & Com. 187, 189–191 (1998).

suspending party to fear a breach,[15] but the idea of limiting the kinds of threatened breaches that justify suspension to those originating from specified causes is unfamiliar to those schooled in U.S. domestic law. Under U.C.C. §2-609, any threatened breach, no matter what its causes, will justify suspension provided the threat creates "reasonable grounds for insecurity."[16] On the other hand, it has been suggested that "[t]he grounds for possible threats to performance are described in such wide terms that they cover practically all grounds of disturbance."[17] (For discussion of this last contention, see §389 infra.)

389   **(d) Comparing Suspension of Performance Under U.S. Domestic Law.**   The (U.S.A.) Uniform Commercial Code provides:

> Section 2-609. Right to Adequate Assurance of Performance.
>   (1) A contract for sale imposes an obligation on each party that the other's expectation of receiving due performance will not be impaired. When reasonable grounds for insecurity arise with respect to the performance of either party the other may in writing demand adequate assurance of due performance and until he receives such assurance may if commercially reasonable suspend any performance for which he has not already received the agreed return...
>   (4) After receipt of a justified demand failure to provide within a reasonable time not exceeding thirty days such assurance of due performance as is adequate under the circumstances of the particular case is a repudiation of the contract.

The provision on suspension in the Uniform Commercial Code (UCC) resembles Article 71 in that it protects both sellers and buyers, but the grounds for suspension are broader than in the Convention since UCC 2-609(1) protects a party's "expectation" of receiving due performance and applies when "reasonable grounds for insecurity arise."[18] *The UCC standard appears to require a less clear and certain threat of a breach than the language in Article 71(1). It should be substantially easier to show grounds — even "reasonable grounds" — for "insecurity" about the other side's performance than to show that it was "apparent" the other side would fail to perform. Indeed, the official comments*

---

15. See Rainer Hornung, Art. 71 para. 10, *in* Schlechtriem & Schwenzer, *CISG Commentary* (2nd English ed. 2005).

16. See Flechtner, Pittsburgh Symposium 95.

17. Rainer Hornung, Art. 71 para. 6, *in* Schlechtriem & Schwenzer, *CISG Commentary* (2nd English ed. 2005). See *also id.* para. 10.

18. See Flechtner, Pittsburgh Symposium 95; White & Summers §6-2; Restatement, Second of Contracts §251; 6 Corbin §§1259, 1260.

to UCC §2-609 suggest that even marketplace rumors concerning the other party's situation can help create the required "reasonable grounds."[19]

There is much to be said for the more liberal suspension standard in the UCC. Suppose, for example, a buyer declares, without justification, that it "might not" accept delivery. Clearly the seller would reasonably feel insecure and could suspend under UCC §2-609, but does such an ambiguous declaration make it "apparent" the other side will not perform so as to justify suspension under Article 71?[20] *Perhaps international transactions require a higher threshold before performance of a transaction can be even temporarily suspended while the buyer's intentions are clarified, but the cost in (possibly) wasted preparation and transport charges can be a stiff one.*[21]

There is another way in which grounds for suspension under UCC §2-609 are broader than those in Article 71. As noted earlier (see §388.2 supra), the UCC, unlike Article 71(1), does not require the threatened breach to arise from specified causes. Certainly the required origins for the threatened breach specified in Article 71(1)(a) and (b) ("a serious deficiency" in a party's "ability to perform" or "creditworthiness," or a party's "conduct in preparing to perform or in performing the contract") are very broad — so broad, in fact, that it has been asserted they encompass "practically all grounds."[22] *There is, however, at least one basis for a threatened breach that, absent a quite liberal interpretation of the phrase "conduct in preparing to perform," might not be covered: a declaration of simple unwillingness (as opposed to inability) to perform, like that described in the previous paragraph. Thus permitting a party to suspend performance in such circumstances — a course that has much to recommend it — faces several roadblocks under Article 71.*[23]

19. (U.S.A.) UCC §2-609 cmt. 4.

20. It is even less likely — and properly so — that such an ambiguous declaration would constitute grounds for avoidance of the contract under Art. 72. See the comparison between the certainty required for a threatened breach in order justify suspension under Art. 71 and final avoidance under Art. 72 in §388 *supra*.

21. See Flechtner, Pittsburgh Symposium 95.

22. See Rainer Hornung, Art. 71 para. 6, *in* Schlechtriem & Schwenzer, *CISG Commentary* (2nd English ed. 2005). See also *id*. para. 10.

23. See Flechtner, Pittsburgh Symposium 95.

390 C. Stoppage of Goods in Transit

Unlike paragraph (1) which is available to both parties, paragraph (2) addresses a special problem that is of concern only to sellers — a threat to payment that becomes evident after the goods have been dispatched. Paragraph (2) provides that in specified circumstances the seller may prevent the carrier from handing over the goods to the buyer.

This right is available without regard to whether risk of loss has passed to the buyer. The reason is that transit risk normally passes to the buyer when the goods are delivered to the carrier (Art. 67(1), §§364–365, *supra*), so that limiting stoppage to the period before risk passes would virtually nullify the Convention's rules on stopping goods in transit; in addition, the Convention's risk rules and Article 71(2) address problems that are functionally distinct. For similar reasons domestic rules that "property" or "title" has passed to the buyer may not undermine the narrow and specific rights conferred by Article 71(2).[24] The Convention has rejected the use of such general concepts in determining the mutual rights and obligations of the seller and buyer (Art. 4(b), §§28, 70, 358); on the other hand, Article 71(2) (last sentence) provides that the seller's right to stop delivery to the buyer does not impair the rights of third persons.

Paragraph (2) will be useful only in an unusual combination of circumstances: (1) The threat of non-payment is discovered after the goods are dispatched and before they are handed over, and (2) The seller has not retained control over the goods, as by the retention of a negotiable bill of lading (Art. 58(2)). Comparable provisions on stoppage in transit are contained in domestic legislation.[25]

The provisions on stoppage in transit in Article 71(2) of the Convention reflect a substantial revision of Uniform Law for the International Sale of Goods (ULIS) Articles 73(2) and (3). ULIS attempted to deal with the effect of stoppage in transit on the rights of a third person who is a "lawful holder" of a document of title. This attempt proved to be inadequate; in contrast, Article 71(2) of the Convention provides that it "relates only to the rights in the goods as between the buyer and the seller." Whether a third person has acquired rights in the goods that

---

24. See Rainer Hornung, Art. 71 para. 29, *in* Schlechtriem & Schwenzer, *CISG Commentary* (2nd English ed. 2005).

25. E.g., (U.K.) SGA (1893) 44–46, preserved in SGA (1979); (U.S.A.) UCC 2-705; see Rainer Hornung, Art. 71 para. 26, *in* Schlechtriem & Schwenzer, *CISG Commentary* (2nd English ed. 2005).

would override the seller's right to prevent delivery to the buyer would depend on applicable domestic law, akin to the rules protecting the property rights of good faith purchasers. As we have seen, Article 4(b) excludes such issues from the scope of the Convention.[26]

The fact that Article 71(2)'s rules on stoppage relate only to rights "as between the buyer and the seller" does not make this provision as feeble as might be supposed.[27] True, the Convention does not state that when Article 71(2) applies the carrier must deliver the goods to the seller; the carrier needs protection lest some third party in good faith might have purchased the goods (or documents representing them) and thereby acquired rights to the goods that are protected by applicable domestic law.[28] On the other hand, Article 71(2) states that the seller may stop delivery "even though the buyer holds a document that entitles him to obtain them"; under this language the seller may stop delivery even though the buyer holds a negotiable bill of lading or other document controlling delivery.[29] In this case, to protect the carrier, the seller by an appropriate proceeding should require the buyer to deliver the documents to the seller or to the carrier. See Arts. 62, 71(2).

Even a third party who holds documents that control delivery may not have rights under domestic law that would cut off the seller's right to the goods. The essential point is that domestic law can be expected to honor the seller's rights against the buyer established by Article 71(2) and give the seller as much protection against third persons as domestic law accords to other persons in the seller's position. The carrier, of course, can have no objection to delivering the goods to the person who is entitled to them if the procedures suggested above protect the carrier against third-party claims.[30] (In any case the carrier is normally entitled to receive any unpaid freight charges before delivering the goods.)

---

26. The UNCITRAL revision was based on *Rep. S-G*, "Issues Presented by Chapters IV to VI of ULIS, paras. 59–61, V *YB* 88–89, *Docy. Hist.* 167–168. Action by UNCITRAL: V *YB* 37–39, *Docy. Hist.* 183–185. Difficulties of interpretation of ULIS 73(3) with respect to the rights of third persons are discussed in Cohn, *The Defence of Uncertainty*, 23 Int. & Comp. L.Q. 520, 536–538 (1974).

27. *Cf.* Bennett, *B-B Commentary* 520–521.

28. See Rainer Hornung, Art. 71 para. 34, *in* Schlechtriem & Schwenzer, *CISG Commentary* (2nd English ed. 2005).

29. See Flechtner, *Pittsburgh Symposium* 97 n.202; Rainer Hornung, Art. 71 para. 29, *in* Schlechtriem & Schwenzer, *CISG Commentary* (2nd English ed. 2005).

30. *Compare* Rainer Hornung, Art. 71 para. 34, *in* Schlechtriem & Schwenzer, *CISG Commentary* (2nd English ed. 2005).

A seller's right to stop delivery is not limited to "suspension" of performance under Article 71(2). Assume that, while the goods are in transit, a buyer commits a fundamental breach (e.g., failure to pay) or it becomes clear that the buyer *will* commit a fundamental breach (e.g., buyer repudiates the contract). The seller may thereupon avoid the contract (Art. 64(1)(a), §354 *supra*; Art. 72(1), §396 *infra*) and may reclaim the goods to enforce the right (Art. 81(2), §444 *infra*) to "claim restitution" of what has been supplied under the contract. Here, as under Article 71, the seller may be subject to the rights of third parties based, for example, on good faith purchase.

391 D. Continuation of Performance on Receipt of Adequate Assurance

Under Article 71(3) a party who has suspended performance "must immediately give notice of the suspension to the other party"[31] and "must continue with performance if the other party provides adequate assurance of performance." *The restoration of performance obligations upon receipt of adequate assurance demonstrates the temporary and contingent nature of suspension under Article 71. The main issue here is, what constitutes adequate assurance of performance? This matter is discussed in the next section.*

392 (1) Examples of "Adequate Assurance" of Performance

Reassuring words alone cannot provide "adequate assurance" of performance: under paragraph (3) a party notified of suspension must provide evidence of concrete facts or action that removes the threat that he "will not perform a substantial part of his obligation" (Art. 71(1)).[32]

Threats of non-performance may develop under a wide variety of circumstances; the range of remedial steps can only be suggested. For example, where a seller has suspended its performance because a buyer has ceased payment of his current obligations, adequate assurance of performance may, in some circumstances, be provided by proof that the

---

31. See Rainer Hornung, Art. 71 paras. 20–21, *in* Schlechtriem & Schwenzer, *CISG Commentary* (2nd English ed. 2005). For decisions on what constitutes adequate notice, as well as the effect of failure to notify, see UNCITRAL Digest Art. 71 para. 10–11.

32. For further general discussion of what constitutes adequate assurance of performance, see Rainer Hornung, Art. 71 paras. 38–39, *in* Schlechtriem & Schwenzer, *CISG Commentary* (2nd English ed. 2005).

buyer has reestablished current payments; in other circumstances "adequate assurance" may call for the issuance by a bank of an irrevocable letter of credit. Threats to a seller's continued performance resulting from a strike or the loss of a source of necessary materials may be removed by showing that the strike has been settled or that a new source of materials has been obtained. Developing an adequate solution to such problems calls for good faith consultation between the parties.[33]

Must a party who is subject to suspension provide assurance of perfect performance? Suppose that the assurance shows that full performance will occur but after a slight delay. Continued suspension of performance is closely akin to avoidance of the contract; the answer to the above question should be consistent with the principles of avoidance in Article 25, 49, 64 and with the rule of Article 71(1) authorizing suspension only when there is a threat of non-performance by the other party of "a *substantial* part of his obligations." An assurance under Article 71(3) should be "adequate" even if it involves an insubstantial non-conformity in performance.[34] Of course, a party in breach must compensate the other party for resulting loss (Art. 74).

393 (2) Extension of Time Because of Suspension

Assume that a party, aggrieved by a threat of non-performance, justifiably suspended performance. The other party then provided "adequate assurance" of performance so that the aggrieved party became obliged to resume performance. Is the aggrieved party held to the initial time-schedule specified in the contract?

The Convention and the rules of domestic law set forth, *supra* at §384, do not address this question. It seems that, at least in some circumstances, the right to "suspend" performance must carry with it an extension of the time for continued performance. Suppose that a contract made on June 1 requires the seller to manufacture goods to the buyer's specifications and deliver them on September 1. On July 1, before the seller has had time to manufacture the goods, the seller justifiably suspends performance under Article 71(1). The seller immediately notifies

---

33. *Accord*, Bennett, *B-B Commentary* 519–521. Art. 7(1) calls for interpretation of the Convention to promote "the observance of good faith in international trade," and Art. 7(2) invokes the "general principles" on which the Convention is based. As has been suggested (Art. 7, *supra* at §100) numerous specific provisions of the Convention seem to illustrate a general duty to communicate needed information to the other party.

34. *Accord*, Bennett, *B-B Commentary* 523; Strub, *supra* note 6, at 496.

the buyer of the suspension but the buyer does not provide adequate assurance of his performance until August 15. If completion of manufacture would require a month, the right of "suspension" would be nullified if the seller must deliver the goods by September 1. The problem calls for a reasonable adjustment to the new situation.[35] The seller may not always need an extension of time that is equivalent to the period of the suspension; helpful suggestions for solving these problems are available in domestic legislation.[36]

394 ## E. Consequences of Failure to Provide Adequate Assurance

Assume that Party A is aggrieved by a threat of non-performance by B and properly suspends performance, but after receiving notice of A's suspension B fails to provide adequate assurance. A may continue to suspend performance, but how will the contract relationship finally be resolved?

If the time for B's performance arrives and B continues to fail to perform, in most cases A may avoid the contract and claim damages for non-performance.[37] Arts. 25, 49, 64 and 81. However, A may not need to wait for the time specified in the contract for performance; B's failure to respond with assurances of performance may make it "clear" that B will commit a fundamental breach of contract[38] — a ground for avoiding the contract under Article 72, which follows. (See §§396 & 398 *infra*.)

---

35. *Accord*, Rainer Hornung, Art. 71 para. 22 & 24, *in* Schlechtriem & Schwenzer, *CISG Commentary* (2nd English ed. 2005); Strub, *supra* note 6, at 495.

36. See *Ont. L. Ref. Com., II Sales* 531 and III *id.* 52: §8.9(4) of draft bill. When adequate assurance is provided, the party's obligation to perform is restored "but he is not liable for any delay *occasioned by his suspension* of performance." Under UCC 2-611(3) if a party repudiates the contract and then retracts the repudiation, the repudiating party's rights are reinstated "with due excuse and allowance to the aggrieved party for *any delay occasioned by the repudiation.*" *Cf. Secretariat Commentary* Art. 62, para. 9, *O.R.* 52; *Docy. Hist.* 442.

37. See UNCITRAL Digest Art. 71 para. 1.

38. *Accord*, Strub, *supra* note 6, at 497 (citing first edition); Flechtner, *Pittsburgh Symposium* 93 (same). *Compare* Rainer Hornung, Art. 71 paras. 23 & 40 and Art. 72 para. 9, *in* Schlechtriem & Schwenzer, *CISG Commentary* (2nd English ed. 2005). The standards of Arts. 71 and 72 are different. See §388.1 *supra*; Rainer Hornung, Art. 71 paras. 8–9, *in* Schlechtriem & Schwenzer, *CISG Commentary* (2nd English ed. 2005). Failure to provide assurances will not always justify avoidance. *Cf.* Ziegel, *Parker Colloq.* 9–35; Rainer Hornung, Art. 71 para. 400, *in* Schlechtriem & Schwenzer, *CISG Commentary* (2nd English ed. 2005); *Schlechtriem, 1986 Commentary* 96.

Article 72.
Avoidance Prior to the Date for Performance

395   Articles 49 and 64, *supra* at §301 and §353, govern the right of an aggrieved party (A) to avoid the contract when the other party (B) has already committed a breach of contract by defective performance or by failing to perform by the date required under the contract. In contrast, Articles 71 and 72 are concerned with situations where breach by B is threatened prior to the date for performance.[1] Article 71 merely permits A to "suspend the performance of his obligations"; A is permanently liberated from its obligation to perform or to accept performance only by avoiding the contract, which A is entitled to do under Article 72, below, when "it is clear" that B "*will commit* a fundamental breach."[2]

Article 72[3]

(1) If prior to the date for performance of the contract it is clear that one of the parties will commit a fundamental breach of contract, the other party may declare the contract avoided.

(2) If time allows, the party intending to declare the contract avoided must give reasonable notice to the other party in order to permit him to provide adequate assurance of his performance.

(3) The requirements of the preceding paragraph do not apply if the other party has declared that he will not perform his obligations.

396 A. Grounds for Avoidance; Hazards

In examining the right to suspend performance under Article 71, we saw that standards for suspension are less rigorous than the standards for avoidance under Article 72. Article 72 authorizes an aggrieved party (A) to avoid the contract prior to the date for performance only when "it is clear" that the other party (B) "will commit a fundamental breach of

---

1. See UNCITRAL Digest Art. 72 para. 1.

2. See Rainer Hornung, Art. 72 para. 9, *in* Schlechtriem & Schwenzer, *CISG Commentary* (2nd English ed. 2005); UNCITRAL Digest Art. 72 para. 2.

3. Paragraph (1) of Art. 72 is substantially the same as Art. 63 of the 1978 Draft and ULIS 76. Paragraphs (2) and (3) were added at the Diplomatic Conference; see §398 *infra*. Other developments at the Diplomatic Conference were linked to Art. 71; see §388 *supra*. For earlier action in UNCITRAL see V *YB* 41–42, 57, VI *YB* 72, 106, VIII *YB* 55, *Docy. Hist.* 150, 187–188, 203, 231, 348.

contract"[4] — a standard requiring great certainty that a threatened breach will occur, and perhaps a threat of a more serious breach, than the standard for "mere" suspension under Article 71. See §§388-388.1 *supra*).[5] Unless B has declared that he will not perform (Art. 72(3)), it may not be clear whether an attempt by A to avoid the contract in advance of the time for performance will overstep the limits set by Article 72. Unless the demanding standards of this provision are met, A still has a duty to accept performance by B. Moreover, a wrongful declaration of avoidance by A may constitute a repudiation giving B the right to avoid the contract under Article 72(1).[6]

What circumstances make it "clear" that a party "will commit a fundamental breach of contract?" Paragraph (3) shows that a party's declaration "that he will not perform his obligations" empowers the aggrieved party to declare the contract avoided, even though such a declaration does not make it absolutely "clear" that the repudiating party will not change his mind and perform by the due date.[7] Schlechtriem notes that "the frequent cases in which a demand for new terms or alleged contract violations by the other side are used as a pretext for not performing ones own obligations" provide "in most cases" a basis for immediate avoidance.[8] This proposition was probably intended to refer to situations in which one party (B) demands new terms from A coupled

---

4. For decisions on the level of probability that a future breach will occur required by Art. 72(1), see UNCITRAL Digest Art. 72 para. 4.

5. *Compare* Rainer Hornung, Art. 72 paras. 11–12, *in* Schlechtriem & Schwenzer, *CISG Commentary* (2nd English ed. 2005).

6. See Rainer Hornung, Art. 72 para. 34, *in* Schlechtriem & Schwenzer, *CISG Commentary* (2nd English ed. 2005). A's hazards would be reduced if A, pursuant to Art. 72(2), notifies B of A's intention and thereby gives B an opportunity to provide assurances of performance. Failure by B to respond effectively to such a notice would make it more difficult for B to challenge a subsequent declaration of avoidance. See also Art. 7(1) (interpretation to promote "the observance of good faith").

7. See UNCITRAL Digest Art. 72 para. 5. See also Rainer Hornung, Art. 72 para. 8, *in* Schlechtriem & Schwenzer, *CISG Commentary* (2nd English ed. 2005) (arguing that avoidance for a repudiation that is governed by Art. 72(3) is, in effect, a "separate remedy" from avoidance under Art. 72 in other circumstances). If the aggrieved party does not respond to repudiation by declaring the contract avoided, he may be obliged to accept performance if the repudiator changes his mind. See Rainer Hornung, Art. 72 para. 27, *in* Schlechtriem & Schwenzer, *CISG Commentary* (2nd English ed. 2005). *Cf.* Art. 81, *infra Treitel, Contract* 653–654, 661. *Cf. also Corbin* §§980–981 (retraction of repudiation may be barred by other party's change of position).

8. See *Schlechtriem, 1986 Commentary* 95. See also Rainer Hornung, Art. 72 paras. 28–29, *in* Schlechtriem & Schwenzer, *CISG Commentary* (2nd English ed. 2005); UNCITRAL Digest Art. 72 para. 5.

with an unconditional declaration that B "will not perform" its obligations. Avoidance by A should not be triggered if B informs A of the need
to negotiate a modification of their agreement (*cf.* Art. 29). In any event,
a response by A that goes beyond a notice of suspension of A's counter-
performance and a request for assurance (Art. 71, *supra*) may be hazardous since it may provide grounds for B to avoid the contract on the
ground that A has repudiated under Art. 72(1).

Actions may give rise to a repudiation — for example, the wrongful
resale to a third person of the goods that the seller had contracted to deliver
to the buyer, or the sale of the manufacturing plant at which the seller had
agreed to produce goods for the buyer. Of course, these are only a few of
the circumstances that might invoke Article 72.[9] *For example, as discussed above in connection with Article 71 (see §394 supra), a party's
failure to provide adequate assurance of its performance after it has
received notice that the other side has justifiably suspended its performance under Article 71 may make it "clear" that the party will commit a
fundamental breach, thus giving the other side a right to avoid under
Article 72. This solution is important to the sensible operation of
Article 71, since it permits a resolution to the state of temporary "suspension" under that provision. As discussed below (see §398 infra),
however, procedural aspects of the right to avoid under Article 72 present challenges in coordinating these two articles.*

397 B. Advantages; Consequences

We have just noted some of the hazards of Article 72 avoidance. Are
there advantages of early avoidance? Where A's avoidance is clearly
justified, A's declaration of avoidance makes it possible for A to resell
(or repurchase) the goods called for by the initial contract; A need not be
concerned lest B change its mind and tender performance.[10] In addition,
by virtue of Article 75, *infra* at §409, a reasonably prompt resale or

---

9. For other examples see Rainer Hornung, Art. 72 paras. 10–12, *in* Schlechtriem & Schwenzer, *CISG Commentary* (2nd English ed. 2005); UNCITRAL Digest Art. 72 paras. 5–7. See
also Gulotta, *Anticipatory Breach — A Comparative Analysis*, 50 Tulane L. Rev. 927, 932
(1976); *Restatement, Second of Contracts* §250, Comments c and d; *Corbin* §§984, 1259;
Treitel, Remedies (1988) 379–381. For the approach of German (FRG) law see *Dölle,
Kommentar* Art. 76, p. 485 at 11–12. On repudiation under the CISG see Stoll, 52 *Rabels
Z* 617 (1988) (in German; English summary).
10. See Rainer Hornung, Art. 72 para. 4, *in* Schlechtriem & Schwenzer, *CISG Commentary*
(2nd English ed. 2005).

repurchase (even prior to the date for performance) may fix the damages for which the repudiating party will be liable. *Indeed, there may be limits on how long A retains the right to avoid under Article 72 once grounds for such avoidance have appeared—although those limits must be worked out by implication since the Convention does not expressly address the issue.*[11]

If A has properly avoided the contract under Article 72 may it bring legal action before the date for B's performance? Such haste in instituting legal proceedings is seldom of practical value, but Articles 75 and 76, *infra* at §409, seem to authorize action immediately on avoidance.[12]

The effects of avoidance in various settings (Arts. 49, 64, and 72) are prescribed in Ch. V, Sec. V (Arts. 81–85) *infra*; these include being released from the obligation to perform the contract, the right of the aggrieved party to recover damages (Arts. 81(1)), and the right to claim restitution of whatever the avoiding party has supplied or paid under the contract (Art. 81(2)).

398 C. The Requirement of Advance Notice

Paragraphs (2) and (3) were added to this article at the Diplomatic Conference. The discussion of Article 71, *supra* at §388, referred to the concern, primarily on behalf of developing countries, that the power of suspension might be abused. Similar concerns were expressed with respect to avoidance under Article 72; the addition of paragraphs (2) and (3) was part of the compromise developed by an *ad hoc* working group with respect to both Articles 71 and 72.[13]

The addition of paragraphs (2) and (3) to Article 72 appears to have been useful. *The purpose of requiring advance notice of an intent to avoid, as provided in Article 72(2), is to permit the other side to respond with "adequate assurance of his performance"—a concept already discussed in connection with Article 71 (see §392 supra).*[14] *Such an*

---

11. See Rainer Hornung, Art. 72 paras. 31–32, *in* Schlechtriem & Schwenzer, *CISG Commentary* (2nd English ed. 2005).

12. The leading English decision authorizing immediate legal action is Hochster v. De la Tour, 118 Eng. Rep. 922 (Q.B. 1853). Recovery of damages, of course, does not present the problem of requiring specific performance before the agreed date. See *Corbin* §961, §962; *Restatement, Second of Contracts* §253.

13. *Com. I* Action: *O.R.* 130–131, *Docy. Hist.* 702–703; discussion: *O.R.* 419–422, 431–433, *Docy. Hist.* 640–643, 652–654, 702–703.

14. See also Rainer Hornung, Art. 72 para. 20, *in* Schlechtriem & Schwenzer, *CISG Commentary* (2nd English ed. 2005).

assurance may remove the grounds that made it "clear" the party would commit a fundamental breach, thus preserving the contract by eliminating the right to avoid it under Article 72.[15] Under paragraph (2), furthermore, advance notice of avoidance is to be "reasonable," and must be given only "if time allows." Modern methods of communication would normally permit such a notice without unduly hampering the aggrieved party's freedom of action.[16] In any event, advance notice "if time allows" would be consistent with good faith and normal commercial practice and, indeed, would reduce the hazards of making a declaration of avoidance.[17]

The advance notice procedure in Article 72(2), however, was not particularly well-drafted—for example, it does not address how long a party has to provide adequate assurance that it will perform.[18] *The procedure also complicates coordination between Article 72 and 71. Suppose a party (A) properly suspends its performance of a contract under Article 71 because it is "apparent" that the other party (B) will not perform a substantial part of its obligations. Article 71(3) provides B an opportunity to provide adequate assurance that it will perform. As noted earlier (see §§394 & 396 supra), it is important for the proper functioning of suspension under Article 71 that, if B fails to provide adequate assurance, A can treat this as grounds for avoidance under Article 72 — that is, the failure to provide adequate assurance as provided in Article 71 may make it "clear" that B will commit a fundamental breach. But if A then wants to avoid does Article 72(2) (assuming "time allows") require A to afford B a second opportunity to provide adequate assurance? As the editor of the current edition has previously opined:*

> That would be absurd. It can be finessed by holding that a demand for assurances under Article 71 satisfies the notice requirement in Article 72(2) [or that the failure to provide adequate assurance under Article 71 constitutes a repudiation under Article 72(3) which obviates the requirements of Article 72(2).] The need to construe around this problem, however, illustrates the clumsy fit between Articles 71 and 72....[19]

---

15. See Rainer Hornung, Art. 72 paras. 13–14 & 21, *in* Schlechtriem & Schwenzer, *CISG Commentary* (2nd English ed. 2005).

16. *Compare* Rainer Hornung, Art. 72 paras. 15–17, *in* Schlechtriem & Schwenzer, *CISG Commentary* (2nd English ed. 2005).

17. See also §396 *supra. Accord*, Bennett, *B-B Commentary* 530. The significance of communications between the parties was discussed under Art. 7, *supra* at §100.

18. See Rainer Hornung, Art. 72 para. 22, *in* Schlechtriem & Schwenzer, *CISG Commentary* (2nd English ed. 2005).

19. Flechtner, *Pittsburgh Symposium* 92 n. 190.

Article 73.
Avoidance in Instalment Contracts

399   A sales contract calls for deliveries in January, February, and March. Article 73, ***which applies to such instalment contracts***,[1] in three paragraphs, addresses seriatim the following three questions: (1) Part of the January delivery is seriously defective — may the buyer refuse to accept the entire delivery? (2) As in (1), the January delivery has serious defects — may the buyer not only refuse that delivery but also the deliveries scheduled for February and March? (3) The buyer receives and accepts the January delivery, which conforms to the contract, but the February delivery is seriously defective — may the buyer not only refuse the February delivery but also return the goods that he received in January and refuse the delivery scheduled for March?

Paragraphs (1) and (2) of Article 73 apply to breach of contract by either the seller or the buyer; examples (1) and (2), above, could be rephrased in terms of failure by the buyer to pay for an instalment.[2]

Article 73[3]

(1) In the case of a contract for delivery of goods by instalments, if the failure of one party to perform any of his obligations in respect of any instalment constitutes a fundamental breach of contract with respect to that instalment, the other party may declare the contract avoided with respect to that instalment.

(2) If one party's failure to perform any of his obligations in respect of any instalment gives the other party good grounds to conclude that a fundamental breach of contract will occur with

---

1. An instalment contract is one calling for more than one delivery of goods, irrespective of how payment is to be made. See Rainer Hornung, Art. 73 paras. 6–8, *in* Schlechtriem & Schwenzer, *CISG Commentary* (2nd English ed. 2005); UNCITRAL Digest Art. 73 paras. 3–4.

2. See Rainer Hornung, Art. 73 paras. 11 & 30, *in* Schlechtriem & Schwenzer, *CISG Commentary* (2nd English ed. 2005).

3. Article 73 is the same as Art. 64 of the 1978 Draft Convention. See *O.R.* 54 (*Sec. Commy. on Art. 64*), *Docy. Hist.* 444. No objections were raised at the Diplomatic Conference. ULIS 75 also dealt with breach in instalment contracts but was substantially redrafted by the Working Group. *W/G 5* paras. 1 16–127, V *YB* 29, 40–41, *Docy. Hist.* 186–187. Further refinements were made in the Commission's 1977 review. VIII *YB* 55, *Docy. Hist.* 348. See Bennett, *B-B Commentary* 532–533. For a careful comparison of CISG 73 with (U.S.A.) UCC 2-612 see Flechtner, *Pittsburgh Symposium* 88–92.

respect to future instalments, he may declare the contract avoided for the future, provided that he does so within a reasonable time.

(3) A buyer who declares the contract avoided in respect of any delivery may, at the same time, declare it avoided in respect of deliveries already made or of future deliveries if, by reason of their interdependence, those deliveries could not be used for the purpose contemplated by the parties at the time of the conclusion of the contract.

400 A. Refusal of the Defective Instalment

As was indicated above, paragraph (1) is directed to the problems that are presented when either party fails to perform his obligations with respect to one instalment of a larger contract. In example (1) described in §399, some of the goods delivered in January are defective. Article 51, as we have seen (§§314–317), permits the buyer to avoid the contract as to the non-conforming goods, provided the defects constitute a fundamental breach with respect to that portion of the delivery.[4] But may the buyer reject the entire January delivery? Or if the buyer fails to provide for paying for the January delivery, may the seller refuse to tender the January instalment?

The approach established by paragraph (1) makes the rules on avoidance for fundamental breach (Arts. 25, 49 and 64) applicable separately to each instalment.[5] The crucial question is this: Was there "a fundamental breach *with respect to that instalment?*" If so, Article 73(1) states that "the other party may declare the contract avoided *with respect to that instalment.*"[6]

The approach of Article 73(1) is thus similar to that established in Article 51 when "the seller delivers only a part of the goods or if only a part of the goods delivered is in conformity with the contract." Article 51 provides that the remedies for breach (including the right to avoid the contract) apply *"in respect of the part* that is missing or which does not conform." As has been noted (Art. 51, *supra* at §315) such explicit

---

4. See UNCITRAL Digest Art. 73 para. 2. *Contrast* Rainer Hornung, Art. 73 para. 13, *in* Schlechtriem & Schwenzer, *CISG Commentary* (2nd English ed. 2005), which appears to assume — inexplicably — that Art. 51 does not apply to a partially non-conforming delivery under an instalment contract.

5. Huber, 43 *Rabels Z* 413, 506 (1979) (comment on Art. 64 of 1978 Draft).

6. For decisions on what constitutes a fundamental breach with respect to an instalment see UNCITRAL Digest Art. 73 para. 5.

provisions are useful to avoid misunderstanding that can result from the concept "avoidance of *the contract*"; when a buyer refuses to receive only a part of the goods covered by the contract he does not avoid *all* of "the contract." Articles 51 and 73 adapt the general concept of "avoidance of the contract" to a narrower issue: What may the aggrieved party do with respect to a specific delivery or the non-conforming portion of a delivery, or a specific payment? Once the issue has been made specific and concrete, the Convention's general rules on avoidance for fundamental breach (Arts. 25, 49 and 64) may be applied without added difficulty.[7] As we have seen in connection with Articles 47 and 49(1)(b), and the similar provisions in Articles 63 and 64(1)(b), in some situations avoidance of contract may be based on the failure of a breaching party to perform in compliance with a notice "fixing an additional period of time of reasonable length" — the so-called *Nachfrist* notice — without a showing that there has been a fundamental breach. Article 73(1), however, states that avoidance as to an instalment of an instalment contract must be based on "a fundamental breach of contract with respect to that instalment." Can *Nachfrist* notice nevertheless be used to establish grounds for avoidance as to an instalment?

The Nachfrist procedure allows a party awaiting late performance to escape the difficult burden of determining when the delay amounts to a fundamental breach. It is thus inapplicable when a buyer wishes to avoid an instalment delivery because it contains non-conforming goods. It is not so clear, however, that Article 73(1) should exclude Nachfrist avoidance as to an instalment when the delivery of that instalment or the establishment of a letter of credit is overdue. Compare the distinction between Article 51(1) & (2), discussed at §317 supra. An analogy to Article 51(1) suggests the Nachfrist avoidance should be available with respect to overdue performance relating to an instalment, *and there is authority supporting that position.*[8] *However, the fact that the drafters of Article 73(1) chose language expressly limiting avoidance to circumstances involving a fundamental breach as to an instalment (contrast the language of Article 51(1)) argues against this result.*[9]

The policy that underlies Article 73(1) (as well as Article 51) is to allow the aggrieved party effective remedies while avoiding

---

7. For discussion of time limits for avoidance under Art. 73(1) see Rainer Hornung, Art. 73 para. 17, *in* Schlechtriem & Schwenzer, *CISG Commentary* (2nd English ed. 2005).

8. See Rainer Hornung, Art. 73 para. 16, *in* Schlechtriem & Schwenzer, *CISG Commentary* (2nd English ed. 2005); UNCITRAL Digest Art. 73 para. 2.

9. Flechtner, *Pittsburgh Symposium* 91–92 n. 182.

unnecessarily drastic consequences from the failure to perform a separable part of the contract. Those circumstances in which breach with respect to a part invoke more drastic remedies with respect to the rest of the contract are defined in paragraphs (2) and (3) of Article 73.

401   ## B. Refusal of Future Instalments

Paragraph (2) provides that seriously defective performance of one part of the contract may empower the aggrieved party to avoid the contract with respect to future performance.[10] The test is whether the initial breach gives "the other party *good grounds to conclude* that a fundamental breach of contract will occur with respect to future instalments." *Article 73(2) is thus concerned with the same problem addressed in Articles 71 and 72 — threat of future breach. Article 73(2) focuses specifically on the threat of future non-conforming instalments that may be implied by delivery of earlier non-conforming instalments.*[11] *The standard for avoidance as to future instalments in Article 73(2), however,* is less strict and more subjective than grounds for suspension under Article 71 or for avoidance under Article 72.[12] This may be explained by the fact that in the setting of Article 73(2) (unlike the situations invoking Articles 71 and 72) an actual breach of contract has already occurred.[13] Under this more flexible standard a single breach or a series of breaches, which would not justify avoidance of the entire contract, may give the other party good grounds to conclude that a "fundamental breach" of the remainder of the contract will occur.[14]

---

10. For discussion of time limits for avoidance under Art. 73(2) see Rainer Hornung, Art. 73 para. 26, *in* Schlechtriem & Schwenzer, *CISG Commentary* (2nd English ed. 2005); UNCITRAL Digest Art. 73 para. 9.

11. See Rainer Hornung, Art. 73 paras. 12 & 28, *in* Schlechtriem & Schwenzer, *CISG Commentary* (2nd English ed. 2005).

12. *Compare* Rainer Hornung, Art. 73 para. 23, *in* Schlechtriem & Schwenzer, *CISG Commentary* (2nd English ed. 2005). For examples of circumstances that will satisfy this standard see *id.* para. 23a; UNCITRAL Digest Art. 73 paras 6–8.

13. Articles 71 and 72, of course, can also be invoked with respect to instalment contracts. See UNCITRAL Digest Art. 72 para. 3 and Art. 73 para. 2.

14. See *Secretariat Commentary* on draft Art. 64(2), para. 6, *O.R.* 54, *Docy. Hist.* 444; Rainer Hornung, Art. 73 paras. 21–22, *in* Schlechtriem & Schwenzer, *CISG Commentary* (2nd English ed. 2005).

402 C. Avoidance of Instalments Based on Interdependence with a Defective Instalment

The situation envisaged by paragraph (3) may be illustrated as follows:

Example 73A. A sales contract called for Seller to deliver one machine in January, a second in February, and a third in March, The three were designed to perform a series of interrelated production operations; none of the machines was compatible with machines made by other manufacturers. In January, Seller delivered a machine that conformed with the contract but the machine delivered in February was so defective that the Seller could not cure the defect. Replacement with a second machine was not possible.

We may assume that, pursuant to paragraph (1), Buyer may reject ("avoid the contract" with respect to) the machine delivered in February. Pursuant to paragraph (3), Buyer may return ("avoid the contract" with respect to) the machine delivered in January and also may refuse to accept the machine to be delivered in March, since "by reason of their interdependence, those deliveries could not be used for the purposes contemplated by the parties at the time of the conclusion of the contract."[15] "Could not be used . . ." is even a stricter standard than for fundamental breach (Art. 25) and reflects the fact that here avoidance extends to goods that are free from defect and can apply to goods (e.g., the machine delivered in January) that have been received without objection. In short, avoidance with respect to the January and March instalments is based solely on their interdependence with the defective machine delivered in February.[16]

15. For discussion of time limits for avoidance under Art. 73(3) see Rainer Hornung, Art. 73 paras. 40–41, *in* Schlechtriem & Schwenzer, *CISG Commentary* (2nd English ed. 2005).
16. The (U.S.A.) Uniform Commercial Code achieves a similar result by providing (§§2-601(c) & 2-608) for rejection or revocation of acceptance of a "commercial unit," which is defined (§2-105(6)) as a unit which "by commercial usage is a single whole for purposes of sale and division of which materially impairs its character or value on the market or in use." For examples in which interdependence among deliveries may result from economic factors contemplated by the parties see Rainer Hornung, Art. 73 para. 32, *in* Schlechtriem & Schwenzer, *CISG Commentary* (2nd English ed. 2005); *Schlechtriem, 1986 Commentary* 96 n. 392; *O.R.* 54, *Docy. Hist.* 444 (*Sec. Comm.* on draft Art. 64(3), para. 8).

SECTION II.

DAMAGES
(Articles 74–77)

Article 74.
General Rule for Measuring Damages

403   Breach of contract can occur in an almost infinite variety of circumstances; no statute can specify detailed rules for measuring damages in all possible cases. All that can be done, and all that is needed, is to state basic principles to govern compensation for breach of contract. This is the role of the present article.

Article 74[1]

Damages for breach of contract by one party consist of a sum equal to the loss, including loss of profit, suffered by the other party as a consequence of the breach. Such damages may not exceed the loss which the party in breach foresaw or ought to have foreseen at the time of the conclusion of the contract, in the light of the facts and matters of which he then knew or ought to have known, as a possible consequence of the breach of contract.

The standard established by Article 74 is brief but powerful. Damages consist of "the loss, including loss of profit suffered . . . as a consequence of the breach" — a standard that is designed to place the aggrieved party in as good a position as if the other party had properly performed the contract — *that is, protection of the aggrieved party's "expectation interest."*[2] We shall have occasion to illustrate this principle in

---

1. Art. 74 is the same as Art. 70 of the 1978 Draft and closely follows ULIS 82. This provision did not provoke significant controversy. See VI *YB* 107, 62, VIII *YB* 59, *O.R.* 394, 131, *Docy. Hist.* 232, 253, 352, 615, 703.

2. See Hans Stoll & Georg Gruber, Art. 74 paras. 2 & 5, *in* Schlechtriem & Schwenzer, *CISG Commentary* (2nd English ed. 2005); Flechtner, *Pittsburgh Symposium* 101; CISG Advisory Council Opinion No. 6, Calculation of Damages under CISG Art. 74 para. 1.1, *available at* http://www.cisg.law.pace.edu/cisg/CISG-AC-op6.html. See *also* Treitel, *Remedies (1988)* 82 (basic principle of remedies).

several settings.[3] *There is also authority for awarding "reliance damages"—that is, costs incurred and gains forgone in reliance upon the contract—under Article 74, although coupled with the suggestion that such recovery cannot be used by the aggrieved party to shift the loss from an unprofitable contract onto the breaching party.[4] A similar approach is followed in U.S. domestic law, which permits recovery of reliance damages but provides that they can be reduced by the amount of loss that the aggrieved party would have incurred had the contract been fully performed on both sides.[5]*

Under U.S. domestic law an aggrieved party may, alternatively, be able to recover "restitutionary damages"—that is, damages measured by the unjust enrichment of the other party that comes at the expense of the aggrieved party—without reduction by the amount that the aggrieved party would have lost under the contract; this can result in shifting the loss from an unprofitable contract onto the breaching party.[6] Suppose, for example,[7] Seller contracts to design and produce five custom machines for Buyer for a price of $20,000 each ($100,000 total) payable upon delivery of the fifth machine. Seller has badly miscalculated its costs under the contract: it has already spent $150,000 to produce the first four machines (which have been delivered to and accepted by Buyer) when Buyer repudiates. Seller's expectation recovery would be, presumably, $80,000. Seller might attempt to recover the $150,000 it spent in producing the machines as reliance damages, but (as noted above) the recovery will be reduced by the amount it would have lost under the contract—$50,000 plus whatever

---

3. Article 74 drives home the Convention's unified approach to the parties' obligations and to remedies for breach. See Ch. 2, *supra* at §26. Intro, to Ch. II, Sec. III at §274. For the fragmented approach of some legal systems see *Treitel, Remedies (Int. Enc.)* §75; *Treitel, Remedies (1988)* Ch. V, 129–131.

4. See Hans Stoll & Georg Gruber, Art. 74 paras. 2 & 5, *in* Schlechtriem & Schwenzer, *CISG Commentary* (2nd English ed. 2005). *Cf.* CISG Advisory Council Opinion No. 6, Calculation of Damages under CISG Art. 74 §9, available at http://www.cisg.law.pace.edu/cisg/CISG-AC-op6.html ("Damages must not place the aggrieved party in a better position than it would have enjoyed if the contract had been properly performed").

5. See American Law Institute, Restatement (2nd) of the Law: Contracts §349.

6. See American Law Institute, *Restatement (2nd) of the Law: Contracts* §373 and cmt. d ("Losing Contracts") thereto.

7. The illustration and discussion in this paragraph is an application of U.S. domestic common law remedy principles to a sales transaction; it is not clear whether this application would be pre-empted by the U.S. domestic statutory sales law — that is, Art. 2 of the U.C.C.

it would have cost to produce the fifth machine. If Seller can show that Buyer would have had to pay another seller $150,000 for the four machines that Seller delivered, however, Seller may be able to recover that amount, unreduced by the losses Seller would have incurred, as restitutionary damages.[8]

Article 81(2) of the Convention provides for restitution when a contract has been avoided (see §444 infra). It makes sense to limit restitution under the Convention to that situation, where it is expressly authorized, and not to allow for recovery of restitutionary damages under Article 74.[9] *Given the comprehensive nature of the Convention's rules on damages for breach, furthermore, those provisions should pre-empt domestic restitutionary rules in a situation like that illustrated in the previous paragraph.*[10]

404   A. Relation Between Article 74 and Remainder of Section II

Article 74, when it applies, specifies the way damages are measured, but it does not itself authorize the recovery of damages — a matter addressed in other provisions of the Convention (see Article 45(1)(b) and 61(1)(b)).[11] The measurement of damages (including damages governed by Article 74) in cases where the contract is avoided can best be considered in the setting of Articles 75 and 76, infra at §409, since these articles are addressed specifically to this problem.[12] Thus, we shall

---

8. The theory supporting such an unreduced recovery is that it prevents the breaching party from being unjustly enriched at the expense of the aggrieved party; the contract price does not limit the restitutionary recovery because, technically, the aggrieved party is not seeking to enforce the contract (as it would be if it sought expectation or reliance damages) but rather is suing "off the contract" under the principle of prevention of unjust enrichment. Interestingly, had Seller in the illustration completed and delivered all five machines, it might have been prevented from pursuing an alternative restitutionary recovery, and thus have been relegated to (lower) expectation or reliance damages.

9. *Accord*, Hans Stoll & Georg Gruber, Art. 74 para. 31, *in* Schlechtriem & Schwenzer, *CISG Commentary* (2nd English ed. 2005).

10. *Accord*, Hans Stoll & Georg Gruber, Art. 74 para. 31, *in* Schlechtriem & Schwenzer, *CISG Commentary* (2nd English ed. 2005).

11. See Hans Stoll & Georg Gruber, Art. 74 paras. 1 & 4, *in* Schlechtriem & Schwenzer, *CISG Commentary* (2nd English ed. 2005); UNCITRAL Digest Art. 74 para. 9.

12. See Hans Stoll & Georg Gruber, Art. 74 para. 4, *in* Schlechtriem & Schwenzer, *CISG Commentary* (2nd English ed. 2005).

temporarily put to one side the following situations: (a) The seller fails to deliver the goods on time or delivers goods that are seriously defective and the buyer declares the contract avoided (i.e., the buyer rejects or returns the goods); (b) The buyer fails to take delivery and pay for the goods and the seller declares the contract avoided (i.e., the seller refuses to deliver or recovers the goods). Nevertheless, the general rules of Article 74 on the recovery of damages are applicable to and supplement the above situations governed by Articles 75 and 76. For example, a failure of performance leading to avoidance of contract may reduce the volume of business of the aggrieved party and thus lead to loss of profit; under these circumstances the damages specified in Article 75 and 76 may be enhanced by the provision of Article 74 that damages may include "loss of profit."[13] This question will be discussed under Articles 75 and 76 at §415.

When the goods are delivered to and retained by the buyer the only breach by the buyer is normally the failure to pay the price. This seldom presents problems of damage measurement; under Article 62, *supra* at §345, the seller "may require the buyer to pay the price," and under Article 78, *infra* at §420, the seller "is entitled to interest" for the period that the payment is in arrears. (As we shall see. Article 78 provides generally for interest on any "sum that is in arrears" from either party. *For discussion of the relationship between Article 74 damages and interest under Article 78, see §§421 & 422 infra.*) Problems invoking the rules of Article 74 can arise changes in exchange rates subsequent to the date when the buyer should have paid.[14] *Some courts have in fact awarded Article 74 damages when currency fluctuations impact the value of late payment, although decisions are not uniform.*[15]

---

13. Knapp, *B-B Commentary* 539. The provision in Art. 74 on unpredictable consequential damages, discussed *infra* at §406, may also apply to damages following avoidance of the contract.

14. See Hans Stoll & Georg Gruber, Art. 74 para. 17, *in* Schlechtriem & Schwenzer, *CISG Commentary* (2nd English ed. 2005); CISG Advisory Council Opinion No. 6, Calculation of Damages under CISG Art. 74 paras. 3.5 through 3.9, *available at* http://www.cisg.law. pace.edu/ cisg/CISG-AC-op6.html. See also Hellner, *The Limits of Contractual Damages in the Scandinavian Law of Sales*, 10 Scan. Stud. in L. 37, 60 (1966); Ziegel, *Parker Colloq.* 9–36, 9–38.

15. See UNCITRAL Digest Art. 74 para. 19; CISG Advisory Council Opinion No. 6, Calculation of Damages under CISG Art. 74 para. 3.8, *available at* http://www.cisg.law. pace.edu/cisg/CISG-AC-op6.html.

405 **B. Damages Caused by Defective Goods and by Delays in Delivery**

There remain cases where the buyer receives, keeps and uses goods that do not conform to the contract. The fact that the buyer retains the goods does not mean that their defects caused no damage. Machinery may fail to function properly; defective raw materials may cause production problems in the buyer's factory; goods purchased for resale may lead to complaints and claims by sub-purchasers. Similar problems may result from the late delivery of machinery or raw materials. For these cases, the primary rule is that of Article 74: The seller is responsible for "the loss ... suffered" by the buyer "as a consequence of the breach." *In the case of non-conforming goods, such damages can include the cost of repairing the lack of conformity[16] or the decrease in the goods' value resulting from the lack of conformity.[17] As has already been noted repeatedly, a showing of fault by the breaching party is not a prerequisite to the recovery of damages under the Convention.[18]*

If the buyer keeps non-conforming goods, it is responsible to the seller for the price. For discussion of whether such a buyer can set-off its damages due to the goods' non-conformity against the obligation for the price, see §444A infra.

406 **(1) Unpredictable Consequential Damages**

Buyers may use or resell defective goods in a wide variety of circumstances; in some circumstances the losses resulting from non-conformity of the goods may be of an unusual nature or unpredictably extreme. This possibility is dealt with in the second sentence

16. See Hans Stoll & Georg Gruber, Art. 74 para. 15, *in* Schlechtriem & Schwenzer, *CISG Commentary* (2nd English ed. 2005); UNCITRAL Digest Art. 74 para. 21; CISG Advisory Council Opinion No. 6, Calculation of Damages under CISG Art. 74 para. 3.2, *available at* http:// www.cisg.law.pace.edu/cisg/CISG-AC-op6.html.

17. See Hans Stoll & Georg Gruber, Art. 74 para. 15, *in* Schlechtriem & Schwenzer, *CISG Commentary* (2nd English ed. 2005); Flechtner, *Pittsburgh Symposium* 106; CISG Advisory Council Opinion No. 6, Calculation of Damages under CISG Art. 74 paras. 3.1 through 3.3, *available at* http://www.cisg.law.pace.edu/cisg/CISG-AC-op6.html.

18. See Hans Stoll & Georg Gruber, Art. 74 paras. 2, 8 & 36, *in* Schlechtriem & Schwenzer, *CISG Commentary* (2nd English ed. 2005).

of Article 74 which sets an outer limit — "the loss which the party in breach foresaw or ought to have foreseen at the time of the conclusion of the contract. . . ."[19] For example, suppose that the non-conformity (or delay in delivery) of a small item interrupts production in the buyer's factory. The seller, of course, is responsible to the buyer for breach of contract. But if the seller did not know and could not have foreseen at the time of contracting that a defect in the goods or a delay in delivery might cause damages of such magnitude as the shut-down of a factory, the above provision of Article 74 could provide a ground for limiting the recoverable damages.[20] *Both the type and the magnitude of the losses suffered by the aggrieved party may make them unforeseeable (and hence non-compensable) for purposes of Article 74.*[21]

407 **(a) Sources in Domestic Law.** This approach is well-known in the common-law world as the "foreseeability" or "improbability" test developed in the name of the 1854 English decision of Hadley v. Baxendale.[22]

The (U.S.A.) Uniform Commercial Code limits the buyer's damages by language derived from the *Hadley* tradition. Where the buyer accepts goods that are non-conforming he may recover "the loss resulting in the *ordinary course of events* from the seller's breach. . ." (§2-714(1)). The UCC also allows the buyer to recover "incidental" and "consequential" damages; the latter are defined (§2-715(2)) with a

---

19. For discussion of the rationale for the foreseeability requirement see Hans Stoll & Georg Gruber, Art. 74 paras. 13 & 38, *in* Schlechtriem & Schwenzer, *CISG Commentary* (2nd English ed. 2005).

20. For decisions addressing when losses are or are not foreseeable see UNCITRAL Digest Art. 74 paras. 33–34.

21. See Hans Stoll & Georg Gruber, Art. 74 para. 39, *in* Schlechtriem & Schwenzer, *CISG Commentary* (2nd English ed. 2005).

22. (1854) 9 Ex. 341, 156 Eng. Rep. 145, discussed in its historical setting in Danzig, 4 J. Legal Studies 249 (1975). See *Benjamin* §1277–1282; *Atiyah*, 417–418; *Farnsworth, Contracts* 873–881; *Bridge, Sale* 743–746; Murphey, 23 Geo. Wash. J. Int. L. & Econ. 415 (1989). Curiously, neither the Hadley judgment nor (U.K.) SGA (1893) explicitly states the rule in terms of "foreseeability", SGA 50(2), 51(2) and 53(2) all refer to "loss *directly and naturally* resulting in the ordinary course of events" from the breach. For a thorough review of rules in the common-law world and an analysis of civil law developments see *Treitel, Remedies (Int. Enc.)* §84 *et seq.* See also *Treitel, Remedies (1988)* 150–173; *Treitel, Contract*, 744–753; Nicholas, French Law of Contract 223–226 (1982).

"foreseeability" limitation that is similar to that of Article 74 of the Convention:[23]

A "foreseeability" limit is also well-known within the domain influenced by French law. The French Civil Code §1150 limits damages to those "which were foreseen or which could have been foreseen at the time of the contract", unless the breach was the result of "willfulness." Indeed, in the 1854 *Hadley* opinion, favorable reference was made to this rule of French law; the extent to which the English court relied on the French approach has been a subject for interesting but inconclusive speculation.[24]

Of course the fact that the foreseeability requirement of Article 74 has roots and analogues in domestic law does not mean the Convention's rule is the same as or even equivalent to any particular domestic foreseeability rule.[25] The assumption that the Convention and particular domestic law are the same conflicts with the international perspective mandated by the methodology of interpretation specified in Article 7(2), and tends to undermine the fundamental purpose of the Convention — to create uniform international sales rules. A U.S. decision that blithely equated the rule of Hadley v. Baxendale with the foreseeability requirement in Article 74 has been strongly and justifiably criticized.[26]

408 **(b) Foreseeable Damages: Lost Profits and Attorney Fees.** *A variety of issues concerning the recovery of Article 74 damages have arisen. A few (beyond those already discussed above) are addressed here.*

Article 74 expressly authorizes the recovery of damages for lost profits. There are various forms of lost profits: compare a "lost volume" seller's lost profits (discussed in §415 infra) with the profits an aggrieved buyer loses because it cannot resell goods or because it received non-conforming machinery that reduced the buyer's own

---

23. For case law under the UCC see *White & Summers* §10-4. See also 5 *Corbin* §§1007–1014.

24. For a careful analysis and critique of the use of German concepts in Scandinavia, see Hellner, The Limits of Contractual Damages in the Scandinavian Law of Sales 10 *Scan. Stud.* 37, 40–79; the author suggests, *inter alia*, wider judicial discretion to limit "consequential" damages. See also Cooke, Remoteness of Damage and Judicial Discretion, [1978] Camb. L.J. 288.

25. See Hans Stoll & Georg Gruber, Art. 74 paras. 34–35 & 37, *in* Schlechtriem & Schwenzer, *CISG Commentary* (2nd English ed. 2005).

26. See V. Susanne Cook, The U.N. Convention on Contracts for the International Sale of Goods: A Mandate to Abandon Legal Ethnocentricity, 16 J.L. & Com. 257, 258–259 (1997).

production. Lost profits, furthermore, can occur in an extraordinarily variety of situations. It is thus not surprising that damage claims for lost profits raise diverse and challenging questions. Can lost profits that are claimed be proven with sufficient certainty?[27] How should lost profits be calculated[28] — should the aggrieved party's fixed costs or overhead be considered?[29] Were claimed lost profits sufficiently fore-seeable at the time the contract was concluded? Could the aggrieved party have mitigated its loss of profits by reasonable measures, as provided in Article 77? In short, the fact that Article 74 expressly authorizes recovery of lost profits raises as many issues as it settles.

Another Article 74 damages issue is of particular interest to those litigating before U.S. courts: if a party successfully sues for breach under the Convention, can it recover the attorney fees incurred during the litigation as damages under Article 74?

Different domestic legal systems handle attorney fees differently. Most systems adopt a "loser-pays" approach under which a party found liable for breach of contract must compensate the aggrieved party for attorney fees the latter incurred.[30] The recovery of attorney costs under such domestic loser-pays rules, however, is often subject to significant limitations, pre-ordained fee schedules, or arbitrary formu-las, often (usually?) resulting in awards significantly less than the actual attorney fees incurred by the prevailing party.[31] Under the

27. See Hans Stoll & Georg Gruber, Art. 74 para. 22, *in* Schlechtriem & Schwenzer, *CISG Commentary* (2nd English ed. 2005); CISG Advisory Council Opinion No. 6, Calculation of Damages under CISG Art. 74 paras. 3.15 through 3.19, available at http:// www.cisg.law. pace.edu/cisg/CISG-AC-op6.html.

28. See CISG Advisory Council Opinion No. 6, Calculation of Damages under CISG Art. 74 paras. 3.12 through 3.14, *available at* http://www.cisg.law.pace.edu/cisg/CISG-AC-op6.html.

29. See Hans Stoll & Georg Gruber, Art. 74 para. 22, *in* Schlechtriem & Schwenzer, *CISG Commentary* (2nd English ed. 2005).

30. See, e.g., §91(1) of the German Code of Civil Procedure ("ZPO"); Chapter 18:1 and 18:8 of the Swedish Code of Judicial Procedures (the *Rattegangsbalk*); Article 696 & 695(7) of the French Code of Civil Procedure. For other examples, see *Joseph Lookofsky, Zapata Hermanos v. Hearthside Baking* [case commentary], 6 Vindobona J. Int'l Com. L. & Arb. 27, 27 n.10 (2002), *available at* http://cisgw3.law.pace.edu/cisg/biblio/lookofsky5.html. For general discussion of this point see John Y. Gotanda, *Awarding Costs and Attorneys' Fees in International Commercial Arbitrations*, 21 Mich. J. Int'l L. 1, 6–10 (1999).

31. See CISG Advisory Council Opinion No. 6, Calculation of Damages under CISG Art. 74 para. 5.4 n. 94, available at http://www.cisg.law.pace.edu/cisg/CISG-AC-op6.html; Harry M. Flechtner, *Recovering Attorneys' Fees as Damages under the U.N. Sales Convention (CISG): The Role of Case Law in the New International Commercial Practice, with Com-ments on* Zapata Hermanos v. Hearthside Baking, 22 Northwestern J. Int'l L. & Bus. 121, 151 (2002), *available at* http://www.cisg.law.pace.edu/cisg/biblio/flechtner4.html#87.

"American rule" applicable in the United States, in contrast, each party shoulders the costs of its own attorneys, win or lose, unless a statute or contract provision specifically provides otherwise.[32]

There is authority for awarding damages under Article 74 for the cost of attorneys employed to litigate a claim, on the footing that such costs are foreseeable losses caused by the breach.[33] *The more sensible and convincing view, however, is that this issue is beyond the scope of the Convention, and is governed by domestic law.*[34]

To the editor of this edition, who (along with Professor Joseph Lookofsky) has weighed in on the issue several times,[35] *leaving the recovery of attorney fees to domestic law is the correct approach: it not*

32. See Harry M. Flechtner, Recovering Attorneys' Fees as Damages under the U.N. Sales Convention (CISG): The Role of Case Law in the New International Commercial Practice, with Comments on *Zapata Hermanos v. Hearthside Baking*, 22 Northwestern J. Int'l L. & Bus. 121, 134–137 (2002), available at http://www.cisg.law.pace.edu/cisg/biblio/flechtner4. html#87.

33. For decisions on this issue see UNCITRAL Digest Art. 74 para. 26. For analysis of decisions awarding attorney fees see Harry M. Flechtner, *Recovering Attorneys' Fees as Damages under the U.N. Sales Convention (CISG): The Role of Case Law in the New International Commercial Practice, with Comments on* Zapata Hermanos v. Hearthside Baking, 22 Northwestern J. Int'l L. & Bus. 121, 126–133 (2002), *available at* http://www.cisg.law.pace.edu/cisg/biblio/flechtner4.html#87. For other authority supporting the proposition that damages for litigation attorney fees incurred by a party are recoverable under Art. 74 see, e.g., John Felemegas, *An Interpretation of Article 74 CISG by the U.S. Circuit Court of Appeals*, 15 Pace Int'l L. Rev. 91 (2003), *available at* http://www.cisg.law. pace.edu/cisg/biblio/felemegas4.html; Bruno Zeller, *Interpretation of Article 74 — Zapata Hermanos v. Hearthside Baking — Where Next?*, 2004 Nordic J. Comm. L. 1, *available at* http://www.njcl.fi/1_2004/commentary1.pdf; Keith William Diener, *Recovering Attorneys' Fees under CISG: An Interpretation of Article 74*, 2008 Nordic J. Comm. L. (Issue 1), *available at* http://www.njcl.fi/1_2008/article3.pdf.

34. See, e.g., Hans Stoll & Georg Gruber, Art. 74 para. 20, *in* Schlechtriem & Schwenzer, CISG Commentary (2nd English ed. 2005); Joseph Lookofsky, *Zapata Hermanos v. Hearthside Baking [case commentary]*, 6 Vindobona J. Int'l Com. L. & Arb. 27 (2002), *available at* http:// cisgw3.law.pace.edu/cisg/biblio/lookofsky5.html; CISG Advisory Council Opinion No. 6, Calculation of Damages under CISG Art. 74 paras. 5.1 through 5.4, *available at* http:// www.cisg.law.pace.edu/cisg/CISG-AC-op6.html. For case law in accord see UNCITRAL Digest Art. 74 para. 26.

35. Harry M. Flechtner, Recovering Attorneys' Fees as Damages under the U.N. Sales Convention (CISG): The Role of Case Law in the New International Commercial Practice, with Comments on Zapata Hermanos v. Hearthside Baking, 22 Northwestern J. Int'l L. & Bus. 121, 126–133 (2002), available at http://www.cisg.law.pace.edu/cisg/biblio/flechtner4. html#87; Joseph Lookofsky & Harry Flechtner, Viva Zapata! American Procedure and CISG Substance in a U.S. Circuit Court of Appeal, 7 Vindobona J. Int'l Com. L. & Arb. 93 (2003); Joseph Lookofsky & Harry Flechtner, Zapata Retold: Attorneys' Fees Are (Still) Not Governed by the CISG, 26 J.L. & Com. 1 (2006–07).

only honors the likely intention of the Convention's drafters, but it also makes the most sense from a policy standpoint. There is nothing in the Convention's travaux préparatoires that indicates the drafters intended Article 74 to address the recovery of attorney fees, or that the drafters even thought about the issue at all. If they did intend to provide for the recovery of attorney fees they certainly went about it an odd, frankly unsupportable way: under Article 74, damages are recoverable only for losses due to a breach, so that only a prevailing claimant who proved it had suffered a breach could recover attorney fees; a party who successfully defended against a claim of breach would have no basis for claiming its attorneys costs under Article 74.[36] Such a bizarre and unfairly one-sided result confirms that Article 74 was never intended to cover the issue of attorney fees.

The likely explanation for why the drafters never contemplated that attorney fees might be covered by Article 74 is that they thought of the recovery of attorney costs as a procedural matter beyond the scope of the substantive sales rules of the Convention; after all the matter is, in domestic law, generally treated as an aspect of procedure.[37] Regulation of the recovery of attorney fees is embedded

36. See, e.g., Hans Stoll & Georg Gruber, Art. 74 para. 20, in Schlechtriem & Schwenzer, CISG Commentary (2nd English ed. 2005); Harry M. Flechtner, Recovering Attorneys' Fees as Damages under the U.N. Sales Convention (CISG): The Role of Case Law in the New International Commercial Practice, with Comments on Zapata Hermanos v. Hearthside Baking, 22 Northwestern J. Int'l L. & Bus. 121, 151 (2002), available at http://www.cisg.law.pace.edu/ cisg/biblio/flechtner4.html#87; CISG Advisory Council Opinion No. 6, Calculation of Damages under CISG Art. 74 para. 5.4, available at http://www.cisg.law.pace.edu/cisg/CISG-AC-op6.html. But see John Felemegas, An Interpretation of Art. 74 CISG by the U.S. Circuit Court of Appeals, 15 Pace Int'l L. Rev. 91, 127 (2003), available at http://www.cisg.law.pace.edu/cisg/biblio/felemegas4.html; Bruno Zeller, Interpretation of Art. 74 — Zapata Hermanos v. Hearthside Baking — Where Next?, 2004 Nordic J. Comm. L. 1, 10, available at http://www.njcl.fi/1_2004/commentary1.pdf.

37. See Harry M. Flechtner, Recovering Attorneys' Fees as Damages under the U.N. Sales Convention (CISG): The Role of Case Law in the New International Commercial Practice, with Comments on Zapata Hermanos v. Hearthside Baking, 22 Northwestern J. Int'l L. & Bus. 121, 153 (2002), available at http://www.cisg.law.pace.edu/cisg/biblio/flechtner4. html#87. Use of the distinction between procedure and substance to determine the scope of the CISG has been criticized. See, e.g., CISG Advisory Council Opinion No. 6, Calculation of Damages under CISG Art. 74 para. 5.2, available at http://www.cisg.law.pace.edu/ cisg/CISG-AC-op6.html. For a response to this criticism see Joseph Lookofsky & Harry Flechtner, Zapata Retold: Attorneys' Fees Are (Still) Not Governed by the CISG, 26 J.L. & Com. 1 (2006–2007).

in and shaped by the procedural system in which the attorney fees are incurred. The U.S. system, with its "American rule" approach to attorney fees, has features that may not fit well with a generalized loser-pays approach, including a tolerance for contingent fees and a distinctly prominent role for private attorneys, often involving functions that in other systems would be considered public (and, therefore, publicly-funded).[38]

In short, the recovery of compensation for the costs of attorneys employed in litigating claims under the Convention should be treated as a question beyond the scope of the Convention, to be handled pursuant to applicable to domestic law. This appears to be exactly the approach adopted to date in virtually all cases.[39]

408.1   Contractual Remedies; Liquidated Damages and Penalties

Article 74 and the other remedy provisions of the Convention are subject to the rule of Article 6 permitting the parties to "derogate from or vary the effect of any of [the Convention's] provisions." The parties can, therefore, shape by agreement the remedies they wish to apply to their transaction. For example, they can agree to exclude liability for specified categories of damages, such as consequential damages, or to provide for an exclusive non-alternative remedy such as repair or replacement of defective goods or parts.[40] *Of course care must be taken to draft such clauses with the Convention's particular substance and terminology in mind.*[41] *Because the Convention does not govern validity issues, furthermore (see Article 4(a), §§64–69 supra), domestic rules going to the validity of such clauses remain applicable.*[42]

---

38. See Ronald A. Brand, *Private Law and Public Regulation in U.S. Courts*, 2 CILE Studies, Private Law, Private International Law, and Judicial Cooperation in the EU-US Relationship 115 (Ronald A. Brand ed., 2005).

39. See Harry M. Flechtner, Recovering Attorneys' Fees as Damages under the U.N. Sales Convention (CISG): The Role of Case Law in the New International Commercial Practice, with Comments on Zapata Hermanos v. Hearthside Baking, 22 Northwestern J. Int'l L. & Bus. 121, 152 (2002), available at http://www.cisg.law.pace.edu/cisg/biblio/flechtner4. html#87.

40. See Hans Stoll & Georg Gruber, Art. 74 paras. 48 & 50, *in* Schlechtriem & Schwenzer, *CISG Commentary* (2nd English ed. 2005); UNCITRAL Digest Art. 74 para. 4.

41. *See* Drafting Contracts Under the CISG (4 CILE Studies) (Harry M. Flechtner, Ronald A. Brand, Mark S. Walter, eds., 2008), in particular the "Sample Agreement of Installment Sale and Purchase" (pp. 7 *ff*).

42. See Hans Stoll & Georg Gruber, Art. 74 para. 50, *in* Schlechtriem & Schwenzer, *CISG Commentary* (2nd English ed. 2005); UNCITRAL Digest Art. 74 para. 4.

The parties' power under Article 6 to derogate from or vary the Convention's remedy provisions obviously extends to contract clauses specifying ("liquidating") damages.[43] There can be many advantages to a well-drafted liquidated damages provision, including minimizing or avoiding difficulties in applying Article 74.[44] *Just as with other contractual remedy provisions, of course, liquidated damages clauses are subject to the validity rules of applicable domestic law.*[45] *Where under private international law (PIL) rules the law of a U.S. state (other than Louisiana) governs questions not governed by the Convention, for example, U.C.C. §2-718(1) would be applicable; it declares that "a term fixing unreasonably large liquidated damages is void as a penalty." Because this approach may differ from that in other domestic laws, the result may be distinctly non-uniform treatment of liquidated damages clauses in transactions governed by the Convention — but that is the inevitable result of leaving validity rules out of the unifying scope of the Convention.*

43. See Hans Stoll & Georg Gruber, Art. 74 paras. 48 & 49, *in* Schlechtriem & Schwenzer, *CISG Commentary* (2nd English ed. 2005); UNCITRAL Digest Art. 74 para. 4.
44. See Kritzer Manual Ch. 6.
45. See Hans Stoll & Georg Gruber, Art. 74 para. 50, *in* Schlechtriem & Schwenzer, *CISG Commentary* (2nd English ed. 2005); UNCITRAL Digest Art. 74 para. 4.

Articles 75 and 76.
Measurement of Damages When
Contract is Avoided

409   Articles 75 and 76 state alternative methods for measuring damages that may be recovered by a seller or buyer who avoids the contract. As we have seen (Arts. 49 and 64, *supra* at §301 and §353), the typical settings for avoidance are these: (a) The seller fails to deliver the goods or delivers seriously defective goods; (b) The buyer fails to pay the price. In these cases the aggrieved party may free itself from duties under the contract by notifying the other party that the contract is avoided (Arts. 26, 81). Thereupon an aggrieved buyer need not accept goods and must return goods that it has received, and an aggrieved seller need not deliver goods to the buyer.[1]

     The Convention's alternative methods for measuring the damages upon avoidance (Arts. 75 and 76) need to be considered together. As we shall see, Article 75 bases damages on a repurchase by the buyer or a resale by the seller, while Article 76 looks to the "current" (or market[2]) price for the goods in question.

410   A. Damages Established by Substitute Transaction: Article 75

Article 75[3]

If the contract is avoided and if, in a reasonable manner and within a reasonable time after avoidance, the buyer has bought goods in replacement or the seller has resold the goods, the party claiming damages may recover the difference between the contract price and the price in the substitute transaction as well as any further damages recoverable under Article 74.

1. As we have seen, avoidance is also possible in more specialized situations. See Art. 72; (anticipatory breach) and Art. 73 (breach with respect to an instalment). For discussion of measuring damages when a contract has been avoided pursuant to Art. 72 see Hans Stoll & Georg Gruber, Art. 76 para. 11, *in* Schlechtriem & Schwenzer, *CISG Commentary* (2nd English ed. 2005).
2. See Hans Stoll & Georg Gruber, Art. 76 para. 4, *in* Schlechtriem & Schwenzer, *CISG Commentary* (2nd English ed. 2005).
3. Article 75 is the same as Art. 71 of the 1978 Draft and is similar to ULIS 85.

The crucial feature of Article 75 is this: Resale by an aggrieved seller or repurchase by an aggrieved buyer *establishes* damages; the aggrieved party "may recover *the difference* between the contract price and the price in the substitute transaction"[4] and need not prove the "current" or market price for the goods.[5] Making (and identifying) a substitute transaction will be especially important when the goods have been specially manufactured or for some other reason are so unique that it will be difficult to establish a "current" price under Article 76.[6] Such "concrete" methods of damage-assessment are available under the domestic laws of many States.[7]

410.1   ## (1) Identifying the Substitute Transaction

If the aggrieved party is constantly in the market for goods of the type in question it may be difficult to determine which purchase or sale was the substitute transaction under Article 75.[8] Since avoidance calls for a declaration made by notice to the other party (Art. 26, §187 *supra*) the aggrieved party may avoid dispute by including in the notice a statement of plans for a substitute transaction, although the Convention does not require that.[9] If this statement is not provided, reference to the aggrieved party's first purchase or sale of comparable goods following

---

4. That is, if an aggrieved buyer pays *more* than the contract price in the substitute transaction, the buyer can recover the difference under Art. 75; and if an aggrieved seller resells the goods for less than the contract price in the substitute transaction, the seller can recover the difference under Art. 75.

5. Prices that were available on the market may be relevant if a dispute arises as to whether the substitute transaction was effected "in a reasonable manner."

6. For situations illustrating difficulties in establishing a current price for the goods see UNCITRAL Digest Art. 76 para. 8.

7. See Hans Stoll & Georg Gruber, Art. 75 para. 1, *in* Schlechtriem & Schwenzer, *CISG Commentary* (2nd English ed. 2005); UNCITRAL Digest Art. 74 para. 9; *Treitel, Remedies (Int. Enc.)* §69; *Treitel, Remedies* (1988) 115–122; U.C.C. (U.S.A.) §§2-706 & 2-712. A "concrete" method based on actual loss is distinguished from an "abstract" measure based on "current" (market) price (see Art. 76 of the Convention). In some systems, the "concrete" approach (*e.g.*, the buyer acquires substitute goods at the expense of the seller) is regarded as a species of specific enforcement.

8. See Hans Stoll & Georg Gruber, Art. 75 para. 3, *in* Schlechtriem & Schwenzer, *CISG Commentary* (2nd English ed. 2005); *B-B Commentary* 554.

9. See Hans Stoll & Georg Gruber, Art. 75 para. 3, *in* Schlechtriem & Schwenzer, *CISG Commentary* (2nd English ed. 2005).

the notice of avoidance seems consistent with the concern to avoid delay, as shown by the "reasonable time" requirement of Article 75.[10]

410.2   **Requirements for a Qualifying Substitute Transaction**   *To qualify as the yardstick for measuring Article 75 damages, a substitute transaction must have been made "in a reasonable manner and within a reasonable time after avoidance." The evident purpose of these requirements is to ensure that the substitute transaction provides both an appropriate and a fair gauge of the aggrieved party's loss. A substantial difference (in a direction that would increase damages) between the price in the substitute transaction and a readily-available contemporaneous market price for the same goods suggests that the substitute transaction may not have been made in a reasonable manner.[11] To accurately measure the aggrieved party's loss, of course, the goods in the substitute contract must be reasonably equivalent to those in the original (breached) contract, and the terms of the two contracts should be comparable.[12] The requirement that the substitute transaction be entered into "within a reasonable time after avoidance" guards against the possibility that delay could allow the aggrieved party to speculate on market changes at the breaching party's expense (cf. §412 infra), although it must be applied in a fashion that permits the aggrieved party a reasonable opportunity to discover and negotiate with alternative suppliers or buyers.[13]*

*   The requirement that a substitute purchase be made "within a reasonable time after avoidance" has been interpreted to disqualify, for Article 75 purposes, replacement sales or purchases made before a contract was declared avoided;[14] where such pre-avoidance substitute transactions are concluded, presumably, the avoiding party is relegated to current price damages under Article 76, to which it is entitled*

---

10. *Compare* Hans Stoll & Georg Gruber, Art. 76 para. 2, *in* Schlechtriem & Schwenzer, *CISG Commentary* (2nd English ed. 2005); UNCITRAL Digest Art. 75 para. 8.

11. See UNCITRAL Digest Art. 75 paras. 9–10; Hans Stoll & Georg Gruber, Art. 75 para. 6, *in* Schlechtriem & Schwenzer, *CISG Commentary* (2nd English ed. 2005).

12. Hans Stoll & Georg Gruber, Art. 75 para. 6, *in* Schlechtriem & Schwenzer, *CISG Commentary* (2nd English ed. 2005).

13. For discussion of the "reasonable time" requirement see Hans Stoll & Georg Gruber, Art. 75 para. 7, *in* Schlechtriem & Schwenzer, *CISG Commentary* (2nd English ed. 2005); UNCITRAL Digest Art. 75 para. 11.

14. See Hans Stoll & Georg Gruber, Art. 75 para. 5, *in* Schlechtriem & Schwenzer, *CISG Commentary* (2nd English ed. 2005); UNCITRAL Digest Art. 75 para. 11; UNCITRAL Digest Art. 75 para. 7.

since it "has not made a purchase or resale under Article 75." Normally, of course, a substitute transaction will be entered into after notice of avoidance is given; the fact that a transaction occurred before avoidance will often suggest that it was not actually intended as a substitute for the avoided contract.[15] Where a reasonable transaction clearly was intended as a substitute for a subsequently avoided contract, however, it seems unnecessarily technical and contrary to the basic principles of the Convention to prevent the avoiding party from using the transaction to measure its damages.

To take an extreme example, suppose an aggrieved buyer is about to dispatch notice of avoidance when it receives a call from another supplier offering a reasonable deal on the very goods it will have to replace. If the buyer accepts the offer on the phone before dispatching the avoidance notice, should that mean the substitute purchase must be ignored in calculating the buyer's damages? Certainly that makes no sense if the price in the substitute purchase is lower than the "current price" on which damages would be calculated under Article 76: it violates a basic principle of the Convention to calculate damages in a way that puts the buyer in a better position than full performance would have. And if Article 76 damages are lower than damages measured by the pre-avoidance substitute purchase it is unjustifiably (indeed, inexplicably) punitive to deny the buyer full protection of its expectation interest because it sensibly and in good faith accepted the offer of replacement goods before declaring the original contract avoided.

A sensible result is possible even if pre-avoidance substitute transactions do not qualify under Article 75: to the extent damages awardable under Article 76 will not fully protect the aggrieved party's expectation as measured by a reasonable pre-avoidance substitute transaction, the necessary further damages can be awarded under Article 74. There is, in fact, authority for awarding damages measured by the difference between the price in a substitute transaction and the contract price under Article 74.[16] Supplementing Article 75 in this fashion makes perfect sense: the underlying principle of all the Convention's damages provisions is the same — to put the aggrieved party in the position it would have been in had the breaching party performed properly.

15. See Delchi Carrier, S.p.A. v. Rotorex Corp., 1994 WL 495787 at *5 (U.S. Dist. Ct. N. Dist. N.Y. 9 September 1994), *available at* cisgw3.law.pace.edu/cases/940909u1.html.

16. See UNCITRAL Digest Art. 75 para. 3; CISG Advisory Council Opinion No. 6, Calculation of Damages under CISG Art. 74 para. 8.1 n. 94, *available at* http://www.cisg.law. pace.edu/cisg/ CISG-AC-op6.html.

411 B. Damages Based on Current Price: Article 76

If the aggrieved party does not fix its damages under Article 75 by a substitute transaction damages may be based on "current" (market) price:

Article 76

(1) If the contract is avoided and there is a current price for the goods, the party claiming damages may, if he has not made a purchase or resale under article 75, recover the difference between the price fixed by the contract and the current price at the time of avoidance as well as any further damages recoverable under article 74. If, however, the party claiming damages has avoided the contract after taking over the goods, the current price at the time of such taking over shall be applied instead of the current price at the time of avoidance.

(2) For the purposes of the preceding paragraph, the current price is the price prevailing at the place where delivery of the goods should have been made or, if there is no current price at that place, the price at such other place as serves as a reasonable substitute, making due allowance for differences in the cost of transporting the goods.

412 (1) The Reference-Point as to Time

When an aggrieved party avoids the contract prior to or at the time the goods are handed over, damages are based on "the current price at the *time of avoidance*" (Para. (1) of Art. 76). This reference-point as to the time for measuring damages was the product of changes made in the closing days of the Diplomatic Conference.[17] Under the UNCITRAL draft, damages were based on the current price at the time the aggrieved party "first had the right to declare the contract avoided" — a point of reference that many delegates feared would be subject to dispute. Consequently, this language was replaced by a reference to "the time

17. *Cf.* ULIS 84. Art. 76 was based on Art. 72 of the 1978 Draft. However, at the Diplomatic Conference changes of substance were made in para. (1): A reference to the time the aggrieved party "first had the *right to declare* the contract avoided" was replaced by "the time of avoidance" and the second sentence was added. Proposals to amend draft Art. 72 were rejected by the First Committee. *O.R.* 132–133, 394–396, *Docy. Hist.* 704–705, 615–617. Later, in Plenary, a modified amendment, leading to the present text, was approved. *O.R.* 172, 222–223, *Docy. Hist.* 730, 757–758.

of avoidance." *Under Article 26, the time of avoidance is when the aggrieved party makes a "declaration of avoidance . . . by notice to the other party."*[18] *The principles adopted in Article 27 for communications under Part III of the Convention suggests that avoidance occurs upon dispatch of such notice by proper means, rather than when the notice is received.*

Article 76 damages are measured by reference to the current price at the time of avoidance in the following situations: (a) The contract is avoided based on anticipatory breach (Art. 72); (b) The seller avoids the contract because the buyer fails to pay (or make the required arrangements for payment, for example, by establishing a letter of credit) prior to or at the time for delivery; (c) The buyer avoids the contract on rejecting a tender of seriously defective goods.

(a) Avoidance after Taking Over the Goods.

Under the second sentence of paragraph (1) damages are not based on the price at the time of avoidance when a party avoids the contract "after taking over the goods." In these cases the reference-point is the current price at a date prior to avoidance — when the goods were taken over.

(i) Avoidance by the Buyer.

At the Diplomatic Conference there was concern that measurement of Article 76 damages at the time of avoidance — a reference point that (as noted above) had been adopted in the final days of the Conference — might be subject to abuse. Specifically, aggrieved parties might be tempted to delay the decision to avoid in order to take advantage of changes in the market price: *if the market price dropped, an aggrieved buyer could then avoid and acquire the goods from another source for less than the contract price, ending up in a better position than if the seller had performed; if the market price rose, the buyer could then avoid and recover enhanced damages because of the higher current price at the time of avoidance. Similar possibilities exist for aggrieved sellers. The time limits on the power to avoid imposed by Articles 49(2) and 64(2) are not sufficient to prevent such unfair speculation at the expense of the breaching party.* To limit the potential for abuse, a second sentence was added to Article 76(1): "If, however, the party claiming damages has avoided the contract *after taking over the goods*" damages would be based on the current price "at the time of such *taking over*" — a definite earlier time not subject to

---

18. See Hans Stoll & Georg Gruber, Art. 76 para. 11, *in* Schlechtriem & Schwenzer, *CISG Commentary* (2nd English ed. 2005).

unilateral postponement.[19] In cases of avoidance by buyers who have received goods this provision seems clear.

(ii) Avoidance by the Seller. The special time for measuring damages provided by the second sentence of Article 76(1) will seldom apply to sellers: sellers seldom avoid the contract "*after* taking over the goods."[20] Avoidance by sellers usually occurs while the seller still has possession of the goods when the buyer commits a fundamental breach by failing to pay or (in more cases) failing to establish a letter of credit. If a seller delivers goods to the buyer on credit (e.g., payment due 60 days after delivery) the buyer's failure to pay will empower a seller to avoid the contract (Art. 64(1)) and "claim restitution" of the goods (Art. 81(2), §444, *infra*). However, in these cases the second sentence does not apply since avoidance will occur *before* rather than "*after* taking over the goods." In all these cases damages under Article 76 would be based on "the current price at the *time of avoidance*."[21]

413 (2) The Reference-Point as to Place

Paragraph (2) of Article 76 points to "the price prevailing at the place where *delivery of the goods* should have been made." This invokes the rules on delivery in Article 31, *supra* at §207. In the most common international sale this is the place for "handing the goods over to the first carrier for transmission to the buyer." This is a convenient place for a seller to measure market price when the buyer's repudiation or breach prevents shipment; on the other hand, when a buyer rightfully rejects ("avoids the contract") after arrival and inspection (Arts. 38, 58) it may be awkward and inadequate for the buyer to prove damages based on market levels in the seller's country.[22] Fortunately, in most situations the

---

19. For discussion of the possibility for abusive speculation where avoidance does not occur "after taking over the goods," see Hans Stoll & Georg Gruber, Art. 76 para. 12, *in* Schlechtriem & Schwenzer, *CISG Commentary* (2nd English ed. 2005).

20. *Compare* Hans Stoll & Georg Gruber, Art. 76 para. 11, *in* Schlechtriem & Schwenzer, *CISG Commentary* (2nd English ed. 2005) ("This provision applies to buyers only").

21. Flechtner, *Pittsburgh Symposium* 99 n. 213, notes that the second sentence could apply to a seller whose goods were wrongfully rejected by the buyer and who took over the goods before avoiding the contract. Favoring damage measurement as of the time of avoidance: Hellner, 22 *Scan. Stud.* 53, 74–75.

22. See Hans Stoll & Georg Gruber, Art. 76 para. 9, *in* Schlechtriem & Schwenzer, *CISG Commentary* (2nd English ed. 2005).

injured party can avoid these problems by making a substitute purchase or a resale under Article 75.

If there is no current price at the place for delivery of the goods, Article 76 damages are calculated by reference to "the price at such other place as serves as a reasonable substitute, making due allowance for differences in the cost of transporting the goods."[23] This provision can ease the evidentiary burden of a party claiming Article 76 damages, and gives a decision-maker necessary flexibility in identifying an appropriate yardstick for measuring an avoiding party's loss. It has not, however, proven of great importance in litigation.

414   C. Election Between Articles 75 and 76

If an aggrieved party does not make a substitute transaction under Article 75 only the "current" (or market) price formula of Article 76 will be available. And the "current" price formula of Article 76 is applicable only if the aggrieved party "has not made a purchase or resale under Article 75" — a rule that was designed to add certainty and prevent abuse.[24]

Under Article 75 the substitute transaction determines damages only if it is effected "in a reasonable manner and within a reasonable time after avoidance." (See §410.2 *supra*.) If the aggrieved party's substitute transaction fails to meet these standards it may be appropriate to adjust the price received to remove the effect of the anomaly.[25] If an adjustment is not feasible damages may be based on the "current price" formula of Article 76; there is no reason to suppose that an aggrieved party who makes an unsuccessful attempt to comply with Article 75 completely loses the right to recover damages.[26]

---

23. For further discussion of this provision see Hans Stoll & Georg Gruber, Art. 76 para. 10, *in* Schlechtriem & Schwenzer, *CISG Commentary* (2nd English ed. 2005). *Compare* U.C.C. (U.S.A.) §2-723(2), which contains a similar rule.

24. See Hans Stoll & Georg Gruber, Art. 75 para. 12 & Art. 76 para. 2, *in* Schlechtriem & Schwenzer, *CISG Commentary* (2nd English ed. 2005); UNCITRAL Digest Art. 75 para. 2 & Art. 76 para. 2.

25. *Cf.* UNCITRAL Digest Art. 75 para. 14 (reduction of Art. 75 damages for aggrieved party's failure to mitigate).

26. See UNCITRAL Digest Art. 75 para. 2. *Compare* Hans Stoll & Georg Gruber, Art. 75 para. 9, *in* Schlechtriem & Schwenzer, *CISG Commentary* (2nd English ed. 2005).

415 D. Recovery of Further Damages: Loss of Profit

Both Article 75 and Article 76 provide that the aggrieved party may also recover "any further damages recoverable under Article 74," that is, "the loss, *including loss of profit* . . . suffered . . . as a consequence of the breach." *Such further damages encompass what, under U.S. law, would be classified as "consequential" and "incidental" damages.*[27] *Such damages might include, for example, compensation for profits that an avoiding buyer expected to earn reselling or using the goods*[28] *— but only if the buyer could not have avoided the loss by reasonable actions, such an entering into a substitute transaction to procure replacement goods (see Article 77).*[29]

A seller's volume of output may be reduced because of the buyer's repudiation, and a buyer's volume of production may be reduced because of the seller's wrongful failure to supply necessary materials. In these situations the reduced level of production may cause loss for which Articles 75 and 76 provide no redress. This problem does not arise when there is ample demand to keep the seller's production at full capacity or when the buyer can procure available supplies elsewhere. In other situations breach of contract may lead to loss of volume which may cause acute loss even when there is little or no change in the level of prices — a setting in which Articles 75 and 76, alone, would not provide adequate redress. *In such circumstances an aggrieved party should be able to recover damages measured by the profits lost because of reduced volume.*[30] Determining the amount of loss of profit may call for accounting procedures to ascertain the contribution that due performance of the contract would have made to the overhead costs of the aggrieved party.[31]

27. See U.C.C. (U.S.A.) §§2-710 & 2-715, defining incidental and consequential damages.
28. See Hans Stoll & Georg Gruber, Art. 75 para. 10 & Art. 76 para. 13, *in* Schlechtriem & Schwenzer, *CISG Commentary* (2nd English ed. 2005); UNCITRAL Digest Art. 75 para. 13.
29. See Hans Stoll & Georg Gruber, Art. 75 para. 11 & Art. 76 para. 13, *in* Schlechtriem & Schwenzer, *CISG Commentary* (2nd English ed. 2005).
30. See UNCITRAL Digest Art. 74 para. 31 & Art. 77 para. 15; CISG Advisory Council Opinion No. 6, Calculation of Damages under CISG Art. 74 paras. 3.20 through 3.22, *available at* http://www.cisg.law.pace.edu/cisg/CISG-AC-op6.html. *Compare* Hans Stoll & Georg Gruber, Art. 75 para. 11 & Art. 76 paras. 2 & 13, *in* Schlechtriem & Schwenzer, *CISG Commentary* (2nd English ed. 2005).
31. See Hans Stoll & Georg Gruber, Art. 74 para. 22, *in* Schlechtriem & Schwenzer, *CISG Commentary* (2nd English ed. 2005).

Article 77.
Mitigation of Damages

416   This article in some situations modifies the remedies provided by other provisions of the Convention.

Article 77[1]

A party who relies on a breach of contract must take such measures as are reasonable in the circumstances to mitigate the loss, including loss of profit, resulting from the breach. If he fails to take such measures, the party in breach may claim a reduction in the damages in the amount by which the loss should have been mitigated.

417 ## A. Varying Concepts of Domestic Law

The principle that a party must mitigate loss that reasonably can be avoided is generally recognized in domestic laws,[2] but is expressed in different ways and is applied with varying degrees of emphasis. Many codes do not explicitly speak of a "duty" to "mitigate" loss. Instead, statutory language that a party is responsible for the damage it "causes" often provides a basis for concluding that some of the damage was caused by the plaintiff rather than the party in breach. Similarly, some systems limit the plaintiff's recovery by principles akin to what other legal systems call contributory negligence — for example, the French doctrine of *faute de la victime*.[3]

As we have seen, in common-law systems one who breaks a contract is responsible for damages without regard to "fault" or "negligence"; in this setting there seems to be a tendency to speak (perhaps imprecisely) of the aggrieved party's "duty" to mitigate loss. Under the Convention, a party is responsible for non-performance of the contract without regard to fault (Arts. 30, 45(1)(b), 53, 61(1)(b); *cf.* Art. 79); consequently, it is not surprising that the Convention states, with some emphasis, that the

---

1. This article is the same as Art. 73 of the 1978 Draft and is substantially the same as ULIS 88. References to the legislative history appear in §419.3, *infra*.
2. See Hans Stoll & Georg Gruber, Art. 77 para. 1, *in* Schlechtriem & Schwenzer, *CISG Commentary* (2nd English ed. 2005).
3. See Treitel, Remedies (1988) 179.

other party "must take" measures to "mitigate the loss . . . resulting from the breach."[4]

Mitigation problems arise in a wide variety of circumstances. In Part B we shall consider mitigation by an aggrieved party (Party A) following failure of performance by the other party (Party X) — a seller's non-delivery, or the delivery of seriously defective goods, or a buyer's failure to receive or pay for goods. In Part C we shall examine the more complex problems of mitigation that arise prior to the time when performance becomes due, as when X repudiates the contract.

418   B. Mitigation following Failure of Performance

When breach by X leads to avoidance by A, Articles 75 and 76, *supra* at §409, restrict the time as of when A's damages may be measured. Resale or repurchase by A (Art. 75) must occur "within a reasonable time after avoidance"; the "current price" (Art. 76) must be ascertained as of the "time of avoidance" or (in some circumstances) at the time of "taking over" the goods. These restrictions prevent an avoiding seller from shifting to the buyer the loss resulting from a subsequent drop in the market price; similarly, an avoiding buyer may not shift a subsequent rise in price to the seller. Thus, claims based on Articles 75 or 76 seldom raise "mitigation" problems under Article 77.

Article 77, enunciating a duty to mitigate loss, becomes important when A relies on the general rule (Art. 74) that damages include loss suffered "as a consequence of the breach." For example, suppose seller X fails to deliver raw materials for use in the buyer A's factory and A fails to purchase substitute materials that are available on the market, with the result that A's production is interrupted. Jurists familiar with the "causation" approach (§417, *supra*) might find it more natural to conclude that Article 74 would suffice: the shut-down by buyer A was a "consequence" of A's conduct rather than X's breach; the explicit mitigation principle in Article 77 strengthens results that some could reach by another route. (See §415 *supra*.) Thus, buyer A could face either the

---

4. *Treitel, Remedies (Int. Enc.)* §§102–106 and *Treitel, Remedies (1988)* 179–192 give an illuminating comparison of the approaches of different legal systems. For discussion of English law see Schmitthoff, The Duty to Mitigate, 1961; J. Bus. L. 361; *Benjamin* §§1283–1286; *Treitel, Contract* 754–758. For U.S.A. rules see UCC 2-704(2), 2-715(2)(a); *White & Summers* §6-7, p. 285, §7-15, §10-4, pp. 451–453; *Farnsworth, Contracts* 858–873.

"causation" approach or the mitigation principle when defective materials or machinery cause "consequential" damages.[5]

419   ## C. Mitigation prior to Date for Performance

In Part B we examined the relatively simple mitigation problems that faced Party A following seriously defective performance by Party X. We now turn to the more complex problems that arise when difficulty, such as repudiation by X, occurs prior to the time for performance. These problems will be introduced in two commercial settings: (1) Goods purchased for resale and (2) Materials needed for production. Perhaps this discussion will help to distinguish these questions:

I. Must an aggrieved party (A) "accept repudiation" by X? In other words does X's repudiation require A to declare the contract avoided and thereupon take action to establish damages? See Example 77A, §419.1, *infra*.

II. Are there situations in which Article 77 requires A to take steps to mitigate loss prior to the date for performance? See Example 77B, §419.2, *infra*.

419.1   ## (1) Goods Purchased for Resale

Example 77A. On June 1, A and X made a contract for A to sell and deliver to X on August 1 1,000 bales of cotton at $50 per bale. Both A and X were merchants engaged in the purchase and resale of cotton. Shortly after June 1 cotton prices fell and on July 1, when the market price was $40 per bale, buyer X repudiated the contract and requested A to resell the cotton before the market could decline further. A replied that A expected X to receive and pay for the cotton in accordance with the contract; X thereupon repeated its repudiation. By August 1, the agreed delivery date, the price had fallen to $30; X again refused to receive and pay for the goods. A thereupon declared the contract avoided, resold the goods for $30 per bale ($30,000) and claimed damages from X of $20,000 ($50,000–$30,000). X contended that on July 1, when X repudiated, A should have mitigated loss by selling the cotton at $40, a step that would have reduced damages from $20,000 to $10,000.

5. For discussion of substitute transactions as a means to mitigate damages see Hans Stoll & Georg Gruber, Art. 75 para. 11, Art. 76 para. 13 & Art. 77 para. 9, *in* Schlechtriem & Schwenzer, *CISG Commentary* (2nd English ed. 2005); UNCITRAL Digest Art. 77 para. 8.

The argument for mitigation should be rejected.

Under Article 72(1) (§§395–397, *supra*), on repudiation by one party (X) "the other party *may* declare the contract avoided"; see also CISG 49(2) and 64(2) (provisions protecting the options of the aggrieved party). Does the mitigation principle of Article 77 create an exception to the option as to avoidance expressed in Article 72(1)? There is nothing unfair or wasteful in A's refusing to accept X's repudiation. No one knows when a "falling" market has reached bottom; if X was confident that the market would continue to fall X could have made a "forward" sale at $40 for delivery on August 1. (The same analysis applies when a seller repudiates prior to the date for delivery followed by a rise in the market price.)[6]

In short, the aggrieved party has no general obligation under Article 77 to attempt to mitigate damages by "accepting repudiation" by the other party.

419.2   (2) Materials Needed for Current Production

Example 77B. On June 1, A and X made a contract for X to produce and deliver to A 10,000 sheets of steel on August 1 at $50 per sheet. Buyer A needed the steel for use in manufacturing. On July 1 Seller X notified A that production difficulties in X's steel mill would prevent delivery of the steel by August 1; X also stated that the production difficulties might persist for an unknown period after August 1 and urged A to obtain the steel elsewhere. Comparable steel was available in A's area; the price at all times remained at $50. For unexplained reasons A did not seek or obtain the steel elsewhere; as a consequence A's production facilities were shut down for the month of August. Buyer A sued X for damages based on shut-down losses (Art. 74, "loss of

---

6. In the United States there is conflict in the case-law and academic writing over whether the aggrieved party has a duty to accept repudiation and to resell (or repurchase) in cases like Example 77A. Favoring this duty: Jackson, 31 Stanf. L. Rev. 69, 75 *et seq.* (1978); *Farnsworth, Contracts* 862. *Contra White & Summers* §6-7 at pp. 278–283. English case-law seems to reject such a duty. *Treitel, Contract* 655 at n. 75; *Benjamin* §§1341–1344, 1755, 1894. This latter position is often put in terms of the aggrieved party's right to press for performance — an approach that is more consistent with a party's right to "require performance" under CISG 46 and 62; *cf.* CISG 28. An aggrieved party who does not respond to repudiation by avoidance places itself in an uncertain position since the repudiating party may still perform. This possibility, *inter alia*, discourages temptation by the aggrieved party to delay a decision as to avoidance in order to speculate, at the other party's expense, on possible changes in the market price.

profit") of $10,000 per day, or $300,000. Seller X argued that, under Article 77, A failed to "take such measures as are reasonable in the circumstances to mitigate the loss" so that there should be a corresponding reduction in the damages.

Seller X's claim for damage-reduction based on Article 77 should prevail. Unlike Example 77A, in this case obtaining available alternative supplies was needed and reasonable to avoid certain loss. In this setting Buyer A's option to avoid or not to avoid is irrelevant. The notice by Seller X would relieve A of concern that Seller X might change its mind and deliver the goods; moreover, A could choose to avoid under Article 72 or, if A wished to press for later delivery by X, A could send X a notice of suspension under Article 71(3). (The effect of a right to require ("specific") performance (Arts. 28, 46), to be considered in the following section, is not relevant here since a court order could not overcome X's production difficulties. In any event, delays intrinsic to legal proceedings could not assure delivery in time to keep A in production.)

419.3   **(3) Mitigation and the Right to Require Performance**

We now meet cases that expose a conflict between two principles: (1) The obligation of an aggrieved party (Party A) to mitigate the loss resulting from breach by the other party (Article 77) and (2) the right of the aggrieved party to "require performance" (Arts. 46(1) and 62, §§280, 349, *supra*, as restricted by Article 28, §§191–199, *supra*).

Example 77C. A sales contract made on June 1 called for A, a producer of steel, to produce and deliver steel girders to X, a building contractor. The contract called for A to cut the girders to special dimensions provided by X for X's use in erecting a building for Owner. The contract price for the girders was $50,000. On July 1, before A had started work on the contract, Owner repudiated its contract with X; X immediately informed A of this and requested A not to cut the girders. Nevertheless, A cut the girders to the specifications stated in the contract. X refused to accept the girders. A sued X in a court in X's State to require X to accept the goods and pay the agreed price. X's State is one of the many common-law jurisdictions that, in cases like the present, does not "require performance" by compelling acceptance and payment of the price, as contrasted with damages. See Art. 28, §§191–199, supra. The court dismissed A's action for the price and permitted A to prove damages. A thereupon resold the girders but they brought only $10,000 because they had been cut in unusual lengths. A claimed damages of

$40,000 (the contract price of $50,000 less $10,000). In response, X requested that damages be reduced by the amount that the value of the girders had been impaired by cutting them to unusual lengths.

In applying Article 77 we must ask this question: Would it have been "reasonable in the circumstances" for A "to mitigate the loss" by honoring X's request of July 1 not to cut the girders? To determine what is "reasonable in the circumstances" one must consider: What would most sellers have done when it is evident that cutting the girders would seriously impair their value? The answer is clear. A's conduct was inconsistent with normal business conduct and the explicit requirement of Article 77. Indeed, A's conduct was foolhardy even by standards of short-term selfishness in view of litigation delays and risks, which were enhanced by increasing the amount at stake by wasteful conduct.

In the above case Seller A's attempt to force X to receive and pay for the girders was doomed to failure by the fact that the legal rules in X's State (the jurisdiction where A would normally need to sue for effective enforcement of a decree requiring performance) rejected this type of action even apart from the mitigation requirement of Article 77. Should the result be different in other jurisdictions? This question is posed by the following case.

Example 77D. The facts are the same as in Example 77C except that the law of X's State generally grants requests to require ("specific") performance of contracts. However, A did not wish to lay out costs for storage of the girders pending litigation; consequently; A resold the girders and requested damages of $40,000 ($50,000–$10,000). Should the court grant X's request to reduce damages, under Article 77, "in the amount by which the loss should have been mitigated?"

The answer, as in Example 77C, turns on whether A failed to take (Art. 77) "such measures as are reasonable in the circumstances to mitigate the loss." The only difference here is that the rules of X's jurisdiction are more favorable to an action to require ("specific") performance. When a seller sues for *damages* Article 77 explicitly requires a "reduction of damages." Clearly, therefore, the request to reduce damages should be granted.[7]

Example 77E. The facts are the same as Example 77D except that Seller A placed the girders in storage and under Article 62 requested the court to "require X" to pay the price [and] take delivery." Buyer X did not object to paying damages but noted that the remedy sought by A

---

7. See Knapp, *B-B Commentary* 564, §§3.1 through 3.3.

would transfer to X the consequences of A's failure to obey the mandate of Article 77 to "take such measures as are reasonable in the circumstances to mitigate the loss..." In the alternative, X claimed that if the court should require X to accept and pay for the girders the court should also award damages to X for the loss ($40,000) that A caused X by A's conduct that violated the mandate of Article 77.

The above case presents a common problem of statutory construction: Two general rules that in most circumstances are compatible in unusual circumstances come into conflict. The appropriate response is to adopt the solution that does the least violence to either principle. Giving effect to the mitigation principle in unusual situations like Example 77E does not make a serious inroad in the general rule requiring performance of contracts; on the other hand, failing to give effect to Article 77 in such cases nullifies the mitigation rule when it is specially appropriate. In short, the mitigation rule is *lex specialis* in relation to the general rule requiring ("specific") performance.

In some cases a party's need for requiring ("specific") performance may be so strong as to outweigh the mitigation principle of Article 77. Such a case is most likely to result when a buyer needs materials that are not available elsewhere. It is difficult to imagine a comparable need when the seller (as in example 77E) sues to force a buyer to accept goods; in these cases the seller usually can be fully compensated by damages.

(a) A Failed Proposal and the Vienna Conference. The

question that remains is whether the above approach to mitigation is foreclosed by the consideration of this provision at the 1980 Conference. The First Committee did not reach this provision (then draft article 73) until the last week of its deliberations. At that stage the Committee took up a suggestion by the present writer prompted by the fact that the first sentence of the article laid down a general rule requiring reasonable steps to mitigate loss while the second sentence mentioned only one sanction — reduction of damages. Out of concern that the article might be construed to exclude application of the mitigation principle to other remedies, an amendment was proposed to add at the end of the second sentence "or a corresponding modification or adjustment of any other remedy."[8]

---

8. Text of the proposal, *O.R.* 133, *Docy. Hist.* 705; discussion in the First Committee, *O.R.* 396–398, *Docy. Hist.* 617–619.

Thirteen delegates addressed the question: Five supported the measure;[9] three were opposed;[10] five were concerned with the drafting — primarily because they felt that the reference to "any other remedy" was too vague or broad.[11] At the conclusion of this discussion a proposal to set up a drafting party to refine the proposal was defeated (24-8).

The above facts present an interesting question concerning the circumstances in which legislative history creates a binding interpretation of the Convention. Some may conclude that the discussion and vote means that in cases like Example 77E a seller's failure to mitigate loss is irrelevant if the seller sues to recover the price in a jurisdiction where domestic law supports this broad approach to "requiring performance" (Art. 62).[12]

The discussion of Article 7 at §91, *supra*, supports the use of legislative history when it reveals the prevailing understanding of the delegates. Did the legislative body face and decide the issue posed by Example 77E? The opinions expressed in the discussion dealt with diverse reasons for not adopting the proposed amendment. This writer (although possibly blinded by interest in the issue) does not see adequate grounds for concluding that a substantial number of delegates would have rejected the mitigation principle in cases like Example 77E.

Emerging from this experience is a lesson: Interpretation based on discussions by a large legislative body is more meaningful for decisions of broad issues of policy than for detailed applications. The present writer surely overlooked this principle in inviting consideration

---

9. *O.R.* 396, *Docy. Hist.* 617, paras. 55 (U.S.A.), 56 (U.K.) and 61 (Ireland, but stating that the principle of the first sentence was sufficiently broad to permit other remedies); *O.R.* 397, *Docy. Hist.* 618, paras. 69 (Australia) and 71 (Netherlands: "something must be done" but more detail needed).

10. *O.R.* 397, *Docy. Hist.* 618, paras. 64–65 (Canada), 66 (Sweden) and 67 (Mexico).

11. *O.R.* 396, *Docy. Hist.* 617, paras. 57 (amendment in wrong section, should not be in section on "Damages") and 60 (useful in theory but reference to "any other remedy" was vague); *O.R.* 397, *Docy. Hist.* 618, paras. 68 (vague), 69 (same) and 73 (too broad).

12. See Hans Stoll & Georg Gruber, Art. 77 para. 4, *in* Schlechtriem & Schwenzer, *CISG Commentary* (2nd English ed. 2005) (stating that Art. 77 restricts only the right to claim damages and is inapplicable to other remedies); UNCITRAL Digest Art. 77 paras. 1 & 2 (indicating that the mitigation principle applies only if a claim for damages is made); *Schlechtriem, 1986 Commentary* 99. But see Hans Stoll & Georg Gruber, Art. 77 para. 5, *in* Schlechtriem & Schwenzer, *CISG Commentary* (2nd English ed. 2005) (suggesting that, in situations resembling Example 77E, a seller does not have "the right to carry out the work and deliver the specific goods that have become useless to the buyer and when doing so is against the buyer's wishes").

(particularly in the closing days of a large diplomatic conference) of complex questions concerning the interplay of competing principles of the Convention—questions that are better left to tribunals for consideration in the light of the precise facts of the case.[13] *Ars longa vita brevis.*

If the verdict of history should be that the mitigation principle is inapplicable to cases like Example 77E one may seek comfort in the hope that few will act like the seller in that case and that, if this should occur, the buyer may be able to show that this conduct is inconsistent with applicable trade usage. See Art. 9(2), §§112–122, *supra.*

---

13. The three concrete cases used as a vehicle for the above discussion were not adequate to expose the factual variations that can be relevant. As was noted above, a party's need for compelling ("specific") performance may be so strong as to override the competing principle calling for mitigation of loss.

Practical problems faced by delegates in obtaining authorization to support changes in a draft in the closing days of a diplomatic conference were discussed under Art. 7, §91, *supra.*

SECTION III.

INTEREST

Article 78.
Interest on Sums in Arrears

420 **A. Legislative History**

In recent decades economic forces, including inflation, have generated sharp increases in interest rates. Uncompensated delay in payment inflicts added loss on the aggrieved party while the party in breach gains from the use of the funds it should have paid. Adequate provision for interest not only compensates the aggrieved party for loss but also encourages voluntary performance.

The most extended delays occur during attempts to reach a settlement and as a result of ponderous judicial processes. Delays in collecting judgments are usually less serious; in any event, post-judgment interest is often provided as part of the forum's general procedural system.[1] We are here concerned with the more serious and intractable problem of prejudgment interest.

Attempts to develop detailed rules in this area encountered sharp differences of view and reversals of position.[2] The UNCITRAL Working Group's Draft Convention (1976), building on Article 83 of ULIS (1964), provided that if the buyer delays in paying the price the seller is entitled to interest based on a two-factor formula — the higher, in seller's country, of (a) the official discount rate plus 1% or (b) the rate for unsecured short-term credits. The full Commission tried unsuccessfully to develop a simpler formula; technical problems included the lack in some countries of an official discount rate or standard rates for short-term credits. In addition, some countries with mandatory rules limiting or prohibiting the charging of interest were opposed to dealing with the

---

1. But see Klaus Bacher, Art. 78 para. 45, *in* Schlechtriem & Schwenzer, *CISG Commentary* (2nd English ed. 2005).
2. For another account of the drafting history of Art. 78 see Klaus Bacher, Art. 78 para. 2, *in* Schlechtriem & Schwenzer, *CISG Commentary* (2nd English ed. 2005).

question. Faced with these difficulties the Commission deleted the draft article on interest.

The comments of governments and international organizations submitted to the Diplomatic Conference included proposals to reintroduce a provision dealing with interest. However, the Conference (like the Commission) found it difficult to agree on a formula to set the interest rate. The Conference finally designated an ad hoc working group to seek a compromise; one of the group's alternative proposals was approved by the First Committee but failed in Plenary to receive the necessary two-thirds majority. A second working group then developed a draft establishing in general terms the right to receive interest on sums in arrears; this was approved (30 to 2, with 12 abstentions) and became Article 78 of the Convention.

Article 78

If a party fails to pay the price or any other sum that is in arrears, the other party is entitled to interest on it, without prejudice to any claim for damages recoverable under Article 74.

One reason for persisting in the effort that produced Article 78 was concern lest the lack of a provision on interest would lead to unintended divergences in the application of the Convention. In some legal systems compensation for lost interest is regarded as an aspect of damage-assessment; this led to concern lest laying down rules for damages (Arts. 74–77) without providing for interest might be understood as barring the recovery of interest. A similar concern resulted from the provision in Article 84(1), *infra* at §450, that a buyer who avoids the contract after paying for the goods may recover interest on the funds that the seller is bound to repay; providing for interest in this one setting might be construed to bar recovery of interest in all other situations.

Unintended intrusions on domestic rules could have been avoided by an express provision that the Convention does not affect any right under domestic law to recover interest. However, such a proposal was not accepted; reasons included the lack of uniformity resulting from the inadequacy or rejection of provision for interest in many countries and the lack of clarity and uniformity of rules of PIL as to which domestic law would be applicable.[3] In sum, Article 78 was designed

3. Proposal: *O.R.* 138, *Docy. Hist.* 710. Discussion in First Committees: *O.R.* 388–392, *O.R.* 415–419, 429–430, *Docy. Hist.* 609–613, 636–640, 650–651 (included discussion of working group alternatives providing formulas for calculating interest, one of which was

to establish a general rule that would be free from the vagaries of domestic law.[4]

421 ## B. The Rate of Interest

As has just been noted, specific formulas for calculating interest were rejected in favor of a general rule that an aggrieved party "is entitled to interest" on "sums in arrears." *The parties may, of course, agree on an interest rate for their transaction — for example, by an express provision addressing the question[5] or through a practice or usage binding under Article 9 of the Convention.[6] (See §422.2 infra.) Absent such an agreement, however, an interest rate must be selected for the parties, and every approach to picking such a rate is subject to the same objection: the drafters could have chosen that solution, but they did not. In such circumstances, little or no guidance can be gleaned from the travaux préparatoires.[7]*

Given the lack of guidance from the express terms or the history of the Convention it should not surprise that a great variety of approaches to the interest rate question have been put forward.[8] These approaches

---

accepted). Compare the proposal for a reservation by Arab countries, *O.R.* 418, *Docy. Hist.* 639. No such provision was made.

4. Nicholas, *B-B Commentary* 570, §2.1 agrees that, under Art. 78, one is entitled to interest even if applicable domestic law makes no provision for interest but adds that domestic law applies if it provides "a relevant formula for calculating interest." The latter suggestion seems difficult to apply when domestic law, through obsolescence or hostility, provides relief that is derisory in relation to the loss of the aggrieved party; in these cases deference to domestic law also seems inconsistent with the policy underlying Article 78 and other articles of the Convention designed to provide compensation for loss resulting from breach of contract.

5. See Klaus Bacher, Art. 78 para. 39, *in* Schlechtriem & Schwenzer, *CISG Commentary* (2nd English ed. 2005); UNCITRAL Digest Art. 78 para. 13.

6. See Klaus Bacher, Art. 78 para. 38, *in* Schlechtriem & Schwenzer, *CISG Commentary* (2nd English ed. 2005); UNCITRAL Digest Art. 78 para. 9.

7. *Contra,* see Franco Ferrari, *CISG Case Law on the Rate of Interest on Sums in Arrears,* 1999 De Droit des Affaires Internationales/International Business Law Journal 86, 89 (criticizing decisions that set a rate of interest by the creditor's cost of funds because a proposal embodying that approach was rejected at the 1980 diplomatic conference).

8. For overviews of the different approaches, see Volker Behr, The Sales Convention in Europe: From Problems in Drafting to Problems in Practice, 17 J.L. & Com. 263, 267–288 (1998); Franco Ferrari, CISG Case Law on the Rate of Interest on Sums in Arrears, 1999 De Droit des Affaires Internationales/International Business Law Journal 86; Klaus Bacher, Art. 78 para. 26–36, in Schlechtriem & Schwenzer, CISG Commentary (2nd English ed. 2005); UNCITRAL Digest Art. 78 para. 7–12.

can generally be divided into two categories[9]: *those favoring a uniform rule based on the general principles of the Convention itself (see Article 7(2)), and those favoring resolution of the interest rate issue by recourse to non-uniform (domestic) law.*

Advocates of the latter approach have suggested consulting the domestic laws of various jurisdictions, including the jurisdiction of the currency of payment, the jurisdiction of the place of payment, the creditor's jurisdiction, the debtor's jurisdiction, or the lex fori.[10] *However the most popular solution — and, apparently, the most commonly adopted approach to the interest rate issue in general — is to refer to the domestic law applicable to the contract under PIL principles.*[11] *Since the drafters were unable to settle on a uniform interest rate, it could be argued, reference to domestic law reflects the drafters' intentions. On the other hand, unlike some other gaps in the Convention, the drafters were certainly aware of — indeed, they grappled mightily with — the interest rate question; if they intended this matter to be beyond the scope of the Convention and to be governed by domestic law, they could have easily have expressly so provided (as they did, for example, with "validity" issues — see Article 4(a)).*

Looking to the general principles of the Convention itself as the source for determining an interest rate — an approach that has also produced a variety of proposed solutions[12] *— has the advantage of*

---

9. See Franco Ferrari, *CISG Case Law on the Rate of Interest on Sums in Arrears*, 1999 De Droit des Affaires Internationales/International Business Law Journal 86, 88–89; Klaus Bacher, Art. 78 para. 27, *in* Schlechtriem & Schwenzer, *CISG Commentary* (2nd English ed. 2005); UNCITRAL Digest Art. 78 para. 8.

10. See Klaus Bacher, Art. 78 paras. 32–33, *in* Schlechtriem & Schwenzer, *CISG Commentary* (2nd English ed. 2005); UNCITRAL Digest Art. 78 para. 10.

11. See Franco Ferrari, *CISG Case Law on the Rate of Interest on Sums in Arrears*, 1999 De Droit des Affaires Internationales/International Business Law Journal 86, 90; Klaus Bacher, Art. 78 para. 32, *in* Schlechtriem & Schwenzer, *CISG Commentary* (2nd English ed. 2005); UNCITRAL Digest Art. 78 para. 12; Volker Behr, *The Sales Convention in Europe: From Problems in Drafting to Problems in Practice*, 17 J.L. & Com. 263, 285–286 (1998).

12. See, e.g., Klaus Bacher, Art. 78 para. 29, *in* Schlechtriem & Schwenzer, *CISG Commentary* (2nd English ed. 2005). Some authorities suggest referring to the interest rate provision (Art. 7.4.9) of the UNIDROIT Principles of International Commercial Contracts. See Klaus Bacher, Art. 78 para. 31a, *in* Schlechtriem & Schwenzer, *CISG Commentary* (2nd English ed. 2005); UNCITRAL Digest Art. 78 para. 11. In the view of the editor of the current edition, however, provisions of the UNIDROIT Principles cannot be applied to supplement the CISG. See Harry M. Flechtner, *The CISG's Impact on International Unification Efforts: The UNIDROIT Principles of International Commercial Contracts and the Principles of European Contract Law*, in *The 1980 Uniform Sales Law: Old Issues Revisited in the Light of Recent Experiences (Verona Conference 2003)* 169, 189–193 (2003). See also

promoting the Convention's fundamental purpose of creating a uniform legal regime for international sales[13] and of avoiding some of the complex problem arising from an application of domestic law to the question.[14] The purpose of Article 78 seems clear: to compensate a party for the lost time value of money that occurs when a sum (like the price) is "in arrears."[15] Although it is placed in its own division of the Convention (Part III, Chapter V, Section III), separate from the provisions on damages, the principle underlying Article 78 is thus akin to that of Article 74, which provides for the recovery of "damages equal to the loss . . . suffered as a consequence of the breach."

In many situations this general rule of Article 74 provides the sole guide for the measurement of damages. However, in some situations Article 74 is supplemented by Articles 75 and 76 which were designed to enhance definiteness in damage measurement. Consideration of these provisions in connection with the present question seems consistent with Article 7(2)'s invitation to settle unresolved questions "in conformity with the general principles" of the Convention (§§96–102, *supra*). Assume that an aggrieved party (A) has been wrongfully deprived of funds by the other party (X) and "in a reasonable manner" (see Art. 75) replaces those funds by borrowing; A's loss may appropriately be measured by the actual cost of the "substitute transaction." In many enterprises, however, there is a constant in-and-out cash flow, supplemented where necessary by a general line of credit or by the diversion of capital; in these settings X's failure to pay may not be matched by a substitute loan. Financial loss from X's failure to pay is none the less real; in these cases the principle underlying Article 76

Franco Ferrari, *CISG Case Law on the Rate of Interest on Sums in Arrears*, 1999 De Droit des Affaires Internationales/International Business Law Journal 86, 89.

13. See Franco Ferrari, *CISG Case Law on the Rate of Interest on Sums in Arrears*, 1999 De Droit des Affaires Internationales/International Business Law Journal 86, 88–89; Klaus Bacher, Art. 78 para. 28, *in* Schlechtriem & Schwenzer, *CISG Commentary* (2nd English ed. 2005); UNCITRAL Digest Art. 78 para. 9.

14. See Klaus Bacher, Art. 78 paras. 32–36, *in* Schlechtriem & Schwenzer, *CISG Commentary* (2nd English ed. 2005); Franco Ferrari, *CISG Case Law on the Rate of Interest on Sums in Arrears*, 1999 De Droit des Affaires Internationales/International Business Law Journal 86, 90. This approach, of course, suffers from the same objection as all other approaches — the drafters could have provided for it but did not.

15. But see Klaus Bacher, Art. 78 para. 29, *in* Schlechtriem & Schwenzer, *CISG Commentary* (2nd English ed. 2005) (citing authority for the proposition that the purpose of Art. 78 is to prevent the unjust enrichment of the party in arrears).

suggests that A's loss may be measured by the "current price" of credit for A (*cf.* Art. 76(3)).[16]

"Simple" or *"compound" interest.* Sharp controversy has developed over whether an award of interest for delayed payment should be compounded at specified intervals (weekly, monthly or yearly) so that interest accumulates on unpaid interest.[17] Fortunately, this problem need not arise under the approach suggested above that the amount of interest should be based on the credit costs faced by the aggrieved party.

422 C. Situations Calling for Interest

The provisions on interest in ULIS and in the draft Convention approved by the Working Group were confined to cases where the buyer delays paying the price. However, Article 78 of the Convention is cast in broader terms and extends to the failure of either party to pay any "sum that is in arrears."[18]

The mandate of Article 7(1) to construe the Convention to promote "uniformity in its *application*" requires us to seek a principle governing the scope of Article 78 that can be considered as a basis for uniform application of the Convention. To this end let us look for situations that are clearly within, and outside, the purpose of Article 78.

16. Articles 75 and 76 strictly apply only when the contract is avoided but they apply to losses that are similar to those where interest is due under Art. 78. This is illustrated by Art. 84 which provides that, when the contract is avoided, "If the seller is bound to refund the price, he must also *pay interest* on it . . ." The reason for this express provision for interest is that the buyer has suffered a loss (the use-value of the funds) which was not part of an agreed exchange. The same is true when a buyer fails to pay the price when it is due (Art. 78). Indeed, as we shall see at §422, *infra*, such an imbalance resulting from the lack of an agreed exchange provides grounds for interest on a "sum in arrears" (Art. 78). Consequently, the loss suffered by a buyer who rightfully avoids the contract and purchases substitute goods at a higher price (Art. 75) is comparable to the loss of a seller who fails to receive the price when it is due. See Klaus Bacher, Art. 78 para. 16, *in* Schlechtriem & Schwenzer, *CISG Commentary* (2nd English ed. 2005). In other words, in situations where interest is due, avoidance is irrelevant since the lost value of the funds is not part of an agreed exchange.

17. *Contrast* the (English) Law Commission, Working Paper No. 80 (1981), discussed in Bowles & Whelan, 45 Mod. L. Rev. 434 (1982) *with* Law Reform Commission of British Columbia, Working Paper No. 49, *discussed in* Bowles & Whelan, 64 Can. Bar Rev. 142 (1986). See also Bowles & Whelan, 1 Int. Rev. L. & Ec. III (1981).

18. See Klaus Bacher, Art. 78 para. 5, *in* Schlechtriem & Schwenzer, *CISG Commentary* (2nd English ed. 2005).

Two specific situations are mentioned in the Convention:

(I) A buyer (X) delays paying the seller (A) for goods A has supplied (Art. 78); (II) A seller (X) delays in refunding to the buyer (A) the price A paid for goods that were so defective as to justify avoidance of the contract (Art. 84(1)).

In both cases the party in breach (X) holds assets for which the aggrieved party (A) has not received the agreed return. In (I) the imbalance results from X's holding goods for which X has not paid; in (II) the imbalance results from X's receipt of funds X should return. In both a sum *of money provided for by the contract* is "in arrears."

In contrast, assume that a seller (X) on June 1 delivered 100 units of goods to a buyer (A) at an agreed price of $1,000 which A agreed to pay on July 1. The goods were defective or, alternatively, consisted of only 800 units. A promptly resold the goods under Article 75 for $800 and paid this sum to X on July 1. Here X was guilty of breach of contract to the extent of $200 but this did not deprive A of funds to which A was entitled. In the language of Article 78 no sum was "in arrears"; no interest should be imposed.

"Liquidated" sums and international trade. Article 78 refers to any "sum" in "arrears." In some jurisdictions interest does not accrue until the amount in arrears has been "liquidated" — that is, made certain; other jurisdictions grant interest even though the sum owed is in dispute.[19]

Let us consider the effect of a strict "liquidated sum" requirement in the most common situation that falls explicitly within Article 78 — the buyer's failure "to pay the price." Deliveries in the large quantities common in international trade often are subject to a shortage in quantity or to a quality defect in a few units. These cases call for a price adjustment; the balance that the buyer must pay is not an agreed or "liquidated" sum. A strict application of a "liquidated sum" requirement would mean that a buyer could delay payment without interest until the precise adjustment is adjudicated; this would create a temptation for intransigence in negotiating an adjustment and dilatory tactics in litigation — a serious impairment of the policies underlying

---

19. *Restatement, Second of Contracts* (U.S.A.) §354. *Interest as Damages*, Paragraph (1), provides that interest is recoverable not only for failure to pay "a definite sum in money" but also for failure to "render a performance with fixed or *ascertainable* monetary value." See Comment C on para. (1): interest is recoverable even though the amount of performance is in dispute and must be proved by evidence extrinsic to the contract. Paragraph (2) provides for allowance of interest in other cases "as justice provides...." Under Comment d, this recovery may extend to interest on consequential loss.

Article 78.[20] On the other hand, it would be reasonable to conclude that no sum is "in arrears" when goods have caused damage that could offset a substantial and undetermined portion of the price.[21] Tribunals and arbitrators are accustomed and qualified to make judgments on such matters in framing a final judgment or award.

A related but distinct question is whether an aggrieved party is entitled interest on damages awarded under Article 74–76.[22] An aggrieved party that suffers damages loses time value just as much as does, for example, an unpaid seller. For example, suppose a seller delivers non-conforming goods that the buyer, acting properly under the Convention and in keeping with the mitigation principle of Article 77, expends funds to repair. As discussed in connection with Article 74 (see §405 supra) the buyer may be entitled to damages measured by the cost of repair; but, in addition to the amounts expended to repair, has not the buyer also lost the value of the use of those funds?[23] On the other hand, the phrasing of the Article 78 requirement of a "sum that is in arrears" may suggest that the drafters did not have damage awards in mind when they promulgated the provision. Certainly the requirement that there be an amount "in arrears" does not fit comfortably with an award of damages for non-conforming goods, although one could easily imply that a breaching party has a duty to reimburse losses caused by the breach as soon as those losses occur.[24] The requirement of a "sum" in arrears also seems an unlikely description of damages resulting from non-conforming goods: this is not just an objection based on the unliquidated amount of such damages, but on the fact that the sums on which the drafters have clearly required interest (e.g., the unpaid price and payments that must be refunded after avoidance of contract) all involve payments of money made or to be made under the contract.

---

20. *Compare* Klaus Bacher, Art. 78 paras. 6, 10–12, & 18, *in* Schlechtriem & Schwenzer, *CISG Commentary* (2nd English ed. 2005).
21. *Compare* Klaus Bacher, Art. 78 para. 20, *in* Schlechtriem & Schwenzer, *CISG Commentary* (2nd English ed. 2005).
22. This question is also distinct from the question of interest on restitutionary obligations triggered by avoidance of contract; the restitutionary issues (as noted above) are governed by Art. 84.
23. *Compare* Klaus Bacher, Art. 78 para. 6, 14–15, & 18, *in* Schlechtriem & Schwenzer, *CISG Commentary* (2nd English ed. 2005).
24. *Cf.* Klaus Bacher, Art. 78 para. 14, *in* Schlechtriem & Schwenzer, *CISG Commentary* (2nd English ed. 2005) (arguing that Art. 78 interest is due on damages "from the time when the loss occurred").

422.1　Relation between Article 78 and Article 74

Under the last clause of Article 78, the right to claim interest is "without prejudice to any claim for damages recoverable under article 74." Thus Article 74 damages can supplement an award of interest under Article 78 and recovery under the two provisions, clearly, is not co-extensive. If the Article 78 interest rate is determined by reference to the legal rate under applicable domestic law — the most popular solution to the interest rate issue (see §421 supra) — Article 74 damages may be awarded if the actual rate that a creditor pays for replacement funds is higher.[25] This commentary concluded (§421 supra) that the interest rate awardable under Article 78 should be based on the general principle underlying Article 74; this suggested an interest rate based on the creditor's cost of borrowing funds. This solution has been criticized as obviating the need for Article 74 damages, thus rendering the final clause of Article 78 meaningless.[26]

Even if the cost-of-funds interest rate solution advocated herein is adopted, additional damages may be recoverable under Article 74. For example, if non-payment of a sum when due foreseeably and unavoidably deprives the creditor of a special investment opportunity or causes losses by disrupting the creditor's operations, damages under Article 74, in additional to interest under Article 78, should be recoverable.[27] Thus the interest-rate solution suggested herein is compatible with the final clause of Article 74.

422.2　Concluding Remarks on Article 78

One may be tempted to regret the inclusion of a provision on interest that can generate so many questions. These questions, however, were not created by Article 78; questions of even larger dimension (e.g., does *any* interest accrue) are now latent in domestic law, and in international trade are compounded by problems of conflict of laws (P.I.L.).

---

25. See Volker Behr, The Sales Convention in Europe: From Problems in Drafting to Problems in Practice, 17 J.L. & Com. 263, 282–283 (1998).

26. See Franco Ferrari, *CISG Case Law on the Rate of Interest on Sums in Arrears*, 1999 De Droit des Affaires Internationales/International Business Law Journal 86, 89.

27. See Hans Stoll & Georg Gruber, Art. 74 para. 16, *in* Schlechtriem & Schwenzer, *CISG Commentary* (2nd English ed. 2005).

One might hope to solve these problems by contract (Art. 6) and this may be possible for a detailed contract prepared for a specific transaction; it will require special skill to prepare a standard clause that will not create difficulties (like clauses on applicable law) in closing the contract.[28]

---

28. A seller with strong bargaining power might propose: "The buyer shall pay interest at—% *per annum* on delay in paying for the goods. In no other situation will either party be liable for interest." Questions that remain might include the reaction of buyers and, under domestic law, challenges to validity. See Art. 4(a), *supra*. For further discussion of the drafting issues see Michael P. Van Alstine, *The UNCITRAL Digest, the Right to Interest, and the Interest Rate Controversy*, in *Drafting Contracts under the CISG (Volume 4, CILE Studies)* 505, 523–528 (Harry M. Flechtner, Ronald A. Brand & Mark S. Walter eds., 2008).

SECTION IV.

EXEMPTIONS
(Articles 79–80)

Article 79.
Impediment Excusing Party From Damages
("Force Majeure")

423 A. Introduction

Even in domestic law it has been difficult to provide coherent answers to the problems that arise when unexpected difficulties prevent or severely impact the performance of a contract. The settings are diverse: war, embargo and other governmental prohibitions, breakdown of transport facilities (e.g., the closing of the Suez Canal), strikes, the shut-down or bankruptcy of a supplier—these are only points on a continuum of difficulties with varying degrees of scope, severity and unpredictability. The applicable legal doctrines go under assorted labels—impossibility, Act of God, frustration, *force majeure*, failure of presupposed conditions.

The legal issue is difficult but narrow: Is the non-performing party liable to the disappointed party for breach of contract? Even the clearest grounds for "excuse" do not permit a party to recover (or keep) the price for performance it has not rendered. The issue is whether the party that fails to perform is liable for damages.

423.1 (1) Varieties of Loss Allocation

Article 79 confronts the thorny problem of determining which party bears the burden of an unexpected barrier to performance. Fortunately, the scope of Article 79 is narrowed by specialized rules on definable types of commercial risks.

423.2 (a) Loss in Transit.   The Convention's rules on loss during transit (Chapter IV, Arts. 66–70, §§358–383 *supra*) apply even though the goods are lost as a consequence of unpredictable disasters such as hurricane, war or government seizure—a point that is relevant to

emphasize the line of demarcation between the risk rules of Chapter IV and the exemption rules of Article 79. Assume that the Chapter IV rules allocate transit risk to the seller and the goods are lost as the result of a hurricane. This disaster may produce two types of loss: (1) Physical loss of the goods and (2) Loss to the buyer because of a rise in price, or because failure to receive the goods (e.g., machinery) interrupts production. Although the seller bears the first type of loss — physical loss of the goods — Article 79 may exempt the seller from liability for breach of contract.

Pragmatic reasons underlie these results. Physical loss during transit is readily and customarily covered by insurance. On the other hand, the buyer's contractual loss from non-arrival, although not so readily or customarily covered by insurance, can be coped with more readily by the buyer than by the seller through insurance or reserves; the seller and seller's insurer will have little or no information about the commercial risks encountered by the various buyers whom the seller supplies.[1]

423.3 **(b) Defective Goods.** Unknown defects in goods also present problems of allocation of loss. Under the Convention the seller is responsible for these losses. (Arts. 35, 45 and 74, §§223, 276, 405, *supra*).[2] Loss to the buyer is placed on the seller even when the seller is not at fault, as when a seller resells defective goods, obtained from a responsible supplier in sealed containers, which the seller has no reasonable opportunity to inspect (§§24–26, 276, *supra*).[3] One pragmatic justification for this result is that the aggrieved buyer (unlike the seller) usually has no practicable recourse against the supplier. As we shall see (§427, *infra*), Article 79 should not be applied to reverse these rules.

Unhappily, there are many types of unexpected loss that fall outside these specialized provisions.

---

1. On commercial losses and insurance see R. Keeton & A. Widiss, *Insurance Law* (1988); R. Holtom, *Underwriting, Principles and Practices* (3d ed. 1987).

2. The scope of damages is limited by the "foreseeability" rule of Art. 74, §406 *supra*, the mitigation principle of Art. 77, §§416–419.3 *supra*, and often is restricted by contract.

3. *Contra*, Hans Stoll & Georg Gruber, Art. 79 para. 40, *in* Schlechtriem & Schwenzer, *CISG Commentary* (2nd English ed. 2005).

423.4 **(2) The Convention**

Article 79[4]

(1) A party is not liable for a failure to perform any of his obligations if he proves that the failure was due to an impediment beyond his control and that he could not reasonably be expected to have taken the impediment into account at the time of the conclusion of the contract or to have avoided or overcome it or its consequences.

(2) If the party's failure is due to the failure by a third person whom he has engaged to perform the whole or a part of the contract, that party is exempt from liability only if:

(a) he is exempt under the preceding paragraph; and

(b) the person whom he has so engaged would be so exempt if the provisions of that paragraph were applied to him.

(3) The exemption provided by this article has effect for the period during which the impediment exists.

(4) The party who fails to perform must give notice to the other party of the impediment and its effect on his ability to perform. If the notice is not received by the other party within a reasonable time after the party who fails to perform knew or ought to have known of the impediment, he is liable for damages resulting from such non-receipt.

(5) Nothing in this article prevents either party from exercising any right other than to claim damages under this Convention.

One notices that the scope of Article 79 is broad: Exemption may be claimed by either party and may apply to "any" of its "obligations."

Analysis of Article 79 can best commence with paragraphs (1) and (5). (Paragraphs (2), (3) and (4) deal with special situations that will be considered *infra* at §§433–435.)

Paragraph (1) states three elements that must be proved by a non-performing party who seeks to establish that it is not "liable for a failure to perform": (a) The failure was "due to an impediment beyond his control"; (b) At the time of the contract the party "could not reasonably be expected to have taken the impediment into account"; and (c) Subsequent to the contract the party could not reasonably be expected "to have avoided or overcome [the obstacle] or its consequences."

---

4. Article 79 is substantially the same as Art. 65 of the 1978 Draft except that, in para. (3), the word "only" that had followed "effect" was deleted. See §435 *infra*. *Cf.* ULIS 74, discussed *infra* §427.

The narrow scope of the statement in paragraph (1) that a party "is not *liable*" for a failure to perform is emphasized in paragraph (5): Nothing in Article 79 "prevents either party from exercising any right *other than to claim damages....*" Confining exemption to "damages" has this important consequence: When one party fails to perform its obligations the other party's right to "avoid the contract" is not impaired. (In non-legal terms, when the seller cannot deliver the buyer need not pay; when the buyer cannot pay the seller need not deliver.) The grounds for avoidance that we have examined (Arts. 25, 47, 49, 63, 64, 72 and 73) remain applicable although the disappointed party may not recover damages. In addition, the parties are subject to the rules in Section V (Arts. 81–84, *infra* at §§437–452) on "Effects of Avoidance" Thus, each party is entitled (Art. 81(2)) to "restitution" of whatever it "has supplied or paid under the contract." Article 84(2) carries this principle further: A buyer who avoids must "account to the seller" for all benefits the buyer has derived from the goods.

424 B. Exemption and the Contract

As we have seen, the Convention (Art. 6) gives overriding effect to the agreement of the parties. Contract provisions on impediments to performance have special value since impediments arise in a countless variety of circumstances and involve infinite gradations of difficulty and unpredictability. General legal rules, domestic or international, can scarcely provide clear and satisfactory answers to all these problems. Consequently, in important transactions and in a wide variety of standard contracts explicit provision is made for the consequences of serious impediments to performance. The contracts can (and do) take account of the conditions and needs presented by various types of transactions. When a commodity (such as grain) is subject to market fluctuations both parties rely heavily on the contract for protection; the grounds for exemption tend to be strict and narrow. When the contract involves construction work or a manufacturing process that requires a substantial period of time, the possibility and seriousness of impediments multiply; these facts are reflected in contracts that call for readjustment of the contract to cope with unanticipated problems.[5]

Principles of efficiency and fairness can best be distilled from contracts prepared with the cooperation of both sellers and buyers; such

5. UNCITRAL, *Legal Guide, Industrial Works*, Ch. XXI (U.N. 1988).

cooperation may be achieved by a trade association that includes both interests or through mediation by international organizations such as the U.N. Economic Commission for Europe (ECE).[6] The solutions provided by some of these contracts will be quoted *infra* at §431 since they may be useful to parties who wish a more definite solution than can be provided by general rules of law; in addition, patterns that emerge from these contracts may provide guidance in applying the general rules of the Convention.

425 **C. The Convention and Domestic Law**

Domestic rules in this area often bear a family resemblance to each other and to Article 79 of the Convention, but a penetrating study by Professor Nicholas exposes the hazards of relying on "superficial harmony which merely mutes a deeper discord."[7] The Convention (Article 7) enjoins us to interpret its provisions "with regard for its international character and . . . the need to promote uniformity in its application." This goal would be served if we could (as by a draft from Lethe) purge our minds of presuppositions derived from domestic traditions and, with innocent eyes, read the language of Article 79 in the light of the practices and needs of international trade. In the absence of such innocence, the preconceptions based on domestic law may be minimized by close attention to the differences between domestic law and the Convention. We turn first to the (U.S.A.) "UCC").

> Section 2-615. Excuse by Failure of Presupposed Conditions
> Except so far as a seller may have assumed a greater obligation and subject to the preceding section on substituted performance:
> (a) Delay in delivery or non-delivery in whole or in part by a seller who complies with paragraph (b) and (c) is not a breach of his duty under a contract for sale if performance as agreed has been made impracticable by the occurrence of a contingency the non-occurrence of which was a basic assumption on which

6. The pioneering work of the ECE is described in *Benjamin. The ECE General Conditions of Sale and Standard Forms of Contract*, [1961] J. Bus. L. 113; II *UNIDROIT YB* 251, 258–267. On the adaptations of the ECE General Conditions to impediments in different contractual settings, see *Force Majeure (I.A.L.S.)* 249–250 (P.I. Benjamin), 305–306 (L. Kopelmanas). 7. Nicholas, *Force Majeure and Frustration*, in 27 Am. J. Comp. L. 231 (1979) (*AJCL UNCITRAL Symposium*). Other comparative studies: *Zweigert & Kotz II (1987)* 179–183; *Treitel, Remedies (1988)* 24–42; Nicholas, *French Law of Contract* (1982) 193–204; Hellner, *The Influence of the German Doctrine of Impossibility on Swedish Sales Law* in *Rheinstein Festschrift* 705; *Force Majeure (I.A.L.S.)*; Dietrich Maskow, *Hardship and Force Majeure*, 1992 Am. J. Comp. L. 657, 658 (1992).

the contract was made or by compliance in good faith with any applicable foreign domestic governmental regulation or order whether or not it later proves to be invalid.

(b) Where the causes mentioned in paragraph (a) affect only a part of the seller's capacity to perform, he must allocate production and deliveries among his customers but may at his option include regular customers not then under contract as well as his own requirements for further manufacture. He may so allocate in any manner which is fair and reasonable.

(c) The seller must notify the buyer seasonably that there will be delay or non-delivery and, when allocation is required under paragraph (b), of the estimated quota thus made available for the buyer.

The Uniform Commercial Code also has rules on the effect of difficulties in specialized situations: casualty to goods identified when the contract was made ("specific" goods) (UCC 2-613), and failure of agreed means of transportation or payment when a "commercially reasonable" or "substantially equivalent" substitute is available (UCC 2-614).[8]

426 (1) Aspects of Performance Subject to Excuse

Article 79 of the Convention follows the approach of important civil law systems in extending the rules on excuse to all aspects of a party's performance. Under paragraph (1) *either party* may be excused from liability "for a failure to perform *any* of his obligations." On the other hand, UCC 2-615 provides excuse *only for the seller*, and then only with respect to *two aspects* of performance — "delay in delivery" and "non-delivery."

427 **(a) Defective Goods.** The differing scope of the provisions on exemption in the Convention and in the UCC leads to this question: May a non-negligent seller be excused from liability when he delivers defective goods? Under the UCC, the answer is No, since the situation involves neither "delay" nor "non-delivery." Under the Convention the answer is not so obvious, since exemption may apply to a party's failure to perform *any* of its obligations.

ULIS. This issue was sharply contested in the preparation of ULIS. At the 1964 Hague Conference, the controversy centered on the choice

---

8. UCC 2-614 requires the disappointed party to accept the substituted performance, and thus is more akin to rules that bar rejection (or "avoidance") for insubstantial breach. See Arts. 49 and 64, *supra* at §301 and §353.

For criticism of English rules on frustration, and a recommendation for reform based on the UCC, see *Ont. Law Ref. Com.*, 11 Sales 365–385.

between two words: "obstacle" v. "circumstances."[9] The 1956 Draft that was brought to the Hague Conference provided that the non-performance must result from an "obstacle." A civil law group, led by the Federal Republic of Germany, feared that this test might refer only to supervening and external events, as contrasted with the more personal issue as to the seller's due care or fault, and might bar excuse based on an extreme and onerous change in economic circumstances. At the insistence of this group, the "obstacle" concept was eliminated. ULIS 74(1) follows:

ULIS Article 74
   1. Where one of the parties has not performed one of his obligations, he shall not be liable for such non-performance if he can prove that it was due to circumstances which according to the intention of the parties at the time of the conclusion of the contract, he was not bound to take into account or to avoid or to overcome; in the absence of any expression of the intention of the parties, regard shall be had to what reasonable persons in the same situation would have intended.

The crucial change was to extend exemption to situations where non-performance "was due to *circumstances....*" "Circumstances" could include a drastic change in costs or other economic conditions. In addition it could be argued that a seller could be freed from liability for defects in the goods that did not result from the seller's fault; such was the interpretation given to the drafting change in Professor Tunc's important commentary.[10]

UNCITRAL and Impediments. UNCITRAL faced this issue and replaced "circumstances" by "impediment" — a word that (like "obstacles") implies a barrier to performance, such as delivery of the goods or transmission of the price rather than an aspect personal to the seller's performance.[11] This decision that exemption applies only to impediments that *prevent* performance (as contrasted with

---

9. See Nicholas, *AJCL UNCITRAL Symposium* 237 *et seq.* The development of the exemption provision (Art. 74) at the 1964 Hague Conference is discussed in Riese, 29 Rabels Z. 79–81 (1965). See also W. Lee, 8 Dickinson J. Int. L. 375 (1990).
10. I *Records 1964 Conf.* 357 at 384; *Dolle, Kommentar* Art. 74(1) p. 456 at 101 (Stoll) (Exemption even for defect in goods existing when the contract is made; regretted deviation from Rabel's broad view of contractual liability and unclear scope of provision).
11. For an example of a decision that fails (apparently) to appreciate the significance of the "impediment" requirement, see Amtsgericht Charlottenburg, Germany, May 4, 1994, English translation available at http://cisgw3.law.pace.edu/cases/940915g1.html. In this case a seller delivered a shipment of shoes that included defective items. The buyer avoided the contract as to the non-conforming shoes (see Art. 51), and paid late for the shoes that it was keeping. Seller demanded, inter alia, interest for this late payment (see Art. 78). The

circumstances that lead to *defective* performance) is supported by the language of paragraph (4): "The party *who fails to perform* must give notice to the other party of the impediment . . ." — a requirement that would be absurd in connection with the delivery of goods with a hidden defect. It is significant that no notice requirement was included in ULIS 74 — a provision that, as we have seen, was understood to permit exemption for the non-negligent delivery of defective goods. This fundamental point — that exemption provided by Article 79 of CISG does not apply to defective performance such as the supply of non-conforming goods — was confirmed by the discussions and by decisions taken at the Diplomatic Conference.[12]

This result is also important to avoid undermining the Convention's contractual approach to the parties' obligations and its unitary approach to the remedies for breach. As we have seen, Article 35(1) provides: "The seller *must deliver* goods which are of the quantity, quality and description required by the contract" and Article 45 provides: "(1) If the seller fails to perform *any* of his obligations under the contract or this Convention" [including, of course, the seller's obligations (Article 35) to supply conforming goods] "the buyer may . . . (b) claim damages. . . . '
A parallel provision on breach by the buyer appears in Article 61(1)(b). The Convention thus is based on a unitary, contractual obligation to perform the contract and be responsible for damages — as contrasted

---

court denied this interest claim on the basis of Art. 79, arguing that the buyer could not be expected to pay promptly at a time when the seller was disputing the claim of partial non-conformity and refusing to take back any goods. The idea that the seller's delivery of non-conforming goods should exempt a buyer who delayed payment for conforming goods that it was keeping evidences a lack of understanding of the "impediment" requirement of Art. 79, and a "fault"-orientation that is inconsistent with the history and proper construction of the provision. Applying Art. 79 to free a party from a claim to interest also shows a failure to understand the effect of exemption under the provision — see Art. 79(5) and §435.6 *infra*. To the extent the seller's actions justified the buyer's late payment, the matter would better be handled under Art. 80.

12. The basic decision narrowing the area of exemption provided by ULIS 74 was taken in UNCITRAL: The Working Group: (1974) V *YB* 39–40, 58, *Docy. Hist.* 185–186, 204; (1975) VI *YB* 60–61, *Docy. ist.* 251–252; The Commission: VIII *YB* 56–57, *Docy. Hist.* 349–350; Diplomatic Conference: *O.R.* 80, 55–56, 378–386, 408–412, 430, 134–136, 227, *Docy. Hist.* 401, 445–446, 599–607, 629–633, 651, 705–708, 762 (adoption by Plenary 42-0). An authoritative analysis of the decision to deny exemption with respect to defects in goods by Professor Nicholas, chairman of the Drafting Party on exemption, appears in *Parker Colloq.* Ch. 5 at §5.02 [2] pp. 5–10–5–14. *Accord*, Tallon, *B-B Commentary* 580; Honnold's explanation at the Vienna Conference, *O.R.* 410–411, *Docy. Hist.* 631–632. *But cf. Schlechtriem 1986 Commentary* 101 n. 416a.

with some legal systems that make liberal use of the idea of fault in dealing with liability for damages for breach of contract.[13]

This decision has important practical consequences for buyers who suffer serious damage from defective goods. Deciding whether the defect resulted from "fault" may call for inquiry into the manufacturing processes of the seller or of a remote supplier.[14] Even when a heavy burden of proof is placed on the seller (or the supplier), a final resolution of the issue is expensive and uncertain. The burdens multiply when the product was manufactured by a remote supplier. As we shall see, exemption under Article 79 (as under most domestic rules) must ordinarily be based on events (e.g., war, embargo, flood, fire) that are widely known. Exemption based on the care taken in a producer's manufacturing processes is anomalous as well as impractical. In addition, the most plausible claim of non-negligence can be made by a seller who resells complex machinery or goods in sealed containers, in circumstances where inspection and testing is impractical. The buyer (unlike the seller) usually has no contractual relationship with the manufacturer who, in any case, may be remote from the buyer. Under these circumstances the only practicable way to transfer liability to the manufacturer is for the buyer to recover from its seller who can more readily secure redress from its supplier.

Despite the foregoing considerations, the discussion of exemption in the leading German commentary (edited by Professor Schlechtriem) argues that Article 79 may exempt a seller that has delivered non-conforming goods,[15] and a number of decisions are in agreement.[16] Of course the line separating failure to deliver because of an impediment

---

13. See Art. 45, *supra* at §276; Treitel, Remedies (Int. Enc.) §§78–79; Treitel Remedies (1988) Ch. II.

14. For an example of the complexity and difficulty of such an inquiry (albeit in the context of Art. 40 — concerning whether the seller "knew or could not have been unaware" of a defect in the goods — rather than Art. 79), see the decision Bundesgerichtshof, Germany, June 30, 2004, English translation available at http://cisgw3.law.pace.edu/cases/040630g1.html.

15. Hans Stoll & Georg Gruber, Art. 79 para. 6, *in* Schlechtriem & Schwenzer, *CISG Commentary* (2nd English ed. 2005). For other commentators who indicate that Art. 79 may exempt a seller that has delivered non-conforming goods see, e.g., Lookofsky, *Understanding CISG in the USA* §6.19 at 127 (although rejecting the specific approach to exemption advocated in the Stoll & Gruber commentary); Bridge, *International Sale of Goods* para. 3.59; Rimke, *Force Majeure and Hardship* 213.

16. See the decisions discussed in UNCITRAL Digest of case law on the United Nations Convention on the International Sale of Goods Art. 79 para. 8. *Cf. also* Oberlandesgericht Zweibrücken, Germany, February 2, 2004, English translation available at http://cisgw3. law.pace.edu/ cases/040202g1.html (apparently entertaining seller's claim to exemption for

and delivery of non-conforming goods because of an impediment can be extremely thin: a good faith seller who is unable to supply conforming goods may choose to withhold delivery, or may choose to ship the non-conforming goods with notice to the buyer of the problem.[17] *Such a choice, of course, arises only if the seller is aware of the lack of conformity.*

The German commentary mentioned above, however, argues that a seller who is reasonably unaware of a lack of conformity in delivered goods should, for that reason alone, be exempted from liability under Article 79.[18] **This position seems to reflect a lack of sympathy with the no-fault approach to liability for damages adopted in CISG.**[19] **That commentary argues, however, that such a seller would remain obligated to repair or provide substitutes for the non-conforming goods under Article 46(2) and (3).**[20] **The result of this approach is a situation that bears a curious resemblance to the traditional civil law approach — a seller that delivers non-conforming goods will not be liable in damages**

---

delivering non-conforming machinery, but denying the claim on the specific facts); Landgericht Freiburg, Germany, August 22, 2002, English translation available at http://cisgw3. law.pace.edu/cases/ 020822g1.html (rejecting seller's claim of exemption for selling a stolen vehicle that was recovered from the buyer; court reasoned that seller's title research was inadequate, perhaps implying that if seller had performed an adequate search and remained ignorant of the problem seller might have been exempt under Art. 79).

17. For the significance of notice, see Art. 79(4). Indeed, an example that has been included in this work since its first edition in 1982 (Example 50A in §310 *supra*), describes a situation in which a seller has an exemption for delivering non-conforming goods (see §311 *supra*).

18. Hans Stoll & Georg Gruber, Art. 79 para. 39, *in* Schlechtriem & Schwenzer, *CISG Commentary* (2nd English ed. 2005) (a seller who delivers goods that were in its possession when the contract was concluded and that had an existing lack of conformity "must therefore be permitted the defence that the defect was hidden and could not have been discovered by methods which a reasonable person in the seller's position could reasonably have been expected to adopt"); *id.* para. 40 ("the seller should be exempted under Art. 79 if he received the goods from a reliable supplier and the defect could not have been discovered using methods which could reasonably be expected of a reasonable person in the seller's position").

19. See, e.g., Hans Stoll & Georg Gruber, Art. 79 para. 40, *in* Schlechtriem & Schwenzer, *CISG Commentary* (2nd English ed. 2005) (responding to the argument that the Convention makes the seller "strictly liable" for delivery of non-conforming goods: "This thesis is open to the criticism that it is practically impossible for the seller to ensure the conformity of the goods with the contract if the goods are directly delivered from the seller's ancillary supplier to the buyer, as is usually the case in international trade").

20. Hans Stoll & Georg Gruber, Art. 79 para. 46, *in* Schlechtriem & Schwenzer, *CISG Commentary* (2nd English ed. 2005). The remedies provided for in Arts. 46(2) & (3) are discussed in §§283 & 284 *supra*. The effect of an Art. 79 exemption on remedies other than damages is discussed in §§435.4 & 435.4 *infra*.

unless it is at fault (i.e., it reasonably should have known of the lack of conformity at the time of delivery), but will remain subject to performance-oriented remedies such as repair and substitute goods.

Such an approach certainly would be awkward in States (such as the United States and other common-law jurisdictions) that, as permitted by Article 28 (see §§191–199 supra), might restrict the availability of specific-performance remedies like repair or replacement of goods; it could well lead to significant differences in outcome in different jurisdictions, with the resulting incentives to forum shop. The position that a seller's reasonable lack of awareness of a non-conformity should exempt it from liability for damages contradicts the structure and drafting history of the Convention, as well as its goal of uniform application. It is important, however, to avoid exaggerating the significance of the different positions on this issue: as the German commentary notes, under its approach a seller who delivers non-conforming goods will be exempted from liability "only . . . in exceptional cases" and "the different approaches will only rarely lead to divergent results."[21]

427.1 Loss-of-Value of Return Performance (Frustration of Purpose) *There are situations in which events occurring (or facts discovered) after a contract is concluded cause the return performance that a party is to receive under the contract to become less valuable. Unexpected technical obsolescence as well as unanticipated market and legal changes, for example, can adversely impact the value of goods that a buyer has contracted to purchase. When the decrease in value is extreme, there is a question whether the buyer must still perform its part of the contract (i.e., whether it will be liable if it does not take and pay for the goods). Domestic law often addresses — and can provide relief — in such situations.*[22] *The issues raised are, obviously, similar to those addressed in CISG Article 79. Article 79, however, provides an exemption when a party "fails to perform any of his obligations . . . due to an impediment," but in this situation the buyer's*

---

21. Hans Stoll & Georg Gruber, Art. 79 paras. 6 & 40, *in* Schlechtriem & Schwenzer, *CISG Commentary* (2nd English ed. 2005). See also Lookofsky, *Understanding CISG in the USA* §6.19 at 127 (the requirements of Art. 79 "reduce the possibility of a non-conformity exemption to something near nil"); Bridge, *International Sale of Goods* para. 3.59 (exemption where the seller has delivered non-conforming goods "should not arise with any frequency").

22. In the United States, such situations are governed by the doctrine of "frustration of purpose" (not to be confused with the similarly-named British doctrine). See *Restatement, Second of Contracts* §265 (1981).

performance of its obligations (i.e., paying the price) has not been prevented by the loss in value.

The issue raised by this situation could well be viewed as falling in a "gap" in the Convention — that is, it is an issue governed by CISG but it is not expressly settled in the Convention. Under Article 7(2) such gaps are to be filled, first, "in conformity with the general principles on which [the CISG] is based."[23] Article 79 contains principles for analyzing what risks the parties to a contract have assumed (and what risks they have not), and these principles are well suited to the loss-of-value situation. The principles underlying Article 79 suggest that exemption from liability for damages should be granted only if a very extreme (bordering on complete) loss-of-value resulted from developments that were beyond the control of the party claiming relief; if those developments were ones that the party could not reasonably be expected to have taken into account at the time of the conclusion of the contract; and if the party could not have avoided or overcome the consequences of the developments. This approach is consistent with the limited case law dealing with the issue.[24]

428   ## D. The Standard for Exemption for Non-Performance

Under Article 79(1), a party who seeks exemption from liability for non-performance must establish (*inter alia*) that the failure to perform "was due to an impediment beyond his control." How high and impenetrable must an "impediment" be to justify non-delivery or non-acceptance? We shall address this question at §432 *infra*. As background for this issue we now consider (1) the hazards of following diverse domestic law and (2) the possible relevance of contract patterns in international trade.

---

23. Only in the absence of such general principles are these gaps to be filled by reference to the (generally domestic) law applicable under rules of private international law. See Art. 7(2), discussed in §§96 ff.

24. See Cour de Cassation, France, June 30, 2004, English translation available at http:// cisgw3.law.pace.edu/cases/040630f1.html (buyer argued that changes in its own customer's requirements, which compelled buyer to use different goods than those buyer had already contracted to purchase from seller, exempted it from liability for failure to take and pay for goods; court applied Art. 79 analysis but rejected exemption argument because buyer failed to show that its customer's changed demands were not foreseeable (i.e., they could have been taken into account at the time the contract was concluded)).

429　**(1) Domestic Law: Hazards; Comparative Law**

Attention has been drawn, *supra* at §425, to the danger that local tribunals may unconsciously read the patterns of their domestic law into the general language of the Convention — an approach that would be inconsistent with the Convention's basic goal of international unification (Article 7(1)). And deliberate recourse to the exemption rules of a single domestic system would flagrantly violate the Convention. As we have seen, Article 7(2) permits recourse to "the law applicable by virtue of the rules of private international law" only as a last resort — that is, when questions are "not expressly settled" by the Convention and cannot be "settled in conformity with the general principles on which it is based" (§102 *supra*). The fact that a provision of the Convention presents problems of application does not authorize recourse to some one system of domestic law since this would undermine the Convention's objective "to promote uniformity in its application" (Article 7(1)). However, no such difficulty arises from a comparative law approach that seeks guidance from the prevailing patterns and trends of modern domestic law.

To be sure, a comparative law approach will be subject to practical limitations. However, comparative studies, stimulated in part by the Convention, are proceeding apace. Moreover, an international body of case law has developed under this and other articles of the Convention. This material would have relatively little value if (in violation of Article 7(2)) tribunals were to resolve ambiguities in the Convention by referring to their own domestic law[25] or to some other legal system indicated by the rules of PIL.

In seeking guidance from a consensus or "common core" of domestic law, certain standards of relevance will be appropriate. The Convention is designated for international trade; the most relevant rules of domestic law are those that reflect the practices and problems of international trade or, at least, grow out of domestic transactions that are comparable to those of international trade. And, akin to this, is the special value of legal trends that reflect a careful reworking and modernization of traditional and archaic legal concepts.

---

25. This has, very unfortunately, occurred in a U.S. court with respect to Art. 79. See Raw Materials, Inc. v. Manfred Forberich GmbH & Co., KG, 2004 WL 1535839 (U.S. District Court for the Northern District of Illinois, July 7, 2004). See also Joseph Lookofsky & Harry Flechtner, *Nominating* Manfred Forberich: *The Worst CISG Decision in 25 Years?*, 9 Vindabona J. Int'l Comm. L. & Arb. 199 (2005).

Professor Tallon, responding to the above suggestion in the first edition, was concerned lest tribunals, after comparing the different domestic approaches to exemption, would conclude that their own system was the most modern and appropriate for international trade.[26] The warning needs to be taken seriously and should lead to withdrawal of the above suggestion if one could believe that tribunals would not, in any case, consider and be influenced by the legal system with which they are familiar; perhaps attention to the approaches of other legal systems could serve as a mild antidote for inevitable national bias. Admittedly, it would be wrong to give weight to domestic legal rules on points where the words of the Convention (in their full legislative context) speak with sufficient clarity to dislodge the natural predilection for familiar domestic law. However, this writer at §432.1, *infra*, confesses to despair over the power of words to communicate answers to the questions of degree that are intrinsic to our current problem. In this situation we need all the help we can get!

The next section suggests yet another unconventional approach. Is it equally dangerous?

430   E. Modern Contract Practices as a Guide

Reference has been made to the widespread use of contract provisions in this area and to the special value of standard terms prepared, for specific types of international transactions, through the collaboration of sellers and buyers. A few examples of contract clauses on exemption will provide a basis for considering the value of contract patterns in applying the Convention.

431   (1) Examples of Exemption Clauses

Over the course of the past decades, the United Nations Economic Commission for Europe (ECE) has supervised and finalized the work of representatives of sellers and buyers and of governmental representatives in preparing general conditions of sale (standard contracts) for a wide variety of transactions. All of these contracts contain provisions on exemption from liability when performance has been prevented by a supervening impediment.

---

26. See Tallon, B-B Commentary 595.

One of the important ECE General Conditions covers the Supply of Plant and Machinery for Export (No. 188); this version was prepared for transactions among countries with market economies. The contract terms on exemption (or "reliefs") are as follows:

General Conditions (ECE) No. 188[27]
10. RELIEFS
10.1. The following shall be considered as cases of relief if they intervene after the formation of the Contract and impede its performance: industrial disputes and any other circumstances (e.g., fire mobilization, requisition, embargo, currency restrictions, insurrection, shortage of transport, general shortage of materials and restrictions in the use of power) when such other circumstances are beyond the control of the parties.
10.2. The party wishing to claim relief by reason of any of the said circumstances shall notify the other party in writing without delay on the intervention and on the cessation thereof.
10.3 The effects of the said circumstances, so far as they affect the timely performance of their obligations by the parties, are defined in Clauses 7 and 8. Save as provided in paragraphs 7.5., 7.7., and 8.7., if, by reason of any of the said circumstances, the performance of the Contract within a reasonable time becomes impossible, either party shall be entitled to terminate the Contract by notice in writing to the other party without requiring the consent of any Court....

The above contract includes (§10.1) a list of specific occurrences that might impede performance, and gives special effect to "industrial disputes."[28]

432 **(a) Use of Contract Patterns in Applying Convention.** The specific provisions of the above General Conditions of Sales and other standard contract terms do not bind the parties unless they have agreed to them. But contracts drafted jointly by sellers and buyers may be useful (along with modern patterns of contract law) to help solve problems of interpreting and applying the general standards of the Convention. A pattern of contracting that is "widely known to, and regularly observed by, parties to contracts of the type involved in the particular trade

27. *General Conditions for the Supply of (ECE) Plant and Machinery* No. 188 (1953) (U.N. Pub. ME/188 bis/53) is reprinted in Sources at 90–97. *General Condition (ECE)* No. 188A: Supply and Erection of Plant and Machinery for Import and Export (1957) (U.N. Pub. 1957, II.E/Min.3) is reprinted in Sources at 98–108. An approach similar to that of ECE No. 188 is followed in General Conditions for the Supply of Machinery and other Mechanical and Electrical Appliances within and between Denmark, Finland, Norway and Sweden §32. (This set of general conditions is reprinted in Sources at 212, 215, 216.).
28. Helpful examples of exemption clauses also are provided in the *Kritzer Guide* at 520–522 (clauses from 7 national settings) and 566 (model export contract, Art. 6 — Excusable Delays) and in the *Kritzer Manual* Ch. 8. Model clauses are also discussed in Rimke, *Force Majeure and Hardship* 232–233.

concerned" may constitute a usage that the parties have "impliedly made applicable to their contract." (See Art. 9, *supra* at §113.) In addition, contract patterns may be useful to inform a tribunal with respect to the practicability and suitability of competing interpretations of the Convention.[29] Professor Nicholas notes that a crucial element in Article 79(1) is whether the party claiming exemption could "reasonably be expected to have taken the impediment into account at the time of the conclusion of the contract" and that patterns of contracting in similar transactions can bear on the "reasonable expectations" of the parties.[30]

It has not been feasible here to reproduce and analyze a sufficient number of contract terms to provide a basis for suggesting patterns of contract practices for various types of international sales. The above examples, however, may provide suggestive leads for further inquiry by those who face problems in this area.

432.1   F. "Impediment" — How Tough a Barrier?

As we have seen (§427 *supra*), paragraph 1 of Article 79 embodies a decision that exemption from liability for a "failure to perform" should be confined to situations in which an "impediment" *prevents* performance — production or delivery of goods, transfer of funds to pay the price. Paragraph 1 also emphasizes that grounds for excusing failure to perform are strict. Thus, the party seeking exemption must prove that its failure to perform (1) "was due to an impediment *beyond his control*" and that the party (2) "could not reasonably be expected to have *taken the impediment into account*" when the contract was made or (3) "to have *avoided* or *overcome* [the impediment] or its consequences."

The nub of our problem is this: It is not practicable to enumerate the circumstances that will excuse a failure to perform. Instead, words must try to express a dividing point on a continuum between "difficult" and "impossible." Even domestic rules cast in terms of "impossibility"

---

29. See Harold J. Berman, *Excuse for Nonperformance in the Light of Contract Practices in International Trade*, 63 Colum. L. Rev. 1413 (1963), and the proceedings of the I.A.L.S. (1960); Helsinki colloquium, *Force Majeure (I.A.L.S.)* 24–29 (Affolter), 37–41 (Berman), 68–81 (Dölle), 145–155 (Schmitthoff). The above approach is supported by the view, which this writer shares, that where the terms of the contract give no guidance, the court should consider what the parties would have provided if they had addressed the question. See Hans Smit, *Frustration of Contract: A Comparative Attempt at* Consolidation, 58 Colum. L. Rev. 287, 313 (1958), *cf. Restatement, Second of Contracts*, Intro. to Ch. 11.
30. See Parker Colloq. 5–9.

conceal questions of degree. Military blockade and government prohibition[31] provide excuse on the grounds of "impossibility" although it may be possible to run a blockade or evade a law. However, the varying concrete results under diverse formulations of domestic law provide a point of reference. Tallon, on the basis of careful study, suggests that the Convention stands somewhere between the most strict and the most liberal of the domestic systems.[32] The discussion in §432.2 *infra* concerning whether economic barriers to performance can constitute an exempting impediment under Article 79 is also relevant here.

In spite of strenuous efforts of legislators and scholars we face the likelihood that Article 79 may be the Convention's least successful part of the half-century of work towards international uniformity.[33] This prospect calls for careful, detailed contract drafting to provide solutions to fit the commercial situation at hand. (Examples of standard contract provisions were set forth at §431 *supra*.) Those who are not able to solve the problem by contract must await the process of mutual criticism and adjustment by tribunals and scholars in the various jurisdictions.

432.2   **(1) Economic Difficulties and Dislocations**

The Convention, as we have seen, narrowed the grounds for exemption in ULIS 74 by replacing exemption based on *"circumstances"* with a provision that failure to perform must be "due to an *impediment*" (§423.3 *supra*). In addition to denying exemption for the delivery of defective goods, this change responded to concerns that the reference to "circumstances" could be a basis for excuse merely because performance became more difficult or unprofitable.[34] However, the language of Article 79(1) seems to leave room for exemptions based on economic dislocations that constitute an "impediment" to performance comparable to non-economic barriers that excuse failure of performance. From this view, which is widely but not universally shared,[35] the standard for

31. Acts of government have been recognized as exempting impediments under Art. 79. See the UNCITRAL Digest Art. 79 para. 16.

32. See Tallon, *B-B Commentary* 592. See also Nicholas, *Parker Colloq.* 5–4 to 5–6 (comparison of domestic approaches) and 5–9 (emphasis on Art. 79(1)'s reference to what a party could "reasonably be expected" to take into account in the light of usages and contract practices in the trade concerned).

33. Accord, Rimke, Force Majeure and Hardship 241–242.

34. See V *YB* 38, *Docy. Hist.* 185 (para. 108).

35. See *Schlechtriem, 1986 Commentary* 101; Enderlein & Maskow, *International Sales Law* Art. 79 §6.3 at 324–325; Rimke, Force Majeure and Hardship 222–223 & 225–226. But see

exemption is not strict impossibility of performance, but rather such extreme difficulty in performance as amounts to impossibility from a practical (although not technical) viewpoint.

Assume that the supply of a material needed to manufacture certain goods unexpectedly becomes so reduced in quantity and inflated in price that only a minority of manufacturers that require this material can continue in production. This situation clearly constitutes an "impediment" rendering performance impossible for most manufacturers whose contracts to sell the goods overlap the onset of the shortage; requiring production by only one (or a minority) unfairly prejudices some in favor of their competitors. Comparable unfairness can result if extreme and unexpected currency dislocations make it impossible for sellers to continue to produce or for buyers to purchase at the monetary values stated in those contracts that overlap the dislocation. *In these situations, of course, the other requirements qualifying the kind of impediment that will satisfy Article 79(1) — that is, that the impediment be beyond the control of the party claiming exemption, and that such party could not reasonably be expected to have taken the impediment into account at the time of contract conclusion or to have later avoided or overcome it — continue to apply.*

The question whether something less than literal impossibility of performance (such as an extreme increase in the cost of performance) can satisfy the requirements of Article 79 raises the question of the applicability of "hardship" doctrine in transactions governed by the CISG. Civil law hardship doctrine requires parties to negotiate an adjustment to a contract — and, if they fail to reach a negotiated adjustment, permits a court to end the contract or even impose a judge-made adjustment — when the contract's economic balance is severely disrupted by unforeseen developments.[36] *The economic imbalance required to invoke*

Hans Stoll & Georg Gruber, Art. 79 paras. 30–32, *in* Schlechtriem & Schwenzer, *CISG Commentary* (2nd English ed. 2005), which advances arguments for the non-applicability of Art. 79 to cases of impracticability or "mere" economic obstacles. The approach by the latter authority rests in part on assumptions that depart sharply from those in the current commentary — specifically, that a party exempt from damages under Art. 79 nevertheless remains obligated to perform under Arts. 46 or 62 (contrast §435.5 *infra*); and that upon a radical change in economic conditions adverse to a promisor the principle of good faith in Art. 7(1) would require the promisee to agree either to adjust the contract terms to reflect the changed conditions or to release the promisor from its obligations (contrast the discussion of "hardship" doctrine in this section *infra*).

36. For a distillation of domestic hardship doctrines in Europe, see Art. 6.111 of the Principles of European Contracts Law (1998). For an internationally-focused hardship doctrine,

hardship, although it must be extreme, is clearly less than would result in impossibility of performance. The distinctive feature of hardship, however, is not the standard that triggers the doctrine; after all, domestic excuse rules such as U.S. impracticability doctrine, as well (as we have seen) as Article 79 itself, do not require literal impossibility, and can be satisfied by "mere" economic dislocations if they are sufficiently extreme. Rather, the distinctive feature of hardship doctrine is its remedy — adaptation of the contract, including the possibility of judge-imposed adjustments. This stands in contrast to the remedy provided by Article 79 — exemption from liability for damages for non-performance. In other words, hardship doctrine looks to continuation of the contract (on new terms affording a just basis) whereas Article 79 exemption contemplates its termination. Proposals to include a hardship-like doctrine aimed at adapted performance of an economically-disrupted contract were rejected during the drafting of Article 79.[37] Thus such doctrines — whether they originate in domestic law invoked to fill a perceived (but actually non-existent) "gap" in the Convention,[38] or are a matter of implied contractual terms where there is no indication that the parties have specifically contemplated such adjustment[39] — should have no application in contracts governed by the CISG.[40] Extreme price and (especially) currency dislocations may be sufficiently widespread to lead to laws or administrative regulations

---

see Arts. 6.2.2 and 6.2.3 of the UNIDROIT Principles of International Commercial Contracts (2004).

37. See Rimke, Force Majeure and Hardship 218–219.

38. See authorities cited in Hans Stoll & Georg Gruber, Art. 79 para. 31 n. 110, *in* Schlechtriem & Schwenzer, *CISG Commentary* (2nd English ed. 2005).

39. Hans Stoll & Georg Gruber, Art. 79 para. 32, *in* Schlechtriem & Schwenzer, *CISG Commentary* (2nd English ed. 2005), suggest that an obligation to renegotiate the terms of a contract if unforeseen difficulties upset the economic balance between the parties can be based either on the principle of good faith stated in Art. 7(2) of the Convention or on a "reasonable interpretation" of the contract. This appears to reflect an outlook shaped by domestic law that includes a hardship doctrine. Tribunals from jurisdictions (like the United States) where the domestic law does not include a hardship-adaptation doctrine are unlikely to see such an approach as obvious (much less required). Incorporating a hardship doctrine in the suggested manner, therefore, might well undermine the uniformity that is a primary goal of the CISG.

40. See Rimke, *Force Majeure and Hardship* 219 ("The problem of hardship has thus been considered during the drafting process of Article 79, but a provision which specifically dealing with it has been deliberately omitted from the CISG. The history of Article 79 excludes the possibility that there is an unstated hardship in the Convention. Article 79's purpose of establishing definite limits as to a promisor's responsibility for breach of contract supports this conclusion. Resort to domestic laws is precluded by Article 7(2).").

that require contract readjustment. Although the Convention does not displace domestic rules of "validity" unless it has "expressly provided" for an issue (Article 4(a), Article 79 comprehensively regulates the impact of changed circumstances on the parties' obligations and should be read to pre-empt domestic rules on this question.[41]

In sum, the application of Article 79 to unanticipated economic difficulties should be consistent with the general principles applicable to this provision: (1) Exemption is confined to barriers to performance (e.g., delivery or payment); (2) An "impediment" to performance may result from general economic difficulties and dislocations only if they constitute a barrier to performance that is comparable to other types of exempting causes.

432.3 **Impediment Existing When Contract Concluded ("Initial Impossibility")** *The most obvious application of Article 79 is in situations where performance is prevented by an impediment that arises after the contract is concluded. Must the impediment arise post-contract to trigger Article 79? Suppose a contract for sale requires specific goods — for example, a particular used piece of heavy industrial machinery, identified in the contract by serial number, which the buyer had inspected and approved before the sale was concluded. After the sale is entered into but before the time for delivery (and before the risk of loss for the goods has passed to the buyer) the goods are struck by a meteorite and destroyed. Because the seller is unable to perform (i.e., it cannot deliver the machinery that the contract specifically required) due to an impediment that was beyond the seller's control, that it could not reasonably be expected to have taken into account when the contract was concluded, and that it could neither have avoided nor overcome, the seller would appear to be exempt from liability for damages under Article 79.*[42] *Now suppose*

---

41. Compare the analysis in §§238 & 240 *supra* concerning the applicability of domestic rules addressing an innocent misrepresentation of the quality of the goods. Schlechtriem makes this significant observation: "It is imperative to treat radically changed circumstances as "impediments' under Article 79 in exceptional cases in order to avoid the danger that courts will find a gap in the Convention and invoke domestic laws with their widely divergent solutions." *1986 Commentary* 102 n. 422a. Domestic rules may not modify CISG provisions dealing with the same problem merely by calling themselves rules of "validity." See §§234, 240, *supra.* CISG Art. 4(a) should apply only to rules of "validity" in the sense that agreement is barred no matter how clearly it is stated. See §234, *supra.*

42. Note, however, that the seller's Art. 79 exemption does not alter the fact that the seller bears risk of loss — that is, the buyer does not have to pay for the destroyed goods. If the

that the meteorite struck shortly before the contract was concluded, but neither party knew (or should have known) of the destruction at that time. Should this difference in timing make a difference in the application of Article 79? Nothing in the provision expressly specifies when the impediment must arise. Of course the requirement that the party claiming exemption "could not reasonably be expected to have taken the impediment into account at the time of the conclusion of the contract" may make it less likely that a pre-existing impediment will satisfy all the requirements of Article 79(1), but it is certainly possible (as in the example above).[43]

In the example above, the pre-existing impediment interfered with (indeed, rendered impossible) the performance of the contract. As was noted in §427.1 supra, however, some impediments affect not a party's ability to perform, but rather the value of the return performance that party is to receive — and this can be just as true for impediments already existing when the contract was formed as for later-arising impediments. For example, suppose that moments before a contract of sale was executed (at a time too close to the execution ceremony to

---

seller tries to deliver the charred and mangled remains of the machinery, the buyer can avoid the contract — see §435.4 *infra*. Thus the seller has lost the value of those goods.

43. Most (but not all) commentators agree that situations involving "initial impossibility" (such as the example in the text) are governed by Art. 79, and domestic doctrines dealing with the question are therefore pre-empted. See, e.g., Hans Stoll & Georg Gruber, Art. 79 paras. 12–13, *in* Schlechtriem & Schwenzer, *CISG Commentary* (2nd English ed. 2005); Enderlein & Maskow, *International Sales Law* Art. 79 §§5.1 & 5.2 at 323; Franco Ferrari, *The Interaction between the United Nations Convention on Contracts for the International Sale of Goods and Domestic Remedies (Rescission for Mistake and Remedies in Torts), in* 71 Rabels Zeitschrift für auslandisches und internationales Privatrecht 52ff. (2007); Rimke, *Force Majeure and Hardship* 213. The counter-argument is based on the idea that the domestic doctrines applicable to this situation (in U.S. domestic law, for example, the situation is likely to be analyzed under the rubric of "mistake") raise issues of "validity" that, under Art. 4(a), are beyond the scope of the CISG. See Lookofsky, *Understanding CISG in the USA* §2.6 at 24; Bridge, *International Sale of Goods* §8.03 at 297–298; Tallon, *B-B Commentary* 578. For an account of this controversy, see Todd Weitzmann, *Validity and Excuse in the U.N. Sales Convention*, 16 J.L. & Com. 265, text accompanying nn. 56–64 (1997). The problem with this latter approach is that, as Art. 4 makes clear, only questions of validity that are not "expressly provided [for] in this Convention" are beyond the scope of the CISG. Thus before one can conclude that initial impossibility is beyond the scope of the CISG (and is therefore governed by domestic law) one must *first* determine whether the issue is governed by Art. 79. Using the validity exclusion to determine the scope of Art. 79 turns this process on its head. See Franco Ferrari, *The Interaction between the United Nations Convention on Contracts for the International Sale of Goods and Domestic Remedies (Rescission for Mistake and Remedies in Torts), in* 71 Rabels Zeitschrift für auslandisches und internationales Privatrecht 52ff. (2007).

permit the parties to learn of it) a completely unanticipated emergency regulation was issued forbidding resale of the goods in the market that was the buyer's target. The regulation does not prevent or even interfere with the buyer's performance of its obligation (to take delivery and pay the price). It thus appears outside the matters expressly addressed in Article 79—just as, it was argued in §427.1 supra, an impediment with similar consequences arising after contract formation would be beyond the express scope of Article 79.

Like the later-arising impediment, the regulation in the example raises a question whether the buyer should be exempt from damages if it refuses to perform in these circumstances. Just as with a post-contract-conclusion impediment that destroys the value of the return performance a party is to receive, there are domestic law doctrines that address this issue.[44] The solution suggested in §427.1 supra for the post-contract conclusion impediment appears equally appropriate here—treat the matter as an "internal gap" under Article 7(2) and use the general principles underlying Article 79 to resolve the situation. The only issue is whether, under applicable non-Convention law, the effect of an existing impediment that destroys the value of the return performance a party is to receive is a question of "validity,"[45] and thus beyond the scope of the Convention (i.e., an "external gap"). In that case, Article 7(2) would not apply, and the issue would not be eligible for resolution by reference to the general principles on which the Convention is based.[46]

433 ## G. Performance Delegated to Third Party

Paragraph (2) addresses cases where a party delegates performance to a third party who fails to perform.

Example 79A. Seller contracted to sell Buyer a machine to be built in accordance with specifications supplied by Buyer. Seller contracted with

---

44. In U.S. law it is likely to be analyzed as a question of excuse for mistake.

45. For discussion of the exclusion of "validity" issues from the Convention, see §§64–69 *supra.*

46. Domestic rules that might "invalidate" contracts based on pre-existing impediments that prevent or burden performance (as opposed to those that undermine the value of return performance) should be pre-empted by the Convention, despite the "validity exclusion" (Art. 4(a)), because the effect of such impediments is expressly provided for in Art. 79. The effect of a post-contract-conclusion impediment that undermines the value of the return performance that a party is to receive (discussed in §427.1 *supra*) should not be seen as an issue of "validity": only rules that render a contract void *ab initio* should be deemed rules of validity. See §64 *supra*; Todd Weitzmann, *Validity and Excuse in the U.N. Sales Convention,* 16 J.L. & Com. 265, text accompanying n. 65 (1997).

Electron to manufacture the machine. Electron had a good reputation for efficiency and responsibility but, in this case, mismanaged production so that it was unable to deliver the machine. At the time of Electron's default, Seller could not obtain the machine from another supplier and was unable to deliver the machine to Buyer.

Under the general rule in paragraph (1), Seller might be able to contend that Electron's failure constituted an "impediment beyond [Seller's] control," and that Seller would therefore be exempt from liability to Buyer. Paragraph (2) restricts exemption in situations like this in which a party (e.g., Seller) has engaged a third person (Electron) "to perform the whole or a part of the contract." The crucial question is posed by paragraph (2)(b): Would the third person (Electron) be exempt from liability to Seller under the rules of paragraph (1)? Here the answer is No. Consequently, Seller cannot be exempt from liability to Buyer. The net effect is that if Seller's default forces it to pay damages to Buyer, Seller must look to Electron for reimbursement. (Under modern procedural systems, if Buyer sues Seller, Seller would bring in Electron as a third-party defendant.) On the other hand, assume that Seller's contract with Electron called for Electron to produce the machine at a specified manufacturing plant, and that, before the date for delivery to Buyer, Electron's plant was destroyed by flood or some other impediment that met the standards of Paragraph (1). Since Electron would be exempt from liability to Seller the barrier to exemption in Paragraph (2)(a) would not apply; Seller could be exempt from liability to Buyer under paragraph (1).

Problems comparable to those posed by Example 79A could also arise if the seller is obliged to deliver the goods to the buyer (as under a quotation *ex ship* Buyer's port) and thus is responsible for transit damage to the goods. If the goods are damaged in transit because of ordinary circumstances (water seepage, improper stowage, or the like), the seller would not only be responsible for the physical damage but also could be liable to the buyer for damages such as production interruption (Art. 74, §§403–408, *supra*). On the other hand, if the goods were lost or seriously damaged as a result of a hurricane, embargo or similar impediment, the seller would bear the loss from physical damage (subject to insurance) but might be exempt from liability for damages to the buyer that resulted from (e.g.) interruption of production.[47]

---

47. Relief of a seller from liability for consequential damages when a ship was interned was illustrated in the setting of Art. 50, *supra* §310. *Cf. Restatement, Second of Contracts* §261, comment e.

434 (1) Default by General Supplier

In Example 79A, *supra*, Seller engaged Electron to manufacture a machine to specifications supplied by Buyer. This case clearly fell within paragraph 2 of Article 79, which applies when a party (P) engages a third person (T) "to perform the whole or a part" of P's contract of sale. The scope of paragraph 2 becomes clearer in the light of its legislative history.

The article on exemption in ULIS (Article 74) had no such provision. However, the UNCITRAL Working Group's 1975 draft (para. 2) was substantially the same as CISG 79(2) except for language that described the third person as a "subcontractor."[48] The report of UNCITRAL's 1977 review in the Committee of the Whole of this language includes the following: "The Committee decided to delete the word "subcontractor." The term was said to be unknown in some legal systems and in others to refer primarily to relationships in the context of construction contracts." In place of this term the Committee decided to substitute "a person whom [*e.g.*] [the seller] has engaged to perform the whole or a part of the contract." The report continued, "It was noted that it would be clear that a seller would not be exempt from liability . . . because of the failure of one of his suppliers to perform since a supplier of the seller could not be considered to be a person the seller had engaged to perform any portion of the seller's contract."[49] At the Diplomatic Conference proposals to include exemption based on defaults by a supplier were not accepted and the UNCITRAL draft was adopted.[50]

This legislative history indicates that narrow scope should be given to the phrase "a third person whom [a party] has engaged to perform the

48. Paragraph (2) of the text approved in 1975 by the Working Group (VI *YB* 60, 61, *Docy. Hist.* 251–252) provided: "2. Where the non-performance of the seller is due to non-performance by a subcontractor, the seller shall be exempt from liability only if he is exempt under the provisions of the preceding paragraph and if the subcontractor would be so exempt if the provisions of that paragraph were applied to him." This language, based on a draft developed at the 1974 session (V *YB* 39–40, *Docy. Hist.* 185–186), responded to views that ULIS 74 provided an area of exemption that was too broad. See *id.* para. 108.

49. VIII *YB* 56, *Docy. Hist.* 349 (para. 448–449). The language resulting from UNCITRAL's 1977 review became Art. 65(2) of the 1978 UNCITRAL draft and in substance was approved as Art. 79(2) of the Convention. The Secretariat Commentary on Art. 65(2) of the 1978 Draft stated: "The third person must be someone who has engaged to perform the whole or part of the contract. It does not include suppliers of the goods or of raw materials to the seller." *O.R.* 56, *Docy. Hist.* 446 (para. 12).

50. *O.R.* 378–381, 408–412, *Docy. Hist.* 599–602, 629–633. For a summary of the conflicting views see *Schlechtriem, 1986 Commentary* 103–104.

whole or part of the contract." In Tallon's words there must be an "organic link" between the main contract and the subcontract.[51] Paragraph (2) would apply, as in Example 79A, §433 *supra*, if a seller (S) turns over to a third party (T) the performance of S's duty to manufacture goods to buyer's (B's) specifications. The paragraph would also seem to apply if S delegates to T S's duty to procure goods and deliver them to B. In both cases S will be exempt from damages for failure to perform the contract only if T was prevented by an impediment that constitutes an excuse under Article 79(1). In short, if under the standard set in Article 79(1) T is liable in damages to S, then S should not be excused from liability to B. (Since T contracted only with S, and S contracted only with B, it would often be difficult or impossible for B to obtain redress directly from T.)[52]

The exclusion of general suppliers from the specialized rule of paragraph (2) does not mean that defaults by a supplier will never lead to exemption for a seller. Assume that a government embargo prevents suppliers from obtaining or selling materials that the seller requires to perform its contract; the embargo could constitute an "impediment" under Article 79(1) exempting the seller from liability to its buyer.[53]

---

51. *B-B Commentary* 585. Tallon also suggests that the third party "should know that his action is a means of performing the main contract" and "must relate only" to the performance of the main contract. For other discussions of the scope of Art. 79(2), see Nicholas, *Parker Colloq.* 5–11 to 23; *Schlechtriem, 1986 Commentary* 104; Hans Stoll & Georg Gruber, Art. 79 para. 26, *in* Schlechtriem & Schwenzer, *CISG Commentary* (2nd English ed. 2005) (arguing that, for Art. 79(2) to apply, the third person must be engaged "after the conclusions of the contract" and must be "aware that he is not acting as a mere supplier"); Bridge, *International Sale of Goods* para. 3.61 (suggesting that Art. 79(2) applies where a party's performance has been delegated to a third party). In the decision of the Tribunal of International Commercial Arbitration at the Russian Federation Chamber of Commerce and Industry, Russian Federation, 30 July 2001, English translation available at http://cisgw3.-law.pace.edu/cases/010730r1.html, the tribunal rejected a buyer's claim that the Russian Central Bank's order forbidding hard currency payments was an impediment that exempted the buyer from damages for failure to pay for delivered goods. The decision appears to indicate that the situation was governed by Art. 79(2) because (according to the English translation) the action of a third party (i.e., the buyer's Russian bank) was "necessary for the performance of the contract" and thus the buyer would be exempt only if its bank would also qualify for exemption under Art. 79(1). For other decisions on the applicability of Art. 79(2), see UNCITRAL Digest of case law on the United Nations Convention on the International Sale of Goods Art. 79 para. 21.

52. Tallon, *B-B Commentary* 584–585.

53. For a decision entertaining the possibility that a seller can be exempt when its general supplier defaulted, see the decision of the Bundesgerichtshof, Switzerland, April 5, 2005, English translation available at http://cisgw3.law.pace.edu/cases/050405s1.html.

Such occurrences, however, are rare;[54] less rare are the situations that fall within Article 79(2) in which a seller engages a third party "to perform the whole or a part" of S's contract with B. Finally, as we have seen (*supra* at §427), Article 79 should not exempt a seller from liability to the buyer for defects in goods; the seller is responsible although the defective goods came from a general supplier or a party to whom the seller has delegated its duty to deliver the goods.

435 **H. Temporary and Partial Impediments**

435.1 **(1) Temporary Impediments**

Paragraph (3) of Article 79 addresses the following situation:

Example 79B. Seller contracted to deliver goods to Buyer on June 1. Before the time for delivery a government embargo (or some comparable impediment) prevented Seller from complying with the contract. On June 30 the embargo (or other impediment) was removed and it was then possible for Seller to deliver the goods to Buyer.

Paragraph (3) leads to the following consequences: (a) Seller is relieved of liability for delay in performing during June; (b) Seller is obliged to deliver to Buyer when the impediment is removed.

The more interesting question is this: Must Buyer accept Seller's delivery on July 1? Answering this question calls for close attention to paragraph (5): "Nothing in this article prevents either party from exercising any right *other than to claim damages* under this Convention." In short, Buyer's right to avoid the contract is not affected by Article 79. If the month's delay in delivery constituted a "fundamental breach" (Article 25), Buyer may avoid the contract (Article 49).[55] If

---

54. See the decision of the Tribunal of International Commercial Arbitration at the Russian Federation Chamber of Commerce and Industry, Russian Federation, April 9, 2004, English translation available at http://cisgw3.law.pace.edu/cases/040409r1.html (summarily rejecting the seller's claim that production difficulties afflicting its supplier should exempt it from damages for failure to deliver).

55. The second ground for avoidance based on a *Nachfrist* notice (Arts. 47(1) and 49(1)(b), §305 *supra*) — an alternative to establishing that the delay constituted a fundamental breach — should not be available to the buyer here. This remedy depends on a notice under Art. 47(1) fixing an additional period "of reasonable length for *performance*," it would be inconsistent with the language and spirit of this provision for the buyer to fix a deadline for performance when the performance demanded is subject to exemption under Art. 79. *Contra* Bridge, *International Sale of Goods* para. 3.58 at 107.

Buyer duly notified Seller of avoidance Seller would have no right to deliver but would not be liable for damages; Buyer would have no obligation to accept the goods. Of course, as we have seen, not every delay (or other non-conformity) in performance justifies avoidance of the contract (Articles 25, 49, 64). If the Convention provided that any delay or other deviation justified avoidance, there might be strong reasons for relaxing such a strict rule when a slight delay is caused by an impediment. But in the context of the Convention's limited right of avoidance, there is no justification for a rule that a party awaiting performance is both (a) deprived of compensation for delay and (b) required to accept the late performance.[56]

The 1978 Draft provided in paragraph (3) that the exemption "has effect *only* for the period during which the impediment exists." At the diplomatic conference it was proposed to add to paragraph (3) a provision that "the party who fails to perform" (i.e., Seller, in Example 79B) is "permanently exempted" if during the period of temporary exemption the circumstances have "so radically changed that it would be manifestly unreasonable to hold him liable." This proposal was rejected but, as an alternative, the word "only" in paragraph (3) was deleted; this change was designed to avoid any impression that paragraph (3) laid down a rigid rule requiring contract relations to resume on the original basis no matter how long the interruption or how great the changes in circumstances.[57]

435.2   **(2) Impediment Preventing Part of Performance**

Example 79C. A contract called for Seller to manufacture for Buyer 1000 units of an alloy that required specified amounts of scarce metal X. Thereafter, government regulations unexpectedly restricted and rationed the use of X; under these regulations Seller could obtain only enough X to manufacture 600 units of the alloy. Seller immediately notified Buyer that Seller would be unable to deliver 400 units. These questions arise: (1) Does Article 79 exempt Seller

---

56. For a similar handling of delay see (U.S.A.) UCC 2–615(l)(a), quoted *supra* §425.

57. See *Com. I* Art. 65, para. (3)(i) *Norway, O.R.* 134, *Docy. Hist.* 706; SK. 27 paras. 52–53, *O.R.* 381, *Docy. Hist.* 602; Hans Stoll & Georg Gruber, Art. 79 para. 42, *in* Schlechtriem & Schwenzer, *CISG Commentary* (2nd English ed. 2005). It may be hoped that this added flexibility will be useful in some of the situations posed by Nicholas in AJCL UNCITRAL Symposium 231 at 242–244.

from damages for failure to deliver the 400 units? (2) What options are open to Buyer?

(a) Exemption for Seller. As Tallon notes, Article 79(3) deals with an impediment for a limited time but makes no provision as to an impediment affecting part of the contract.[58] Nevertheless, Seller is entitled to exemption as to the 400 units. Unlike some legal systems. Article 79 does not speak of nullity of "the contract" but instead provides that a party is not liable for failure to perform "any" of its "obligations" — language that permits exemption to the extent that the impediment applies. Article 51(1), §316 *supra*, reflects a policy that is consistent with this result: "(1) If the seller delivers only a part of the goods . . . articles 46–50 [provisions on remedies for breach] apply in respect of the part that is missing. . . ." There is no reason to suppose that this policy was rejected for Article 79.

(b) Options Available to Buyer. Analyzing Buyer's options gives us an opportunity further to explore the applicability of various remedial provisions of the Convention; some of these apply directly and others (like Article 51(1)) may be helpful as analogies.

(i) Requiring Performance. Since Article 79 exempted Seller from only part of its obligations, under Article 46(1) (§§279–286; *cf.* Art. 28, §194, *supra*) Buyer may "require performance by the seller" with respect to the 600 units or, if Seller fails to deliver, may avoid the contract pursuant to Article 64(1)(a) or (b) and may also recover damages for Buyer's wrongful failure to deliver the 600 units. (See Arts. 74 and 75 or 76, §§353–354, 409–415, 402–406, *supra*).

(ii) Reduction of Price. *If Seller delivers the 600 units (either voluntarily or because of an action by the buyer to "require performance"), how much should the buyer pay? The Article 50 price-reduction formula (see §§309 ff. supra) is available to address this problem, since that provision does not involve "damages" from which the seller is exempt under Article 79(5) (see §§311 & 313 supra). The result would be a price reduced in proportion to the value that Buyer did not receive. Assuming that the 1000 units of alloy in Example 79C were all fungible and independently usable, the likely price reduction would be 40% (i.e., Buyer did not receive 400 of the 1000 units covered by the*

---

58. Tallon, *B-B Commentary* 588, §2.9.

contract), so that Buyer would be responsible to pay 60% of the contract price.

(iii) Avoidance.   Although Buyer may insist on delivery of the 600 units, under some circumstances Buyer may have the option to avoid the contract and refuse to accept any of the units. The Seller, of course, is not liable for damages for failure to deliver the 400 units, but exemption from damages does not impair Buyer's right to avoid the contract (Article 79(5)). Under Article 49(1)(a) Buyer may declare the contract avoided if the seller's failure to perform "*any* of his *obligations . . .* amounts to a *fundamental breach*" as defined in Article 25. If (surprisingly) Seller should refuse to deliver the 600 units Seller has produced, Seller's repudiation (Article 72) would unquestionably justify avoidance.

What circumstances would permit Buyer to refuse the 600 units because of the failure to receive the remaining 400? Suppose that Buyer could use or resell the alloy only in 1000-unit quantities. In these circumstances Seller's delivery of "only a part of the goods" (Art. 51(1), quoted *supra*) could cause such serious detriment (Article 25) that Buyer, under Article 51(2) (§317, *supra*), could declare "the contract avoided in its entirety." Giving legal effect to the linkage between the 600 and the 400 units is also reinforced by Article 73(3) on deliveries by installments (§402, *supra*): failure with respect to a part authorizes avoidance "in respect of deliveries already made or of future deliveries if, by reason of their *interdependence*," these other deliveries could not be used for their intended purpose.[59]

In sum, the Convention provides ample resources for solving problems posed when only part of performance is prevented by an Article 79 impediment.

---

59. It was argued above (n. 54 *supra*) that a buyer facing delayed delivery by a seller who is entitled to exemption under Art. 79 for the delay should not be permitted to use the *Nachfrist* procedure to establish grounds for avoidance where there was no fundamental breach of contract. Where an exempting impediment impacts the delivery of only a part of the goods, there is an additional reason for preventing buyers from using a *Nachfrist* notice to set a deadline for delivery of the missing portion of the goods and then claiming the right to avoid the entire contract if the deadline is missed: in cases of partial delivery, Art. 51(2) precludes the use of *Nachfrist* to avoid the entire contract, requiring instead that the buyer establish a fundamental breach of the entire contract before such avoidance is permitted. See §317 *supra*.

435.3 **I. Remedies other than Damages**

435.4 **(1) Avoidance**

Paragraph (5) states: "Nothing in this article prevents either party from exercising any remedy other than to claim damages under this Convention." This provision is important: a party who may not recover damages for failure of performance may still avoid the contract (Art. 79(5), §§423.4, 435.05, *supra*) and has the rights granted in CISG Section V, *infra* at §437, on "Effects of avoidance."[60]

Consider these cases: (1) A seller delivers goods to buyer but exchange restrictions prevent the buyer from paying. (2) A buyer pays in advance for goods but export controls prevent the seller from delivering goods. In each case the party who is prevented from performing may be exempt from liability for damages. However, the party who has performed without receiving the agreed return is entitled to redress. This is provided by the right of avoidance which carries with it (Art. 81(2)) the right to "restitution" of whatever the party "has supplied or paid under the contract" (§444, *infra*).

The discussion of paragraph (3) of Article 79 (temporary impediments, §435.05, *supra*) shows the importance of avoidance to resolve the question whether performance may be resumed after a "temporary" impediment. Indeed, interruptions of performance that turn out to be permanent at their onset may appear to be temporary. How long must the other party wait before making alternative arrangements by resale or repurchase? The right of avoidance preserved by Article 79(5) provides a means of resolving this problem: when the delay constitutes a "fundamental breach," the buyer can avoid the contract.[61] Indeed,

---

60. *Accord*, Hans Stoll & Georg Gruber, Art. 79 para. 45, *in* Schlechtriem & Schwenzer, *CISG Commentary* (2nd English ed. 2005); Bridge, *International Sale of Goods* para. 3.58 at 107; Enderlein & Maskow, *International Sales Law* Art. 79 §13.2. A decision by the Tribunal de commerce de Besançon, France, January 19, 1998, English translation available at http://cisgw3.law.pace.edu/ cases/980119f1.html, appears to deny a buyer the right to avoid the contract on the basis that the seller was exempt under Art. 79 (although the court permitted the buyer to reduce the price). This decision should be viewed as an incorrect aberration.

61. As was argued in note 54 *supra*, the *Nachfrist* procedure — a basis for avoiding a contract that is an alternative to establishing a fundamental breach (see Arts. 47(1) and 49(1)(b), §305 *supra*) — should not be available to a buyer where the seller has an exemption for its failure to perform.

without the right of avoidance, "temporary" impediments would be unmanageable.[62]

435.5 (2) Specific Performance

The statement in paragraph (5) that nothing in Article 79 affects "any right other than to claim damages" could be read to say that a party who is entitled to exemption from damages could nevertheless be "required to perform" (Arts. 28, 46, 62, §§191–199, 279–285, 345–349, *supra*). This conclusion would be inconsistent with the basic provision that a party "is not liable" when performance is barred by an impediment. In many cases an action to "require" performance would call for an impossibility and in other cases the sanctions to compel performance (e.g., money penalties such as *astreinte*) could be at least as onerous as damages. There is no indication that the legislators intended such an absurd result.[63] It seems probable that queries about the overbreadth of paragraph (5) were dismissed on the ground that an absurd construction

---

62. Tallon, *B-B Commentary* 589–590, §2.10.2, must have been referring to an unusual situation in which delayed performance was impossible and restitutionary problems were absent in referring to avoidance as "useless." Indeed, the view that in some Art. 79 situations the contract would "disappear" (an echo of ULIS *ipso facto* avoidance discarded in CISG (Art. 26, §187.1, *supra*)) is not helpful to parties who need to know what to do following an impediment.

63. *Accord*, Tallon, *B-B Commentary* 590, §2.10.2; *Schlechtriem, 1986 Commentary* 102: A general belief at the Diplomatic Conference that a judgment for specific performance would neither be sought nor obtained. In any event a German court would deny relief under Art. 28. In French procedure the penalty payments to coerce performance (*astreint*) go to the plaintiff — a result that in substance resembles damages, which are barred by Art. 79(5). See *Zweigert & Kotz II (1987)* 165. The argument advanced in Hans Stoll & Georg Gruber, Art. 79 paras. 46–48, *in* Schlechtriem & Schwenzer, *CISG Commentary* (2nd English ed. 2005), that specific performance remains available despite exemption under Art. 79 appears confined (as there described) primarily to situations involving delay in delivery due to a temporary impediment (see §435.1 *supra*) and delivery of non-conforming goods. See Stoll & Gruber, Art. 79 para. 46, *in* Schlechtriem & Schwenzer, *CISG Commentary* (2nd English ed. 2005). As was demonstrated above (§427 *supra*), a seller that delivers non-conforming goods should not be able to claim exemption under Art. 79. Except with respect to situations involving non-conforming goods, the approach of Stoll and Gruber appears consistent with the argument that a party exempt under Art. 79 is not subject to a claim for specific performance while the exemption continues. See Stoll & Gruber, Art. 79 paras. 47–48, *in* Schlechtriem & Schwenzer, *CISG Commentary* (2nd English ed. 2005). See also Enderlein & Maskow, *International Sales Law* Art. 79 §§13.3 & 13.6 (noting that under Art. 79(5) a party's right to demand performance appears to continue to exist even though the other party is exempt under Art. 79 for its non-performance, but noting that "[t]his seems to amount to an obvious contradiction because it is supposed that performance is not possible"

did not justify the complications of producing a revised text. The legislative background is relegated to a footnote.[64] In short, the broad language of paragraph (5) was retained because of the possibility that remedies other than damages might be needed in special circumstances, such as the ending of a temporary impediment or failure to pay the price for goods received when the agreed mode of payment was blocked temporarily (e.g.) by exchange controls. In any event, specific performance in situations excused by Article 79 would be inconsistent with domestic law in many jurisdictions. Consequently, under Article 28 (§§194–199, *supra*) these jurisdictions would be free to follow their own rules on specific performance.

435.6 (3) Price-Reduction and Interest

As mentioned in the discussion of impediments preventing part of performance (§435.2 supra), reduction of price pursuant to Article 50

---

and suggesting that the "optimum solution" is "that a right to performance must not be awarded insofar as the grounds of exemption are in effect").

64. ULIS 74(3) stated that exemption "shall not exclude the avoidance of the contract" or the right of the other party "to reduce the price." This latter alternative reflects the understanding that under ULIS 74(1) lack of fault could exempt the seller from *damages* for defects in the goods, but did not entitle the seller to recover the full price.

The UNCITRAL Working Party draft provided that an exempt party "shall not be liable in damages" but included no provision like ULIS 74(3) or CISG 79(5). V *YB* 39–40, *Docy. Hist.* 185–186; VI *YB* 60–61, *Docy. Hist.* 251–252. The language that became CISG 79(5) was prepared during UNCITRAL's 1977 review (in a Committee of the Whole) of the Working Group Draft. There was "general agreement that" [under this provision the party expecting performance] "should have the right to avoid the contract if the failure to perform amounted to a fundamental breach" and that "he should have the right to reduce the price in appropriate circumstances." (This right would be appropriate if the seller, after an excused delay, delivered defective goods.) In response to an objection that paragraph (5) might authorize specific performance and that "the law should not purport to give the expecting party a right which he could not exercise" it was noted that "a temporary impediment would cease and at such time a right to specific performance should not be precluded." VIII *YB* 56–57, *Docy. Hist.* 349–350 at para. 455a.

A similar discussion occurred at the Diplomatic Conference. *O.R.* 383–385, *Docy. Hist.* 604–606. Proposals to exclude specific performance (*O.R.* 134–135, *Docy. Hist.* 706–707) were rejected in response to concerns that the proposed language might bar remedies to require payment for goods received (USSR, para. 23) or to require performance after the termination of a temporary impediment (Sweden, para. 25). Analysis of these comments show that they do not support coerced performance of the acts for which exemption is provided by Art. 79(1).

is a non-damages remedy available to a buyer even if the seller has an exemption for its failure to perform.[65] *The right to interest (see Art. 78, §§420 ff. supra, and Art. 84, §§450 ff. infra) similarly is not a matter of damages, and remains applicable even where one's counter-party qualifies for an exemption under Article 79.*[66]

65. *Accord*, Hans Stoll & Georg Gruber, Art. 79 para. 45, *in* Schlechtriem & Schwenzer, *CISG Commentary* (2nd English ed. 2005); Enderlein & Maskow, *International Sales Law* Art. 79 §13.4; Lookofsky, *Understanding CISG in the USA* §6.19 at 130; Bridge, *International Sale of Goods* para. 3.59; Tribunal de commerce de Besançon, France, January 19, 1998, English translation available at http://cisgw3.law.pace.edu/cases/980119f1.html.

66. *Accord*, Hans Stoll & Georg Gruber, Art. 79 para. 45, *in* Schlechtriem & Schwenzer, *CISG Commentary* (2nd English ed. 2005); Enderlein & Maskow, *International Sales Law* Art. 78 §2.1 & Art. 79 §13.1; Lookofsky, *Understanding CISG in the USA* §6.19 at 130; Amtsgericht Willisau, Switzerland, March 12, 2004, English translation available at http://cisgw3.law.pace.edu/cases/040312s1.html.

Article 80.
Failure of Performance Caused by Other Party

436   This second (and last) article in Section IV. *Exemptions* has the seduc-
tive charm of a self-evident statement. Our principal problem is to find
its appropriate role in the statutory structure: Does Article 80 govern
only problems of exemption from liability (Article 79, *supra*) or does it
modify all of the remedial provisions of the Convention?

Article 80[1]

**A party may not rely on a failure of the other party to perform, to
the extent that such failure was caused by the first party's act or
omission.**

436.1   A. Relationship to Article 79 on Exemptions

The legislative history of Article 80 links it closely to the rules on
exemption in Article 79. *When it applies, however, Article 80 — unlike
Article 79 — eliminates not only a party's right to claim damages for
non-performance but also the right to avoid the contract.*[2] The idea
expressed in Article 80 appeared as part of the article of ULIS (1964)
that dealt with exemptions. Article 74(3) of ULIS stated that relief from
liability did not exclude avoidance of the contract or reduction of the
price "unless the circumstances which entitled the first party to relief
were caused by the act of the other party...." No such provision was
included in the drafts approved by the UNCITRAL Working Group or
by the Commission.[3]

The language that had been omitted from ULIS 74(3) reappeared at
the Diplomatic Conference in a proposal that the article on exemptions
be followed by an article substantially like Article 80.[4] Some delegates

---

1. The 1978 Draft had no provision like Art. 80; this article resulted from an amendment
proposed at the Diplomatic Conference. *Cf.* ULIS 74(3) (final clause).
2. See Hans Stoll & Georg Gruber, Art. 80 paras. 2 & 9, *in* Schlechtriem & Schwenzer, *CISG
Commentary* (2nd English ed. 2005); UNCITRAL Digest Art. 80 para. 7.
3. W. G. Sess. No. 5, Jan. 1974: V *YB* 39–40, 58 *Docy. Hist.* 185–86, 204 (draft Article 74).
The omitted language did appear in an alternative proposal submitted by an observer. W. G.
Sess. No. 6, Jan. 1975: VI *YB* 60–61, *Docy. Hist.* 251–252.
4. The proposal (by G.D.R.) was labelled Art. 65 *bis*. Text of the proposal: *O.R.* 135–136, *Docy.
Hist.* 707–708. First Committee Deliberations: *O.R.* 386–387, 393 *Docy. Hist.* 607–608, 614.

stated that the proposal expressed the important general principle that one should not gain by a wrongful act; others noted that such a statement was unnecessary and, in any event, followed from the good faith requirement of Art. 7(1), §§94–95, *supra*.[5] Most delegates seemed to feel that there might be some value and, at any rate, no danger in stating the obvious; the provision was approved. The Conference authorized the Drafting Committee to place the new article either in Ch. V Sec. IV, *Exemptions*, or in Part III, Ch. 1, *General Provisions*; the Drafting Committee chose the former and the provision as so structured was approved by the Plenary.[6] Placing Article 80 in the section entitled "Exemptions" is significant since chapter and section headings were regarded as parts of the Convention and were considered and approved by UNCITRAL and the Diplomatic Conference.[7]

436.2   (1) Article 80 and the Exemption Rules of Article 79

The role of Article 80 in exemption cases can be examined in the following case.

Example 80A. A contract called for Seller to deliver goods to Buyer in State X. State X required sellers to obtain a license for the importation of such goods. Seller made an appropriate application but Buyer persuaded the officials of State X to deny the license; as a result Seller could not deliver the goods. Buyer, in a remarkable display of nerve, sued Seller for damages for failure to deliver.[8]

---

5. *In support*: *O.R.* 386–387, *Docy. Hist.* 607–608, at paras. 50, 52, 53, 54, 56, 61, *Opposed*: *Id.* at paras. 55, 57, 60.

6. *First Committee*: *O.R.* 393, *Docy. Hist.* 614. *Plenary*: *O.R.* 227, *Docy. Hist.* 762. The Title of, Sec. III, *Exemptions*, containing Arts. 79 and 80 (then 65 and 65 *bis*) appeared in the draft that was submitted to the Plenary but, unlike some of the headings, was not the subject of a separate vote.

7. The Drafting Committee was generally not authorized to make substantive decisions. However, the First Committee in this case authorized the Drafting Committee to decide where the new article should be placed and this decision was not challenged when the Conference reviewed the final text including the titles of sections and chapters. The names for individual articles in this book were supplied by the present writer for ease of identification and, like the names of articles in the Secretary's Commentary, have no legislative significance. See *O.R.* 14, note 1, *Docy. Hist.* 404.

8. The example is abnormal in several respects. It would be more usual for the buyer to obtain the import license. In such cases a buyer who regrets making the contract might well either make a feeble attempt to obtain the license or induce its government to deny the license. In this setting, as in the above example, a buyer who regrets making the contract would usually be satisfied to be rid of the contract and would not sue for damages; apart from loss of

The denial of a government license normally would constitute an "impediment" to performance and would exempt Seller from liability for damages (Art. 79(5)). Suppose, however, Buyer argues that, under Article 79(1), Seller should have "taken the impediment into account" or should have "avoided or overcome it or its consequences." In these circumstances Seller can invoke Article 80 to bar Buyer's damage claim; the failure to overcome the impediment "was caused by [Buyer's] act or omission" and Seller is exempt from damages under Article 79.

436.3 **(a) Resources apart from Article 80.** In the above case, Article 80 may not be needed to defeat Buyer's outrageous claim. Article 60(a) (§§342–343, *supra*) states that the buyer's obligation to "take delivery" (Art. 53) includes "doing all the acts which could reasonably be expected of him in order to *enable the seller to make delivery.*" — a requirement that, at the very least, prevents the buyer from placing obstacles in the seller's path. One might conceive of cases where an obligation not to block the other party's performance is not stated so explicitly in the Convention; however, a comparable obligation may be fairly implied (as in Example 80A) from normal expectations implied from the contract (Art. 8) and from the parties' practices and trade usages (Art. 9), construed with regard (Art. 7(1)) for "the observance of good faith in international trade."

The possibility of achieving the objectives of Article 80 by other provisions of the Convention does not mean that Article 80 is wholly without value; in some situations Article 80 may provide the clearest basis for a just result.

436.4 **B. Article 80 as a General Obligation**

Article 80, apart from its position in Part III, Chapter V, Section IV (*Exemptions*) might be read as a rule of general applicability and, as we have seen (§436.1 *supra*), both supporters and opponents of this provision claimed that it embodied self-evident truth. Does it follow

---

good-will and the danger of a defense exposing the buyer's machinations, it would be difficult to prove damages from the loss of undesired performance. The difficulty in finding a more normal example illustrates the narrow scope intended for Art. 80. For further discussion of situations in which Art. 80 applies see Hans Stoll & Georg Gruber, Art. 80 paras. 3–5, *in* Schlechtriem & Schwenzer, *CISG Commentary* (2nd English ed. 2005); UNCITRAL Digest Art. 80 paras. 2–6.

that Article 80 is technically applicable to all of the many provisions on remedies, as if it had been placed in Part III, Chapter 1, *General Provisions* (Arts. 25–29)? For reasons set forth at §436.1, placing Article 80 in the exemption section should be respected in determining whether the article technically has the same general operative effect as the articles in Chapter 1, *General Provisions*. On the other hand, the principle expressed in Article 80 and its relationship to other provisions of the Convention that call for cooperation between the parties in the performance of their contract make it suitable for analogical use under Article 7(2) for questions "not expressly settled" by the Convention (§§96–102, *supra*).

This approach seems advisable since, as Tallon demonstrates, Article 80 is not well-drafted to serve as an operative rule supplementing or modifying the many remedial rules provided by the Convention[9] — a deficiency that should not be surprising since (§436.1, *supra*) this provision was prepared in relation to the exemption rules of Article 79. In this setting Article 80 can give a quick answer to an outrageous claim for damages by a party (e.g., Party A) who has prevented performance by Party B. However, in these cases the more important question is this: Can *B recover damages from A* for the loss A's conduct inflicted on B by preventing B's performance of the contract? The language of Article 80 does not address this question; it merely states that A (who prevented performance by B) "may not rely" on B's failure to perform. Read literally, Article 80 gives B only a shield when B needs a sword.

Fortunately, it is not necessary to distort the language of Article 80 to deal with problems for which it was not designed. As §436.3 *supra* indicates, the Convention provides more suitable tools (e.g., Art. 60(a)) for handling these problems.[10] In addition, these provisions are supplemented (Art. 7(2)) by the "general principles on which [the Convention] is based" — that is, the premises underlying various provisions calling for cooperation in performance, including, of course, Article 80.

Finally, the obstructive conduct which Article 80 addresses (albeit inadequately) is governed by this fundamental principle: the making of a contract necessarily implies an expectation of performance; action by one party to prevent performance by the other is clearly inconsistent

---

9. Tallon, *B-B Commentary* §2.5, at 598–599.
10. Hans Stoll & Georg Gruber, Art. 80 para. 11, *in* Schlechtriem & Schwenzer, *CISG Commentary* (2nd English ed. 2005).

with their mutual expectations.[11] For such breaches of contract the Convention provides a wide range of remedies: Arts. 45–52, 61–65, 71–78.

436.5 ## C. The Causation requirement: Reacting to the Other Party's Breach

In several instances tribunals have applied Article 80 to sort out rights where both parties have failed to perform.[12] Some of these decisions have applied Article 80 where a party's action did not create an "impediment" to performance in the sense of Article 79 (and as illustrated in Example 80A). Specifically, Article 80 has been applied to shield a party who decides not to perform, even though performance remains perfectly practicable, if that decision was prompted the other party's non-performance or defective performance. For example, a German appeals court has held that, where a seller refused to deliver some goods because the buyer had refused to pay for earlier deliveries, Article 80 prevented the buyer from claiming (as a set-off defense) damages for the non-delivery: the court reasoned that the buyer's own actions (non-payment) had caused the seller's non-performance.[13]

The result (denial of the buyer's damage claim) may well be correct, but not on the basis of Article 80. Withholding later deliveries as a response to the buyer's failure to pay for earlier deliveries is a perfectly understandable response by the seller, but the provisions of the Convention that properly govern the situation are those dealing with the consequences of the buyer's non-payment — for example, Article 64(1)(a) — and with the threat of future breach — Articles 71, 72 and 73(2). Those provisions may allow a seller who has not been paid for earlier deliveries to escape its obligation to make later deliveries — that is, by suspending performance or by avoiding the contract (or that part of the contract relating to future deliveries). Those provisions, however, impose standards and notice requirements not found in Article 80. Allowing a seller to use Article 80 to justify its own refusal to perform in response to the buyer's breach, even if the seller has not given notice of avoidance or suspension, in effect reinstitutes the ipso

11. Cf. Farnsworth, Contracts, 610–611 at n. 23; Treitel, Remedies (1988) 296.
12. See UNCITRAL Digest Art. 80 paras. 2–3.
13. Oberlandesgericht München, Germany, July 9, 1997, CLOUT case No. 273, English translation available at http://cisgw3.law.pace.edu/cases/970709g1.html.

facto avoidance doctrine of ULIS that was excluded from the Convention (see §187.1 supra).

The drafting history of Article 80 (recounted in §436.1 supra) as well as placement of the provision in the "Exemption" section (Part III, Chapter 5, Section IV, along with Article 79) suggests that the applications described in the previous paragraph are improper. Article 80 should apply only when one party's actions created an impediment or obstacle that prevented or interfered with the other party's performance, as in Example 80A — not when it merely creates a reason for the other side to wish not to perform.[14] As Professors Stoll and Gruber have stated

> Nor can the cause of the promisor's failure to perform be attributed to the promisee's conduct if that conduct has not impaired the promisor's ability to fulfill the contract. If, for example, the buyer, without cause, refuses payment of the due price or refuses payment for previous obligations, the seller is not entitled to refuse delivery of the goods under Article 80. The breach of contract on the part of the promisee is the occasion but not the cause of the non-performance.[15]

---

14. Of course a breach by one party may create an impediment to the other party's performance that invokes Art. 80. For example, where a seller's failure to designate the port of shipment prevented the buyer from opening a letter of credit as contemplated by the contract, the court properly ruled that Art. 80 prevent the seller from relying on the buyer's failure to open the letter of credit. Oberster Gerichtshof, Austria, February 6, 1996, CLOUT case No. 176, English translation available at http://cisgw3.law.pace.edu/cases/960206a3.html.

15. Hans Stoll & Georg Gruber, Art. 80 para. 6, *in* Schlechtriem & Schwenzer, *CISG Commentary* (2nd English ed. 2005.

SECTION V.

Effects of Avoidance
((Articles 81–84)

Introduction to Section V

437   A. Avoidance in Earlier Parts of the Convention

Part III, Chapter II (Obligations of the Seller) stated the grounds for avoidance of the contract by the buyer (Art. 49); Chapter III (Obligations of the Buyer) included corresponding provisions on avoidance by the seller (Art. 64). Chapter IV (Risk of Loss) in Article 70 dealt with the effect of avoidance of the contract on risk. Earlier in the present chapter there were rules on avoidance for anticipatory breach (Art. 72), and for breach in installment contracts (Art. 73). All these provide background for the present section on the effects of avoidance.[1]

438   B. Overview of Section V

Article 81 specifies the effect of avoidance on the parties' rights and obligations under the contract — that it releases both parties from their obligations (although it does not affect obligations to pay damages or to arbitrate) and that each party must return what it has received under the contract. Article 82 governs whether an aggrieved buyer may avoid the contract when it cannot return the goods in the same condition in which they were received. Articles 83 and 84 are concerned with cleaning up the aftermath of undoing a transaction.

---

1. See also Art. 25 (definition of fundamental breach); Art. 26 (avoidance requires notice to the other party); Arts. 51–52 (remedies applicable with respect to partial breach).

Article 81.
Effect of Avoidance on Obligations: Arbitration; Restitution

439   As we have just seen, Articles 81–84 assumes that a right of avoidance exists and has been exercised under provisions set forth in earlier parts of the Convention. Article 81 states the basic consequences of avoidance.

Article 81[1]

(1) Avoidance of the contract releases both parties from their obligations under it, subject to any damages which may be due. Avoidance does not affect any provision of the contract for the settlement of disputes or any other provision of the contract governing the rights and obligations of the parties consequent upon the avoidance of the contract.

(2) A party who has performed the contract either wholly or in part may claim restitution from the other party of whatever the first party has supplied or paid under the contract. If both parties are bound to make restitution, they must do so concurrently.

440   A. Obligations Terminated by Avoidance

440.1   (1) Avoidance and Performance

Article 81 applies to several types of situations, but the most important can be illustrated by a series of four examples. The situations can become complex; we start with the simplest.

Example 81A. The time for performance by the seller and the buyer had not yet arrived and neither had performed when one of the parties (Party X) repudiated its contract with the other party (Party A). This gave the aggrieved party (A) the right to avoid the contract (Art. 72); party A declared avoidance. What are the legal consequences of A's avoidance?

Article 81(1) states that avoidance "releases both parties" from their contractual obligations "subject to any damages that may be due."

---

1. This article is substantially the same as Art. 66 of the 1978 Draft Convention, and is similar to Art. 78 of ULIS except that the latter does not contain the provision on settlement of disputes in Art. 81(1) (second sentence).

Consequently, the aggrieved party (A) is released from its obligation to perform the contract (e.g., for a seller, to deliver the goods; for a buyer, to pay the price[2]) and is also released from the obligation to accept performance from the other party (X). As we shall see more fully (§440.2, *infra*), A also loses the right (Art. 46, 62) to "require" X to perform, but A can recover damages from X for breach of contract (Arts. 74–76).

Example 81B. One of the parties (A) has performed. (E.g., the seller has delivered or the buyer has paid.) The other party (X) repudiated the contract or committed a serious breach that empowered A to avoid (Arts. 49, 64); A declared avoidance. What are the legal consequences?

The effects of avoidance are the same is in Example 81A, with one added feature — X has received assets (goods or funds) from A. As we shall see (§§444–448, *infra*), under Articles 81(2) and 82, Party A may recover what X received and also any damages caused by X's breach of contract.

440.2 ## (2) Requiring Performance: Substitute Goods; Price Recovery

Example 81C. A seller (Party X) delivered goods to a buyer (Party A) that were so defective as to constitute a fundamental breach. Buyer A demands that X accept return of the defective goods. May A also require X to supply substitute goods?

Is A's demand that X accept return of the defective goods an "avoidance?" If so, the statement in Article 81(1) that avoidance "releases both parties from their obligations" under the contract might suggest that A may not require X to deliver substitute goods. However, as we have seen, this specific situation is addressed by Article 46(2) (§283, *supra*) which provides that when non-conforming goods constitute a fundamental breach the buyer, "may *require* delivery of *substitute* goods." This narrow and specific provision excludes any inference that might be drawn from the general language of Article 81(1) that the buyer's sole remedy is a claim for damages. (See the fuller discussion under Article 46 at §283, *supra*).

Example 81D. Seller delivered goods that conformed to the contract. Buyer failed to pay for the goods, which Buyer promptly resold. Seller rightfully declared the contract avoided and under Article 81(2) (§444, *infra*) has the right to "claim restitution" of the goods, but reclamation is

---

not possible since Buyer had resold the goods. What is the impact of avoidance on Seller's rights?

Seller under Article 81(2) may "claim restitution...*of whatever* [Seller] *has supplied*" but, because of Buyer's resale of the goods there is no specific asset to which this remedy can be applied; consequently. Seller probably has no remedy (comparable to Article 46(2) or 62)) to compel (specific) performance.[3] However, under Article 81(1) avoidance releases both parties from their obligations "subject to any *damages* that may be due." In this setting *damages* would normally consist of the unpaid price plus interest (Arts. 74 and 78). This result seems comparable to an action under Article 62 to "*require* the buyer to pay the price" (§§345–349, *supra*) but the "damage" approach set forth in Article 81(1) seems to remit the seller to normal collection procedures by execution of a judgment, rather than the coercive measures available under some domestic systems. In any event, if a tribunal were to conclude that the seller could invoke Article 62 to "*require* the buyer to pay," domestic rules rejecting coercive enforcement would be applicable by virtue of Article 28 (§§191–199, *supra*).

441   B. Obligations not Terminated by Avoidance

The phrase "avoidance of the contract," standing alone, overstates the consequences of this remedy.[4] As we have seen, avoidance does not release a party from the obligation to pay damages for breach of contract (Arts. 74–76, 81(1)).[5] The consequences of "avoidance" are narrowed further by the second sentence of Paragraph (1), as we shall now see.

---

3. *Cf.* Rainer Hornung, Art. 81 para. 20, *in* Schlechtriem & Schwenzer, *CISG Commentary* (2nd English ed. 2005) ("Particular problems are raised when an innocent seller declares the contract avoided in order to recover goods which have already been delivered; the general rules are ill-suited to this particular situation"). If Buyer resold the goods for more than the price owed to Seller, Seller's right to recover the goods may justify recovery of the larger sum that Buyer received. If the proceeds of the resale can be traced — that is, if the price for the resale has not been paid — Seller's specific right to recover the goods might be transferred to a specific right to recover the asset that Buyer wrongfully obtained. *Cf.* Daniel Friedmann, *Restitution of Profits Gained by Party in Breach of Contract*, 104 L.Q.R. 383, 388 (1988).

4. *Compare* Rainer Hornung, *Introduction to* Arts. 81–84 para. 8, and Art. 81 paras. 9–9d, *in* Schlechtriem & Schwenzer, *CISG Commentary* (2nd English ed. 2005).

5. See UNCITRAL Digest Art. 81 para. 4. For domestic law approaches see *Treitel, Remedies (1988)* 392–396. In the United States, barriers to damages were removed by the UCC 2–711(1), 2–720.

442 **(1) Arbitration Clauses**

The sales contract may contain an agreement to arbitrate any dispute that may arise under the contract. Assume that a party to the contract notifies the other party that the contract is avoided and a dispute arises over the justification for the avoidance, or the amount of damages resulting from breach. Does "avoidance of the contract" release either party from the arbitration clause?

In most situations the answer is No: Article 81(1) states: "Avoidance of the contract does not affect any provision of the contract for the *settlement of disputes....*"[6] Avoidance (Arts. 49, 64) is a remedy based on breach of contract; agreements to arbitrate are designed to supply a way to resolve such disputes.

The UNCITRAL Arbitration Rules (1976) in Article 21(2) protect this basic function by providing that an arbitration clause, although included in the contract, "shall be treated as an agreement *independent of the other terms* of the contract"; the arbitrators "have the power to determine the *existence or the validity* of the contract of which an arbitration clause forms a part."[7] Complex questions may, however, be posed by claims that a sales contract containing an arbitration clause was executed as a result of fraud. The effect of such a claim on the authority of the arbitrators will depend, in the first instance, on the breadth of the parties' agreement to arbitrate — for example, by the incorporation of the UNCITRAL Arbitration Rules which includes Article 21, *supra*. A second factor in some jurisdictions is whether the alleged fraud is confined to the sales transaction (e.g., a fraudulent statement as to the quality of the goods or the buyer's solvency) and thus is severable from the agreement to arbitrate.[8] Of course, the validity of the scope of the parties' agreement to arbitrate may be controlled by domestic law (*cf.* CISG 4(a)).

A current approach to these questions is reflected in the UNCITRAL Model Law on International Commercial Arbitration (1985).[9]

---

6. See UNCITRAL Digest Art. 81 para. 4.

7. For the text of the UNCITRAL Arbitration Rules see *AJCL UNCITRAL Symposium*, 27 Am. J. Comp. L. 489, 496; VII *YB* 22. Art. 21(1) of the Rules: "The arbitral tribunal shall have the power to rule on objections ... with respect to the *existence or validity* of the arbitration clause or the separate arbitration agreement."

8. See Sanders, *AJCL UNCITRAL Symposium, supra*, at 462–463.

9. See H. Holtzmann & I. Neuhaus, Guide to the UNCFTRAL Model Law on International Commercial Arbitration (Kluwer, 1989) 478–480. Art. 16(1) of the Model Law is similar to Art. 21(1) & (2) of the UNCITRAL Rules, *supra*. To permit a unified and uninterrupted

443   (2) Other Obligations Unaffected by Avoidance

Paragraph (1) of Article 81 states that avoidance does not affect any "provision of the contract governing the rights and obligations of the contract *consequent upon the avoidance of the contract*" — for example, a contract provision governing the amount of damages or the handling of rejected goods.[10] In addition, Articles 85–88, *infra* at §454–457, requiring a party who rejects goods to take steps to preserve them, apply regardless of avoidance; as we shall see, these requirements have their most significant applications when a party avoids the contract.[11]

444   C. Restitution of What has been Supplied or Paid

Paragraph (2) has implications that may be surprising to those schooled in the common law.

Example 81E. A contract called for Seller to deliver goods on June 1; Buyer's payment was due on July 1. The goods were delivered on schedule but Buyer failed to pay on July 1 or thereafter. Seller avoided the contract based on Buyer's fundamental breach and brought an action to require Buyer to return the goods.

Paragraph (2) states that a seller who avoids a contract "may claim restitution . . . of whatever [the seller] has supplied . . . under the contract." The language calls for recovery of goods, and not merely an action for the price[12] — a reading that can invoke the seller's right under Article 62 to "*require* the buyer to . . . perform his . . . obligations."

Some legal systems similarly give effect to the principle of "avoidance" (*résolution*) by permitting a seller to recover the goods when the buyer fails to pay.[13] On the other hand, the common law and the (U.S.A.)

---

arbitral proceeding the arbitrators may have jurisdiction to decide basic questions like the existence and validity of the agreement to arbitrate even though these questions, unlike the merits of the award, may be subject to judicial review. On CISG and Arbitration see Thomas E. Carbonneau & Marc S. Firestone, *Transnational Law-Making: Assessing the Impact of the Vienna Convention and the Viability of Arbitral Adjudication*, 1 Emory J. Int'l. Dispute Res. 51 (1986).

10. See UNCITRAL Digest Art. 81 para. 4.

11. See *Secretariat Commentary* Art. 66 para. 6, *O.R.* 57, *Docy. Hist.* 447; Rainer Hornung, Art. 81 para. 10, *in* Schlechtriem & Schwenzer, *CISG Commentary* (2nd English ed. 2005).

12. See UNCITRAL Digest Art. 81 paras. 5–6.

13. See, e.g., Houin, Sale of Goods in French Law, *Comp. Sales (I.C.I.Q.)* 16, 28; Vaisse, Rights and Remedies available to an Unpaid Seller under French Law, 4 Int. Bus. Lawyer 379 (1976). *Cf.* Kjelstrup, The Unpaid Seller Under Norwegian Law *id.* at 375.

Uniform Commercial Code do not carry the concept of "avoidance" or "rescission" this far. When goods have been delivered on credit the unpaid seller has only the general claim of a creditor to the price of the goods; in general, recovery of the goods must be based on wrongful (e.g., fraudulent) conduct of the buyer in obtaining the goods, or on his signed agreement that the seller retains a property (or "security") interest in the goods.[14]

The seller's right under the Convention to recover the goods is subject to practical limitations. This remedy is of special importance when the buyer is insolvent; in this setting the rights of creditors are likely to intervene by levy of execution or by the designation of a receiver or trustee in bankruptcy. The Convention will not override the rights of creditors, purchasers and other third persons granted by domestic law; under Article 4, the Convention "governs only . . . the rights . . . *of the seller and the buyer . . .*"[15]

(For discussion of responsibility for damage to goods following avoidance of contract, see §§448.1A & 448.1B infra.)

444A **Concurrent Restitution; Set-off and Recoupment under the Convention**

The Convention (unlike some domestic rules) does not confine the obligation to make restitution to the party in breach; under paragraph (2) each party is entitled to restitution.[16] But if both parties are bound to make restitution "they must do so concurrently."[17] *That certainly means, for example, that an avoiding buyer that has paid (in whole or in part) for the goods need not return them to the seller except in exchange for a refund, along with payment of the buyer's reasonable expenses in preserving the goods (see Article 86(1)). If the seller refuses such a refund the buyer should eventually be entitled to sell*

14. *Honnold, Sales* 343–345. *Cf.* UCC 2–702 (recovery within 10 days when buyer "has received goods on credit while insolvent"); UCC 9–203(1)(a) (security interest against debtor in possession must be based on a "security agreement" signed by debtor). A similar approach is proposed in Hellner 22 *Scan. Stud.* 53.69. See also Hellner, Contracts and Sales, *Intro. Swedish L.* 201, 217.

15. See *Secretariat Commentary* Art. 66 para. 10, *O.R.* 57, *Docy. Hist.* 447. For protection of third parties under French law see Houin, Sale of Goods in French Law, *Comp. Sales (I.C.I.Q.)* 16, 29.

16. See UNCITRAL Digest Art. 81 para. 6.

17. See UNCITRAL Digest Art. 81 para. 8.

the goods for the seller's account under Article 88(1).[18] *(See §457 supra.) In that event Article 88(3) makes clear that the buyer can retain its expenses of preserving and selling the goods from the proceeds of that sale. Can the avoiding buyer also escape (or at least reduce its stake in) the mutual restitution stalemate by setting off the amount that the seller owes buyer in restitution against the proceeds of the sale of the goods? That would certainly be possible under U.S. domestic sales law,*[19] *but the Convention does not specify whether mutual obligations to make concurrent restitution are (if both have become monetary obligations) subject to set-off*[20] *(or, more accurately in U.S. legal usage, "recoupment"*[21]*).*

Indeed the Convention does not expressly address any of the many broader issues of set-off or recoupment that can arise in connection with a sales transaction. Can an avoiding buyer that has resold goods under Article 88(1) deduct the amount of its damages under Article 74–76 from the proceeds of resale?[22] *If the contract is not avoided, can a buyer that receives non-conforming goods set off its Article 74 damages against its obligation to pay the price?*[23] *Suppose a buyer has claims against the seller in connection with another transaction — can those claims be set-off against what the buyer owes the seller on the price or for restitution? Should it matter whether the other transaction was governed by the Convention? Suppose the claims against the seller that the buyer wishes to set off are tort claims?*

Because Article 81(2) expressly provides that mutual restitution is to be made "concurrently" it has been suggested that the narrow question of recouping mutual claims of restitution is governed, pursuant to Article 7(2), by the Convention's general principles[24]*; however, other*

---

18. See Flechtner, Pittsburgh Symposium at 81.

19. See (U.S.A.) UCC §2–711(3) ("On rightful rejection [of goods] or justifiable revocation of acceptance a buyer has a security interest in goods in his possession or control for any payments made on their price … ").

20. This situation is discussed in Flechtner, *Pittsburgh Symposium* at 81–82.

21. "Recoupment" is the setting off of mutual claims that arise from the same transaction, whereas set-off involves the netting of claims from different transactions. See the entries for these terms in *Black's Law Dictionary* (8th ed. 2004).

22. See Klaus Bacher, Art. 88 para. 18, *in* Schlechtriem & Schwenzer, *CISG Commentary* (2nd English ed. 2005).

23. *Compare* (U.S.A.) UCC §2–717 ("The buyer on notifying the seller of his intention to do so may deduct all or any part of the damages resulting from any breach of the contract from any part of the price still due under the same contract").

24. See Rainer Hornung, Art. 81 para. 16, *in* Schlechtriem & Schwenzer, *CISG Commentary* (2nd English ed. 2005).

authority — including the Secretariat's Commentary — suggests that the matter is subject to applicable domestic law.[25] Since the Convention contains nothing even indirectly addressing recoupment or set-off of claims other than mutual claims to restitution, the argument that domestic law governs this issue is very strong, particularly where the claims arise out of different transactions. The effect of set-off or recoupment on the rights of third parties, furthermore, is clearly beyond the scope of the Convention (see Article 4). Thus applicable domestic law surely determines, for example, whether a right to set-off or recoupment takes priority over the right of a creditor to garnish a buyer or seller's Article 81(2) restitution claims.[26]

444.1 (1) Reclamation based on Contract

Interesting issues on the interplay between the uniform international rules and domestic law may be explored in the setting of the following case.

Example 81F. The contract of sale provided that Buyer would pay the price within 30 days after delivery and added that if Buyer failed to pay the price at the agreed time Seller, without further notice, had the right to repossess the goods. Buyer failed to pay and Seller brought an action in Buyer's jurisdiction to recover the goods.

Buyer might oppose reclamation on the ground that Seller's rights are governed by Article 81 of the Convention, which provides for restitution based on avoidance of the contract; Seller had not declared avoidance by the notice as required by Article 26.

Seller may reply that its action to repossess is asserting a property right in the goods. Under Article 4(a) the Convention "is not concerned" with the effect of the contract on "property in the goods sold" and therefore the Convention's rules on avoidance are not applicable. To support this argument Seller may be able to point to a provision in the

---

25. See *Secretariat Commentary* Art. 77 para. 9, *O.R.* 63, *Docy. Hist.* 453; Flechtner, *Pittsburgh Symposium* at 81–83. See also Handelsgericht, Switzerland, December 3, 2002, English translation *available at* http://cisgw3.law.pace.edu/cases/021203s1.html (http://cisgw3.law.pace.edu/cases/021203s1.htmlset-off of restitutionary obligations governed by domestic law).

26. See Flechtner, *Pittsburgh Symposium* at 82–83. *Cf. Secretariat Commentary* Art. 66 para. 10, *O.R.* 57, *Docy. Hist.* 447 (noting that a claim to restitution under the Convention may be thwarted by domestic bankruptcy or insolvency rules). Set-off rights asserted against a debtor in U.S. federal bankruptcy proceedings are governed by §553 of the U.S. Federal Bankruptcy Code, 11 U.S.C. §553.

contract (often found in sales contracts) that property in the goods is retained by the seller until the price is paid; even if the contract did not include this clause Seller could argue that the contract clause permitting reclamation in substance gives Seller a property interest in the goods.[27]

This argument for excluding the Convention is subject to a strong objection: The Convention in Article 81 *is* "concerned with" reclamation of goods when the buyer fails to pay.[28] If the contract had contained no provision for reclamation Seller, with appropriate notice, would have the right under Article 81(2) to recover the goods. To meet the argument that under Article 81(2) recovery of the goods rests on avoidance, Seller could invoke the parties' right under Article 6 to derogate from the Convention's provisions, including the provision that reclamation must be based on a notice of avoidance. In short, the parties have exercised their right under Article 6 to reshape the Convention's rules on remedies for breach.[29] On the basis of this line of reasoning Seller should prevail.

One question remains: Does applicable domestic law invalidate (Art. 4(a)) a contractual provision allowing reclamation of the goods on non-payment? Such a rule of invalidity is conceivable but seems unlikely.[30] However, as we have seen, the Convention's rules are limited (Art. 4) to the rights "of the seller and the buyer" and yield to the rights of third persons such as creditors and purchasers. (See §444A *supra*.)

27. See UNCITRAL Digest Art. 81 para. 9.

28. See Rainer Hornung, *Introduction to* Arts. 81–84 para. 5, *in* Schlechtriem & Schwenzer, *CISG Commentary* (2nd English ed. 2005).

29. *Compare* Rainer Hornung, *Introduction to* Arts. 81–84 para. 6, *in* Schlechtriem & Schwenzer, *CISG Commentary* (2nd English ed. 2005).

30. See, e.g., (U.S.A.) UCC 9–503: A "secured party has on default the right to take possession of the collateral." A seller's interest in the goods after delivery is limited to a "security interest" (UCC 1–201(37)) and is not enforceable unless the debtor (here, the buyer) "*has signed* a security agreement."

Article 82.
Buyer's Inability to Return Goods
in Same Condition

445 ## A. The Factual Setting for Article 82

The present article addresses the following situation: a buyer receives goods which he discovers are subject to serious defects and elects to avoid the contract (Art. 49(1)(a)) or to require the seller to deliver substitute goods (Art. 46(2)).[1] In either event, the buyer is obliged to return the goods he has received (Art. 81(2)). But suppose that before the buyer avoids the contract, a part (or even all) of the goods have been damaged or have disappeared. Paragraph (1) of Article 82 states the general rule that the two remedies mentioned above are not available if the buyer cannot return the goods "substantially in the condition in which he received them." Paragraph (2) states three exceptions that make deep inroads on this general rule.[2]

446 ## B. Effect of Article 82

Article 82[3]

(1) The buyer loses the right to declare the contract avoided or to require the seller to deliver substitute goods if it is impossible for him to make restitution of the goods substantially in the condition in which he received them.

(2) The preceding paragraph does not apply:

(a) If the impossibility of making restitution of the goods or of making restitution of the goods substantially in the condition in which the buyer received them is not due to his act or omission;

---

1. As has been noted under Art. 47 at §288 and under Art. 49 at §305, when the seller has delivered the goods the buyer may avoid only in the event of a fundamental breach; avoidance based on failure to comply with a *Nachfrist* notice applies only to non-delivery. Similarly, the buyer may compel the seller to deliver substitute goods (Art. 46(2)) only "if the lack of conformity constitutes a fundamental breach of contract."

2. See Rainer Hornung, Art. 82 para. 12 (stating that the exceptions in Art. 82(2) restrict the general rule of Art. 82(1) "in such a fundamental way that the rule becomes the exception") and 16 (same), *in* Schlechtriem & Schwenzer, *CISG Commentary* (2nd English ed. 2005).

3. This article is the same as Art. 67 of the 1978 Draft and is similar to ULIS 79.

(b) if the goods or part of the goods have perished or deteriorated as a result of the examination provided for in article 38; or

(c) if the goods or part of the goods have been sold in the normal course of business or have been consumed or transformed by the buyer in the course of normal use before he discovered or ought to have discovered the lack of conformity.

447   (1) The General Rule Barring Avoidance or Compulsory Substitution

Paragraph (1) embodies a principle, generally accepted in domestic law, that a transaction may only be "avoided" if assets received under the transaction can be returned in substantially the same condition.[4] This restriction does not lead to serious injustice to an aggrieved buyer: Even if the buyer may not avoid the contract or require the seller to deliver substitute goods the buyer may recover damages resulting from the seller's breach of contract (Art. 74).

448   (2) Exceptions to the General Rule

Paragraph (2) is designed to preserve the avoidance and substitute goods remedies of buyers who have received seriously defective goods even when the buyer cannot return the goods in "substantially" the same condition. Under subparagraph (2)(b) the buyer's remedies are preserved if a major part (or even all) of the goods have perished as a result of the examination required by Article 38.[5] Subparagraph (2)(c) preserves the buyer's remedies when the buyer has sold or consumed the goods[6] — a result that may seem surprising since the buyer may have

---

4. See *Treitel, Remedies (Int. Enc.)* §181; (U.S.A.) UCC 2–608(2) (revocation of acceptance). For decisions in which this principle precluded an aggrieved buyer from avoiding the contract see UNCITRAL Digest Art. 82 para. 3. For discussion of when a change in the condition of the goods is "substantial" see Rainer Hornung, Art. 82 para. 11, *in* Schlechtriem & Schwenzer, *CISG Commentary* (2nd English ed. 2005).

5. For decisions on this exception see UNCITRAL Digest Art. 82 para. 5. For discussion of the exception see Rainer Hornung, Art. 82 para. 22, *in* Schlechtriem & Schwenzer, *CISG Commentary* (2nd English ed. 2005).

6. For decisions on this exception see UNCITRAL Digest Art. 82 para. 6. For discussion of the exception see Rainer Hornung, Art. 82 paras. 23–29, *in* Schlechtriem & Schwenzer, *CISG Commentary* (2nd English ed. 2005).

received benefits from the goods. However, under Article 84(2), *infra* at §450, the buyer "must account to the seller" for the benefits it has received.[7]

Article 82(2)(a) is more complex. As we have seen, under Article 82(1) the buyer may not avoid the contract or require the seller to deliver substitute goods if the buyer cannot return the goods in "substantially" the same condition. Under Article 82(2)(a) this restriction on the buyer's remedies does not apply when the change in the condition of the goods is not due to the buyer's "act or omission"[8] — a phrase that calls for close attention.

448.1   **(a) "Act or Omission."**   This phrase also appears in Articles 66 and 80 and in each setting poses this question: What standard governs whether consequences, such as damage to goods, are "due to" a party's "act or omission"?

Violations of obligations imposed by the contract and the Convention clearly make one responsible for the consequences. In the setting of Article 82, when a buyer has received seriously defective goods does the "act or omission" standard make the buyer responsible whenever the goods (e.g.) are stolen or are damaged by fire or storm? Can the answer be developed from inferences drawn from the Convention or does domestic tort law apply?

Invoking domestic law can undermine choices that are implicit in Article 82. Suppose, for example, that domestic tort law makes one absolutely responsible for damage to goods while in one's custody or possession. This result may be appropriate for commercial warehouses or operators of motor vehicles but would be inconsistent with decisions of the Convention on the rights of a buyer who has received seriously defective goods.[9] As we have seen, subparagraphs (2)(b) and (2)(c) are based on the premise that the aggrieved buyer's remedies should be

---

7. For discussion of the relationship between the exception in Art. 82(2)(c) and the rule of Art. 84(2) see Rainer Hornung, Art. 82 para. 23, *in* Schlechtriem & Schwenzer, *CISG Commentary* (2nd English ed. 2005).

8. For decisions on this exception see UNCITRAL Digest Art. 82 para 7.

9. See Rainer Hornung, Art. 82 para. 19, *in* Schlechtriem & Schwenzer, *CISG Commentary* (2nd English ed. 2005) (Art. 82(2)(a) provides for "the general principle governing the division of risks, namely that the seller is responsible for all consequences ensuing from a lack of conformity of the goods or from faulty delivery, save where they are due to the buyer's act or omission").

strongly protected.[10] This concern is also suggested by the nuanced language of subparagraph (2)(a); if the buyer's remedies were to be foreclosed whenever the defective goods are subject to casualty this sweeping result could have been stated simply and clearly. A less strict standard with respect to a buyer's responsibility for defective goods is also evidenced by the closely comparable provision of Article 86(1): "If the buyer has received the goods and intends to exercise any right under the contract or the Convention to reject them, he must take *such steps to preserve them as are reasonable in the circumstances"* — a duty of reasonable care but not a standard of absolute liability for loss.

On the other hand, suppose that domestic tort law imposes little or no responsibility for care. This approach may be appropriate when one is asked gratuitously to hold another's goods but is not appropriate to the duties owed to the other party to a consensual transaction — especially in an international sale when the party whose goods are at risk is in another country.[11]

Basing the standard on provisions of the Convention rather than domestic tort law supports these values: (1) The solution is more likely to be appropriate to the needs of international sales. (2) In addition, this approach conforms to Article 7(1)'s mandate to interpret the Convention with regard "to its international character and to the need to promote uniformity in its application," and responds to Article 7(2)'s invitation to settle questions not expressly settled in the Convention "in conformity with the general principles on which it is based . . ." (§§85–102, *supra*).

448.1A   Damage to Goods after the Buyer Validly Avoids the Contract

The Convention does not clearly address responsibility for loss, damage or destruction of goods that occurs after a buyer has validly avoided the contract or otherwise rejected the goods.[12] *(Convention*

---

10. *Cf.* Rainer Hornung, Art. 82 para. 19, *in* Schlechtriem & Schwenzer, *CISG Commentary* (2nd English ed. 2005) ("the exceptions in Art. 82(2) should be expanded as widely as legally possible").

11. Tallon, *B-B Commentary* 608, states that if the goods "disappear owing to the buyer's *negligence*" the buyer cannot avoid the contract. *Accord,* Rainer Hornung, Art. 82 para. 20, *in* Schlechtriem & Schwenzer, *CISG Commentary* (2nd English ed. 2005).

12. See UNCITRAL Digest Art. 66 Intro to Ch. IV para. 13, Art. 81 para. 7. For discussion of what is encompassed by "rejection" of goods see §455.1 *infra*, where the use of the concept in Art. 86 is discussed.

rules affecting responsibility for damage that occurs before a buyer avoids the contract are discussed in connection with Articles 70, 82 and 86.) As noted earlier (§359.1 supra), a decision of the highest court of Austria — the Oberster Gerichtshof — held that, where the buyer had borne transit risk when the goods were shipped to it, a breaching seller bore the risk for goods as they were transported back to the seller after the contract had been "consensually" avoided.[13] *Placing the risks for returning goods on the seller was justified, the court explained, by the principle underlying Article 82(2)(a) — a provision that limits an avoiding buyer's responsibility for pre-avoidance damage to that caused by the buyer's own "act or omission" — and because the seller "caused these risks with his breach of contract."*

It has been argued, however, that this approach "unduly penalize[s] . . . the seller in breach," and that the seller's fundamental breach does not "justify the seller's additional one-sided risk-bearing for the fate of goods which are not in his possession." It is asserted, therefore, that a buyer who justifiably avoids the contract "becomes responsible for the goods he has received."[14] *That argument is — at the least — counter-intuitive. Under Article 82(2)(a) an avoiding buyer is only responsible for pre-avoidance damage or loss if it is caused by the buyer's own act or omission; and under Article 86 a buyer who intends to reject goods is merely required to employ "reasonable" steps to preserve them. Thus a buyer is responsible for pre-avoidance damage only if it has acted unreasonably — that is, the damage results from its fault. It is bizarre to suggest that the buyer takes on greater responsibility for the goods — responsibility for damage or loss not caused by its own fault or actions — when the buyer justifiably avoids. Such a rule would create wasteful arguments about whether damage occurred before or after avoidance, and perverse incentives to delay avoidance as long as possible.*

The best approach is that suggested by the Austrian court: an avoiding buyer's liability for returning the goods after avoidance should mirror its responsibility under Articles 82 and 86 for pre-avoidance damage. A buyer who justifiably avoids the contract should be liable

---

13. Oberster Gerichtshof, Austria, June 29, 1999, English translation *available at* http://cisgw3.law.pace.edu/cases/990629a3.html.

14. See Rainer Hornung, Art. 82 para. 13, *in* Schlechtriem & Schwenzer, *CISG Commentary* (2nd English ed. 2005).

for damage occurring as the goods are being returned to the seller only if the buyer's fault caused the damage.[15]

48.1B Damage to Returned and Rejected Goods in Other Circumstances

Beyond the question of risk for goods being returned after a buyer's justifiable avoidance of contract, there are also no clear rules in the Convention to resolve broader issues of risk of loss for goods following justified or unjustified rejection or return of the goods. In general, the editor of this third edition suggests that the principle employed in the previous section should be followed: subject to certain limitations, the risk should be shouldered by the party in breach; otherwise, the party who would bear risk under the rules in Article 66–70 should continue to bear the risk.

Thus if, after delivery has been made (and risk has passed) to the buyer, the seller justifiably avoids the contract (e.g., because the buyer refuses to pay the price — see §§356.1 & 444 supra), the risk of trans- porting the goods back to the seller should be borne by the buyer.[16] *Similarly, if the buyer improperly attempts to avoid the contract after receiving the goods — for example, the buyer gives notice of avoidance even though the breach (if any) by the seller is not fundamental, or after the buyer lost the right to avoid under Article 82 or Article 49(2) — the buyer should continue to bear the risk for damage to the goods. Of course if the seller acquiesces in the buyer's improper avoidance by accepting the return of the goods, there will come a point at which risk must return to the seller — for example, when the seller, after accepting the returned goods, itself avoids the contract because of the buyer's breach.*

Suppose the buyer, after risk has passed to it, breaches by refusing delivery and the goods remain in the seller's control. In these circum- stances the seller is obligated under Article 85 to take "reasonable"

---

15. As argued in §359.1 *supra*, the Oberster Gerichtshof's alternative theory for imposing the risk of transporting the goods on the breaching seller — that the buyer had borne transit risk when it received the goods, and transit risk in returning the goods should be allocated on a mirror image basis — probably reflects invalid jurisdictional considerations deriving from regional law, and should not be followed.

16. *Contrast* Rainer Hornung, Art. 82 para. 8, *in* Schlechtriem & Schwenzer, *CISG Com- mentary* (2nd English ed. 2005).

steps to preserve the goods, at least until it avoids the contract. If the goods suffer casualty despite the seller's reasonable attempts to preserve, the seller could still require the buyer to take delivery and pay the price pursuant to Article 62. And since risk had passed to the buyer, the buyer should not be able to deduct anything for the damage that has occurred. But should this result obtain no matter when the damage occurred? There must come a point at which risk of damage to goods in the control of seller reverts back to the seller. The seller should not be able hold on to the goods indefinitely at the risk of the buyer. As noted earlier (see §348 supra), domestic restrictions apply in a seller's action to recover the price for goods. Under U.S. domestic sales law, for example, a seller can recover the price of goods that the buyer has not accepted and that have suffered casualty after risk of loss passed to the buyer, but only if the casualty occurred within a "reasonable time" after the buyer received the risk[17]; in other words, after passage of the reasonable time the risk for damage to goods that the seller holds because the buyer has refused delivery reverts back to the seller.[18]

448.2   **(b) "Avoidance" when the Goods are Gone.**   In unusual circumstances, paragraph (2) may permit a buyer to "avoid" a contract when the buyer has nothing to return. The major practical justification for avoidance (and similar remedies under domestic law) is to shift the burden of disposing of defective goods to the party who is in breach of contract. When the buyer no longer has the goods in question, one may ask why he would elect "avoidance" rather than recovery of damages under Article 74.

The answer lies in the fact that under Article 81, *supra* at §439, avoidance releases the buyer from his obligation to pay the price and entitles him to recover any payments on the price. Recovery of the price may relieve the buyer of the burden of proving the scope of his damages — a justifiable protection for the aggrieved party. But in some cases choosing avoidance may be prompted by the fact that the market level has fallen; in this setting the recovery of the agreed price (or freedom from paying the price) shifts to the seller the loss of the market decline, although the contract contemplated that this loss would fall on the buyer in exchange for the chance of gain from a rise in price. To minimize speculation by the buyer at the seller's expense it will be

---

17. (U.S.A.) U.C.C. 2–709(1)(a).
18. See Günter Hager, Art. 66 para. 7a, *in* Schlechtriem & Schwenzer, *CISG Commentary* (2nd English ed. 2005).

important to give full effect to the limits on the time for avoidance set out in Article 49(2) — an approach that is consistent with the mandate of Article 7(1) requiring the Convention to be interpreted with regard to "the need to promote . . . the observance of good faith in international trade" (see Art. 49, *supra* at §308).

Article 83.
Preservation of Other Remedies

449   This article, like Article 82 (§445, *supra*), addresses the relationship among different remedies. Article 82 dealt with the effect of substantial changes in the condition of goods after their receipt by the buyer, and provided that in specified circumstances these changes made it inappropriate for the buyer to exercise two of the remedies provided by the Convention — the right to avoid the contract (Art. 49) and the right to require the seller to deliver substitute goods (Art. 46(2)). Article 83, perhaps unnecessarily, states that Article 82 does not prevent buyers from exercising their other remedies.

Article 83[1]

A buyer who has lost the right to declare the contract avoided or to require the seller to deliver substitute goods in accordance with article 82 retains all other remedies under the contract and this Convention.

449.1   Article 83 states that although a buyer, because of changes in the condition of delivered goods, has lost two remedies as provided in Article 82 (§§445–448.2, *supra*), the buyer "retains *all other* remedies under the contract and this Convention." Remedies that are clearly preserved, without regard to changes in the condition of the goods after their receipt, include the buyer's right to recover damages (Arts. 45(1)(b), 74–76) and to reduce the price (Art. 50);[2] the buyer's right to require the seller to "remedy the lack of conformity by repair" (Art. 46(3)) (unless resale, consumption, processing or other change in the condition of the goods makes repair "unreasonable having regard to all the circumstances" (Art. 46(3), first sentence); *and remedies provided for in the contract, provided those remedies are consistent with the buyer's inability to return*

---

1. This article is substantially the same as Art. 68 of the 1978 Draft and ULIS 80.
2. See Oberlandesgericht Stuttgart, Germany, 12 Mar. 2001, English translation *available at* http://cisgw3.law.pace.edu/cases/010312g1.html.

the goods substantially in the condition in which they were received as per Article 82.[3]

Is a buyer's right to "require performance by the seller" under Article 46(1) a remedy distinct from the buyer's right under Article 46(2) to "require delivery of substitute goods" when their "lack of conformity constitutes a fundamental breach of contract?" To answer this question we need to examine situations in which Article 82 bars the buyer from requiring the delivery "of substitute goods" (Art. 46(2)). For example, assume that the buyer resells, consumes or otherwise transforms the goods *after* the buyer discovers their lack of conformity. Under these circumstances the exception provided by Article 82(2)(c) is inapplicable; consequently, Article 82(1) provides that the buyer has lost its right under Article 46(1) to require the seller to deliver substitute goods. In this setting there are few situations in which the buyer may (Art. 46(1)) "require performance" by the seller without contravening the more specific rules of Article 46(2) and 82 defining the circumstances in which the buyer may *not* require the "delivery of substitute goods."[4]

Of course, the buyer's right under Article 46(1) to "require performance," and the more specific right under Article 46(2) to require the delivery of substitute goods, are unimpaired in the many situations that lie outside the narrow scope of Article 82. (As we have seen, Article 82 preserves these two remedies when the condition of the defective goods has not "substantially" changed after their receipt (Art. 82(1)) and also in the cases described in Article 82(2)(a), (b) and (c).) For example, assume that the buyer has resold, consumed or transformed the goods *before* discovering their lack of conformity; here, as we have seen, Article 82(2)(c) preserves the buyer's right to avoid the contract (and claim restitution of payments made) or to require the seller to deliver substitute goods. The buyer will not be able to make restitution to the seller of the goods that were delivered (in the case of avoidance) or exchange the initial shipment for "substitute goods," but under Article

3. See Rainer Hornung, Art. 83 para. 3, *in* Schlechtriem & Schwenzer, *CISG Commentary* (2nd English ed. 2005).
4. Assume that a buyer has processed or sold goods after knowledge of a third-party claim of ownership (Art. 41) or infringement of intellectual property (Art. 42). Art. 82(2)(c) may bar the buyer from avoiding the contract or requiring the seller to deliver substitute goods but should not bar the buyer from "requiring performance" by the seller (Art. 46(1)) of an implied obligation under Arts. 41 or 42 to remove or defend the third-party claim. See §270.1, *supra. Accord*, Rainer Hornung, Art. 83 para. 3, *in* Schlechtriem & Schwenzer, *CISG Commentary* (2nd English ed. 2005).

84(2)(b), *infra*, the buyer "must account to the seller for all benefits he has derived from the goods." Of course, the sum for which the aggrieved buyer must "account" will be reduced or extinguished (Art. 74) by the "loss, including loss of profit, suffered by" the buyer "as a consequence of the breach."[5]

5. The right to recover damages for breach of contract under Art. 74 when the buyer requires the delivery of substitute goods (Art. 46(1) is preserved by the general language of Art. 83; the obligation to account for benefits received from goods under Art. 84 is made specifically applicable (subpara. (2)(b)) when the buyer has "declared the contract avoided or *required the seller to deliver substitute goods.*" Avoidance of the contract and requiring the delivery of substitute goods present similar problems and are expressly linked in Arts. 82(1), 83 and 84(2)(b).

Article 84.
Restitution of Benefits Received

450　　Under Article 81(2), *supra* at §444, a party who has performed by supplying goods or paying under a contract that is later avoided, may recover whatever it "has supplied or paid." Under Article 82 a buyer who receives seriously non-conforming goods and requires the seller to deliver substitutes (Article 46(3) must return the original goods). Article 84 supplements these provisions by requiring compensation for delay in recovering the price paid or the goods supplied.

Article 84[1]

(1) If the seller is bound to refund the price, he must also pay interest on it, from the date on which the price was paid.

(2) The buyer must account to the seller for all benefits which he has derived from the goods or part of them:

　　(a) if he must make restitution of the goods or part of them; or

　　(b) if it is impossible for him to make restitution of all or part of the goods or to make restitution of all or part of the goods substantially in the condition in which he received them, but he has nevertheless declared the contract avoided or required the seller to deliver substitute goods.

451　## A. Introduction

Under Article 78, *supra* at §420, a party is entitled to interest when the other party "fails to pay the price or any other sum that is in arrears." In that setting, interest is designed to compensate one party for the other's breach of contract — the "failure" to pay a "sum in arrears." Consequently, in considering the rate of interest attention was directed to the loss suffered by the person who should have received the payment. See Art. 78, *supra* at §421. *Article 84(1) also provides for the recovery of interest, and like Article 78 it does not specify a rate of interest; as*

---

1. This article is the same as Art. 69 of the 1978 Draft Convention and is substantially the same as ULIS 81.

shown below, however, a claim for interest under Article 84 may be made by an aggrieved party or by a breaching party.[2]

Article 84(2) may require a buyer — whether it is an aggrieved party or a breaching party — to "account to the seller for all benefits" that the buyer has derived from goods that have been delivered under a contract.

451.1   B. Scope of Article 84

Article 84, the final provision in Section V, and to the obligation of a buyer to return the original non-conforming goods if it requires the seller to deliver substitutes under Article 46(2). *Effects of Avoidance*, states obligations that are ancillary to the obligations of each party, upon avoidance of the contract, to return whatever it has received (Art. 81(2)). In spite of the relatively narrow scope of Article 84 it embraces a surprisingly wide variety of situations. Obligations under *each* of these two paragraphs can arise when there has been a fundamental breach by *either* party (Art. 81(1), *supra*) because either party (or *both* parties) may be obliged to make restitution. It will not be feasible to address all of these permutations but it seems advisable to examine the operation of Article 84 in a few specific cases.

451.2   (1) Interest on Sums Received by the Seller; Article 84(1)

Example 84A. Pursuant to the contract Buyer paid for the goods shortly prior to delivery but Seller failed to deliver. Buyer declared the contract avoided and sued to recover the price plus (Art. 84(1)) "interest on it from the date on which the price was paid."[3] How should the tribunal compute the interest owed to the buyer?

As we have already seen (Art. 78, §421, *supra*), even where the Convention provides for the recovery of interest neither UNCITRAL nor the Diplomatic Conference found it feasible to specify the rate of interest; the earlier discussion of Article 78 suggested that the solution should be

---

2. UNCITRAL Digest Art. 84 para. 2.

3. Buyer under Art. 74 could also claim damages resulting from the failure to receive the goods when promised (e.g., interruption of production) and at the agreed price (e.g., the effect of a rise in the market price).

derived by analogy to the Convention's rules on compensation for breach of contract (Arts. 74, 75 and 76).[4]

A seller's obligation to refund the price usually (as in Example 84A) can result from its breach of contract — that is, when the buyer avoids the contract because the seller failed to deliver or (more frequently) when the seller delivered goods that were seriously defective. In these cases it seems appropriate to base interest on the loss suffered by the aggrieved buyer rather than on a restitutionary approach to prevent unjust enrichment of the seller.[5] The approach based on damage for breach of contract, developed by analogy to the Convention's rules on damage measurement in Articles 74, 75 and 76, was discussed under Article 78 (§421, *supra*) and need not be repeated here. On the other hand, recovery based on the restitution of benefits received does seem appropriate for claims against a party who is not in breach of contract.[6] This approach will be illustrated *infra* at §452 in Example 84C.

451.3 (2) Benefits Derived from Goods; Article 84(2)

We now turn from Article 84(1) ("interest on" the *price*) to Article 84(2), which addresses "benefits derived" from *goods* that have been delivered. *Article 84(2) provides that the buyer must account to the seller for such benefits in two situations. First, under Article 84(2)(a) the buyer must do so if it "must make restitution of the goods or part of them." This rule applies where the seller has properly avoided the contract (see Article 81(2)); it also applies where the buyer has properly avoided the contract (see Article 81(2)) or required the seller to deliver substitute goods under Article 46(2), as long as the buyer can return the original goods "substantially in the condition in which he received them" as provided in Article 82(1). Article 84(2)(b), on the*

---

4. *But cf.* Rainer Hornung, Art. 84 para. 13, *in* Schlechtriem & Schwenzer, *CISG Commentary* (2nd English ed. 2005); Tallon in *B-B Commentary* §2.1, p. 612.

5. The reference in Art. 81(2) to "restitution of what a party has *supplied* or *paid*" seems to refer to the *payment* or the *goods* that must be returned, rather than to Interest. The term "restitution" is not used in Art. 84(1) in providing for the recovery of interest; on the other hand, Art. 84(2) calls for a restitutionary approach in requiring a buyer "to account" for "benefits" derived from the goods. In this latter setting there seems to be no practicable alternative to restitution. See §451.3, *infra*.

6. For discussion of the interest rate issue and of alternative approaches to it see Rainer Hornung, Art. 84 para. 13, *in* Schlechtriem & Schwenzer, *CISG Commentary* (2nd English ed. 2005). For decisions on the rate of interest payable under Art. 84(1) see UNCITRAL Digest Art. 84 para. 3.

other hand, requires the buyer to compensate the seller for benefits derived from the goods if, under Article 82(2), the buyer has avoided the contract or required delivery of substitute goods even though it could not return the original goods substantially in the condition in which they were received.

We turn first to the buyer's obligation under Article 84(2)(a). To facilitate comparison the following illustration is similar to Example 84A, except that the party in breach is the buyer rather than the seller.

Example 84B. Seller delivered goods to Buyer under a contract that called for payment 30 days after delivery. Buyer failed to pay and Seller declared the contract avoided. Seller brought an action to reclaim the goods (Art. 81(2) and also demanded (Art. 84(2)) that Buyer "account to the seller for all benefits which he has derived from the goods. . . ."

Seller, who could have pursued an action for the price under Article 62 had it not avoided the contract, will be fortunate if it can reclaim the goods before Buyer resells or consumes them or (in view of Buyer's failure to pay Seller) before Buyer's creditors seize the goods. See the discussion of Article 81(2) at §444, *supra.*[7] Our concern now is application of Seller's claim under Article 84(2) for the "benefits" Buyer "has derived from the goods."

The Article 84(2)(a) claim for the value of benefits that the buyer derived from the goods may be helpful to Seller if Buyer has resold the goods at a higher price.[8] *If the buyer has not resold the goods the seller's Article 84(2)(a) claim will be for, for example, the value that the buyer obtained from using the goods.* However, when (as in this case) the buyer has failed to pay, a seller may face serious difficulty collecting any claim.[9]

---

7. In view of the hazards confronting an attempt to recover the goods, the seller should demand, as alternative relief, that Buyer pay the price (Art. 62).

8. *Cf.* Rainer Hornung, Art. 84 para. 27, *in* Schlechtriem & Schwenzer, *CISG Commentary* (2nd English ed. 2005) (recovery of price that the buyer received for reselling goods under Art. 84(2)(b)). But see Oberlandesgericht Oldensburg, Germany, February 1, 1995, CLOUT case No. 165, English translation *available at* http://cisgw3.law.pace.edu/cases/950201g1. html (buyer resold goods, then discovered that they were non-conforming and avoided the contract; seller could not recover under Art. 84(2) because it failed to prove that buyer received benefits for the goods). Presumably, the buyer could deduct the cost of redisposition; a similar adjustment would be appropriate when the goods have been processed. See Rainer Hornung, Art. 84 para. 28, *in* Schlechtriem & Schwenzer, *CISG Commentary* (2nd English ed. 2005).

9. When the buyer has resold the goods to a customer who has not yet paid for them the seller will find it useful to ascertain whether applicable domestic law defers the claims of creditors

Under Article 84(2)(b), a buyer who — as provided in Article 82(2) — properly avoids the contract even though it cannot make restitution of the goods substantially in the condition in which they were received must also account to the seller for the benefits it derived from the goods. For example, the buyer may have resold the goods in the ordinary course of business (Article 82(2)(c)), in which case the buyer's benefit is the price received in the resale, less the costs associated with the resale. This has been characterized as a substitute or "surrogate" for restitution of the goods.

452 (3) Cross-Claims; Rights of Party in Breach

Example 84A and Example 84B illustrated the relatively simple situation when only one party performs and that party avoids the contract because of non-performance by the other party. Our final example faces a more complex situation: Both parties have performed at least in part; avoidance in this setting presents a new feature — recovery by a party who is *in breach of contract* from the aggrieved party.

Example 84C. On June 1 Buyer paid one-half of the price for a machine which Seller, in accordance with the contract, delivered on July 1. The balance of the price was due thirty days after delivery but Buyer failed to pay. Seller promptly avoided the contract for fundamental breach and obtained a court order impounding the machine for delivery to Seller. Buyer, invoking Article 81, noted that on avoidance both parties must make concurrent restitution of whatever they have received; consequently, Seller must refund the payment Buyer made on June 1. In addition, Buyer noted that under Article 84(1) Buyer was entitled to interest "from the date on which the price was paid."

How should the interest on Buyer's payment be measured? In Example 84A (§451.2, *supra*) a buyer claimed interest on a payment from a seller who had committed a fundamental breach by failing to deliver the goods. In that setting it was suggested that interest should be allowed, by analogy to Articles 74, 75 and 76, on the basis of the loss to the aggrieved party. That approach would not be appropriate here since

---

to the seller's right to recover the goods (*cf.* (U.S.A.) UCC 2–402(1)) and also whether a right to recover goods extends to specific proceeds like the customer's unpaid debt for the goods. See also Daniel Friedmann, *Restitution of Profits Gained by Party in Breach of Contract*, 104 L.Q. Rev. 383 (1988).

interest is claimed by the party in breach. In this case a restitutionary approach seems more appropriate; recovery should be based on the benefit Seller received from the use of the money. Of course, Buyer's claim may be reduced or eliminated by Seller's right to recover damages resulting from Buyer's breach as well as Buyer's obligation under Article 84(2) to account for benefits it derived from the goods. (For discussion of the parties' right to set-off or recoup mutual claims, see §444A *supra*.)

SECTION VI.

PRESERVATION OF THE GOODS
(Articles 85–88)

INTRODUCTION TO THE SECTION

453   This concluding section is designed to prevent the loss or deterioration of goods when a dispute prevents their acceptance or retention by the buyer. To this end, a party who is in the best position to care for the goods is given the responsibility to do so, regardless of whether this party is in breach of contract.

The Convention's provisions on the passing of risk (Ch. IV, Arts. 66–70) were similarly designed to minimize loss — by placing responsibility for the safety of the goods on the person who was in the best position to prevent casualty or other loss. (See Art. 67, *supra* at §367 and Art. 69, *supra* at §375.)

In some situations uncertainties about one's legal position may interfere with achieving this ideal. Honest differences may arise over whether the goods fail to conform to the contract, and whether nonconformity of the goods or the conduct of one party frees the other party from its duty to perform the contract. One might imagine that a superhuman Being, omniscient as to both facts and law, would be free from doubt — but such an omniscient Being might be disappointed in the positions taken by well-meaning merchants and even by able tribunals.

In response to these practical difficulties, Section VI, in limited circumstances, prescribes duties to care for goods on grounds that do not turn on legal issues such as fundamental breach and avoidance of the contract. Of course, the party in breach is responsible for damages resulting from the breach, including any costs incurred by the other party in preserving the goods.

The seller's duties are defined in Article 85 and the buyer's duties in Article 86. Articles 87 and 88 apply to both parties.

[677]

Article 85.
Seller's Duty to Preserve Goods

454   The present article applies only when the seller has the goods in its possession or control. For reasons summarized in the Introduction, the seller may have a duty to preserve the goods even though the buyer's failure to take delivery is a breach of contract.

Article 85[1]

If the buyer is in delay in taking delivery of the goods or, where payment of the price and delivery of the goods are to be made concurrently, if he fails to pay the price, and the seller is either in possession of the goods or otherwise able to control their disposition, the seller must take such steps as are reasonable in the circumstances to preserve them. He is entitled to retain them until he has been reimbursed his reasonable expenses by the buyer.

This article has its simplest (but not its most significant) application when the buyer should take delivery at the seller's place of business but fails to come for the goods by the date specified in the contract.[2] Under the rules on risk (Ch. IV, Art. 69, *supra* at §373) the risk of loss passes to the buyer on the date when "he commits a breach of contract by failing to take delivery." Suppose that, after risk has passed to the buyer, the seller leaves perishable goods out in the rain or discontinues necessary refrigeration. In such situations, Article 85 — which applies if "the buyer is in delay in taking delivery" and the seller "is either in possession of the goods or otherwise able to control their disposition" — requires the seller to "take such steps as are reasonable in the circumstances to preserve" the goods. The seller is responsible for loss to the goods that results from his failure to comply with this duty.[3]

---

1. This article is substantially the same as Art. 74 of the 1978 Draft. The addition of the "or where payment..." phrase in para. (1) was a clarifying amendment. See *O.R.* 398, *Docy. Hist.* 619. *Cf.* ULIS 91.

2. See Klaus Bacher, Art. 85 paras. 4–5 and 9, *in* Schlechtriem & Schwenzer, *CISG Commentary* (2nd English ed. 2005).

3. See *Secretariat Comm., O.R.* 62, *Docy. Hist.* 452 (Ex. 74A); Klaus Bacher, *Introduction to Arts. 85–88* para. 4, *in* Schlechtriem & Schwenzer, *CISG Commentary* (2nd English ed. 2005) ("If a party infringes a duty laid down in Articles 85–88, the other side in general is entitled to claim damages"); Barrera Graf in *B-B Commentary* 616.

Another application of Article 85 may be illustrated as follows:

Example 85A. A sales contract called for Seller to send the goods to Buyer by carrier. The contract did not require Seller to deliver the goods to Buyer on credit, so Seller properly shipped the goods under a bill of lading that called for delivery to "Seller or order" (a "negotiable" or "order" bill of lading); Seller retained possession of this document through banks acting on Seller's behalf and thereby controlled disposition of the goods (Art. 58). When the goods reached their destination. Seller (acting through a correspondent hank) offered to deliver the document to Buyer in exchange for payment. Buyer failed to pay. (For purposes of this illustration it does not matter whether Buyer attempted to avoid the contract because of an erroneous view that the goods were seriously defective (Art. 25) or repudiated the contract without any reason). The goods remain in the possession of the carrier. High demurrage charges are accruing and there is danger that the goods will be stolen. Has Seller any duties with respect to the goods?

Seller would be correct in pointing out that risk of loss had passed to Buyer under the general rules of Chapter IV. In the absence of agreement, and under most trade terms (e.g., F.O.B., C & F, C.I.F.) risk passed to Buyer at the beginning of transit (Art. 67). And even if the contract provided that transit risks fall on Seller (e.g., "delivery *ex ship* Buyer's city") risk passed to Buyer when the goods were placed at its disposal and it failed to take delivery (Art. 69).

Article 85 applies "where payment of the price and delivery of the goods are to be made concurrently, if [the buyer] fails to pay the price." Thus it requires action by Seller in the circumstances of Example 85A.[4] Since Buyer did not pay, Seller retains control over the negotiable bill of lading and thereby has control over the disposition of the goods. Hence, under Article 85 "the seller must take such steps as are reasonable in the circumstance to preserve" the goods. These steps might well involve depositing the goods in a warehouse (Art. 87) or reselling them (Art. 88).[5] *For further discussion of risk of loss to goods in situations like Example 85A, see §448.1B supra.*

The duties imposed by Article 85 are of special importance under the Convention because of the broad scope of the seller's right to recover the

---

4. See Klaus Bacher, Art. 85 paras. 6 & 10, *in* Schlechtriem & Schwenzer, *CISG Commentary* (2nd English ed. 2005); *Schlechtriem, 1986 Commentary* 109.

5. For discussion of steps to preserve goods that the seller may be required to take under Art. 85 see Klaus Bacher, Art. 85 paras. 12–14, *in* Schlechtriem & Schwenzer, *CISG Commentary* (2nd English ed. 2005).

full price (Art. 62) — a remedy that has practical consequences that are very different from liability for damages.[6] Under legal systems influenced by the common law and the (U.K.) Sale of Goods Act (1893), a seller who remains in possession of the goods seldom is entitled to force the goods on the buyer by recovering the full contract price (§346, *supra*). Of course, the seller may recover damages for breach of contract but this remedy calls for the seller to redispose of the goods. In the above legal setting, there is little need for rules specifically requiring the seller to protect the goods from damage since the seller cannot transfer this loss to the buyer.[7]

A seller's obligation under Article 85 to preserve the goods does not end if the seller brings an action (Art. 62) to require the buyer to pay the price. The seller is not required to hand over the goods before the buyer pays (Art. 58(1)) and, for various reasons, will need to retain control of the goods. *The seller's Article 85 obligations, however, should cease upon avoidance of the contract[8]: avoidance puts an end to the seller's right to require the buyer to take the goods and pay the price under Article 62, leaving the seller in much the same position as under common-law systems, as described in the previous paragraph.*

A seller who incurs expenses in fulfilling its obligations under Article 85 is entitled, pursuant to the last sentence of Article 85, to reimbursement by the buyer, and can retain the goods until such reimbursement is given.[9] This protection, however, may not be sufficient to motivate an aggrieved seller to pursue an action requiring the buyer to take delivery and pay the price, as opposed to avoiding the contract and pursuing damages under Articles 74–76. Bringing a legal action for the price under Article 62, and thus retaining an obligation to preserve the goods under Article 85, does not assure payment. The seller's suit may fail — the buyer may interpose a defense based on seller's breach; an

---

6. For discussion of steps to preserve goods that the seller may be required to take under Art. 85 see Klaus Bacher, Art. 85 para. 1, *in* Schlechtriem & Schwenzer, *CISG Commentary* (2nd English ed. 2005).

7. *Atiyah* 365–371 (the remedy is complicated by use of the "properly" concept): *Benjamin* §§1241–1257; *Bridge, Sale* 719–727. See (U.S.A.) UCC 2–709(1)(a): Seller may recover the price of goods the buyer has "accepted"; *cf.* 2–709(1)(b) (price recovery "if the seller is unable after reasonable effort" to resell the goods).

8. See Klaus Bacher, Art. 85 para. 15, *in* Schlechtriem & Schwenzer, *CISG Commentary* (2nd English ed. 2005); Flechtner, *Pittsburgh Symposium* 104–105.

9. For discussion of these rights see Klaus Bacher, Art. 85 para. 16–18, *in* Schlechtriem & Schwenzer, *CISG Commentary* (2nd English ed. 2005). For decisions on the seller's right to recover the costs of preserving the goods see UNCITRAL Digest Art. 85 para. 3.

action to require payment of the price may be rejected by the forum (Art. 28 and §§197, 348–349, supra). Moreover, at the end of the legal road the buyer may not be able to satisfy a judgment. There are other practical considerations of even greater weight. The seller usually will not wish to maintain control over the goods during the extended time that may be required to bring the case to trial and final judgment. Warehouse costs and deterioration of the goods may substantially reduce the seller's security interest and make it prudent for the seller to redispose of the goods and claim damages for breach of contract. In any event, if substantial warehouse costs and deterioration occur the buyer may claim that the seller failed under Article 88(2), infra, to take "reasonable measures to sell" the goods — a specific provision that reinforces the general obligation under Article 77 (§§416–419, supra) to "mitigate the loss" resulting from breach. *These considerations may well counsel an aggrieved seller who has control of the goods to relieve itself of Article 85 obligations by avoiding the contract, disposing of the goods, and seeking damages (e.g., under Article 75).*

Article 86.
Buyer's Duty to Preserve Goods

455   Article 85 dealt with the seller's duty to preserve the goods; the present article is concerned with the duty of the buyer.

Article 86[1]

(1) If the buyer has received the goods and intends to exercise any right under the contract or this Convention to reject them, he must take such steps to preserve them as are reasonable in the circumstances. He is entitled to retain them until he has been reimbursed his reasonable expenses by the seller.

(2) If goods dispatched to the buyer have been placed at his disposal at their destination and he exercises the right to reject them, he must take possession of them on behalf of the seller, provided that this can be done without payment of the price and without unreasonable inconvenience or unreasonable expense. This provision does not apply if the seller or a person authorized to take charge of the goods on his behalf is present at the destination. If the buyer takes possession of the goods under this paragraph, his rights and obligations are governed by the preceding paragraph.

There have been decades of experience with rules similar to Article 86. See, for example, (U.S.A.) Uniform Commercial Code §2–603.

455.1   **The Duty to Preserve Goods under Article 86(1); "Receipt" of Goods and the Intent to "Reject" Them**

Article 86(1) requires the buyer take reasonable steps to preserve goods that it has "received" if the buyer intends "to exercise any right ... to reject them." "Receiving" goods has been equated to acquiring possession of them.[2] The term "reject" (with reference to goods) also appears in Article 86(2), but has not appeared earlier in the Convention; this broad term is used here to assure that the buyer's duty to preserve the goods will apply whenever the buyer exercises a right to refuse to accept the goods or to return them to the seller after receiving them.

1. This article is substantially the same as Art. 75 of the 1978 Draft. The last sentence of para. (2) was added for clarity. *O.R.* 399–400, *Docy. Hist.* 620–621. *Cf.* ULIS 92.
2. See Klaus Bacher, Art. 86 para. 3, *in* Schlechtriem & Schwenzer, *CISG Commentary* (2nd English ed. 2005).

Thus a buyer's justified declaration that the contract is avoided because of the tender of seriously defective goods (Arts. 25, 26, 49) terminates the obligation to "take delivery" of the goods (Arts. 53, 60(b)); in other words, the buyer may "reject" the goods. Similar consequences follow from avoidance after the buyer has received the goods (Art. 81(2)). Under Article 46(2), when non-conformity of delivered goods constitutes a fundamental breach the buyer may "require delivery of *substitute* goods," a remedy that involves rejection and return of the initial delivery. Pursuant to Article 51 these remedies that involve "rejection" of goods may be applied to a "part of the goods." *In addition, under Article 52 a buyer may refuse to take an early delivery or a tendered quantity that is "greater than that provided for in the contract"—further instances of "rejection."*[3] Article 86, in referring to the right to "reject" goods in both subparts (1) and (2), refers to all these remedies regardless of whether the buyer "has received" the goods (Art. 86(1)), or whether goods, after dispatch to the buyer, have been placed at the buyer's "disposal" (Art. 86(2)).

The buyer's obligation to preserve goods under Article 86(1) would come into play, for example, where the buyer has had possession of the goods for some time (and perhaps has put them into use), then discovers a latent defect that constitutes a fundamental breach and decides to avoid the contract. The buyer has clearly "received" the goods and intends to "reject" them, thus triggering the duty to preserve the goods.

Article 86(1) states that the buyer must protect the goods if the buyer "intends to" reject them. This language could be read to mean that there is no duty to protect the goods before the buyer forms an intent to reject — for example, a buyer receives the goods on Monday, leaves them in the rain on Tuesday and forms (and/or declares) an intent to reject them on Wednesday.[4] In spite of awkward drafting, Article 86(1) should require reasonable steps to preserve goods while they are in the buyer's possession during the period leading up to a decision to reject.[5] In any event, under Article 82(1) a buyer loses its right to avoid the

---

3. See Klaus Bacher, Art. 86 para. 5, *in* Schlechtriem & Schwenzer, *CISG Commentary* (2nd English ed. 2005). *Cf.* Cour de Cassation, France, January 4, 1995, CLOUT case No. 155, English translation available at http://cisgw3.law.pace.edu/cases/950104f1.html (http://cisgw3.law.pace.edu/cases/950104f1.htmlbuyer (buyer who was attempting to reject excess goods denied right to expenses of preservation under Art. 86 because it failed to prove any such expenses).

4. *Cf.* Barrera Graf, *B-B Commentary* §2.3, p. 622.

5. See Klaus Bacher, Art. 86 para. 7, *in* Schlechtriem & Schwenzer, *CISG Commentary* (2nd English ed. 2005).

contract (Art. 49) or to require the delivery of substitute goods (Art. 46(2)), if the buyer cannot return the goods "in substantially the same condition" as when they were received; as we have seen, inability so to return the goods is not excused by Article 82(2)(c) since the damage to the goods would be due to the buyer's "act or omission."[6] This result is reinforced by the Convention's rules on risk of loss. Under nearly all of the situations envisaged in Article 86, risk has passed to the buyer under Articles 67 (handing over to the carrier), 68 (making of contract or handing over to the carrier), or 69 (buyer's taking over the goods). *(For discussion of responsibility for damage to goods after a buyer's rejection of the goods, see §448.1A supra.)*

455.2   The Duty to Take Possession of Goods under Article 86(2)
       The buyer's duty under Article 86(2) has its clearest application in cases like the following:
       Example 86A. Seller shipped to a distant Buyer; the bill of lading called for delivery to "Buyer," not to "order of Seller" or to "Seller." Thus, Seller did not retain control over the goods by a negotiable bill of lading (contrast Example 85A, supra §454). When the goods reached Buyer it rightfully rejected them on the ground that they were seriously defective.
       In such cases Buyer might "receive" (take possession) the goods for inspection, in which case it will be subject to Article 86(1) and the duty to preserve it imposes. Even if the goods are still in the possession of the carrier, the goods were consigned to Buyer; he did not need the bill of lading to take delivery. Thus, under Article 86(2), the goods were at Buyer's "disposal at their destination." *Furthermore, Buyer did not have to pay the price or, evidently, undergo any other "unreasonable inconvenience or unreasonable expense" in order to take possession of the goods*. If Seller has no agent in or near Buyer's city, Article 86(2) requires Buyer *to take possession of the goods; when it does so, Buyer is subject to the Article 86(a) obligation* to take reasonable steps to preserve the goods. **The rationale for this rule is clear:** it is difficult for a seller to preserve and dispose of the goods that have been rejected at a remote destination.
       Some of the limits set by Article 86(2) may be illustrated as follows:
       Example 86B. The transaction called for payment at destination in exchange for a bill of lading made out to the "order of Seller," a

---

6. See Klaus Bacher, Art. 86 para. 7, *in* Schlechtriem & Schwenzer, *CISG Commentary* (2nd English ed. 2005); *Schlechtriem, 1986 Commentary* 109.

document that, as in Example 85A (Article 85 at §454, supra), controlled the disposition of the goods. Buyer refused to accept and pay for the goods.

Example 85A posed the question whether the seller had a duty to preserve the goods in similar circumstances. Does Article 86 place such a duty on the buyer? The answer is No. Paragraph (1) is not applicable since the buyer has not "received" the goods. And paragraph (2) is not applicable since the buyer can only get possession by paying the price. In the prior example (Example 86A), the duties imposed by Article 86 apply since the rejected goods are in the buyer's "possession or control"; on the other hand, this standard shields the buyer from such duties in Example 86B.

455.3   Retention of Goods and Reimbursement of Expenses of Preservation

A buyer who incurs expenses in performing its Article 86(1) duty to preserve goods — a duty that, as we saw (§455.2 supra), is also imposed on a buyer who takes possession of goods pursuant to Article 86(2) — may "retain them until he has been reimbursed his reasonable expenses by the seller." This right to retain goods and recover reasonable expenses mirrors the right of a seller that has incurred expenses to preserve goods pursuant to Article 85.[7] The right to retain goods until reimbursed applies even though (as must be the case for Article 86 to come into play) the buyer intends to reject the goods or has already done so. Unsurprisingly, much of the reported litigation on Article 86 involves a buyer's claim for the expenses of preservation.[8]

7. See Klaus Bacher, Art. 86 para. 18, *in* Schlechtriem & Schwenzer, *CISG Commentary* (2nd English ed. 2005).
8. See UNCITRAL Digest Art. 86 para. 2.

Article 87.
Deposit in Warehouse

456   Article 85 and 86, *supra*, established a duty "to preserve" goods. The two provisions that follow authorize two specific types of action that may fulfill this duty — storage in a warehouse (Art. 87) and sale of the goods (Art. 88).

Article 87[1]

A party who is bound to take steps to preserve the goods may deposit them in a warehouse of a third person at the expense of the other party provided that the expense incurred is not unreasonable.

Deposit of goods in a warehouse is such a common way to "preserve goods" that this article might seem unnecessary, except for doubt as to whether storage by one party would authorize the warehouse to assert a possessory lien for storage charges and recover those charges from the other party to the sales contract. The rights of the warehouse, which is not a party to the contract of sale, are not governed by the Convention. See Articles 1 and 4. Unless the storage contract provides otherwise, the party who deposits the goods is primarily liable to the warehouse. The depositing party, however, may seek reimbursement from the other party to the sales contract for storage charges that are "not unreasonable," as expenses of preserving the goods recoverable under Articles 85 or 86.[2] A party who preserves the goods by depositing them in a warehouse can stop the accumulation of storage charges by selling the goods, as authorized by Article 88, which follows.[3]

For discussion of risk of loss in the kinds of circumstances in which Article 87 might come into play, see §448.1A and §448.1B supra.[4]

---

1. This article is the same as Art. 76 of the 1978 Draft. *Cf.* ULIS 93.

2. See Klaus Bacher, Art. 87 paras. 8–9, *in* Schlechtriem & Schwenzer, *CISG Commentary* (2nd English ed. 2005). For decisions on recovering the expenses of warehousing goods see UNCITRAL Digest Art. 87 para. 2.

3. (U.S.A.) UCC §2–604 gives a rejecting buyer the option to "store the rejected goods for the seller's account." UCC §7–209 gives the warehouseman a lien against (sub (1)) "the bailor" and (sub (3)) certain third persons.

4. See also Klaus Bacher, Art. 87 paras. 5–6, *in* Schlechtriem & Schwenzer, *CISG Commentary* (2nd English ed. 2005).

Article 88.
Sale of the Goods

457   Placing perishable goods in a warehouse (Art. 87) may not be adequate to fulfill a party's duty under Articles 85 or 86 to "preserve" goods. Even if goods that a party has a duty to preserve are not perishable, warehouse charges for an extended period may become excessive, perhaps even exceeding the value of the goods; in some cases the bailor may not be confident of recouping these charges from the other party to the sales contract.[1] Consequently, the bailor may need to sell the goods and put an end to accumulating storage charges. Article 88 addresses these possibilities.

Article 88[2]

(1) A party who is bound to preserve the goods in accordance with article 85 or 86 may sell them by any appropriate means if there has been an unreasonable delay by the other party in taking possession of the goods or in taking them back or in paying the price or the cost of preservation, provided that reasonable notice of the intention to sell has been given to the other party.

(2) If the goods are subject to rapid deterioration or their preservation would involve unreasonable expense, a party who is bound to preserve the goods in accordance with article 85 or 86 must take reasonable measures to sell them. To the extent possible he must give notice to the other party of his intention to sell.

(3) A party selling the goods has the right to retain out of the proceeds of sale an amount equal to the reasonable expenses of preserving the goods and of selling them. He must account to the other party for the balance.

---

1. See Klaus Bacher, Art. 88 para. 5, *in* Schlechtriem & Schwenzer, *CISG Commentary* (2nd English ed. 2005); China International Economic and Trade Arbitration Commission [CIETAC], People's Republic of China, June 6, 1991, English translation *available at* http://cisgw3.law.pace.edu/cases/910606c1.html.
2. This article is closely based on Art. 77 of the 1978 Draft. In para. (1) "the price or" was inserted to conform to the addition of a reference to the price in Art. 85, *supra* at §454. In addition, in para. (1) "reasonable" was inserted before "notice." *O.R.* 413–414, *Docy. Hist.* 634–635. *Cf.* ULIS 94, 95.

Option to Sell. Paragraph (1) provides *authority* (not an obligation) to sell. In view of the optional character of this paragraph, the standard is flexible: "unreasonable delay" by the other party in taking the actions specified in Article 88(1).[3] *Those actions — taking (or taking back) possession of the goods, paying the price or the first party's costs of preserving the goods — would end the first party's obligation to preserve the goods; that, of course, is why unreasonable delay in taking the actions justifies sale of the goods by the party with the obligation to preserve. On that principle, the right to sell the goods should also be available to a buyer when a seller unreasonably delays making restitution of the buyer's payments following avoidance of the contract (see Art. 81(2), §444A supra).[4] A sale under Article 88(1) must be by "appropriate means"[5] and must be accompanied by "reasonable notice [to the other party] of the intention sell."[6]*

Duty to Sell. Paragraph (2) imposes a duty to "take reasonable measures to sell"[7] when "the goods are subject to rapid deterioration or their preservation would involve unreasonable expense."[8] *As with optional sales under Article 88(1), notice of the intention to sell is required for mandatory sales under Article 88(2), but only "[t]o the extent possible."[9]*

The present article applies to any party who is "bound to preserve the goods" — a *seller* in possession of goods when the buyer fails to pay or to take delivery (Art. 85), or a *buyer* who receives goods which he has

---

3. See Klaus Bacher, Art. 88 para. 4, *in* Schlechtriem & Schwenzer, *CISG Commentary* (2nd English ed. 2005). For decisions applying Art. 88(1), see UNCITRAL Digest Art. 88 para. 2.

4. *Accord*, Klaus Bacher, Art. 88 para. 4, *in* Schlechtriem & Schwenzer, *CISG Commentary* (2nd English ed. 2005).

5. See Klaus Bacher, Art. 88 para. 9, *in* Schlechtriem & Schwenzer, *CISG Commentary* (2nd English ed. 2005); *Oberlandesgericht* Hamburg, Germany, November 26, 1999, CLOUT case No. 348, English translation *available at* <http://cisgw3.law.pace.edu/cases/991126g1. html; Iran-U.S. Claims Tribunal, July 28, 1989, *available online at* http://www.unilex.info/ case.cfm?pid=1&do=case&id=38&step=FullText.

6. See Klaus Bacher, Art. 88 paras. 6–8, *in* Schlechtriem & Schwenzer, *CISG Commentary* (2nd English ed. 2005).

7. See Klaus Bacher, Art. 88 para. 14, *in* Schlechtriem & Schwenzer, *CISG Commentary* (2nd English ed. 2005).

8. See Klaus Bacher, Art. 88 paras. 11–12, *in* Schlechtriem & Schwenzer, *CISG Commentary* (2nd English ed. 2005). For decisions applying Art. 88(2) see UNCITRAL Digest Art. 88 para. 4.

9. See Klaus Bacher, Art. 88 para. 13, *in* Schlechtriem & Schwenzer, *CISG Commentary* (2nd English ed. 2005).

the right to reject (Art. 86).[10] And, as has been noted, paragraph (1) of Article 88 grants a *privilege* to sell while paragraph (2) imposes a *duty* to sell.

A seller's *duty* to sell goods in its possession (Art. 88(2)) needs to be considered in relationship to the seller's right under Article 62 to "require the buyer to pay the price." In discussing Article 62 (§§346, 348, *supra*) we saw that requiring payment by one who has not received the goods is subject under Article 28 to the remedial approach of *fora* in many States where such "specific performance" is compelled only if damages do not provides an adequate remedy (§§194–199, *supra*). In discussing Article 62 we also noted (§349) that Article 88(2), by requiring the seller to resell goods held for the buyer, in substance creates an exception to the rule (Art. 62) that the seller may force acceptance of goods by requiring the buyer to pay the price. However, this exception under Article 88(2), is limited to cases under 85 where the seller is "either in possession of the goods or otherwise able to control their disposition"[11] and, unhappily, does not solve the disputed issue whether a seller may engage in wasteful production, free of the loss-mitigation rule of Article 77, if the seller sues for the price (Art. 62) rather than damages.

457.1   Article 88(3): Proceeds of Sale

Article 88(3) prescribes disposition of the proceeds of a sale con-ducted under Article 88(1) or Article 88(2): it permits the selling party to retain the "reasonable expenses" of preserving and selling the goods, but requires the selling party to "account to the other party" for the balance of the proceeds.[12] For discussion of whether the selling party can set-off other claims against the proceeds, see §444A supra.[13]

---

10. See Klaus Bacher, Art. 88 para. 4, *in* Schlechtriem & Schwenzer, *CISG Commentary* (2nd English ed. 2005); UNCITRAL Digest Art. 88 para. 2.

11. The language just quoted limits the scope of the seller's obligation under Art. 85 to take steps to preserve the goods and thereby also limits the situations in which Art. 88(2) requires the seller to take reasonable measures to sell the goods.

12. See Klaus Bacher, Art. 88 paras. 17–19, *in* Schlechtriem & Schwenzer, *CISG Commentary* (2nd English ed. 2005); UNCITRAL Digest Art. 88 para. 5.

13. See also Klaus Bacher, Art. 88 para. 18, *in* Schlechtriem & Schwenzer, *CISG Commentary* (2nd English ed. 2005).

Part IV.

FINAL PROVISIONS

(Articles 89–101)

INTRODUCTION TO PART IV OF THE CONVENTION

458   **A. Overview of Part IV**[1]

Sellers and buyers will rarely be concerned with some of the articles of Part IV — that is, Articles 91 and 99 on procedures for bringing the Convention into force and for making the transition between the 1964 Hague Sales Conventions (Uniform Law on the Formation of Contracts for the International Sale of Goods (ULF) & Uniform Law for the International Sale of Goods (ULIS)) and the present Convention. These matters are handled by government officers who have experience with similar provisions in other conventions.

Other provisions have wider applicability. Five Articles (92–96) authorize States to declare that they will not be bound by specified provisions. Some of these "declarations" (commonly called "reservations") were considered in connection with the articles which they modify: E.g., Article 1(1)(b) on the Convention's sphere of application — subject to reservation under Article 95 (§47, *supra*); Article 11 rejecting domestic formal requirements (e.g., Statutes of Frauds) — subject to reservation under Article 96 (§§128–129, *supra*).

Other articles in Part IV need attention here. For example, the Scandinavian States have invoked Article 92 to exclude Part II on Formation; these reservations, important for parties in States that have made the reservation, also need to be noted by their trading partners (see §467, *infra*). *The Scandinavian States have also made the reservation authorized by Article 94, declaring the Convention inapplicable to international sales between parties located in those States (see §469, infra).* During a limited period following the Convention's entry into force in each Contracting State, sellers and buyers may need to know

---

1. For general commentary on Part IV see Peter Schlechtriem, *Part IV, Final Provisions* paras. 1–11, *in* Schlechtriem & Schwenzer, *CISG Commentary* (2nd English ed. 2005); Peter Winship, *Final Provisions*, 24 Int'l Law. 711 (1990); Evans, Preamble, *B-B Commentary* 633.

whether the Convention applies to them and may need help in untangling the compact language of Article 100 (see §473, *infra*). The role of other articles will be examined at §§461–474, *infra*.

459　**B. Development of Part IV**

The Final Provisions (with one exception — Article 96) were not developed in United Nations Commission on International Trade Law (UNCITRAL). The General Assembly's resolution providing for the 1980 Diplomatic Conference requested the Secretary General to prepare and circulate a draft of proposed final provisions; this draft appears in the Convention's *Official Records* at 66–70. For reasons explained in Chapter 1, §10, *supra*, the Conference did most of its work in two "committees": While the First Committee prepared Parts I–III of the Convention, the Second Committee prepared the Final Provisions.[2]

460　**(3) Method of Presentation**

The full texts of most of the articles of Part IV will not be reproduced here; these articles appear in the full text of the Convention, reproduced in the Appendix. In addition, the crucial language of these articles will be quoted in the discussion which follows.

461　**C. Discussion of Salient Provisions**

461　**(1) Article 89: Depositary**

Designating the Secretary-General of the United Nations as depositary is customary for conventions prepared by the United Nations. Except for one brief reference in Article 99(6), Part IV does not set forth the duties of a depositary. A detailed list of these duties appears in Article 77(1) of the Vienna Treaty on Treaties (1969) and presumably is generally applicable

---

2. The Second Committee's deliberations are recorded in the *Official Records* (*O.R.*) at 434–474 and 479; the resulting draft as reviewed by the Drafting Committee appears at *O.R.* 165–167, *Docy. Hist.* 165–167. This draft was then submitted to the Plenary Conference for final action; the deliberations and decisions (at this stage requiring a two-thirds majority) are recorded at *O.R.* 228–230. A careful study by Professor Winship of the final provisions of the UNCITRAL Conventions appears in 24 Int. Law. 711 (1990).

to this Convention.[3] Under Article 77(1)(a) of the Vienna Treaty these duties include "preparing certified copies of the original" — a service that may be important to parties engaged in litigation.

The Secretary-General's depositary functions are performed by the following office: Depositary Functions of the Treaty Section, Office of Legal Affairs, United Nations, New York, 10017.

462   (2) Article 90: Relation to Other Conventions

This article is important and deserves quotation:

Article 90[4]

This Convention does not prevail over any international agreement which has already been or may be entered into and which contains provisions concerning the matters governed by this Convention, provided that the parties have their places of business in States parties to such agreement.

463   **(a) Basis for Future Amendment.**   The present Convention does not contain any provision that expressly provides for amendment. However, under the Vienna Treaty on Treaties (1969) (Arts. 40(4), 41(1)(b)) the lack of an express provision for amendment does not bar amendment — and an amendment will be effective for the parties who agree without the concurrence of all parties to the original treaty.[5] Article 90 of CSIG, by providing that it "does not prevail over any international agreement which . . . *may be entered into* and which contains provisions concerning *the matters governed by the Convention*," should avoid any doubt that this Convention is subject to amendment by the flexible procedures provided by the Vienna Treaty on Treaties. This is fortunate since amendment by denunciation (Article 101, *infra*) and readoption would be difficult for a widely-adopted treaty like the Sales

---

3. *See* Peter Schlechtriem, Article 89 paragraph 2, *in* Schlechtriem & Schwenzer, *CISG Commentary* (2nd English ed. 2005); Evans, *B-B Commentary* 634.

4. Article 90 is substantially the same as Article 37 of the 1974 Convention on the Limitation Period in the International Sale of Goods (A/Conf. 63/15). There was little discussion of Article 90 at the 1980 Vienna Conference. See *O.R.* 439–440, 479.

5. I. Sinclair, *The Vienna Convention on the Law of Treaties* 106–109 (2nd ed. 1984). Article 40(2) & (3) of the Vienna Treaty on Treaties prescribes procedures for amending a multinational treaty — for example, all parties to the treaty must be noticed of the proposal to amend and have the right to take part in the decision on whether to amend.

Convention; in the absence of extraordinary precautions the cumbersome character of adoption procedures coupled, with the preoccupation or neglect by officials and legislatures, could produce unintended gaps in the applicability of the uniform law.[6] It should also be reassuring to note that the 1974 Convention on the Limitation Period in the International Sale of Goods, containing a provision substantially the same as CISG Article 90 and no other provision relating to amendment, was amended without objection or mishap by a Protocol approved at the 1980 Conference that finalized the Sales Convention.[7]

464 **(b) Relation to Past Conventions.** Article 90 states that the Sales Convention does not prevail over any international agreement "which *already has been* or may be entered into ..." Since Article 1 of the Convention contains rules governing its applicability we need to consider the relationship between the 1980 Sales Convention and the 1955 Hague Convention on the Law Applicable [P.L.I.] to International Sales of Goods ("1955 Hague P.I.L. Convention")[8] — a Convention that has been adopted by some States that have adopted the 1980 Convention.[9] Article 1(1)(b) of the Sales Convention (CISG) and the 1955 Hague P.I.L. Convention are complementary rather than in conflict. CISG 1(1)(b) (§47, *supra*) provides that the Sales Convention is applicable "when the rules of private international law lead to the application of the law of a Contracting State," and thus invites the use of "conflicts"

6. CISG Article 101(2) provides that a denunciation may provide a longer delay before effectiveness than the twelve-month delay specified in this article. Delicate handling of this provision could minimize the danger of gaps but it would be hazardous to rely on inclusion of the same flexible period in the instruments of denunciation filed by all Contracting States.

7. The Protocol amended the 1974 provisions on sphere of application to conform to the approach that had developed in preparing the 1980 Convention. The Protocol appears in the *Official Records* of the 1980 Conference at p. 191. The 1974 Limitation Convention, as amended, entered into force on August 1, 1988. See also Winship, n. 1 *supra* at 731–732.

8. U.N. Treaty Series, vol. 510, p. 149, No. 7411 (1964); UNCITRAL *Register* vol. 1. p. 5. See also, generally, Peter Schlechtriem, *Article 90* paras. 3–8, *in* Schlechtriem & Schwenzer, *CISG Commentary* (2nd English ed. 2005). Detailed procedures for replacement of the 1964 Hague Conventions on Sales (ULF & ULIS) are specified in CISG Article 99(3)–(6). The text of Article 99 appears in the full text of the Convention in the Appendix.

9. See the 1955 Hague P.I.L. Status Table *available at* <http://hcch.e-vision.nl/index_en. php?act=conventions.status&cid=31>. The question whether CISG yields to the Hague PIL Convention when the Hague PIL rules conflict with the rules of applicability in CISG is deferred to §§464.3–464.5 so that the question can be considered in a setting where such a conflict may occur.

(P.I.L.) rules of the 1955 Hague Convention or any other applicable convention.

A more interesting question is presented by CISG 1(1)(a), which provides an additional basis for applicability when the places of business of the seller and buyer are in different "Contracting States." Under unusual circumstances (e.g., contracting and performance do not take place in the States of either the seller or buyer but in a third-non-Contracting State) Article 1(1)(a) could call for applicability of the Convention although the forum's rules of private international law designate the law of a non-Contracting State.

Happily, such a conflict with the 1955 Hague P.I.L. Convention will be rare. The general P.I.L. rules in Article 3 of the 1955 Convention designate the law of the State where the seller has its residence subject to a narrow exception designating the State where the buyer has its residence. Thus, in the cases to which CISG 1(1)(a) applies (seller and buyer are in different Contracting States), both CISG and Article 3 of the 1955 Hague Convention point to the Convention. In unusual cases where law under the Convention on the point in controversy is different in these two States (e.g., because only one has exercised a permitted reservation or there is an irreconcilable conflict in interpreting a relevant provision of the Convention) the rule of the Contracting State designated by Article 3 of 1955 Hague P.I.L. would be applicable.

464.1   **(i) CISG Rules on Inspection and Notification.**   Another provision of the 1955 Hague P.I.L. Convention, while narrow in scope, raises significant questions concerning the application of Article 90 to conventions on private international law ("conflicts"). Article 4, as an exception to the above general rules of Article 3, provides that "... the domestic law of the country in which inspection of goods delivered pursuant to a sale is to take place shall apply in respect of ... *the periods within which the inspection shall take place, the notifications concerning the inspection and the measures to be taken in case of refusal of the goods.*"[10] This problem can be illustrated as follows:

    Example 90A. Seller and Buyer have their places of business, respectively, in States A and B. Both States have adopted the Sales Convention

---

10. For simplicity, the impact of this provision on CISG is discussed in terms of its rules in inspection and notification. However, the reference in Hague Article 4 to "measures to be taken in case of refusal of the goods" could supersede Articles 85–88 that deal specifically with this question and, to an uncertain extent, the applicability of general rules on rejection and avoidance with respect to defective goods (Arts. 49, 81–84).

and the 1955 Hague P.I.L. Convention. A contract made by the parties called for delivery of a machine to Buyer in State C; this State had not adopted the Sales Convention. The domestic law of State C provides that a buyer may not recover for loss or damage resulting from defects in the goods if the buyer fails to notify the seller of the defects within six months following delivery with no exception when latent defects are discovered at a later date. The machine delivered to Buyer had a serious latent defect that Buyer, in spite of appropriate inspection, did not discover until eight months following delivery. Buyer immediately notified Seller and made a claim for damages. Seller rejected the claim, relying on the above rules of State C, the place of delivery. Buyer brings an action against Seller in State A, a Contracting State.

Deciding which law applies touches sensitive nerves. Time limits for inspection of goods and notification of defects are of great practical importance and were the subject of extended debate and hard-fought compromises embodied in Articles 39 and 44, §§254–261, *supra.* Happily, as we shall see, conflicts between domestic rules designated by Article 4 of the Hague P.I.L. Convention and the substantive rules of the Sales Convention (CISG) can arise only in unusual circumstances.

464.2 **(ii) The Scope of the Problem.** One factor limiting the scope of the problem results from the provision of CISG 90 that the Sales Convention yields to another convention (e.g., the Hague Convention) only when the seller and buyer "have their places of business" in different States both of which are parties to the Hague Convention. A second limitation on the scope of our problem results from the fact that conflict between the two conventions can arise only when an international sale subject to the Sales Convention calls for delivery in a non-contracting State. As we have seen, the Hague Convention (Art. 4) states that the law applicable to inspection and notification is that of the place of delivery; when the place of delivery is in a Contracting State the law of that State for a contract governed by the Sales Convention is, of course, the law of the Convention, including its rules on inspection and notification.

In view of these practical limitations one may well wonder whether the problem is worth the bother; however, working with this issue in one specific setting may make it easier to cope with similar problems in other settings.[11]

---

11. I Sinclair, *The Vienna Convention on the Law of Treaties* 93 (2nd ed. 1984), describes this area as a "particularly obscure aspect" of treaty law. Nothing that follows contradicts this view.

464.3   **(ii) Does CISG yield to Hague (1955)?**   Example 90A posed this question: Which rules on inspection and notification apply — the rules of non-contracting State C *via* Hague (Art. 4) or the rules of the Sales Convention (Arts. 39 & 44)? Since this sale is in general governed by the Sales Convention the application of other rules depends on the interpretation of Article 90.[12] The crucial language of Article 90 is this: The Sales Convention yields only to another treaty "which *contains provisions concerning the matters governed by this Convention.*" The Hague Convention, of course, does not "contain provisions" on inspection, notification and related rules of the law of sales (n. 8, *supra*). The only possible overlap could be between the P.I.L. rules of Hague Article 4 and the rules of CISG 1(1) that govern the applicability of the Convention.

Both of these provisions address the general question of the applicability of law. However, we can conclude that Hague Article 4 governs the same "matter" as Article 1 of the Sales Convention only if we forget that Article 1 is an integral part of a Convention to unify a large and interconnected body of substantive law. Article 1(1) states that it determines when "this Convention applies" — this means *all* of the Convention subject only to those reservations specified in Articles 92–96.[13]

Whether Article 90 was intended to yield to another treaty in the setting of Example 90A can be tested by asking: Suppose that a delegate to the Vienna Sales Conference had proposed an amendment that the Convention's provisions on inspection of the goods, notification of defects and related provisions would not apply when a contract governed by the Convention called for delivery in a non-Contracting State. This participant in the legislative process has no doubt that any such proposal would have been rejected out of hand. If this is correct, it seems difficult to construe Article 90 so broadly as to reach this unacceptable result.

12. Article 30 of the Vienna Treaty on Treaties provides that when successive treaties have incompatible provisions the earlier Treaty yields (para. 3) unless the later treaty provides otherwise (para. 2) — that is, the 1955 Hague Convention would yield to the 1980 Sales Convention.
13. The 1955 Hague P.I.L. Convention was not designed to intrude on a Convention establishing uniform law for sales; the first such convention (ULIS) was adopted in 1964. The care taken to avoid such intrusion in the 1986 Hague P.I.L. Convention is described *infra* at §464.4.

464.4 **(iii) CISG and Hague (1986).** The problem posed by Example
90A would be moot under the 1986 Hague Convention on the Law
Applicable [P.I.L.] to Contracts for the International Sale of Goods
(15 Int. Leg. Mat. 1575).[14] Article 23 provides: "This Convention
does not prejudice the application of the U.N. Convention on contracts
for the international sale of goods." Similar deference to the 1980 Sales
Convention results from Articles 8(5) and 22(1). The specificity on these
points of the 1986 Hague convention compared with the generality of
CISG 90 avoids any impasse between the two Conventions based on
Alphonse-Gaston *politesse*.

465 **Other Article 90 Issues**

   *Article 90 raises other important issues, including the relationship
between the Convention and directives and regulations of the
European Union.*[15]

466 **(3) Article 91: Signature, Ratification and Accession**

   Article 91(1) provided that the Convention would be "open for signature" from the conclusion of the Vienna Conference (April 11, 1980)
"until September 1981." Within this eighteen-month period twenty-one
States signed the Convention.[16]
   What is the significance, if any, of "signature" of the Convention?
Article 91(2) provides that signature "is subject to ratification, acceptance or approval" (herein termed "ratification") and that only after this
second step does a State become a Contracting State. See also the Vienna
Treaty on Treaties (1969) Articles 12, 14(1)(a). The obligations if any,
undertaken by signature are unclear;[17] the practical significance of the

14. For Contracting States to the 1986 Hague P.I.L. Convention see the Status Table *available at* <http://hcch.e-vision.nl/index_en.php?act=conventions.status&cid=61>.
15. For discussion of this matter see Peter Schlechtriem, *Article 90* paras. 3 and 9–13, *in*
Schlechtriem & Schwenzer, *CISG Commentary* (2nd English ed. 2005).
16. For simplicity "ratification" herein includes acceptance and approval. All three terms
(Art. 91(2)) refer to domestic constitutional procedures by which signatory States adopt the
Convention.
17. See the Vienna Treaty on Treaties (1969) Art. 18: Signature subject to ratification creates
an obligation "to refrain from acts which would defeat the object and purpose of the treaty."
It is sometimes said that such signature implies an obligation to submit the treaty to the
ratification process. By analogy to the courting customs of this writer's youth, signature
implies less than engagement and perhaps is similar to "going steady" or a promise to "think
it over."

signature process is to provide a convenient means by which States can learn from each other whether there is sufficient interest in the Convention to justify launching the cumbersome legislative processes required for final adoption.

The other provisions of Article 91 are self-evident.

467 (4) Article 92: Reservation to Exclude Part II or Part III of the Convention

In 1964 separate conventions were adopted on formation of contracts for international sales (ULF) and on obligations under the contract (ULIS). Following this pattern, the UNCITRAL Working Group prepared separate draft conventions. However, the full Commission in 1978 merged the two drafts into a single draft convention but provided (Article 92) that Contracting States may declare that they will not be bound by Part II (Formation) or by Part III (Obligations under the contract).[18]

Interest in this option was shown primarily by the Scandinavian States, based on their satisfaction with their uniform law on contract formation.[19] In fact, Denmark, Finland, Iceland, Norway and Sweden have all ratified the Convention subject to a declaration under Article 92 not to be bound by Part II: Formation of the Contract. At the time this is written, no other State has made a declaration under Article 92.

The application of Article 92 in most situations presents little difficulty. However, it may be useful to illustrate the interplay of a reservation excluding Part II and the alternative grounds for applicability in Article 1(1)(a) and (b).

Example 92A. Seller (in State A) and Buyer (in State B) communicated with each other in a manner that raised a question as to whether they had made a contract. Both States had adopted the Convention but State B had also made declaration under Article 92 excluding Part II of the Convention on formation of the contract. Under what circumstances will Part II apply to this question?

This question calls for an application of Article 1 of the Convention (§§44–47, *supra*). Applicability cannot be based on Article 1(1)(a). Under Article 92(2) "in respect of the matters governed by" Part II,

---

18. See §9, *supra* and UNCITRAL, Report of the Eleventh Session (1978), paras. 20–22, IX *YB* 13–14.

19. See Peter Schlechtriem, *Article 92* para. 1, *in* Schlechtriem & Schwenzer, *CISG Commentary* (2nd English ed. 2005).

State B "is not to be considered a Contracting State" within Article 1(1). Consequently, with respect to Part II on Formation the places of business of *both* parties are *not* in "Contracting States."[20] Under Article 1(1)(b), Part II will apply if the rules of private international law lead to the application of the law of State A but not if the rules of Private International Law (PIL) point to State B. *According to both leading commentators[21] and decisions,[22] if PIL rules lead to the application of the law of State A the forum should apply Part II even if it is located in State B (or any other State that has made the Article 92 reservation).*

468   **(5) Article 93: Application to Part of a State**

Article 93 is of interest to relatively few States — federal systems where the central government lacks treaty power to establish uniform law for international sales. The United States, fortunately, is not in this position. On the other hand e.g., Canada's treaty power was crippled by a 1937 decision of the (British) Privy Council, a restriction, that now is moot.[23] Article 93 responds to this difficulty by providing that a State may declare that the Convention will apply "only to one or more" of its territorial units — an option that permits a State to adopt the Convention with its applicability limited to those units (e.g., Provinces) that have enacted legislation to implement the Convention.[24] The effect of a declaration under Article 93 may be illustrated as follows:

Example 93A. State C ratified the Convention subject to a declaration under Article 93 that the Convention will apply to its territorial unit Y

---

20. See Peter Schlechtriem, *Article 92* para. 3, *in* Schlechtriem & Schwenzer, *CISG Commentary* (2nd English ed. 2005).

21. See Joseph Lookofsky, *Understanding the CISG in Scandinavia: A Compact Guide to the 1980 United Nations Convention on Contracts for the International Sale of Goods* §8.4 (2nd ed. 2002); Peter Schlechtriem, *Introduction to Articles 14–24* para. 10 and Art. 92 para. 3, *in* Schlechtriem & Schwenzer, *CISG Commentary* 176 (2nd English ed. 2005).

22. See the decisions cited in UNCITRAL Digest Part 2 para. 3 n. 6.

23. See Jacob S. Ziegel, *Canada and the Vienna Sales Convention*, 12 Can. Bus. L.J. 366, 368–369 (1986–1987). For the treaty power of the United States in relation a convention establishing uniform law for international sales see Honnold, 107 U. Pa. L. Rev. 207, 304–199 (1959).

24. Canada had earlier availed itself of this provision but has since extended the Convention to all constituent units. See footnote (d) in UNCITRAL's Status Table for the Convention, *available at* <www.uncitral.org/uncitral/en/uncitral_texts/sale_goods/1980CISG_status. html>. Canada's role in securing adoption of such a federal state provision is described in H. Allan Leal, *Federal State Clauses and the Conventions of the Hague Conference on Private International Law*, 8 Dalh. L.J. 257 (1984).

but not to territorial unit Z. Seller A, whose place of business is in Y, and also Seller B, whose place of business is in Z, make sales contracts with Buyer, whose place of business is in State D, a Contracting State that has made no such reservation.

Article 93(3) provides that only the contract made by Seller A, located in territorial unit Y, will be governed by the Convention.[25] If Seller had multiple places of business, some in Y and some in Z, the contracts subject to the Convention will those in which Seller's place of business in Y (rather than Z) "has the closest relationship to the contract and its performance." See Art. 10(a), §§42, 123–124, *supra* (In some cases the Convention may apply to international sales involving parties with places of business in Z when the forum's rules on conflicts (P.I.L.) designate the law of a Contracting State.)

469   (6) Article 94: States With the Same or Closely Related Law

The Nordic States have a long and successful history of cooperation in developing the same or similar laws for sales of goods and many other subjects. Article 94 authorizes such States to declare that the Convention will not apply to contracts between parties who "have their places of business in those States."[26] Denmark, Finland, Iceland, Norway and Sweden, in ratifying the Convention, have made the declaration authorized by Article 94.

470   (7) Article 95: Exclusion of Article 1(1)(b)

Article 95 permits a State to declare "that it will not be bound by subparagraph (1)(b) of article 1 . . ." Article 1(1) provides for two cumulative grounds for applicability: Sub (1)(a) — when the places of business of the parties are indifferent Contracting States, and Sub(1)(b) — "when the rules of private international law lead to the application of the law of a Contracting State." The effect of the Article 95 reservation — which has been adopted by the United States, China, the Czech Republic, Singapore and Slovakia — is explored in connection with Article 1 (see §47 *supra*).

---

25. See Peter Schlechtriem, *Article 93* para. 3, *in* Schlechtriem & Schwenzer, *CISG Commentary* (2nd English ed. 2005).

26. See Peter Schlechtriem, *Article 94* para. 9, *in* Schlechtriem & Schwenzer, *CISG Commentary* (2nd English ed. 2005).

471 (8) Article 96: Preservation of Domestic Rule requiring a Writing or other Formalities

Article 96 permits a declaration excluding Article 11 — a provision that rejects domestic requirements as to form, often called Statutes of Frauds. This reservation was discussed in connection with Articles 11 and 12, §§126–129 *supra*.

472 (9) Article 97: Formalities and Effective Date for Declaration Effecting Reservations; Article 98: No Reservations Permitted except those Expressly Authorized; Article 99: Initial Entry into Force and Transition Procedures involving the 1964 Hague Convention (ULF and ULIS)

These three articles govern in detail formal matters of concern primarily to Foreign Ministries who have had extensive experience with these questions.[27]

In connection with Article 99(1) it may be noted that the Convention entered into force among the first eleven Contracting States on January 1, 1988.[28]

473 (10) Article 100: Effective Date as to Offers and Contracts

The Convention does not have retroactive effect. Under Article 100(1) the rules on formation of the contract (Parts I and II of the Convention) are applicable only when "the proposal for concluding the contract" is made on or after the Convention enters into force for the relevant Contracting State or States. Under Article 100(2) the rules governing the rights and obligations under contracts (Parts I and III of the Convention) are applicable "only to contracts concluded after the date when the Convention enters into force" for the relevant Contracting State or States.

---

27. For discussion of these articles see Evans, *B-B Commentary* 661–671.

28. For information on adherences — as well as reservations, dates of entry into force, and other information related to ratification of the Convention — see UNCITRAL's Status Table for the Convention, *available at* <www.uncitral.org/uncitral/en/uncitral_texts/sale_goods/1980CISG_status.html>.

Paragraphs (1) and (2) both refer to entry into force "in respect of the Contracting States referred to in subparagraph (1)(a) or the Contracting State referred to in subparagraph (1)(b) of article 1." The effect of this dense language can be understood with the help of an example.[29]

Example 100A. The Convention entered into force for State A on March 1, 1990 and for State B on May 1, 1990. (These dates reflect the twelve-month period following the deposit of the instrument of adoption specified in Article 99). On April 20 Seller in State A by email made a "proposal" (which for the present we will assume was an "offer") for a sales contract to Buyer in State B. On May 10 Buyer byemail transmitted an "acceptance" to Seller. Does the Convention (Parts I and II) govern the question whether these communications concluded a contract?

The problem is complex since Article 100(1) provides that applicability may be derived from *either* (A) Article 1(1)(a) ("Sub (1)(a)") *or* (B) Article 1(1)(b) ("Sub(1)(b)").

(A) Can applicability of the Convention be *based on Article (1)(a)?* The answer is No since the Convention had not entered into force "in respect of the Contracting States referred to" in Sub(1)(a). Article (1)(a) makes the Convention applicable only when the States of *both* parties "are Contracting States"; at the time of the offer the Convention was effective only in State A.[30]

(B) However, the formation rules of the Convention may yet apply if the Convention was in force on April 20 (the date of the offer) "in the Contracting State referred to" in Sub (1)(b) — that is, the Contracting State designated by "the rules of private international law." If these rules designate State B the answer is still No, since the Convention became effective in State B only on May 1; if the rules designate State A (effective date March 1) the Convention applies.[31]

Paragraph (2) of Article 100 on the effective date for obligations under the contract (Part III of the Convention) uses the same approach

---

29. The example is suggested by the helpful discussion in Evans, *B-B Commentary* 673–674.
30. If the States in question had both made a declaration under Article 95 excluding Sub (1)(b) the answer could end here.
31. In Example 100A the communications were transmitted by email. If the communications (e.g.,) went by post and were subject to delay it may be necessary to refer to Article 15(1) (an offer "becomes effective when it *reaches* the offeree") and Article 18(2) (an acceptance becomes effective when it "*reaches* the offeror"). Although these rules may lead to the conclusion that the Convention does not apply it seems necessary to use the Convention's own rules to apply its rules on applicability.

as paragraph (1) on formation; the above illustrations based on paragraph (1) apply to paragraph (2), *mutatis mutandis.*

474 **(11) Article 101: Denunciation**

The language of this article seems clear. In any event, denunciation would be handled by a foreign ministry which should be familiar with this process. The Secretary-General as depositary can be expected to notify Contracting States of important acts such as a denunciation. See Vienna Treaty on Treaties (1969) Article 77(1)(e).

475 **D. Postscript: The Preamble**

This postscript is out of order but (as a lame excuse) so was preparation of the Preamble. UNCITRAL did not prepare a preamble nor was this matter considered by the committees of the Vienna Conference that considered the Convention's substantive provisions (see §10, *supra*). Instead, a preamble was first considered and prepared by the Drafting Committee on April 9, two days before adjournment of the Conference (*O.R.* 154); by this time discussion of the Convention's substantive provisions had been completed. On April 10 the Drafting Committee's proposal was adopted by the Conference Plenary without substantive discussion (*O.R.* 219–220, 231). At this point only formalities remained and the Conference adjourned on April 11.

Under these circumstances the Preamble serves as a hortatory statement of reasons for accepting the uniform law but can hardly be given weight in construing its provisions. The Convention sets forth the rules for interpreting its provisions (Art. 7, §§85–103.1, *supra*). Article 7 and the other provisions of the Convention were discussed at length in UNCITRAL and at the Diplomatic Conference; the Preamble scarcely provides a basis for modifying the understandings embodied in the Convention's provisions. *Language from the Preamble has been cited in several cases in support of holdings that, to achieve the Convention's purposes, the CISG must pre-empt claims based on domestic law to the extent such claims are within the scope of the Convention.*[32] *The Preamble is cited in these decisions as authority for very general and*

---

32. See Asante Technologies, Inc. v. PMC-Sierra, Inc., 164 F. Supp. 2d 1142, 1151 (N.D. Cal. 2001), where the court cited Preamble language ("the development of international trade on the basis of equality and mutual benefit" and "the adoption of uniform rules which

unexceptional — even obvious — propositions: that the CISG was meant to create uniform international sales law and to promote the development of international trade. The citations might almost be characterized as "make-weight" authority for undisputed contentions, and in the view of the editor of the current edition do not signal a significant role for the Preamble in resolving specific challenging issues under the Convention.

govern contracts for the international sale of goods and take into account the different social, economic and legal systems would contribute to the removal of legal barriers in international trade and promote the development of international trade") in concluding that "the expressly stated goal of developing uniform international contract law to promote international trade indicates the intent of the parties to the treaty to have the treaty pre-empt state law causes of action." See also Geneva Pharmaceuticals Technology Corp. v. Barr Laboratories, Inc., 201 F. Supp. 2d 236, 285–286 (S.D.N.Y. 2002), where the court cited the same Preamble language (as well as the Asante case itself) in support of the proposition that, where the Convention governed a transaction, the CISG pre-empted contract causes of action (although not tort claims) founded on non-CISG domestic law. It is also interesting to note that, in confronting the far less obvious issue of whether the CISG pre-empted a party's claim based on domestic law promissory estoppel doctrine, the court did not resort to the Preamble for assistance. Id., at 286–287.

INDEX

References are to section numbers.

A

Acceptance of offer   22, 157–78
Act or omission   360, 362, 381, 436–6.4, 446, 448–448.1A, 455.1
Additional period of time fixed, *see* Nachfrist
Adequate assurance   385, 388, 389, 391–6, 398
Agency   41, 66, 127, 132
Agreement, *see* Contract
Aircraft   49, 54
Aliud   223, 256.1, 289
Amendment of Sales Convention   463
Anticipatory breach   180, 273, 356.1, 384, 388, 395–8, 412, 437
Arbitration agreement   442
Assurance of performance, *see* Adequate assurance
Attorney fees, recovery of   98, 408
Auction sales   51
Avoidance of contract   181–7.2, 246–7, 282–2.1, 287–91, 296, 301–8.2, 314–7, 345, 350–6.1, 379–83, 395–402, 404, 409–15, 435.4, 437–52, 454–5.3

B

Barter Transactions   56.1
Battle of the forms   165–70.4
Brussels Convention   207–8, 332
Burden-of-proof   50–1, 59.1, 60.7, 70.1
Buyer's obligations   321–57

C

Cancellation, *see* Avoidance of contract
Carriage of goods   208, 212–5, 359.1, 363–71, 390
Case law under the Sales Convention   14, 21, 90, 92–3
Checks, notes and other money paper   53
Communicating with other party   95, 100, 134, 248
Compelling performance (specific performance)   191–9.1, 277, 279–86, 345–9, 419.3, 454
Conclusion of contract   22, 108, 157–79
Confirmation agreements   160
Conflict of laws, *see* Private International Law

R

Receipt of
  acceptance   170, 179
  communications   138, 140, 161–2, 179, 190, 357
Recoupment   444A
Rejection of
  goods   272, 277, 306, 455.1-.2 (*see also* Avoidance of contract)
  offer   152–6, 165–70.4
Reliance damages   403
Remedies for
  buyer's breach   26, 344–57
  seller's breach   26, 275–320
Repair   244–7, 279, 284–6, 296–8, 368.2, 382.1, 449.1
Repudiation   150, 385–98, 413, 419–419.2
Requirements contracts   137.3
Requiring performance   191–9.1, 259, 279–86, 345–9
Reservations   1, 10, 46.1–7.6, 103, 127.1, 128–9, 131, 372.3, 458, 467–72
Restitution   70, 438, 444–8.2, 449.1–52
Revocation of acceptance of goods, *see* Avoidance of contract
Revocation of Offer   22, 138–51, 179
Risk of loss, *see* Passing of risk

S

Sale of goods during transit   372–2.3
Sample or model of goods   227
Scope of application of Sales Convention   35–37, 61–74, 408
Services, *see* Mixed contracts
Software   56, 56.4
Specific performance, *see* Compelling performance
Sphere of application of Sales Convention   12–15, 35–37, 39–60.7
Statute of Frauds, *see* Contracts, oral
Subjective intent   106–107, 110
Suspension of performance   384–94

T

Take delivery, buyer's obligation to   321–2, 341–3
Temporary impediments   435.1
Tort claims   65, 70.1–73
Trade usage, *see* Custom
Travaux préparatoires   70.1, 88–91, 93, 372.3, 408, 420–1

U

UNCITRAL   5–10, 32–3, 92–6
UNIDROIT Principles of International Commercial Contracts   21.1, 65, 93, 169, 170.4, 281.1, 421, 432.2
Uniform Law for the International Sale of Goods (ULIS), *see* Hague Conventions
Uniform Law on the Formation of Contracts for the International Sale of Goods (ULF), *see* Hague Conventions
UNILEX   24, 63, 67, 93, 127.2, 281.1
Usage of trade, *see* Custom

V

Validity   64
Vienna Convention on the Law of Treaties   90, 103, 372

W

Waiver   204, 257.3, 291
Warsaw Convention   89–90, 92
Withdrawal of offer   138, 179
Written form, *see* Contracts, oral

Z

Zapata Hermanos case   408